Dante Beyond Borders
Contexts and Reception

LEGENDA

LEGENDA is the Modern Humanities Research Association's book imprint for new research in the Humanities. Founded in 1995 by Malcolm Bowie and others within the University of Oxford, Legenda has always been a collaborative publishing enterprise, directly governed by scholars. The Modern Humanities Research Association (MHRA) joined this collaboration in 1998, became half-owner in 2004, in partnership with Maney Publishing and then Routledge, and has since 2016 been sole owner. Titles range from medieval texts to contemporary cinema and form a widely comparative view of the modern humanities, including works on Arabic, Catalan, English, French, German, Greek, Italian, Portuguese, Russian, Spanish, and Yiddish literature. Editorial boards and committees of more than 60 leading academic specialists work in collaboration with bodies such as the Society for French Studies, the British Comparative Literature Association and the Association of Hispanists of Great Britain & Ireland.

The MHRA encourages and promotes advanced study and research in the field of the modern humanities, especially modern European languages and literature, including English, and also cinema. It aims to break down the barriers between scholars working in different disciplines and to maintain the unity of humanistic scholarship. The Association fulfils this purpose through the publication of journals, bibliographies, monographs, critical editions, and the MHRA Style Guide, and by making grants in support of research. Membership is open to all who work in the Humanities, whether independent or in a University post, and the participation of younger colleagues entering the field is especially welcomed.

ALSO PUBLISHED BY THE ASSOCIATION

Critical Texts

Tudor and Stuart Translations • *New Translations* • *European Translations*

MHRA Library of Medieval Welsh Literature

MHRA Bibliographies

Publications of the Modern Humanities Research Association

The Annual Bibliography of English Language & Literature

Austrian Studies

Modern Language Review

Portuguese Studies

The Slavonic and East European Review

Working Papers in the Humanities

The Yearbook of English Studies

www.mhra.org.uk

www.legendabooks.com

ITALIAN PERSPECTIVES

Editorial Committee
Professor Simon Gilson, University of Oxford (General Editor)
Dr Francesca Billiani, University of Manchester
Professor Manuele Gragnolati, Université Paris-Sorbonne
Dr Catherine Keen, University College London
Professor Martin McLaughlin, Magdalen College, Oxford

Founding Editors
Professor Zygmunt Barański and Professor Anna Laura Lepschy

In the light of growing academic interest in Italy and the reorganization of many university courses in Italian along interdisciplinary lines, this book series, founded by Maney Publishing under the imprint of the Northern Universities Press and now continuing under the Legenda imprint, aims to bring together different scholarly perspectives on Italy and its culture. *Italian Perspectives* publishes books and collections of essays on any period of Italian literature, language, history, culture, politics, art, and media, as well as studies which take an interdisciplinary approach and are methodologically innovative.

APPEARING IN THIS SERIES

20. *Ugo Foscolo and English Culture*, by Sandra Parmegiani
21. *The Printed Media in Fin-de-siècle Italy: Publishers, Writers, and Readers*, ed. by Ann Hallamore Caesar, Gabriella Romani, and Jennifer Burns
22. *Giraffes in the Garden of Italian Literature: Modernist Embodiment in Italo Svevo, Federigo Tozzi and Carlo Emilio Gadda*, by Deborah Amberson
23. *Remembering Aldo Moro: The Cultural Legacy of the 1978 Kidnapping and Murder*, ed. by Ruth Glynn and Giancarlo Lombardi
24. *Disrupted Narratives: Illness, Silence and Identity in Svevo, Pressburger and Morandini*, by Emma Bond
25. *Dante and Epicurus: A Dualistic Vision of Secular and Spiritual Fulfilment*, by George Corbett
26. *Edoardo Sanguineti: Literature, Ideology and the Avant-Garde*, ed. by Paolo Chirumbolo and John Picchione
27. *The Tradition of the Actor-Author in Italian Theatre*, ed. by Donatella Fischer
28. *Leopardi's Nymphs: Grace, Melancholy, and the Uncanny*, by Fabio A. Camilletti
29. *Gadda and Beckett: Storytelling, Subjectivity and Fracture*, by Katrin Wehling-Giorgi
30. *Caravaggio in Film and Literature: Popular Culture's Appropriation of a Baroque Genius*, by Laura Rorato
31. *The Italian Academies 1525-1700: Networks of Culture, Innovation and Dissent*, ed. by Jane E. Everson, Denis V. Reidy and Lisa Sampson
32. *Rome Eternal: The City As Fatherland*, by Guy Lanoue
33. *The Somali Within: Language, Race and Belonging in 'Minor' Italian Literature*, by Simone Brioni
34. *Laughter from Realism to Modernism: Misfits and Humorists in Pirandello, Svevo, Palazzeschi, and Gadda*, by Alberto Godioli
35. *Pasolini after Dante: The 'Divine Mimesis' and the Politics of Representation*, by Emanuela Patti

Managing Editor
Dr Graham Nelson, 41 Wellington Square, Oxford OX1 2JF, UK
www.legendabooks.com

Dante Beyond Borders

Contexts and Reception

EDITED BY NICK HAVELY AND JONATHAN KATZ
WITH RICHARD COOPER

Italian Perspectives 52
Modern Humanities Research Association
2021

Published by Legenda
an imprint of the Modern Humanities Research Association
Salisbury House, Station Road, Cambridge CB1 2LA

ISBN 978-1-78188-830-8 (HB)
ISBN 978-1-78188-834-6 (PB)

First published 2021

All rights reserved. No part of this publication may be reproduced or disseminated or transmitted in any form or by any means, electronic, mechanical, photocopying, recording or otherwise, or stored in any retrieval system, or otherwise used in any manner whatsoever without written permission of the copyright owner, except in accordance with the provisions of the Copyright, Designs and Patents Act 1988, or under the terms of a licence permitting restricted copying issued in the UK by the Copyright Licensing Agency Ltd, Saffron House, 6–10 Kirby Street, London EC1N 8TS, England, or in the USA by the Copyright Clearance Center, 222 Rosewood Drive, Danvers MA 01923. Application for the written permission of the copyright owner to reproduce any part of this publication must be made by email to legenda@mhra.org.uk.

Disclaimer: Statements of fact and opinion contained in this book are those of the author and not of the editors or the Modern Humanities Research Association. The publisher makes no representation, express or implied, in respect of the accuracy of the material in this book and cannot accept any legal responsibility or liability for any errors or omissions that may be made.

Trademark notice: Product or corporate names may be trademarks or registered trademarks, and are used only for identification and explanation without intent to infringe.

© Modern Humanities Research Association 2021

Copy-Editor: Dr Nigel Hope

CONTENTS

Acknowledgements   xi
Select List of Abbreviations   xii
List of Figures   xiii
Notes on Contributors   xv

Three Dante Societies: Historical Notes   xxi
CHRISTIAN Y. DUPONT, FEDERICA COLUZZI, RICHARD COOPER, ANDREA RENKER

Introduction   1
NICK HAVELY

PART I: CULTURE AND POLITICS

1   The Eclogues of Giovanni del Virgilio and Dante in Classical Perspective   9
MATTHEW LEIGH AND JONATHAN KATZ

2   Measuring the Divine by Geometry and Feeling: Canto 33 of Dante's *Paradiso*   21
CORNELIA KLETTKE

3   Speaking to the Citizen: Urban Identity, Ethics, and Politics in Tuscan Vernacular Literature and Dante   35
JOHANNES BARTUSCHAT

4   Dante's Lamentations: The History of Exile and the Politics of Restoration   47
MATTHEW S. KEMPSHALL

PART II: VISUAL AND PERFORMING ARTS

5   Transitional Narrative Strategies and the Art of Usury in Dante's *Commedia*   63
CHRISTOPHER KLEINHENZ

6   Form and Freedom in the Dante Series Prints of Geoff MacEwan   74
GERVASE ROSSER

7   Psalms, Ecclesiastical Chant and Healing in the *Purgatorio*   88
FRANCESCO CIABATTONI

8   'Che cosa è questa, Amor?': Cavalcanti and *Paradiso* in a Ballata by Francesco Landini   100
PEDRO MEMELSDORFF

PART III: ITALY AND BEYOND

9 *Un grido di sì alto suono*: Voicing the *Commedia*   119
   NICK HAVELY

10 Who Could Understand the *Commedia*? Multilingualism, Comprehension and Oral Communication in Medieval Italy   132
   ALESSANDRO CARLUCCI

11 Notes on the Presence of Petrarch in the Dante Commentaries of Cristoforo Landino (1481) and Trifone Gabriele (1525–1527)   145
   SIMON GILSON

12 Dante and Islam, Islam and Dante   157
   VALERIO CAPPOZZO

13 Dante in Spain: Translations, Literary Theory and Canonizations   169
   PAUL CARRANZA

14 Dante and Death in Late Medieval France   180
   HELEN SWIFT

15 Illustrating editions of Dante in France before Gustave Doré   193
   RICHARD COOPER

16 A Poor Relation among French Dante Scholars: Abel-François Villemain's Public Classes at the Sorbonne 1828–1830   215
   FRANZISKA MEIER

17 Dante Alighieri and German Romanticism   228
   ALFRED NOE

18 Dante's Presence in Weimar around 1800   240
   KARL PHILIPP ELLERBROCK

19 'How the Young Women Take to It!': Italian Exiles and Women Readers of Dante in Nineteenth-Century New England   252
   CHRISTIAN Y. DUPONT

20 'Why Do You Rend Me?' Dante and the Pain of James Russell Lowell   265
   KATHLEEN VERDUIN

21 Dante for Mothers   277
   CAROL CHIODO

PART IV: MODERN AND CONTEMPORARY PRESENCE

22 Hidden Presence: Dante's *Commedia* in Proust's *À la recherche du temps perdu*   289
   KARLHEINZ STIERLE

23 Allen Tate's Flight from Racism: Dante and 'The Swimmers'   299
   DENNIS LOONEY

24 'Maintaining Neutrality in a Period of Moral Crisis': Appropriations of *Inferno* 3 in Twentieth- and Twenty-First-Century America 311
KRISTINA M. OLSON

25 *Dante Today*: Tracking the Global Resonance of the *Commedia* 324
ELIZABETH COGGESHALL

26 Vernacular Hybridity Across Borders: Dante, Amīr Khusrau, Sandow Birk 338
AKASH KUMAR

27 Translating Dante 1966–2019 349
PETER HAINSWORTH AND DAVID ROBEY

General Index 363
References to Dante's Works 377

ACKNOWLEDGEMENTS

This being a volume involving partnership between Dante Societies, the editors are especially indebted to the President, Vice-President and Secretary of the Dante Society of America (Albert Ascoli, Kristina Olson, Christian Dupont) and the President of the Deutsche Dante-Gesellschaft (Rainer Stillers). Their assistance in identifying potential contributors among their membership has been invaluable, as has been their support for the project throughout.

We are grateful to the copyright owners who have given permission for illustrations to be reproduced here. The sources for the latter, where relevant, are indicated in the 'List of Figures', above. Thanks are due to the artist Geoff MacEwan for his collaboration and for his permission to reproduce his work in Chapter 6 and on the cover of this volume.

At Legenda, the publisher (Graham Nelson) and the General Editor of the series (Simon Gilson) have been constantly helpful, prompt to deal with questions, and generous with guidance and advice. Catherine Keen, as external reader of the volume's first draft, provided many helpful comments and useful suggestions for improvement. At a later stage, Nigel Hope conducted the copy-editing process with exemplary skill, greatly enhancing the clarity and consistency of the various contributions.

Among the friends and colleagues who have advised, assisted and encouraged in various ways, we should particularly like to thank Teodolinda Barolini, Marina Brownlee, Margaret Bent, Peter Hawkins, Chris Kleinhenz, Giorgio Monari and Helen Swift. And throughout the process we have been fortunate to have worked with such a creative and collaborative group of contributors.

Nick Havely
Jonathan Katz
Richard Cooper

SELECT LIST OF ABBREVIATIONS

Aen.   Virgil, *Aeneid*
Conv.   Dante, *Convivio* (editions as specified in individual chapters)
DBI   *Dizionario biografico degli italiani*, c. 92 vols, ed. by R. Romanelli (Rome: Istituto della Enciclopedia Italiana, 1960-)
DVE   Dante, *De Vulgari Eloquentia* (editions as specified in individual chapters)
Ecl.   Dante & Giovanni del Virgilio, *Eclogues* (editions as specified in Chapter 1, n. 1)
ED   *Enciclopedia Dantesca*, dir. U. Bosco, ed. G. Petrocchi, 6 vols (Rome: Istituto della Enciclopedia Italiana, 1970–78)
GDLI   *Grande dizionario della lingua italiana*, ed. S. Battaglia, 25 vols, incl. supplements and indexes (Turin: UTET, 1961–2009)
Inf.   Dante, *Inferno* (editions as specified in individual chapters)
Mon.   Dante, *Monarchia* (editions as specified in individual chapters)
Par.   Dante, *Paradiso* (editions as specified in individual chapters)
PL   *Patrologiae Cursus Completus, Series Latina*, ed. J. P. Migne, 221 vols (Paris: Garnier, 1865)
Purg.   Dante, *Purgatorio* (editions as specified in individual chapters)
VN   Dante, *Vita Nuova* (editions as specified in individual chapters)

LIST OF FIGURES

FIG. P.1. Portrait of Henry Wadsworth Longfellow in 1862, by George Peter Alexander Healy, now in the Bowdoin College Museum of Art

FIG. P.2. Portrait of the Rev. Edward Moore (artist unknown): by kind permission of the Principal and Fellows of St Edmund Hall

FIG. 2.1. Gioacchino da Fiore, *Liber figurarum*, Reggio Emilia, MS R1, f. 12r, in Leone Tondelli, Marjorie Reeves and Beatrice Hirsch-Reich, *Il libro delle figure dell'Abate Gioachino da Fiore*, 2nd edn, II (Turin: Società Editrice Internazionale, 1953), pl. II. © Staatsbibliothek zu Berlin — Preußischer Kulturbesitz.

FIG. 6.1. William Blake, *Beatrice Addressing Dante from the Car*. Ink and watercolour on paper. 1824–27. 37.2 × 52.7 cm.. Tate Gallery, London. Photo © Tate

FIG. 6.2. Geoff MacEwan, *Beatrice* from the *Purgatorio* series. Print dimensions: 24.7 × 29.4 cm. Photo © Geoff MacEwan

FIG. 6.3. Geoff MacEwan, *The Reed Bed* from the *Purgatorio* series. Print dimensions: 24.7 × 29.4 cm. Photo © Geoff MacEwan

FIG. 6.4. Geoff MacEwan, *The Earthly Paradise* from the *Purgatorio* series. Print dimensions: 24.7 × 29.4 cm. Photo © Geoff MacEwan

FIG. 6.5. Geoff MacEwan, *The Garden* from the *Purgatorio* series. Pring dimensions: 24. × 29.4 cm. Photo © Geoff MacEwan

FIG. 6.6. Geoff MacEwan, *The Dark Wood* from the *Inferno* series. Print dimensions: 36 × 30.5 cm. Photo © Geoff MacEwan

FIG. 6.7. Geoff MacEwan, *Exit from Hell* from the *Inferno* series. Print dimensions: 36 × 30.5 cm. Photo © Geoff MacEwan

FIG. 6.8. Geoff MacEwan, Plate 7 from the *Paradiso* series. Print dimensions: 24.6 × 32.5 cm. Photo © Geoff MacEwan

FIG. 6.9. Geoff MacEwan, Plate 8 from the *Paradiso* series. Print dimensions: 24.5 × 32.5 cm. Photo © Geoff MacEwan

FIG. 6.10. Geoff MacEwan, *Bruno Latini* from the *Inferno* series. Print dimensions: 36.2 × 30.2 cm. Photo © Geoff MacEwan

FIG. 6.11. Geoff MacEwan, *Oderisi da Gubbio* from the *Purgatorio* series. Print dimensions: 24.7 × 29.4 cm. Photo © Geoff MacEwan

FIG. 8.1. Landini, *Che cosa è questa, Amor*, tenor *tempora* 1–21 (Sq, fol. 163r)

FIG. 8.2. Landini, *Che cosa è questa, Amor*, tenor *tempora* 7–15 (Sq, fol. 163r)

FIG. 8.3. Numeric implications of Landini, *Che cosa è questa, Amor*, tenor *tempora* 1–21

FIG. 8.4. Landini, *Che cosa è questa, Amor*, tenor *tempora* 22–27 (Sq, fol. 163r)

FIG. 8.5. Jacopo di Cione (attr.), *Paradiso*, Florence, Monastero della Vergine Maria e di Santa Brigida

FIG. 15.1. Turin, BNU, MS L.III. 17; *La Commedia* (Venice: Petrus de Plasiis, 1491), fol. i.1

FIG. 15.2. Turin, BNU, MS L.III. 17; *La Commedia* (Venice: Petrus de Quarengiis, 1497), fol. xviii^v

FIG. 15.3. Turin, BNU, MS L.III. 17; *La Commedia* (Venice: Petrus de Quarengiis, 1497), fol. xxiv^r

Fig. 15.4. *Il Dante* (Lyon: J. de Tournes, 1547); *Lo amoroso Convivio*, Venice Z. A. da Sabio, 1521; *Comedia*, (Venice: Bernardino Stagnino, 1536)
Fig. 15.5. *Dante, con nuove et utili ispositioni* (Lyon: G. Roville, 1551), pp. 11, 232, 442
Fig. 15.6. *La Divina Commedia* (Paris: Marcel Prault, 1768)
Fig. 15.7. Mme Giacomelli, *La Divina Comedia* (Paris: Salomon [1813]), *Inf.* 3 and 12
Fig. 15.8. Mme Giacomelli, *La Divina Comedia* (Paris: Salomon [1813]), *Inf.* 21 and 24
Fig. 15.9. Mme Giacomelli, *La Divina Comedia* (Paris: Salomon [1813]), *Purg.* 8; *Par.* 27
Fig. 15.10. Sébastien Rhéal, *Inferno* (Paris: À la Direction, 1843), last two prints
Fig. 15.11. Antoine Étex, *La Divine Comédie* (Paris: J. Bry aîné, 1854), pp. 41 and 46–47
Fig. 15.12. Antoine Étex, *La Divine Comédie* (Paris: J. Bry aîné, 1854), pp. 69 and 82–83
Fig. 15.13. Antoine Étex, *La Divine Comédie* (Paris: J. Bry aîné, 1854), pp. 105 and 132–33
Fig. 15.14. Antoine Étex, *La Divine Comédie* (Paris: J. Bry aîné, 1854), pp. 156 and 165
Fig. 15.15. Antoine Étex, *La Divine Comédie* (Paris: J. Bry aîné, 1854), p. 161
Fig. 15.16. Adolf von Stürler, *L'Enfer de Dante Alighieri*, canto 5
Fig. 15.17. Adolf von Stürler, *L'Enfer de Dante Alighieri*, cantos 16 and 20
Fig. 15.18. Adolf von Stürler, *L'Enfer de Dante Alighieri*, cantos 22 and 27
Fig. 15.19. Adolf von Stürler, *L'Enfer de Dante Alighieri*, cantos 30 and 33
Fig. 25.1. Tag Cloud, *Dante Today* [image captured 2 October 2020]
Fig. 25.2. Map of Sightings, *Dante Today* [image captured 2 October 2020]

NOTES ON CONTRIBUTORS

Johannes Bartuschat is Professor of Italian at the University of Zurich. He specializes in Italian Literature of the Middle Ages and the Renaissance. His publications include essays on Dante, Brunetto Latini, Boccaccio, the history of Dante criticism, the relationship between literature and figurative arts, and the book *Les 'Vies' de Dante, Pétrarque et Boccace en Italie (XIV–XV siècles): contribution à l'histoire du genre biographique* (Longo Angelo, 2007). He is the chief editor of *La Rassegna Europea della Letteratura Italiana*. He has recently co-edited with Elisa Brilli and Delphine Carron *The Dominicans and the Making of Florentine Cultural Identity* (Firenze University Press, 2020).

Valerio Cappozzo is Associate Professor and Director of the Italian Program at the University of Mississippi, co-Editor-in-Chief of «Annali d'Italianistica», member of the MLA Forum Executive Committee (LLC Medieval and Renaissance Italian), and he currently is the Vice President of the American Boccaccio Association. His monograph, *Dizionario dei sogni nel Medioevo. Il* Somniale Danielis *in manoscritti letterari* was published in 2018 by Olschki in Florence. Cappozzo's forthcoming publications include an edited volume on *Boccaccio and Islam* (Olschki), and he is also editing the volume *Predicting the Past: Dream Interpretation in the Global Middle Ages*, for Brill's series 'Reading Medieval Sources'.

Alessandro Carlucci is a research fellow in Italian linguistics at the University of Bergen and an honorary fellow of the Faculty of Medieval and Modern Languages at the University of Oxford. His articles have appeared in *Language Sciences*, *Zeitschrift für romanische Philologie*, *Modern Language Review*, *Rivista italiana di dialettologia* and several other journals. He is the author of *The Impact of the English Language in Italy* (Lincom, 2018) and *Gramsci and Languages* (Brill, 2013; Haymarket, 2015), the latter of which was awarded the Giuseppe Sormani International Prize for the best monograph on Antonio Gramsci (2017).

Paul Carranza is a senior lecturer in Spanish at Dartmouth College, where he specializes in the areas of late medieval and Renaissance Spanish poetry. He has published articles on Garcilaso de la Vega and Cervantes and contributed articles on Spanish literature to the *Virgil Encyclopedia*. He has also published an essay on the Vergilian sources of *Inferno* 5 in *Dante Studies*. He is currently working on a book project on the role of Roman inscriptions in Renaissance Spanish literature.

Carol Chiodo is the inaugural Librarian for Collections and Digital Scholarship at Harvard University Library. A scholar of medieval and Renaissance Italian literature, she is the editor of the book, *Dante's Volume from Alpha to Omega* (2021). She has also recently contributed essays on the history of Dante's reception in North America (**NEMLA** *Italian Studies*, 2019) and on teaching Dante in the virtual classroom for the MLA 'Approaches to Teaching World Literature' series. In 2020, she was awarded a grant from the Andrew W. Mellon Foundation for her work at Harvard College Library on collections as data. A lifetime member of the Dante Society of America, she chairs the organizing committee for the 700th anniversary celebration of Dante at Harvard in 2021.

Francesco Ciabattoni (PhD, Johns Hopkins University, 2006) is Full Professor and Term Professor of Italian Literature at Georgetown University. He has received prestigious awards including a Mellon and a Fulbright scholarship. Among his publications are *Dante's Journey to Polyphony* (Toronto University Press, 2010), *The Decameron Third Day in Perspective: Volume Three of Lectura Boccaccii* (Toronto University Press, 2014, edited with Pier Massimo Forni), *La citazione è sintomo d'amore* (Carocci, 2016), and *Tradition and the Individual Text: Essays in Memory of Pier Massimo Forni* (*MLN*, 2020, edited with Federica Deigan and Stefano Giannini). Professor Ciabattoni is the founder and director of <https://theitaliansong.com>.

Elizabeth Coggeshall is assistant professor of Italian in the department of Modern Languages and Linguistics at Florida State University. She specializes in the literature and culture of medieval Italy, with a particular focus on Dante. Her research centres on the intersections of literature, ethics, and cultural identity; medievalism and popular culture; and the transmedia reception of Dante's works. Since 2012 she has been the co-director (with Arielle Saiber) of the website *Dante Today: Citings and Sightings of Dante's Works in Contemporary Culture*, a curated, crowd-sourced digital archive that showcases Dante's sustained presence in contemporary culture. She currently serves on the Council of the Dante Society of America.

Federica Coluzzi is Leverhulme Early Career Fellow at the University of Warwick, working on the project *Dante's Transnational Female Public in the Long Nineteenth Century (1789–1921)* and co-editing a volume of essays titled *The English Life of the Vita Nova: Translation and Reception from the Victorians to the Present* for the Routledge Series in Translation Studies. Her first monograph, *Dante Beyond Influence*, is forthcoming with Manchester University Press (2021). Her work has been featured (published and forthcoming) in *Dante Studies*, *Tre Corone*, *Nineteenth-Century Prose*, *Studium* and *Strumenti Critici*, as well as in the *Palgrave Encyclopedia of Victorian Women's Writing*.

Richard Cooper is Emeritus Professor of French at Brasenose College and Master of St Benet's Hall, Oxford. He works on Franco-Italian relations in the Renaissance. Publications include Marguerite de Navarre, *Chrétiens et mondains, poèmes épars* (Champion, 2007); *Histoire et ancienne cronique de Gerard d'Euphrate, duc de Bourgogne* (Garnier, 2012); *Roman Antiquities in Renaissance France* (Ashgate, 2013). Forthcoming publications include Marguerite de Navarre, *Les Tombeaux* (Champion, 2021); and Maurice Scève, *Œuvres Complètes*, vol. IV (Garnier, 2021). He holds a Leverhulme Emeritus Fellowship, and is Secretary of the Oxford Dante Society.

Christian Y. Dupont has served as Burns Librarian and Associate University Librarian for Special Collections at Boston College since 2014, and as secretary and librarian for the Dante Society of America for as many years. He began his career as a rare books and manuscripts curator at the University of Notre Dame, where he also earned a doctorate in theology. Among his publications in various disciplines are studies of the formation of major American Dante collections and associated figures. Forthcoming essays include 'From Poetics to Phenomenology: Consciousness in Dante's *Divine Comedy*' and a history of the illustration of *Inferno* 33.

Karl Philipp Ellerbrock is *Akademischer Rat* at the University of Jena, where he teaches French and Italian literature. He is the editor, with Edoardo Costadura, of *Dante, ein offenes Buch* (Deutscher Kunstverlag, 2015). His study *Die Poetik des Ungesagten in Dantes Commedia* was published by Wilhelm Fink Verlag in 2021.

Simon Gilson is Agnelli-Serena Professor of Italian at the University of Oxford and Fellow of Magdalen College. He is the author of *Dante and Renaissance Florence* (Cambridge University Press, 2005) and *Reading Dante in Renaissance Italy: Florence, Venice and the 'Divine Poet* (Cambridge University Press, 2018). With Dario Brancato he is currently working on a multi-volume critical edition of selected philosophical translations and commentaries by Benedetto Varchi.

Peter Hainsworth is an Emeritus Fellow of Lady Margaret Hall, Oxford. After lectureships at Hull and Kent Universities, he taught at Oxford until retiring in 2003. As well as *Petrarch the Poet* (Routledge, 1986), he has written widely on other Italian authors, medieval and modern. He co-edited with David Robey *The Oxford Companion to Italian Literature* (Oxford University Press, 2002) and co-authored with him a *Very Short Introduction to Italian Literature* (Oxford University Press, 2012) and a *Very Short Introduction to Dante* (Oxford University Press, 2012). He has also published two volumes of translations: *The Essential Petrarch* (Hackett, 2012) and *Tales from the Decameron* (Penguin, 2015).

Nick Havely (co-editor) is Emeritus Professor of English and Related Literature at the University of York and is an Honorary Member of the Dante Society of America. His recent publications include *Dante* (Blackwell Guides to Literature, 2007), *Chaucer: 'The House of Fame'* (PIMS/Durham Medieval Texts, 2013) and *Dante's British Public: Readers and Texts, from the Fourteenth Century to the Present* (Oxford University Press, 2014, repr. 2017). With Bernard O'Donoghue he has co-edited a translation of the *Purgatorio* by sixteen contemporary poets (Arc Publications, 2021), and he is currently working on a book about travellers in the Tuscan Apennines.

Jonathan Katz (co-editor) teaches Latin, Greek and Sanskrit languages and literatures at the University of Oxford, where he is a Fellow of St Anne's College and the University's Public Orator. He also has research interests in musicology and ancient philosophy, and has published many translations from nineteenth- and twentieth-century German literature.

Matthew Kempshall is the Cliff Davies Fellow and Clarendon Associate Professor in History at Wadham College, University of Oxford. He is the author of *The Common Good in Late Medieval Political Thought* (Oxford University Press, 1999), and *Rhetoric and the Writing of History 400–1500* (Manchester University Press, 2011).

Christopher Kleinhenz is Carol Mason Kirk Professor Emeritus of Italian at the University of Wisconsin-Madison. He served as President of the American Association of Teachers of Italian and the American Boccaccio Association and as Editor of *Dante Studies* (1988–2002). He is currently a Director of the *Rivista internazionale di ricerche dantesche*. Recent publications include *Dante intertestuale e interdisciplinare: saggi sulla 'Commedia'* (Aracne, 2015), *The 'Decameron': A Critical Lexicon* (Arizona CMRS, 2019), and *Approaches to Teaching Dante's 'Divine Comedy'* (MLA, 2020). He was awarded the *Fiorino d'oro* by the Società Dantesca Italiana (2008) and is a Fellow of the Medieval Academy of America (2009).

Cornelia Klettke, Professor at the Universities of Rostock, Cologne and Potsdam, has published studies of French, Italian, Spanish and Portuguese literature from Dante to the present day and arranged exhibitions on Dante and Botticelli in collaboration with the Kupferstichkabinett Preußischer Kulturbesitz Berlin. Forthcoming are *Dante e Botticelli* (Carte Ridenti — Dante visualizzato, vol. 4, Cesati); Akten der Jahrestagung der Deutschen Dante-Gesellschaft in Potsdam 'Die vier Elemente und ihre Kodierung in der *Commedia*' (*Deutsches Dante-Jahrbuch*); *La Poétique du simulacre et les grands modèles* (Classiques Garnier); editor of the commented German complete edition of the *Zibaldone* by Leopardi (Matthes & Seitz).

Akash Kumar is a Visiting Assistant Professor of Italian at Indiana University, Bloomington. His research focuses on issues of translation, science, and intercultural mingling in medieval Italian literature, especially Dante. As an Associate Editor of Digital Dante, he is also active in the field of Digital Humanities. Recent work includes collaborating with Richard Lansing on *The Complete Poetry of Giacomo da Lentini* (University of Toronto Press, 2018) and the essay "Walls of Inclusivity: Dante's *Divine Comedy* and World Literature' (2019), <https://doi.org/10.1002/9781118635193.ctwl0057>.

Matthew Leigh is Professor of Classical Languages and Literature in the University of Oxford and a Fellow of St Anne's College. He has written widely on topics in Latin literature. His forays into Italian literature include essays on Petrarch and Goldoni and a translation of three eighteenth-century comedies on the craze for Freemasonry.

Dennis Looney has, since 2014, served as Director of Programs and Director of the Association of Departments of Foreign Languages at the Modern Language Association. From 1986 to 2013, he taught Italian at the University of Pittsburgh, with secondary appointments in classics and philosophy. Publications include *Compromising the Classics: Romance Epic Narrative in the Italian Renaissance* (1996), which received the MLA's Marraro/Scaglione Award in Italian Studies, honorable mention, and *Freedom Readers: The African American Reception of Dante Alighieri and* *the* Divine Comedy (2011), which received the AAIS Book Prize. He co-edited and co-translated *Ariosto's Latin Poetry* (2018) with Mark Possanza.

Franziska Meier is Professor of French and Italian Literature at the Georgia-Augusta-University in Göttingen. Her research focuses on French post-revolutionary autobiographical writing in the first half of the nineteenth century as well as on Dante and Dante reception. Her book *Dantes Besuch in der Hölle: Dantes Göttliche Komödie. Biographie eines unwahrscheinlichen Erfolgs* is forthcoming (C. H. Beck, 2021).

Pedro Memelsdorff is a performer and musicologist who in 1987 founded Mala Punica, an ensemble specializing in late-medieval polyphony and recipient of numerous awards. A former fellow of Villa I Tatti, a Bloch lecturer at Berkeley, and a Blodgett Distinguished Artist at Harvard, he is now an Affiliate Researcher at the University of Tours and a member of the college of the Swiss Graduate School in Italian Civilization. A guest lecturer at Oxford and Pisa, he authored a monograph and twenty essays on late-medieval music, co-directs the Early-Music Master programmes at ESMUC-Barcelona and directs the Early Music Seminars at the Fondazione Cini-Venice. He also served as the Director of the Schola Cantorum in Basel.

Alfred Noe retired recently as Professor in the Department of Romance Languages at the University of Vienna. He obtained his habilitation in Romance literatures in 1988 and in comparative literature in 1996. His main research interests are the works of Johann Rist, the Italian libretto in the seventeenth and eighteenth centuries, and the works of the Italian poets laureate at the imperial court in Austria. He is a corresponding member of the Accademia Galileiana in Padua and a member of the scientific advisory board of the *Giornale storico della letteratura italiana*. He was awarded the Premio Flaiano di Italianistica in 2012.

Kristina M. Olson (PhD, Columbia University, 2006) is an Associate Professor of Italian in the Department of Modern and Classical Languages at George Mason University. She is the author of *Courtesy Lost: Dante, Boccaccio and the Literature of History* (University of Toronto Press, 2014) and several articles on Dante, Boccaccio and Petrarch. She has co-edited three volumes: *Open City: Seven Writers in Postwar Rome* (Steerforth Press, 1997); *Boccaccio 1313–2013* (Longo Editore, 2015); and *Approaches to Teaching Dante's* Divine Comedy (second edition) with the Modern Language Association (2020). She is the President of the American Boccaccio Association (2020–23).

Andrea Renker is a research assistant at the University of Konstanz. She studied Latin and French philology in Hamburg and Aix-en-Provence. Her fields of research are Dante studies, European Enlightenment discourses and classical reception. Her recent publications include *Streit um Vergil: Eine poetologische Lektüre der Eklogen Giovanni del Virgilios und Dante Alighieris* (Franz Steiner, 2020). She is the editor of *Lettere Aperte* 5: 'Ciao, Gideon! Gideon Bachmann e la sua opera: riletture critiche e ricordi' (2018).

David Robey is an Emeritus Fellow of Wolfson College, Oxford, and Emeritus Professor of Italian at Reading University. He was also Professor of Italian at Manchester University. He is the author of a computer-based study of the language and metre of the *Divine Comedy* (*Sound and Structure in the 'Divine Comedy'* (Oxford University Press, 2000)), and, with Peter Hainsworth, joint editor of *The Oxford Companion to Italian Literature* (OUP, 2002) and joint author of *Italian Literature: A Very Short Introduction* (OUP, 2012) and *Dante: A Very Short Introduction* (OUP, 2015).

Karlheinz Stierle is Professor Emeritus of Romance Philology and Theory of Literature at Constance University. Member of the Heidelberger Akademie der Wissenschaften, Membro Straniero dell'Academia Nazionale dei Lincei, and Correspondant de l'Académie des Sciences Morales et Politiques. Currently Honorarprofessor at the Universität des Saarlands, Saarbrücken, Commendatore nell'ordine del merito della Repubblica Italiana and Commandeur dans l'Ordre des Palmes Académiques. He recently published *Dante Alighieri: Dichter im Exil, Dichter der Welt* (C. H. Beck, 2014) and *Montaigne und die Moralisten: Klassische Moralistik — Moralistische Klassik* (Wilhelm Fink, 2016). Forthcoming is his *Paris denken — Penser Paris* (Suhrkamp, 2021).

Helen Swift is Associate Professor of Medieval French and Tutorial Fellow of St Hilda's College, Oxford. Having focused for several years on the fifteenth-century *querelle des femmes* (including *Gender, Writing and Performance: Men Defending Women in Late Medieval France* (Oxford University Press, 2008)), she now explores more broadly questions of narrative voice and identity, from Guillaume de Machaut to Jean Bouchet. *Representing the Dead: Epitaph Fictions in Late-Medieval France* (D. S. Brewer, 2016; runner-up, Society for French Studies R. Gapper Book Prize) examined challenges to the construction of identity in the context of voices and bodies speaking from beyond the grave.

Kathleen Verduin (BA Hope College, MA The George Washington University, PhD Indiana University) is a professor of English at Hope College in Holland, Michigan. She studies American literature and modern fiction, and she has published ten essays on the modern reception of Dante. She is currently at work on a project on nineteenth-century American responses to the *Vita Nuova*. From 1982 to 1998 she served as Associate Editor of the series 'Studies in Medievalism'.

THREE DANTE SOCIETIES: HISTORICAL NOTES

1. *The Deutsche Dante-Gesellschaft*

Andrea Renker

At some point in the post-war Germany of the late 1940s, two strangers met on a train and quickly discovered their unusual shared passion for Dante Alighieri. One of these was Walter Goetz, who between 1927 and 1949 was President of the Weimar-based Deutsche Dante-Gesellschaft (DDG). The other was Friedrich Schlüter, a regular participant member of a group of Dante enthusiasts in Krefeld, a small town close to the Belgian border. When Goetz lamented the dire state of the DDG in the repressive atmosphere of the Soviet occupation zone, Schlüter's generous and open-minded response was a pragmatic offer to host future gatherings of the society in Krefeld. It was this encounter that enabled the DDG, which was under increasing political pressure at its then home in Weimar, to find a second home, and hold its meetings, in Krefeld. It was not until 2016 that the DDG returned to its official seat (having been transferred during German partition to Munich) in Weimar. At the same time the Krefeld connection came to an end.[1]

Far from being of mere anecdotal interest, this episode from the rather turbulent history of the DDG exemplifies how the society has always been marked by strong individual engagement as well as historical contingencies. Founded in 1865 by the jurist and Dante scholar Karl Witte, and under the patronage of King John of Saxony (himself a distinguished translator of the *Commedia*), the world's oldest Dante Society was intended to be a German platform of international standing for Dante studies, combining the various activities of local groups of Dante scholars, readers and translators. The DDG's wide and diverse membership now ranges from academic scholars to interested amateurs, and finds in Dante a key to Italian language and culture, which at least since the publication of Goethe's *Italian Journey* has been a constant element of German *Sehnsucht* ('longing').

Despite its many vicissitudes, including two World Wars and the post-war Division of Germany, the DDG can look back on an almost continuous history. The initial enthusiasm suffered a setback with Witte's death in 1883, and there followed a thirty-year hiatus in the society's activities. It was the musicologist and composer Hugo Daffner who revived the society in 1914 and acted as its president until 1927. Resisting the ideology of the Third Reich by remaining politically neutral, the DDG became the target of the *Klassenkampf* [class struggle] during the period of German division; from a Marxist point of view the society was criticized for pursuing *bürgerliche Literaturwissenschaft* [bourgeois literary studies]. After cooperation between the citizens of East and West was officially prohibited in 1968, these hostile conditions nearly led to the disintegration of the DGG into two separate societies (a fate the German Shakespeare-Gesellschaft was unable to escape). Once again it was due to individual commitment, especially that of Hans Rheinfelder in the West (President of the DDG between 1949 and 1971) and Otto Riedel in the East (Vice-President between 1962 and 1983), that the DDG prevailed as a single coherent entity. But it was only after the fall of the Berlin Wall in 1989 that a true reunification of the western DDG with those Dante friends and scholars who remained in the East became conceivable.

Under the succeeding presidents August Buck (1972–93), Bernhard König (1993–2005), Winfried Wehle (2006–13) and Rainer Stillers (since 2013), routine activities long in abeyance, and long missed, were re-established, and nowadays annual conferences, organized in cooperation with different universities and taking place in different locations all over Germany, serve as opportunities for cooperation and exchanges between members and internationally renowned researchers. The society's contributions are regularly collected in its annual *Deutsches Dante-Jahrbuch*, which contains reviews of recent publications on Dante and a current bibliography. Another annual publication, the newsletter *Il Novo Giorno*, provides information on activities concerning Dante and his works.

Combining high scholarly standards with the enthusiasm of individual members, 155 years after its foundation the DDG continues to pursue its goal of fostering and spreading critical understanding and appreciation of Dante, or, as the first statutes from 1865 read, 'die Liebe zu demselben' ('the love of the same').

2. The Dante Society of America

Christian Y. Dupont

Though founded sixteen years after the Deutsche Dante-Gesellschaft, the Dante Society that was established in Cambridge, Massachusetts, in 1881, with America's most famous poet as its first president, may lay claim to being the oldest continually active society with a mission to 'encourage the study and appreciation of the time, life, works, and cultural legacy of Dante Alighieri', according to its present formulation.

The inspiration for the Society is often traced, not unjustly, to the fabled 'Dante Club', a circle of friends whom Henry Wadsworth Longfellow regulary invited to his home on Wednesday evenings between 1865 and 1867 to help him revise his translation of the *Commedia* — the first to be completed by an American. Most notable among them were James Russell Lowell and Charles Eliot Norton, who continued, in turn, the tradition of teaching Dante at Harvard University that Longfellow, and before him, George Ticknor, had inaugurated.

A suggestion that Norton made to his students in 1880 regarding 'the possible service which a club for the promotion of Dante studies might render' led to its formation the following year with the adoption of by-laws and the election of Longfellow as president, more for honour than duty. Longfellow died before the second annual meeting of the society, held in May 1882, observing the supposed month of Dante's birth. Lowell succeeded him as president, but Norton was the main driver and organizer, eventually serving as president after Lowell's death until his own. Of the forty-nine members listed in the first annual report, many had read Dante with Norton at Harvard or in social groups. Nearly half lived outside Massachusetts; six were women.

A primary purpose of the society from the beginning was the 'purchase of books of Dantesque interest' for Harvard College Library'. Harvard librarian William Coolidge Lane was appointed the Society's librarian in 1888. In 1890, he published a catalogue of *The Dante Collections in the Harvard College and Boston Public Libraries*, which included some 1,200 entries. He also compiled an American Dante bibliography for publication in the Society's annual reports, but discontinued the practice in 1891, when the newly formed Società Dantesca Italiana launched its bibliography. It was revived in 1953, and since 2016, the societies have partnered to maintain the online *Bibliografia Dantesca Internazionale*.

Another original purpose of the Society has been to contribute to Dante scholarship. By the end of the nineteenth century, the Society had published a series of concordances and indexes to Dante's works that were acclaimed for their usefulness and purchased by scholars in Europe. Beginning in 1886, members funded an undergraduate essay prize, at first for Harvard students but soon opened to students from other American universities. Some of the best were published as 'accompanying papers' to the Society's annual reports alongside contributions by

Fig. p.1. Portrait of Henry Wadsworth Longfellow in 1862, by George Peter Alexander Healy, now in the Bowdoin College Museum of Art

prominent scholars, including the Englishmen Paget Toynbee and Edward Moore, who had been named one of the Society's first honorary members in 1889.

Annual reports and accompanying papers were published irregularly in clusters from the mid-1920s to the mid-1930s, and not at all between 1936 and 1950. The Society continued to meet annually, however, except in 1939, and published separately during those years three essays and a book.

When Ernest Hatch Wilkins retired from the presidency of Oberlin College and returned to the Boston area in the late 1940s, he undertook to reinvigorate the Society by publishing the backlog of annual reports, drumming up library subscriptions and supporting its incorporation, in 1954, as the Dante Society of America, whereupon he was elected president.

The Society's efforts to commemorate the 600th anniversary of Dante's death in 1921 had been meagre, but it engaged in many well-publicized activities around the 700th anniversary of his birth in 1965, including the issuance of a commemorative postage stamp, the publication of an updated concordance to the *Commedia*, the coordination of symposia and exhibits, and the organization of a speakers' bureau. The scope of the Dante Prize was enlarged to include Canadian students, and a graduate student essay prize was established in honour of former president Charles Hall Grandgent. In addition, the Society began to hold a second yearly meeting in conjunction with the annual meeting of the Modern Language Association. Today, the Society organizes panel sessions on Dante at the annual meetings of the MLA, the Renaissance Society of America, and International Congress of Medieval Studies.

Still more consequential for the Society's integration with broader American academic life was the initiative to expand its annual report and accompanying papers into a full-fledged annual journal. Under the editorship of Anthony L. Pellegrini, *Dante Studies* was published by the State University of New York Press beginning in 1966. In 1997, it moved to Fordham University Press, and then to Johns Hopkins University Press in 2014.

Also in 2014, under the leadership of president Nancy J. Vickers, the Society's bylaws and mission were updated to accentuate its outreach to non-academic audiences, who have always represented a segment of its overall membership, which has ranged from around 100 during the first part of the twentieth century to a peak of approximately 450 by its end, and around 425 since.

Succeeding Vickers, Albert R. Ascoli for the first time invited universities outside Massachusetts, including Canadian institutions, to host the Society's annual meetings and to organize a symposium co-sponsored by the Society. He also led a fundraising campaign to endow an annual prize named in honour of Robert M. Durling to recognize excellence in teaching Dante at the secondary level. An online forum for publishing short commentaries and notes on Dante's works inaugurated by former president Robert Hollander in 1995, the *Electronic Bulletin of the Dante Society of America* was rebranded in 2016 as *Dante Notes* and expanded to include sections on pedagogy and 'student enounters' — essays contributed by secondary students and readers who have encountered his texts in non-traditional academic contexts.

In the preparation for the 700th anniversary of Dante's death in 2021, the Dante Speakers Bureau has been revived, and under the leadership of its nineteenth president, Alison Cornish, the Society is planning — the after-effects of the pandemic allowing — to return to its birthplace in Cambridge to hold a conference in partnership with Harvard University that will explore the lively and distinct reception of Dante in America, and indeed the Americas, reflecting its reinvigorated and expanded mission.

Bibliography

DUPONT, CHRISTIAN Y., 'Reading and Collecting Dante in America: Harvard College Library and the Dante Society', *Harvard Library Bulletin*, 22.1 (2011), 1–57, <https://nrs.harvard.edu/urn-3:FHCL.HOUGH:33026942>.

GIFFORD, GEORGE H., 'A History of the Dante Society', *Annual Reports of the Dante Society, with Accompanying Papers*, 74 (1956), 3–27, <http://www.jstor.org/stable/40165964>.

DE VITO, ANTHONY J., 'The First Hundred Years of the Dante Society', *Dante Studies, with the Annual Report of the Dante Society*, 100 (1982), 99–132, <http://www.jstor.org/stable/40166321>.

3. The Oxford Dante Society: Early Years (1876–1921)

Federica Coluzzi

The material memory of the Oxford Dante Society (ODS) survives in the dark and sinuous calligraphy of its founder and President, Rev. Edward Moore Principal of St. Edmund Hall, and the minute, delicate script of its first honorary secretary, Paget Toynbee. Preserved at the Taylorian Institution Library, their manuscripts record the first forty years in the life of the ODS as the first of its kind to be instituted on British soil, and the driving force of the academic formation, promotion and institutionalization of Dante studies in Britain at the turn of the twentieth century.

The ODS was formally established in the autumn of 1876, a few months after the foundation of the Barlow lectureship on the *Divina Commedia* at University College London. Although its activities were separated from 'the normal studies of the University', the founding members were all part of the Oxonian academic body, with the inclusion of a good number of members of the Anglican clergy.[2]

The foundational objective was that of 'stimulat[ing] and forward[ing] the study of the *Divina Commedia*' as well as 'encourag[ing] mutual inquiry as to critical, historical, and other points relating to [Dante's] works' and 'his age'.[3] As a knowledge-making institution, the ODS sought to bring order and discipline, structure and method to amateur endeavours through rigid criteria of organization, participation and registration of its scholarly activities. Unlike its sister institutions — the London and the Manchester Dante Societies, established in 1904 and 1906 — the ODS remained exclusive in terms of admission, counting a maximum of fifteen ordinary members joined by few invited visitors (A. J. Butler and William Michael Rossetti), and honorary members, including William W. Vernon, William Gladstone and John Ruskin, along with American *dantisti* Charles Eliot Norton and James Russell Lowell, establishing through them a transatlantic network bridging the nascent American and British traditions of studies.

Held once a term, the meetings opened with the members' reading of a paper or essay followed by a plenary commentary of two or three passages from Dante's works, one of which at least had to be supplied by the host. The evening closed with the exchange of news about recent Dantean publications, research trips and discoveries, and communications to the ODS. On occasions, members participated in collection-encounters: on 25 May 1880, Moore exhibited two fifteenth-century MSS acquired in Rome, of the *Commedia* (*c.* 1400) and of the *Convivio* (1465). The lists of papers presented and passages read show the far-reaching variety and sophistication of topics discussed, extending beyond the *Commedia* to encompass *Convivio*, *Epistolae* and *Vita Nuova* and *De Vulgari Eloquentia*, *Quaestio de Aqua et Terra*, and *Eclogae*. These tackled issues of transmission, editing and emendation of the manuscripts; the ancient and modern commentary tradition; biographical and historical discussions of the poetic, theological or political systems; and questions

Fig. p.2. Portrait of the Rev. Edward Moore (artist unknown): by kind permission of the Principal and Fellows of St Edmund Hall

of translation and reception, influence and intertextuality. The interleaved abstracts testify to the 'perpetual refinement of approaches and methods, of structures and lexicon' of their Dantean scholarship.[4]

From the semi-private space of the ODS, the papers reached the (national and international) public sphere and wider dissemination on the pages of periodicals and specialized journals such as the *Athenaeum*, the *Academy* and the *Modern Language Review*. Often the discussions led to larger scholarly endeavours like Henry F. Tozer's *English Commentary to Dante's* Divina Commedia (1901), and Charles L. Shadwell's translations *Purgatory* (1892–99), *Paradise* (1915) and the edition of the *Quaestio de Aqua et Terra* (1909). The most prolific member of the Society, however, was Paget J. Toynbee, who first joined as an occasional visitor, then became ordinary member in 1895, and was ultimately elected Honorary Secretary in 1916.[5]

The occasion for a collaborative project presented itself on 22 November 1892, the night in which 'Mr. Shadwell explained to the Society the intention of the Clarendon Press to issue the complete works of Dante in one volume'.[6] Moore presided over the project, selecting collaborators and prescribing textual criticism as the only methodological approach for dealing scientifically with the complicated problems presented by the text of Dante's works. Ideologically, the *Oxford Dante* sought to surpass Giovanni Scartazzini's *Enciclopedia Dantesca* (1896), harshly criticized for its cumbersome commentary, and for its arbitrary selection and organization of references. The new concise edition prioritized Dante's texts, philologically reconstructed and systematically presented as a whole, and 'did not admit of an *apparatus criticus*, or of notes, in which attention could be drawn to corrections'.[7] Along with Toynbee's *Index of Proper Names and Notable Matters*, the volume included Witte's edition of *De Monarchia* (1874) and Pio Rajna's edition of *Vita Nuova* (1876). The result was a volume of 'immense convenience' which soon became 'the standard of reference, not only in [Britain], but also throughout the Continent, and in America'.[8] The strict principles of collation, edition and emendation turned Dante's magnum opus into a manageable and intelligible object designed as a reference book for a broader audience of students and amateurs.

The volume was issued in 1894, presented in two different formats: an ordinary paper edition at the cost of six shillings and a compact eight-shilling volume offering a veritable 'edizione tascabile' of what had previously been unobtainable in less than four volumes. Its publication marked a watershed moment in the history of Dante reception in Britain. The second edition in 1,000 copies appeared in 1897. In 1904, the third edition with a print-run of 3,000 copies brought the volume 'up to the level of contemporary scholarship', including Rajna's edition of the *De Vulgari Eloquentia* ('the first-fruits of the *Società Dantesca Italiana*'), Friederich Beck's critical edition of the *Vita Nuova*, and the *Eclogae* edited by Philip H. Wicksteed and Edmund Gardner.[9] In 1909, the Ashendene Press produced a monumental large folio edition printed in 111 numbered copies and including eight decorative wood-carved plates: a work soon valued as one of the three greatest fine-press books, alongside the Doves Bible and the Kelmscott Chaucer. The 1924 fourth edition curated by Toynbee included also Michele Barbi's revision of the *Vita Nuova* and Professor Santi's notes on the *Canzoniere*.

The true 'offspring of the Oxford Dante Society', the *Oxford Dante* stood as the enduring evidence of the crucial role that the Society performed in fostering the specialization and academization of Dante Studies in Britain between the mid-1870s and the early twentieth century. Setting an example of scholarly professionalism and scientific rigour, the ODS acted as a catalyst for the institution of the Taylorian Dante Lectures at Oxford, the creation of Dante collections and the production of a wide-ranging body of publications for specialized students and researchers in this burgeoning field.[10]

The Last Hundred Years (1921–2020)

Richard Cooper

When in 1921 the 45-year-old Oxford Dante Society marked both its 134th meeting and the Sixth Centenary of the Poet's death by sending greetings to its younger fellow society, the Società Dantesca Italiana, it remained a small and exclusive dining club of a maximum of twelve members, meeting three times a year to hear and discuss papers. Its members included Heads of Oxford Colleges and Divines such as the Dean of Winchester or the Bishops of Oxford and Ripon, but also the Poet Laureate, Robert Bridges. The meetings were always held in Oxford, with the exception of an outing to Winchester in 1923, hosted by the Dean. It continued to bathe in the glory of the *Oxford Dante*, of which a new edition was published in 1924, and celebrated its Jubilee in 1926, soon followed by the resignation in 1928 of its Secretary, Paget Toynbee, whose legacy to the Bodleian and to Balliol of 4,000 volumes was to enrich resources for Dantean scholarship. The pattern of meetings was also enhanced by the election of Italian members like Cesare Foligno, who introduced live readings from the *Commedia*, which continue today. Membership was never narrowly limited to Italianists, however, as witness the election of the Regius Professor of Hebrew, G. A. Cooke (1927), of the future Nobel Prize in Chemistry, Sir Cyril Hinshelwood (1939), of C. S. Lewis (1937), of Charles Williams (1944), and of J. R. R. Tolkien (1945), three Inklings. Lewis gave papers on Dante's use of Simile, on Imagery in *Paradiso* and on Statius and Dante, before resigning in 1957 when resident in Cambridge. He had proposed the name of Tolkien, who remained a member until 1955, having given a paper on *Lusinghe*.

The Society had long numbered Italians among members and guests, including a founder member, Vitale de Tivoli, who had taught Italian to Lewis Carroll and was instrumental in the Society acquiring a deathmask of the poet; Italian links were pursued by the election of successive Serena Professors of Italian, and by the invitation to the Italian ambassador, Duke Tommaso Gallarati-Scotti, who gave a paper in 1948 on the Pietra poems. The Society participated in the Seventh Centenary celebrations of the poet's birth by inviting to Oxford three major Dante scholars: first Professor Bruno Nardi, who received an honorary doctorate for his eightieth birthday in 1964; then Professor Natalino Sapegno, who attended a meeting in February 1965; then the President of the Società Dantesca Italiana, Professor Gianfranco Contini, who gave a lecture on *Il Fiore* before attending an extraordinary meeting of the Society on the eve of his honorary doctorate in June 1965. The Secretary, Colin Hardie, represented the Society at the 1965 celebrations in Florence, Verona and Ravenna and at the Dante-Woche in Munich of the Deutsche Dante-Gesellschaft. That same year the Society published a volume of seven *Centenary Essays on Dante*, the royalties from which were then sent to help salvage documents damaged in the terrible floods in Florence of November 1966.

In 1951 Tolkien had supported increasing the limited membership, but was defeated, and it was not raised to fifteen until 1966, soon after which women members were elected, and the Society began to invite scholars from other universities to join members in giving papers. The format of meetings was changed, so that instead of the paper being given after dinner by candlelight, and the meetings finishing near midnight, the Society continues to gather before dinner to hear and discuss the paper.

In order to celebrate its own centenary, the Society gave a series of lectures in 1976–77, which were then published as the successful volume, *The World of Dante* (1980). The Secretary, Cecil Grayson, was invited to Florence in November 1988 to represent Oxford at the centenary of the Società Dantesca Italiana. Close Italian links were pursued with the election as Honorary Member in 1990 of President Francesco Cossiga, and then of the Italian Ambassador, Luigi Amaduzzi, who entertained the Society at the Italian Embassy.

Members of the Society collaborated in publishing lecture series: firstly *Dante and Governance* (1997), and then a collection of the Paget Toynbee Lectures given in Oxford (1995–2003), *Dante in Oxford* (2017); members also reached a broader public with David Robey and Peter Hainsworth's *Dante: A Very Short Introduction* (2015), and with Nick Havely's *Dante's British Public* (2014). In anticipation of the forthcoming Seventh Centenary in 2021, the Society is planning a major celebration in Oxford with exhibitions at the Ashmolean and the Bodleian, a Dante concert at the Holywell Music Room, public lectures, and the present volume of essays on *Dante Beyond Borders*. As it approaches its 430th meeting, the Oxford Dante Society is delighted to join forces with its historic partners in Germany and the United States to ONORARE IL SOMMO POETA.

Notes

1. On this and other aspects of the society's history, see the monograph by Frank-Rutger Hausmann: *Die Deutsche Dante-Gesellschaft im geteilten Deutschland* (Stuttgart: Hauswedell, 2012).
2. See John Lindon, 'Gli apporti del metodo di Edward Moore nei primi decenni della Società Dantesca Italiana, in *La Società Dantesca Italiana, 1888–1898: Convegno Internazionale, Firenze 24–26 Novembre 1988* (Milan and Naples: Ricciardi, 1995), pp. 37–53.
3. *Records of the Oxford Dante Society*, 24 November 1876. University of Oxford, Taylorian Institution Library, Papers relating to the Oxford Dante Society, vol. 1, GB 486 MSS. Octavo It. 18–20.
4. Harrison R. Sleeves, *Learned Societies and English Literary Scholarship in Great Britain and the United States* (New York: Columbia University Press, 1913), p. xiii.

5. Among Toynbee's major contributions, we find: *A Dictionary of Proper Names and Notable Matters in the Works of Dante* (Oxford: Clarendon Press, 1898), *Dante Studies and Researches* (London: Methuen,1902), *Dante in English Literature from Chaucer to Cary (1380–1844)*, 2 vols (London: Methuen, 1909), as well as studies and translations of Dante's works, such as *Dante Alighieri: His Life and Works* (London: Methuen, 1900) to his edition of Henry F. Cary's *A Vision*, 3 vols (London: Methuen, 1900). After his death, Toynbee bestowed his Dante collection consisting of books and rare editions, papers and press cuttings to the library of Balliol College as well as to the Bodleian Libraries. For further information, see Diego Zancani, 'Una biblioteca di cent'anni fa: la "Dante Collection" di Paget Toynbee (1855–1932)', *Bibliofilia*, 100 (1998), 495–512.
6. *Records*, p. 20.
7. Paget Toynbee, 'The Oxford Dante', *Annual Reports of the Dante Society*, 42–44 (1926), 19–44 (p. 27).
8. Ibid., p. 25.
9. Ibid., p. 27.
10. On the occasion of the 1921 Centenary, Toynbee and other members of the Society contributed chapters to *Dante: Essays in Commemoration 1321–1921* (London: University of London Press, 1921). For more recent publications by members of the Society, see the first paragraph of the Introduction to this volume.

INTRODUCTION

Dante Beyond Borders is an international collaborative project to mark the 700th anniversary of the poet's death. It originated with and is edited by members of the Oxford Dante Society, which was founded in 1876 and with the intention 'to forward the study of the *Divina Commedia* and other works of Dante and his age'. During the later twentieth century that purpose was partly fulfilled through the publication of collections of essays by members. In 1965 *Centenary Essays on Dante* appeared, followed in 1980 by *The World of Dante* and in 1997 by *Dante and Governance*.[1]

Now, in the third decade of the twenty-first century, it seems appropriate to extend the range of this enterprise in several ways. The collection that follows draws upon both the diverse strengths of the present Oxford Dante Society membership and those of the wider world of Dante scholarship. For this new centenary volume we have invited contributions from members of other historic Dante Societies: in America (founded in 1881) and in Germany (founded in 1865).

The international response to the call for contributions from members of these Dante Societies has been impressive, yielding a collection of twenty-seven essays. It has enabled us to present a variety of interdisciplinary and cross-cultural approaches to the *Commedia* and other works. Such approaches feature innovative work not only by established Dante scholars but also by a number of those at a relatively early stage in their academic careers; indeed, around a third of the contributions represent the work of a new generation of researchers.

Those contributions are organized in a way that provides overall thematic coherence while throughout aiming to encourage thinking beyond chronological, disciplinary and territorial borders. Some of the chapters in the first part of the collection (sections I–II) will thus focus upon specific traditions and disciplines (classical, philosophical, political) and on certain significant media (the visual arts, music, drama) with which Dante engaged. Other chapters in these initial two sections look beyond the poet's time and consider how his work has featured in, for example, later visual art, music and performance. The reader will thus at an early stage in the collection be invited to think about contexts *alongside* reception — engaging not only with 'Dante *and*' but also with 'Dante *in*' such traditions. These two sections also serve to prepare for the more sustained emphasis on reception in the later part of the volume (sections III–IV), where the chapters address the vast variety of cultures, genres and media within and beyond Europe which received Dante's work: from Spain, France and Germany to North America and the Indian sub-continent; and from medieval multilingualism and early modern humanism to present-day politics, graphics and databases.

First in the collection is a section focusing broadly on the contexts of 'Culture and Politics'. It begins with an account by Jonathan Katz and Matthew Leigh of Dante's Latin epistolary exchange with his friend Giovanni del Vergilio, Professor at the University of Bologna, arguing that Dante's '2nd' and '4th' Eclogues should be read not only in the context of his wider discourse on language but also as a significant final interaction with Latin tradition and with Vergil in particular. Other aspects of the medieval context are then explored by Cornelia Klettke through a discussion of theological and scientific traditions behind the last canto of the *Paradiso*, in 'Measuring the Divine by Geometry and Feeling', thus engaging with 'vision' as both eyesight and *raptus*, as well as with the influence of medieval mathematics, meteorology and technology. The other two chapters in this section address political issues in Dante's time and their relevance to his work. In 'Speaking to the Citizen' Johannes Bartuschat analyses some examples of didactic texts (Brunetto Latini, Bono Giamboni) and of political poetry from the second half of the thirteenth century in order to illustrate these new forms of literary communication and to show how such Tuscan texts are important for Dante as examples of the relationship between poetry and philosophy, the choice of the vernacular, the role of literature as tool of the divulgation of knowledge and as a kind of teaching intrinsically tied to the life in the city. In 'Dante's Lamentations', Matthew Kempshall then analyses the connection between exile and political prophecy though Dante's understanding of the Book of Lamentations, arguing that because of the way in which this scriptural text was applied, at one and the same time, to the suffering of an individual soul, to ecclesiastical corruption, and to the vicissitudes of politics, the poet was able to present his own revelation of theodicy and providential justice.

The second group of chapters in this volume — on the 'Visual and Performing Arts' — combines attention to both context and reception by illustrating how these arts related to and have in turn responded to Dante's work. In 'Transitional Narrative Strategies and the Art of Usury in Dante's *Commedia*' Christopher Kleinhenz focuses on the family crests on the money bags hanging around the necks of Dante's usurers, examining the historical nature of heraldic emblems and the nature and depiction of usury in medieval art, along with the poet's purpose in using these artistic images at this particular place in the poem, namely to underline the role of deceptive appearances and to explore the web of connections that join usury to the sins of fraud. Turning to Dante's presence in contemporary visual art, Gervase Rosser's chapter engages critically with the three sets of prints made in response to the *Divine Comedy* by the living Scottish artist Geoff MacEwan — *The Inferno* (1992), *The Purgatorio* (2010) and *Paradise* (2012) — showing how the balance between form and freedom, structure and flow which characterizes all of the images is a faithful response to the poem, and how, by the way in which they require the viewer's engagement and responsible attention, they lend fresh energy to the political and social imperatives of Dante's vision.

Along with visual art, music is also in various ways reflected and appreciated in the *Commedia*, as well as playing a significant part in the poem's later reception. Literary and musical echoes of hymns and psalms punctuate the poem itself. Francesco Ciabattoni's chapter illustrates the tradition of ascribing corrective and healing function to psalms and shows how in the *Purgatorio* the musical exercise to which the penitents are subjected functions as spiritual and choral refinement. Connections between Dante's work and the music of the *duecento* and *trecento* have long puzzled commentators, and Pedro Memelsdorff's chapter on Cavalcanti and *Paradiso* in a ballata by Francesco Landini reconsiders a group of late fourteenth-century musical compositions by Landini, Paolo da Firenze and Lorenzo Masini as related to each other, to Dante's *Paradiso* and to Gherardi da Prato's *Paradiso degli Alberti*.

Through translation and other forms of diffusion Dante has become one of the most transnational of poets, and the chapters in the third part of this volume address a wide span of reception in 'Italy and Beyond', from the *trecento* to the nineteenth century. Nick Havely's chapter on 'Voicing the *Commedia*' considers the poem's relationships to a long tradition of performing the text and investigates features of its oral/aural presence in private and public, from the medieval and early modern periods to the twenty-first century, in and beyond Italy. Also focusing upon the spoken as well as the written word, Alessandro Carlucci poses the question 'Who could understand the *Commedia*?' — engaging with multilingualism, comprehension, and oral communication in medieval Italy, and showing how the recent expansion of linguistic research on mutual intelligibility between closely related languages can help us to redefine and better understand some long-standing questions concerning the circulation and recitation of Dante's *Commedia* outside Florence. Moving on to early modern Italian reception — and recognizing that comparisons between Dante and Petrarch have played an integral part in some of the most celebrated interventions in Italian literary criticism — Simon Gilson's 'Notes on the Presence of Petrarch in the Dante Commentaries of Cristoforo Landino (1481) and Trifone Gabriele (1525–27)' show that the history of such comparisons, from the 1370s to the early seventeenth century, offers us a rich series of entry points by means of which to consider how Dante and Petrarch were interpreted, and to evaluate the broader critical and cultural dynamics of their reception.

Looking beyond Italy, several notable scholars have commented on the influence of Muslim religious literature on episodes in the *Commedia*, but an in-depth analysis of Dante's reception in the Islamic world and its literature has yet to be ventured. Valerio Cappozzo's account of 'Dante and Islam, Islam and Dante' examines how Islamic dream sciences and divination are reflected in the *Vita Nuova* and *Commedia* and how the Italian author has been received in the Middle Eastern world. Turning then to Dante in Spain: in 'Translations, Literary Theory, and Canonizations', Paul Carranza argues that engagement with the *Commedia* was a key factor in the development of Spanish humanism and that by not trying to engage with its larger themes of salvific history and empire, Spanish fifteenth-century authors (such as the Marquis of Santillana, Juan de Mena and Francisco Imperial) were able to take elements of the poem for their own needs, which ranged from reflections on Fortune, to love as an *infierno de amor*.

Three further chapters in this section address various aspects of Dante's presence from the late Middle Ages to the nineteenth century in another Romance culture: France. Helen Swift's chapter on 'Dante and Death in Late-Medieval France' reviews the evidence for the early reception of the *Commedia* in the fourteenth century and explores how we might discern the poem's influence in infernal-type landscapes and in perceptions of the dead by the living in French literature of the fifteenth century. In 'Illustrating Editions of Dante in France before Gustave Doré', Richard Cooper surveys what publishers in France had offered to their readers before Doré swept the board, giving attention to illuminated manuscripts and early modern woodcuts, as well as to editions and translations of the eighteenth and early nineteenth centuries. Focusing on a key moment for the poet's reception in nineteenth-century France, Franziska Meier's discussion of Dante and French medievalism in the 1820s and 1830s then considers the responses of French historians and philologists, in particular the public classes of Abel-François Villemain, professor of rhetoric at the Sorbonne, whose 'cours de littérature francaise' features Dante and was closely followed by intellectuals and writers such as Balzac.

For Dante scholarship in Germany, the early nineteenth century was also a highly fruitful period — yielding, for example, the translations and critical studies by Karl Ludwig Kannegießer, Adolf Friedrich Streckfuß, Karl Witte and Prince John of Saxony.[2] Two chapters in the third section of the present volume deal with this key period in German reception. In 'Dante Alighieri and German Romanticism', Alfred Noe illustrates the contexts within which Dante's *Commedia* was perceived during the period, giving attention to travel writing, the reception of the Italian classics, contemporary translations and dramatic texts. Karl Philipp Ellerbrock's 'Dante on Display in Weimar' offers a synthetic account of Dante's entrance into German letters around 1800, describing the key role played by Weimar and Jena in his reinvention as a 'modern poet' and raises the question of how the cultural heritage of Dante's poetry can be made accessible to a wider present-day public.

One absence from this stage of the volume's representation of nineteenth-century reception is Britain (except for the observations in the second half of Chapter 9) — largely because the history of British responses in that period has been well-served by chapters, monographs and anthologies.[3] Conversely, the United States lacks a comprehensive monographic survey of the subject, powerful though Dante's presence has been in its literature and culture.[4] Hence, in the final part of this volume's third section three chapters chart directions for exploring aspects of that presence in nineteenth-century American culture. In 'Italian Exiles and Women Readers of Dante in New England' Christian Y. Dupont extends the lines of inquiry into the reading of Dante by women from prominent New England families, focusing ultimately on those — such as Margaret Fuller and Kate Sedgwick — who discovered him earlier in the century through their encounters with exiled Italian revolutionaries who tutored them in their language and literature. Kathleen Verduin's chapter, '"Why Do You Rend Me?" Dante and the Pain of James Russell Lowell' surveys Lowell's writings on Dante, both professional and private, and trace his suicidal reflections — inextricable, of course, from the contemporary influence of Goethe's *Sorrows of Young Werther* — especially as they cluster around *Inferno* 13 and the Circle of the Suicides. Finally in this section, Carol Chiodo's 'Dante for Mothers' investigates a small, but influential group of female readers whose contributions to the reception of Dante's work in North America have not been previously recognized: the women of the St. Louis Movement, who maintained that reading Dante could contribute to a number of fields of thought, at a time when the barriers to women's education were many, and whose eagerness to apply Dante's philosophical ideas to the social and political concerns that preoccupied them — including children's education — is an untold chapter in Dante's reception in North America.[5]

The fourth and last section of this volume comprises a group of six modern and contemporary readings, exploring more recent aspects of Dante's cross-cultural presence 'beyond borders'. It begins with two chapters on French and American modernist writers. Karlheinz Stierle's chapter shows how the presence of Dante's *Commedia* in Marcel Proust's *À la recherche du temps perdu*, his saga of time lost and time refound, is of a particular quality both in the originality of its intertextual references and through its affinity to the narrative structure of Dante's work. In 'Allen Tate's Flight from Racism: Dante and "The Swimmers"' Dennis Looney traces Tate's early engagement with Dante and then shows how, like the African American authors discussed in Looney's own 2011 study *Freedom Readers*, he came to use the Italian poet to critique the dominant culture of a racist past. The presence of Dante in more recent American political writing and discourse is the subject of Kristina M. Olson's discussion of contemporary appropriations of *Inferno* 3, which shows how President Kennedy's creative mistranslation of Dante's punishment of cowardice from 1963 has, up to the very recent present reverberated within the circles of political activism and discussions of human rights, establishing the idea of neutrality in moral crisis as the worst civic sin.

Three more chapters conclude the collection with a cross-cultural approach to contemporary reception. In '*Dante Today*: Tracking the Global Resonance of the *Commedia*' Elizabeth Coggeshall uses the holdings of the digital archive *Dante Today: Citings and Sightings of Dante's Works in Contemporary Culture* to read the echoes of the *Commedia* in the twenty-first century, analysing the 'resonance' of the *Commedia* against the background noise of contemporary culture and considering the intersection between the reference and its genre, medium and context. Akash Kumar then proposes two modes of reading Dante across cultural and temporal borders: first, a consideration of the principle of vernacular hybridity as something that binds the poet of the *Commedia* to the medieval Delhi poet Amīr Khusrau (1253–1325); and secondly, a look at the contemporary American yet multicultural vision of the *Commedia* by the artist Sandow Birk. Finally, Peter Hainsworth and David Robey compare British, American, French and German translation practice from 1966 to 2019, considering differences and convergences, along with such issues as the potential reading public, the identity and position of translators, and the general question of differing national cultures.

The aim of this collection is, therefore, to present a multi-faceted, interdisciplinary and cross-cultural approach to a poet whose sources, skills and concerns were in his own time multifarious and internationally minded and whose work has subsequently been more transnational than most in its range and impact — with the *Commedia* having been rendered into about fifty different national and ethnic languages: from Afrikaans to Welsh and from Arabic to Yiddish. 'Reading mocks the borders of the nation' was an assertion made in a paper on Dante during a conference on global literary studies at the beginning of the millennium.[6] Despite the subsequent crises of confidence about globalization and internationalism, it still seems appropriate, as we approach a landmark anniversary of a poet whose work has been in circulation for over 700 years, to engage again with the origins and effects of that work beyond disciplinary and cultural borders.

Notes to the Introduction

1. On both periods of the Society's activities, see the historical notes, below, pp. 000–000.
2. On these German translators and critics, see W. P. Friederich, *Dante's Fame Abroad* (Chapel Hill, NC: UNC Studies in Comparative Literature, 1950), pp. 390–440, and more recently, Ernst Behler's chapter on 'Dante in Germany' in *The Dante Encyclopedia*, ed. Richard Lansing (New York: Garland, 2000), pp. 262–69.
3. For example: Paget Toynbee, *Dante in English Literature*, 2 vols (London: Methuen, 1909); Steve Ellis, *Dante and English Poetry* (Cambridge: Cambridge University Press); Valeria Tinkler-Villani, *Visions of Dante in English Poetry* (Amsterdam: Rodopi, 1989); David Wallace, 'Dante in English', in *The Cambridge Companion to Dante*, ed. Rachel Jacoff (Cambridge: Cambridge University Press, 1993), pp. 237–58, and pp. 281–304 in the revised 2007 edition; Ralph Pite, *The Circle of Our Vision: Dante's Presence in English Romantic Poetry* (Oxford: Clarendon Press, 1994); Alison Milbank, *Dante and the Victorians* (Manchester: Manchester University Press, 1998); Antonella Braida, *Dante and the Romantics* (Basingstoke: Palgrave Macmillan, 2004); Julia Straub, *A Victorian Muse: The Afterlife of Dante's Beatrice in Nineteenth-Century Literature* (London: Continuum, 2009); Nick Havely, *Dante's British Public: Readers and Texts, from the Fourteenth-Century to the Present* (Oxford: Oxford University Press, 2014, 2nd edn 2017), chapters 5–7; and Federica Coluzzi, *Beyond Influence: Rethinking Dante Reception in Victorian Literary Culture* (Manchester: Manchester University Press, forthcoming, 2021).
4. An important mid twentieth-century monograph is Angelina La Piana's *Dante's American Pilgrimage* (New Haven, CT: Yale University Press, 1948); a collection of essays dealing with *Dante in America* from 1813 to 1981 was edited by A. B. Giamatti (Binghamton, NY: Center for Medieval and Renaissance Studies/Dante Society of America, 1983); and African-American reception from the nineteenth century to the present has more recently been the subject of a pioneering study by Dennis Looney, *Freedom Readers* (Notre Dame, IN: Notre Dame University Press, 2011); while there have also been monographs on the responses of individual American authors, such as Longfellow, Eliot and Pound. The *Dante Encyclopedia* does not feature 'America' (or 'the USA') in its group of 'Dante in' articles, perhaps because of the enormity of the task, although pieces on the Dante Society of America and on individual American *dantisti* (Longfellow, Norton, Singleton and others) are included. For further guidance on this subject, see notes 4–6 in Christian Dupont's essay in this volume (Chapter 19) and the essays by Dupont, Kathleen Verduin and Dennis Looney in Aida Audeh and Nick Havely (eds), *Dante in the Long Nineteenth Century: Nationality, Identity, and Appropriation* (Oxford: Oxford University Press, 2012), pp. 248–301.
5. For British works by women writers on Dante for children around the turn of the nineteenth and twentieth centuries, see Anne Laurence, 'Exploiting Dante: Dante and his Women Popularizers, 1850–1910', in *Dante in the Nineteenth Century: Reception, Canonicity, Popularization*, ed. by Nick Havely (Oxford and Berne: Peter Lang, 2011), pp. 281–301 (pp. 290–92).
6. Wai Chee Dimock, 'Literature for the Planet', *PMLA* 116.1 (2001), 173–88 (178).

PART I

Culture and Politics

CHAPTER 1

The Eclogues of Giovanni del Virgilio and Dante in Classical Perspective

Matthew Leigh and Jonathan Katz

The four-poem correspondence between Giovanni del Virgilio and Dante composed between 1319 and 1321 and collectively known as the *Eclogues* (*Ecl.*) is a fitting topic for a volume on *Dante beyond Borders*.[1] For Giovanni's advocacy of Latin as the language of literature and Dante's surprising reply to him in that same language enrols both men in a linguistic community that transcends the barriers of space and time.[2] In addition, the pastoral turn effected by Dante's first reply to Giovanni temporarily removes both men from the cities where currently they reside and transports them to a world known only through the literary imagination.

Giovanni del Virgilio was educated in Bologna. An exponent both of the medieval *ars dictaminis* tradition of rhetorically structured letter-writing championed in that city by such figures as Bene da Firenze and Giovanni di Bonandrea and of the proto-humanist engagement with classical Latin literature of figures such as Lovato Lovati and Albertino Mussato in Padova,[3] he appears to have given private lessons in Latin before being employed by the city's university in November 1321 to take courses on Vergil, Ovid, Lucan, and Statius.[4] It was to his devotion to Vergil that he owed his surname and in his first letter to Dante he describes himself as 'the house-bred slave of the tuneful Maro' (*Ecl.* 1. 36 *vocalis verna Maronis*). This devotion shows through as his first letter opens, as do both the *Aeneid* and the *Bellum Civile*, with a single seven-line period; but whereas the proems of Vergil and Lucan set out the subject matter of their poems, Giovanni instead offers a Latin paraphrase of Dante's still incomplete *Commedia* and asks him why he offers up matters of such grandeur and seriousness to the common people while leaving nothing to scholars such as himself to read (*Ecl.* 1. 6–7). The reference to the common people (*vulgus*) is the first of a series of phrases deprecating Dante's decision to compose the *Commedia* in the *volgare*; when Giovanni talks of himself and his associates as pallid, he draws on conceptions of the scholarly life that go back to antiquity.[5] He further develops this theme over the next nine lines, identifying the Latinless reader of the *Commedia* with Davus the slave of comedy, the unlettered tribe, and the comically coiffed fool who would drive out Horace.[6] To this Giovanni imagines Dante replying that he writes not for such people but rather for those sophisticated in study (*Ecl.* 1. 14); but this will not pass, for Dante does so in the language of the people while the man of learning scorns the speech of the crowd; this would be the case even if it were not subject to variation when, in fact, it is divided into a thousand separate idioms (*Ecl.* 1. 15–16: *clerus vulgaria tempnit, | et si non varient, cum sint ydiomata mille*).[7]

Developing this dismissive attitude to the people, Giovanni criticises Dante's employment of Italian as casting pearls before swine and dressing the Muses in unworthy garb (*Ecl.* 1. 21–22: *nec margaritas profliga prodigus apris, | nec preme Castalias indigna veste sorores*). Yet this is not just the snobbery of one imprisoned by his own learning, and two particular formulations have a bearing on the theme of Dante beyond borders. The first is the complaint that neither those among whom Dante is numbered sixth nor he whom Dante follows in heaven wrote in the *volgare* (*Ecl.* 1. 17–19).[8] Here Giovanni refers back to *Inferno* 4. 101–02, where Homer, Horace, Ovid, Lucan and Vergil admit Dante to their ranks, and to the *Purgatorio*, in which Statius succeeds Vergil as the poet's guide. Yet for these lines to be meaningful, the poets named must have had a choice of languages in which to compose: by opting for Greek in the case of Homer and Latin in that of the other five poets, they also rejected their own contemporary *volgare*. What that *volgare* was Giovanni is in no position to reconstruct, but he implies that it must have been very different from the language in which they actually wrote.[9] Yet what he feels able to claim is that, for all ages, to write in the language of the ancient poets is to join a linguistic community that transcends the borders of place and time.

At vv. 23–29 Giovanni sets out his positive prescription for the next stage of Dante's career, arguing that he will only achieve true distinction by tackling different themes and in the song of the Roman *vates* (*Ecl.* 1. 23–24).[10] There are many topics ripe for treatment in epic verse (*Ecl.* 1. 25) and Giovanni sets out some of these in four lines each beginning with the same imperative form (*Ecl.* 1. 26–29: *dic* [...] *dic* [...] *dic* [...] *dic*). Only such Latin epic will ensure Dante an audience from Cadiz in the West to the mouth of the Danube in the East, in Egypt and in Libya (*Ecl.* 1. 30–32), and, if he cares for fame, he will not be content to be hemmed in by small boundaries or to be celebrated in the judgement of the crowd (*Ecl.* 1. 33–34).[11]

The remainder of Giovanni's letter first sets out his own credentials as a teacher and critic and looks forward to awarding Dante the laurel crown (*Ecl.* 1. 35–40).[12] In elaborately figured terms Giovanni next tells of war and war's alarms and makes two separate suggestions: first that Dante's lyre can quell the troubles of men; second, that all other poets will wait on his word and, should he not recount the coming wars, they will remain untold (*Ecl.* 1. 41–46). A duly obsequious *envoi* restores to Dante his proper position of teacher, casts Giovanni as his inferior, and prays that the great man will quit Ravenna and make the writer's prayers come true (*Ecl.* 1. 47–51). Throughout one may note Giovanni's debt to the Latin poets,[13] but this emerges most significantly at v. 50: in referring to his verses as those that the goose squawks at the clear-voiced swan, Giovanni borrows a motif from Vergil's 9th *Eclogue* as the young Lycidas says just the same of his own verse in relation to that of Varius and Cinna (Verg. *Ecl.* 9. 35–36). Perhaps it was this that inspired Dante to cast his reply in the terms of Latin pastoral.

To Dante the terms of Giovanni's letter must have seemed amusingly familiar. For, as is commonly believed, it was in 1304–06 and while resident in Bologna that Dante set to writing two works that engaged closely with the theory of language and that were still to remain incomplete and unpublished at the time of his death: the *De Vulgari Eloquentia* and the *Convivio*.[14] In these works Dante establishes the nature of the two linguistic systems that he names *volgare* and *gramatica*. The former arose from the Babylonian confusion and is characterized by the multiplication of local variations in language and by the change in those individual languages across time. The latter was an artificial construction designed to reintroduce stability and regularity, so that those acquainted with it could communicate with one another across the divide of space and time.[15] While the speaker of any local *volgare* would be baffled by that of the same community a thousand years before or even by that of closely neighbouring communities in his own time, one immersed in *gramatica* can communicate with writers born centuries before or active in lands as distant as Britain and Germany.[16] Yet still Dante embraces his mother tongue as the most effective vehicle for poetry; he surveys the poetic production of all the regions of Italy and argues that the writers of the peninsula should adopt a *volgare illustre* to be formed out of the finest features of them all.[17]

The distinction between *gramatica* and the *volgare* is evident in other writers of Dante's period and it is clear that it also underpins Giovanni's observation that none of the great poets of antiquity chose to write in their equivalent of the *volgare* of the *Commedia*.[18] While both Giovanni and Dante acknowledge that what are now called classical Greek and Latin are forms of *gramatica*, in general Dante applies the term to Latin, and it is clearly in Latin that Giovanni expects Dante to write.[19] Giovanni is thus arguing with Dante in terms that the latter knew all too well. This relationship extends even as far as individual words and figures.[20]

It would therefore appear that Dante composed his answer well over a decade before Giovanni made bold to put the question to him. This, however, is less surprising if we recall one common factor in the lives and studies of both men: the city of Bologna and the activities of the scholars at work in the local university.[21] Giovanni's views are not so much his own as those of his teachers, views that Dante will have encountered at first hand during his Bolognese sojourn and while composing his own deeply original accounts of the Italian and the Latin languages.

The poem with which Dante answers Giovanni's challenge pays scant attention to the younger man's critique of poetry in the *volgare*. Here Tityrus (i.e. Dante) suggests that, once he has completed the composition of the *Paradiso*, Mopsus (i.e. Giovanni) should then yield to him.[22] Only after his companion Melibeus has asked what exactly Mopsus writes does Tityrus summarize his complaints:

> 'comica nonne vides ipsum reprehendere verba,
> tum quia femineo resonant ut trita labello,
> tum quia Castalias pudet acceptare sorores?'

> ['Do you not see him criticise comic words, first because they resound as if rubbed on a woman's lips, then because the Castalian sisters are ashamed to accept them?']

This is a somewhat imprecise summary of Giovanni's letter, for it nowhere suggests that poetry written in the *volgare* makes a womanly sound.[23] Yet the reference to the Muses' sense of shame in accepting Dante's linguistic choices clearly picks up on Giovanni's complaint that Dante dresses the Castalian sisters in an unworthy garb (*Ecl.* 1. 22: *nec preme Castalias indigna veste sorores*);[24] and, in his reference to the criticism of comic words (*Ecl.* 2. 52), Dante both echoes Giovanni on the comically coiffed fool (*Ecl.* 1. 13: *comicomus nebulo*) and sums up his argument that Dante cannot produce truly sublime verse if he writes in Italian.[25]

Troubled by this critique, Melibeus asks what they can do to win Mopsus round (*Ecl.* 2. 56–57). Tityrus' reply develops a figured identification introduced as early as the second line of the poem. There he refers to Giovanni's verse epistle as songs drawn for us like milk from the bosom of the Pierides (*Ecl.* 2. 2) and later Tityrus describes its author as bearing guts full of the milk of song (*Ecl.* 2. 31–32). Now Tityrus reminds Melibeus of a sheep in his own possession, as delightful as it is fecund, and promises to fill ten small vessels with its milk and send them to Mopsus (*Ecl.* 2. 58–64). What part of Dante's oeuvre this most singular sheep stands for is debated. To many the sheep is the *Paradiso* and the ten vessels are ten cantos from this poem.[26] Yet consensus on the identity of these cantos is elusive: Raffa argues for *Paradiso* 1–10, and Annett for the eleven canti of *Paradiso* 15–25, while Pertile points to the reference to the milk of the Muses at *Paradiso* 23. 57 and observes that from *Paradiso* 24–33 there are ten cantos of the great work still to come.[27] Others emphasize the significance of the number 10 for Vergil's *Eclogues* and take it that Dante is promising to emulate the productivity of his master.[28] When Tityrus states that Melibeus knows the sheep, he may imply that Mopsus as yet does not. Inasmuch as Giovanni himself has referred to the *Paradiso* in the opening lines of his own letter, a notional collection of ten pastoral songs would better match this pattern.[29]

However we understand this sheep of song, the essence of Dante's response is to write in Latin but most certainly not on those epic themes that Giovanni had recommended. Instead, Dante adopts a form that bears some of the very characteristics that could be held against the Italian of the *Commedia*. For, in the dedicatory epistle to the *Paradiso* addressed to Can Grande, Dante explains the title *Commedia* both in terms of the trajectory of the narrative from misery to happiness and in terms of style.[30] As comedy speaks modestly and in a humble manner (*Epist.* 10. 30: *remisse et humiliter*), so the manner of the *Commedia* is modest and humble because the speech is that of the people in which women also communicate (*Epist.* 10. 31: *si ad modum loquendi, remissus est modus et humilis, quia locutio vulgaris, in qua et muliercule comunicant*).[31] Pastoral, meanwhile, was the lowly first stage of the famous *rota Virgiliana* and Servius emphasises its humble character (*humilis character*) in the preface to his commentary on the *Eclogues* as a whole.[32] Vergil himself employs various motifs in order to signal the inherent modesty of the genre and its links to comedy.[33]

Giovanni's first letter to Dante recasts the *Commedia* in terms appropriate to Roman epic: hell becomes Orcus and Tartarus (*Ecl.* 1. 4, 10); purgatory is cast as Lethe (*Ecl.* 1. 5); Padova is named by reference to its Trojan ancestors (*Ecl.* 1. 28); Naples is dubbed Parthenope (*Ecl.* 1. 29). Other references to the Ligurian mountains, to 'father Apenninus', and to the Tyrrhenian Sea pose no challenges at all (*Ecl.* 1. 29 and 42–43). Though Giovanni does not specify his own residence in Bologna, he does offer a tortured periphrasis of Ravenna as the city encircled by the Eridanus, that is to say by the Po (*Ecl.* 1. 47). In other words, he finds more or less obscure ways to refer to places that, once deciphered, retain their familiar position on the map. Dante's reply, by contrast, makes only one such reference: declining Giovanni's offer of the laurel crown, he refers to his longing to do so by the Arno of his ancestors (*Ecl.* 2. 43–44: *patrio* [. . .] *Sarno*).[34] In all other cases the world that both he and Giovanni (or rather Tityrus and Mopsus) inhabit is that of pastoral and resists any attempt to fix it on the map: when first sighted, Tityrus and Melibeus are under an oak tree (*Ecl.* 2. 4, 67: *sub quercu*); Mopsus inhabits pastures shaded by Mount Menalus (*Ecl.* 2. 11, 23) or the hills of Aonia (*Ecl.* 2. 28);[35] and the place to which he invites Tityrus is recast as woods and countryside ignorant of the gods (*Ecl.* 2. 41).[36] When Tityrus breaks into indignation at thoughts of the Arno, urges Melibeus to learn to fix his teeth on hard crusts, or describes the cramped huts cooking the spelt soup that will sustain them, the privations of Dante's life in exile come to the surface (*Ecl.* 2. 38, 42–44, 66, 68).[37] Yet overall the places of pastoral and the life lived in them draw both Dante and Giovanni away from the confines of the real and set them free in a world that cannot be reinscribed in any map of Italy or anywhere else.[38]

This aspect of Dante's pastoral turn extends to his use of names. The medieval tradition of allegorical writing and interpretation can encourage an almost mechanical unmasking of the characters of literary works, and much criticism appears to read Dante's *Eclogues* as if supplemented from the first by the identifications supplied by the glossator in the Zibaldone Laurenziano: Melibeus just *is* Ser. Dino Perini, Alphesibeus *must* be the doctor Fiducio de' Milotti.[39] Yet the ancient pastoral tradition to which Dante responds is significantly subtler in its use of such masks.[40] For while there is an obvious sense in which Dante does refer to himself by the name Tityrus and to Giovanni by the name Mopsus, the role played by names in Vergil's poems is distinctly more complicated. Consider the comment of Servius at Vergil, *Eclogue* 1. 1:

> et hoc loco Tityri sub persona Vergilium debemus accipere, non tamen ubique, sed tantum ubi exigit ratio.
>
> [And in this passage we must understand Vergil under the mask of Tityrus, yet not everywhere, but only where the rationale demands.][41]

The warning is that, while here Tityrus is to be identified with Vergil himself, this does not entitle us to treat every aspect of this character in the *Eclogues* as a reflection of the author's own life.[42] Servius himself equates Vergil with Corydon in *Eclogue* 2 and with the master of Moeris in *Eclogue* 9,[43] while Vergil implicitly places himself in the pastoral world when the Menalcas of *Eclogue* 5 points to the hemlock stalk on which he learned the first lines of *Eclogues* 2 and 3.[44] On occasion even modern scholars strip away the masks of Vergil's pastoral characters and identify precise one-on-one correspondences, but few are convinced.[45] Others emphasise the elusiveness of Vergilian identifications even when what is at issue is correspondence between shepherds and contemporary social types rather than specific individuals.[46] That this aspect of Vergilian bucolic was not lost on Dante will become ever clearer through analysis of his second contribution to this exchange.[47]

Dante's pastoral strategies have an obvious and immediate impact on Giovanni's reply to him. Delighted that the master deigns to answer him with a Latin poem, Giovanni abandons all thought of a Latin epic and embraces the bucolic mode. This he expresses in the claim to have laid aside greater reeds and to have grasped slender ones instead (*Ecl.* 3. 31–32: *nec mora, depostis calamis maioribus, inter | arripio tenues et labris flantibus hysco* [And straight away putting aside the larger reeds I took up the more delicate ones and opened my breathing lips]). Here the adjective *tenuis* echoes two key statements of Vergil's poetic programme in the *Eclogues* as first Meliboeus describes Tityrus as playing on a slender oat (Verg. *Ecl.* 1. 2: *tenui . . . auena*) and then Tityrus himself proclaims his intention to contemplate the rustic muse on a slender reed (Verg. *Ecl.* 6. 8: *tenui . . . harundine*). The second statement comes amidst a passage in which Tityrus politely declines to compose an epic in celebration of the martial exploits of P. Alfenus Varus and renders into Latin the scene in the preface to the *Aetia* of Callimachus in which Apollo instructs the poet to feed fat the sacrificial sheep but to keep the muse slender.[48] In the Latin poets of the Augustan age, such passages proliferate and the poet's polite refusal to write in the epic genre on the grounds of Apollo's veto or some personal incapacity is known as the *recusatio*.[49] Dante is writing in this mode and Giovanni is alert to the fact. There will be no more talk of epic.

Giovanni also responds to Dante's invocation of the transcendent geography of pastoral. He has yet to abandon all hope of bringing Dante to Bologna and where first we find him is at the meeting point of the Reno and the Savena (*Ecl.* 3. 1–2). There he hears Tityrus singing in the shade of the Adriatic shore (*Ecl.* 3. 11) and this clearly places Dante in Ravenna in the same way as did Giovanni's first letter when it referred to his residence by the branches of the Po (*Ecl.* 1. 47). As Dante refers to his exile from Florence and yearning to be crowned by his native river, so Giovanni acknowledges the bitterness of exile, the ingratitude of Florence, and the call of the Arno (*Ecl.* 2. 42–44, 3. 36–38). When he indicates that a further refusal will lead him to slake his thirst in the Phrygian Muso, this is clearly a threat to offer the crown instead to the Paduan Albertino Mussato (*Ecl.* 3. 88).[50] Yet Giovanni is no longer simply dealing in learned periphrases for real cities, regions, and people of Italy. He follows Vergil into the world of pastoral and more specifically into Arcadia, talking of Mount Menalus, of the joy inspired in the shepherds and nymphs of Arcadia by the song of Tityrus, of the Fauns who leap down from Mount Lyceum (*Ecl.* 3. 18, 21–22, 25), and of the youths and veterans of Parrhasia (*Ecl.* 3. 68).[51] His own position has also changed significantly. For though the meeting point of the Reno and the Savena places him near Bologna, he is beneath well-watered hills in his native cave while his cattle, lambs, and goats take to pasture (*Ecl.* 3. 1–5). He himself is left the sole inhabitant of the woods (*Ecl.* 3. 6) while his peers hurry into the city to take up the legal training that Dante described in his earlier poem (*Ecl.* 3. 7: *causis*, cf.

2. 29: *causarum*). Inspired by Dante's pastoral turn, he reconsiders his first effort and asks why he sat in the city and sang a civil song (*Ecl.* 3. 26–28: *si cantat oues et Tityrus hircos | aut armenta trahit, quianam ciuile canebas | urbe sedens carmen?* [If Tityrus too is singing of the sheep and the goats, or draws to him the herds, why, pray, did you sit in the city and sing your urban strains?]). Instead, he will do as Dante has done and sing a pastoral song on a reed derived from Lake Benacus (*Ecl.* 28–30).[52] His verse is now liberally scattered with motifs drawn from the *Eclogues* and his companions include the thoroughly Vergilian Alexis, Corydon, Nisa, Testilis and Melibeus.[53] The invitation of Giovanni's first letter is not rescinded, but now it is the place itself that bids Tityrus come (*Ecl.* 3. 53: *ut uenias, locus ipse uocat*).

Dante's second reply has no little fun with the younger man's effort. Writing now in the third person, he places Tityrus in company with another figure from Vergilian pastoral, Alphesibeus, and describes how the pair take their herds to the woods in order to seek shelter from the heat (*Ecl.* 4. 1–9).[54] Here the hot and panting Melibeus, the interlocutor of Tityrus in Dante's initial reply to Giovanni, joins them (*Ecl.* 4. 29–30). He rushes to find them because he is now the bearer of Giovanni's message in the previous poem, and his pipe miraculously performs the poem in its entirety. This Dante states by quoting the very first line of Giovanni's poem (*Ecl.* 3. 1, cf. 4. 41) and then noting that, had be but taken three more breaths, he would have soothed the silent rustics with one hundred verses (*Ecl.* 4. 42–43). Conscious surely of the one hundred cantos of his own *Commedia*, Dante is clearly amused at the fact that Giovanni's poem lasts only 97 lines, and he underlines the point by restricting his own reply to the exact same number of verses.[55]

There is also something thoroughly playful about this poem's sense of place.[56] First Tityrus refers to Mopsus' mistaken belief that he is living on the right bank of the Po and the left of the Rubicon, where Emilia meets the limits of the Adriatic (*Ecl.* 4. 68–69) when in fact he resides in Pelorus, the north-eastern promontory of Sicily (*Ecl.* 4. 26, 46, 73). What is more, Mopsus seems rather unaware of where he himself is to be found. For far from residing at the meeting point of the Savena and the Reno, he is actually in the vicinity of Mount Etna and invites Tityrus to a region made terrifying by the Cyclops Poliphemus (*Ecl.* 4. 27, 73–75).[57] Dante has not read Theocritus, *Idylls* 6 and 11, both of which feature the Cyclops and his hopeless love for Galatea, but Servius makes clear that Vergil, *Eclogue* 2 models the lovelorn Corydon on this figure, and the Cyclops sings a thoroughly pastoral song at Ovid, *Metamorphoses* 13. 789–869.[58] Yet Ovid's Polyphemus finally subjects his rival Acis to a brutal assault and Ovid later reminds the reader of the testimony of the lost companion of Ulysses, Achaemenides, who, in Book 3 of the *Aeneid*, warns Aeneas and his men of the threat of the Cyclops.[59] Dante's Alphesibeus recalls both these narratives as he urges Tityrus to decline the invitation of Mopsus if it means going anywhere near this monster (*Ecl.* 4. 76–87).[60] Only now does he also warn Tityrus against allowing his head to be confined by what he calls "Rhenus and that famous Naiad" (*Ecl.* 4. 85: *Rhenus et Nayas illa*) and associate this hazard with the prospect of coronation with a laurel wreath (*Ecl.* 4. 86–87). If the "famous Naiad" is a periphrasis for the Savena, then Alphesibeus is drawing Dante's Sicilian fantasy back into the reality of contemporary Bologna, and those who identify the Cyclops with figures such as Romeo de' Pepoli and Fulcieri da Calboli have good grounds for their theories.[61] All this is undeniable, but what makes this poem exciting is how far Dante has gone in his pastoral geography in order to escape the real world before eventually surrendering to it.

Nor has Dante yet abandoned the more playful effects of ancient pastoral. For the *envoi* to the poem introduces a play with names that leaves much that has come before rather harder to decipher than previously it might have appeared:

> callidus interea iuxta latitavit Iolas,
> omnia qui didicit, qui retulit omnia nobis:
> ille quidem nobis; et nos tibi, Mopse, poymus.

[Meanwhile crafty Iolas lay close by in hiding, who heard all, who told us all. 'Twas he who created the song for us, and we, Mopsus, for you.][62]

Here Dante embraces the distancing capacity of a poem written in the third person. For whereas in his first contribution, the speaking 'I' of the poem was named Tityrus, now the narrator is anonymous and stands at two degrees of separation from the events recorded; the previously unmentioned Iolas overhears the conversation of Tityrus and Alphesibeus and reports it to the narrator, who then turns it into verse for the benefit of Mopsus. This is as subtle an effect as Vergil's avoidance of direct identification of his own voice with that of any of the shepherds of his own collection.

Dante has to make clear to Giovanni that he is not going to turn to Latin epic on contemporary themes or come to Bologna to accept the laurel crown. Yet rather than simply write back in the *volgare* and give his correspondent the short shrift that his strictures on the *Commedia* rather deserve, Dante offers up a different version of Giovanni's beloved Vergil and takes him on an increasingly intricate journey among the people and the places of pastoral. Though finally his poetic geography arrives back in Bologna and in Giovanni's chosen way of describing the city, the places in-between have led him far away from mundane reality, and the final reference to the characters encountered along the way baffles any routine identification of the contemporary figures lurking beneath the masks of pastoral. This is a true tribute to the genius of Vergilian bucolic.

Notes to Chapter 1

1. For purposes of clarity, we refer to these four poems in footnotes as *Ecl.* 1–4. In preparing this chapter we have consulted the following editions: P. H. Wicksteed and E. G. Gardner (1902) *Dante and Giovanni del Virgilio* (Westminster: Constable, 1902); E. Cecchini, *Dante Alighieri: Opere Minori*, III (Milan: Ricciardi, 1979), pp. 645–89; Giorgio Brugnoli, and Riccardo Scarcia, *Dante Alighieri: Le Egloghe, testo, traduzione e note* (Milan: Ricciardi, 1980); Manlio Pastore Stocchi, *Dante Alighieri: Epistole, Egloge, Questio de situ et forma aque et terre* (Rome and Padua: Antenori, 2012). All translations are our own.
2. For time in Dante's *Eclogues*, see esp. the excellent Sabrina Ferrara, 'Il senso del tempo nelle *Egloghe* di Dante, uomo e poeta', *Italianistica*, 44 (2015), 199–208.
3. For Giovanni del Virgilio's association with both traditions, see G. Vecchi, 'Giovanni del Virgilio e Dante: la polemica tra latino e volgare nella corrispondenza poetica', in *Dante e Bologna nei tempi di Dante*, VII centenario della nascita di Dante, II (Bologna: Commissione per i testi di

lingua, 1967), pp. 61–76; Ronald Witt, ' "Ars Dictaminis" and the Beginnings of Humanism: A New Construction of the Problem', *Renaissance Quarterly*, 35 (1982), 1–35, esp. 21–22, 25–27. He structures his first missive to Dante according to the rules of the *ars dictaminis*, but it is written in the dactylic hexameters of Horace's *Epistles* and includes many imitations of the ancient Latin poets. For the life and career of Giovanni, see *DBI*, xxxviii. 404–09 and Giuseppe Indizio, 'Giovanni del Virgilio maestro e dantista minore', *Studi Danteschi*, 77 (2012), 311–39, esp. 311–27. For the *ars dictaminis*, see also Rita Copeland and Ineke Sluiter, *Medieval Grammar and Rhetoric: Language Arts and Literary Theory, AD 300–1475* (Oxford: Oxford University Press, 2009), pp. 685–87.

4. Contrast this syllabus with that of Giovanni di Bonandrea, who taught at Bologna until 1321, devoting half the year to the *ars dictaminis* and the other half to the *Rhetorica ad Herennium*. Though Giovanni himself also composed an *ars dictaminis*, his interests went beyond this tradition. See Witt, art. cit. (n. 3), p. 35.
5. For scholarly pallor, see Quint. *Inst.* 7. 10. 14; Plin. *Ep.* 6. 2. 2; *TLL*, X.1.124.47–55; *Purg.* 31. 14; Sabrina Ferrara, 'Ethical Distance and Political Resonance in the *Eclogues* of Dante', in *Ethics, Politics and Justice in Dante*, ed. by Giulia Gaimari and Catherine Keen (London: UCL Press, 2019), pp. 111–26 (p. 114). See also Dante's description of Giovanni at *Ecl.* 2. 30 ('sacri nemoris perpalluit umbra') and at 2. 37 ('insomnem . . . Mopsum').
6. Davus is the name of a comic slave in Terence, *Andria* and *Phormio*. For this name as a cipher for the slave of comedy, cf. Hor. *Serm.* 1. 10. 40, 2. 5. 91, *AP* 237; for the 'gens ydiota', cf. Lucil. fr. 649 M: 'inlitteratum [...] atque idiotam'. For more on 'comicomus', see below, p. 11–12.
7. For the phrase 'clerus vulgaria tempnit', cf. Hor. *Carm.* 3. 1. 1: 'odi profanum vulgus et arceo'. Horace goes on to make the ritual bid for silence and presents himself as a priest of the Muses singing new songs to boys and girls. We may compare *Ecl.* 1. 36–37 in which Giovanni dubs himself 'clericus Aonidum' and promises to expound Dante's works in the schools ('promere gimnasiis').
8. 'forensi' is glossed in L as 'vulgari'.
9. For more on this notion, see below, p. 11.
10. For the Augustan poets' adoption of the term *vates* and its lofty connotations of priest and prophet as well as poet, see Verg. *Aen.* 7. 41; Hor. *Carm.* 1. 1. 35; Prop. 4. 6. 1; Hellfried Dahlmann, 'Vates', *Philologus*, 97 (1948), 337–53; J. K. Newman, *Augustus and the New Poetry* (Brussels: Latomus, 1967), pp. 99–206.
11. For a parallel argument in classical Latin, see Cic. *Arch.* 23 claiming that works in Greek have a far greater spread than those in Latin. The *Pro Archia* was only rediscovered by Petrarch in Liège in 1333.
12. In 1315 the city of Padova had presented Albertino Mussato with the laurel crown in recognition of his tragedy, *Ecerinis*, on the sufferings of the city at the hands of Ezzelino III da Romano. For more on the laurel crown, see below, p. 13.
13. Note in particular *Ecl.* 1. 41: 'iam michi bellisonis horrent clangoribus aures' [Already my ears ring with the war-sounding din]; cf. Hor. *Carm.* 2. 1. 17–18: 'iam nunc minaci murmure cornuum | perstringis auris' [Already now you assail our ears with the threatening clamour of horns]. What already touches the ears of Giovanni both as event and as the subject for Dante's epic verse could still touch those of Horace as an event recalled through the famously vivid works of Asinius Pollio.
14. Marco Santagata, *Dante: The Story of his Life*, trans. by R. Dixon, (Cambridge, MA: Harvard University Press, 2016), pp. 174–86. For more detailed discussion, see *Dante Alighieri, De vulgari eloquentia*, ed. by Mirko Tavoni (Milan: Mondadori, 2011), pp. 1113–16; E. Fenzi ed., *Dante: De vulgari eloquentia* (Rome; Salerno, 2012), pp. xxiii–xxiv.
15. For the *volgare* and *gramatica* distinguished, see *DVE* 1. 2–4; for the multiplicity of forms of the *volgare*, see *DVE* 1. 6. 1, 1. 7. 7; for the stability of *gramatica*, see *DVE* 1. 9. 11, 2. 8. 7, *Conv.* 1. 5. 10; for the geographical spread of *gramatica*, see *Conv.* 1. 7. 13; for the limited number of speakers of *gramatica*, see *Conv.* 1. 8. 2. In neither of these works does Dante explicitly state that the ancient Latin writers chose *gramatica* over the *volgare*, but he does express this view elsewhere, at *VN* 25. 3–4.

16. For change across time in local variants of the *volgare*, see *DVE* 1. 9. 9–10; for variety even within the same city, see *DVE* 1. 9. 5. For change in the local *volgare* from that of fifty and 1,000 years before, see *Conv.* 1. 5. 9; for the realization that one's own local *volgare* is not the language of Adam, see *DVE* 1. 6. 2–3; for communication with and separation from speakers of English and German, see *Conv.* 1. 6. 8, 1. 7. 13. For scholarship on these topics, see esp. G. Vinay, 'Ricerche sul De Vulgari Eloquentia I: Lingua "artificiale", "naturale" e letteraria', *Giornale Storico della Letteratura Latina*, 136 (1959), 236–58; Giorgio Brugnoli, 'Il latino dei dettatori e quello di Dante', in *Dante e Bologna*, pp. 113–26; P. V. Mengaldo, *Linguistica e retorica di Dante*, Saggi di varia umanita, 2 (Pisa: Nistri-Lischi, 1978), pp. 60–76; idem at *ED* iii. 259–65; Angelo Mazzocco, *Linguistic Theories in Dante and the Humanists* (Leiden: Brill, 1993), esp. pp. 159–79.
17. For the 'vulgare illustre', see *DVE* 1. 17–19.
18. *ED* iii. 259–65, esp. 260 quoting the fourteenth-century scholar Henri de Crissey; Mengaldo, op. cit. (n. 16), pp. 65–66 and n. 68 citing Egidio Colonna, *De regimine* II. 2. 7.
19. For Greek — a language to which neither neither Dante nor Giovanni had any access — as a form of *gramatica*, see *DVE* 1. 1. 2, *Conv.* 1. 11. 14. To others Hebrew was also a form of *gramatica*, but *DVE* 1. 6. 4–7 suggests that Hebrew is a divinely created tongue and one that has endured unchanged because the Jews had no role in the building of the tower of Babel; but later in Canto 26 of the *Paradiso*, Adam represents the language as his own creation and acknowledges that it too has been subject to the same mutability as the *volgare*. Mazzocco, op. cit. (n. 16), pp. 159–79.
20. See e.g. *DVE* 2. 6. 3 'ydiotas' for the unlettered and 2. 4. 9 on geese imitating eagles.
21. For the *DVE* as evidence of Dante's engagement with the university culture of Bologna, 'roccaforte latina', see Mengaldo, op. cit. (n. 16), p. 64.
22. Note *Ecl.* 2. 48–51, esp. 51: 'concedat Mopsus'.
23. For more on this issue, see below, p. 12.
24. Contrast the more flattering *Ecl.* 1. 1, in which Giovanni addresses Dante as the 'nourishing voice of the Pierides', i.e. of the Muses.
25. Mark Davie, 'Dante's Latin Eclogues', *PLLS* 1 (1976), 183–98, esp. 190 argues that *Ecl.* 2. 52 attributes to Giovanni the view that 'any composition in the *sermo forensis* must . . . necessarily be *comicus*'.
26. Giovanni Reggio, *Le Egloghe di Dante* (Florence: Olschki, 1969), pp. 21–31 argues this case and offers a detailed account of previous views on either side of the case.
27. G. P. Raffa, 'Dante's Mocking Pastoral', *Dante Studies*, 114 (1996), 271–91, esp. 274; Scott Annett, 'Una veritate ascosa sotto bella menzogna: Dante's *Eclogues* and the World Beyond the Text', *Italian Studies*, 68 (2013), 36–56; Lino Pertile, 'Le *Egloghe* di Dante e l'antro di Polifemo', in *Dante the Lyric and Ethical Poet*, ed. Z. G. Baránski and Martin McLaughlin (Oxford: Legenda, 2010), pp. 153–67, esp. 155–56.
28. Eugenio Chiarini, 'I "Decem Vascula" della prima ecloga dantesca', in *Dante e Bologna*, pp. 77–88.
29. Verg. Ecl. 3. 71 has Menalcas describe his gifts to his lover: 'aurea mala decem misi; cras altera mittam' [I have sent ten golden apples; tomorrow I shall send a second lot]. For contestation over whether the ten apples should be equated with the collection of *Eclogues*, see Serv. at Verg. *Ecl.* 3. 71.
30. Space forbids discussion of the disputed authenticity of this work. For an account of the *status quaestionis* with ample bibliography, see Paolo De Ventura, 'Dante tra Cangrande e i falsari: gli ultimi vent'anni dell' Epistola XIII', *Critica Letteraria*, 40 (2012), 3–21.
31. See *ED* ii. 78–81 on the various meanings of the title *Commedia*.
32. Traugott Lawler, *The Parisiana Poetria of John of Garland* (New Haven: Yale University Press, 1974), pp. 40–41 and 103.
33. Note esp. Verg. *Ecl.* 6. 1–2, where Thalia is the Muse of Comedy and the verb *ludere* implies a modest artistic undertaking antecedent to something greater to come. Note also *Ecl.* 10. 75: 'surgamus' [let us arise], which simultaneously calls time on the play of pastoral and points to higher works to come. For both passages, see *Publio Virgilio Marone. Le Bucoliche. Introduzione e commento*, ed. by Andrea Cucchiarelli (Rome: Carrocci, 2012), ad loc.
34. Though Dante declines to come to Bologna to accept the laurel crown, he is far from indifferent

to the idea of his own coronation. See esp. *Par.* 1. 13–15 and 22–33 and esp. 25. 1–9, where he makes clear that he yearns to be crowned but only in his native Florence.
35. While Aonia is a region of Boeotia containing the poetically significant Mount Helicon and Mount Cithaeron, Mount Menalus (Maenalus in classical Latin) is located in Arcadia and associated by Vergil with the god Pan (see esp. Verg. *Ecl.* 8. 21–25).
36. For similar reflections on time in Dante's *Eclogues*, see Ferrara, art cit. (n. 2), p. 200. For space, see ibid., pp. 203–04, 206.
37. For the bread of exile, cf. *Par.* 17. 58–60.
38. For not dissimilar views of what the bucolic turn means for Dante, see Ferrara, art. cit. (n. 5), esp. pp. 120–21.
39. For the allegorical interpretation of Dante and Giovanni's *Eclogues* and their deployment of the *modus transumptivus*, see Mauda Bregoli-Russo, 'Le Egloghe di Dante: un'analisi', *Italica*, 62 (1985), 34–40. For what both Dante (see *Ep.* 3. 2, 13. 9) and the Bolognese scholars influenced by the *Poetria Nova* of Geoffrey of Vinsauf and the *Candelabrum* of Bene da Firenze understood by this category, see Fiorenzo Forti, 'La "transumptio" nei dettatori bolognesi e in Dante', in *Dante e Bologna*, pp. 127–49, esp. 128–34. Note esp. Forti's distinction between allegory as merely an extended set of metaphors and what ibid., p. 132 calls the 'rigoroso parallelismo concettuale e moralizzante dell'allegoria dei teologi'.
40. Jonathan Combs-Schilling, 'Tityrus in Limbo: Figures of the Author in Dante's Eclogues', *Dante Studies*, 133 (2015), 1–26; Elisabetta Bartoli, 'Le *poetrie* e la bucolica medievale latina', in *Le poetrie del medioevo latino. Modelli, fortuna, commenti*, ed. G. C. Alessio and Domenico Losappio (Venice; Ca' Foscari, 2018), pp. 15–44, esp. 18.
41. For a medieval reader's response to this passage, see Bartoli, art, cit. (n. 40), p. 32 n. 76 quoting Bernard of Utrecht, *Commentum*, 64, l. 166: 'Bucolici enim carminis non est teste Servio ubique allegoriam habere' [A bucolic poem need not everywhere contain allegory, as we know from Servius].
42. Servius refers to 'allegoria' and its cognates 27 times in relation to the *Eclogues*, 4 times in relation to the *Georgics*, and not at all in relation to the *Aeneid*. Frequently he comments on, even deprecates, allegories claimed by others (at Verg. *Ecl.* 1. 5, 2. 73, 3. 20, 3. 71, 3. 74, 5. 20, 5. 56, 7. 21). In general he limits allegorical reading to Vergil's relations with the great men of Rome and the matter of the land confiscations (at Verg. *Ecl.* 1. 29, 2. 6, 3. 74, 3. 93 and 94, 8. 12, 9. 23), but he also describes as allegory figures for poetic composition and closure (at Verg. *Ecl.* 3. 111, 10. 17, 10. 31, 10. 71, *G.* 2. 541, 3. 291, 4. 117).
43. Serv. at Verg. *Ecl.* 2. 1, 9. 1. Quint. *Inst.* 8. 6. 46 identifies Vergil with Menalcas.
44. Verg. *Ecl.* 5. 85–87.
45. L. Herrmann, *Les masques et les visages dans les Bucoliques de Virgile*, (Brussels; University of Brussels, 1930).
46. R. O. A. M. Lyne, *Collected Papers on Latin Poetry* (Oxford; Oxford University Press, 2007), pp. 103–06.
47. See below, p. 15–16.
48. Verg. *Ecl.* 6. 3–8; Call. *Aet.* fr. 1. 21–24 Pf.
49. See e.g. Hor. *Carm.* 1. 6; Prop. 2. 1, 3. 3; Ov. *Am.* 1. 1.
50. The legendary foundation of Padova by the Trojan Antenor underpins the reference to the Muso as Phrygian.
51. Mount Lyceum is located in Arcadia and closely connected to the cult of Zeus. Parrhasia is a region of southern Arcadian and often a metonym for Arcadia as a whole.
52. Verg. *Ecl.* 7. 13 places the events described by the river Mincius, which flows from Lake Benacus (now Lake Garda) into the poet's native Mantua. For Benacus and Mincius figured as father and son, see Verg. *Aen.* 10. 205–06.
53. *Ecl.* 3. 8, 55–56, 58, 61. Meliboeus appears first in Verg. *Ecl.* 1, Corydon, Alexis, and Thestylis in Verg. *Ecl.* 2, and Nysa in Verg. *Ecl.* 8.
54. For Alphesiboeus, see Verg. *Ecl.* 5. 73 and 8. 1.
55. E. R. Curtius, *European Literature and the Latin Middle Ages*, trans. by W. R. Trask (London: Routledge, 1953), p. 508.

56. For the geography of *Ecl.* 4, see also Pertile.
57. For the Cyclops and Sicily in ancient pastoral, see Theoc. *Id.* 11. 7 and 47. Dante will have been familiar with this tradition from the Achaemenides episode at Verg. *Aen.* 3. 588–691, which contains five references to Mount Etna.
58. Joseph Farrell, 'Dialogues of Genre in Ovid's "Lovesong of Polyphemus" (*Metamorphoses* 13. 719–897)', *American Journal of Philology*, 113 (1992), 235–68.
59. Verg. *Aen.* 3. 588–691; Ov. *Met.* 14. 158–222.
60. For Ovidian influence, note esp. *Ecl.* 4. 77: 'assuetum rictus humano sanguine tingui' [[Polyphemus,] wont as he is to stain his jaws in human blood]; cf. Ov. *Met.* 14. 168: 'aspiciam fluidos humano sanguine rictus' [May I look on [Polyphemus'] jaws dripping with human blood].
61. Mark Davie, 'Patterns in Dante's Imagery', in *Patterns in Dante: Nine Literary Essays*, ed. C. Ó Cuilleanáin and Jennifer Petrie (Dublin: Four Courts Press, 2005), pp. 207–34, esp. 231.
62. *Ecl.* 4. 95–97.

CHAPTER 2

Measuring the Divine by Geometry and Feeling: Canto 33 of Dante's *Paradiso*

Cornelia Klettke

Intellect and Feeling: The Description of the Divine According to Earthly Standards

Dante's *Commedia* at its core represents and illustrates Christian world knowledge of the period around 1300. In poetic language, knowledge of arithmetic, geometry, astronomy, myth, philosophy, theology, and Christian tradition equally merge into a universal world-view. This study of the closing canto examines how Dante stages the fusion of intellect, will, and feeling as well as their relationship to divine truth in the medium of poetry.

The Empyrean as the kingdom of God's omnipotence lies beyond the physical experiences of man. It is based solely on the emotional values of faith, love, and hope. In the divine authority, the *Unam Sanctam*, the devout Christian sees ultimate perfection. In order to be able to grasp this perfection conceptually, Dante relies on standards that can be derived from the experiences and intellectual achievements of mankind and come from the fields of physics and philosophy. These ideas, which arise from the human mind, are transferred to the Divine as metaphors. Dante's work shows a total interconnection of perspectives in all conceivable directions. According to physical and mathematical laws, everything is connected with everything else and subordinated to the principle of symmetry, so that at the end of the poem the idea of harmony, which pervades the *Paradiso*, seems to be the highest balance in the cosmos (cf. already *Par.* 15. 73–75). The harmony that is found in the highest degree in God includes, by definition, knowledge *and* feeling. And feeling is at least on an equal level with the intellect.

In Dante's text, algebra and Christology coalesce indissolubly. As an essential structural element, numerical symbolism or mysticism confers on the number three a unique virulence in all areas — from the outer structure of the work to the most profound religious content. The closing canto of *Paradiso* culminates in a vision of the Trinity in the form of three coloured circles (*Par.* 33. 115–17), the last metaphor for knowledge that is accessible to sensory perception.

The number three also appears in the identification of the Dante figure with Aeneas and Paul. All three are connected by a mortal's 'transgression'[1] into, and return from, the afterlife. Aeneas returns from Hades. Paul could have had experiences of both hell and heaven; according to a medieval legend,[2] he visited the underworld (cf. *Inf.* 2. 28 ff., and 32). Dante also refers to the second letter to the Corinthians, in which Paul writes about an experience that is interpreted as a 'rapture' (*raptus*) (2 Cor. 12, 2–4).[3]

Paul confines himself to hermetic and ambiguous allusions to an otherworldly experience attributed to him by the biblical exegesis. These somewhat incoherent expressions of the apostle have been compared with the stammering of later mystics after a *raptus*, and it has been judged that Dante's language in *Par.* 33 does not exhibit this incoherence, although the repeated reference[4] to speechlessness in the face of the unspeakable reflects the experience of a vision. This has repeatedly misled readers of the *Commedia* to plead for the authenticity of the vision.[5] It is more likely, however, that Dante only seemingly gives the experience of a vision to his figure of the otherworldly pilgrim, who reaches the most sacred areas of Paradise and finds himself in a world of departed souls, a vision that simulates the mode of immersion[6] over several phases and describes ethereal phenomena. In this staging of the vision of the pilgrim we recognize reminiscences of various religious teachers, in particular Bernard of Clairvaux, to whom Beatrice had given ultimate responsibility as a teacher for the seeker of God.

Dante's journey through Paradise is, despite some inferior precedents, ultimately unparalleled. The beginning of *Par.* 2. 1–7 evokes the extraordinary and unique character of this journey. Addressing his readers, Dante chooses the metaphor of the boat and the sea voyage for his poetry and his work. In agreement with Curtius,[7] we may see the sea voyage as an autoreflexive text metaphor. More allusions to the legend of the Argonauts arise. Jason's activity of ploughing (*Par.* 2. 18) can also be related to the trace ('solco', v. 14) left by a ship in the water and transferred to the flowing dynamics of writing.[8] Through the allusions to the legend of the Argonauts, Dante stages his poem as a pioneer voyage — one that also distantly echoes Ulysses, who had been shipwrecked close to Mount Purgatory (*Inf.* 26). Dante could see himself not only as a 'New Jason', but also as a 'nuovo Ulisse'[9] who, instead of exploring the land and the oceans beyond the pillars of Hercules, has a single greater goal in mind, namely the heavenly kingdom. Mythical geography gives way to a journey into a utopian hereafter.

In this pioneer journey the aim and the destination are an empire that exists only in the beliefs of humanity, which is only imaginable *meta*-physically, an empire that is inaccessible to mortals. The great adventure of the author Dante is that in his fiction he sends a man of flesh and blood, his double, into the immaterial world in which all the laws of nature are suspended, and which can exist only in imagination. The hereafter as a utopian space, the duration of the journey as immeasurable, overstrain human powers of representation. The poet expresses the mental process in non-communicable metaphorical language. The pilgrim, endowed with natural human abilities, fails as a witness to the transcendental, unimaginable, and unspeakable:

> La concreata e perpetüa sete
> del deïforme regno cen portava
> veloci quasi come 'l ciel vedete. (*Par.* 2. 19–21)

Dante leaves the elements of earth and water behind. Evoking the speed of the celestial journey, he enters the field of astronomy. The statement is grounded in the contemporary knowledge of the movement of the celestial bodies, and thus expresses the utmost degree of cosmic speed. The goal expressed at the beginning of the *Paradiso* is picked up again in *Par.* 33, when Dante illustrates the events of the universe in all their diversity over the millennia, with the metaphor of the knot ('nodo') as an indecipherable universal form (*Par.* 33. 88–96).

On the journey through Paradise the seafaring metaphor is sidelined, even though its repercussions can be noticed time and again until the end (see *Par.* 33. 96). Another idea comes to the fore: flight. This replaces seafaring and especially wandering. The gravity of the earthly gives way to lightness. On the journey of the pilgrim through the starry sky to the Empyrean, comparisons with lightning and with the bow and arrow (e.g. *Par.* 1)[10] as human standards in the pre-technical age visualize the unimaginable speed and the movement in time lapse. The aim and duration of the journey through paradise coincide in a single point:

> the point as a sign of light (*Par.* 28. 16–18; 41–42)
>
> the point as a moment (*Par.* 33. 94–96)

With a single blink of an eye, the mental imagination brings about the experience of space (point of light) and time (moment).

Dante's unique image of the central point of light in the depths of the Empyrean has attracted the attention of physicists.[11] Dante arrives at this statement through the combination of the human faculty of vision and the mental power of the imagination, that is, the power of judgment. When measuring space and time, Dante assumes the archaic myth (the legend of the Argonauts) as the only earthly impetus comparable to his journey into the cosmos. In the context of the abstractions imagined as the metaphysics of light based on the element of fire,[12] Dante, in his search for God, intuitively prefigures modern astrophysics in the run-up to Planck and Einstein.

Dante feels transported and uplifted by unknown energies (of light), which initially emerge from the eyes of Beatrice, and from eye contact, and are later increasingly replaced by a concentrated vision, a contemplation fed by the burning *disio* of the devout mortal and his unwavering will to carry out such a feat of strength. After all, the journey of the seeker of God is based on the constancy of this will-power (*Par.* 33. 143). The metaphor of vision is presented as an interaction of divine power and human will and aspiration. Having arrived in the heavenly paradise, Beatrice leaves her protégé to take her place among the blessed in the celestial rose. With the fire of her eyes she had guided the pilgrim, inspired him, given him orientation and support. Here the otherworldly pilgrim experiences a brief moment of being lost (*Par.* 31. 55–57).

The Model Function of the Theology of Saint Bernard of Clairvaux for the Mystical Immersion

For the next phase of contemplation, Saint Bernard takes over the function of teacher (*Par.* 32. 2–3) and the role of the helper. It is not by chance that the poet brings Saint Bernard into play in order to initiate the visionary act in Canto 33. He makes the saint appear as the 'servant' of the Virgin Mary (*Par.* 31. 102), for Bernard had, as a religious teacher, redefined the concept of the Blessed Mother about 150 years before Dante's time. The spirit of Bernard's theological writings shines through in the last canti of *Paradiso*. In his work *De Diligendo Deo* (written between 1130 and 1141), the theologian had proposed a particular conception of God's image which places the loving God in the foreground above the punitive, bringing love into the centre of the relationship between God and mankind. Related to this are his discourses on contemplation, that is to say the immersion in God, which, as the mystical experience of rapture, can bring about a momentary vision of the Divine: 'I would call him blessed and holy to whom it has been vouchsafed to experience such rapture in this mortal life [...] for even an instant.'[13]

The contemplative vision which the poet Dante made the subject of Canto 33 stages this sacred moment as an 'alta fantasia' (*Par.* 33. 142) of his character. Among other reminiscences, it exhibits certain echoes of the views of Saint Bernard. For example, at the end of the long preliminaries in Canto 32, the poet has the experienced mentor and counsellor of the soul see that, for the mortal who is ready for ecstasy and yearns for the mystical vision of God, now is the crucial time:

> Ma perché 'l tempo fugge che t'assonna (*Par.* 32. 139)

Dante describes the mental state of the pilgrim, when looking at the celestial rose, as a kind of waking dream. In order to be able to rise to the highest spheres, the seeker of God needs an emotional and spiritual act of strength. However, this degree of will-power cannot be achieved by mortals without the intercession of Saint Bernard and without the act of mercy of the Queen of Heaven. The elevation to the highest spheres, which merely takes place through the eyes, happens only with the consent and mediation of Mary (*Par.* 33. 25–27).

Here, the author Dante evokes an echo of the daring of the Argonaut with the idea of a mortal's crossing into the realm of eternal bliss. Mary's intercession is to make the impossible possible. She is supposed to ensure that a mortal can be vouchsafed the sacred act of looking up and seeing the Divine/truth. This 'transgression' promises the highest feelings of bliss, but no intellectual knowledge of what it is:

> cotal son io, ché quasi tutta cessa
> mia visïone, e ancor mi distilla
> nel core il dolce che nacque da essa. (*Par.* 33. 61–63)

Once the vision has passed, all that remains is a feeling described by the *pharmakon* metaphor as a 'dolce' on which otherwise angels feed.[14] The Dante character thus partakes of heavenly food. The metaphor is based on the sensual perception of taste. The 'dolce' describes the very first impression of the awakened. Through the connotations of honey we also see a reference to Bernardus as *doctor mellifluus*. The metaphor of honey, which has figured in the 'quintessence of all sweetness' ever since Origen, undergoes an internalization with Bernard.[15] The food metaphor here describes the extremity of feeling, the highest bliss that stands above everything. It appears as the most powerful reaction to the state of rapture; a mortal has *felt* God's presence.

The conditions evoked by Bernard for the experience of ecstasy appear fulfilled in Dante's text. Through the references to the apostle Paul, whom Dante joins, the criterion of exception has already been fulfilled. The seeker of God may consider himself blessed. The vision also takes place 'in a single moment' ('unius vix momenti spatio'), the speed of which is illustrated in the relativization of the sense of time when one dreams:

> Un punto solo m'è maggior letargo
> che venticinque secoli a la 'mpresa
> che fé Nettuno ammirar l'ombra d'Argo. (*Par.* 33. 94–96)

Experience or Fiction? The Staging of Mystical Images

The poetic representation of the visions in the final canto of the *Commedia* reflects the ineffability of the event. The truth remains closely sealed. Correspondingly, the creator of the poem continues to hide behind his mask as otherworldly pilgrim. At least he does not explicitly set it aside, although the reader is always tempted to understand the last great images as a vision experienced by the author himself. It seems impossible to answer definitively the question of whether the poet and pilgrim merge in the end. We can observe signals in the text which are to be regarded as self-references on the author's part, namely the reference to the text ('e per sonare un poco in questi versi', *Par.* 33. 74), the evocation of future generations reading the text (vv. 71–72), and the expressions of speechlessness and inability to verbalize what has been seen.[16] Time and again, a meta-level is established which stands at a distance from the visions and approximates to a commentary on the mystical experience.

I tend to assume that, for the poet Dante, the masking eventually loses its initial meaning. As if under the direction of a leader, the persona recedes from that of observer, learner, and wonderer into the role of the directly affected individual without a mediator, through a minimization of the gap between experiencer and the writer.[17] The illusion of duality dissolves. What remains is an ambivalence that makes it difficult to decide whether the final sequences are real visions or stagings, whether they are inspirations and intuitions of Dante himself in an effort to come closer to the Divine, or images and pictures which the author Dante drew from other sources. This ambivalence prompts the suspicion of fictionalization, namely that the imagery culminates in a poetic condensation of mystical experiences of *others* against the background of theological doctrines of the twelfth and thirteenth centuries. In that sense, the last cantos appear to be a performance by the poet, in which Dante seems to be resorting to practices and more or less up-to-date accounts of mystical rapture.

The mystery of the divine vision is reproduced in the text in a continuous circling around the centre — the truth, that is, God. There is no linear representation of the act, no beginning and no end, but a continuous approach through repetitions. This refers both to the process of vision and to the metaphors of the phenomena of light, to the modalities of perception, the lack of capacity of memory, and the powerlessness of language in relation to the ineffable, as well as to the feelings of astonishment, emotion, excitement, happiness, bliss, and the all-embracing power of love. Truth itself, that is, the Trinity, is first depicted as a super-dimensional source of light whose intense radiance blinds and injures the mortal's eye to the point of intolerability, so that the light at the same time conceals it, rendering the viewer incapable of seeing (*Par.* 33. 76–78), a reminiscence of Paul's Damascus experience (Acts 22, 11). In order to withstand this divine radiance, great energy is required by the individual this immersed, and this is achieved by the will and by desire. If the will subsides, man is lost. This interpretation results from the idea of equating the divine essence with the principle of the good. In terms of the moral concepts of Thomas Aquinas, only the will directed towards the good can lead to the vision of God.

Images as Visions of Geometrizations of the Divine: The Three Important Images of Intertwining

Dante transforms the experience of God, or divine vision, through a number of comparisons which, while not providing any concrete image, convey a vague impression of the perceived majesty of the Divine through an imagery that can be understood by common sense. By means of modified repetition, the text tries to convey to the reader that what has been seen in the vision, and what the text has captured in words, is only a faint reflection of the sensed infinity of the Divine:

> sustanze e accidenti e lor costume[18]
> quasi conflati insieme, per tal modo
> che ciò ch'i' dico è un semplice lume. (*Par.* 33. 88–90)

The closeness to God, which an enraptured person may have experienced in his vision, can be reproduced only indirectly by the writer. We can see how the author tries to touch upon the essence of God with three important images, and we may examine their structural similarities. All three images are geometrized representations of the Divine. In each, the intertwining of the visual imagination with the inexpressible and unrepresentable feeling of love is emphasized, and the truth is drawn into a sphere of inaccessibility.

First Image: The 'nodo'

This metaphor stands for the unity of an inextricable multiplicity. The picture, which is called a 'basic form' ('forma universal', *Par.* 33. 91) corresponds, as an abstract idea, more to an effort of philosophical-theological thinking than to an optical perception in the stage rapture:

> La forma universal di questo nodo
> credo ch'i' vidi (*Par.* 33. 91–92)

The poet's statement about the 'node' metaphor as a basic form is not absolute; the word 'credo' indicates some tentativeness. Dante does not presume to state the ultimate in all certainty.

The concept of the 'nodo' finds a correspondence, as it were a further illustration, in the verses:

> O luce etterna che sola in te sidi,
> sola t'intendi, e da te intelletta
> e intendente te ami e arridi! (*Par.* 33. 124–26)

The text imitates the labyrinthine figure of the knot, an inextricability, even an inaccessibility that makes penetration impossible. The impenetrability of this picture is underlined in another figure:

> Nel suo profondo vidi che s'interna,
> legato con amore in un volume,
> ciò che per l'universo si squaderna (*Par.* 33. 85–87)

The book ('volume') is another metaphor for the 'nodo', in which the multiple phenomena of the universe are bound together. What holds the conglomerate inseparably together is love. The book that captures and binds the scattered elements symbolizes the entity that orders the universe. As a metaphor of the Holy Scripture, the book forms a counterpart to the wind-driven leaves bearing the prophecies of the archaic Sibyl (*Par.* 33. 65–66) and is differentiated from them through its own meaning, namely Christian love.

Second Image: The 'cerchi trinitari'

While the approach of the mystic to the 'forma universal' of the 'nodo' evokes the internalization of the Divine in its essential principle following the model of Bernard, the second figure turns to another kind of imagery, that of mystical union with the Trinity through the form of geometric encryption and colour symbolism. This attempt by the religious teachers to explain the mystery of the Divine Sonship and of the Holy Spirit, based on an older medieval tradition,[19] was taken up by the theologian Gioacchino da Fiore — like Bernard a Cistercian — in the twelfth century and charged with a religiosity mysticism; the teaching of Fiore initiated a new mystical movement. In *Par.* 33. 115–20, Dante evokes one of the most familiar paintings (Fig. 2.1) from the *Liber figurarum* attributed to Gioacchino, and presents it as a vision of his Dante figure.

It is quite possible that Dante studied the *Liber figurarum* in the codex at Reggio Emilia.[20] Ciccia points out that Dante may also already have acquainted himself with this copy in the convent of Santa Croce in Florence.[21] The codex is considered the best, especially in terms of the quality of its miniatures, that is, the intensity of their colours, more specifically the iridescent glow of the green, blue and red, overpainted with a subtle white serpent line, as well as the interaction with the

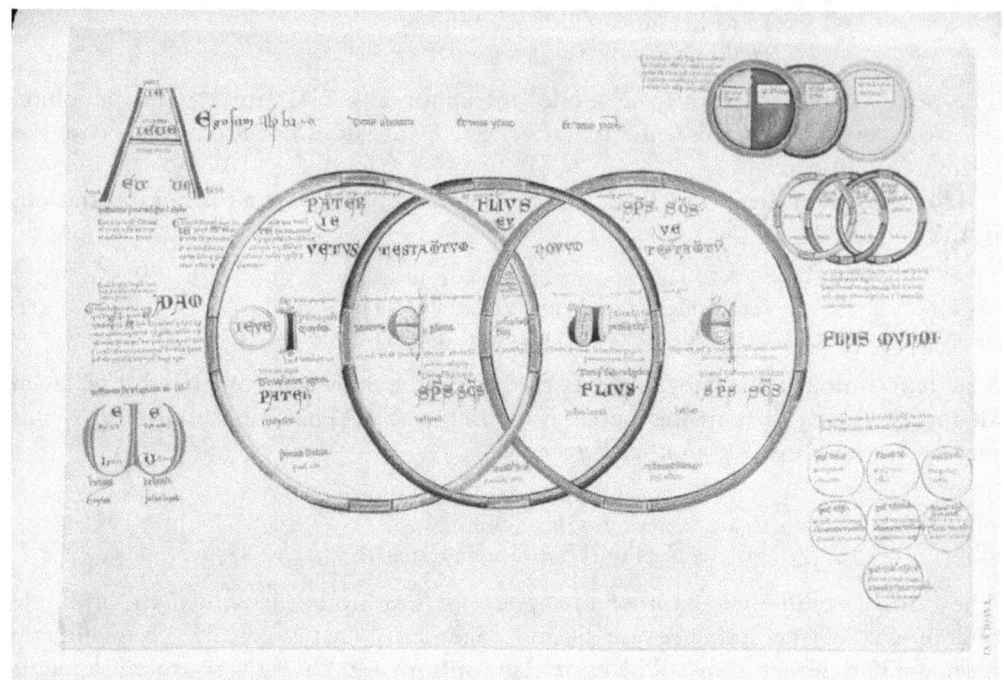

Fig. 2.1. Gioacchino da Fiore, *Liber figurarum*, Reggio Emilia, MS R1, f. 12r, in Leone Tondelli, Marjorie Reeves and Beatrice Hirsch-Reich, *Il libro delle figure dell'Abate Gioachino da Fiore*, 2nd edn, II (Turin: Società Editrice Internazionale, 1953), pl. 11. © Staatsbibliothek zu Berlin — Preußischer Kulturbesitz.

gold.[22] If we follow Tondelli's argument, it would seem that, in the 'vision' of the three 'giri' evoked in *Par.* 33. 116, Dante has this impressive folio illustration in mind and recreates it from memory in his language.

A closer comparison of *Par.* 33. 115–20 with Fiore's figures shows what narrow ground it is that the poet treads when he approaches the doctrine of Gioacchino, condemned for heresy at the Lateran Council (1215). Dante has allowed a momentary appearance by this gifted theologian by dedicating an entire tercet of praise to him in the speech of Bonaventura (*Par.* 12. 139–41).[23] Without subscribing to Fiore's doctrine — Tondelli draws attention to Dante's consistent adherence to orthodoxy[24] — the poet has found inspiration in the formative imagery of Gioacchino, and has translated it into his own symbolic language.[25] Accordingly, the playing with the letters of the Tetragrammaton in *Par.* 26 also finds its roots in the illustrations of the *Liber figurarum*.[26] If the idea of the celestial rose does indeed refer to the imagery of Fiore,[27] we may associate the importance of geometrization, and above all the figure of the circle, as an abstract symbol for the eternal/the Divine in Dante's poem, with the mystic's realm of thought. The following image, appearing as a vision, stages the 'teologia figurativa'[28] of Gioacchino in the language of the poet:

> Ne la profonda e chiara sussistenza
> de l'alto lume parvermi tre giri
> di tre colori e d'una contenenza;
>
> e l'un da l'altro come iri da iri
> parea reflesso, e 'l terzo parea foco
> che quinci e quindi igualmente si spiri. (*Par.* 33. 115–20)

Already in the first verse Dante uses the term 'sussistenza' to clarify the unity of substance of the three circles as symbols of the Trinity, thus departing from Gioacchino's heretical conception.[29] Also different from Gioacchino's depiction is the composition of the circles. In the second tercet the poet turns the image of the interaction and the relation of the parts of the Trinity into language through an ingenious compression. In doing so, Dante distances himself almost imperceptibly from Gioacchino's idea of two adjacent circles, father and son, by placing the reflection of two circles into the sphere of the apparent ('parea') and at the same time including a comparison of the two circles with two rainbows ('come iri da iri'). Through this rhetorical device, the poet obscures the imagery of the painter. By adding a comparison which refers to Aristotle,[30] he softens the sensually conceivable image of Gioacchino, and with the complexity of pure poetry, he transfers it into the ambiguity of the inexpressible.[31] The 'teologia figurativa' based on mathematical calculation is thus surpassed by poetry.

The position of the third, fiery circle remains vague and indefinite, unlike the interlacement in Gioacchino's painting. What is emphasized is the inspiring and invigorating effect that the circles of father and son alike exert on the circle of the Holy Spirit. Fire, as a symbol of love, with its circular form points to the intertwining of the parts of the Trinity through love. Dante's two tercets strongly suggest the imagery of Gioacchino's glowing colour plates, even though Dante's text dispenses with the specific deployments of green, sky blue, and red. In the medieval commentaries on Aristotle's *Meteorologica*, a rainbow contained three colours, to which could be added a fourth colour.[32] The attribution of the colours green (God the Father), sky blue (Christ) and red (Holy Ghost) to the three circles symbolizing the Trinity can be regarded as an innovation by Gioacchino.[33] We may question whether the delicate white serpentine lines over which in the manuscript at Reggio Emilia the respective circles are painted bring into play the fourth colour or, what is more likely, symbolize an element of *unity* linking the three colour circles; the latter view would be supported by the four gold segments observed on each circle, which indicate a reciprocal anchorage. Dante does not reproduce Gioacchino's geometric intertwining of the circles. He allows the intricate complexity of the Trinity to merge as unity through love, and to appear indissoluble. Gioacchino's luminous and precisely calculated colour model appears in Dante's text as an approximate reminiscence and remains vague and enigmatic.

Dante's comparison of the Trinity with the three colours of the rainbow can already be seen prefigured by Basil of Caesarea.[34] With the evocation of the rainbow, a kind of echo structure emerges, which is reminiscent of the covenant of Noah after the Flood (Genesis 9. 13–14). The covenant, concluded after the great catastrophe in the phase of renewal of mankind, is echoed in Fiore's theory of the three ages. This so-called chronometric reading seems to be also encrypted in Gioacchino's illustration. The three circles are projected onto three ages, with the third age, the breakthrough of true love,[35] attributed to the Holy Spirit and promising, in Fiore's prophecy, a renewal of humanity.

This controversial hypothesis was responsible for tainting Gioacchino with the charge of heresy shortly after his death. The content of the allegation related, among other things, to his idea of the Second Coming of the Holy Spirit.[36] Dante's text deftly bypasses the dangerous cliffs of suspicion of heresy by not further elaborating the 'seen' with the argument of ineffability (vv. 121–23). With the smile attributed to the Divine, the poet places a poetic 'seal' on the mystery of the Trinity in the next tercet: 'Dante aggiunge un verbo — *arridi* — che non è nei teologi. Quel divino riso irradiato sul mondo, per cui esso vive, è il sigillo del poeta del *Paradiso* al mistero della Trinità'.[37] The smile, as a metaphor for the communicative mediation of divine love, is purely an invention of Dante. In its inexplicability, it refers to Christ and prefigures the idea of squaring the circle.[38]

Third Image: The Squaring of the Circle

The third image (*Par.* 33. 127–38) also creates the illusion of an ecstatic vision. Unlike the previous image, this one is concerned with the double nature of Christ:

> Quella circulazion che sì concetta
> pareva in te come lume reflesso,
> da li occhi miei alquanto circunspetta,
>
> dentro da sé, del suo colore stesso,
> mi parve pinta de la nostra effige:
> per che 'l mio viso in lei tutto era messo.
>
> Qual è 'l geomètra che tutto s'affige
> per misurar lo cerchio, e non ritrova,
> pensando, quel principio ond' elli indige,
>
> tal era io a quella vista nova:
> veder voleva come si convenne
> l'imago al cerchio e come vi s'indova; (*Par.* 33. 127–38)

As in the image of the Trinity, the author seems to start from Fiore's illustration (vv. 127–28). At the same time, he imagines the human face of the Son of God, through the sight of which he comes to understand the mystery of the double nature. The vision of the human face appears, in the present interpretation, as an echo of the evocation of the Veil of Saint Veronica (*Par.* 31. 103–08), which was first exhibited in St Peter's Basilica in the holy year 1300 as the most precious relic and true image (*vera icona*): 'molta gente va per vedere quella immagine benedetta la quale Iesu Cristo lasciò a noi per essemplo de la sua bellissima figura'.[39] The Dante figure had previously been admonished by Bernard following the mention of this sacred relic as a material image of Christ (*Par.* 31. 103–17), emphasizing instead the immateriality of the transcendental. The icon lays a claim to truth, and thus represents a transition between reality and fiction. The seeker of truth and God feels himself left alone with the problem of the essence of Christ. He formulates his cardinal question as follows:

> veder voleva come si convenne
> l'imago al cerchio e come vi s'indova; (*Par.* 33. 137–38)

Here too Dante, following a medieval tradition, brings geometrization into play. He compares this insolubility with the mathematical problem of squaring the circle. We may interpret the evocation of this classic geometrical problem as a denial of the claim that the double nature of Christ can be calculated or measured. The square integrated into the circle enclosing the Trinity with its finite lines symbolizes mortality. This indissoluble contradiction is inherent in Christian doctrine, a contradiction that, as *Coincidentia oppositorum*, merges only in faith in the divine mystery of the double nature of Christ.

New Time Measurement by the Mechanical Clock: The Two Speeds as a Symbol of Temporality and Eternity

The author concedes his inability to grasp the truth through the figure of wings ('penne', *Par.* 33. 139), a polysemic metaphor which, in an autoreflexive sense, refers both to writing, and to the superhuman speed of flight.

This agonizing question of knowledge becomes redundant through the occurrence of 'fulgore', which may be interpreted as a counterpart of the Damascus experience of the Apostle Paul:[40]

> se non che la mia mente fu percossa
> da un fulgore in che sua voglia venne. (*Par.* 33. 140–41)

Another way of interpreting 'fulgore' would be to simulate a *raptus* that enlightens one who is immersed in the human face of Christ, following Bernard's model. In any case, the search for truth culminates in the blissful feeling of closeness to God, which is, and gives, pure energy, that is, love:

> ma già volgeva il mio disio e'l velle,
> sì come rota ch'igualmente è mossa,
> l'amor che move il sole e l'altre stelle. (*Par.* 33. 143–45)

In accordance with the creed of the Dante character (*Par.* 24. 130–32), Dante the author ends his poem in ultimate, consummate devotion to divine love. Like Christ in the veil of Veronica, Dante himself is immersed in the sacred texture of his 'poema sacro' (*Par.* 25. 1).

In the euphoria of *Unio mystica*, the poet ultimately expresses confidence in the moving omnipotence of the Divine in an almost solemn gesture. As a symbol of the infinite, the image of the wheel ('rota') is added to the metaphor of the circle and circling.[41] Dante appears to convey his idea of temporality and eternity by using the model of the technical invention of the workings of tower clocks. This invention was contemporary with the creation of Dante's poem: the invention of clocks with gears can be dated to around 1300. Dante evokes clockwork mechanism, by way of comparison, in a few places in *Paradiso*. The *Commedia* is considered to be the first poem to mention this innovation.[42] Dante's allusions to the different speeds of the gears and movements ('E come cerchi in tempra d'orïuoli | si giran sì, che 'l primo a chi pon mente | quïeto pare, e l'ultimo che voli'; *Par.* 24. 13–15) and as a measure of the duration of an hour (*Par.* 10. 139–40) lead to his view of an equilibrium inherent in creation. This harmony of temporality and eternity, which arises from the moving force of the Divine, has no physical grounding — as a driving energy, it is based solely on love as *movens* of the universe, a feeling that may also allow mortals to participate in eternity. Dante compares the mechanical movements of the man-made technical timepiece with the divine activity in space.

The seeker of truth experiences God through the moving forces of the cosmos. He recognizes the divine principle of symmetry and harmony in technical achievement. In doing so, he submits in astonishment to the divine will.

Notes to Chapter 2

1. This term (see William Franke, *Dante and the Sense of Transgression: The Trespass of the Sign* (London: Bloomsbury Academic, 2012) is here used in the sense of a transition involving an element of 'taboo-breaking'.
2. On the vision of Saint Paul, see August Rüegg, *Die Jenseitsvorstellungen vor Dante*, 2 vols (Einsiedeln/Cologne: Benzinger, 1945), I, 255–91.
3. See Anna Maria Chiavacci Leonardi, commentary on *Inf.* 2. 28, 'lo Vas d'elezïone', in Dante Alighieri, *Commedia con il commento di Anna Maria Chiavacci Leonardi* (Bologna: Zanichelli, 2001), La prima cantica, p. 29. The quote from Paul is also found in *Epistula* 13, § 79.
4. In *Par.* 33. 55–56, 90, 106–08, 121–23.
5. The prototype of this tendency is embodied by Bruno Nardi, for whom Dante represents an enlightened being on the same level with the biblical prophets and who understands the *Commedia* as the manifestation of a religious revelation. On 'Dante profeta' see Bruno Nardi, *Dante e la cultura medioevale* (Bari: Laterza, 1949), pp. 336–416 (pp. 392–93).
6. Charles S. Singleton (*Dante Studies I: Commedia. Elements of Structure* (Cambridge, MA: Harvard University Press, 1954, p. 62) already pleads for the falseness of the vision and its poetic fiction.
7. See 'Das Schiff der Argonauten', in Ernst Robert Curtius, *Kritische Essays zur europäischen Literatur*, 3rd edn (Berne: Francke, 1963), pp. 412–37 (p. 430).
8. On the poetological potency of the myth of the Argonauts for the *Commedia*, see Michelangelo Picone, 'Dante argonauta. La ricezione dei miti ovidiani nella *Commedia*', in *Ovidius redivivus: von Ovid zu Dante*, ed. by Bernhard Zimmermann and Michelangelo Picone (Stuttgart: Metzler, 1994), pp. 173–202 (pp. 199–200).
9. Michelangelo Picone, 'Dante, Ovidio e il mito di Ulisse', in *Lettere Italiane*, 43 (1991), 500–16 (p. 515).
10. See Cornelia Klettke, 'Disegnare gli spazi del limite nel *Paradiso* di Dante: Botticelli tra immaterialità, *trasumanar* e *alta fantasia*', in *Dante visualizzato. Carte ridenti IV: Dante e Botticelli*, ed. by Cornelia Klettke (Florence: Cesati, 2021), pp. 261–80 (p. 271).
11. For more details, see Robert Osserman, *Poetry of the Universe* (New York: Anchor, 1995), p. 117 (to Bernhard Riemann's theories of the retroverse and the hypersphere as well as to the astrophysical notions of the Big Bang).
12. See Cornelia Klettke, 'Feuer und Flamme: Die Lichtmetaphysik in Dantes *Commedia*', in *Deutsches Dante-Jahrbuch*, 95 (2020), 3–21.
13. 'Beatum dixerim et sanctum, cui tale aliquid in hac mortali vita raro interdum, aut vel semel, et hoc ipsum raptim atque unius vix momenti spatio, experiri donatum est' [That person I would count blessed and holy to whom some such experience has been granted in this mortal life, be it rarely, or but once even, and this but fleetingly and in scarcely a single passing moment],

De diligendo Deo, in Bernard of Clairvaux, *Sämtliche Werke*, 10 vols (Innsbruck: Tyrolia, 2002), I, x.27, pp. 120–21.
14. It is reminiscent of *Par.* 31. 1–9, especially verse 9 ('là dove suo laboro s'insapora'), the 'sweet work' of the bees in the celestial rose.
15. See Klaus Lange, 'Geistliche Speise: Untersuchungen zur Metaphorik der Bibelhermeneutik', *Zeitschrift für deutsches Altertum und deutsche Literatur*, 95 (1966), 81–122 (p. 95). On the tropological meaning of honey in Bernard, see 'Doctor mellifluus', in Henri de Lubac, *Exégèse médiévale: les quatre sens de l'écriture*, 2 vols (Paris: Aubier, 1959), I, 599–620; also Christine Ott, 'Brot und Milch: Die Metaphorik der geistigen Speise im *Paradiso*', in *Neue Interpretationsansätze zu Dantes Commedia*, special issue ed. by Cornelia Klettke, *Deutsches Dante-Jahrbuch*, 91 (2016), 95–113 (pp. 102–05).
16. See above, note 4.
17. See also the opposite opinion of Georges Güntert, 'Canto XXXIII', in *Lectura Dantis Turicensis*, ed. Georges Güntert and Michelangelo Picone, 3 vols (Florence: Cesati, 2002), III, 505–18 (pp. 507–08).
18. After Thomas Aquinas.
19. See Salvatore Battaglia, *Il canto XXXIII del Paradiso* (Turin: Società Editrice Internazionale, 1965), pp. 18–19.
20. See Carmelo Ciccia, *Dante e Gioacchino da Fiore* (Cosenza: Pellegrini, 1997), pp. 53, 55.
21. See ibid., p. 55. See Leone Tondelli, *Il libro delle figure dell'Abate Gioachino da Fiore*, 2nd edn, 2 vols (Turin: Società Editrice Internazionale, 1953), I, p. 219.
22. See Tondelli, I, 223–24.
23. For further details see Peter Dronke, *The Medieval Poet and his World* (Rome: Edizioni di storia e letteratura, 1984), p. 99.
24. See Tondelli, I, p. 224.
25. Ciccia (p. 34) points to various other plates from the *Liber figurarum*, which have served as models for symbolic codes in Dante's text.
26. See ibid., pp. 86–93.
27. See ibid., p. 34.
28. Marco Rainini, *Disegni dei tempi: Il Liber Figurarum e la teologia figurativa di Gioacchino da Fiore* (Rome: Viella, 2006), pp. 24–25.
29. See Tondelli's discourse (I, 224, 379–81) on the substance.
30. According to Simon A. Gilson, 'Dante's Meteorological Optics: Refraction, Reflection, and the Rainbow', *Italian Studies*, 52 (1997), 51–62 (p. 61), the comparison 'come iri da iri | parea reflesso' refers to the idea of the reflection of two rainbows into one another, which can be traced back to Aristotle's *Meteorologia*. See reference to this in *Par.* 12. 10–11 (p. 59).
31. See also Donato Pirovano, 'Dante e la visione di Dio', in *Rivista di Letteratura italiana*, 37 (2019), 9–19 (p. 14).
32. See Gilson, p. 58.
33. Tondelli, I, 223.
34. See Tondelli (ibid.), who refers to Giovanni Busnelli, *Il concetto e l'ordine del 'Paradiso' dantesco*, 2 vols (Citta di Castello: S. Lapi, 1911–12); also Ciccia, p. 86.
35. See Ciccia, p. 33.
36. See ibid., p. 34, p. 14.
37. See Chiavacci Leonardi, 'La terza Cantica', p. 605, note 126.
38. Giulia Gaimari, 'Il sorriso dei beati nella *Commedia*: Un'interpretazione letterale', *Lettere italiane*, 66 (2014), 469–95, ignores this last smile.
39. Dante, *Vita Nuova* (40. 1), cit. after Chiavacci Leonardi, 'La terza Cantica', p. 566, 'Veronica'.
40. See also Chiavacci Leonardi, 'un fulgore', p. 606, notes 140–41.
41. On the reference of the wheel to Ezekiel and to Plato's *Timaeus*, see 'L'immagine finale: *Paradiso* XXXIII, 144', in John Freccero, *Dante: la poetica della conversione* (Bologna: Il Mulino, 1989), pp. 319–34. On the problem of interpretation of the verse 'sì come rota ch'igualmente è mossa' (*Par.* 33. 144) and the proposals on how to interpret it thus far in detail, see Lino Pertile, 'Poesia e scienza nell'ultima immagine del Paradiso', in *Dante e la scienza*, ed. by Patrick Boyde and Vittorio Russo (Ravenna: Longo, 1995), pp. 133–46.

42. With reference to *Par.* 10. 139ff., see Thomas Reid, *Treatise on Clock and Watch Making: Theoretical and Practical* (Philadelphia: Carey & Lea, 1832), p. 4; on the two gears of the mechanical clock, see *Par.* 24. 13ff.

CHAPTER 3

Speaking to the Citizen: Urban Identity, Ethics, and Politics in Tuscan Vernacular Literature and Dante

Johannes Bartuschat

In the last strophe of his *Le dolci rime*, commented in the fourth book of the *Convivio*, Dante addresses the poem itself by calling it 'Contra-li-erranti mia' ('Against-the-mistaken'); in the commentary he explains himself that this 'title' is an allusion to a treatise of Thomas Aquinas:

> Questo 'Contra-li-erranti' è tutto una parola, ed è nome d'esta canzone, tolto per essempio dal buono frate Tommaso d'Aquino, che a un suo libro, che fece a confusione di tutti quelli che disviano da nostra Fede, puose nome 'Contra li Gentili'. (*Conv*. 4. 30. 3)

Through this passage, Dante not only ennobles his *canzone*, but highlights also two of its main features: first, that an essential part of his demonstration resides in the confutation of widespread but false ideas, and that consequently his *canzone* is part of a wider debate; and secondly, that this poetic text written in the vernacular claims for itself the properties and dignity of a philosophical text. In his *canzone*, Dante addresses a question often debated in his time, the definition of true nobility, and he deems it necessary to give a theoretical basis to his answer. We should recall that the question of nobility has its roots in social conflicts of the time and that it concerns both literature and philosophy, since it is at the centre of Guinizzelli's renowned *canzone*, *Al cor gentil*.

I want to analyse through a few examples (chiefly from Bono Giamboni and Brunetto Latini) the elements which I have just underscored, in Tuscan literature of the preceding decades (from 1260 to the end of the century) and indicate their importance for Dante: namely, the relationship between poetry and philosophy, the choice of the vernacular, and the role of literature as a tool for disseminating knowledge and as a kind of teaching intrinsically tied to the life in the city.

Let us start with a text that summarizes well the tendencies I have just mentioned: the *Fiore di Rettorica* by Bono Giamboni, a free translation of the *Rhetorica ad Herennium*, with borrowings from other rhetorical treatises, most notably *De inventione*.[1] Its prologue is an excellent introduction to our topic:

> Questo libro tratta degl'amaestramenti dati da' savi a' dicitori che voglion parlare con parola buona, composta, ordinata e ornata, e in su le proposte sapere consigliare, il detto suo piacevolmente profferere: recati a certo ordine per messer Bono Giamboni, ad utilità di coloro a cui piacerà di legger in volgare.
> E comincia il prologo. Per manifeste ragioni pruovano i savi filosofi che scrissero dottrina di parlare che la vertù che diede Idio a l'uomo nella lingua di sapere favellare è la cagion perché avanza tutte le bestie; e, quanto per la detta cagione è maggiore e migliore che gl'altri animali, cotanto l'uno uomo è maggiore e migliore che l'altro in ciò che sa favellare meglio e più saviamente. E io, veggendo nella favella cotanta utilitade, sì mi venne in talento, a priego di certe persone, della Rettorica di Tulio e d'altri detti di savi cogliere certi fiori, per li quali del modo del favellare desse alcuna dottrina. (1. 1–8)[2]

Bono bases his praise of rhetoric on the definition of 'man' as a being with language faculty, and thus superior to animals. Rhetoric is therefore, as a science and a praxis, an expression of human reason. Bono defines rhetoric as the art of expression and of counsel. Through its double nature as verbal skill and tool of communication in the city, rhetoric has a particular 'usefulness'. This approach explains why Bono does not consider it a specialist subject and, as he uses the vernacular, he broadens his audience by talking not to clerks, but rather to people engaged in the life of the city. He specifies that this work has been commissioned by 'some people' and that therefore he is answering a specific demand of his audience.

The *Fiore di Rettorica* is representative of the cultural life of Tuscany in the second half of the thirteenth century in two ways. On the one hand, it participates in the vulgarization of rhetorical doctrine, which enjoyed a great success, not only for its practical importance in juridical and political life, but also because of a profound conviction, distinctive of communal culture: that eloquence is essential for the life of the city and that rhetoric is therefore an ethical and political discipline.[3] On the other hand, it is part of the very rich Tuscan production of *volgarizzamenti*, free translations that are also always rearrangements and adaptations.[4] Starting from 1250, not only Latin is being translated, but also French; contemporary works are translated along with classical ones. Thanks to the *volgarizzamenti*, and to original works as well, a great process of vulgarization of knowledge takes place in Tuscany in the thirteenth century. A new audience calls for texts which make historical, rhetorical and philosophical knowledge accessible by linking them to the realities of the city.

In the thirteenth century, translation concerns mostly texts of a theoretical nature (literary texts such as Ovid and Virgil are translated from the beginning of the fourteenth century). Among the *volgarizzamenti*, a significant number pertain to the field of moral instruction and are conceived within an explicitly civic context and for an urban audience; we may recall for example the translations of Albertano da Brescia's works.

The association between ethics and politics also explains the rise of historiography in the vernacular, in terms of both the diffusion of knowledge on Roman history and the writing of contemporary historical works. The important production of chronicles that will lead to the masterpieces by Dino Compagni and by Giovanni

Villani, is centred around the city and the values which should support it: hence the appeal for unity among the citizens is the true driving force of the chronicle of Compagni. There is also a strong interest in political theory; we only mention here the Sienese version of the *De regimine principium* by Giles of Rome, drawn up from the French version in an extremely short time after its composition. This 'civil' orientation of culture does not only concern vernacular works; see, for example, the treatises and sermons of the Dominican Remigio de' Girolami, whose links to the political realities of the time are extremely close and numerous.[5] The project to devise a doctrine of the city able to call for citizens to identify themselves with their city and with its values is also present in figurative arts, for instance in the production of frescoes.[6]

Hence the beginnings of narrative literature, specifically of the short story, are part of this cultural configuration, since we find works which mix narration and teaching, such as the *Fiori e vita di filosafi*, which celebrate the character and wisdom of philosophers; the *Conti d'antichi cavalieri*, which extol the heroes of Roman history, and the *Novellino*, whose prologue emphasizes the utility of knowledge and literature.

In the field of poetry, after the absence of political themes that characterizes the Sicilian school, Tuscan writers develop, alongside love poetry, a political poetry, which is profoundly different from the Provençal *sirventes*.[7] The poet intervenes as a moral instructor; he addresses his fellow citizens in order to remind them of the core values of life in the city. In this kind of poetry, which is thus also always moral poetry, the call to principles that must govern the city is accompanied by numerous references to the realities of the life of the cities, most notably economic realities.[8]

The absolutely central place of the city, which brings together authors and audience, determines a new circuit of communication and a new role for the author: that of instructing his fellow citizens. In fact, a new type of author emerges in this new cultural context: a secular author and citizen who belongs to the same social context as his audience. These authors are often engaged in the life of the city; in this case, they are jurists and public office holders. They acquire and claim an authority of a new type, which is not based on clerical status, but which rather results from their ability to connect their teaching to the realities of the city.[9] All our authors are convinced that acquisition and dissemination of knowledge are the basis of reform of the city. It is significant that they frequently employ the term 'philosophy' to designate the knowledge they are displaying.[10]

These new conceptions of 'philosophy' and of authorship can also be found in the most significant work of Bono Giamboni, the *Libro de' vizî e delle virtudi*. Its beginning is inspired by Boethius' *De consolatione philosophiae*: the author is in a state of moral torpor and complaining about his misfortune. It is the intervention of Philosophy that makes him understand that his is a moral crisis. The author is presented as the disciple and the son of Philosophy. The idea of a spiritual awakening is tied to the idea of teaching and the relationship between the student and his master. Philosophy takes the protagonist on an allegorical journey. At the end of the journey, she leads him to the five Virtues which 'open the doors of Paradise', namely Faith and the four cardinal Virtues which instruct him. Thus educated and strengthened, the author-protagonist is admitted to the circle of Virtues. This ritual is authenticated as a judicial act by a notary present, who inserts the name of 'Bono Giamboni' in the register of members. It is at this point — through this signature — that the name of the author is revealed.[11] In the *Libro*, the allegorical narration is both the progressive exposition of a doctrine and the story of the moral 'rebirth' of the persona and his education.

Bono conceives his 'education' as related to the ethical and political problems of communal society. Enrico Faini has recently shown how Bono Giamboni has introduced in his otherwise faithful translation of Vegetius significant references to the realities of Florentine communal society.[12] In his *Libro*, Bono combines very singularly the schema of the allegorical journey with the topic, inherited from Prudentius, of the battle between vices and virtues. The narration of this allegorical battle not only contains numerous allusions to the realities of the time, but also appears in its entirety as a political allegory. The moral opposition that is attached to personifications is charged with strong political connotations.[13] In chapter 58, *Superbia* addresses the virtues as 'cavalier di popolo'.

> — O misera gente, non vi vergognate voi, con cosí cattivi cavalieri di popolo, e con cosí misero popolazzo e uomini tutti poveri e brolli, di richiedere di battaglia i re e' baroni e tutta la gentilezza del mondo, a' quali, per li gran fatti di loro antecessori, è dato tutto 'l mondo a segnoreggiare e a godere? (58. 1)

The two 'armies' which face each other therefore reflect the opposition between the 'nobles' and the *popolo*. The Vices, whose army is guided by Pride, embody violence and abuse of power, the characteristics of a nobility which refuses to integrate into communal society and to renounce its prerogatives.

The *Libro* offers a project for a profound reform of the city. At the end of the battles, the goods belonging to the Vices are distributed to the poor. The Vices have indeed wrongly appropriated these riches. Bono rebukes the nobility for its *avarizia* [greed], the accumulation which amasses riches in the hands of the same few and prohibits their circulation. Bono opposes to this a distributive justice, embodied by the act of charity. The Virtues then decide to build a hospice and a temple, a project which symbolises the two essential dimensions of the new society being built: charity and faith. It is Philosophy who draws the plans of the buildings on the sand (63. 6–10). The originality of this part of the *Libro*, in which the call for a necessary social reform takes on an almost 'utopia'-like character, cannot be stressed enough. The *Libro* is the story of a moral regeneration that reaches a collective dimension. The conversion of the individual becomes the model for a collective conversion. It is Philosophy who enables the city to be born again, and the author is its voice.

This new role of the author in the city also informs the works of Brunetto Latini. In the *Rettorica*, an amply commentated translation of the seventeen first chapters of Cicero's *De inventione*, Brunetto develops a complete theory of rhetoric and its role in the political life of the city. He presents himself as a new Cicero, defending the republic and its values with the strength of eloquence.[14] His commentary claims a civic role for rhetoric, an indispensable tool for the preservation of peace. The faculty of speech defines man and his rational nature, as well as his social nature. It is constitutive of the city, since it is the fundamental link between men; that is why the city is governed by speech and why rhetoric is a properly political art, destined to restore the sense of the common good. This conception is most empathetically formulated when Brunetto Latini comments extensively on the Ciceronian passage on the *vir bonus et sapiens* [good and wise man] who, thanks to his eloquence, leads humanity from a primitive state of savagery, in which it lives without laws, to civilization (*De inventione* 1. 2; *Rettorica* 2. 1–2).[15] Brunetto, however, gives a more political interpretation of the Ciceronian ideal of the union of wisdom and eloquence: the orator is the *rettore*, into whom the roles of *rector* [guide/leader] and *rhetor* [orator] are conflated. For Brunetto, rhetoric as a 'civic science' is part of a system of sciences to which he gives the name of 'philosophy' and whose parts he lists in the *Rettorica* (17. 6–18).

Brunetto's great encyclopaedia written in *langue d'oïl*, the *Tresor*, accomplishes this programme.[16] In the first part, the author displays theological, historical, and scientific knowledge; the second part focuses on ethics, the third on rhetoric and the art of governing. This encyclopaedia distinguishes itself from all previous and contemporary works in the genre, both by the use of the vernacular and by its political and civic orientation.[17] The *Tresor* contains all necessary knowledge for government and its theoretical foundations, and confirms once again the strong link — which characterizes vulgarization in thirteenth-century Tuscany — between theory and its application. The *Tresor* addresses the elites who have to administer Florence, but not exclusively; it is not a *Fürstenspiegel*, but a true encyclopaedia, which encompasses the totality of knowledge, valuable and precious (as the title indicates) to all.

After the *Tresor*, Brunetto Latini wrote an allegorical poem where he transposed part of his doctrinal content into a literary form: the *Tesoretto*. Brunetto is here inspired by the genre of the allegorical journey poem, which he bends to a purpose of secular instruction without an edifying goal and without a link to the afterlife. At the beginning, the author meets at Roncesvalles a *scolaro*, who informs him of the defeat at Montaperti (vv. 113–62). When he learns this news, which for him means exile, the 'I' of the text falls into a state of bewilderment and errancy (this motif might have influenced Dante at the beginning of the *Comedy*) that he will be able to escape only through an allegorical journey, by means of which he will acquire the necessary knowledge to overcome this hardship. The figure of the author is twofold: the protagonist of the poem is both its historical author, Brunetto Latini — since the initial scene evokes Brunetto's embassy to Spain in 1260 — and a character of an allegorical journey.[18]

Brunetto expresses his pain as an exile, but most importantly he laments the situation in Florence, of which his banishment is a consequence: the loss of unity and civil concord. He does not simply wish to see his political party triumph, which would allow him to come back, but mostly wants to restore the unity of the city: only when concord prevails over factionalism will Florence have a future.

> tutti per comune
> tirassero una fune
> di pace e di benfare
> ché già non può scampare
> terra rotta di parte. (vv. 175–79)[19]

In the scientific part of the poem, Brunetto asserts that the creation principle of Nature is that of concord, of which he gives a social and political interpretation:

> Ogn'omo ha sua natura
> e diversa fattura,
> e son talor dispàri:
> ma io li faccio pari,
> e tutta lor discordia
> ritorno in tal concordia. (vv. 827–32)

Moral philosophy centred around the notion of the common good forms the foundation of all Brunetto Latini's works, but it undergoes different developments, reflecting the complementarity between theory and practice, which is, as we have seen, typical of this period. Before treating rhetoric and politics in the third book, in the second book of the *Tresor* Brunetto develops a complete moral doctrine based on the widespread twelfth-century treatise *Moralium dogma philosophorum* and on a 'compendium' of the *Nicomachean Ethics*, the *Summa Alexandrinorum*. The *Tesoretto* by contrast abandons the exposition of the theoretical basis of ethics. In the part of the poem devoted to the virtues, Brunetto's argument concerns the concrete situations of social life, and essentially consists of precepts and prohibitions. His teaching must answer to the challenges of urban society by establishing norms of behaviour. The protagonist of the poem visits the country of Justice, where she resides with the other virtues she commands; Brunetto says that there are about twenty, without naming them all, specifies that he will only speak about four of them, and adds that a full exposition, which includes the other virtues, can be found in the *gran Tesoro* instead:

> Però più non ne dico;
> ma sì pensai con meco
> che quattro n'ha tra loro
> cu' i' credo ed adoro
> assai più coralmente,
> perché 'l lor convenente
> mi par più grazïoso
> e a la gente in uso:
> Cortesia e Larghezza
> e Leanza e Prodezza.
> Di tutte e quattro queste
> il puro sanza veste
> dirò in questo libretto;
> dell'altre non prometto
> di dir né di ritrare;
> ma chi 'l vorrà trovare
> cerchi nel gran Tesoro

> ch'io fatt'ho per coloro
> c'hanno il core più alto:
> là farò grande salto
> per dirle piú distese
> ne la lingua franzese. (v. 1335–56)

Brunetto thus clearly distinguishes the two works: to the complete theory expounded in the encyclopaedia he opposes the form of practical teaching of the *Tesoretto* (called *libretto*), whose main characteristic is clarity ('il puro sanza veste dirò').

The personifications of the chosen virtues — *Cortesia, Larghezza, Leanza*, and *Prodezza* — direct their teachings not to the protagonist, but to a knight (v. 1367), and we notice that these four virtues are typically courtly or noble. This part of the *Tesoretto* is directed specifically towards the nobility inasmuch as Brunetto intends to censure the activities of that class, which is considered harmful to the common good, and wants to compel noblemen to be loyal to the *comune*. It is, however, necessary to add that Brunetto also addresses the mercantile classes, which on a cultural and ideological level largely adhered/subscribed to aristocratic and courtly values. In other words: Brunetto warns them against the imitation of poorly understood courtly values.[20]

The teaching of largesse (*Larghezza*) can serve as an example to illustrate how Brunetto reinterprets courtly values following a pragmatic approach. He wants to transform the aristocratic ideal of largesse into a socially useful attitude. In the first place, he rejects the idea that largesse could make one poor. By opposing the idea of a boundless largesse, Brunetto not only calls for reasonable behaviour, but also modifies the status of ethical discourse: virtue is not an absolute ideal any more — as it was in an aristocratic world, in which the noble class defined itself by means of certain virtues — but rather a line of conduct to interpret in a pragmatic manner. On this basis, the citizen is invited to spend so that his riches may benefit all. We should note that this was also the central tenet of the contemporary theological justification of economic activity, which shows that Brunetto addresses the merchant class, worried by the moral condemnation of its activity.

The central value exalted by his teaching is, for largesse as for all the other virtues, measure. This is not the Aristotelian concept of virtue as a mean between two extremes, but a means of avoiding excess and unreasonable behaviour. This recommendation acknowledges a danger, which Brunetto's ethos is designed to prevent and which he often mentions using the term *follia* ('madness'). This word does not indicate a simple excess, but the very loss of reason: an irrationality that releases destructive and anti-social forces.

In the section dedicated to the *cortesia*, it is not at all surprising that Brunetto intervenes on the question of nobility, which he considers a form of social prestige that does not necessarily correspond with the real merit of people but is based on reputation. To define real nobility, Brunetto does not bring forward the notion of an elite, be it social or spiritual, but that of 'honest living' that pleases others (vv. 1725–46). Being useful to others and displaying behaviour which can please them is at the heart of Brunetto's ethos, a strongly *social* ethos. In the teaching of Courtesy, as with the other virtues, practical advice prevails and it reveals social tensions and conflicts peculiar to the life of the commune. Thus, we find recommendations on how to ride on horseback in town, alone or in *brigata* (vv.1803–20): the knight should avoid any form of arrogance or flaunting of his social status. The underlying logic is that of the integration of the nobility into urban society. Aristocratic culture, as a class culture, must yield its place to a communal culture. It is highly significant that Courtesy condemns erotic passion: she prohibits the knight from courting women and warns him against the ravages of passion (vv. 1831ff.). To assert that love is not a form of *cortesia* is obviously a frontal attack on noble and courtly culture.

The advice dispensed by Loyalty (*Lealtade*) emphasises the loyalty of the citizen towards the city:

> E vo' ch'al tuo Comune,
> rimossa ogne cagione,
> sie diritto e leale,
> e già per nullo male
> che ne poss'avenire
> no·llo lasciar perire; (vv. 1939–44)

Loyalty towards one's city is for Brunetto more than a simple rule of conduct: it is the basis of his anthropology, which he formulates in the opening of the *Tesoretto*, quoting a famous sentence of Cicero:[21]

> Ogn'om, ch'al mondo vene:
> nasce prim\<er\>amente
> Al padre e a' parenti,
> e poi al suo Comuno; (vv. 166–69)

A civic perspective also imbues the lines dedicated to *prodezza*, which is here considered as a typically chivalric virtue. According to Brunetto, the virtue of *prodezza* can give rise to reckless acts that fall under the 'madness' we have already described, in other words to anti-social forms of behaviour (vv. 1985–93). He urges the nobles to renounce violence; violence perpetrated by the nobles was endemic in the Tuscan towns of the time and was almost 'a class privilege'. Brunetto therefore criticizes the cult of 'prowess', which for him is intrinsically tied to violence and responsible for numerous disorders in the city. *Prodezza* thus refutes the idea that acts of violence are a manifestation of bravery. However, she states explicitly that participation in military actions of the communal militia is not 'madness', and that in this context one can, and indeed should, risk one's life. The recommendation to serve the *comune* leads therefore to the exaltation of the supreme sacrifice: to die for the fatherland.[22] In the midst of a passage dominated by practical considerations, this assertion stands out and demonstrates that the doctrine of the social and political nature of humankind is at the heart of Brunetto's philosophy.

Reinterpreting the categories of noble ethics, Dante will take up a similar enterprise in his moral *canzoni* on nobility, *Le dolce rime*, on the 'leggiadria' ('Poscia ch'Amor m'ha del tutto lasciato') and against greed ('Doglia mi reca'). As Enrico Fenzi has shown,[23] these poems represent a decisive turn in Dante's career: the former love poet conceives for himself a radically new identity — that of the author as teacher of citizenship — and places himself in the tradition of communal writers such as Guittone d'Arezzo and Brunetto. As for these authors, Dante's starting point is the observation and criticism of contemporary society. However, Dante does not only wish to regulate the citizens' behaviour, as Brunetto did; he seeks to establish a true philosophical foundation for moral discourse as well, discussing its categories with the goal of restoring its profound meaning. But — as we know — that is only a stage in Dante's career, the chronologically last echo of this orientation being his self-presentation in the *De vulgari eloquentia* as *cantor rectitudinis* (2. 2. 9). The condemnation of Brunetto in *canto* 15 of the *Inferno* — even if he is, in a dialectic typical of the *Comedy*, recognized as a master — and the violent rejection of Guittone, mentioned with disdain already in the *De vulgari* and excluded from the canon of the vernacular poets of the *Purgatory*, are clear testimonies to the fact that Dante was developing a new conception of literature. The reasons are many and both conceptual and, so to speak, historical: in the *Comedy*, Dante does not share Brunetto's faith in public eloquence as a fundamental of civic life any longer, and he implies more broadly that education through literature, as endorsed by the Florentine intellectuals, is out of its depth; it is responsible for failing to stop Florence's moral decline. In his opinion, 'civic' literary culture is insufficient with regard to both its cultural means and its moral and philosophical conceptions.

The *Comedy*, which sublimates and broadens the concept of poetry speaking to citizens into a poem endowed with a prophetical force and written 'in pro del mondo che mal vive' (*Purg.* 32. 103), would not have been possible without the intermediary phase of the *Convivio*, a work profoundly inscribed within the cultural constellation I have analysed in this essay. The *Convivio* — which is, we may recall, the first philosophical treatise in the vernacular in medieval Europe — is a project of divulgation of knowledge of a new kind. It is not a selective adaptation of useful content for a city-dweller audience; Dante wishes to educate his audience in philosophy in all its depth and extension. The Aristotelian maxim which opens the *Convivio*, that all men by nature desire to know, inspires a revolutionary concept: that of a philosophy for all, written in the vernacular, and the basis of a culture which deserves to be called 'a new sun' (*Conv.* 1. 13. 12). An innovation of great importance is evident in the autobiographical dimension of the treatise. The story of Dante's conversion to philosophy gives substance to his conception of philosophy, which is defined as the search for truth and the love of wisdom. The allegory that is the basis of the second and third books of the *Convivio* — namely that love for a woman is tantamount to love for Philosophy — far from being simply a strategy of auto-exegesis, reveals a profound truth: Dante is Philosophy's lover.[24] In Brunetto's works the strong role given to the author reinforces his 'authority'; in Dante's treatise, the 'I' projects itself in the text as the subject that Philosophy needs. The *Convivio* is the fruit of Dante's conversion to philosophy. In the light of the author's exile, evoked in an important passage of the first book (1. 3), this conversion acquires a new meaning, since it confers upon Dante the authority to overcome the shame of exile, which unjustly diminishes his reputation. At the same time, the solitude of exile allows Dante to detach himself from the mistaken conceptions which dominate the life of cities and to re-found ethics on authentically philosophical bases.

In his famous exposition of the correspondence between the heavens and the sciences (*Conv.* 2. 13), Dante takes up Brunetto's encyclopaedic project, but radically reworks it. Dante's system of knowledge distinguishes itself remarkably in the panorama of the time through the pre-eminence of moral philosophy. The value of rhetoric no longer resides, as it did for Brunetto, in its civic purpose, but in its role of propaedeutic knowledge, as introduction to the study of philosophy. But above all, rhetoric can no longer be thought of as separate from poetry.

The praise of Cicero and Boethius, *movitori* of the third heaven, the heaven of rhetoric (*Conv.* 2. 12. 9), is the legitimation of a work composed of philosophical poetry and prose, and of the author's role as a poet philosopher. The same basis underpins the *Comedy*, which however Dante does not any longer conceive as philosophical teaching, but as a mission of moral and spiritual awakening. The author-protagonist is not a teacher of philosophy any more, but a humble *viator* who must purify himself and become worthy of the vision Providence allows him to access. The link between ethics and politics remains vital for the *Comedy*, but the city is not its ideal horizon any longer, since Florence in Hell becomes the emblem of human corruption, a true *civitas diaboli* [city of the devil]. I do not have the space to illustrate how the condemnation of Florence does not imply a rejection of the terrestrial city. Let us only notice that Dante presents himself in the *Comedy* still as a citizen, and as an exile he embodies even more the positive values of common life which the city of Florence has forgotten.[25] Dante recalls frequently the ideal of the terrestrial city, the last time in *Paradiso* 31, where the astonishment of the pilgrim Dante facing the vision of eternity is compared to the astonishment that overwhelms the barbarians entering Rome at the sight of 'l'ardua sua opra | [...] quando Laterano/ a le cose mortali andò di sopra' ['her mighty works, [...] when the Lateran rose above all mortal things'] (vv. 35–37). It is highly significant that Dante does not call the Paradise the 'heavenly Jerusalem', but 'quella Roma onde Cristo è romano' ['that Rome where Christ is Roman'] (*Purg.* 32. 102). In canto 32 of the *Paradiso*, we find a particularly striking example of the sublimation and reinterpretation of terrestrial values in the light of heaven: the ineffable beauty of the archangel Gabriel is evoked by courtly language; he is, among other things, an incarnation of *leggiadria* (v. 109), a celestial example of this virtue, the essence of which Dante had attempted to define in both a philosophical and a civic perspective in his 'Poscia ch'Amor m'ha del tutto lasciato'. The context of the city is not erased, but reappears in the light of a truth accessible only to one who has ascended to heaven and can therefore become a truly new kind of teacher for his fellow citizens.

Notes to Chapter 3

1. The *Fiore* was long attributed to Fra Guidotto da Bologna, but Giambattista Speroni demonstrated convincingly that it is by Bono Giamboni (see the introduction to Speroni's edition of Bono Giamboni, *Fiore di rettorica* (Pavia: Università degli Studi di Pavia, 1994).
2. I quote redaction β; ed. Speroni, p. 3.
3. On the link between rhetoric, politics and ethic in the thirteenth century in Italy, there is much literature; see for example Enrico Artifoni, 'Preistorie del bene comune: tre prospettive sulla cultura retorica e didattica del Duecento', in *Il Bene comune: forme di governo e gerarchie sociali nel*

Basso medioevo (Spoleto: C.I.S.A.M., 2012), pp. 63–87 and recently Sara Bischetti and Antonio Montefuso, 'Prime osservazioni su ars dictaminis, cultura volgare e distribuzione sociale dei saperi nella Toscana medievale', *Carte romanze*, 6.1 (2018), 163–240.

4. Cesare Segre, 'I volgarizzamenti del Due e Trecento', in *Lingua, stile e società* (Milan: Feltrinelli, 1963), pp. 49–78; Alison Cornish, *Vernacular Translation in Dante's Italy: Illiterate Literature* (Cambridge: Cambridge University Press, 2011).
5. See Charles Till Davis, 'An Early Florentine Political Theorist: Fra Remigio de' Girolami', in *Dante's Italy* (Philadelphia: University of Pennsylvania Press, 1984), pp. 198–223; but all the essays in this volume are of the greatest interest for our topic).
6. Maria Monica Donato, '"Cose morali, e anche appartenenti secondo e' luoghi": per lo studio della pittura politica nel tardo Medioevo toscano', in *Le forme della propaganda politica* (Rome: Ecole Française de Rome, 1994), pp. 491–571. Quentin Skinner, 'Ambrogio Lorenzetti: The Artist as Political Philosopher', *Proceedings of the British Academy*, 72 (1986), 1–56.
7. Paolo Borsa, *Poesia politica nell'Italia di Dante* (Milan: Ledizioni, 2017).
8. Marco Berisso, '"Secondo il corso del mondo mess'ò 'n rima!": Le canzoni socio-economiche di Monte Andrea', in *La poesia in Italia prima di Dante*, ed. by Franco Suitner (Ravenna: Longo, 2017), pp. 49–64.
9. Enrico Artifoni, *Tra etica e professionalità politica: la riflessione sulle forme di vita in alcuni intellettuali pragmatici del Duecento italiano*, in *Vie active et vie contemplative au Moyen Age et au seuil de la Renaissance*, ed. by Christian Trottmann (Rome: Ecole Française de Rome, 2009), pp. 403–23.
10. See Ruedi Imbach, *Dante, la philosophie et les laïcs. Initiation à la philosophie médiévale* (Paris: Cerf, 1996); Sonia Gentili, *L'uomo aristotelico alle origini della letteratura italiana* (Rome: Carocci, 2005).
11. Bono Giamboni, *Il libro de' vizî e delle virtudi; Il trattato di virtù e di vizî*, ed. by Cesare Segre (Turin: Einaudi, 1968), 76. 13–19: 'E le Virtù, vogliendo le dette cose di mia bocca sapere, dissero: — Vuo' tu, figliuolo, diventare nostro fedele? — Ed io, ch'era già rassicurato per li buoni conforti che la Filosofia m'avea dati, dissi: — Sí voglio molto volontieri –. Ed elle dissero: — E vuo' promettere d'osservare i nostri ammonimenti? — E io dissi: — Sí prometto co l'aiuto e a la speranza di Dio — . Ed elle allotta sí mi benedissero e segnaronmi ciascuna per sé, e dissero: — E noi t'amettiamo per fedele e compagno; e fedelmente ti serviremo, e promettiamo in questo mondo di darti la grazia delle genti, e nell'altro paradiso e 'l regno di Cielo: nel quale luogo ti farai glorioso e beato e partefice co li angeli della gloria e della beatitudine di Dio onnipotente. E dacché m'ebbero benedetto e segnato e ricevuto per fedele, scrissero BONO GIAMBONI nella matricola loro, secondo che la Filosofia disse ch'io era chiamato.'
12. Silvia Diacciati and Enrico Faini, 'Ricerche sulla formazione dei laici a Firenze nel tardo Duecento', *Archivio Storico Italiano*, 175 (2017), 205–37 (pp. 208–19).
13. Guido Castelnuovo, *Etre noble dans la cité: Les noblesses italiennes en quête d'identité (XIIIe–XVe siècle)* (Paris: Classiques Garnier, 2014), pp. 197–98.
14. In addition, Brunetto himself translated three of Cicero's speeches: *Cicerone, Pro Ligario, Pro Marcello, Pro rege Deiotaro (orazioni cesariane). Volgarizzamento di Brunetto Latini*, ed. by C. Lorenzi (Pisa: Edizione della Normale, 2018).
15. See Cary J. Nederman, 'Nature, Sin and the Origins of Society: The Ciceronian Tradition in Medieval Political Thought', *Journal of the History of Ideas*, 49 (1988), 3–26.
16. *Tresor*, ed. by Pietro Beltrami and others (Turin: Einaudi, 2007).
17. Christel Meier, '*Cosmos politicus*: Der Funktionswandel der Enzyklopädie bei Brunetto Latini', *Frühmittelalterliche Studien*, 22 (1988), 315–56.
18. Johannes Bartuschat, 'Brunetto Latini, Dante e la figura dell'autore', *Studi Danteschi*, 83 (2018), 95–116.
19. *Tesoretto*, in Brunetto Latini, *Poesie*, ed. by S. Carrai (Turin: Einaudi, 2016), p. 000.
20. On the political and social implications of the *Tesoretto*, see, from a somewhat different perspective, the recent article by Ginaluca Briguglia, '"Io Burnetto Latini": Considerazioni su cultura e identità politica di Brunetto Latini e il *Tesoretto*', *Philosophical Readings*, 10.3 (2018), 176–85.
21. *De officiis*, 1. 22: 'Non nobis solum nati sumus, ortusque nostri partem patria vindicat, partem amici'[We are not born for ourselves alone; our country claims a share in our origin, as do

our friends]; on the importance of this maxim for Brunetto and on his civic philosophy, see Enrico Fenzi, 'Brunetto Latini, ovvero il fondamento politico dell'arte della parola e il potere dell'intellettuale', in *A scuola con ser Brunetto: indagini sulla ricezione di Brunetto Latini dal Medioevo al Rinascimento: atti del convegno internazionali di studi (Basilea 8–10 giugno 2006)*, ed. by Irene Maffia Scariati (Florence: Sismel: 2008), pp. 323–69.

22. Vv. 2146–2166; for the medieval genesis of the ideal of sacrifice for the fatherland, see the seminal study by Ernst H. Kantorowicz, '"Pro patria mori" in Medieval Political Thought', *The American Historical Review*, 56 (1951), 472–92.
23. Enrico Fenzi, '"Sollazzo" e "Leggiadria": un'interpretazione della canzone dantesca *Poscia ch'amor*', in *Le canzoni di Dante: interpretazioni e letture* (Florence: Le Lettere, 2017), pp. 263–336.
24. See Peter Dronke, *Dante's Second Love: The Originality and the Contexts of the 'Convivio'*, The Barlow Dante Lectures, delivered at University College London, 1–2 November 1995 (Leeds: Society for Italian Studies, 1997).
25. Catherine Keen, *Dante and the City* (Stroud; Tempus, 2003); Claire Honess, *From Florence to the Heavenly City: The Poetry of Citizenship in Dante* (Oxford: Legenda, 2006).

CHAPTER 4

Dante's Lamentations: The History of Exile and the Politics of Restoration

Matthew S. Kempshall

> How the city sits alone, once so full of people. How like a widow, she who once had lordship over peoples, she who was ruler of provinces now pays tribute.[1]

Jeremiah's threnody on the desolation of Jerusalem in 586 BC opens with an encapsulation of his lament on the exile of the people of Judah into captivity in Babylon. Alone, grieving and bereft of consolation, a personification of present tribulation is contrasted with prosperity in the past, as a penitential call to understand the justice of God's chastisement opens at least the possibility for redemption through reform. The impact on Dante's representation of his own suffering and exile, from the death of Beatrice in the *Vita Nuova* to a lament for Rome in *Purgatorio* 6 to the plea to Italian cardinals in *Letter* 11, was marked. So too was the impact of the deeper meanings with which this biblical text had been invested by patristic and medieval exegesis. In part, this was a matter of form — the first three chapters of Lamentations followed an acrostic of the Hebrew alphabet such that each verse could be read across to its equivalent in order to provide 'vertical' readings of the whole; the first verse of each chapter, for example, opened with the letter 'aleph' and each of them therefore summarized the 'teaching' (*doctrina*) of what followed. In part, this was a matter of interpretative approach — the suffering of Jerusalem and its people was expounded at the literal level of historical narrative, but was also understood as a moral or tropological account of the individual soul and an allegorical account of the Christian Church. Placed fictively in the midst of the penitential Jubilee at Rome in 1300, as well as the ritual of the Easter liturgy itself (Lamentations formed part of matins on Thursday, Friday and Saturday of Holy Week), this one scriptural text accordingly provides a natural starting-point for examining the nature and purpose of the *Commedia*.[2] The destruction of Jerusalem evoked the stubbornness of a rebellious people scourged by God's retributive justice, but also the failure of its spiritual and political leaders to heed those prophetic voices who had admonished them to correct the sins that made such chastisement necessary. A penitential lament on personal and collective suffering necessarily called forth bitter denunciation of the moral, spiritual and political corruption which had caused it. Dante's *Commedia*, in this respect, was consciously aligned with an exegetical tradition stretching back to the ecclesiastical and political critiques of Hrabanus Maurus and Paschasius Radbertus in the ninth century and calls for spiritual restoration and reformation in the twelfth.[3]

Dante's understanding of Lamentations extended to how it was read, not in isolation, but in conjunction with other scriptural texts and thereby as part of a broader historical narrative of theodicy and providential justice. In the first instance, this involved the book of Jeremiah, a work for which, according to patristic and medieval commentators, Lamentations acted as a formal conclusion, a quasi-judicial reprise (*more iuridico*) of a case which had just been put forward and at much greater length. Integration within this fuller narrative, as part of the same text, invited its exposition as a rhetorical *conquestio* — a peroration to elicit both pity and indignation from its audience. Again, the impact on Dante's charge-sheet is marked: the negligence and oppression of kings; the pride and avarice of priests; the deceit of false prophets; the hypocrisy of scribes and Pharisees; the shamelessness of spiritual prostitution; triple condemnation of the house of God; concern over the justice in good people suffering.[4] Correspondence with the book of Jeremiah invited, in turn, correlation with Ezekiel, the prophet whom Jeremiah mirrored — both of them lived through the events of 586, one writing in Judah in internal exile from Jerusalem, the other in captivity at Babylon.[5] This chronological conjunction connected the content of their respective texts more closely to one another than with Isaiah or Job, books which otherwise offered comparable reflections on the operation of divine justice and the vicissitudes of temporal prosperity. The significance in Dante adapting Ezekiel's more striking visions therefore goes beyond the imagery itself: the analogy between the prophet's loss of his wife and God's grief at the loss of the Temple; the metaphorical encounter with lion, wolf and leopard in a forest; the despoliation of the tree by a feathered eagle; spiritual prostitution with other nations; location of the Earthly Paradise on the holy mountain of God; the vision of an eternal peace in a new Jerusalem. Indeed, Ezekiel's summary of the tripartite contents of the scroll he was commanded to eat (*comedere*), as 'woe, lamentation and song' (Ezekiel 2. 9), quite apart from giving Dante a threefold structure for his own *Commedia* (*vae* describes the punishment of the wicked, *lamentatio* the suffering of the good, *carmen* the glory of the just), drew attention to the most immediate literary corollary for Jeremiah's verse *planctus*. Lamentations, it was argued, should really be entitled 'Lamentation of Lamentations' in order to highlight its position as the scriptural antonym to the Song of Songs (*Cantica Cantorum*).

Like Lamentations, the Song of Songs was read literally but also tropologically — as an account of the union of the individual soul with God — and allegorically — as the love of Christ (the Bridegroom) and the Church (the Bride). Patristic and medieval commentators therefore analysed its nature and purpose not only as a rhetorical *epithalamium* but also as a narrative of separation and return which would culminate in the marriage of the heavenly Jerusalem in Revelation.[6] This 'apocalyptic' reading of the Song of Songs accordingly shaped much of Dante's imagery for the procession in the Earthly Paradise, including its inversion by the harlot disporting with the giant.[7] A historicized reading, however, also offered an interpretation of the text as a narrative of four brides of Solomon, each of whom represented a different stage in the history of God's relationship with His people.[8] On this reading, the critical figure for the Christian Church, living under grace in the old age of the world, was the Sunamite (I Kings 1. 3, 2. 17). Arriving from the west, this Bride is called — four times — to 'turn back' to the Bridegroom, a summons which immediately follows the observation 'I did not know: I am troubled by the chariots of Aminadab'.[9] This last cross-reference accordingly presented a second point of reference for Dante's procession in the Earthly Paradise and, just as significantly, a second narrative of exile and return, that of the Ark of the Covenant — captured by the Philistines, returned on a chariot drawn by oxen, stationed in the house of Aminadab 'on the hill' and in the 'city of forests' (*civitas silvarum*) or 'assembly of peoples' (*conventus gentium*), and then taken, finally, on a new chariot to Jerusalem at the head of a triumphal procession led by David.[10] As the physical symbol of the relationship between God and His people, the sign of His presence which would ultimately cause Ezekiel to rename a restored Jerusalem 'the Lord is there' (*dominus ibidem*), the nature and form of the ark (in the Tabernacle and in the Temple), its removal and return, and its supersession (by the new covenant of Christ) were all read allegorically as prefigurements of the structures of the Church. The physical transportation of the ark to Jerusalem, however, not on poles carried by priests (as Exodus required), but on the chariot of Aminadab and then a new chariot by David, presented a very specific subject for interpretation. In this narrative ark, the chariot was the bearer of God's presence, connected by its wood, first, to the cross of the Crucifixion and, ultimately, to the heavenly throne above the wheels of the four living creatures (Ezekiel 1. 4–28). The chariot of Aminadab, in short, was the people of God — first, the people of Israel and of Judah, and then, like St Christopher, those amongst the Gentiles who 'carried' Christ.[11]

Lamentations, and the scripture on which its exposition depended (Jeremiah, Ezekiel and the Song of Songs), furnished Dante with a precise range of references through which to present the desolation of his own exile as a moral and political commentary on contemporary Christendom. Tropological and allegorical exegesis of historical events yielded a prophetic register of penitence and redemption in which a literal narrative of individual and collective suffering could be set against an explanation of divine justice in the providential unfolding of God's covenant with His people. When Dante invokes Lamentations 1. 1 at the very start of his letter to the Italian cardinals in May–June 1314, it therefore constituted more than just a strategy of self-authorization. His citation is immediately followed by a summary of Jeremiah's central charge against Jerusalem — the cupidity of the princes of the Pharisees had corrupted the priesthood and brought destruction upon the city of David. God commanded his prophet who, in his opening cry and with words 'that are repeated, alas, too often' (*et nimium, proh dolor, iterata*), wept for the holy city of Jerusalem. Dante's own lament was for the funeral of the

Church (*in matris ecclesiae quasi funere*).¹² Like Jeremiah, he finds himself compelled to weep for Rome as a 'widowed and deserted' city; he grieves at the 'lamentable scourge' (*plagam lamentabilem*) which has left enemies of the Church 'mocking our Sabbaths' (Lamentations 1. 7) and shouting 'where is their God?' (Psalm 78. 10). Culpability, Dante observes, lies with leaders of the Church neglecting to conduct (*regere*) the chariot of the Bride of Christ along its destined orbit. Rather than light a way for their faithful flock through the 'wood' of this earthly pilgrimage (*per saltus peregrinationis huius*), they have guided their sheep, and themselves, to the edge of a precipice, turning their backs on the Bride's chariot just like men with their backs towards the Temple (Ezekiel 8. 16). The role of shepherd has been usurped; sheep are not only neglected but driven away (Jeremiah 10. 21; Ezekiel 34. 1–16). Cupidity has replaced charity and justice with immorality and injustice, as leaders of the Church pursue wealth and influence through reading canon law rather than the Fathers. Dante's call to shame and repentance concludes with an exhortation to return to Rome, by invoking 'Gloria in excelsis' (Luke 19. 38), that is, Christ's entry into Jerusalem.

Dante's use of Lamentations to criticize the venality and corruption of the institutional Church may have been rooted in his own reading of the Fathers but it had an immediate, and urgent, source of inspiration in the way in which this text was also being read by members of the Franciscan Order.¹³ John Pecham's commentary from *c*. 1270, for example, demonstrated the force with which it could be invested. While echoing the exegesis of Hrabanus Maurus and the *Glossa Ordinaria* (literal, tropological and allegorical application to Temple, Church and individual soul; formal analysis as a *conquestio*; juxtaposition with the Song of Songs; threefold division of woe, lamentation and song), Pecham reserved his sharpest criticism for leadership of the Church. Jeremiah, he observed, spoke literally about the devastation of the Temple by the Babylonians, but his words are understood more truly (*verius*) if they are applied to the devastation wrought on the Church by worldly men, that is, by leaders who have been subverted by prosperity. Pecham accordingly divided Lamentations into two parts — the first two chapters apply literally to the Temple and allegorically to the whole Church, but chapters three and four are directed specifically towards the corruption and negligence of individuals in positions of authority.¹⁴ Pecham's critique gives Dante's own concentration on Jeremiah's text an even sharper resonance and sets his citation within a particular language of thirteenth-century ecclesiastical reform. As Dante himself warns, *everyone* is murmuring or muttering or thinking or dreaming (*murmurant aut mussant aut cogitant aut somniant*) what he is himself saying out loud and even if, for the moment, these people are not speaking out on what they have seen, they will not keep silent forever.

Even within a Franciscan context, however, there are two elements to Dante's upbraiding of the Italian cardinals which still strike a distinctive note. First, when Dante warns the cardinals not to try God's patience, he invokes the retributive actions of Elijah — bringing down flames to destroy the priests of Baal and their idols of gold (I Kings 18. 20–40) — and Christ — cleansing the Temple of those who had turned it into a market-place and a 'den of thieves' (Jeremiah 7. 11). 'Beware of the whip', Dante writes, 'beware of the fire' (*attendatis ad funiculum, attendatis ad ignem*). The second occurs when Dante anticipates the charge that he has no authority himself to speak in such terms: 'will you perhaps reproach me indignantly, asking "who is this who does not fear the sudden punishment of Uzzah, but sets himself up as the protector of the ark, no matter how unsteady it may be?".' Dante's reference here is, again, to the chariot of Aminadab and, more specifically, to the moment at the 'threshing floor' (*area*) of Nachon when Aminadab's son placed his hand on the ark to stop it from falling and was struck dead by God for his presumption in usurping the role of a priest (II Kings 6). Dante's defence is that, whereas Uzzah reached out to touch the ark of the covenant, he is merely reaching out to the oxen who are pulling the chariot off its course. In contrast to Elijah, who ascended to heaven in the fiery chariot of the sun (II Kings 2. 11), the leaders of the Church are like the false charioteer Phaeton, plunging it into the sea. Dante's primary target, in other words, is those yoked together to lead the Church who have allowed the chariot of the Bride of Christ to err. The precipice on which they teeter is an alliance of king (Demetrius) and high priest (Alcimus) which will destroy the people of Israel.[15]

Dante's anticipation of God's retributive justice as the purification of the Temple by Elijah and by Christ, together with his concern for the chariot of Aminadab led astray on its journey to Jerusalem, open up perhaps the most controversial aspect of his interpretation and application of Lamentations. If Pecham's exposition had demonstrated how Jeremiah could be deployed as a call to reform, castigating the sins of cupidity and immorality within the institutional Church, then circulation of another commentary, *Super Ieremiam*, drew out the radical implications of this agenda further still. Composed in the 1240s, but attributed directly to Joachim of Fiore, *Super Ieremiam* became a hugely influential text after it was circulated and expanded by Florensians, Cistercians and Franciscans. By identifying wealth and property as defining sins of the contemporary Church (a charge extended to the Donation of Constantine), *Super Ieremiam* heralded a reform to be driven by a new monasticism based on the *vita apostolica*. The Roman Church was another Jerusalem (*altera Jerusalem*) which could be restored only through devotion to poverty and contemplation by 'spiritual men'. Crucially, these *viri spirituales* were to be identified as the mendicant orders, and central to their characterization was the figure of Elijah in a second coming which would itself be preceded by a second Jeremiah.[16] What gave this reading such polemical force was its basis in the approach to the history of the Old Testament which Joachim had himself elaborated in the *Liber de Concordia Novi ac Veteris Testamenti*.[17]

Joachim of Fiore's interpretation of scripture literally turned on Ezekiel's vision of a wheel within wheels (1. 15–16), whereby Revelation served as the small wheel to the big wheel of Scripture, providing the key to understanding the providential order of history. The result was a Trinitarian division of three *status* — of the Father, the Son and the Holy Spirit — where the double procession of the Holy Spirit, from *both* the Father *and* the Son, meant that the age of the Spirit appeared under the dispensation of *both* the Old Testament *and* the New. The figures of Elijah and Benedict accordingly provided Joachim with the twin sources for this new age of spiritual liberty, as the herald(s) of the third *status*.[18] In demonstrating that the second and third *status* were not discrete periodizations but had overlapping borders, Joachim retained the significance of the Incarnation as the central moment in the relationship between God and humankind. The Annunciation therefore remained the most important chronological pivot, even though Elijah continued to be present at both the First and the Second Coming of Christ, returning, first in the spirit as John the Baptist, and then in person as a precursor to the Last Judgment. The closeness of this association was continued when Joachim correlated each of the Gospels with a period of world history: Matthew covers the time from Abraham to the Annunciation; Mark from John the Baptist to the present; Luke from the return of Elijah to the end of the world; John the heavenly kingdom.[19] What gave Joachim's general schematization of three *status* such potential for controversy, however, was the way in which he mapped onto this pattern of threes and twos a pattern of sevens from Revelation.

A tradition of reading events in the Old Testament typologically, prefiguring history since the Ascension, did not, of course, originate with Joachim. However, his identification of detailed harmonies between two sets of ages — seven periods in the Old Testament mirroring seven periods in the New — provided a more systematic key to the providential sequence of history than any which had existed before. This was the import of his *Concordia*, whose first four books set out the literal correspondences between individual events, *singula ad singula*, while the fifth book explored their spiritual significance. The result was an approach to contemporary history, not only as fulfilment of the transition from the *status* of the Son to the *status* of the Spirit, but also as a reiteration of those events which marked the transition from the Fifth to the Sixth Age in the Old Testament. Those events began with the destruction of Jerusalem and the exile of the people of Judah and they ended with return from captivity under Cyrus and the restoration of the Temple under Darius. The exactness with which this historical moment of renewal could now be applied to the present, in other words, provided a very clear political and ecclesiastical agenda. In itself, the rebuilding of Jerusalem had been a long-standing source of figurative language for the moral and spiritual regeneration of the Church — if Ezekiel and Jeremiah described the causes and consequences of its corruption, then Ezra and Nehemiah described the course of its renewal. This was why Bede, for example, commented on the latter as a continuation of his works on the Tabernacle and the Temple. This was also why Ezekiel's vision of a rebuilt Jerusalem and restored Temple was so resonant for reform movements from the ninth century to the twelfth. What changed with Joachim's *Concordia* was the immediacy and precision with which the Old Testament narrative could now be read. However complex the spiritual interpretation which was extrapolated from his two models of periodization — three *status* and two sets of Seven Ages — the key to understanding the trajectory of contemporary events was provided by return from captivity under Cyrus, king of Babylon, and then restoration under Zerubbabel, the governor (*dux*) of Judah, and Jesus/Jeshua, the high priest, and at the prompting of the prophets Haggai and Zachariah (Ezra 1–6). While the general permeation of the third *status* could be explained through the prism of Elijah, in other words, its immediate manifestation would take the form of a recapitulation of the restoration of the Temple.

The exegetical approach of the *Concordia* meant that, after Joachim's death, interpretation of his writings became increasingly tied to specific historical events, most notably to the conflicts between Frederick II and the papacy and to divisions within the Franciscan Order over the nature of apostolic poverty and obedience to Francis' *Rule*. What gave the *Concordia* its radicalizing potential was the way in which Joachim's harmonies were read against the eschatology of the Seven Seals from Revelation 6–8. According to this scheme, the first advent of Elijah in the Old Testament marked the transition from the Third Seal to the Fourth — under the dispensation of the New Testament, this corresponded to Justinian. The reign of Hezekiah, meanwhile, marked the transition from the Fourth Seal to the Fifth — this corresponded to Charlemagne. To understand events in his own lifetime, Joachim himself concentrated on the transition from the Fifth Age to the Sixth and, as a result, on the tribulations accompanying the opening of the Sixth Seal and the deliverance prefigured by Judith and Esther. Following his death, however, these same concordances demonstrated where the next generation should focus its attention. In particular, once Bonaventure had sanctioned the identification of Francis as the Angel of the Sixth Seal, coming in the spirit of Elijah, it became open season on reading contemporary history as the Sixth Age of tribulation and persecution which would culminate in the advent and destruction of Antichrist and precipitate the eternal peace of the Seventh.

While the heterogeneity of 'spiritual Franciscanism' militates against any one specific reading of Joachim providing a single tradition, let alone accepting the retrospective construction made by Angelo of Clareno, it remains a striking consequence of Bonaventure's teaching just how much of Joachim's approach to history could be endorsed within the Franciscan Order.[20] Pierre de Jean Olivi, in particular, used Bonaventure's authority to read both the *Concordia* and *Super Ieremiam* as guides to the significance of contemporary events, interpreting the transition from the second to the third *status* as Christ's second coming in the Spirit and the transition from the Fifth to the Sixth Age of the Church as the key to understanding the present.[21] Olivi's corresponding emphasis on the second coming of Elijah and the restoration of Jerusalem was bound up with an exposition of Revelation but, like Joachim's, it would be misleading to excerpt the latter in isolation from the former. The concrete identification of a mystical Antichrist and the great Antichrist, therefore, or the actual arrival of the end of the Sixth Age in the 1300s, were extrapolations which often went beyond what Olivi himself actually wrote and taught, not least at Santa Croce between 1287 and 1289. Ubertino da Casale's fixation on Boniface VIII and Benedict XI, for example, or the *Vaticinia de Summi Pontificibus*' identification of Angelic Popes and pseudo-Methodian Last World Emperors, should not be read back into Olivi's teaching in the 1280s. The official examination (1310–12), and ultimate condemnation (1318), of Olivi's commentary on Revelation may have made such re-readings more prevalent but, in the 1290s at least, renewal under Elijah and restoration under Zerubbabel and Jesus/Jeshua were more pressing themes than the imminence of persecution by Antichrist. Matthew 17. 11 ('Elijah will come and restore all things') remained, first and foremost, a clarion call for reform.[22]

Where, then, does a 'Joachimist' or 'Franciscan' or 'Joachite' approach to Old Testament history leave Dante's particular use of Lamentations (and, with it, of Jeremiah, Ezekiel and the Song of Songs) in the *Commedia*? The explicit elision of Elijah, *viri spirituales* and the mendicant orders, and their central role in the transition from the second *status* to the third, certainly helps clarify Dante's opening anticipation of the Veltro and its hounding of the sin of cupidity. While Elijah could actually be depicted as a hunting dog in illustrations of the Haggadah, running before the trumpet of the Lord, he is explicitly identified (II Kings 1.8) by two types of animal pelt — he was a hairy man (*vir pelosus*) and he wore a leather belt (*zona pellicia accinctis renibus*). Given the tradition of embodying Elijah's spiritual return in Franciscans and Dominicans, and equating them with the 'two witnesses' of Revelation 11:3, this dovetails neatly with Dante's statement that the Veltro's 'birth' is 'between felt and felt', where 'nazion' refers both to birth and the collective identity of 'nation'.[23] When the focus of spiritual renewal shifts from the three *status* to the Seven Ages, Dante's imagery for the procession in the Earthly Paradise also comes into much sharper relief. The triumphal procession of the ark of the covenant is initially highlighted at the gate of Purgatory in the second of three sculpted tableaux illustrating humility: Mary at the Annunciation; David before the Ark; Trajan and the widow. In itself, this tripartite sequence marks a strikingly historicized juxtaposition of, first, the Incarnation of Christ, then the journey of God's presence amongst His people to Jerusalem, and, finally, the provision of justice by a temporal ruler for a weeping and grieving widow. Dante also pointedly refers in his description, once again, to the presumption of Uzzah: 'the cart and the oxen drawing the holy ark, because of which people fear an office not committed to them' (*Purgatorio* 10. 56–57). When Dante subsequently encounters Beatrice's Bridal chariot in *Purgatorio* 29, it is therefore a natural extension for him to be faced, even troubled, by the chariot(s) of Aminadab. Dante sees a triumphal chariot on two wheels (that is, the people of God — Jews and Gentiles), surrounded by the winged cherubim of Ezekiel's four wheels with symbols of the evangelists (10. 4–14). The chariot itself is described as surpassing anything offered to Scipio or Augustus, but also the chariot of the sun — another allusion to Elijah which is immediately tied, once again, to its deviation and destruction under Phaeton when Jove was (with deliberate wordplay) 'arcanamente giusto' (*Purgatorio* 29. 106–20). Dante's vision in the Earthly Paradise, in other words, is of the presence of God being restored to Jerusalem, the covenant being renewed when the chariot of His people is attached to the 'despoiled' and 'widowed' tree of Jesse, 'the seed of all righteousness'. What is different is that, rather than reach out to a pair of oxen, Dante now presents a chariot drawn, and protected, by a griffin.

Ezekiel is quite clear in his symbolism for the power of the ruler of Babylon when the feathered eagle which despoils the cedar of Lebanon is explicitly identified as Nebuchadnezzar (Ezekiel 17). Ezra is equally clear on the symbolism of the lion when he sees a despoiling eagle being checked by the lion of Judah (II Esdras 11). Within these terms of reference, Dante's choice of a draught animal that combines the natures of eagle and lion is all the more striking. And yet, as medieval commentators recognized, the historical role of Babylon in the destruction and restoration of Jerusalem was more complex than such a bald antithesis might imply. Nebuchadnezzar, for example, is described by God as 'my servant' (*servus meus*) when destroying Jerusalem and leading the people of Judah into captivity (Jeremiah 27. 6).[24] When his successor, Cyrus, delivers the decree that ends this captivity and permits the restoration of the Temple, God describes him as 'my anointed' (*christus meus*).[25] The respective roles of Nebuchadnezzar and Cyrus, in other words, offered a more ambivalent characterization of temporal authority. This extended to Egypt and Assyria, but also to Rome — not only as the continuation of the sequence of Daniel's world monarchies (Daniel 2. 31–45), but also as a power responsible both for the divine retribution of the destruction of Jerusalem (under Titus and Vespasian)[26] and for the peace which enabled the establishment of a universal Christian Church (under Augustus).[27] According to Hrabanus Maurus, therefore, the eagle should be understood as a symbol of temporal power in general, be it Babylon or Rome (*aquilae vocabulo potestas terrena figuratur*).[28] Dante acknowledges the same ambivalence in the form of the griffin. Traditionally a cruel and predatory beast which fights for gold, in the Earthly Paradise it retains the capacity to tear at the tree of divine justice with its eagle's beak. Indeed, once it has departed, it is an eagle which despoils the tree and another which scatters its feathers to ill effect.[29]

By securing peace for the people of God, both Cyrus and Augustus may have been positive agents of God's providential justice, but neither was himself a righteous ruler. The equivocal function of temporal power which these rulers exemplify was a subject central to Dante's political theology. It is reflected, for example, in the distinction between the temporal justice that regulates relations between individuals in the human community and the general justice that comprises every virtue. This twofold conception of *iustitia* is the reason why, in *Paradiso*, Justinian describes the historical and providential role of the Roman Empire in the circle of Mercury, but individually righteous rulers are depicted separately in the circle of the Sun. In *Monarchia*, the goal of the universal monarchy is to direct its justice to secure a peace and liberty within which individual humans are then free to be guided by the teachings of philosophers in order to perfect their own righteousness through their moral and intellectual virtues. Dante's conception of the peace and justice secured by temporal rulers, in other words, takes the form of an Augustinian framework of utility and order, restraining the worst aspects of sinful human behaviour in order to make a life of virtue possible, rather than a means of directly instituting it through laws.[30] In *Monarchia*, Dante's primary motivation is polemical. His concern is to demarcate responsibility for the life of virtue and thereby resolve a question which had recently rendered the relationship between the spiritual power and the temporal such a bitter source of contention. If moral virtue is a good of the soul, and the spiritual power guides the soul, then any Aristotelian definition of the goal of the temporal power, not as peace, but as the life of virtue, would necessarily make temporal authority subordinate to the power of the Church. Dante's solution in *Monarchia* is to distinguish between a hierarchy of dignity and a hierarchy of authority, but also to appeal to an 'accidental' perfection of nature by grace. The moon, he explains, does not derive its existence, power or function from the sun, but it is still enabled to function 'more virtuously' when it is illuminated by the light of the sun. The temporal power, likewise, does not derive its existence, power or function from the spiritual power, but it can nonetheless receive a paternal blessing of grace from showing reverence to the Church. Dante never denies the superiority of the spiritual power in terms of the dignity of its office; what he vigorously aims to refute is the translation of this superiority into an authority to command.[31]

In the *Commedia*, Dante makes the same theological point about the accidental perfection of natural moral virtue by grace with his distinctive treatment of the justification of Trajan, Cato and Ripheus. The political consequences for the relationship between the temporal and the spiritual power, however, are no less striking. In the *Commedia*, Dante's analysis depends on the sequential connection between the chariot of Aminadab in the Earthly Paradise and the 'two suns' of Marco Lombardo which precede it. By replacing the oxen with a griffin, Dante is not side-stepping the question of the relationship between the spiritual and the temporal power. On the contrary, he has already tackled it and in a place which made it literally central to the *Commedia* — in *Purgatorio* 16. Dante's critique of the negligence and corruption of the leadership of the Church is necessarily couched, in the first instance, in negative terms. As an exchange between the blind man whose truth is not accepted by the Pharisees (*Purgatorio* 16. 1–15; *Ep.* 11) and the angry man whose speech begins with 'Agnus Dei' (*Purgatorio* 16. 19–21; *Ep.* 6), the conversation with Marco Lombardo is devoted to locating the cause of the world going astray. Dante finds the reason why it has been completely deserted by every virtue in the failure of spiritual and political guidance within the Church. Law serves as a bridle and the world therefore requires a ruler to hold the reins in his hands. Instead, the shepherd does not exhibit the requisite separation of powers — in Dante's image, divided hoofs ('unghie fesse'). Rome used to have two suns, he explains, which made visible the two roads, that of the world and that of God, but the sword has now been joined to the crook and, as a result, the Church of Rome has confused in itself the 'due reggimenti' which should otherwise be governing those two paths.

If Dante's solution to the world's iniquity is to disentangle the crook and the staff, therefore, his first step was to emphasize the function of peace. In *Monarchia*, the demarcation of the two powers was made clearer by limiting temporal power to the provision of material peace and order, and the function of spiritual power to poverty, preaching and the sacraments. Peace was thus the providential function of Augustus and the *praeparatio evangelica*, but also of Cyrus and the return from Babylon. The restoration of the Temple required Cyrus to issue a decree for its construction, but also to protect it against both external and internal opposition.

This served as a prefiguration of how the Church required peace, legal support against greed and oppression, and defence from heretics and false Catholics. While the role of the temporal power was to secure such peace, however, this did not preclude a righteous ruler also listening to, and acting upon, the teaching of the Church, as Justinian did with Pope Agapetus. This was the difference between Cyrus and Augustus, on the one hand, and David or Constantine on the other. The temporal and the spiritual powers could still have a mutual relationship — this was the importance of 'accidental' perfection of nature by grace, the blessing of a father for his son. In *Purgatorio*, this was also the symbolic role of the griffin, as its twin form is revealed in a significantly indirect manner. What enables Dante to see, in this 'animal binato' and 'doppia fiera', the alternating 'reggimenti' of eagle and lion is their reflection in the mirror of Beatrice's emerald eyes of justice (*Purgatorio* 31. 118–23). It is only the accidental perfection brought by the light of grace which reveals when the exercise of temporal power is righteous.

Once Dante has reached the Earthly Paradise, he has himself been explicitly freed from the necessity of the bridle of temporal and ecclesiastical law — his own will is free and just, now that he has been 'crowned and mitred' over himself' by Virgil (cf. *Purgatorio* 27. 140–42). This does not mean, however, that the original symbolism of the chariot of Aminadab has been abandoned. Cyrus and Darius may have provided the temporal peace which was required for return and reconstruction, but the task of moral and spiritual restoration would be achieved under the direction of Zerubbabel and in partnership with Jesus/Jeshua. Zerubbabel, the 'master of Babylon' (*magister Babylonis*), is God's 'servant' (*servus*) and 'seal' (*signaculum*), born in Babylon and of royal stock. His relationship with the high priest Jesus/Jeshua, however, is explicitly equal: they are two olive trees (*duae olivae*), two sons of oil (*filii olei*), serving the Lord as two olive branches (*duae spicae olivarum*), on the right and the left of the lampstand (Haggai 1–2; Zachariah 4). This same equality had been emphasized by Joachim of Fiore when he had identified the Seven Seals with a pair of figures from the Old Testament, each of them typifying the presence of both Christ (Elijah) and the Holy Spirit (Elisha). According to Joachim's scheme, the first six pairs presented an alternating pattern of precedence but, in the seventh pair, Christ and the Holy Spirit are equal. Thus, while the Sixth Seal is represented by Ezekiel and Daniel (the former taking precedence over the latter), the Seventh Seal is represented by Jesus/Jeshua and Zerubbabel, their equality symbolized by their joint responsibility for the rebuilding of the Temple.[32] Dante follows suit. Patristic and medieval exegesis of Zerubbabel and Jesus/Jeshua saw them, like Melchisedek, as the prefiguration of a kingship and priesthood which was united in Christ. As the temporal and spiritual leaders responsible for the restoration of the Temple, Dante therefore saw in their equality, as he did in the griffin, 'one person in two natures' (*Purgatorio* 31. 81).

Reading the *Commedia* from the starting-point of Lamentations suggests that Dante's use of Jeremiah, Ezekiel and the Song of Songs was a careful, even systematic, commentary on the failure of spiritual and political leadership within the Christian Church. An analysis of that failure is made literally and figuratively central in *Purgatorio* 16 and a response to that failure is spelled out in *Purgatorio* 29–32. His penitential understanding of the concordance of the destruction and restoration of Jerusalem with the corruption and renewal of contemporary Christendom depended on a particular understanding of the retributive nature of divine justice but also on the identification of a distinctive pattern to the harmonies of providential history. What gave him hope in the desolation of exile — his own and that of the Church — was the prospect of divine mercy and redemption. Spiritual renewal would come in the form of Elijah, embodied in the preaching and contemplation of *viri spirituales* — this was the general transition from the second to the third *status* which is anticipated with the Veltro. However, it would also take a more immediate form in the rebuilding of Jerusalem and the restoration of the Temple in the Sixth Age — facilitated by the temporal power of a universal monarch but engineered by the equal partnership of Zerubbabel and Jesus/Jeshua.

The *pax Augusta* would not be repeated in the Sixth Age and the griffin accordingly departs once the people of God have been reunited with the tree of righteousness. If this universal peace was a type, then, as Bonaventure argued, it primarily prefigured the peace that would accompany the Second Coming of Christ. However, in the Earthly Paradise, the temporal power whose eagle left its feathers on the chariot will not be, in Dante's words, without an heir ('reda') or branch (*Purgatorio* 33. 37–39). Dante's historical frame of reference remains Lamentations (Psalm 78 is sung at the very start of canto 33, immediately before the prophecy of restoration). For readers of Joachim's *Concordia*, calculations of the number of generations which separated events in the Old Testament from their parallel events in the New carried a literal as well as figurative significance. Dante accordingly concludes *Purgatorio* with the imminence of God's vengeance (Jeremiah 51), a time ('tempo') in which the thieving woman ('la fuia') and her accomplice will be slain. While the formal date for regeneration under Zerubbabel and Jesus/Jeshua was given as the second to the sixth years of the reign of Darius, a more significant chronology was provided, first, by the number of years that separated the rebuilding of the Temple from destruction and captivity under Nebuchadnezzar and, second, by the number of years that then separated its restoration from the First Coming of Christ. The first figure was given as seventy years (Jeremiah 23, 25; Daniel 9. 2), a penitential number which could also be matched to the exile of the ark of the covenant from the time of its capture by the Philistines to its restoration to Jerusalem by David. The second number had been calculated differently by Eusebius, Bede and Petrus Comestor, depending on whether the *terminus ad quem* was Christ's birth, the beginning of His ministry, or His passion. For Joachim, the critical moment was the Annunciation. A chronological calculation of the period from the restoration of the Temple specifically to the Annunciation accordingly provided Dante with its own numerological sign: a time of 515 years, 'un cinquecento diece e cinque', DXV.

Notes to Chapter 4

1. Lamentations 1. 1. Scriptural references are to the *Biblia Sacra Vulgata*, ed. by B. Fischer, R. Weber and R. Gryson, 4th edn (Stuttgart: Deutsche Bibelgesellschaft, 1994), read through the *Glossa Ordinaria* (Strassburg, 1480–81) and Petrus Comestor, *Historia Scholastica* (*Patrologia Latina* 198). What follows is a summary of a longer study on Dante's political thought; it owes its existence to the inspiration and encouragement of George Holmes, John Barnes and Kirstin Gwyer.
2. R. L. Martinez, 'Lament and Lamentations in *Purgatorio* and the Case of Dante's Statius', *Dante Studies*, 115 (1997), 45–88; idem, 'Dante between Hope and Despair: The Tradition of Lamentations in the *Divine Comedy*', *Logos*, 5 (2002), 45–76.
3. Hrabanus Maurus, *Expositio super Ieremiam* (*PL* 111); Paschasius Radbertus, *Expositio in Lamentationes Ieremiae* (*PL* 120); Gilbertus Universalis, *Glossa Ordinaria in Lamentationes Ieremie: Prothemata et Liber I*, ed. by Alexander Andrée (Acta Universitatis Stockholmiensis: Studia Latina Stockholmiensia, 52 (Stockholm: Almqvist & Wiksell International, 2005).
4. Rachel Jacoff, 'Dante, Geremia e la Problematica Profetica', in *Dante e la Bibbia*, ed. by Giovanni Barblan (Florence: Olschki, 1988), pp. 113–23; R. L. Martinez, 'Dante's Jeremiads: The Fall of Jerusalem and the Burden of the New Pharisees, the Capetians and Florence', in *Dante for the New Millennium*, ed. by Teodolinda Barolini and H. W. Storey (New York: Fordham University Press, 2003), pp. 301–19.
5. Jerome, *Prologus Hiezechielis* (ed. Weber), p. 1266; Josephus, *Antiquitates* (Venice, 1486), X. v. 1, vii. 2, ix. 1.
6. E. A. Matter, *'The Voice of My Beloved': The Song of Songs in Medieval Christianity* (Philadelphia: University of Pennsylvania Press, 1990).
7. Lino Pertile, *La puttana e il gigante: Dal Cantico dei cantici al Paradiso Terrestre di Dante* (Ravenna: Longo, 1998); E. A. Matter, 'The Love Song of the Millennium: Medieval Christian Apocalyptic and the Song of Songs', in *Scrolls of Love: Reading Ruth and the Song of Songs*, ed. by P. S. Hawkins and L. C. Stahlberg (New York: Fordham University Press, 2006), pp. 228–43.
8. Honorius Augustodunensis, *Expositio in Cantica Canticorum* (*PL* 172).
9. Song of Songs 6. 11–12: *nescivi anima mea conturbavit me propter quadrigas Aminadab*. Cf. Jeremiah 3. 14, 31. 21; Ezekiel 14. 6, 18. 30, 33. 11.
10. 1 Samuel 6. 1–7. 1. cf. 1 Chronicles 13; Josephus, *Antiquitates*, 7. iv. 1–2.
11. Raymond Tournay, 'Les Chariots d'Aminadab (Cant. vi.12): Israël, Peuple théophore', *Vetus Testamentum*, 9 (1959), 288–309.
12. *Ep.* 11, ed. by Edward Moore (Oxford: Clarendon Press, 1924); trans. by C. E. Honess, *Four Political Letters* (London: Modern Humanities Research Association, 2007), pp. 83–97.
13. Cf. Nick Havely, *Dante and the Franciscans: Poverty and the Papacy in the Commedia* (Cambridge: Cambridge University Press, 2004).
14. John Pecham, *Expositio Threnorum* (Bonaventure, *Opera Omnia* VII (Quaracchi, Florence: Collegium S. Bonaventurae ad Claras Aquas, 1895), pp. 607–51).
15. I Maccabees 7. 9. cf. *Inferno* 19. 85–86, quoting II Maccabees 4. 7–9 (Antiochus and Jason).
16. *Super Ieremiam* (Venice, 1516); S. E. Wessley, *Joachim of Fiore and Monastic Reform* (New York: Peter Lang, 1990), ch. 5.
17. *Liber de Concordia Novi ac Veteris Testamenti I–IV*, ed. by E. R. Daniel, *Transactions of the American Philosophical Society*, 73 (1983); *Concordia Novi ac Veteris Testamenti*, ed. by Alexander Patschovsky, 4 vols, MGH Quellen zur Geistesgeschichte des Mittelalters, 28 (Wiesbaden: Harrassowitz Verlag, 2017).
18. *Expositio in Apocalypsim* (Venice, 1527); Marjorie Reeves, *The Influence of Prophecy in the Later Middle Ages: A Study in Joachimism* (Oxford: Clarendon Press, 1969).
19. *Tractatus super Quatuor Evangelia*, ed. by Francesco Santi (Rome: Istituto storico italiano per il Medio Evo, 2002).
20. Bonaventure, *Collationes in Hexaëmeron* (*Opera Omnia*, v (Ad Claras Aquas: Quaracchi, 1891), pp. 329–449); cf. Bernard McGinn, 'The Significance of Bonaventure's Theology of History', *Journal of Religion*, 58 (1978), 64–81; David Burr, *Spiritual Franciscanism: From Protest to Persecution in the Century after Saint Francis* (University Park, PA: Pennsylvania State University Press, 2001).

21. David Burr, *Olivi's Peaceable Kingdom: A Reading of the Apocalypse Commentary* (Philadelphia: University of Pennsylvania Press, 1993). Cf. Olivi, *Expositio in Canticum Canticorum*, VI, ed. by Johannes Schlageter, Collectio Oliviana, 2 (Rome: Grottaferrata, 1999), p. 266.
22. Cf. Malachi 3. 1, 4. 5.
23. J. A. Scott, *Dante's Political Purgatory* (Philadelphia: University of Pennsylvania Press, 1996). For the conflation of Francis with Dominic *quasi unus homo*, and for the pairing of Elijah (as the symbol of *caritas* and the Holy Spirit) with Jeremiah (as the symbol of hope and the prophet who reveals the mysteries of the Fifth Age for both the Synagogue and the Church), see Angelo of Clareno, *Epistola* 30, in *Opera*, I, ed. by Lydia von Auw, Fonti per la storia d'Italia, 103 (Rome: Istituto storico italiano per il Medio Evo, 1980), pp. 155–66 (pp. 164–66). Elijah returns first in the spirit (in the monasticism of Benedict, Bernard and, ultimately, Francis and Dominic) and then in person (preparing the way for Christ's Second Coming, like John the Baptist).
24. Jeremiah 43. 10; cf. Habbakuk 1. 12, 2. 1.
25. Isaiah 45. 1.
26. *Paradiso* 7. 50–51; cf. *Purgatorio* 21. 82–84, 23. 28–30; *Paradiso* 6. 91–93.
27. *Paradiso* 6. 55–56, 80–81; *Monarchia* I. xvi. Cf. Orosius, *Historiae Adversum Paganos*, ed. by M.-P. Arnaud-Lindet, 3 vols (Paris: Belles Lettres, 1990–91), III. viii, 148–50, VI. xxii, 234–37.
28. Hrabanus Maurus, *Expositio super Ieremiam*, XIX. iv, cols. 1258–59.
29. *Purgatorio* 32. 43–45, 115, 126. Cf. Peter Armour, *Dante's Griffin and the History of the World* (Oxford: Clarendon Press, 1989).
30. M. S. Kempshall, 'The Utility of Peace in *Monarchia*', in *War and Peace in Dante*, ed. by J. C. Barnes and Daragh O'Connell (Dublin: Four Courts Press, 2015), pp. 141–72.
31. *Monarchia* 3. 4, 3. 16; cf. M. S. Kempshall, 'Accidental Perfection: Ecclesiology and Political Thought in *Monarchia*', in *Dante and the Church: Literary and Historical Essays*, ed. by Paolo Acquaviva and Jennifer Petrie (Dublin: Four Courts Press, 2007), pp. 127–71.
32. *Concordia*, III. i (ed. Daniel), pp. 208–84 (ed. Patschovsky), pp. 203–302. Cf. D. C. West and Sandra Zimdars-Swartz, *Joachim of Fiore: A Study in Spiritual Perception and History* (Bloomington: Indiana University Press, 1983), pp. 83–94.

PART II

Visual and Performing Arts

CHAPTER 5

Transitional Narrative Strategies and the Art of Usury in Dante's *Commedia*

Christopher Kleinhenz

At the end of canto 17, the midpoint of the *Inferno*, Dante the Pilgrim and Virgil make the fearsome journey downward on the back of Geryon from the seventh to the eighth circle, from the sins of violence to those of simple fraud. Here, as well as throughout the *Comedy*, Dante the Poet takes especial care in organizing his other world so that transitions between cantos, sins and circles are precise and often effected through a variety of devices intended to foreshadow these movements from one part of Hell to another.[1] Dante's divisions between cantos and circles are, however, not generally rigid, there being no 'one sin per canto rule'. While the first six cantos of *Inferno* are carefully ordered as discrete units, more fluid 'borders' exist between cantos and places, as, for example, in canto 7, where movement towards the fifth circle (the marsh of the Styx and the sin of anger) begins in verse 97. This narrative strategy continues in canto 8, which divides into two equal parts (1–64, 65–130), the second half beginning with the forward look towards the towers of the City of Dis and the sixth circle (heresy). Subsequent cantos (9–15) are generally self-contained, but the opening verses of canto 16 announce the end of the seventh circle and the sins of violence by noting the cascade of the rivulet into the eighth circle ('Già era in loco onde s'udia 'l rimbombo | de l'acqua che cadea ne l' altro giro', 1–2) before proceeding to the Pilgrim's meeting with the three Florentine sodomites.[2] In verse 91 of canto 16 the deafening sound of the falling water (''l suon de l'acqua n'era sì vicino, | che per parlar saremmo a pena uditi', 92–93) returns to set the stage for the last part of the seventh circle: the description of Virgil's mysterious actions and the equally unsettling arrival of (the still unidentified) Geryon.

The preparation for the appearance of the tripartite beast and the encounter with the usurers has been enhanced by a careful process of foreshadowing and retrospection, a process that in many ways reflects the poem's rhyme scheme, *terza rima*, that moves us inexorably both forward and backward in its intricate three-step movement: first anticipating the next two rhymes, then reaching a medial state of equilibrium looking in both directions, and finally achieving fulfilment in its final moment of reflection.[3] We could argue that the poem, through its rhyme scheme, teaches us how to read the text and approach its wealth of meanings and narrative strategies as integral parts of an interpretative dance that moves both backward and forward, anticipating and reflecting.

Hell is divided into three broad categories of sin — incontinence, violence and fraud — and their subdivisions.[4] Incontinence is defined as the lack of control over the passions, the failure to observe moderation in one's desires and appetites. Both Aristotle and Thomas Aquinas divide appetites into two categories (concupiscible and irascible), and anger is an excess of this irascible element, which destroys the individual.[5] The transition from incontinence to violence is effected literally in the passage across the Styx and morally as a reflection of Aquinas's definition of the dual nature of wrath, both as a sin of incontinence, when occasioned by an external element and committed through weakness and excess of passion, and as a sin of violence, when caused by an intrinsic disorder and committed through deliberate intention and choice.[6] Thus, in his arrangement of the infernal circles Dante carefully shows the transitional nature of anger, which links the realm of incontinence (circles 2–5) — Upper Hell — with that of violence (circle 7) — the first major division of Lower Hell.[7] Through use of similar narrative strategies the poet will also provide for a seamless transition in moving from the seventh (violence) to the eighth circle (simple fraud) through the sin of usury.[8]

The third zone of the seventh circle, the sterile desert pelted by the constant rain of fire, divides into three sections: the violent toward God who lie supine on the sand (blasphemers, canto 14); the violent against nature who are in constant motion (sodomites, cantos 15–16); and the violent against human industry who sit in crouched position at the edge of the precipice (usurers, canto 17).[9]

Among these categories usury[10] is considered the worst; thus, the usurers have the most extreme position, precisely at the edge of the chasm, at the bottom of which lies the eighth circle, that of simple fraud.[11] Just as anger was seen as the transitional element between the sins of incontinence and violence, so usury performs the same function here in the seventh circle, serving as the link to fraud.[12] In canto 11 after describing the structure of Hell, Virgil responds to the Pilgrim's question regarding usury and explains how that sin combines two aspects of violence toward God (97–111): it is against both nature (the child of God) and nature's offspring (art or human industry).[13]

At the end of canto 16 Dante the Poet introduces the mysterious figure of Geryon rising from the depths in the final verses (121–36) and begins canto 17 with an elaborate description of this attractively decorated tripartite beast, described succinctly as the 'sozza immagine di froda' (7). As the presiding genius of the eighth circle, Geryon has the 'face of an honest man' ('la faccia [...] d'uom giusto', 10), attractive visual adornments (13–14), and a deadly stinger (26–27). In short, this beast is the embodiment of the con man, one who exudes honesty to establish an atmosphere of trust, who presents an attractive appearance, but who is ready to strike the fatal blow with the carefully concealed 'venenosa forca' (26). The poet reinforces the constant play on the deceptive nature of appearances through references to the wondrous nature of Geryon's bodily decoration, more pleasing than the legendary fabrics of the beguiling, stereotypically perfidious 'Tartari' and

'Turchi' (17) and the beautiful woven art of Arachne (18), all examples that suggest the seductive nature of human art and the deceptions it can foster. Appropriately Geryon does not fully enter the seventh circle, but remains at its perimeter, the scorpion-like tail swinging in the void, much like the boat half in and half out of the water (19–20) or the beaver with tail in water and the rest of its body on shore (22). Geryon's dramatic entrance combines the threat of violence and the subversive, deceptive nature of superficial artistic beauty. This introduction underscores the relationship between violence and fraud and leads to the encounter with the usurers and the eventual passage to the eighth circle:

>   Così ancor su per la strema testa
> di quel settimo cerchio tutto solo
> andai, dove sedea la gente mesta.
>   Per li occhi fora scoppiava lor duolo;
> di qua, di là soccorrien con le mani
> quando a' vapori, e quando al caldo suolo:
>   non altrimenti fan di state i cani
> or col ceffo or col piè, quando son morsi
> o da pulci o da mosche o da tafani.
>   Poi che nel viso a certi li occhi porsi,
> ne' quali 'l doloroso foco casca,
> non ne conobbi alcun; ma io m' accorsi
>   che dal collo a ciascun pendea una tasca
> ch' avea certo colore e certo segno,
> e quindi par che 'l loro occhio si pasca.
>   E com' io riguardando tra lor vegno,
> in una borsa gialla vidi azzurro
> che d' un leone avea faccia e contegno.
>   Poi, procedendo di mio sguardo il curro,
> vidine un' altra come sangue rossa,
> mostrando un'oca bianca più che burro.
>   E un che d'una scrofa azzurra e grossa
> segnato avea lo suo sacchetto bianco,
> mi disse: 'Che fai tu in questa fossa?
>   Or te ne va; e perché se' vivo anco,
> sappi che 'l mio vicin Vitalïano
> sederà qui dal mio sinistro fianco.
>   Con questi Fiorentin son padoano:
> spesse fïate mi 'ntronan li orecchi
> gridando: "Vegna 'l cavalier sovrano,
>   che recherà la tasca con tre becchi!".'
> Qui distorse la bocca e di fuor trasse
> la lingua, come bue che 'l naso lecchi. (17.43–75)

Visual artistry comes to the fore when the Pilgrim sees a group of Florentine moneylenders with one Paduan — Reginaldo (Rinaldo) degli Scrovegni — among them.[14] Because the falling fire has disfigured their faces, Dante can identify them only through the colourful family crest on the moneybags that hang around their necks.[15] The anonymity of the usurers, together with their intense sinful desire for material wealth, looks back to the avaricious souls in canto 7.[16] Indeed, the usurers' lack of a specific identity — they are known only through their crest — would suggest that the condemnation extends to the entire family.[17]

Sitting on the edge of the chasm, pelted by the rain of fire, and weeping, the usurers fix their gaze on the emblazoned money pouch hanging around their necks.[18] This particular detail of the moneybag as punishment for usury is noted in the statutes adopted in Padua in the thirteenth century[19] and represented in the visual arts,[20] notably in the Arena Chapel[21] in Padua. The heraldic imagery on the bags provides the only clue to the usurers' identity.[22] The crest of the Black Guelf Gianfigliazzi family presents a blue lion on a gold background (59–60),[23] and that of the Ghibelline Obriachi family is a white goose on a red field (62–63).[24] The third usurer, the Paduan Reginaldo degli Scrovegni, is easily identifiable by his crest displaying a pregnant blue sow on a silver field (64–65).[25] Recognizing the Pilgrim as still living, he rudely orders him to leave (66–67), but first he foretells the arrival of a fellow Paduan citizen, Vitaliano (68–69),[26] and then relates what the Florentine usurers shout about the awaited arrival in this part of Hell of the 'cavalier sovrano who the will wear the purse with the three goats' (72–73),[27] their compatriot Gianni Buiamonte de' Becchi.[28] As Momigliano has noted, this announcement of the eventual presence in Hell of two still-living individuals is a first in the poem and serves to foreshadow similar pronouncements in the eighth and ninth circles.[29]

Several themes pervade canto 17 and contribute to its overall meaning. One is the emphasis on animals, those present on the scene — both real (Geryon) and in artistic representations (the images on the crests) — and those present in allusions (the beaver, 21–22) and in descriptive passages, such as those employed in the first and final parts of the canto to describe both the figure of Geryon ('serpente', 12, and 'scorpion', 27) and the descent to the eighth circle ('anguilla', 104, and 'falcon', 127). The souls of the usurers, tormented by fire, are also described as acting like dogs bitten by fleas and other insects (47–51), and, after his words to the Pilgrim, Reginaldo sticks out his tongue like an ox licking its nose (74–75). The use of this sort of animal imagery to describe the usurers is intended to show their base characteristics, their venal actions that undermine whatever 'nobility' they might have enjoyed in Florence or Padua. Indeed, they tarnished whatever veneer of urban 'nobility' they attempted to forge for themselves through their family crests.[30] Given Dante's views on the nature of true nobility, the fact that his father and grandfather were moneylenders[31] may have made this episode in the poem particularly troubling for him.[32]

Another theme that emerges in this canto is the deceptive nature of appearances, a particular element that serves to foreshadow the sins punished in the eighth circle, all of which depend on some sort of fraud, some kind of misrepresentation. Dante the Poet underlines this idea by presenting the money pouches emblazoned with the family crests. Given that in the Middle Ages art performed a variety of purposes, in canto 17 it is used to identify the usurers and their family, and it further reminds us that medieval artistic representation can serve radically different ends: both to praise and to condemn.[33] The reference to Arachne in the description of

Geryon's decorated body suggests how art can serve a deceptive purpose,[34] just as the accompanying allusion to the 'drappi' of the Tartars and Turks would appear to indicate the commonly, if wrongly held, notion of their treacherous nature and dubious reputation as truth tellers.[35] Similarly, one motive for the invention of a heraldic device may be to present a positive but perhaps aggrandized image of a family and its 'noble' history. In other cases it may be to imitate such images in an attempt to give one's lineage a certain social standing. In the former instance, a wealthy, socially or politically prominent family might adopt an emblematic figure, such as an eagle or a lion that would suggest a noble heritage.[36] In the latter case, the family would propose inventing a crest based on the family name,[37] such as the Scrovegni's use of a sow ('scrofa') or the Becchi's incorporation of a goat ('becco'), both of which are domestic animals that do not rank very high in the hierarchy of beasts.[38] These crests might be the perfect emblems of the 'gente nuova' (16.73) who with their 'sùbiti guadagni' (16.73) have generated 'orgoglio e dismisura' in Florence (74–75).[39] Nevertheless, the mere designing and adopting of a particular crest would also serve to confer a certain prestige on the family, which could be considered a deceptive practice, a stratagem perhaps confirmed by the usurers' symbolic position in the topography of *Inferno* — literally on the verge of the circle of fraud. The Poet's narrative strategy here is to use Geryon — the 'sozza imagine di frode' — as the element whose physical description and arrival in the seventh circle serve both to interrupt the narrative and to separate the usurers from the other violent souls. The usurers whose sin involves deceptive/fraudulent practices then mirror Geryon's characteristics, thus establishing their pivotal role in anticipating the next major division of Hell.[40]

Dante makes many connections between usury and the sins of the eighth circle and particularly to those found in the first three *bolge* ('ditches').[41] The constant movement of the panders and seducers (canto 18) may have been anticipated by that of the sodomites (and also the lustful in canto 5), and the close relationship between the sin of sodomy and usury is well established. The comparison of the panders and seducers, who run in opposite directions around the circular track, to the traffic pattern devised during the Roman Jubilee of 1300 when the large crowds of pilgrims were routed in two directions across the bridge toward and away from the Castel Sant'Angelo and St Peter's basilica (18. 28–33), may be more than merely descriptive. It may be a pointed criticism of Pope Boniface VIII, Dante's arch-nemesis, who proclaimed the Jubilee and offered plenary indulgences to those pilgrims who fulfilled certain requirements. Given his unrelenting criticism of ecclesiastical corruption, Dante may be suggesting that Boniface and other wayward clerics may be in some ways similar to these sinners in Hell, in that they are 'pandering' the Church by 'selling' indulgences and 'seducing' the faithful by their 'marketing' of the Jubilee.[42]

The Jubilee of 1300 was also important for the Scrovegni in Padua, for in that year Enrico (Reginaldo's son) ceased his usurious practices and set in motion his plan to build the Arena Chapel, which Giotto decorated in 1303–05.[43] In the fresco depicting Enrico's offering of the chapel to the Virgin Mary, Giotto depicts the donor 'as a penitent: he wears a robe of violet, a colour liturgically associated with the penitential seasons of Advent or Lent'.[44] Since Dante was probably in Padua at some point in this period, he would have viewed Giotto's visual images, whose specific meaning and extended analogies he would later incorporate to facilitate the transition from the sin of usury to the sins of fraud. The moneybags, which hang from the usurers' necks in the *Comedy*, reflect an artistic tradition that ranges from sculptural programmes to Last Judgment frescoes and defamatory paintings (*pitture infamanti*).[45] Giotto uses images of moneybags in the Arena Chapel frescoes, specifically in relation to the following figures in the Last Judgment:[46] the avaricious and usurers; a simoniac bishop and a prostitute receiving a moneybag; and Judas,[47] who is in proximate position to three avaricious souls hanging by the strings of their sacks.[48] In addition to Judas's general characterization in the Middle Ages as the personification of avarice, he is also depicted in various medieval texts as a usurer.[49] Moreover, the common association in the Middle Ages between usury and prostitution[50] would strengthen these ties, for in canto 18 we find Thaïs, the prostitute and flatterer, who is befouled with human excrement, providing yet another connection with usury.[51] Moreover, additional links between usury and simony and prostitution[52] would anticipate the events in the third *bolgia* (canto 19), where the simoniacs are described as prostituting the Church (19. 106–08), and Dante adapts and conflates the images of the harlot and the beast from Apocalypse 17 to inveigh against the Donation of Constantine as the 'conversion' of the Church to earthly riches (19. 109–17).[53]

In conclusion, the web of connections that join usury to the sins of fraud allows the reader to move progressively and seamlessly from the seventh to the eighth circle and to appreciate the pivotal nature of Dante's consummate narrative art, which, as noted at the beginning of this chapter, relies on the pattern of anticipation and retrospection. Dante's depiction of usury and usurers focuses on the art of the heraldic images emblazoned on the bags hanging around the sinners' necks and draws on and complements them with similar images of corruption, violence and eternal judgment so aptly presented by Giotto in the Arena Chapel frescoes. With this rich palette of colours the Poet demonstrates his keen artistic sensitivity and presents a vivid portrait of the evils of usury besetting both the noble classes and the ascendant bourgeoisie who, through their fraudulent and (non-physically) violent activities, were eroding the very fabric of society. Dante's knowledge of and close attention to the visual arts and his formidable narrative skills enable him to present the usurers as crucial figures whose presence and web of associations aid both his and our journey through the *Inferno*.

Notes to Chapter 5

1. Teodolinda Barolini has made insightful comments on these matters in *The Undivine 'Comedy': Detheologizing Dante* (Princeton: Princeton University Press, 1992), pp. 21–47, 67–73, 257–65.
2. All citations from the *Comedy* follow Petrocchi's edition: Dante Alighieri, *La Commedia secondo l'antica vulgate*, 2nd edn (Florence: Le Lettere, 1994).
3. For *terza rima* see, among others, Freccero, 'The Significance of *Terza Rima*', in *Dante: The Poetics of Conversion*, ed. by Rachel Jacoff (Cambridge, MA: Harvard University Press, 1986), pp. 258–71.
4. For a detailed study of these categories see, among others, Marc Cogan, *The Design in the Wax: The Structure of the 'Divine Comedy' and its Meaning* (Notre Dame, IN: University of Notre Dame Press, 1999).
5. *Summa Theologiae*, $1^a\, 2^{ae}$ quaes. 46, art. 8, and $2^a\, 2^{ae}$ quaes. 158, art. 5, resp. See the Latin text and English translation of the *Summa* by Thomas Gilby, O.P., *Summa Theologiae*, XLIV (New York and London: McGraw-Hill and Eyre and Spottiswoode, 1972). For the nature of wrath in canto 8 see my essay, '*Inferno* VIII', in *Dante's 'Divine Comedy': Introductory Readings. I: Inferno*, ed. by Tibor Wlassics (Charlottesville: University of Virginia, 1990), pp. 93–109.
6. For these matters and appropriate references to St. Thomas, see Charles S. Singleton's notes to his translation/commentary: Dante Alighieri, *The Divine Comedy: Inferno, II: Commentary* (Princeton: Princeton University Press, 1970), notes to vv. 23–24 (pp. 165–66) and notes to vv. 83–84 (pp. 176–78).
7. Circle 6 is reserved for heresy, a sin of the intellect.
8. Simon Ravenscroft makes this same point in 'Usury in the *Inferno*: Auditing Dante's Debt to the Scholastics', *Comitatus*, 42 (2011), 89–113 (p. 110).
9. The sterility of the desert is most suitable for these souls whose sins are unproductive and unnatural and are punished by the unnatural fall of fire, which reflects the destruction of Sodom and Gomorrah (Genesis 19. 24).
10. Among medieval treatments of usury see the treatise (*De peccato usure*) by the Florentine Dominican Remigio dei Girolami: Ovidio Capitani, 'Il *De peccato usure* di Remigio de' Girolami', *Studi medievali*, ser. 3, 6.2 (1965), 537–662. Among modern discussions of usury see Odd Langholm, 'Three Italian Advocates of Aquinas: Tolomeo of Lucca, Remigio of Florence, John of Naples', in his *Economics in the Medieval Schools: Wealth, Exchange, Value, Money and Usury according to the Paris Theological Tradition 1200–1350* (Leiden: Brill, 1992), pp. 454–78, and idem, *The Aristotelian Analysis of Usury* (Oslo: Universitetsforlaget, 1984).
11. For usury in the *Comedy* see Ovidio Capitani, *ED*, V, 852–53; Joan M. Ferrante, *The Political Vision of the* Divine Comedy (Princeton: Princeton University Press, 1984), pp. 316–24, 343–44; and Giuseppe Garrani, *Il Pensiero di Dante in tema di economia monetaria e creditizia*, 2nd edn (Palermo: Fondazione Culturale 'Lauro Chiazzese', 1967), pp. 70–90. For usurers see Stefano Jacomuzzi, 'Usurai', in *ED*, V, 853–54.
12. This sort of spatial organization has been noted by earlier critics: Cogan, *Design*, pp. 48–54; Guy Raffa, 'Usury', in *The Dante Encyclopedia*, ed. by Richard Lansing (New York: Garland, 2000), pp. 847–49; and Maria Francesca Rossetti, *A Shadow of Dante* (London: Rivingston, 1871), p. 56.
13. Indeed, in his study on Dante's reception of Aristotelian-Thomist views on usury and the nature of money, Ravenscroft points to links that join usury to both blasphemy and sodomy ('Usury', pp. 96–100). In the first part of his treatise Remigio dei Girolami focuses on the links between usury and sodomy.
14. For the joining here of Florence and Padua, two major centers of usury, see Giorgio Padoan, *Il lungo cammino del 'poema sacro'. Studi danteschi* (Florence: Olschki, 1993), pp. 54–56, and Garrani, p. 72.
15. The moneybag is also the common visual sign of avarice, to which usury is linked.
16. This obsession with wealth is present in the usurers' constant gaze on their moneybags (17. 57). For additional similarities between the avaricious and the usurers see Ravenscroft, 'Usury', pp. 106–11.
17. This has been suggested by some critics, such as Arnaldo d'Addario, "Obriachi", in *ED*, IV, 110–11 (p. 110): 'un giudizio di condanna morale valido per l'intera casata'.

18. Their seated position would also suggest and mirror their usual working condition, sitting behind a table at the market. See Natalino Sapegno's commentary to Dante Alighieri, *La Divina commedia: Inferno*, 3rd edn (Florence: La Nuova Italia, 1985), n. to v. 55 (p. 196), and Singleton's commentary on the *Inferno*, n. to v. 55 (pp. 300–01).
19. For this historical detail see Anne Derbes and Mark Sandona, *The Usurer's Heart: Giotto, Enrico Scrovegni and the Arena Chapel in Padua* (University Park: Pennsylvania State University Press, 2008), pp. 36, 52.
20. For a richly detailed and nuanced study of the history and significance of this motif in medieval art see Giuliano Milani, *L'uomo con la borsa al collo: genealogia e uso di un'immagine medievale* (Rome: Viella, 2017).
21. The fact that Enrico, the son of Reginaldo degli Scrovegni (the usurer in canto 17), commissioned the building of the chapel is important for this particular image.
22. Often heraldic imagery reflects the family name, and thus, these 'insegne parlanti' 'speak' their identity: for example, the device of a ladder 'scala' for the Scaligeri (Verona) or that of a tower 'torre' for the Della Torre/Torriani (Milan). For this practice and for valuable commentary on Italian heraldic crests in general see the monumental volume by Giacomo Bascapé and Marcello Del Piazzo, *Insegne e simboli. Araldica pubblica e private medievale e moderna* (Rome: Ministero per i beni e le attività culturali, Ufficio centrale per i beni archivistici, 1991), pp. 199–208. For general studies of medieval heraldry see the following works by Michel Pastoureau: *Figures et couleurs: Études sur la symbolique et la sensibilité médiévales* (Paris: Le Léopard d'Or, 1986), and *Traité d'héraldique*, 3rd edn (Paris: Picard, 1997). In this canto two animals on the crests stem from the family name: the sow 'scrofa' for the Scrovegni and the goats 'becchi' for that of Gianni di Buiamonte de' Becchi. The crests of the other two families — the Ubriachi (the goose) and the Gianfigliazzi (the lion) — do not follow this model. Our information about these two families comes primarily from the early commentators on the poem, for which see the texts contained in the Dartmouth Dante Project, <https://Dante.Dartmouth.EDU>.
23. This usurer is perhaps Catello di Rosso Gianfigliazzi. See d'Addario, 'Gianfigliazzi, Catello', in *ED*, III, 153, and 'Gianfigliazzi', in *ED*, III, 153; see also Vanna Arrighi, 'Gianfigliazzi, Catello (Castello)', *Dizionario biografico degli italiani*, LIV (Rome: Istituto della Enciclopedia Italiana, 2000), pp. 354–55. The Gianfigliazzi family demonstrates the extensive international dimension of Italian banks and other merchants in the Middle Ages, for they had an office in Vienne (France). On this general point see also Ferrante, *Political Vision*, p. 313.
24. This usurer is perhaps Ciapo Obriachi. The family name has also been given as Ebriachi, Imbriachi, and Ubriachi. See d'Addario, 'Obriachi'.
25. For the family and Reginaldo/Rinaldo see, respectively, Gabriella De Biasi, 'Scrovegni', in *ED*, V, 103–04, and 'Scrovegni, Rinaldo degli', in *ED*, V, 104–05; and Chiara Frugoni and Reinhold C. Mueller, 'Scrovegni', in *Dizionario biografico*, 91 (2018), 680–85.
26. This sinner is generally thought to be Vitaliano del Dente, although a certain Vitaliano Vitaliani has been proposed. For a discussion of this question, see Nicolò Mineo, 'Vitaliani, Vitaliano', in *ED*, V, 1085–86. According to Derbes and Sandona, Vitaliano was listed in historical records as a 'vicino' ('neighbour') of Reginaldo (*The Usurer's Heart*, p. 166, n. 85).
27. There has been much discussion in the commentaries as to whether the crest displays three goats or three eagles' heads in profile (with beaks, 'Becchi'). The early Florentine commentators generally consider the crest as having three black goats on a gold field (Jacopo Alighieri, Pietro Alighieri, L'Ottimo, and the Anonimo Fiorentino, as well as Guido da Pisa and Benvenuto da Imola), while others (e.g. Graziolo dei Bambaglioli, Jacopo della Lana, Francesco da Buti) suggest three gold eagles' heads with prominent beaks in profile on a blue field. For this question and other matters related to the Becchi family (including historical documents), see Michele Barbi, '"Vegna il cavalier sovrano . . ." (*Inf.*, XVII, 72)', *Studi danteschi*, 10 (1925), 55–80, as well as Federigo Tollemache ('Becco', in *ED*, I, 554–55), who concludes that it is probably wise to accept the Florentines' identification, since they would be closer to the historical truth than the others. If this interpretation of the family crest is correct — three black goats on a yellow background — the chromatic symbolism reinforces the proclamation that the representative of the Becchi family is the 'cavalier sovrano', because black (and red) in this period play 'le rôle de

couleur mauvaise, de couleur du péché, de l'enfer, du paganism ou de la mort' [the role of evil colours: those of sin, hell, paganism or death] (Pastoureau, *Figures et couleurs*, p. 198), and yellow, which assumed a more negative connotation after 1250, signifying 'la cupidité ou la trahison' [greed or treachery] (p. 199), would be its appropriate companion.
28. Gianni Buiamonti, a wealthy banker/usurer, served as Gonfaloniere di Giustizia in 1293. He died in 1310 following the collapse of his banking empire and the subsequent public shame. The fact that he was named a 'cavaliere' in 1297–98 makes the Florentine usurers' 'celebration' of his imminent arrival as the 'cavalier sovrano' especially sarcastic. For the Becchi family see Franco Cardini, 'Buiamonti, Giovanni', in *ED*, I, 715.
29. Disclosures of the identity of other souls, either already present or soon to arrive in Hell, are made by Venedico Caccianemico (canto 18), Pier da Medicina (canto 28), and Bocca degli Abati (canto 32). See Dante Alighieri, *La Divina Commedia: Inferno*, con i commenti di Tommaso Casini-Silvio Adrasto Barbi e di Attilio Momigliano (Florence: Sansoni, 1979), pp. 332–34.
30. As Tommaseo notes in his commentary on the *Inferno*: 'La tasca portava l'arma del casato: ingegnoso per dar a conoscere que' dannati senza lungo discorso, e per portare in Inferno lo scherno della sudicia nobiltà.' Cited from the commentary to *Inferno*, 17. 55–57 by Niccolò Tommaseo (Torino, UTET, 1927), as found in the Dartmouth Dante Project, <https://Dante.Dartmouth.EDU>. Umberto Bosco and Giovanni Reggio note that by means of the crests '[f]orse Dante vuole colpire la nobiltà degenere, più che i singoli individui' (Dante Alighieri, *La Divina Commedia: Inferno* (Florence: Le Monnier, 1979), n. to vv. 59–60 (p. 254)).
31. The poet's grandfather (Bellincione) and father (Alighiero) were moneylenders. See Simonetta Saffiotti Bernardi, 'Alighieri, Alighiero II', in *ED*, I, 132; d'Addario, 'Alighieri, Alighiero', in *Dizionario biografico*, 2 (1960), 383, and 'Alighieri, Bellincione', in *Dizionario biografico*, 2 (1960), 383–84; Renato Piattoli, 'Alighiero, Bellincione', *ED*, I, 134.
32. For Dante's sense of nobility see, among many others, Domenico Consoli, 'Nobiltà e nobile', in *ED*, IV, 58–62, and the wide-ranging two volumes by Umberto Carpi, *La nobiltà di Dante* (Florence: Polistampa, 2004). Dante the Pilgrim's fear in certain parts of the poem may be generated by his potential 'culpability', as, for example, in canto 21 (the barrators) where the devils show a particular interest in him, an obvious reference to the false charges of corruption brought after his term as prior, which led to his exile. Therefore, mindful of his family's involvement with this particular sin, the Pilgrim's fear in this episode is not limited to the downward flight on Geryon's back, but is also generated by his familial usurious circumstances.
33. Religious art is intended to glorify the divine and sacred, as well as to instruct the general populace on a variety of subjects. For example, representations of the Last Judgment show not only the delights of Paradise but also the torments of Hell, thus serving as a guide to human activity concerning the consequences of virtue and vice. It is not by accident that artistic representations of the Last Judgment are depicted on the inside west wall of churches as a reminder to those parishioners, who leave the sanctuary, of the worldly temptations that await them in the world and the horrific consequences of errant behaviour, as well as the heavenly rewards for virtuous earthly conduct.
34. See Barolini, *Undivine 'Comedy'*, pp. 63–64, and Kristina M. Olson, 'The Ethical and Sartorial Geography of the Far East: Tartar Textiles in Boccaccio's *Decameron* and *Esposizioni*', *Le Tre Corone*, 6 (1999), 125–39 (pp. 132, 138).
35. See Singleton's commentary on the *Inferno*, vv. 17 and 18 (pp. 297–98).
36. For a discussion of the hierarchy of these animals, see the chapter, 'Quel est le roi des animaux?' (in Pastoureau, *Figures et couleurs*, pp. 159–73), which concludes that the lion is king of animals and the eagle is the king of kings ('le roi des rois,' p. 173).
37. On this point Pastoureau writes that 'l'écu armorié est un insigne familial, souvent assimilable au nom' [the armorial shield is a family insignia, often similar to the name] (*Figures et couleurs*, p. 127). He examines the notion of the 'figure parlante' to a greater extent in *Traité d'Héraldique*, pp. 251–53.
38. On this point Pastoureau offers a gentle corrective, noting that: 'Il a ainsi été amusant d'observer que parmi les familles dont le nom était construit sur le mot 'porc', celles qui étaient nobles prenaient volontiers comme figure héraldique un simple cochon domestique, tandis que celles

qui ne l'étaient pas adoptaient un sanglier, meuble parlant mais jugé plus honorifique qu'un vulgaire cochon.' (*Traité d'héraldique*, p. 253) [It was thus interesting to note that, among the families whose names were associated with the word 'porc', those who were noble readily adopted the ordinary domestic pig as a heraldic device, while those who were not adopted the boar, overstated but thought to be more honourable than the common pig.] While to our modern sensibility the figures of a sow and a goat might evoke derision, for the families concerned these animals were their apt and able representations. In the moralistic tradition pigs and sows have negative connotations; see Stéphanie le Briz-Orgeur, 'La truie, ses pourceaux . . . et le cochon dans la *Moralité de Bien Advisé Mal Advisé*', in *Le Bestiaire, Le Lapidaire, La Flore. Actes du Colloque international Université McGill, Montréal, 7–8–9 octobre 2002*, ed. by Giuseppe Di Stefano and Rose M. Bidler, Le moyen français, 55–56 (Montréal: Ceres, 2004–05), pp. 219–44. Conversely, the lion and the goose have a distinguished history, the former as the king of the beasts and the latter as the saviour of Rome. The Black Guelf Gianfigliazzi were a magnate family (noted in the *Ordinamenti di Giustizia* of 1293), and their crest with the lion reflects their noble standing. The Ghibelline Ubriachi family with the goose on its crest was prominent in the knightly class in Florence from the twelfth century to 1267, after which they had to forge a new identity and conduct business away from Florence, in France (Gap) and elsewhere. We recognize the importance of these images in establishing the status of these individual families as prominent actors in the everyday communal life of their respective cities. That being said, the use of these blazons, noble or common as they may be, does not diminish Dante's basic message: that whatever prominence these families have or had on earth, in the afterlife the souls of the usurers weep and focus their greedy, ravenous eyes on the emblazoned moneybags hanging from their neck, recognizing in its deceptive appearance their own transgressions. The bags and crests signalling family honour represent for these sinners an eternal source of sadness and a constant reminder of their duplicitous activity. Garrani calls them the 'stemmi di una degenere pervertita nobiltà' (*Pensiero*, p. 71). In his 'Lettura del canto XVII dell'Inferno' (*Letterature moderne*, 3 (1952), 276–88 (p. 282)), Giovanni Getto notes the downward arc of the heraldic figures from 'quella ancora nobile del leone a quella meno nobile dell'oca bianca più che burro, a quella turpe della scrofa "grossa" (cioè gravida)'.

39. See Guglielmo Gorni's pertinent commentary on this topic ('Canto XVII', in *Lectura Dantis Turicensis: Inferno*, ed. by Georges Güntert and Michelangelo Picone (Florence: Franco Cesati, 2000), 233–41 (p. 240)): 'È una nobiltà nuova cresciuta con sùbiti guadagni, che ostenta stemmi, figure e colori di varia natura e origine. Usurai nobilitati, scandalosamente. O viceversa nobili dediti all'usura, che hanno degradato la loro nobiltà di sangue in pratiche vili, alla ricerca di facili guadagni.' On the deleterious effects of usury on society Ravenscroft notes: 'Perhaps the most fundamental of all the scholastic arguments against usury, however, shared with patristic sources, was the notion that usury was a sin against society, constituting an exploitation of the poor, and a practice incompatible with the principal Christian virtue of charity' ('Usury', p. 106). See also Franco Lanza, 'Il canto XVII dell'*Inferno*', in *Nuove letture dantesche*, II (Florence: Le Monnier, 1968), pp. 117–35 (p. 129).
40. In his commentary Giuseppe Giacalone notes that the 'linea di deformazione umana, che riduce al livello animalesco la vita morale degli usurai anche attraverso i loro stemmi (oca, scrofa), s'accorda in fondo e si armonizza con tutta la linea deformata e mostruosa della vitalità animalesca di Gerione. Al punto [...] che la posizione stessa degli usurai non poteva non essere se non in questa zona di passaggio tra il peccato di violenza alla natura e quello della frode, dato che l'usura in certo senso è un po' anche peccato della mente frodolenta.' (Dante Alighieri, *La Divina Commedia* (Rome: Signorelli, 1988), p. 346) On this point see Ravenscroft, 'Usury', pp. 110–12; Cogan, *Design*, p. 59; Ferrante, *Political Vision*, p. 344; and Garrani, *Pensiero*, p. 70.
41. Barolini notes the affinity between the usurers and fraud and particularly the language and gestures of the eighth circle (*Undivine 'Comedy'*, pp. 72, 76–79).
42. For the Jubilee see, among others, Herbert L. Kessler and Johanna Zacharias, *Rome 1300: On the Path of the Pilgrim* (New Haven: Yale University Press, 2000).
43. See Derbes and Sandona's discussion of these events (*The Usurer's Heart*, pp. 40–43). On the much-debated question of whether Enrico Scrovegni had the chapel built to expiate his father's

sin of usury, Derbes and Sandona argue that this was, indeed, the case (*The Usurer's Heart*, pp. 31–35).

44. Derbes and Sandona argue that in the donor fresco the inclusion of the cleric, whom they identify as Altegrado Cattaneo, 'only intensifies the penitential significance of the image', for 'Altegrado was very probably Enrico's confessor, and he was the trusted agent of Benedict XI, the pope who absolved Enrico' (*The Usurer's Heart*, p. 41).

45. For the general presence of this image in medieval art see Giuliano Milani, *L'uomo*, and 'The Ban and the Bag: How Defamatory Paintings Worked in Medieval Italy', in *Images of Shame: Infamy, Defamation and the Ethics of* oeconomia, ed. by Carolin Behrmann (Berlin: De Gruyter, 2016), pp. 119–40; and Gherardo Ortalli, 'Pittura Infamante: Practices, Genres and Connections', in *Images of Shame*, ed. by Behrmann, pp. 29–47.

46. For the image of the moneybags hanging from the necks of usurers, see the discussion by Derbes and Sandona, *The Usurer's Heart*, pp. 36–40, 48–52. See also their discussion of Last Judgment imagery in '*Triplex Periculum*: The Moral Topography of Giotto's Hell in the Arena Chapel, Padua', *Journal of the Warburg and Courtauld Institutes*, 78 (2015), 41–70.

47. For Judas as a usurer, see Derbes and Sandona, *The Usurer's Heart*, pp. 45–48, 59–65.

48. Furthermore, the *Pact of Judas* in the chancel depicts him with a moneybag in hand, and the image of Envy ('Invidia') at the dado level presents her with a moneybag in hand opposite Charity ('Karitas'), who shows contempt for earthly riches by standing on moneybags. See Derbes and Sandona, *The Usurer's Heart*, pp. 48–51.

49. See the discussion and bibliography in Derbes and Sandona, *The Usurer's Heart*, pp. 45–48, 176–77.

50. There are also visual associations in Giotto's Last Judgment. See Derbes and Sandona, *The Usurer's Heart*, pp. 67–70.

51. See Derbes and Sandona for the association of excrement and usury (*The Usurer's Heart*, p. 69 and n. 102 (p. 183).

52. See the discussion by Derbes and Sandona (*The Usurer's Heart*, pp. 67–69). Milani ('The Ban', p. 136) also notes the association in the medieval mind between Judas and Simon Magus.

53. Other sins in the eighth circle associated with usury are barratry (cantos 21–22), thievery (cantos 24–25) and sowing scandal (canto 28). See Ferrante *Political Vision*, pp. 348–51, 353, and Lanza, 'Il canto XVII', p. 125.

CHAPTER 6

Form and Freedom in the Dante Series Prints of Geoff MacEwan

Gervase Rosser

The paths which have led a myriad of readers to the *Divine Comedy* have shaped, in just so many diverse ways, the nature of each first encounter. For most, that first rapture is later overlaid by widening knowledge both of the poem and of the world — a dynamic and enriching process which, however, obscures the vividness of the initial meeting. Three series of prints by Geoff MacEwan after *Inferno* (1991), *Purgatorio* (2010), and *Paradiso* (2012) capture in its freshness one reader's first response to the strange landscapes of Dante's vision. These — forty-four in total — are among the most significant images of the *Divine Comedy* to be made in modern times. They are, moreover, unlike any others. Illustration of the *Divine Comedy* began as soon as the poem began to circulate in the fourteenth century. Amongst the galaxy of artistic responses which have appeared during seven centuries, MacEwan's joins a small number which have resisted the temptation to depict the scenes and characters of Dante's narrative, in favour of a treatment which is largely abstract. Yet the further, paradoxical, achievement of these prints is that by their refusal of either a literal re-presentation or a comfortingly aestheticized complement to the poem, and by the way in which they require the viewer's engagement and responsible attention, MacEwan lends fresh energy to the political and social imperatives of Dante's vision.[1]

Geoff MacEwan's path to Dante passed through the culture wars of the 1960s. A child of the Second World War, brought up by adoptive parents, MacEwan found himself, as a student in the 1960s at Goldsmiths' College and the Slade School, at a time of artistic crisis.[2] The ascendancy of the New York School was in question. Early influences on MacEwan had been the paintings of Francis Bacon, Mark Rothko and Philip Guston; but the Vietnam War cast a pall over the prestige of the generation of American Abstract Expressionists. And what, in any case, was the purpose of art in the late twentieth century? The dominant view in the art schools at that moment was purist: a painting was just that and nothing more — any hint of illustration, of dependence on external models, was anathema to the Modernist creed. Interested as he was both in literature and in the world around him, MacEwan was unable to find a place in this environment, and opted instead for artistic exile:

he worked as a technical illustrator, drawing screws and electrical diagrams for industry. Returning after some years to paint, he felt the necessity to make work which would be engaged and ideological, with the capacity to make a difference. This impulse found expression in a large and ponderous painting of 1981 (since lost), *O Clouds Unfold*: a landscape incorporating a map of Europe showing Russian troops massing on the border of Poland, framed by quotations from Thoreau and Engels. The title, from Blake's 'Jerusalem', conveyed the momentousness of the artist's solemn message. This heavily freighted work led MacEwan to question again how art might be political without making speeches. And at this juncture William Blake, whose biography he had been reading, took him to Dante.

As the artist has said more recently, 'the turn to Dante was an attempt to resolve the question of political art'. The outcome, in MacEwan's case, was a series of images whose abstraction deliberately eschews explicit and contemporary political commentary. In the artist's own account, the journey became one, rather, of self-exploration: 'by choosing to work from Dante, I was moving away from any direct socio-political critique and was engaged instead with the conflicts within my own psyche. In fact, I'd embarked on a spiritual journey.' This trajectory was in marked divergence from that of another artist of the same generation and similar formation, Tom Phillips.[3] Both MacEwan and Phillips rejected what they saw as the narrow literalism of much Dante illustration, including the famous depictions by Gustave Doré (1855–68). But where Phillips's reappropriation of Dante incorporated visual quotations drawn from twentieth-century cinema, television and poster propaganda in order to reinject the poetic imagery with immediacy for a contemporary readership, MacEwan pursued a more reflective and psychological path. By his development of a personal imagery MacEwan equally (although unconsciously) distanced himself from another significant modern artistic response to Dante, that of Robert Rauschenberg. Over two years from 1958, Rauschenberg used a solvent technique to transfer dozens of images of sportsmen, politicians and slogans from popular magazines in order to create plates corresponding to each of the thirty-four cantos of *Inferno*. The viewer able to identify athletes, tyrants and grafters from the celebrity listings and rogues' galleries of the contemporary media was thereby prompted to muse on Dante's continuing relevance. By working with current characters and imagery Rauschenberg responded to what he recognized to have been a feature of the original poem. This historical immediacy was not to be part of MacEwan's approach. However, despite their differences of content and technique, the respective Dante series of Rauschenberg and MacEwan share a significant quality: a degree of deliberate indeterminacy, which leaves the reader to work at and to reflect on the hints provided by the images.[4] And in the responsibility which is left to the viewer of both sets of images, there lies a transformative potential which may be described, in either case, as political. Both are the work of artists who read the *Divine Comedy* as a call to action.

MacEwan first responded to the *Divine Comedy* in a series of twenty-five oil paintings commissioned in 1982 for the 369 Gallery in Edinburgh.[5] The print series of *Inferno* followed in response to a commission from the Edinburgh University

FIG. 6.1. William Blake, *Beatrice Addressing Dante from the Car*. Ink and watercolour on paper. 1824–27. 37.2 × 52.7 cm. Tate Gallery, London. Photo © Tate.

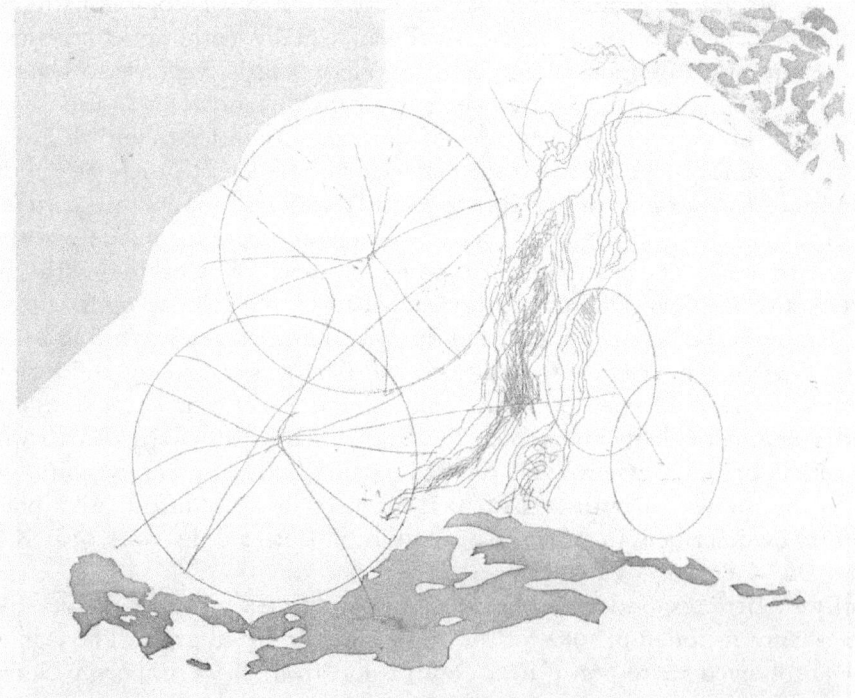

FIG. 6.2. Geoff MacEwan, *Beatrice* from the *Purgatorio* series.
Print dimensions: 24.7 × 29.4 cm. Photo © Geoff MacEwan.

Library in 1990. *Purgatorio* in turn was a commission from the artist's *gallerista*, Juan Oliver Maneu, director of Cán Prunera, the gallery of modern art in Sóller, on the island of Mallorca where MacEwan has lived and worked for a quarter of a century. Eventually, in 2012, the same gallery was able to mount an exhibition of the *Inferno* and *Purgatorio* prints together with *Paradiso*.[6]

The artist worked on the poem 'page by page, just as if I was experiencing the poem as a journey in real time: I simply read the poem and whenever I felt an image rise I painted.' Although, when he embarked on the prints of *Inferno* in 1990, he was returning to a text already read, he remained concerned that his images should not anticipate the conclusion of the poem but should convey at each stage of the unfolding story the impact of its startling strangeness. Having begun with the English translation by Cary — with results which MacEwan has described as 'terrible' — he moved on to the sparer, less orotund prose version by Sinclair. While sharing with every other reader of Dante an interest in the human stories of the characters encountered in the poetic journey, MacEwan has ignored the infinite rabbit-holes of scholarly references. His avoidance of academic scholarship on Dante has been equalled by his freedom from detailed awareness of his artistic predecessors. A partial exception is William Blake, whose image of *Beatrice Addressing Dante from the Car* MacEwan recalled from youthful visits to the Tate Gallery (Fig. 6.1). A formal, although distant, debt to that image is evident in MacEwan's own print of *Beatrice* from his *Purgatorio* series (Fig. 6.2). But MacEwan's entire Dante project is blessedly free of pre-existing artistic models — while the real connection to Blake lies, rather, in MacEwan's affinity with the earlier poet-artist's combination of personal vision, artistic originality and political engagement.

Geoff MacEwan's artistic formation took place under the sign of Expressionism, and his engagement with all of his many projects as a printmaker has been mediated through active exploration of his own psyche. The artist's lifelong concerns both to come to terms with his own demons, and to catalyse in his audience a sense of political commitment and social ethics, resonate very closely with the aspirations of the poet of the *Divine Comedy*. An acknowledged influence has been Anton Ehrenzweig's *The Hidden Order of Art: A Study in the Psychology of Artistic Imagination* (published in 1967, after the author's death), of which book MacEwan has remarked: 'It taught me to accept confusion as a necessary stage in the process of arriving at an image and its completion. In other words, it taught me not to be fearful.' Characteristic of all MacEwan's printmaking has been a willingness to take risks: working directly on the plates, he has consistently treated the design process as a creative act of uncertain outcome.[7] The result is an art which is not — and cannot be — didactic or banner-waving. Indeed, within the Dante series, MacEwan can be seen moving — perhaps quite unconsciously: he has spoken of his own surprise, looking back, at the way each stage of the project had evolved — away from the rigidity of a formal framework, in the direction of a more fluid and open-ended design. This movement also corresponds to the pilgrim-poet's own transition from the constraints of this-worldly human perception to the infinitely labile connectedness of the celestial state. The transitional *cantica* of *Purgatorio*, in MacEwan's version, opens with a plate characterized by a strict geometry which

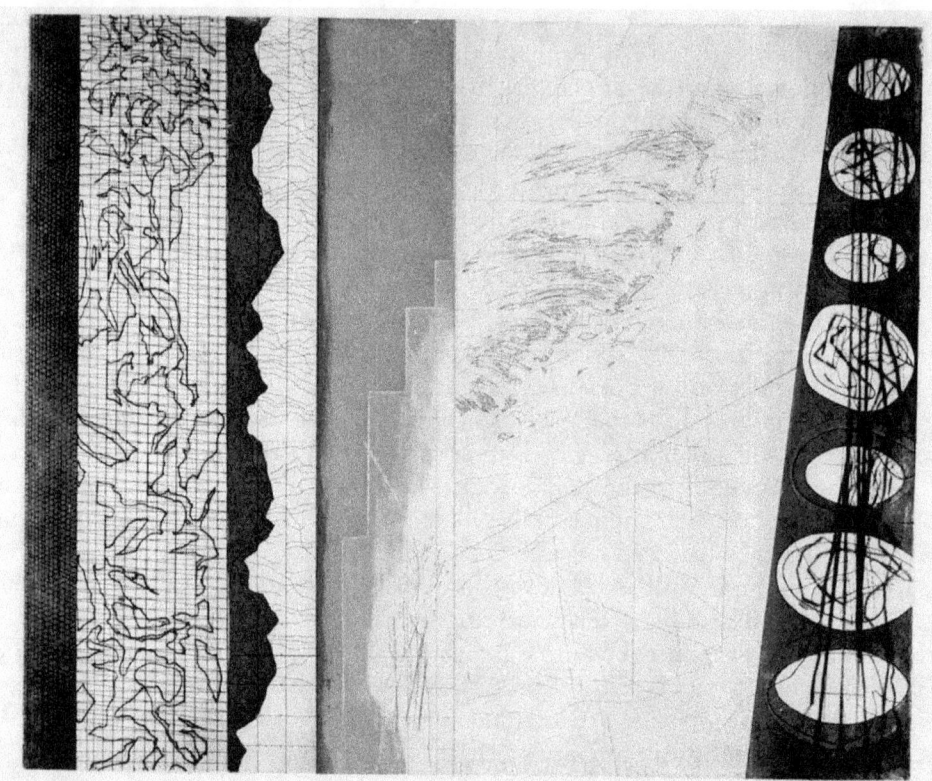

Fig. 6.3. Geoff MacEwan, *The Reed Bed* from the *Purgatorio* series. Print dimensions: 24.7 × 29.4 cm. Photo © Geoff MacEwan.

suggests the rectitude of the path of purgation which must be taken, if a higher level of consciousness is to be reached (Fig. 6.3). The poetic passage to which the image relates describes the ritual, at the foot of the mountain of Purgatory, in which the pilgrim must kneel while Virgil uses the morning dew to wipe his face clean of the sinful traces of Hell (*Purgatorio* 1. 121–29). The heavenly presence of the angel bringing new souls to begin their purgatorial ascent is surely alluded to in the loose and dynamic lines to the right of the centre of the image (*Purgatorio* 2. 10–50). The remaining pictorial elements, however, communicate a call to order, as the viewer — or Dante's reader — prepares for the trials ahead. By complete contrast, the final plate of the *Purgatorio* series — although significantly linked to the first by its cerulean blue colour, also used in a small part of the otherwise monochrome first engraving — is altogether free in its composition (Fig. 6.4). To the tight control, verging on claustrophobia, of the first image succeeds this pair of morning glory flowers, unconstrained and open upon the whiteness of infinity. Their placement in the sequence corresponds to the appearance in the poem of Beatrice, and they are suggestive both of the poet's reunion with his beloved, and of the ever-widening experience of confraternity which opens up to the virtuous soul in Dante's vision of *Paradiso*. Another image occurring late in the *Purgatorio* series is *The Garden* (Fig.

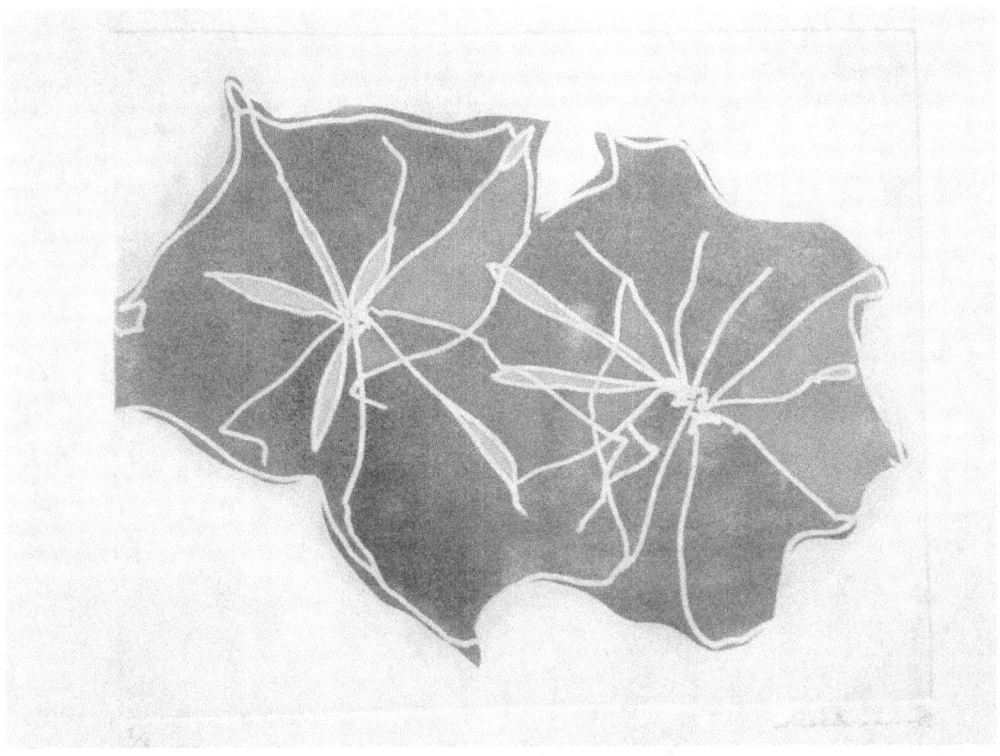

Fig. 6.4. Geoff MacEwan, *The Earthly Paradise* from the *Purgatorio* series. Print dimensions: 24.7 × 29.4 cm. Photo © Geoff MacEwan.

6.5), which corresponds to the pilgrim's passage, at the summit of the mountain of Purgatory, to the Earthly Paradise. To accede to the garden, the penitent must pass through a wall of purging fire: an ordeal at which the Dante character initially balks, until Virgil points out to him that on the other side is Beatrice (*Purgatorio* 27–28). MacEwan's beautiful image radically shifts the perspective to a celestial vision from above the mountain, so that the Garden of Eden is perceived as laid out to view, ringed by the purgatorial flame. It is as though, in this imaginary, the whole mountain is seen in a heavenly gaze, surrounded by the blue ocean of the Southern Hemisphere. The fire here stands not only for the particular threshold at the apex of the mountain but for the purifying function of the ascent in its entirety. The green form of the garden resembles a leaf without precisely identifying itself as such; the surrounding flames, likewise, evoke rather than depict their subject. Such images as these of *Purgatorio* are not illustrations of the text: instead they are ethical statements in their own right, offered as reflections on and complements to the poem.

The balance between form and freedom, structure and flow, which characterises all of these images is a faithful response to a poem which similarly offsets against the absolutes of divine authority the indeterminacy of human free will. That freedom to roam carries a responsibility which extends to every reader of the *Divine*

Fig. 6.5. Geoff MacEwan, *The Garden* from the *Purgatorio* series. Print dimensions: 24.7 × 29.4 cm. Photo © Geoff MacEwan.

Comedy; MacEwan's plates convey the burden of that responsibility. Each image, indeed, bears the weight of experience, offering not merely a symbolical reflection on the poetry but a physical movement which calls for the viewer's cooperation. MacEwan's *Inferno*, monochrome in its entirety, invests the drypoint graphic line with infinite kinetic energy, charting the passages and dead ends of Hell with a combination of linear gestures and cross-hatched passages from dark to light. *The Dark Wood*, corresponding to the opening canto of the poem, may read as a series of incomplete and partially blocked trial runs, openings onto an unidentified beyond (Fig. 6.6). The nature of the medium, which in its unforgiving way makes it impossible for the artist to conceal the trace of a mark once made on the zinc surface, speaks to the tension of this initial passage into the vision. At the other end of the hellish sequence, *Exit from Hell* uses cross-hatching with such dramatic effect that the image, once again, does not merely represent the action of the poem (*Inferno* 34. 70–139) but draws the viewer physically up and around the liberating passage which will give out upon the shore of the mountain of Purgatory and the sight of the stars (Fig. 6.7). The *Inferno* series (unlike *Purgatorio* and *Paradiso*) was

Fig. 6.6. Geoff MacEwan, *The Dark Wood* from the *Inferno* series. Print dimensions: 36 × 30.5 cm. Photo © Geoff MacEwan.

Fig. 6.7. Geoff MacEwan, *Exit from Hell* from the *Inferno* series. Print dimensions: 36 × 30.5 cm. Photo © Geoff MacEwan.

Fig. 6.8. Geoff MacEwan, Plate 7 from the *Paradiso* series.
Print dimensions: 24.6 × 32.5 cm. Photo © Geoff MacEwan.

designed as an artist's book, with a transparent overlay for each plate bearing labels for characters and locations: a form of laconic commentary on the images. In the case of *The Dark Wood*, these notes include a reference, at the bottom left-hand corner of the image, to a sea and a beach. In the last plate, *Exit from Hell*, the same indication appears again in the transparency on the left-hand side of the print. These two signposts, referring to the sea and the shore of Purgatory, indicate the artist's idea that the thought of repentance was already in the pilgrim Dante's mind at the outset of his journey into Hell.

Paradoxically, for all the strangeness of this psychological journey, we recognize what is required of us at each passage of the itinerary. This is partly due to signposts given by the artist in the form of line and light (in addition, in *Inferno*, to written labels on the transparent overlays), such as in the entrance to and exit from Hell just discussed. Formal pointers to meaning can work powerfully upon us even — or perhaps especially — where the artist was unconscious of their presence until after the moment of creation. The final two images of *Paradiso* are revelatory in this respect. For this series MacEwan reverted to monochrome: a practical choice determined by the far greater expense of coloured monoprints, but one to which his artistic ambition was successfully reconciled. Stripped of the distraction of colour, the tonal progression from dark to light in the etchings of *Paradiso* conveys the more

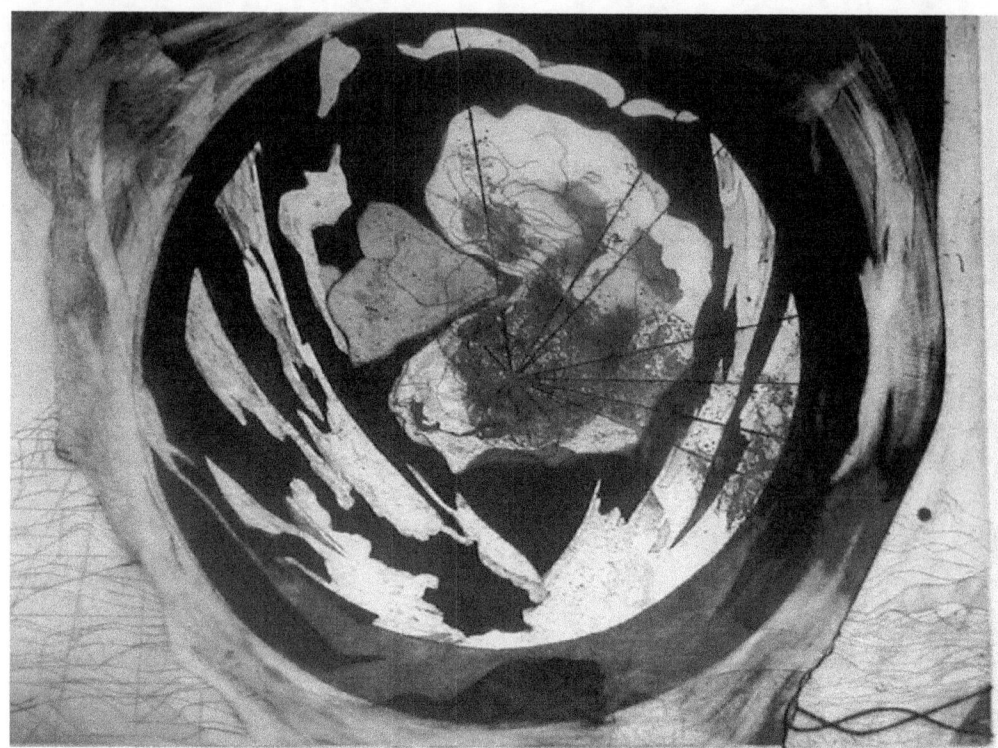

Fig. 6.9. Geoff MacEwan, Plate 8 from the *Paradiso* series. Print dimensions: 24.5 × 32.5 cm. Photo © Geoff MacEwan.

powerfully the sense, unimaginable in the terrestrial realm, of order in infinity. The penultimate plate evokes a cosmic setting (Fig. 6.8). Graphic waves at the outer edges suggest a sea of infinite space, within which more definite forces circulate around a still centre. From here emanate, like the beams of a lighthouse, a trinity of bright rays which guide the viewer, and the poem's reader, to the heart of things. The same framework is repeated in the ultimate image of the Empyrean, which since we have now passed the lighthouse can now be seen directly: it is revealed to resemble a womb (Fig. 6.9). The journey has thus been a pilgrimage towards home. As Dante had put it (in Sinclair's translation): 'From His hand who regards it fondly before it is, comes forth, like a child that sports, tearful and smiling, the little simple soul' (*Purgatorio* 16. 85–88); human life is a quest to return to that point of origin. The artist has stated that the powerful symbolism of this final image was an altogether unintentional outcome: a serendipitous combination of formal experiment and the ascent to the surface of a subconscious force.

Subconscious forces take their cue from diverse points of origin, whether catalysed by our personal lives or entering from the common culture. So does history creep in, to complicate the apparent naïveté of that initial encounter with Dante. For all the originality of MacEwan's images of the *Divine Comedy*, their designer worked in the knowledge that others had explored this terrain before. Just twice in the entire

Fig. 6.10. Geoff MacEwan, *Bruno Latini* from the *Inferno* series. Print dimensions: 36.2 × 30.2 cm. Photo © Geoff MacEwan.

FIG. 6.11. Geoff MacEwan, *Oderisi da Gubbio* from the *Purgatorio* series.
Print dimensions: 24.7 × 29.4 cm. Photo © Geoff MacEwan.

project, MacEwan includes a fully realized human portrait, and each acknowledges the weight of a cultural tradition. Brunetto Latini (*Inferno* 15. 22–124) appears in MacEwan's realization as the shadowy yet authoritative presence remembered also in Eliot's *Little Gidding* (Fig. 6.10). Just as the poets, in their visionary encounters with 'familiar compound ghosts', did not simply recall particular mentors but saw reflected in them the authority of language and art transmitted by history, so the engraver here — without explicit citation, as we have seen, of artistic forbears — nods to the ever-present past. Equally significant is MacEwan's singling out — among a total of just fourteen plates on *Purgatorio* — of Oderisi da Gubbio for representation in the circle of the Proud (Fig. 6.11). The former star amongst the manuscript illuminators of Paris purges his hubris, stooping as he bears around the mountain of Purgatory a penitential rock. To the pilgrim Dante, Oderisi's shade willingly acknowledges that now 'the pages smile brighter from the brush' of another artist (*Purgatorio* 11. 82–83). MacEwan has said that 'Oderisi is a sort of alter ego for me: I've felt a little like him from time to time.' Brunetto and Oderisi — whose heads, moreover, resemble one another in MacEwan's rendition — both stand for the modern artist, as they did also for Dante, as metonyms for a cultural tradition which, even as it constantly evolved, remained inescapable. The presence of the cultural past is the ultimate reason why, as the surprised viewers of MacEwan's images, we realize that the way being indicated is strangely familiar.

Notes to Chapter 6

1. A set of each series is held by the Print Room of the Ashmolean Museum, Oxford. I am grateful to the Print Room Supervisors, Dr Caroline Palmer and Katherine Wodehouse, for their kind assistance. My thanks also to Geoff MacEwan for his collaboration. The artist's images are reproduced with his permission.
2. Unless otherwise stated, the sources for factual statements and quotations in this essay are: Nicholas Campion, 'Celestial art: An Interview with Geoff MacEwan', *Culture and Cosmos*, 18.1 (2014), 55–70; and interview with Geoff MacEwan by the author, 19 December 2018, at the Royal Academy, London.
3. Tom Phillips, *Dante's Inferno* (London: Talfourd Press, 1983).
4. For Rauschenberg see Ed Krčma, *Rauschenberg/Dante: Drawing a Modern Inferno* (New Haven and London: Yale University Press, 2017), p. 158.
5. There were two exhibitions of these works: *Dante's Inferno: Paintings by Geoffrey MacEwan* (Edinburgh: 369 Gallery, *c.* 1982); *Dante's Divine Comedy: Paintings by Geoffrey MacEwan* (Edinburgh: Talbot Rice Gallery, 1986). The paintings were later sold; their present location is unknown.
6. *Geoff MacEwan: Visitations*, Cán Prunera Museu Modernista, 2012.
7. MacEwan reiterated this in a talk about his Dante prints delivered at the Ashmolean Museum, Oxford, on 31 May 2018.

CHAPTER 7

Psalms, Ecclesiastical Chant and Healing in the *Purgatorio*

Francesco Ciabattoni

In genuinely liturgical music — plainsong as well as polyphonic music — the text has a mystic significance which elevates it beyond criteria such as 'clear pronunciation' or similar requirements of modern singing. Its existence, like that of God, is eternal and independent of actual apperception on the part of men.[1]

In a papal *constitutio* probably issued around 1324,[2] John XXII denounced and limited the excessive use of musical embellishments, especially polyphonic ones, in liturgical chants:

nonnulli novellae scholae discipuli, dum temporibus mensurandis invigilant, novis notis intendunt, fingere suas quam antiquas cantare malunt, [...] melodias hoquetis intersecant, discantibus lubricant [...] Currunt enim, et non quiescunt; aures inebriant, et non medentur;

[some disciples of the new school, while keeping the vigil to measure the hours, occupy themselves with new songs. They prefer inventing their own to singing the old ones [...] They strip the melodies of hockets, slide on the descants; [...] These notes go too fast, never rest, inebriate the ears and *do not heal*.][3]

These latest words of the pontifex from Cahors, *né* Jacques Duèse, reflect a concern that is not merely theological or musical, but medical in a broader sense, because plainchant, with its monophonic and steady emission, the specific frequency and rumination of words, was credited with a healing power that acted on the soul and on the body. The exorcising power of music is, after all, attested in the Book of Kings (Samuel) by the well-known episode of David delivering Saul from a haunting demon, a story that acts as a counterpoint to that of classical tradition, in which Pythagoras soothes the heated temperament of a jealous young man by changing the musical key from Phrygian to Lydian.[4] The tale was also quoted by Basil of Caesarea,[5] who in his *Homilies on the Psalms* claims that music 'reprimit excandescentiam et animi concitationem' [softens the rage and agitation of the mind] and that the psalms, precisely in their musical performance, are a medicine capable of healing the wound of sin, to calm tumultuous souls and repress exuberance and lust, generating friendship among the singers:[6]

Omnis Scriptura est divinitus inspirata atque utilis, ideo a Spiritu sancto conscripta, velut in communi animarum curandarum officina nos omnes quotquot sumus homines ad nostrum morbum sanandum medelam seligere possimus. *Medicina* enim, inquit Scriptura, sedabit peccata magna [...] *Nam antiquis animarum vulnus medetur*: promptam nuper vulneratio sanitatem reddit; quod agrum est fovet; quod vero incolumen et integrum, conservat. [...] *Ideo concinni illi psalmorum concentus excogitati nobis sunt*, ut ii qui pueri sunt aetate, aut etiam omnino moribus sunt juvenes dum in speciem *quidem cantant, reipsa tamen animas erudiant suas* [...]. Psalmus tranquillitatis est animarum, pacis arbiter, tumultuosas turbulentasque cogitationes comescit. Ut reprimit excandescentiam et animi concitationem, ita lasciviam refrenat. *Amicitias conciliat psalmus*: consociat dissidentes, inter inimicos gratiam componit. Quis enim adhuc eum quocum unam ad Deum vocem emisit, loco inimici habere possit? Itaque et bonorum maximum charitatem conciliat *psalmorum cantus, qui concentum ceu quoddam vinculum ad concordiam ineundam adiuvenit, populumque ad chori unius symphoniam congregat*. Daemones psalmus fugat, accersit angelorum patrocinium; ministrat arma contra nocturnos timores, diurnorum laborum est requies [...].[7]

[All scripture is inspired by God and is useful, composed by the Spirit for this reason, namely, that we men, each and all of us, as if in a general hospital for souls, may select the remedy for his own condition. Medicine, the Scripture says, will sooth even the greatest sins [...] *The old wounds of souls it cures*, and to the recently wounded it brings speedy restoration of health; the diseased it treats and the unharmed it preserves [...]. *He devised for us these harmonious melodies of the psalms*, that they who are children in age or, even those who are youthful in disposition might to all appearances *chant but, in reality, become trained in soul* [...] A psalm imparts serenity of soul; it is the author of peace, which calms bewildering and seething thoughts. For, it softens the rage and agitation of the mind, and what is unbridled it chastens. *A psalm forms friendships*, unites those separated, conciliates those at enmity. Who, indeed, can still consider as an enemy him with whom he has uttered the same prayer to God? So that *psalmody, bringing about choral singing, a bond, as it were, toward unity, and joining the people into a harmonious union of one choir, produces also the greatest of blessings, charity*. A psalm is a city of refuge from the demons; a means of inducing help from the angels, a weapon in fears by night, a rest from toils by day [...].]

It is the effort of singing 'ad chori unius symphoniam' — that is, in the monophony of plainchant — that favours spiritual healing, acts as a *pharmakon*, and builds concord among the singers, calming bewildering and seething thoughts, and training the souls. Basil wrote in Greek and, although his homilies were translated into Latin by Rufinus of Aquileia as early as the fourth century, it would be hard to establish whether Dante might have known him, but the comparison between sin and sickness, which can be cured by singing psalms, was spread in the Middle Ages especially through the works of Saint Augustine, and the principle is quite similar to Dante's own in the *Purgatorio*: he makes the singing of psalms and chants a spiritual benefit activated through musical performance. Let us take, for example, the effect of 'Agnus dei', a prayer from the litany of the saints, over the wrathful in *Purgatorio* 16:

> Pur 'Agnus Dei' eran le loro essordia:
> una parola in tutte era e un modo
> sì che parea tra esse ogni concordia (*Purgatorio* 16. 19–21)

In a context of complete obscurity, the pilgrim and his guide must wander, searching for the way up, wrapped in a thick, dark fog which blinds just like anger, the sin that is being purged on this layer. Suddenly, the wayfarers hear the well-known 'Agnus dei', a wonderful evocation of ecclesial communion performed chorally — and monophonically as suggested by 'una parola [...] e un modo' — by the wrathful, signifying the reacquisition of the concord they failed to possess in their physical lives. Since plainchant rhythm was based on syllabication, 'parola' and 'modo' seem to indicate more than just lyrics and mood: they suggest that the souls' singing is tuned together and they sing *a tempo* together. Thus, the litany — in both the text and the mode of performance — leads the repenting wrathful towards a communal effort aimed at remedying their sin through the musical exercise of its opposite: peaceful and productive cooperation. The sung prayer therefore performs the corrective and healing function which the Bishop of Caesarea had described. Basil is sometimes invoked by Dante scholars, though in relation to his conception of the Empyrean, associated with the *Anima Mundi* which Plotinus and Proclus passed on to the Fathers of the Church (among whose number is Basil) and down to Peter Lombard.[8] Closer to Dante's day, William of Auvergne's *De universo* (1231–36) included an entire chapter on music's healing capacities, especially efficacious against spiritual illnesses such as depression, phobias, and melancholy: 'Manifestum est etiam multos *morbos spirituales* musicis interdum fuisse curatum concentibus sicut insania, melancholia et alias quasdam alienationes' ['It is evident that music performance healed many *spiritual illnesses* such as folly, melancholy and several other ailments'; *De Universo*, II. 3. 20. 996E]. William conceded that in some cases, based on ancient beliefs, music could even alter the senses with the same efficacy as an opioid,[9] and induce a metaphysical experience such as the *excessus mentis*.

But among the doctors of the church who capitalized on the figure of sin as malady, Augustine was certainly the most influential. He developed a veritable *theologia medicinalis* in which the incarnation of Christ constituted a form of medicine for original sin, with the ability to cure man. Augustine often compares sin to a pestilence of the soul and liturgical singing to a medicine.[10] In *De natura et gratia* (13, 34, 53–54) the saint explicitly equates sin with a sickness, calling it a spiritual wound, and, on the basis of Jesus's words to the Pharisees in Matthew 9. 12–13 ('Non est opus valentibus medicus, sed male habentibus'; 'They that are in health need not a physician, but they that are ill'), describing Christ as a physician who treats man, who suffers from the malady of sin and therefore 'iam medico indiget' ('needs a doctor', *De natura et gratia* 13). Quoting Psalm 40 in *Sermones ad populum*, Augustine then compares the sinner to the sick who asks the Lord for help. God is therefore the doctor of the soul, and the medicine consists of singing the psalm: 'Voce consona, corde concordi, pro ipso corde nostro Dominum deprecantes [...] Ut autem sanetur, medicum quaerimus' ('With voices in harmony and hearts in concord we have begged the Lord [...] but to heal it we look for a doctor').[11]

Thus, Augustine states that a physician is necessary for the patient to heal from the malady of sin, and our request for metaphysical help must take place in an appropriate voice. Elsewhere — also quoting the same verse of Psalm 40 — he introduces the importance of choral psalmody to obtain healing: 'Una voce multi cantavimus, quia in Christo unum sumus [...] *Domine, miserere mei, sana animam meam quoniam peccavi tibi*' ('We all sang in one voice because we are one in Christ [...] Lord, have mercy on me, heal my soul since I have sinned against you', *Sermo*, 16. B. 1). The saint comments on the psalmodic line explaining that 'Clamat aeger ad medicum' ('The sick person invokes the physician'; *Expositiones in psalmos 31*, 2. 16. 36),[12] and Psalm 6. 3–4 reads: 'Miserere mei, Domine, quoniam infirmus sum: sana me, Domine, quoniam conturbata sunt ossa mea' ('Have mercy on me, O Lord, for I am weak: heal me, O Lord, for my bones are troubled'), on which Augustine comments by saying: 'quis non intelligat significari animam luctantem cum morbis suis, diu autem dilatam a medico' ('who does not see represented here a soul struggling with her diseases; but long kept back by the physician'; *Enarratio in Psalmum* 6, 4). Thus, if the notion of sin as a disease is already implicit in the text of the psalms, the bishop of Hippo takes advantage of that rhetorical emphasis and proposes the Psalter, the most intrinsically musical book of the Bible, as the remedy. It is this repertoire that functions as medicine sung in Dante's *Purgatorio*: psalm singing as a spiritual cure for sin, and monophonic performance acquires a central role, as appears clear when the newcomers to purgatory intone 'In exitu Isräel de Aegypto' (Psalm 113) 'tutti insieme ad una voce'.

We should not be surprised that the therapeutic properties of monophonic and choral chant continue to be recognized even today. In addition to the amazing accounts of how music healed serious brain injuries and diseases, as told in Oliver Sacks's *Musicophilia: Tales of Music and the Brain*, one can refer to Peregrine Horden's collected volume *Music as Medicine*, which details the uses of musicotherapy through the centuries. And with regard to a specific example concerning Gregorian chant (which is essentially monophonic psalm singing), there exists a 'Tomatis method' for the treatment of neuropsychological and physiological pathologies, which consists in listening for an extended period of time to music, especially Mozart and Gregorian chant. The Tomatis method has been applied with positive results to speech disorders, anxiety, depression and stress, and learning problems (dyslexia and dyscalculia).[13] The therapeutic method in question is named after Alfred Tomatis, a French otolaryngologist who visited the monks of the abbey of Saint-Benoît d'En Calcat, 45 miles east of Toulouse, in June 1967. When the monks abandoned the practice of singing Gregorian chant for six hours a day on the orders of the abbot, many of them showed signs of fatigue and depression.[14] They restored good energy levels after resuming singing on the advice of Dr Tomatis. Today, a whole new branch of medicine, called Medical Humanities, explores the intersections of music and medicine, often citing Dante's *Purgatorio* as an eminent example of psalm-singing enacting spiritual healing.[15]

The preoccupation of John XXII, then, appears to be well founded, when considered in light of modern medical science. Since, in the *Purgatorio*, Dante has so many different psalms performed, it is appropriate to investigate the curative aspects of this musical practice in his poem. Purgatory is a place of spiritual convalescence, 'dove l'umano spirito si purga' (*Purgatorio* 1. 11), and its denizens are already destined for salvation but need a *pharmakon* that allows them to complete their purification. The musical practice of singing the penitential psalms (or psalmody, as Dante writes in *Purgatorio* 33. 2) is also part of this spiritual medicine.

The pilgrim is also here in search of *salute* — the Italian word means both physical health and spiritual salvation: the loss of Beatrice's greeting in the *Vita nuova* had caused the loss of salvation and the right path, but also the beginning of a profound psycho-physical anxiety. Even on the day of Beatrice's birth, the infant Dante underwent a 'passïon nova' ('E' m'increscie di me sì duramente'; *Rime*, LXVII) which Claudio Giunta linked — with due caution — to descriptions of epilepsy found in medieval medical treatises, a notion later followed by Marco Santagata.[16] But for the penitents of Dante's *Purgatorio* to reach a spiritual tuning, they must perform the prayers chorally, often under duress or while undergoing a punishment. The sweetness of heavenly music, which we read about in the *Paradiso*, is obviously denied in the context of profitable suffering in the *Purgatorio*: the penitents must perform the songs while simultaneously carrying weights, being forced into painful postures or suffering torments as the time is not yet ripe for the aesthetic, soothing pleasure of paradisal music. In purgatory penitential songs often 'diletto e doglia parturie' (*Purgatorio* 23. 12), and herein lies its spiritual and medicinal efficacy, utilizing a sort of homeopathic approach. Augustine in the *Confessions* discusses his own delight in chanting, while denouncing the risks of abandoning oneself to excessive aesthetic pleasure during the performance of church songs.[17] Elsewhere Augustine warned against excessive enjoyment and recommended sobriety in singing so that the voice would not sound coarse or subdued, stressing the importance of the performance over the melody itself.[18]

Dante's second canticle presents a number of hymns and psalms sung by the souls. These chants can be of two types: glorifying (such as the 'Gloria in excelsis deo' of *Purgatorio* 20) and penitential (for example the 'Miserere' of *Purgatorio* 5). The latter type, performed in chorus monophonically, reflects the effort of penitent souls to gain spiritual harmony through choral prayer, a yearning that moves from musical to metaphysical and from metaphysical to social, since attuning with other singing souls is necessary for spiritual progress. Erminia Ardissino observes that 'le anime cantano in coro in unisono realizzando una perfetta unità d'intendimenti':[19] it is a unity of faith that fosters healing through the mortification of the tendency towards individualism. The meaning of purgatory is, therefore, metaphysical, social and political all at once, and the musical exercise to which the penitents are subjected functions as a spiritual and choral refinement. It is the choral tuning process that cements the singers' friendship, as Basil expounded, and as William Peter Mahrt remarks:

> unison singing is a communal act that binds the singers in a common enterprise; because it is unison, the bond is most intimate, as Dante suggests in the *Purgatorio*. In unison or in monophonic performance the singers can perfect elements of tuning, timbre, diction, rhythm, and expression in common.[20]

In the Middle Ages, the psalms were considered a specifically musical genre, as noted by biblical scholars and musicologists[21] and distinct from other types of prayer: 'The psalms, in contrast to the prayers and readings of the Office, were performed nearly always in a manner resembling singing rather than non-musical recitation.'[22] Not surprisingly, the Book of Psalms was seen, among all the parts of the Bible, as the most intrinsically musical, and David as the sacred poet-musician par excellence. Unlike other parts of the liturgy which were also chanted or read with a sustained voice, the psalms had a distinctly melodic aspect; in fact, 'lectio dicitur quia non cantatur, ut psalmus et hymnus, sed legitur tantum' ('A lectio is so called because it is not sung like a psalm or hymn but merely read').[23] If the singing of the psalms initially had an individual or soloist character, towards the second half of the eighth century choral performance took over in all monasteries.[24]

Let us return to Dante. If we consider only direct quotations and exclude allusions, echoes and oblique references, in the *Purgatorio* we count ten psalms plus four hymns, in contrast to only two psalms in *Paradiso*.[25] As Enrico Malato notes, the 'Miserere' (Psalm 50) stands out, with three occurrences, as

> la prima parola che Dante personaggio pronuncia nel poema e sarà anche l'ultima evocata prima della sua immersione nel tripudio della candida rosa, attraverso un'allusione, nel discorso di san Bernardo, 'al cantor [David] che per doglia / del fallo disse: Miserere mei.'[26]

Conversely, in songs of expiation, the audience experiences an oxymoronic mixture of pleasure and pain, providing the basis of the healing principle of purgatory, already foregrounded by Virgil's words at the onset of the journey: 'E vederai color che son contenti | nel foco, perché speran di venire, | quando che sia, alle beate genti' (*Inferno* 1. 118–20). This principle is reaffirmed by Forese Donati, who happily drinks 'lo dolce assenzio de' martiri' (*Purgatorio* 23. 86) and calls it a solace ('io dico pena e dovria dir sollazzo', *Purgatorio* 23. 72). Furthermore, Augustine, arguing against Pelagianism in *De natura et gratia*, underscores the necessity of a painful cure to extirpate the disease:

> Quasi non et ulcus in dolore est et sectio dolorem operatur, ut dolor dolore tollatur. Hoc si experti non essemus et in aliquibus terris, ubi ista numquam contigerant, audiremus, sine dubio utique deridentes fortassis etiam verbis huius uteremur et diceremus: 'Absurdissimum est dolorem necessarium fuisse, ne ulceris dolor esset'. (*De natura et gratia*, 27)

> [As if a sore were not attended with pain, and an operation did not produce pain, that pain might be taken away by pain. If we had not experienced any such treatment, but were only to hear about it in some parts of the world where these things had never happened, we might perhaps use this man's words, and say, 'It is the height of absurdity that pain should have been necessary in order that a sore should have no pain.']'[27]

This pain can take the form of a musical oxymoron, as we can imagine when the doors of purgatory are thrown open (*Purgatorio* 9. 133–45). I have written elsewhere about this often commented-upon passage regarding medieval organology;[28] here I am interested in underscoring the acoustic oxymoron that mixes the metallic roar of the hinges with the 'sweet sound' of the 'Te Deum'. This paradoxical mixture is an example of the necessary concomitance of pain and benefit in medicine found in Augustine's and William of Auvergne's writings. The apparent contradiction is resolved from a purgatorial perspective, to which the roar of the opening gate alludes: healing is achieved through the experience of pain,[29] which reflects the key event of Christian history, the redemption of humankind through the suffering of Christ on the cross. The words of the 'Te Deum' appropriately reference the redemption and salvation obtained by the torture of the crucifixion: 'Te ergo quaesumus, tuis famulis subveni, quos pretioso sanguine redemisti' ('Therefore, we pray, help your servants, whom you have redeemed with your precious blood').[30] This, of course, is just the beginning of the penitential journey, since the pilgrim, on whose forehead the guardian angel has now engraved the seven 'Ps', enters the realm of atonement which will climax in the baptism of fire and then in the waters of Lethe in the earthly paradise.

The avaricious must sing Psalm 118 among tears and sighs: '*Adhesit pavimento anima mea* | sentìa dir lor con sì alti sospiri | che la parola a pena s'intendea' ("Adhaesit pavimento anima mea' | I heard them say with such deep sighs | the words could hardly be distinguished'; *Purgatorio* 19. 73–75). The episode appears as an accurate dramatization of the Psalm, reiterating all the elements of suffering and pathos, including prayer against avarice and the penitent's request to avert his eyes so that they will not witness vanity, ropes, tears and sighs:

> Adhesit pavimento anima mea [. . .]
> Inclina cor meum in testimonia tua et non in avaritiam:
> Averte oculos meos ne videant vanitatem; in via tua vivifica me. [...]
> Funes peccatorum circumplexi sunt me et legem tuam non sum oblitus [...]
> Exitus aquarum deduxerunt oculi mei quia non custodierunt legem tuam [...].
> Os meum aperui et adtraxi spiritum quia mandata tua desiderabam [...].
> (Psalm 118. 25, 36–37, 61, 131, 136)

> [My soul hath cleaved to the pavement [...]
> Incline my heart into thy testimonies and not to covetousness.
> Turn away my eyes that they may not behold vanity: quicken me in thy way. [...]
> The cords of the wicked have encompassed me: but I have not forgotten thy law [...]
> My eyes have sent forth springs of water: because they have not kept thy law [...].
> I opened my mouth and panted: because I longed for thy commandments [...].]

Similarly pronounced in a fashion that is barely comprehensible, because it is interrupted by sobs and sighs, is the psalm from the lips of the gluttonous:

> Ed ecco piangere e cantare s'udie
> 'Labia mea, Domine', per modo
> tal, che diletto e doglia parturie. (*Purgatorio* 23. 10–12)

For these sinners, the oxymoric coexistence of delight and grief emphasizes the biblical quotation. Here too the performance is dramatized and performed in explicitly musical form, interspersed with tears. The gluttons appear so thin, haggard and pale 'che dall'ossa la pelle s'informava' (*Purgatorio* 23. 23–24), and their song begs the Lord to open their lips in order to sing the praise of God ('Domine, labia mea aperies, et os meum annuntiabit laudem tuam' ('O Lord, open my lips: and my mouth shall declare thy praise'; Psalm 50. 17), thus invoking an appropriate use of the mouth, the organ with which the gluttons sin. Perhaps we can perceive in another verse of the psalm — 'Auditui meo dabis gaudium et laetitiam, et exsultabunt ossa humiliata' ('To my hearing thou shalt give joy and gladness: and the bones that have been humbled shall rejoice'; Psalm 50. 10) — a reference to the 'bones' of Dante's line 24 as much as to the promise of full auditory satisfaction in the joyful songs of paradise. Their song must, for now, be one of delight and tears together, so as to enact spiritual healing.

As one progresses up the mountain, the traumatic and frightening passage through the wall of flames which separates the reign of penance from the earthly paradise can only take place through a trial by fire, a cauterization of the sin of the lustful, who here in purgatory also include sodomites ('si parton "Soddoma" gridando'; *Purgatorio* 26. 79). Among the lustful are many poets, and even Dante will have to purify himself of the poetic sin of his youth, when he was too inclined towards courtly and Cavalcantian love. Only in this way can the pilgrim gain the pure heart sanctioned by the beatitude sung by the last guardian angel ('Beati mundo corde'; *Purgatorio* 27. 8). The song of the lustful who burn in the flames resounds with these words:

> 'Summae Deus clementiae' nel seno
> al grande ardore allora udì cantando
> che di volger mi fe caler non meno; (*Purgatorio* 25. 121–23)

which reprise a hymn for Saturday Matins, with an emphasis on anatomical features specifically relevant to the sin of lust. Here musical healing is accompanied by fire, and the request of setting 'our loins on fire' fits the retaliation for carnal sin. Finally, the narrative macrosequence of the earthly paradise abounds with musical moments of amazing beauty and unsustainable intensity. One in particular, Dante's confession of his sin in earthly paradise, is emphatically accompanied by singing angels, who ease the meltdown of the frozen knot ('[...] li angeli cantaro | di sùbito 'In te, Domine, speravi'; | ma oltre 'pedes meos' non passaro'; *Purgatorio* 30. 82–83) so that Dante can bathe in the Lethe (*Purgatorio* 30. 91–99). During Dante's baptism in the Lethe, Psalm 50 resumes with 'Asperges me' (*Purgatorio* 31. 98), a chant which most commentators believe is performed by the angels, who had previously acted as a theatrical 'chorus' (*Purgatorio* 30. 19, 21, 83–84) providing musical commentary and support to the drama of the encounter/confrontation between Dante and Beatrice.[31] This verse ('Asperges me') from the 'Miserere' — also very familiar to medieval Christians as a self-contained antiphon, although Dante commentators refer specifically to the psalm — is naturally appropriate to the context, since, as already noted by Landino and the Ottimo Commento, and more recently by Chiavacci Leonardi, 'si recitava nella liturgia della penitenza, quando il sacerdote spargeva l'acqua benedetta sul peccatore.'[32]

All of this psalmodic and musical construction, in which Beatrice's triumphant return takes place, culminates in the double baptism of Dante, but the emotional fulcrum of the episode is the confession which Beatrice draws from the pilgrim, now ready to face the painful admission of his sins. Here again returns the concept of spiritual medicine associated with the use of speech and song, which has a profound theological basis because the confession was described as a medicinal act by the Lateran IV Council of 1215:

> Sacerdos autem sit discretus et cautus ut, more periti medici, superinfundat vinum et oleum vulneribus sauciati, diligenter inquirens et peccatoris circumstantias et peccati, per quas prudenter intelligat quale illi consilium debeat exhibere et cujusmodi remedium adhibere, diversis experimentis utendo *ad sanandum aegrotum*.
>
> [The priest should be discerning and prudent, so that like a skilled doctor he may pour wine and oil over the wounds of the injured one. Let him carefully inquire about the circumstances of both the sinner and the sin, so that he may prudently discern what sort of advice he ought to give and what remedy to apply, using various means *to heal the sick person*.][33]

The musical journey of *Purgatorio* ends with a baptism that cures the pilgrim as Matelda sings and dances along with the angels and finally the theological virtues (*Purgatorio* 31. 132): the musical and choreographic context of the ritual effect a fundamental function in the purification and healing process, connecting the inner world of emotions, feelings and profound psychic experience to the outer world of signs. Without dance and music, which combine gestures, words and sounds into an organic patterns of meaning, there would be no spiritual growth and no chance of salvation.

Notes to Chapter 7

1. Willi Apel, *The Notation of Polyphonic Music, 900–1600* (Cambridge, MA: The Medieval Academy of America, 1949), p. 217.
2. Three hypotheses have been proposed for the dating of the *Constitutio Docta sanctorum Patrum*: 1317–18, 1320–21 and 1324. Michael Klaper considers the latest date to be most likely correct; see Michael Klaper, '"Verbindliches kirchenmusikalisches Gesetz" oder belanglose Augenblickseingebung? Zur Constitutio "Docta sanctorum patrum" Papst Johannes' XXII', *Archiv für Musikwissenschaft*, 60 (2003), 69–95 (p. 80). On this complex matter see also Margaret Bent, *Magister Jacobus de Ispania, Author of the 'Speculum musicae'*, Royal Musical Association Monographs, 28 (Farnham: Ashgate, 2015), pp. 54–56.
3. My translation. Latin text from Michael Klaper, 'Liturgia e polifonia all'inizio del Trecento: appunti sulla genesi, trasmissione e ricezione della constitutio Docta sanctorum di papa Giovanni XXII', in *'Deo è lo scrivano ch'el canto à ensegnato'. Segni e simboli nella musica al tempo di Iacopone. Atti del Convegno internazionale, Collazzone, 7–8 luglio 2006*, ed. by Ernesto Sergio Mainoldi and Stefania Vitale (= *Philomusica on-line*, 9.3 (2010)), pp. 135–48 (p. 147) <http://www.riviste.paviauniversitypress.it/index.php/phi/article/view/613/pdf_2>. See also Karl Gustav Fellerer, 'Zur Constitutio "Docta SS. Patrum"', in *Speculum musicae artis. Festgabe für Heinrich Husmann zum 60. Geburstag*, ed. by Heinz Becker and Reinhard Gerlach (Munich: Fink, 1970), pp. 125–52; Helmut Hucke, 'Das Dekret Docta sanctorum patrum Papst Johannes XXII', *Musica disciplina*, 38 (1984), 119–31.
4. 'Igitur quandocumque spiritus Domini malus arripiebat Saul, David tollebat citharam, et percutiebat manu sua, et refocillabatur Saul, et levius habebat: recedebat enim ab eo spiritus malus' [So whensoever the evil spirit from the Lord was upon Saul, David took his harp, and

played with his hand, and Saul was refreshed, and was better, for the evil spirit departed from him]. 1 Kings (Samuel) 16. 23. Quotations and translations from the Bible are taken from <http://www.drbo.org>.

5. 'Vulgatum quippe est, quam saepe iracundias cantilena represserit, quam multa vel in corporum, vel in animorum affectionibus miranda perfecerit. Cui enim est illud ignotum, quod Pythagoras ebrium adolescentem Taurominitanum sub Phrygii modi sono incitatum, spondeo succinente reddiderit mitiorem et sui compotem' [It is told that music often soothed anger, and that it performed wonders for the afflictions of both the body and the soul. Indeed, who does not know that Pythagoras first excited a drunken youth from Taormina and then calmed him by singing a spondaic rhythm?] (Boethius, *De institutione arithmetica libri duo, De institutione musica libri quinque*, 1.1, ed. By Godofredus Friedlein (Leipzig: Teubner, 1867), pp. 184–85).

6. I quote here the Latin text translated from the Greek, as printed by J. P. Migne in volume XXIX of his *Patrologia Graeca*. See also Saint Basil, *Tou en hagiois patros hemon Basileiou archiepiskopou Kaesareias Kappadokias ta heuriskomena panta: Sancti patris nostri Basilii Caesareae Cappadociae archiepiscopi opera omnia, quae exstant, vel quae ejus nomine circumferuntur*, ed. by Julianus Garnier (Paris: Joannis Baptistae Coignard, 1721–30). English translation from Basil the Great, *Exegetic Homilies*, trans. by Sister Agnes Clare Way (Washington, DC: The Catholic University of America Press, 1963), pp. 151–52 (with amendments).

7. Basilius, *Homiliae in Psalmos*, I. 1–2, 90A–91C, cols. 210–11.

8. See Bruno Nardi, *Saggi di filosofia dantesca* (Milan: Società Anonima Editrice Dante Alighieri, 1930; Florence: La Nuova Italia, 1967), p. 183; and Dante Alighieri, *La Commedia di Dante raccontata da Vittorio Sermonti*, ed. by Vittorio Sermonti, 3 vols (Florence: Giunti, 2012), III, 597.

9. Brenno Boccadoro, 'L'Inferno e il Paradiso della musica: l'etica musicale in Guglielmo d'Alvernia', *Musica e storia*, 15.2 (2007): 259–78 (p. 259). On this subject see also Boccadoro, 'La musique, les passions, l'âme et le corps', in *Autour de Guillaume d'Auvergne (†1249)*, ed. by Franco Morenzoni and Jean-Yves Tilliette (Turnhout: Brepols, 2005), pp. 75–92; and Christopher Page, 'Music and Medicine in the Thirteenth Century', in *Music as Medicine: The History of Music Therapy Since Antiquity*, ed. by Peregrine Horden (London: Ashgate, 2000), pp. 109–19 (p. 113).

10. See, for example, *De natura et gratia* 34 and 53; *Exposition on Ps*.1 and 7. In *Ps*. 87 Augustine notes 'chorus autem concordiam significat' [But the choir signifies concord], echoing Basil and anticipating Dante's line in *Purgatorio*, XVI. 21. For a summary of Augustine's rhetoric of sin as sickness, see Gerard Lukken, *Original Sin in the Roman Liturgy: Research into the Theology of Original Sin in the Roman Sacramentaria and the Early Baptismal Liturgy* (Leiden: Brill, 1973), esp. pp. 311–17.

11. Psalm 40. 5. Augustine, *Sermones ad populum, classis prima: Sermo XX*. 1 (*PL*, XXXVIII, col. 137). Translation by E. Hill, in Augustine, *The Works of Saint Augustine, A translation for the 21st Century*, ed. by John E. Rotelle, trans. by Edmund Hill (New York: New City Press, 1990–2003), III: *Sermons, vol. II (20–50) on the Old Testament*, p. 15.

12. Translation by Philip Schaff, *Nicene and Post-Nicene Fathers of the Christian Church* (Buffalo: The Christian Literature Company, 1886–1900). Quoted at <http://www.ccel.org/ccel/schaff/npnf108.i.html>.

13. See Tim Gilmore, 'The Efficacy of the Tomatis Method for Children with Learning and Communication Disorders: A Meta-Analysis', *International Journal of Listening*, 13 (1999), 12–23; Carmela Stillitano and others, 'The Effects Of The Tomatis Method On Tinnitus', *International Journal of Research In Medical and Health Sciences*, 4.2 (2014), 2307–83; Billie Thompson and Susan Andrews, 'An Historical Commentary on the Physiological Effects of Music: Tomatis, Mozart and Neuropsychology', *Integrative Physiological and Behavioral Science*, 35.3 (2012), 174–88; Alfred Tomatis, *The Ear and Language* (Norval, Ont.: Moulin, 1996).

14. I draw the anecdote from Norman Doidge, *The Brain's Way of Healing: Remarkable Discoveries and Recoveries from the Frontiers of Neuroplasticity* (New York: Penguin, 2015), pp. 449–51.

15. See Donatella Lippi and others, 'Music and medicine', *Journal of Multidisciplinary Health*, 3 (2010), 137–41 (p. 140), available at <https://www.ncbi.nlm.nih.gov/pmc/articles/PMC3004608/>.

16. This association, first proposed by Cesare Lombroso, has a long and heavily debated history. See Cesare Lombroso, 'La nevrosi in Dante e Michelangelo', *Gazzetta Letteraria*, 25 November

1893; and Giunta's comment in Dante Alighieri, *Rime*, in *Opere*, ed. by Claudio Giunta (Milan: Mondadori, 2011), p. 234. On Dante's supposed epilepsy and narcolepsy see Giuseppe Plazzi, 'Dante's Description of Narcolepsy', *Sleep medicine*, 14 (2013), 1221–23; Francesco Maria Galassi, Michael Habicht and Frank Rühli, 'Dante Alighieri's Narcolepsy', *The Lancet Neurology*, 15 (2016), 245; Marco Grimaldi, 'Dalla *science fiction* alla *fiction science*: Dante narcolettico', *Le parole e le cose* <http://www.leparoleelecose.it/?p=22253>; Marco Santagata, *Dante: il romanzo della sua vita* (Milan: Mondadori, 2012), p. 32. Perhaps Dante's most eloquent reference to epilepsy is found in his description of Vanni Fucci's torment (*Inferno*, XXIV. 112–18). For an account of Lombroso and his critics, see Spencer Pearce, 'Dante and Psychology in the Late Nineteenth Century', in *Dante in the Nineteenth Century: Reception, Canonicity*, ed. by Nick Havely (Oxford and Bern: Peter Lang, 2011), esp. pp. 221–26; and for a balanced approach to such contemporary 'retrospective diagnosis' in Plazzi, Santagata and others, see Sarah Bakewell, 'If Dante Was a Narcoleptic, Why Should It Matter?', in *Guardian: Books*, Sat. 28 Sept, 2013, <https://www.theguardian.com/commentisfree/2013/sep/27/dante-narcoleptic-creativity> [accessed 15 January 2020].

17. See Augustine, *Confessions*, 10. 33, trans. by Albert C. Outler (Philadelphia: Westminster Press, 1955) and Francesco Ciabattoni, *Dante's Journey to Polyphony* (Toronto: University of Toronto Press, 2010), p. 112.
18. Augustine, *De Musica*, 6. 13. 38, Trans. by R. Catesby Taliaferro (Portsmouth, RI: Portsmouth Priory School, 1939); see also Ciabattoni, *Dante's Journey*, pp. 104–05.
19. Erminia Ardissino, 'I canti liturgici nel Purgatorio dantesco', *Dante Studies*, 108 (1990), 39–65 (p. 43).
20. William P. Mahrt, 'Chant', *A Performer's Guide to Medieval Music*, ed. by Ross W. Duffin (Bloomington: Indiana University Press, 2000), p. 2.
21. See Gianfranco Ravasi, *I Salmi nella Divina Commedia* (Rome: Salerno, 2013), p. 9; Piero Weiss and Richard Taruskin, *Music in the Western World: A History in Documents* (Belmont, CA: Schirmer, 2008), p. 19.
22. Joseph Dyer, 'The Singing of Psalms in the Early-Medieval Office', *Speculum*, 64 (1989), 535–78 (p. 538).
23. Isidore of Seville, *Etymologiae*, 6. 19. 9, ed. by W. Lindsay (Oxford: Clarendon Press, 1911). Translation from Dyer, p. 538, fn. 14.
24. See Dyer, p. 546, 568.
25. The Psalms performed in the *Purgatorio* are: (1) *Purgatorio* 3. 46: 'In exitu Israel de Aegypto' [When Israel went out of Egypt]: Psalm 113. 1; (2) *Purgatorio* 5. 24: 'cantando "Miserere" a verso a verso' [chanting *Miserere* line by line]: Psalm 50. 3; (3) *Purgatorio* 19. 73: 'Adhaesit pavimento anima mea' [My soul hath cleaved to the pavement]: Psalm 118. 25; (4) *Purgatorio* 23. 11: 'Labia mia, Domine' [O Lord, thou wilt open my lips]: Psalm 50. 17; (5) *Purgatorio* 28. 80: 'ma luce rende il salmo Delectasti' [but the psalm *Delectasti* offers light]: Psalm 91. 5; (6) *Purgatorio* 29. 3: 'Beati quorum tecta sunt peccata' [Blessed are they whose sins are covered]: Psalm 31. 1; (7) *Purgatorio* 30. 19: 'Tutti dicean: "Benedictus qui venis"' [They all said: 'Blessed be you that come']: Psalm 117. 26 (but also Luke 19. 38 and Matthew 21. 9, although in the scripture the verb is in the third person: 'Benedictus, qui venit'. This text was also sung in the Sanctus as part of the liturgy); (8) *Purgatorio* 30. 83–84: '"In te, Domine, speravi" | ma oltre "pedes meos" non passaro' [In thee, O Lord, have I hoped', | but did not sing past 'my feet']: Psalm 30. 2–9; (9) *Purgatorio* 31. 98: '"Asperges me" sì dolcemente udissi' [I heard 'Thou shalt sprinkle me' so sweetly sung]: Psalm 50. 9; (10) *Purgatorio* 33. 1–2: '"Deus venerunt gentes", alternando | or tre or quattro dolce salmodia' ['O God, the heathens are come' the ladies, | now three, now four, in alternation sang, | beginning their sweet psalmody in tears]: Psalm 78. 1.
26. Enrico Malato, *Saggio di una nuova edizione commentata delle Opere di Dante: il canto I dell'Inferno* (Rome: Salerno, 2007), p. 39.
27. Translation from Augustine, *De Natura et gratia*, trans. by Peter Holmes and Robert Ernest Wallis, in *Nicene and Post-Nicene Fathers*, ed. by Philip Schaff (Buffalo, NY: Christian Literature Publishing Co., 1887), first series, V. Found online at: <http://www.newadvent.org/fathers/1503.htm>.

28. Francesco Ciabattoni, '"Temprando col dolce l'acerbo": Instrumental and Vocal Polyphony in the "Commedia"', *Bibliotheca Dantesca*, 1 (2018), 108–26, <https://www.repository.upenn.edu/bibdant/vol1/iss1/6/>.
29. See Denise Heilbronn, '*Concentus Musicus*: The Creaking Hinges of Dante's Gate of Purgatory', *Rivista di Studi Italiani*, 2.1 (1984), 1–15. See also Francesco Ciabattoni, *Dante's Journey to Polyphony* (Toronto: University of Toronto Press, 2010), pp. 122–29; and Francesco Ciabattoni, '"Temprando col dolce l'acerbo": Instrumental and Vocal Polyphony in the "Commedia"', *Bibliotheca Dantesca: Journal of Dante Studies*, 1 (2018), Article 6. Available at: <https://www.repository.upenn.edu/bibdant/vol1/iss1/6 Download>.
30. Translation from Gunilla Iversen, 'Pax et Sapientia: A Thematic Study on Tropes from Different Traditions', in *Embellishing the Liturgy: Tropes and Polyphony*, ed. by Alejandro Enrique Planchart (New York: Routledge 2009), pp. 449–84 (p. 478).
31. In his commentary on this passage, however, Singleton underscores the difference between this rite and the true baptismal sacrament, which only cleanses away original sin. See Dante Alighieri, *The Divine Comedy*, ed. and trans. by Charles S. Singleton, 6 vols (Princeton, NJ: Princeton University Press, 1970–75).
32. See note on *Purgatorio* 30, in Dante Alighieri, *Commedia*, ed. by Anna Maria Chiavacci Leonardi (Milan: Mondadori, 2012), p. 922.
33. *Sacrorum Conciliorum Nova et Amplissima Collectio*, ed. by Joannes Dominicus Mansi, 53 vols (Venice: Antonio Zatta, 1769–1969), XXII, cols 953–1086 (1009 B). English translation from *Decrees of the Ecumenical Councils*, ed. by Norman Tanner and Giuseppe Alberigo, 2 vols (Washington, DC: Georgetown University Press, 1990), I, 245 (with amendments).

CHAPTER 8

❖

'Che cosa è questa, Amor?': Cavalcanti and *Paradiso* in a Ballata by Francesco Landini

Pedro Memelsdorff

Much has been said and written about the disambiguation strategies used by Dante's early commentators, or by rhymers and *novellieri* of the Italian Trecento; and similar strategies have been discerned in the iconographic programmes of illuminated manuscripts, paintings and fresco cycles of the time. In the present study I will focus on a *musical* setting instead, whose text — as I believe — operates as a disambiguation of *Par* 31 and 33: a ballata composed by Francesco Landini probably in Florence in the 1380s and opening with the words 'Che cosa è questa, Amor'.[1] The piece will be discussed from three points of view: first, in its relationship to a group of contemporary texts set to music; second, in its possible relationship to a momentous poetic *auctoritas*, a sonnet by Guido Cavalcanti; and third, in its link to Dante's *Paradiso*. By extension, the following reflections aim at reconsidering the reception of the *Commedia* in late-Trecento Florentine musical repertoires.

The Context: Landini's *Cosa*

A few words may suffice to sketch the possible historical context of the piece's origin. Around 1425 or 1426 (or perhaps already in 1415, or even in the last years of the fourteenth century, depending on the different dating suggested by scholars ranging from Alessandro Wesselofsky to Elisabetta Guerrieri) Francesco Gherardi da Prato wrote a celebrated narrative work in five books known as *Il Paradiso degli Alberti*.[2] In its last three books he describes a group of intellectuals meeting in a villa outside Florence in 1389 where, as in Boccaccio's *Decameron*, different characters present short stories to be heard and eventually discussed by the entire *brigata*.

Skipping the thorny transmission — and disputed ascription — of Gherardi's works, as well as the modern criticism of *Il Paradiso degli Alberti*'s exceedingly rich frame narrative,[3] I will only mention that one of the villa's guests was a female philosopher named Niccolosa (abbreviated as *Cosa*);[4] and that in the frame narrative two young women are told to sing a ballata quoting her name:

> Or su, gentili spiriti ad amar pronti,
> volete voi vedere il paradiso?
> Mirate d'esta *Cosa* suo bel viso.[5]

As musicologists know, another copy of the same ballata — this time ascribed to Francesco Landini — survives on fol. 163 of the Florentine musical manuscript Sq.[6] In it the word *Cosa* is replaced by the name *Petra*, confirming that in Gherardi's narrative *Cosa* stands indeed for the *senhal* of the piece's addressee.[7] Moreover, '*Cosa*' is quoted in two further works by Gherardi: *Trattato d'una angelica Cosa*, and *Il giuoco d'amore*, where *Cosa* is described as 'lucente più ch'altra damigella al mondo sola'.[8] Finally, it is also used in a rather large number of contemporary musical settings.[9] These include, but are certainly not limited to, four ballatas by Francesco Landini, one or two by his younger contemporary Paolo da Firenze, one by Andrea da Firenze, one anonymous setting now in London, and one madrigal by Lorenzo Masini:

Author of setting	Incipit	Sources	Form
Francesco Landini	'Che cosa è questa, Amor'	Sq 163; Pan 36v–37	ballata
Francesco Landini	'Chi pregio vuol'	Sq 157; Pan 11v; Pit 69v; Rei 51; F.5.5. 137v	ballata
—	'Deh pon quest'amor'	Sq 144; Pan, 2	ballata
—	'Or su gentili spirti'	Sq 142	ballata
—	'Cosa null' à più fé'	Sq 132; Pan 35v; Pit 87v–88; F.5.5. 138	ballata
Paolo da Firenze	'Uom c'osa di veder'	Pit 82; SL cxxxviiiv/108v	ballata
—	'Or sia che può'	Pit 82v; SL cxxxvi/105; Magl. 22v; Chig. 135v	ballata
Andrea da Firenze	'Cosa crudel m'ancide'	Sq 185v	ballata
Anon.	'Cosa non è ch'a sé'[a]	Lo 169v–170/72v–73	ballata
Lorenzo Masini	'Vidi nell'ombra'	Sq 47v–48; Pan 78v–79; Pit 23v–24; Lo 129v–130/32v–33; cantus fragm. in Ott. 77	madrigal

[a] Agostino Ziino ascribed the piece to Francesco Landini in 'Chosa non è ch'a sé tanto mi tiri: una ballata anonima nello stile di Landini', in Sergio Gensini (ed.), *La Toscana nel secolo XIV* (Lucca: Pacini, 1988), pp. 519–38

TABLE 1. Sample of musical settings mentioning *Cosa*

All of these pieces, except Andrea da Firenze's and perhaps Landini's 'Cosa null' à più fé', share a lofty register and a series of common themes, such as beauty, radiance, loving eyes, perfect heart, divine splendour, God or the gods, or *Amore*.[10] Two of them also share Dante's topos of special status, the fixation in God's regard ('Uom c'osa' and 'Che cosa è questa, Amor'), the second of which quite literally reworks the celebrated trope *Quae est ista* from the Solomonic Song of Songs (6:10 and 8:5), or perhaps the trope *Quis est iste* from Isaiah (63:1), possibly mediated by Dante's quote 'Chi è questa che ascende del diserto' (*Conv.* 2. 5. 5), or perhaps — as will be discussed here — by Cavalcanti's sonnet 'Chi è questa che vèn'.[11]

This is the core piece of the present study: Landini's ballata opening with the question:

> Che cosa è questa, Amor, che 'l ciel produce
> per far più manifesta la tuo luce?

Reasons of space prevent comparing it to a neo-stilnovo reworking of Cavalcanti's sonnet, 'Chi è costei, Amor, che quando appare' by Landini's contemporary Cino Rinuccini — another member of Gherardi's *brigata* witnessing the circulation of the *senhal Cosa*.[12] It seems relevant to point out, however, that the biographical connections between at least some of these poet-musicians, and the intertextual web between all of them, not only reveal a generic affinity due to shared cultural backgrounds, but also support the hypothesis of some sort of *puy* or poetical/musical contest.[13] This may have occurred within, or related to, some literary meeting similar or perhaps even identical to that described by Gherardi; and it may have consisted either in linking Niccolosa's name to an authoritative source, for instance Dante (as seems the case in Paolo's 'Uom c'osa' and Landini's 'Che cosa' to be explored in the following), and/or intertwining it with the biblical (Cavalcantian?) question (as in Landini's *Che cosa* and the London anonymous).[14] Landini's possible relationship with both *auctoritates*, Cavalcanti and Dante, will therefore be explored in the next sections.

Landini and Cavalcanti

Before embarking on a comparison between Landini's 'Che cosa è questa, Amor' and Cavalcanti's 'Chi è questa che vèn', a preliminary reflection seems necessary.

Scholars have long addressed the question of the authorship of the texts set to music by Landini, which in many cases — including ours — allows for no definitive answer.[15] It seems possible, however, to assess interactions between texts and settings as significant, though by no means unproblematic, markers of Landini's ideological involvement with — or at least awareness of — the issues raised by the poems he sets to music. To consider them in the case of 'Che cosa è questa, Amor', a few words on its musical setting are needed.[16]

Landini's piece, a ballata mezzana with a two-line ripresa and cross-rhymed piedi, survives in two musical manuscripts. One of them (Pan) was partially copied late in Landini's life; the other one (Sq) is datable to *c.* 1415 and shares with Gherardi's *Paradiso* the characteristics of a retrospective, traditionalist, and self-monumentalizing collection.[17] In both sources the piece is in three voices, with a fully texted cantus–tenor dyad and a contratenor bearing no text in Pan (where the second stanza is missing altogether). While the cantus and the contratenor basically share the same pitch range and melodic profile, the tenor is slower and less ornate (which is usual) and it also starts declaiming the text on a single pitch repeated seven times (which in turn is highly unusual, indeed a hapax in the whole of Landini's works; see Figure 8.1).[18]

Given that the same music is sung on the words 'e a cui lice star fiso a vederla' (in the first volta) and on the words 'e qual nel sommo Iddio ficcar gli occhi osa' (in the second volta), this pitch repetition may refer to the aforementioned topos of special status, here pointed towards *Cosa* or God, perhaps alluding to Stilnovo stereotypes[19]

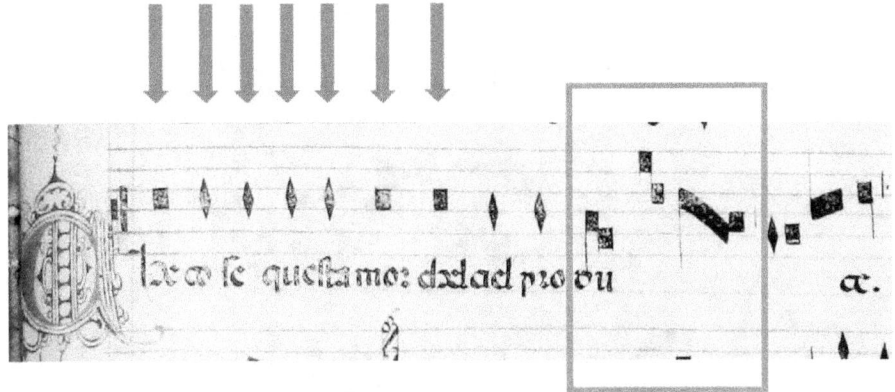

Fig. 8.1. Landini, 'Che cosa è questa, Amor', tenor *tempora* 1–21 (Sq, fol. 163r).

or to *Paradiso* 33 (to be explored below). Conversely, it may allude to *Paradiso* 8. 16–21, that is to Dante's description of fixed lights surrounded by circulating sparks in the Heaven of Venus: early (and modern) commentators have compared them with polyrhythmic musical settings in which a slow tenor — thus 'un tenore fermo', as worded by Francesco de Buti[20] — is combined with rapid melismas in other voices, precisely what occurs in 'Che cosa è questa, Amor'.

The deliberateness of the tenor's opening gesture seems confirmed by the contrast with its own continuation, for the construct 'il ciel produce' is set to music in both manuscripts with a long melisma on the syllable *du*, made up of an unusual series of seven pitches, E-D-d-a-G-D-E. These produce the following intervals: a descending major second, an upward leap of an octave, two separate descending fourths or descending *interruptae* fifths, which in turn form a twice *interrupta* descending octave (that is, a falling octave broken by two intermediate pitches), and, finally, an ascending major second. Figure 8.2 highlights them with coloured rectangles.

If we consider the dichotomy between descending and ascending intervals, on the one hand, and that between *disgregati* and *interrupti* intervals, on the other (as stated by Marchetto da Padova or Johannes Ciconia in Trecento Italy), Landini's series consists in fact of a mirror figure or palindrome.[21] Moreover, the unusual series of melodic intervals — second, fourth, fifth and octave — may also express a theoretical reflection, in that throughout medieval theory their Pythagorean superparticular proportions (respectively 9:8, 4:3, 3:2, and 2:1) corresponded to those constituting the celestial harmony.[22] In other words, it is as if the melisma on *produce*, made of seven different pitches representing the *summa* of the heavenly proportions, was meant both as an astronomical allusion to *ciel* and as a symmetrical response to the question 'Che cosa è questa, Amor', recited on seven equal pitches at the beginning (Figure 8.3). The rest of the melisma functions as a *verto* clause (made of the pitches D-F-G-a), indeed paralleled by its *chiuso* variant at the end of the second line (with the pitches D-F-G-a/G-F-E-D).

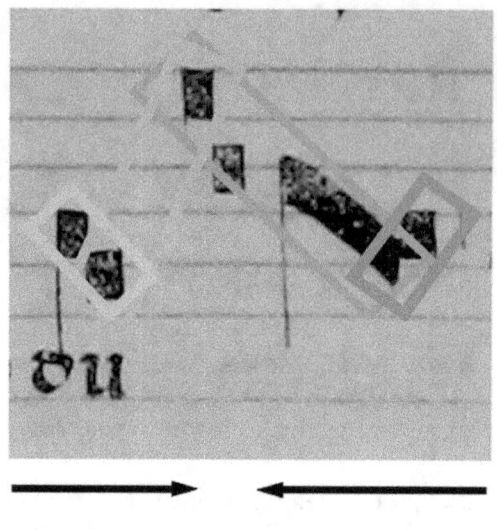

Fig. 8.2. Landini, 'Che cosa è questa, Amor', tenor *tempora* 7–15 (Sq, fol. 163r).

Fig. 8.3. Numeric implications of Landini, 'Che cosa è questa, Amor', tenor *tempora* 1–21.

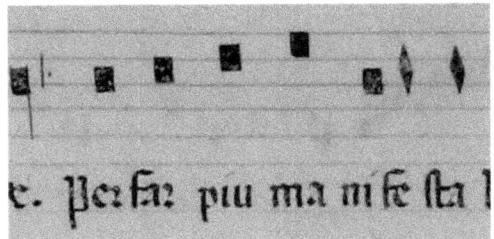

Fig. 8.4. Landini, 'Che cosa è questa, Amor', tenor *tempora* 22–27 (Sq, fol. 163r).

Similar links between text and music return in the second line of the ripresa, for instance in the musical treatment of the construct 'per far più manifesta', which brings into play further theoretical connotations. In fact, the increasing *manifestatio* described by the poetic text ('per far più manifesta la tuo luce') seems to be alluded to by the rising musical scale a-b-c-d (see Figure 8.4), which provides the first full exposure of the inner organization of the upper species of fourth of the tenor's melodic mode. Thus — in medieval terms — it provides its explanation, revelation, or indeed *manifestatio*.[23] On the very word *manifesta*, finally, the same upper fourth is restated as a leap, followed by the repeated — and thus emphasized — pitch b. In its two possible readings (as b-fa, i.e. B flat or, more likely, b-mi, B natural) this pitch determines, reveals, *manifests* the tenor's first mode as including, respectively, a second or first upper species of fourth (or, using just for clarity a somewhat later term, its Aeolian or Dorian propensity).[24] Summarizing then, on the word *manifesta* the tenor's melodic mode is unambiguously 'revealed'.

Further musical correspondences characterize the piedi — for instance the treatment of the words *vezzosa* and *subito*, which for reasons of space cannot be discussed here. I believe that they add to the aforementioned correspondences in the ripresa and, once again, suggest Landini's awareness of, and indeed deliberate interaction with, the poetic issues raised by the text. Therefore, whoever was the author of the text, 'Che cosa è questa, Amor' may well be placed with those pieces set by Landini that have been described as having a philosophical-theological connotation — such as his celebrated Ockhamist eulogy, or the ballata 'Contemplar le gran cose' — in order to assess his cultural and ideological background.[25]

Finally, these correspondences also allow for a relevant comparison between 'Landini's' and Cavalcanti's poems:[26]

Cavalcanti, *Rime*, IV[27]

Chi è questa che vèn, ch'ogn'om la mira,
che fa tremar di chiaritate l'âre
e mena seco Amor, sì che parlare
null'omo pote, ma ciascun sospira?

O Deo, che sembra quando li occhi gira,
dical' Amor, ch'i nol savria contare:
cotanto d'umiltà donna mi pare,
ch'ogn'altra ver' di lei i' la chiam' ira.

> Non si poria contar la sua piagenza,
> ch'a le' s'inchin' ogni gentil vertute,
> e la beltate per sua dea la mostra.
>
> Non fu sì alta già la mente nostra
> e non si pose 'n noi tanta salute,
> che propiamente n'aviàn conoscenza.

Landini, ballata 33[28]

> Che cosa è questa, Amor, che 'l ciel produce,
> per far più manifesta la tuo luce?
>
> Ell'è tanto vezzosa, onest'e vaga,
> leggiadr'e graziosa, adorn'e bella,
>
> ch'a chi la guarda subito 'l cor piaga
> con gli occhi bel che lucon più che stella,
>
> e a cui lice star fiso a vederla,
> tutta gioia e virtù in sé conduce.
>
> Che cosa [...]
>
> Ancor l'alme beate che in ciel sono,
> guardan questa perfetta e gentil cosa,
>
> dicendo: [quando] fia che in questo trono
> segga costei dov'ogni ben si posa?
>
> E qual nel sommo Iddio ficcar gli occhi osa
> vede come esso ogni virtù in lei induce.
>
> Che cosa [...]

A first glimpse suffices to show that 'Chi è questa' and 'Che cosa è questa' display almost no formal similarities: a different poetic form, no common rhymes or rhyme words, and few — and perhaps barely characterizing — shared terms, such as *Amor*, *occhi*, *virtù*, *gentile*. Conversely, single verses or formal features such as rhymes or rhyme–word pairings appear to link Landini to Dantesque or Petrarchan models. Landini's line 1, for instance, blends the Solomonic quote with Petrarch's *RVF* 132 ('s'egli è amor, che cosa e quale?'); his line 6 hints at *Inf.* 2. 55, and his rhyme-pairing *produce–luce* at *Par.* 2. 147 or 25. 68. More generally speaking, finally, the raw material of 'Che cosa è questa, Amor' seems heavily indebted to various passages in *Vn* (to be thoroughly discussed below).

However, a closer scrutiny also reveals a number of *thematic* correspondences with 'Chi è questa che vèn', located almost precisely at parallel places along the twofold structured narrative of both poems (Cavalcanti's two quatrains and Landini's first stanza, on the one hand, and Cavalcanti's tercets and Landini's second stanza, on the other).[29] Considering this shared order together with the rarity of thirteenth- and fourteenth-century poems *opening* with questions like *Chi è questa/questo*, despite the high diffusion of Solomonic *themes*,[30] a direct or perhaps indirect relationship between Landini's and Cavalcanti's texts seems plausible. Indeed, a possible mediator between them may have been Rinuccini, whose poems mentioned earlier,

'Chi è costei, Amor, che quando appare' and 'Chi guarderà mia donna', contain blatant formal links to Cavalcanti's 'Chi è questa che vèn' and Landini's 'Che cosa è questa, Amor' respectively.

This said, however, it appears that Landini's text, while basically agreeing with, or adding detail to the thematic content of Cavalcanti's first section (his two quatrains, corresponding to Landini's stanza 1), totally contradicts Cavalcanti's second section (that is, his tercets, corresponding to Landini's stanza 2). Here are some details:

- Cavalcanti's Solomonic opening 'Chi è questa' is nuanced by Landini's 'Che cosa è questa', where *cosa* informs the *senhal* and at the same time activates an allusion to *Conv.* 2. 5. 5 and *VN* XIX ('Donne ch'avete', 43–46), confirmed by Landini's line 10, 'questa perfetta e gentil cosa', which adds a further allusion to *VN* XXXI ('Li occhi dolenti', 28).[31] Therefore, already here the word *cosa* signals — if only *in nuce* — the connection between Niccolosa and the reflection on love's *quidditas* inherent in both Cavalcanti's sonnet and Landini's ballata. Moreover, in Gherardi's *Paradiso* the character Niccolosa (*Cosa*) discusses a question of (parental) love, adducing philosophical arguments to claim her point: that 'amare non solamente istia nella perfezzione, ma più tosto nella affezione'.[32] Thus, *mutatis mutandis*, she addresses a question similar to Cavalcanti's and Landini's.

- Cavalcanti's apparently unaddressed initial question (or object clause?) is clearly addressed to *Amor* through Landini's possessive *tuo* [i.e. *di Amor*] in line 2 (trivialized as *sua* by both Cappelli and Corsi).[33] While this possessive clarifies *ex post* the sense of the clause as 'Che cosa è questa, Amor, che 'l ciel produce' (hence the modern editorial commas), the lack of syntactic punctuation in the original sources enhances a transient equivocal perception of *Amor* as subject ('Amor produce il ciel') or object ('il ciel produce Amor'), allowing for an implicit answer to the question to be gradually decoded while the ripresa is repeatedly heard during a musical performance of the piece.[34]

- Cavalcanti's much discussed — and ambiguous — 'fa tremar di chiaritate l'âre'[35] is paralleled by Landini's explicatory 'per far più manifesta la tuo luce', further 'revealed' or 'clarified', as mentioned before, by the musical setting.

- The inexpressible effect of the lady's regard on Cavalcanti ('quando li occhi gira, dical' Amor'[36]) is paralleled — and disclosed — by Landini's straightforward 'a chi la guarda subito 'l cor piagha'.

- Cavalcanti's dichotomy *umiltà–ira*, finally, is amplified by Landini's catalogue of seven courtly virtues in lines 3–4 (perhaps allusive of Dante's sonnet 'Due donne in cima de la mente mia'), where the words *vezzosa, onesta, vaga, leggiadra, graziosa, adorna e bella* are suddenly contrasted with the verb *piaga* in line 5: a traumatic disappointment describing the lady's regard, at once bright and devastating.[37]

From here on, however, things dramatically change: for, while Cavalcanti's quatrains and Landini's first stanza describe the earthly encounter with the lady, their second sections are philosophical and theological in nature respectively. Moreover, they fundamentally disagree with each other, displaying striking differences in all the parallel places:

§ Cavalcanti's 'virtù gentili', perhaps adding to the conventional meaning ('noble qualities') a further one (*virtù dei gentili*, that is antique, heathen virtues) become Landini's *anime beate*, thus (Christian) blessed souls.[38] Interestingly, both poems resort — in corresponding positions — to the theatricalization of personifications: *virtù gentili* bending over *dea di beltate*, *anime beate* speaking about *Cosa*.

§ Cavalcanti's 'dea di beltate' (goddess of *beauty*) becomes Landini's 'perfetta e gentil cosa dove ogni ben si posa' (that is, the repository of every *good*), a shift adding an ethical dimension to the scene, while once again hinting at Dante (*VN* 31, 'Li occhi dolenti', 28).[39]

§ Finally, Cavalcanti's lady is inscrutable to our mind ('Non fu sì alta già la mente nostra', 'non aviàn [noi] conoscenza'), while Landini *sees*, thus understands how (*vede come*) it is God who induces every virtue in her.[40]

By so doing, however, Landini opposes, perhaps even reverses, Cavalcanti's main arguments: the limitation of the human mind resulting in the inexplicability and inscrutability of love. Space and thematic constraints prevent any detailed discussion of these much commented on arguments here; but given the context, a short historiographical review seems necessary.

As is well known, Cavalcanti's philosophical stance concerning love has prompted countless discussions, from the early commentaries on his manifesto canzone 'Donna me prega' throughout the fourteenth, fifteenth and sixteenth centuries, up to the philological reconstruction of the poem in the 1940s[41] and its ensuing reconsideration in the twentieth and twenty-first centuries. Modern scholars have evoked a number of possible ideological imprints on his works, such as Neoplatonism or scholastic Neoplatonism, respectively suggested by Pietro Ercole and James E. Shaw, the Scholasticism and 'loose' Thomism suggested by Carlo Calcaterra and Guido Favati, or the Thomism-Augustinism proposed by Mario Casella — just to mention few authors. Islamic Scholastic Aristotelianism, and indeed Averroism, has been advocated as early as 1895 by Giulio Salvadori and further nuanced by Karl Vossler and Ezra Pound; and finally, from the 1940s on, Bruno Nardi's clear-cut Averroistic reading has mainly influenced the debate. Therefore, 'radical Aristotelianism' or concealed Averroism has since been accepted by a number of scholars including Mario Marti, Paul Oskar Kristeller, Maria Corti, Antonio Gagliardi, and Zygmunt Barański. More recently, however, Epicurean readings have re-emerged, which include Barański's 'Christian-Epicureanism' (mediated by Seneca) and, above all, Rossana Sodano's claim of Cavalcanti's Epicurean atheism (mediated by Alexander of Aphrodisias).[42]

As for Cavalcanti's reception history in the fourteenth century, I will again only hint at it briefly. Early glossators such as Dino del Garbo and important (though arguable) references to Cavalcanti's Epicureanism and/or Averroism in works by Jacopo da Pistoia, Dante, or Boccaccio, as well as in Filippo Villani's *De famosis civibus*, produced a fair consensus on the heterodox philosophical background of Cavalcanti's lyrics.[43] That is, Guido's suspected heretical sympathies — and indeed atheism — circulated with these writings in and beyond the fourteenth century.

In short, Rinuccini and Landini, as well as any intellectuals witnessing literary discussions at Gherardi's villa in 1389 (or reading about them in the early fifteenth century), must have been aware of at least part of these debates: for reworking Cavalcanti must have entailed both the resort to an accepted *auctoritas*, on the one hand, and the attitude to Dante's and Villani's criticism, or Boccaccio's possible rehabilitation, on the other.[44]

Returning to Cavalcanti's text, then, it seems relevant to interpret his *mente* as the rational soul that tries in vain to moderate the effect of the *veduta forma* stored as a *phantasma* in the memorative faculties of the sensitive soul, as taught by Aristotelians of his time. Or one could interpret his much-commented 'pessimism' (*non si poria, non fu sì alta, non si pose in noi*), following Nardi, Contini, or Marti, as a consequence of his alleged 'radical Aristotelian' or indeed Averroistic approach to psychology and metaphysics. Conversely, it could reflect the Alexandrist approach described by Sodano, that is the inability of human intellect, capable of abstraction and yet corruptible and unholy ('non si pose 'n noi tanta salute'), to rationally explain love ('che propiamente n'aviàn conoscenza').[45]

Landini, for his part, answers his own initial question, first, by stating that earthly lovers receive joy and virtue by looking at the lady's eyes ('a cui lice star fiso a vederla tutta gioia e virtù in sé conduce') and, second, explaining that who dares to gaze into God's light sees how it is He who induces every virtue in her ('vede come esso ogni virtù in lei induce'). This last statement definitively requalifies the equivocal double metonymy *ciel/Amor* = *God* embedded in Landini's opening ('Che cosa è questa, Amor, che 'l ciel produce'), ultimately linking it to the close of *Par.* 33 ('Amor che move il sol e l'altre stelle'). For in fact — concluding with a further musical observation — 'move il sol' could also be alluded to by the aforementioned fixed pitch in the tenor's opening, where *Amor* = God moves the fixed pitch G-sol ('move il sol') to form all other celestial proportions ('l'altre stelle'). If so, it would be Landini's *music* that provides the key to unlock the equivocal question and answer it with Dante's ultimate revelation.

In other words, and simplifying, Landini's text *and* setting outline an ascetic process from earthly love to Salvation through the reconceptualization of love as (God-mediated) wisdom, thus providing an orthodox answer to both his own and Cavalcanti's questions at once.

Landini's 'Paradiso'

To do so, however, Landini significantly distances himself from Cavalcanti's topics and terminology *mente, ira* or *non propiamente aviàn conoscenza* and resorts to a wording and imagery quite frequent in Dante's *Paradiso*. In fact, references such as the choice of the *dramatis personae* of stanza 2 suggest that Landini migrated the whole scene into the context of Dante's *Paradiso* 31 (2, 66–69), that is, to the Empyrean's *Candida Rosa*. All the characterizing elements are indeed mentioned: the sky, the light, the empty throne, and the *milizia santa* of the blessed souls — whom Dante describes as absorbed in their ineffability, but Landini as *dicendo 'quando fia'*, speaking and asking when she (*Cosa*, the lady addressed) will finally occupy the seat that awaits her. This seat, as I believe, is Dante's throne of *Paradiso* 31. 69, a passage variously discussed by early and modern critics: 'la rivedrai/nel trono che i suoi merti le sortiro'. In other words: by depicting the blessed souls' impatience before the (still) empty throne Landini stages the very moment of Beatrice's ultimate assumption in the seat of the blessed.[46]

However, quite a crucial clarification seems necessary here: in Landini's heaven *Cosa* replaces Beatrice, and so, in the last instance, Landini replaces Dante. It is no longer Dante-*philomythes* but Landini who, hinting at *VN* 19 and 31, contradicts Cavalcanti's alleged radical pessimism and gazes into the eternal light of God.[47] He is the one who sees and understands — with Dante and Augustine, but also through his own, apophatic theology — that it is God in His ineffable luminosity, in His unbearable, ultimately blinding brightness (*Par* 33. 84), who induces light, joy, and all possible virtues in her, thus in him.[48]

★ ★ ★ ★ ★

Landini, as is well known, was blind. Perhaps not surprisingly, he seems to have been obsessed with the topic of sight, an issue discussed in almost a century of Italian Ars nova studies.[49] Three of his madrigals and over thirty of his ballatas thematize in some way the problem of light, sometimes (perhaps) referring to his own, physical blindness, sometimes to mystical or Stilnovo related matrices. To the autobiographical type may belong cases such as the madrigal 'Mostrommi amore', in which Landini compares himself to a blindfolded falcon, or the ballata 'Occhi dolenti miei', in which he speaks directly to his own eyes to comfort them. To the second type belongs the piece discussed here, 'Che cosa è questa, Amor', not yet analysed in this sense. In fact, in front of the apotheosis of the beloved, Landini interrogates himself again about light: not about earthly light, however, but about the heavenly light that Niccolosa (or *Cosa*) enhances in *Amore* and which *is in itself* (divine) *Amore*. One could say, summarizing, that Landini adds a mystical gloss to Cavalcanti's alleged heterodoxy, resorting to *Paradiso* 31 and 33, and concluding with his pervasive word *luce*, the same that dominates Dante's Empyrean when music falls silent.[50]

A final footnote may provide a further hint at the historical context and open new lines of research. While the title of Gherardi da Prato's work is conjectural, the name of the villa where its frame narrative takes place is notoriously historical: *Paradiso*. Owned by Niccolò degli Alberti and passed to his son Antonio, it included the chapel of Santi Maria e Zanobi a Fabroro, which was entirely decorated with frescoes.[51] Those at its apse wall, recently ascribed to Jacopo di Cione — a member of the Orcagna *bottega* — and dated to *c.* 1385, represent a *Paradiso* or *Candida Rosa* (see Figure 8.5).[52]

Forgoing any detailed discussion of the cycle, it may nonetheless be useful to reflect on its possible interaction with Gherardi's and Landini's works. If Landini — as it seems likely — witnessed any discussion about the new cycle in the late 1380s, it seems tantalizing to ascribe to this event his setting of 'Che cosa è questa, Amor'.

Fig. 8.5. Jacopo di Cione (attr.), *Paradiso*, Florence, Monastero della Vergine Maria e di Santa Brigida, chapel of Santi Maria e Zenobi a Fabroro.
Photo: Wikimedia Commons user Sailko; Creative Commons Attribution 3.0 Unported

For his *vede come* would then have acquired one more double sense, his vision of the heavenly invisible being ironically paralleled by his incapacity to see its earthly depiction. At the same time his question 'Che cosa è questa, Amor' would have acquired new depth, as it would have even more blatantly disambiguated *Cosa–Beatrice* as the very means produced by God–Love to make His own (non-earthly) light revealing to both Landini and Dante.

> *I wish to thank Stefano Carrai, Francesco Ciabattoni, and Lino Pertile for their invaluable Dantesque expertise, Carlo Ginzburg for his always generous advice, and Elena Abramov-van Rijk, Margaret Bent, Maria Caraci Vela, and Dorit Tanay for their music-historical remarks.*

Notes to Chapter 8

The following abbreviations of MS sources are used:

Chig.	Vatican City, BAV, MS Chigiano M.IV,79
F.5.5.	Florence, BNC, Incunab. 5.5
Lo	London, BL, MS Add. 29987
Magl.	Florence, BNC, MS Magliabechiano VII 1041
Ott.	Vatican City, BAV, MS Ottoboniano 1790
Pan	Florence, BNC, MS Panciatichiano 26
Pit	Paris, BNF, MS f. it. 568
Rei	Paris, BNF, MS n.a.fr. 6771 (Codex Reina)
SL	Florence, Archivio del Capitolo di San Lorenzo, MS 2211
Sq	Florence, BML, MS Mediceo-Palatino 87 (Codex Squarcialupi)

1. Standard bibliographies on Landini include Lucia Marchi's 'Bibliografia', in *Col dolce suon che da te piove*, ed. by Antonio Delfino and Maria Teresa Rosa Barezzani (Florence: Galluzzo, 1999), pp. 619–34, and Alessandra Fiori's *Francesco Landini* (Palermo: L'Epos, 2004), pp. 171–78.
2. The (non-original) title was conjectured in the pioneering edition of Giovanni Gherardi da Prato, *Il Paradiso degli Alberti*, by Alessandro Wesselofsky, 3 vols (Bologna: Romagnoli, 1867) (henceforth *Wesselofsky*). I will use the edition by Antonio Lanza (Rome: Salerno, 1975) (henceforth *PdA*). Wesselofsky dated the work to 1389, Hans Baron to 1425–26. Francesco Bausi, 'Gherardi, Giovanni', in *Dizionario Biografico degli Italiani* (henceforth *DBI*), LIII (Rome: Istituto della Enciclopedia Italiana, 2000), pp. 559–68 suggested a redactional process spanning from 1415 to the mid-third decade of the century. Guerrieri suggests an even longer process, from the last years of the fourteenth century until the fourth decade of the fifteenth. A longer version of the present study, with extensively detailed bibliography, is in preparation.
3. *PdA*, IX–XI; Bausi, 'Gherardi', pp. 559 and 564. See also Elisabetta Guerrieri 'Il *Paradiso degli Alberti* di Giovanni Gherardi da Prato: il modello decameroniano e altri archetipi letterari', *Heliotropia*, 14 (2017), 265–82.
4. Gherardi praises her as 'donna di grande intelletto e di costumi molto gentile': *PdA*, p. 180.
5. *PdA*, pp. 176–77.
6. See MSS sigla before note 1. The Sq MS is reproduced in *Il codice Squarcialupi: MS. Mediceo Palatino 87, Biblioteca Medicea Laurenziana di Firenze*, ed. by F. Alberto Gallo (Lucca: LIM, 1993).
7. On the text of this ballata, see Giovanni Tavani, 'The Poetic Texts', ibid., pp. 223–42 (pp. 232–34) and Giuseppe Corsi, *Poesie musicali del Trecento* (Bologna: Commissione per i testi di lingua, 1970), pp. 204–05.
8. The *Trattato d'una angelica cosa* was published in *Wesselofsky*, I, pt. 2, pp. 385–435, *Il giuoco d'amore*, in *Lirici toscani del Quattrocento*, ed. by Antonio Lanza, 2 vols (Rome: Bulzoni, 1973), I, 611–38 (quotation from p. 634).
9. See Giuseppe Corsi, review of Wolf's *Der Squarcialupi Codex Pal. 87*, *Belfagor*, 12 (1957), 213–24 (p. 223n.); Nigel Wilkins, *Music in the Age of Chaucer* (Cambridge: Brewer, 1979), pp. 51–52. The topic is also mentioned in *PdA*, p. xi; Fiori, *Francesco Landini*, p. 32; and Gianluca D'Agostino, 'Some Musical Data from Literary Sources of the Late Middle Ages', *L'Ars Nova italiana del Trecento*, 7 (2009), 209–36 (p. 220).
10. Andrea da Firenze's is a satiric *ballata piccola* with monostich, heptasyllabic *piedi* and *ripresa*; Landini's 'Cosa null' à più fé' praises fidelity.
11. My references to the *Convivio* follow Dante Alighieri, *Opere minori*, ed. by Cesare Vasoli and Domenico De Robertis (Milan and Naples: Ricciardi, 1988). Cavalcanti's *Rime* were edited by Gianfranco Contini, Giulio Cattaneo, Marcello Ciccuto, Domenico De Robertis, Letterio Cassata, Tommaso Gurrieri, Roberto Rea and Giorgio Inglese, most of whom noticed the parallels between Cavalcanti's sonnet, the Solomonic Song, and Isaiah. But see especially Lino Pertile, *La puttana e il gigante* (Ravenna: Longo, 1998), pp. 26–36.
12. Cino Rinuccini, *Rime*, ed. by Giovanna Balbi (Florence: Le Lettere, 1995), pp. 91–93 (like Cassata, Balbi signals the Cavalcantian derivation of the poem, not, however, its possible relation to Landini's ballata). The *senhal Cosa* concludes Rinuccini's 'Chi guarderà mia donna', ibid., pp. 165–66, a poem that shares with Landini's ballata two rhyme words, two verse openings, and terms such as *fiso* and *produsse*.
13. Pioneering musicological studies by Ursula Günther, F. Alberto Gallo and Leonard Ellinwood have long since disclosed some of the intertextual and/or biographical connections between these authors.
14. On the 'gare dei partiti letterari' (literary contests) see *Wesselofsky*, I, pt. 2, pp. 50–51 and Balbi, pp. 33–34. On their ideological background see Antonio Lanza, *Polemiche e berte letterarie nella Firenze del primo Quattrocento* (Rome: Bulzoni, 1971); Michael Long, 'Musical Tastes in Fourteenth-Century Italy' (PhD diss., Princeton University, 1981); and idem, 'Francesco Landini and the Florentine Cultural Elite', *Early Music History*, 3 (1983), 83–99. Both have more recently been confuted by Elena Abramov-van Rijk, 'Who was Francesco Landini's Antagonist in his Defense of Ockham?', *Philomusica on-line*, 14 (2015), 1–23.
15. Landini is known to have written two Latin and one or two Italian poems not set to music. One of the Latin ones is the much discussed *Versus in laude Ioyce Ocham*, an invective against

humanism published by both Wesselofsky and Lanza (*Polemiche*, pp. 233–38); the other is 'Quidam terrenis curis', first commented on by Lorenzo Mehus in *Ambrosii Traversarii* [...] *Latinae epistolae* (Florence: Typographio Caesareo, 1759), p. 325. The two Italian ones are sonnets: 'Chi cerca possedere', an Italian paraphrase of 'Quidam terrenis curis', and 'Se, per segno mirar', a response to Franco Sacchetti, published by *Wesselofsky*. See also Davide Daolmi, *Francesco Landini*, <http://www.examenapium.it/meri/landini/index.html>. Regarding the non-ascribed texts set to music by Landini, some have been suspected to be autobiographical and thus possibly his own. See, for instance, Hélène Nolthenius, 'Een autobiographisch madrigal van Francesco Landini', *Tijdschrift voor Muziekwetenschap*, 17 (1955), 237–41.

16. The piece is transcribed in *Polyphonic Music of the Fourteenth Century* (henceforth *PMFC*), vol. IV (Monaco: L'Oiseau-Lyre, 1958), pp. 164–65.
17. On Pan see *Il codice musicale 'Panciatichi 26' della Biblioteca Nazionale di Firenze*, ed. by F. Alberto Gallo (Florence: Olschki, 1981); John Nádas, 'The Structure of MS Panciatichi 26 and the Transmission of Trecento Polyphony', *Journal of the American Musicological Society*, 34 (1981), 393–427; and Stefano Campagnolo, 'Il codice Panciatichi 26 della Biblioteca Nazionale di Firenze', in *Col dolce suon*, ed. by Delfino and Barezzani, pp. 77–119. On Sq see *Il codice Squarcialupi*, ed. by Gallo.
18. Pitches are here indicated following the Guidonian Gamut (where modern G-A-B-c-d-e-f-g/a-b-c'-d'-e'-f'-g'/a'-b'-c''-d''-e'' correspond respectively to Guidonian Γ-A-B-C-D-E-F-G/a-b-c-d-e-f-g/aa-bb-cc-dd-ee).
19. Countless examples of 'fiso' include lines by Cavalcanti, Lapo Gianni, Dino Frescobaldi, and Cino da Pistoia.
20. Francesco de Buti, commentary on Dante's *DC* (1385–95). Early commentaries can be consulted at the *Dartmouth Dante Project*, https://dante.dartmouth.edu/commentaries.php. See also Alessandra Fiori's 'Discorsi sulla musica nei commenti medievali alla "Commedia" dantesca', *Studi e problemi di critica testuale*, 59 (1999), 67–102 (pp. 78–79); and Antonella Puca, 'Astronomia e *musica mundana* nella *Commedia* di Dante', in *La musica nel pensiero medievale*, ed. by Letterio Mauro (Ravenna: Longo, 2001), pp. 217–43 (pp. 241–42).
21. Jan W. Herlinger, *The Lucidarium of Marchetto of Padua* (Chicago: University of Chicago Press, 1985), pp. 306–67 and 508–16; *The Berkeley Manuscript*, ed. by Oliver B. Ellsworth (Lincoln: University of Nebraska Press, 1984), pp. 88–94; Johannes Ciconia, *Nova Musica* and *De Proportionibus*, ed. by Oliver B. Ellsworth (Lincoln: University of Nebraska Press, 1993), pp. 306–09.
22. Notoriously, Boethius' *De institutione musica*, 1, 20 and 27 reworks Plato's *Timaeus* and *Republic*, comparing the sound of planets with the strings of a (Pythagorean-tuned) lyre. His influence on the medieval notion of music of the spheres reaches Dante's *note de li eterni giri* (*Purg.* 30. 93) or *dolce lira* (*Par.* 15. 4).
23. Matthias Hochadel, *Commentum Oxoniense in musicam Boethii* (Munich: Bayerische Akademie der Wissenschaften, 2002), pp. 300–02.
24. See the analysis of Zacara da Teramo's *Deduto sei* provided by the anonymous *Trattato di Vercelli* (c. 1420) witnessing the contemporary use of (church?) modes to describe and classify secular polyphony: Anna Cornagliotti and Maria Caraci Vela, *Un inedito trattato musicale del Medioevo, Vercelli, Biblioteca Agnesiana, cod. 11* (Florence: Sismel, 1998), p. 77.
25. On the Ockhamist eulogy see above, nn. 14–15. On 'Contemplar le gran cose' see Daniele Sabaino, 'Per un'analisi delle strutture compositive nella musica di Francesco Landini', in *Col dolce suon*, ed. by Delfino and Barezzani, pp. 260–321.
26. For the sake of practicality, I will henceforth label the text of 'Che cosa è questa, Amor' as Landini's.
27. After Marcello Ciccuto (ed.), *Guido Cavalcanti: Rime* (Milan: Rizzoli, 1978), pp. 9–10.
28. After Natalino Sapegno, *Poeti minori del Trecento* (Milan and Naples: Ricciardi, 1952), p. 498, except for three places where I follow the MSS: 7: *vederla*; 11: *che in*; 14: *virtù in lei*. The number of the ballata follows the order in *PMFC*, vol. IV.
29. For the articulation of sonnets in two sections (piedi and volte) see Gidino da Sommacampagna's *Trattato e arte deli Rithimi volgari*, ed. by Gian Paolo Caprettini (Verona: La Grafica, 1993), p. 69.

30. The scrutiny of a high number of inventories and repertoires including standard works such as Marco Santagata (ed.), *Incipitario unificato della poesia italiana*, 2 vols (Modena: Panini, 1988) and Giuseppe Mazzatinti, *Inventari dei manoscritti delle biblioteche d'Italia*, 101 vols (Florence: Olschki, 1890–1982) shows that besides the poems cited here (Cavalcanti, Landini, and Rinuccini), only one or perhaps two further contemporary vernacular ones share similar incipits.
31. Quotes from the edition of *VN* of Domenico De Robertis (Milan and Naples: Ricciardi, 1980).
32. *PdA*, pp. 180–83 (p. 182).
33. Antonio Cappelli, *Ballate del secolo XIV tratte da due codici musicali* (Modena: Cappelli, 1869), p. 10; Corsi, *Poesie musicali*, p. 144.
34. On cases similar to Landini's equivocal formulation see Pedro Memelsdorff, 'Equivocus', *L'Ars nova italiana del Trecento*, 7 (2009), 143–87 (p. 174 and 181).
35. De Robertis recalls its influence on Dante's *Inf.* 1. 48, *Purg.* 1. 117, and *Par.* 2. 110–11 (Guido Cavalcanti, *Rime* (Milan: Ledizioni, 2012), p. 17). See also Roberto Rea's and Giorgio Inglese's comparison with Guinizzelli's *donna-luce* (Guido Cavalcanti, *Rime* (Rome: Carocci, 2011), p. 57).
36. De Robertis (Cavalcanti, *Rime*, p. 18), sees in 'quando gli occhi gira' a further allusion to the Song of Songs.
37. Dante Alighieri, *Rime*, ed. by Domenico De Robertis (Florence: Galluzzo, 2005), pp. 332–34 (p. 333). On Cavalcanti's use of the dichotomy *umiltà–ira* see the comments to his *Rime* by Cattaneo (Guido Cavalcanti, *Rime* (Turin: Einaudi, 1967), p. 23), Ciccuto (p. 75), and De Robertis (p. 18). Pertile, pp. 74–76, points out the influence of the Solomonic dichotomy between *pulchra-suavis-decora* and *terribilis* (Song of Songs 6:3) on Dante's perception of Beatrice in *Purg.* 30. 58–71.
38. On a possible use of *gentili* as 'pertaining to the Gentiles' see, for instance, Boccaccio's *filosofi gentili*, and *poeti gentili*, occurring in *Comento alla Divina Commedia*, and in *Redazioni compendiose della vita di Dante*. Modern commentators on Cavalcanti's passage such as De Robertis, Cassata, or Rea only stress the conventional sense.
39. While Rea acknowledges *bellezza*'s apology for, but not deification of, *madonna*, De Robertis rejects any reference to Venus.
40. Modern commentaries on Cavalcanti's last three lines are countless and vary according to the ideological standpoint of their authors. See, nevertheless, the commentary on Cavalcanti's use of *vedere* in De Robertis, 'L'altro Cavalcanti', in *Guido Cavalcanti tra i suoi lettori*, ed. by Maria Luisa Ardizzone (Fiesole: Cadmo, 2003), pp. 149–75 (p. 20).
41. Mario Casella, 'La canzone d'amore di Guido Cavalcanti', *Studi di filologia italiana*, 7 (1944), 97–160.
42. Cf. the historiographic summary by Zygmunt G. Barański, 'Guido Cavalcanti and his First Readers', in *Guido Cavalcanti*, ed. by Ardizzone, pp. 174–75 (p. 150, n. 5), and idem, '*Alquanto tenea della oppinione degli Epicuri*: The Auctoritas of Boccaccio's Cavalcanti (and Dante)', in *Mittelalterliche Novellistik im europäischen Kontext*, ed. by Mark Chinca and Timo Reuvekamp-Felber (Berlin: Young, 2006), pp. 280–325 (p. 285, n. 17), updated by Rossana Sodano, *Cavalcanti restituito agli epicurei* (Rome: Vecchiarelli, 2018), pp. 456–57.
43. 'Incroyance religieuse (conventionnellement rangée sous l'étiquette d'épicurisme), que les sources du XIVe siècle attribuent unanimement à Guido' [Religious unbelief (usually labelled as Epicureanism) which fourteenth-century sources all attribute to Guido]; Paolo Falzone, 'L'averroisme du "premier ami" de Dante? Relecture critique d'une vulgate historiographique', in *Dante et l'averroisme*, ed. by Alain de Libera and others (Paris: Les Belles Lettres, 2019), pp. 235–68 (p. 236). Falzone's 'sources unanimes du XIVe siècle' [all fourteenth-century sources] seem limited to Boccaccio's *Decameron* 6. 9 and Filippo Villani, *De origine civitatis Florentie et de eiusdem famosis civibus*, ed. by Giuliano Tanturli (Padua: Antenore, 1997), p. 146, while he wonders about the heterodoxy of Dino del Garbo's *Scriptum super cantilena Guidonis de Cavalcantibus* and Jacopo da Pistoia's *Quaestio de felicitate*, as well as about Dante's anti-Cavalcantism in *Inf.* 10. 52–72 and *Purg.* 11. 97–99.
44. Barański, 'Guido Cavalcanti and his First Readers', pp. 174–75; idem, '*Alquanto tenea*', pp. 323–24.
45. Sodano, *Cavalcanti restituito*, pp. 176–77.
46. Note that Landini's cantus further emphasizes *trono* with a melisma lasting two *tempora*, including the top pitch of the piece twice.

47. On Dante-*philomythes* see Zygmunt G. Barański, ' "Per similitudine di abito scientifico": Dante, Cavalcanti and the Sources of Medieval "Philosophical" Poetry', in *Science and Literature in Italian Culture: From Dante to Calvino*, ed. by Pier Paolo Antonello and Simon A. Gilson (Oxford: EHRC, 2004), pp. 14–52 (pp. 14–15).
48. Nino Pirrotta, 'Francesco Landini: I lumi della mente', in *Dolcissime armonie*, ed. by Piero Gargiulo (Florence: Cadmo, 1997), pp. 3–11.
49. Fiori, *Francesco Landini*, pp. 19–21; Daolmi.
50. On the silence at the end of Dante's journey see Corrado Bologna, *Il ritorno di Beatrice: Simmetrie dantesche fra* Vita nova, 'Petrose' e Commedia (Rome: Salerno, 1998), pp. 116–19; Claudia Elisabeth Schurr, *Dante e la musica* (Perugia: USP, 1994), p. 79; Marco Cerocchi, *Funzioni semantiche e metatestuali della musica in Dante, Petrarca e Boccaccio* (Florence: Olschki, 2010), p. 45.
51. *Il Paradiso degli Alberti*, ed. by Daniele Rapino (Florence: Polistampa, 2014), in particular the chapter by Fabrizio Iacopini and Daniela Valentini, 'Il restauro del ciclo decorativo', pp. 47–56.
52. Eleonora Pecchioli, 'La storia del complesso, l'iconografia e gli autori della decorazione della Sala del Capitolo', ibid., pp. 19–37.

PART III

Italy and Beyond

CHAPTER 9

Un grido di sì alto suono: Voicing the *Commedia*

Nick Havely

> Mi sono sempre chiesto come si fa a leggere Dante. Pagherei qualsiasi cosa per sentirlo leggere da Boccaccio.
>
> [I keep wondering how you set about reading Dante. I'd give anything to hear Boccaccio reading him.][1]

Between 1998 and 2013 Roberto Benigni performed cantos from *Inferno* for crowds in their thousands on the Piazza Santa Croce at Florence and at venues elsewhere (including London in 2009). Unlike some Italian performers, Benigni recites from memory, and in his recent collection of interviews he cites Dante's own *memoria di ferro*, along with the advice of Benigni's mentor Umberto Eco that students should learn poetry by heart and perform it *ad alta voce*.[2]

This chapter will turn later to how (as Benigni asks) Boccaccio might have given voice to Dante in his last major work (the *Esposizioni sopra la Commedia di Dante*), as well as to the wider issue of orality as a feature of the poem's transmission and reputation during the *trecento*.[3] It will also consider some examples of when and where Dante was staged and read aloud from the early modern period through to the nineteenth and twentieth centuries, along with the contexts and possible impact of such performances.

'Nuovo ludo': The *Poema* and the Piazza

We begin, however with voices, 'cries and shrieks' in the city: a performance in early *trecento* Florence that might in some ways have anticipated the *Commedia*. On May Day in 1304 — a few years before Dante's *Inferno* was begun — an elaborate staging of Hell was enacted near the Ponte alla Carraia, as later described in Giovanni Villani's *Cronica*.[4] Villani records how this representation (*somiglianza e figura*) of the afterlife was set up on floating stages in the Arno with impressive audiovisual effects: *fuochi . . . uomini contrafatti a demonia . . . figure d'anime ignude . . . diversi tormenti con grandissime grida, e strida, e tempesta . . .* This 'unusual show' (*nuovo giuoco*) attracted a large audience crowding on to the Ponte alla Carraia during that May Day's festivities. However, the wooden bridge then collapsed in a number of places, turning the *giuoco*, as Villani points out, from jest into grim reality by sending many of the spectators to experience the afterlife for themselves. By this time Dante had been in exile from Florence for over two years, but the irony of his home city's over-ambitious display and its disastrous conclusion would not have been lost on him.

What would the *Commedia* owe to such traditions? What precisely Dante meant by calling his whole poem a *Commedia* has been and continues to be much disputed. In Dante's usage it also indicates aspects of his poem's project: treating an encyclopaedic range of topics in a wide-ranging 'middle style' appropriate to the vernacular and making them accessible to lay readers and audiences.[5] But 'comedy' also invokes traditions of early theatre, and particularly the Latin plays that continued to be familiar as 'schoolroom texts' in Dante's time.[6]

One of the two uses of *comedìa* in Dante's poem occurs at the start of an episode which has itself been linked in several ways to traditions of medieval popular theatre.[7] In the midst of the *Inferno*'s circles of deception (the *Malebolge*) two cantos are devoted to the games played by a group of devils — the *Malebranche* — with the souls of corrupt officials who now inhabit a river of boiling pitch. At the beginning of *Inferno* 21, as Dante and Virgil enter this dark scene, the grim naturalism of the episode and the pace of the narrative are reinforced by a rhetorical device (*occupatio*) that cuts short the conversation between the two travellers, since it involves matters of which *mia comedìa cantar non cura*. Instead Dante's comedy here turns to more obviously comic narrative and to the 'grotesque' tradition in medieval popular culture.[8] Yet those comic elements, outrageous as they are, also carry a larger significance: the devils, with all their ferocious behaviour and bestial names, are serving a providential purpose. The disastrous outcome of their final game — when two of the over-excited devils fall into the boiling pitch as Dante and Virgil make their exit — also reflects the ultimate impotence of their designs upon humanity and the pilgrim poets. That final twist in the diabolical comedy is introduced and underlined by one of Dante's addresses to the reader, whom at this stage the poet also invites to become an 'audience' (*o tu che leggi, udirai nuovo ludo*). Even the word *ludo* that Dante uses to describe the 'game' or spectacle played by the devils and the damned soul at the end of *Inf.* 22 — a game whose conclusion parallels that of the Florentine May Day *giuoco* — is closely related to the Latin term *ludus* which was applied to various types of medieval drama.[9]

As a number of critics have noted, dramatic features abound throughout Dante's *Commedia*: the shaping of life-stories; the structure of encounters and dialogues of the *Inferno*; the more formal and liturgical performances and processions of the *Purgatorio*; the patterned and at times balletic movement of souls in the *Paradiso*.[10] Some episodes in the poem point back to the tropes and liturgical drama of the medieval Church; some have parallels in medieval Italian devotional writing: the *contrasti* and the dramatic *laude* which originated with the religious confraternities and were most fully developed by Dante's contemporary the Franciscan Jacopone da Todi.[11] To such features could also be added the extraordinary range and contrast of vocal sound in the *Commedia* — from the measured tones of Dante's guides and mentors, and the quiet voices of such as Francesca, La Pia and Piccarda, to the fractured babble of the *Inferno* and the violent bursts of invective and outcry that continue to be heard even in the outer reaches of the *Paradiso*.[12] *Grido* and *gridare* continue through the poem to characterize the raising of its voice — and perhaps, also, to appeal to performers.

How much did Dante and his *trecento* promoters highlight such features by performing the *Commedia*? As Ahern suggests, 'oral performance afforded enormous publicity and the chance of winning readers from the marginally literate who rarely read vernacular texts'.[13] There are some examples, too, of *trecento* authors promoting their work *in publicum* by reading it aloud to a select audience.[14]

This is not, of course, to deny the ambitious 'bookishness' of Dante's poem. Its sense of words being formed on the page (even at moments in the vision itself), then transmitted to an imagined reader, is undeniable; indeed, we may well wonder what, in an oral performance, could be the effect of its twenty or so 'addresses to the *reader*'.[15] Yet relatively few of those addresses specifically focus on visual reading, and in several cases the addressee is one who is also explicitly 'hearing' the text (*udire*, *ascoltare*).[16] This suggests that voicing the text and reading it silently are, as they continued to be, considered not as exclusive alternatives but as complementary and mutually enriching experiences. Hence that Dantean address to *lettori* as *uditori* in *Inferno* 22; hence also, at the end of *trecento*, Chaucer's mischievous advice to the reader to turn over the page if s/he is getting worried about 'hearing' *harlotrye* in the *Miller's Tale*.[17] In such passages reading thus invokes voicing, which can in turn offer, for example, heightened grotesquerie and 'comedy' (Dante's devils' game) or the prospect of acute embarrassment or enjoyment (Chaucer's churls' tales).

It has also been pointed out that Dante himself envisages his role in the *Commedia* as not only that of the 'scribe' but also as 'the singer of his themes'; that the work is very likely to have been introduced to its audience through being 'recited in public by Dante or by someone else to his patrons and their courts and to other circles of more educated hearers'; and that on such occasions a particularly powerful effect would have been that 'for the only time ever, the two Dantes, the living poet and the traveller back from the realms of the dead, converged in the person of the reciter'.[18] We do not have written documentation of such 'publication' by Dante himself, but such a supposition seems reasonable, given, for example, contemporary concerns about the *Commedia*'s vernacularity rendering it susceptible to debasement through performance.[19]

Twenty years or so after the poet's death, there is evidence of the poem actually being presented to a wider audience through a performance at Verona by Dante's son (and commentator) Pietro Alighieri. A description of that event is in a Latin poem by the scholar, grammar-teacher and friend of Petrarch, Moggio de' Moggi (b. 1325), who is likely to have been in Verona to witness the occasion around 1346 or 1347.[20] Moggio's 51-line account is studded with compliments to 'Judge Pietro di Dante' (*Petro Dantis iudici*) and with allusions to gods and muses, so that it is quite difficult to determine precisely what kind of performance was going on or how much Moggio himself was actually able to grasp about the *Commedia*'s basic features.

As the first seven lines of Moggio's poem indicate, Pietro's performance took place on the evening of a festival in the old *forum* of Verona, now the Piazza delle Erbe, near the stalls of the goldsmiths and cup-makers, and in the presence of an audience that included the grammarian Rinaldo Cavalchini (lines 1–6). Pietro Alighieri is said to have delivered a version of his father's poem with skill and grace, taking his audience beyond the Acheron with Charon's boat and across the other infernal rivers and torments of the underworld (19–29); then, 'having crossed Hell' (*Dite pererrato*), Pietro's pilgrim arrives at the 'Elysian fields' and prostrates himself before the throne of God (32–33). What kind of summary is being summarized here remains uncertain. Moggio's modern editor suggests that it might have been along the lines of the vernacular outlines of synoptic cantos (*capitoli*) composed by one of Dante's other sons, Jacopo, or by Bosone da Gubbio;[21] but neither the content of Pietro's putative *capitolo* nor the form of its language is more fully described. Ahern states — perhaps on the basis of this speculation — that Pietro 'performed a vernacular verse summary of the *Commedia*'.[22] That seems possible, perhaps as a gesture towards those Veronese goldsmiths and cup-makers; on the other hand, given Pietro's pre-eminence and linguistic preferences as commentator and the presence of illustrious grammarians in his audience, he could equally well have chosen to perform in Latin. In either case, apart from Moggio's effusive concluding tribute to Pietro and his *fama*, there is little to indicate what the audience at any level thought about the performance.

In Moggio's poem — as earlier in Giovanni del Virgilio's verse letter — elaborate Latin is the medium for describing the *Commedia*'s potential or actual orality. Less illustrious vernacular performers of the poem — such as the 'Lombard comedians' mentioned by Alberigo da Rosciate — are unlikely to have left accounts of their activities.[23] Later in the Trecento, however, a prominent Florentine author writing in the vernacular would engage in an actual public performance of what the Comune would call El Dante.

Giovanni Boccaccio's *lettura* of Dante in 1373–74 — the *Esposizioni sopra la Commedia di Dante* — was, at least in its planning and advertising, a significant public event. Earlier in 1373 the Florentine Priors and Council of Twelve had approved a proposal to appoint 'a worthy and wise man, learned in the art of poetry [...] to read the book that is commonly known as *Dante* in the city of Florence to all who wish to hear' (*ad legendum librum qui vulgariter appellatur* El Dante, *in civitate Florentie omnibus audire volentibus*).[24] The petition's emphasis on the civic benefits of such an event echoes Boccaccio's own arguments some twenty years earlier about the purpose of the poem's *fiorentino idioma* being 'to make it more generally useful' (*fare utilità più commune*) to Florentines and other Italians.[25]

The publicity for Boccaccio's 1373 *lettura* — with its emphasis on making the poem available to 'all who wish to hear' — was to some extent driven by local politics: aiming to rescue for the city the bones of its now famous poet who had died in exile to be buried at Ravenna, and in the absence of those to embody him in Florence in the form of the 'book that is commonly known as *Dante*'.[26] But although Boccaccio's *lettura* broke off in the middle of the *Inferno*, its broader cultural purpose of making the text accessible to a wider audience would have been served not only by the speaker's literal and allegorical *esposizioni* but also by substantial recitation of the poem itself which appears to be signalled at a number of points, for instance at the start of the 'allegorical exposition' of *Inferno* 1 and the 'literal exposition' of *Inferno* 2.[27]

Boccaccio's subsequent regrets about exposing Dante's poem to the *vulgo indegno* reflect his long-standing ambivalence about the use of the vernacular for such a project; yet such anxieties amongst the *literatissimi* of the *trecento*, from Giovanni del Virgilio to Petrarch, themselves reflect the extent to which Dante was indeed becoming (to quote Giovanni's epitaph for Dante) *vulgo gratissimus auctor*.[28] So also, at a less august level do Sachetti's apocryphal stories about the blacksmith and the donkey-driver mangling the *Commedia*'s verse in the presence of the indignant poet.[29] Evidence of the ownership and proliferation of *Commedia* manuscripts during the fourteenth and fifteenth centuries moreover indicates the poem's increasing circulation at least amongst a mercantile readership, and such a readership would have provided an audience for the public lectures on Dante that continued in Florence after Boccaccio and on into the fifteenth century.[30] It is highly likely, too, that promoters of Dante — such as the grain-merchant Domenico Lenzi and the auditor and town-crier Antonio Pucci — would not only have read the poem for themselves but communicated them through 'prelection' in their respective domestic and social contexts.[31] As Michael Clanchy observed, in such contexts 'books were scarce and it was ordinary good manners to share their contents among a group by reading aloud'; and as Mary Carruthers has recently reminded us, premodern literary cultures were 'complex mixtures of oral and written materials'.[32]

Renaissance Orality

Such sharing — and the complementarity of reading and voicing the text — continued to be an important feature of the circulation of the *Commedia* during its early modern afterlife. Even when, with the advent of printing, books became less scarce, sharing of them through oral delivery continued alongside and cross-fertilized solitary and silent reading. Key characteristics of Renaissance culture, Brian Richardson notes, were 'the ability to hold texts in one's memory and a deep appreciation of the aural qualities that the human voice could add to texts'; and it has also been proposed that furthermore 'the physical voice [...] should be integral to how we understand writing in this period, not least because it informed how men and, in a different way, women, both learned to read *and* to perform'.[33] As Roger Chartier has suggested, in the early modern period such voicing of the word on the page in both domestic or more formal contexts could reinforce social bonds: 'it was around a text being read aloud, a book leafed through and then discussed that the various forms of intellectual sociability were constructed: the sociability of the *salon*, the more regulated form typical of the academy, the casual sociability of the unannounced visit'.[34]

Chartier's evidence was drawn chiefly from sixteenth- and seventeenth-century France, Spain and Britain, but Italian examples are not hard to find. Richardson has emphasised that, at a variety of levels and contexts, 'Renaissance Italy was a deeply hybrid oral/written culture'.[35] Within that culture, reading Dante's *Commedia* (by now available in a variety of printed editions) was a striking example of what Chartier called 'sociability'. A celebrity performance that Benigni would also (probably) have given much to have heard was the recitation of Dante at Bologna in 1494–95 by the young Michelangelo. According to Vasari, a prominent member of the Bolognese nobility, the diplomat and art patron Giovanni Francesco Aldrovandi assisted the impoverished painter on his arrival from Venice: not only providing him with painting commissions but also employing him to read poetry, so that he (Aldrovandi) and his household could hear 'le cose di Dante, del Petrarca e del Boccaccio' voiced with a proper Tuscan accent.[36]

As Chartier suggested, the purpose of such readings could be served 'in a more regulated form' by academies.[37] In the mid *cinquecento* the Florentine scholar and printer Antonio Francesco Doni (1513–74?) published a work which reflects, amongst other things, the presence of an oral Dante in Florentine academic culture.[38] Doni had become secretary of the Accademia Fiorentina (previously the Accademia degli Umidi) early in 1546, and on 28 June 1547 he dedicated a series of *Lettioni d'academici fiorentini sopra Dante* to a fellow academician, the humanist and politician Bartolomeo Panciatichi, who came from a Florentine mercantile family. The volume contained addresses by a variety of speakers, several of whom — such as Giovan Battista Gelli and Pier Francesco Giambullari — would become well known as promoters of Dante.[39]

The Florentine Academy — like its predecessor organization (the Umidi) — was committed to the vernacular: its mission included 'the promotion, explication and dissemination of the Florentine literary classics, notably Dante and Petrarch, the defence of the Florentine language, and the translation of Latin texts into the vernacular'.[40] The first of the contributors to Doni's *Lettioni* — Francesco Verini — highlights his use of that vernacular (the *lingua Toscana*) for several reasons: because it is 'easier, more natural and closer to me' (*più agevole, più naturale & a me più vicina*) and enabled him 'by that means to be of use to more people' (*con essa giouare a più*) — the latter being a reminder that along with the *nobili ascoltatori* mentioned by Verini, the general public were admitted to the *lezioni* in the Sala del Papa at Santa Maria Novella on Sundays.[41] Bearing in mind his mixed audience, Giambullari opens his *lezione* by addressing both the academicians and *voi altri benignissimi uditori*.[42] Those listeners could expect to hear generous amounts of reading aloud from the *Commedia*: for instance, among a multitude of shorter passages, Gelli quotes fifteen lines of Adam's response to Dante in *Paradiso* 26, and Giambullari includes passages of similar length from the *Purgatorio*, while shorter quotations are frequent throughout the *Lettioni*.[43] The Accademia's public presentation of Dante and the *Commedia* is thus a striking example of 'the complex interaction of degrees of orality and literacy as well as of popular and elite cultures'.[44]

Along with such public and private readings — quotation, allusion and adaptation also gave the *Commedia* a continuing oral presence in early modern theatre. Despite the claim of a character in an early seventeenth-century English comedy that '*Dante* is hard, and few can vnderstand him', at around that very time such understanding was in fact beginning to be exploited in a number of ways on the Italian stage.[45] For example, among the six interludes presented in the court theatre of the Uffizi Palace, Florence, on the occasion of the wedding of Ferdinando I de' Medici, Grand Duke of Tuscany, to Christine of Lorraine on 2 May 1589, the fourth represented 'the triumph over Hell of a new Golden Age' and its scenery 'involved an elaborate representation of the classical Hades, which burst on to the stage out of a rocky landscape'. As the modern editors of the text suggest, 'Its imagery was clearly inspired by Dante's *Inferno*, and so continued the "Dantean-Christian" framework which [...] had previously been applied to the pagan underworld by Poliziano [in his *Fabula* of *Orfeo*].'[46]

Within a few years of Lady Pol's pronouncement about Dantean difficulty in *Volpone*, several very different underworld rescue narratives with obvious Dantean resonances were being staged in Italy. The *Orfeo* of 1607, with text by Alessandro Striggio, court secretary to the Duke of Mantua and music by Claudio Monteverdi, has Orpheus at the beginning of Act 3 being literally abandoned by the allegorical figure of Hope as she contemplates the *orribil soglia* of Hell and repeats the inscription of *Inf.* 3. 9 (accompanied by ominous blasts of brass); while later in the same Act the hero will couch his main appeal to the spirits of the underworld ('Possente Spirto') in Dantean *terza rima*. A few years later in 1614, Giovanni Briccio's *Tartarea: Commedia Infernale* follows a fallible hero and his two unruly servants as they seek to rescue a lady (Albina) who 'signifies virtue' and who in the last act addresses the somewhat feckless pilgrim (Domitio) in terms which recall Beatrice's reproachful greeting of 'Dante' in the *Paradiso terrestre*.[47]

Theatrical voicing of the *Commedia* through the representation of major characters, such as Ugolino, on stage was also already under way in the seventeenth century, although it becomes more frequent with the recovering status of Dante in the later eighteenth.[48] And as Dante becomes established as national and international poet during the latter period, performance, recitation, reading aloud all proliferate alongside the multitude of illustrations, adaptations and translations of the *Commedia*.[49]

Stage, Study, Stadium

A notable example of recitation in the early and mid-nineteenth century was the career of the tragedian Gustavo Modena (1803–61), an eccentric who can in several ways be seen as a predecessor of Roberto Benigni. Modena, who had made a hit performing the lead in a stage version of a Dantean tragedy (Silvio Pellico's *Francesca da Rimini*), began to develop what would become his *dantate* recitations during his years of political exile in the 1830s, and his first stage performance of episodes from the *Commedia* took place in London in 1839. Subsequently, from his return to Italy in the 1840s until his death in 1861, the *dantate* continued to form part of his prominent theatrical, political and educational activities.[50]

A striking feature of Modena's Dante readings is the considerable amount of evidence about them, not only in his own letters but from the reactions of those who witnessed the performances. Thus comments from fellow political exiles, such as Agostino Ruffini and Giuseppe Mazzini, give some impression of how the performances developed from drawing-room recitations in Switzerland and Paris to the 1839 stage show at Her Majesty's Theatre in London. Views on Modena's 'attitudes, gestures and declamation' on the latter occasion can be found in some of the London journals; the political activist Carlo Bini and the novelist and travel-writer Frances Trollope were both strongly impressed by the 'eeriness' of his oral performances in the early 1840s back in Italy. Late in his career, Modena himself perhaps echoes his style of delivery when he speaks self-mockingly of putting on 'Dante's gown, to 'bark' (*abbaiare*) for an evening'.[51]

Evidence about reading Dante aloud in less public contexts is somewhat harder to assess, since it often appears incidentally or ambiguously in letters and journals. Reading aloud to a small group or a single person continues to be frequent at all levels of society in the nineteenth century; so also does memorizing large amounts of verse for recitation.[52] Some examples of Dante being delivered in this form involve well-known literary or political figures, such as Shelley or Gladstone, presenting the text to their partners.[53] They may also speak of reading Dante *with* (as opposed to *to*) another person.[54] Such reading appears to be a significant feature of the reception of the *Commedia* in the nineteenth century, and it might have taken several forms: reading a text aloud, translating it, agreeing to discuss it, or perhaps a mixture of all three. During the early decades of the century, for example, the journals of Mountstuart Elphinstone — a prominent East India Company 'scholar-administrator' — refer frequently to the process of 'reading *with*' friends (my italics).[55] For example, following a visit from an adventurous young Scottish aristocrat (Lady Hood) Elphinstone looks back wistfully to 'our readings of Dante & our innumerable digressions', while recollections of those readings continue to be one of the subjects of conversation in his letters to her.[56] The contexts and dynamics of such shared but private experiences of the *Commedia* would be worth investigating further — in both Italian and wider global contexts — as a feature of the poem's oral history during the nineteenth century and beyond.

The *Commedia*'s public performance on stage and screen has been quite fully explored in recent studies, although there is more yet to be learned about the contexts and impact of public readings, recitations and recordings — as well as the forms of *echi danteschi* in Italian popular culture.[57] At the academic level, the poem's voice has been heard from the podium over seven centuries in various accents and languages: for example, in Boccaccio's *esposizioni*, in the Florentine Academy's *lettioni*, and in Coleridge's and Foscolo's lectures to London audiences in 1818 and 1823 — as well as in the modern *lectura Dantis*, where the convention of reading the canto aloud continues to be observed in various forms; and a contemporary debate about the *lectura* convention has recently served to highlight the function of such voicing. Most of the participants in the recent series of *lectura Dantis* at the University of St Andrews, for example, have followed the practice of reading the text before commenting on it so as to introduce the audience to the lecture's material; however, a case has also been made for reading the canto *afterwards*, in order to test the validity of the *lectura*'s argument.[58]

Returning to the point where this chapter began — with a contemporary presence of the poem in the piazza — Roberto Benigni's *TuttoDante* performances themselves raise issues about the voicing of the *Commedia*. Unlike the orotund style of delivery adopted by a number of Italian performers such as Carmelo Bene, Benigni's treatment of the text is restrained and focused.[59] As in one version of the *lectura*, his reading followed his own 'commentary': a personal (and often satirical) meditation on Dante and on contemporary culture and politics.[60] And the carnivalesque context of such occasions — compared by one commentator to 'football fever' (*tifo di stadio*) — is a reminder of how oral performance has become a key feature of commemorative Dante festivals: from Tommaso Salvini's show-stopping rendition of *Inferno* 1 at the 1865 Florence *festa* to events presently being planned for the centenary year of 2021.[61] At such events — and in the cultural contexts outlined in this chapter — voicing the *Commedia* in the original or in translation is one way in which Dante has crossed and will continue to cross linguistic, cultural and social borders.

Notes to Chapter 9

1. Roberto Benigni, *Il mio Dante: con un scritto di Umberto Eco* (Turin: Einaudi, 2008), p. 15.
2. Ibid., pp. 23–25. See also p. 8 for Eco's insistence on poetry being 'la più popolare delle arti, [...] nata per essere recitata a voce alta e mandata a memoria' (the most popular of the arts [...] naturally suited to being recited aloud and committed to memory').
3. As will be apparent, this part of the chapter is much indebted to two important articles on orality and performance in and around the *Commedia* in the *trecento*: John Ahern, 'Singing the Book: Orality in the Reception of Dante's *Comedy*', published first in *Annals of Scholarship* 2.4 (1982), 17–40, then in *Dante: Contemporary Perspectives*, ed. by A. Iannucci (Toronto and London: University of Toronto Press, 1997), pp. 214–39 (subsequent references are to the later version); and Peter Armour, 'Comedy and the Origins of Italian Theatre around the Time of Dante', in *Writers and Performers in Italian Drama from the Time of Dante to Pirandello: Essays in Honour of G. H. McWilliam*, ed. by J. R. Dashwood and J. E. Everson (Lewiston, Queenston and Lampeter: Edwin Mellen Press, 1991), pp. 1–31.
4. Giovanni Villani, *Nuova Cronica*, II, ed. by Giuseppe Porta (Parma: Guanda, 1990–91), pp. 131–32. See also Armour, 'Comedy and the Origins of Italian Theatre', pp. 8–9 and n. 21. As Armour points out (pp. 8–9 and n. 21), the later version of the scene by Antonio Pucci (*c.* 1310–88) in his *Cronica di Giovanni Villani ridotta in terza rima* (canto 41, terzine 72–100) includes 'several Dantesque effects and phrasings'.
5. See for example Zygmunt Barański's article sub-section on '*Commedia*: Title and Form' in *The Dante Encyclopedia*, ed. by Richard Lansing (New York and London: Garland, 2000), pp. 184–88.
6. Armour, 'Comedy and the Origins of Italian Theatre', pp. 2–3, 5 and n. 13.
7. Umberto Bosco, 'Dante e il teatro medievale', in *Studi filologici, letterari e storici in memoria di Guido Favati*, I, ed. by Giorgio Varanini and Palmiro Pinagli (Padua: Antenore, 1977), pp. 144–46; also Armour, 'Comedy and the Origins of Italian Theatre', p. 8.
8. Aaron Gurevich, *Medieval Popular Culture: Problems of Belief and Perception*, trans. by J. M. Bak and P. A. Hollingsworth (Cambridge: Cambridge University Press, 1988); see ch. 6 and especially pp. 184–94, on 'the medieval perception of demons'.
9. See Umberto Bosco, 'Il ludo dantesco dei barattieri', in *Essays in Honour of John Humphreys Whitfield*, ed. by H. C. Davies and others (London: St George's Press, 1975), esp. pp. 39–40.
10. See Bosco, 'Dante e il teatro medievale', pp. 138–44, and Armour, 'Comedy and the Origins of Italian Theatre', pp. 6–12.
11. Bosco, 'Dante e il teatro medievale', p. 136; Armour, 'Comedy and the Origins of Italian

Theatre', pp. 10–12.

12. Striking examples in the later cantos of the *Paradiso* are the deafening 'grido di sì alto suono' uttered by the 'contemplative' souls (21. 140–42) and the change of tone accompanying St Peter's speech at the beginning of canto 27.
13. Ahern, 'Singing the Book', pp. 228–29.
14. See R. K. Root, 'Publication before Printing', *PMLA/Proceedings of the Modern Language Association of America*, 28 (1913), 417–31; R. M. Walker, 'Oral Delivery or Private Reading? A Contribution to the Debate on the Dissemination of Medieval Literature', *Forum for Modern Language Studies*, 7 (1971), 36–42, esp. pp. 39–41. The question of what it meant to 'publish' a book in Western Europe between 1000 and 1500 is currently under investigation by a European Research Council funded project at the University of Helsinki; see <https://www.helsinki.fi/en/researchgroups/medieval-publishing/the-project>.
15. On the addresses to the reader in the *Commedia*, see the classic articles by Hermann Gmelin, in *Deutsches Dante-Jahrbuch*, 29/30 (1951), 130–40; Erich Auerbach, *Romance Philology*, 7 (1953–54), 268–78; and Leo Spitzer, *Italica*, 32 (1955), 143–65; also the more recent discussion in William Franke, *Dante's Interpretive Journey* (Chicago and London: University of Chicago Press, 1996), pp. 37–81.
16. See *Inf.* 22. 118 (*tu che leggi, udirai*) and *Par.* 2. 2 (*desiderosi d'ascoltar*). For examples of comparable complexities in medieval addresses to the reader and in the 'social context of medieval aurality', see Joyce Coleman, *Public Reading and the Reading Public in Late Medieval England and France* (Cambridge: Cambridge University Press, 1996), pp. 63–66 and 76–108.
17. Chaucer, *The Miller's Prologue*, 3176–77, in *The Riverside Chaucer*, ed. by L. D. Benson, 3rd edn (Oxford: Oxford University Press, 2008), p. 67.
18. Armour, 'Comedy and the Origins of Italian Theatre', pp. 19–20 and 23.
19. Presentation of ten canti from the *Paradiso* are mentioned in Dante's first epistle to Giovanni del Virgilio; see *Dante and Giovanni del Virgilio*, ed. by P. H. Wicksteed and E. G. Gardner (London: Constable, 1902), p. 156, lines 58–64; and on the identity of those ten canti, see the chapter by Matthew Leigh and Jonathan Katz in this volume. See also the reference to dedicating the *Paradiso* in the 'Epistle to Cangrande': P. J. Toynbee, *Dantis Alagherii Epistolae*, 2nd edn (Oxford: Clarendon Press, 1966), p. 170, lines 56–59.
20. See Marco Vatasso, *Del Petrarca e di alcuni suoi amici* (Rome: Typografia Vaticana, 1904), esp. pp. 72–74 and 100–02. A more recent edition is by Paolo Garbani, *Moggio Moggi: carmi e epistole* (Padua: Antenore, 1996).
21. Vatasso, *Del Petrarca e di alcuni suoi amici*, p. 100 (headnote).
22. Ahern, 'Singing the Book', p. 227.
23. In the preface to Alberigo's Latin version of Jacopo della Lana's commentary on the *Commedia*; see Henry A. Kelly, *Tragedy and Comedy from Dante to Pseudo-Dante* (Berkeley and Los Angeles: University of California Press), pp. 32–33.
24. For the text of the petition, see Isidoro Del Lungo, *Dell'esilio di Dante: discorso commemorativo del 27 gennaio 1881* (Florence: Le Monnier, 1881), pp. 164–65.
25. Boccaccio, *Trattatello in laude di Dante*, ed. by P. G. Ricci in *Tutte le opere di Giovanni Boccaccio*, III (Milan: Mondadori, 1974), pp. 486–87 (paragraphs 190–92).
26. Not long after this (in 1396) the Florentine Commune would make one of several attempts to have the poet's body itself returned from Ravenna.
27. Reading the text aloud before commenting on it was standard medieval academic practice; see Hastings Rashdall, *The Universities of Europe*, I (Oxford: Clarendon Press, 1936), pp. 216–21, and R. S. Raitt, *Life in the Medieval University* (Cambridge: Cambridge University Press, 1912), pp. 140–44).
28. For Boccaccio's regrets about the *Esposizioni*, see sonnets 122 and 123 in *Giovanni Boccaccio: opere minori in volgare*, IV, ed. by Mario Marti (Milan: Rizzoli, 1972), pp. 134–35; for Petrarch's comments on Dante (and the mangling of vernacular poems 'by the tongues of the vulgar'), see his 1359 letter to Boccaccio (*Familiares* 21. 15) in *Petrarca: Prose*, ed. by Guido Martellotti (Milan and Naples: Ricciardi, 1956), pp. 1002–10; see also Leonardo Bruni, *Ad Petrum Paulum Histrum Dialogus* (c. 1401–07), in *Prosatori latini del quattrocento*, ed. by Eugenio Garin (Milan and Naples:

Ricciardi, 1956), p. 70. Giovanni del Virgilio's reference to Dante's popularity is in the epitaph he composed for the poet; see *Dante and Giovanni del Virgilio*, ed. by P. H. Wicksteed and E. G. Gardner (London: Constable, 1902), p. 174.

29. Franco Sacchetti, *Il Trecentonovelle*, ed. by Emilio Faccioli (Turin: Einaudi, 1970), especially nos 114 and 115. Dante as popular hero and source of folk-wisdom is referred to frequently in the *Trecentonovelle*, viz.: nos 4, 8, 15, 121, 175, 193, 208, 210.
30. On the continuation of Dante lectures after Boccaccio, see Simon Gilson, *Dante and Renaissance Florence* (Cambridge: Cambridge University Press, 2005), pp. 11–12 with n. 43.
31. On mercantile ownership of *Commedia* manuscripts, see Luisa Miglio, 'Lettori della *Commedia*: i manoscritti', in *Per correr miglior acque: bilanci e prospettive degli studi danteschi sulle soglie del nuovo millennio*, I, ed. by Lucia Battaglia Ricci (Rome: Salerno, 2001), pp. 295–323. For Lenzi, see *Il libro del biadaiolo*, ed. by Guiliano Pinto (Florence: Olschki, 1978) and Vittore Branca, 'Un biadaiolo lettore di Dante', in *Studi in onore di Alfredo Schiaffini*, ed. by Ettore Paratore, *Rivista di Cultura Classica e Medievale*, 7 (1965), 200–08. On Pucci's popularizing work in his *Libro di varie storie* (c. 1362?) and *Centiloquio* (c. 1373–76?), see Kathleen Speight, '*Vox populi* in Antonio Pucci', in *Italian Studies Presented to E.R. Vincent*, ed. by C. P. Brand and others (Cambridge: Cambridge University Press, 1962), pp. 76–91.
32. Michael Clanchy, *From Memory to Written Record: England 1066–1307*, 2nd edn (Oxford: Blackwell, 1993), p. 198; Mary Carruthers, 'Reading', in *The Oxford Handbook of Dante*, ed. by Manuele Gragnolati, Elena Lombardi and Francesca Southerden (Oxford: Oxford University Press, 2021), pp. 34–48 (p. 38).
33. Brian Richardson, 'Reciting Petrarchan verse in Renaissance Italy', in Stefano Jossa and Giuliana Pieri, *Chivalry, Academy and Cultural Dialogues* (Oxford: Legenda, 2016), p. 167; and Jennifer Richards and Richard Wistreich, 'Introduction: Voicing Text 1500–1700', *Huntington Library Quarterly*, 82.1 (2019), 3–16 (p. 6).
34. Roger Chartier, 'Leisure and Sociability: Reading Aloud in Early Modern Europe', in *Urban Life in the Renaissance*, ed. by Susan Zimmerman and R. F. E. Weissman, (Newark, DE, London and Toronto: University of Delaware Press, 1989), pp. 103–20 (p. 107).
35. See *Voices and Texts in Early Modern Italian Society*, ed. by S. Dall'Aglio, Brian Richardson and Massimo Rospocher (Abingdon: Routledge, 2016), p. 2.
36. Giorgio Vasari, *Le Vite de' più eccelenti pittori, scultori e arcitettori nelle redazioni del 1550 e 1568*, ed. by Rosanna Bettarini and Paola Barocchi, 6 vols (Florence: Sansoni, 1966–87), IV, 79–80.
37. Chartier, 'Leisure and Sociability', p. 107.
38. On Doni's career as *academico pellegrino* through various Italian cities and the scope of his interests (he claimed expertise in *scrivere ... cantare, sonare, disegnare e poetizzare*), see http://www.treccani.it/enciclopedia/anton-francesco-doni_(Dizionario-Biografico)/; also, on Doni's 'variegated oeuvre', Anna Tedesco's article in *The Encyclopedia of Italian Literary Studies*, ed. by Gaetana Marrone and Paolo Puppa, 2 vols (Abingdon and New York: Taylor & Francis, 2006), I, 645–47.
39. On Giambullari, see Konrad Eisenbichler's article in *The Encyclopedia of Italian Literary Studies*, I, 839–42; and on Gelli (who was appointed as 'lettore di Dante at the universities of Florence and Pisa in the mid-1550s), see Judith Bryce, 'The Oral World of the Early Accademia Fiorentina', *Renaissance Studies*, 9.1 (1995), pp. 83–85 and 88.
40. Judith Bryce, 'The Oral World of the Early Accademia', p. 77.
41. Verini in *Lettioni d'academici fiorentini sopra Dante* (Florence: Doni, 1547), p. 9. On the Sunday and Thursday sessions of the Academy and the public attendance at Verini's own Dante lectures (said to have drawn 'crowds of two thousand people'), see Bryce, 'The Oral World of the Early Accademia', pp. 80–81, 86 and 88.
42. Giambullari in *Lettioni*, p. 53.
43. Gelli and Giambullari in the *Lettioni*, pp. 26, 91 and 94.
44. Bryce, 'The Oral World of the Early Accademia', p. 79.
45. Ben Jonson, *Volpone or the Foxe* (London: Thomas Thorppe, 1607), sig. G2r (Act 3, scene 2).
46. See *Overture to the Opera: Italian Pastoral Drama in the Renaissance*, ed. by C. Salvadori Lonergan and P. Brand (Dublin: UCD Foundation for Italian Studies, 2013), pp. 4–5. I am grateful to Prof. Richard Andrews for drawing my attention to this text and edition.

47. Giovanni Briccio *La Tartarea: Commedia Infernale* (Viterbo: Girolamo Discepolo, 1614), pp. 7 and 101 ('mirami che son Albina').
48. Giovanni Leone Semproni's tragedy *Il Conte Ugolino* was composed in the first half of the seventeenth century though not published till much later (Rome: Giovan Maria Salvioni, 1724). Examples in the eighteenth century are Heinrich Wilhelm von Gerstenberg's influential *Ugolino; eine Tragödie in fünf Aufzügen* (Hamburg and Bremen: Cramer, 1768) performed at Berlin in 1769; and Andrea Rubbi's *Ugolino, Conte de' Gherardeschi* (Bassano: Remondi, 1779).
49. For Dante's presence on the nineteenth-century stage, see, for example: Beatrice Corrigan, 'Dante and Italian Theater: A Study in Dramatic Fashions', *Dante Studies*, 89 (1971), 93–105; Letizia Putignano, 'Francesca da Rimini sulle scene del teatro d'opera italiano', in *Sventurati amanti: Il mito di Paolo e Francesca nell' 800*, ed. by Claudio Poppi (Milan: Mazzotta, 1994), pp. 39–44; Richard Cooper, 'Dante on the Nineteenth-Century Stage', in *Dante on View: The Reception of Dante in the Visual and Performing Arts*, ed. by Antonella Braida and Luisa Calè (Aldershot and Burlington VT: Ashgate, 2007), pp. 22–37.
50. See Michael Caesar and Nick Havely, 'Politics and Performance: Gustavo Modena's *dantate*', in *Dante in the Long Nineteenth Century: Nationality, Identity and Appropriation*, ed. by Aida Audeh and Nick Havely (Oxford: Oxford University Press, 2012), pp. 111–37; and more recently, Rossella Bonfatti, 'Performing Dante or Building the Nation? The *Divine Comedy* between Dramaturgy of Exile and Public Festivities', *Medievalia*, 38 (2017), 37–67.
51. Caesar and Havely, 'Politics and Performance', pp. 114–15 (Mazzini and Ruffini); 116–24 (on the 1839 London show, quoting the review in *Athenaeum* 604, p. 397); 124–27 (on Bini's and Trollope's reactions); and 130 (on the final *dantate* at Bologna and Turin in 1860).
52. See, for example, William St Clair, *The Reading Nation in the Romantic Period* (Cambridge: Cambridge University Press, 2004), pp. 394–95.
53. The Shelleys were reading the *Commedia* between December 1818 and September 1819; see *The Journals of Mary Shelley, 1814–1844*, ed. by Paula R. Feldman and Diana Scott-Kilvert, 2 vols (Oxford: Oxford University Press, 1987), I, 246 (with n. 2), 247 (*Inferno*), 293–95 (*Purgatorio*) and 295–97 (*Paradiso*). More specifically, Mary notes on 31 January 1819 that 'Shelley reads the "Vita Nuova" *aloud* to me in the evening' (p. 351, my italics), and that reading appears to have continued at intervals into mid-February (p. 353); while her husband notes at around the same time that he 'read Dante *with* Mary' (*Letters of Percy Bysshe Shelley*, ed. F. L. Jones, 2 vols (Oxford: Oxford University Press, 1964), II, 114). Gladstone when rereading the *Inferno* at Hawarden in the summer of 1841 records reaching 'Inferno IV–VII: some aloud to C.', that is, to Catherine Glynne, his wife; see *The Gladstone Diaries*, III, ed. by M. R. D. Foot and H. C. G. Matthew (Oxford: Clarendon Press, 1974), p. 127 (29 July 1941).
54. See *The Gladstone Diaries*, II, ed. by M. R. D. Foot (Oxford: Clarendon Press, 1968), pp. 204–07 (13, 14 and 17 November, 1835) and 328 (13 June 1838).
55. On Elphinstone and Dante, see Nick Havely, *Dante's British Public: Readers and Texts, from the Fourteenth Century to the Present* (Oxford: Oxford University Press, 2014), pp. 194–211; on the references to shared reading in his journals, see p. 201 with n. 34.
56. Elphinstone Journals, British Library MSS Eur F88/370, pp. 140–41 (23 March 1813; for his letters to Lady Hood, see National Archives of Scotland (Edinburgh), GD 46/17/42, especially the letters of 16 and 24 March 1813). Their shared reading may well have reached the end of the *Inferno*, since in the letter of 24 March he reminds Lady Hood of the rhyme between *Tambernicchi* and *cricchi* (*Inf.* 32. 28–30).
57. Nineteenth-century folklorist scholars, such as Giuseppe Pitré, Giovanni Papanti (e.g. in *Dante secondo la tradizione e i novellatori* of 1873) and Alessandro D'Ancona, detected such echoes in popular oral traditions and performance; and for evidence about such traditions, see Giovanni Bronzini, 'Prospetto critico delle tradizioni popolari dantesche', in *Studi filologici, letterari e storici in memoria di Guido Favati*, ed. by Giorgio Varanini and Palmiro Pinagli (Padua: Antenore, 1977), pp. 149–75 (I am grateful to Dr Alessandro Carlucci for drawing these sources to my attention). For accounts of Dante on stage and screen, see especially: Corrigan, 'Dante and Italian Theater'; Gianfranco Casadio (ed.), *Dante nel Cinema* (Ravenna: Longo, 1996); *Dante, Cinema and Television*, ed. by Amilcare Iannucci (Toronto, Buffalo and London: University of

Toronto Press, 2004); and *Dante on View: The Reception of Dante in the Visual and Performing Arts*, ed. by Antonella Braida and Luisa Calè (Aldershot and Burlington VT: Ashgate, 2007), parts I and III. The impact and status of recorded and online readings and presentations of the text on radio and TV should also be taken into account. For example: the Princeton Dante Project includes a complete audio version of the *Commedia* in Italian (Lino Pertile) and selected cantos from the *Inferno* in translation (Robert and Jean Hollander); at http://etcweb.princeton.edu/dante/pdp/; a complete Italian recording was produced by Audio-libri and a complete English version (Benedict Flynn's) by Naxos.

58. As a contributor to the St Andrews series, I am grateful to Prof. Corinna Salvadori of the Dept of Italian, Trinity College Dublin for her perceptive arguments in favour of the latter procedure.
59. On the various styles of modern Italian performance, see Rino Caputo's excellent chapter 'Dante by Heart and Dante Declaimed: The "Realization" of the *Comedy* on Italian Radio and Television', in *Dante, Cinema and Television*, ed. by Iannucci, pp. 213–33.
60. See the account of Benigni's one-night *TuttoDante* performance at the Theatre Royal Drury Lane (5 April 2009) in Havely, *Dante's British Public*, p. 282.
61. On Salvini's 1865 performance at the Teatro Pagliano in Florence, see Caesar and Havely, 'Politics and Performance', pp. 131–33. On the 1865 *festa di Dante*, see Anne O'Connor, *Florence: City and Memory in the Nineteenth Century* (Florence: Città di Vita, 2008), pp. 65–81 and Mahnaz Yousefzadeh, *The City and the Nation in the Italian Unification: The National Festivals of Dante Alighieri* (Basingstoke: Palgrave Macmillan, 2011). On the wider subject of commemoration, a collaborative study of contemporary political, cultural and literary anniversaries and their transformations, see Céline Sabiron and Jeremy Tranmer, '"Decentering Commemorations": Literary, Cultural, Historical and Political Commemorations across and beyond the British Isles', *European Journal of English Studies*, 24 (2020), 105–14.

CHAPTER 10

Who Could Understand the *Commedia*? Multilingualism, Comprehension and Oral Communication in Medieval Italy

Alessandro Carlucci

Ignazio Baldelli, a major expert on the linguistic situation in medieval Italy, once asked the following question about Saint Francis of Assisi:

> Quale lingua avrà usato Francesco a Bologna nel 1222 per farsi capire dal popolo di Bologna e da uomini di diversa origine regionale e nazionale come Federico Visconti da Pisa e Tommaso da Spalato? Non certo il suo volgare assisano, non comprensibile appunto dai popolani di Bologna o da gente come Tommaso da Spalato. Eppure il tono e lo stesso svolgimento della predica, pur se da lasciare ammirati i dotti, erano appunto 'popolari'.[1]

The same question can be asked about Dante and his most popular work, the *Commedia*. This poem is written in Tuscan, and many scholars have claimed that — in its core linguistic features — it is Dante's most Florentine work. But despite 'the extraordinary amount of erudition that has been devoted to clarifying every detail of Dante's life and works', the question of how intelligible his language was outside Florence, in different parts of medieval Italy, has never been systematically addressed — let alone fully answered. 'The degree of our ignorance is especially worrying if we try to take into account not only literate people [...] but also illiterate speakers of local varieties.'[2]

The dominant view among linguists and historians of the Italian language, which I shall discuss later in this chapter, rests on two points which need to be recalled right away. First, the Romance varieties of Italy — also known as 'vernaculars' or 'dialects' — 'are very different from each other, and mostly unintelligible to speakers of other dialects'.[3] Second, when Italy became a unified country, only a small minority of its population spoke Italian, which is largely based on Dante's Florentine. The number of people who confidently controlled Italian was even smaller between the sixteenth and the nineteenth century, when its use was mostly confined to literature and official communication.[4] As far as earlier periods are concerned, we know that some members of the educated elites (especially those who had literary inclinations) were increasingly exposed to the prestige of Tuscan and were perhaps able to understand it, if not to use it actively. We also know that, during the fifteenth century, convergence on Latin or Tuscan models and avoidance of the most idiosyncratic local features led to the emergence of regionally shared vernacular varieties (also known as 'koiné languages'), which were used in particular domains and especially in written texts, such as chancery documents. But what about further back in time and on lower rungs of the socio-cultural ladder?

Fully solving this historical problem is a task that goes beyond the scope of this chapter, and given the well-known difficulty of studying orality with regard to linguistic situations of the past (lacking audio recordings and other crucial evidence) it is, in part, an impossible task. However, in what follows I shall try to verify Tavoni's recent suggestion that comprehension across different vernaculars may have been 'greater than we today consider possible'.[5] In doing so, I also intend to counter the increasing, and, in my opinion, damaging, separation between two previously interconnected disciplines such as linguistics and literary studies. Thanks precisely to the exceptional 'amount of erudition' which we can rely on when it comes to Dante's poem, the written and oral circulation of the *Commedia* is a promising case for the historical study of mutual intelligibility between closely related languages — an area of modern linguistic research which has substantially expanded in recent years.[6] At the same time, from the point of view of literary research, an up-to-date linguistic perspective may help us to redefine and better understand some topics within Dante studies — such as Dante's linguistic choices, the popularity of the *Commedia* among illiterate audiences, or the function of the early commentaries — for which the question of linguistic intelligibility has been raised,[7] but not specifically analysed.[8]

'Vulgo gratissimus auctor'

In the works of historians who are not specifically interested in language, the main distinction is normally between Latin and vernacular. Latin is seen as a barrier to intelligibility, but the possibility that the different Romance varieties of Italy could also create barriers to intelligibility is rarely considered, for instance, by historians of preaching and economic historians. The latter have recently explored the difficulties of Italian merchants who had to learn and use languages other than their native varieties, but these languages are Catalan, French, German and other non-Italian varieties.[9] The dominant view — or, in some cases, the implicit assumption — seems to be that most of the inhabitants of medieval and early modern Italy could understand each other by using some sort of common vernacular language, as long as their culture and experience of the world was not tied to a purely local dimension.[10]

A particularly relevant example is offered by Peter Armour's research on the recitation of the *Commedia* and its 'popularity [...] among the people in general'.[11] He writes:

> In an age like Dante's, only professionals — churchmen, lawyers, scholars — were truly literate in the official language of writing, Latin; some of the upper

classes and rising bourgeoisie (though not, according to *Vita nuova*, XXV, their womenfolk) might have retained a smattering of schoolboy Latin and could have read a vernacular text. In this society, the principal means of diffusion of a poem such as the *Comedy* among the people as a whole would have been by public recitation or by public reading out loud, perhaps with some commentary. Until the invention of printing put copies of the poem into many private hands, the vast majority of the earliest receptors of Dante's masterpiece would have experienced it as an oral-aural work, and its recitation would have been a public, indeed a social, act.[12]

Armour introduces comparisons with other genres in verse, which circulated 'in the streets' and 'reached most of the people by some form of performance'. He then goes on to argue that, in the same way,

> the *Comedy*, also a great vernacular narrative in verse, was capable of being diffused at all levels of society, among the educated, the ecclesiastical and secular leaders, the merchants and middle classes, and even [...] those members of society who were least likely to have any literacy at all. For all its hearers, when recited or read out loud and in public, the poem was in the *volgare*, their mother tongue, and though its language is mostly removed from the everyday and the colloquial, it would nevertheless have been immediately familiar to them in its basic structure and modes of expression in the context of their own daily means of communication.[13]

These modern arguments are rooted in a conceptual framework which has a long tradition. The distinction between Latin and vernacular was already a fundamental dichotomy for some of those who first referred to public performances of Dante's work. Most notably, Petrarch complained that Dante's poetry was altered, mispronounced and not fully understood 'in tabernis et in foro' [in taverns and piazzas] (*Familiares* 21. 15), and Giovanni del Virgilio reproached Dante for enabling the uneducated ('gens ydiota', 'vulgus') to access the complex contents of the *Commedia* — often, to make it worse, through the distorting performances of street entertainers (*Egloge* 1. 12).[14] These authors, as well as later humanists, frowned upon Dante's choice of the vernacular instead of Latin. Echoes of this dissatisfaction may be read between the lines even in the famous celebratory epitaph which Giovanni del Virgilio wrote on the death of Dante, where the latter is called 'vulgo gratissimus auctor' [best loved author of the common people].[15]

Whether in a similarly negative vein or in more positive terms, allusions to a popular, predominantly oral diffusion of the *Commedia* would continue to appear for centuries. In two of Franco Sacchetti's novellas, the poem is sung by people from relatively low social backgrounds — a blacksmith and a mule-driver respectively.[16] But this literary source is not particularly interesting from a linguistic point of view, given that both episodes are set in Florence, where good understanding of Dante's language is usually expected. At any rate, not only in Florence but also in other Italian cities, various secular and religious events involved some form of public performance of parts of Dante's poem. Already in the fourteenth century, itinerant preachers and other clerics took an interest in the *Commedia* and 'continued to quote Dante's poem in their sermons well into the next century, as confirmed by the testimony of illustrious witnesses such as Lorenzo de' Medici and Erasmus of Rotterdam'.[17] Skipping over to our age, we can mention a song by the singer-songwriter Francesco Guccini, in which he sketches his humble childhood in an Emiliano-speaking village, in the Apennines, 'fra i saggi ignoranti di montagna che sapevano Dante a memoria e improvvisavano di poesia'.[18]

Italo-Romance Intercomprehension in Modern Linguistics

What we have seen in the previous section is difficult to reconcile with the standard scholarly view that a common language had not yet emerged among ordinary speakers in medieval Italy, and that Italo-Romance varieties were 'incomunicabili ieri come oggi da un capo all'altro d'Italia'.[19] Even when medieval literary works represent communication between speakers of different vernaculars, and therefore seem to point towards relatively good levels of Italo-Romance intercomprehension, most linguists remain sceptical. For instance, Serianni doubts that one of Boccaccio's characters, a woman from Genoa, could really have conversations with 'molti mercatanti e ciciliani e pisani e genovesi e viniziani e altri italiani' (*Decameron* 2. 9. 47).[20]

In recent years, however, a few linguists have begun to question this idea of radical unintelligibility and have called for a less conventional interpretation of the extant medieval evidence.[21] In the following three sections of this chapter I shall test the two views — the traditional one, and the one suggesting instead higher levels of intercomprehension — by making use of three types of evidence: speakers' judgements about the intelligibility of Tuscan varieties; linguistic explanations contained in the early commentaries to the *Commedia*; and, finally, a textual sample from the poem (which I shall briefly analyse by applying a similar methodology to that used by Wright in his study of the comprehensibility of the Strasbourg Oaths, and by Vincent in his discussion of the first few lines of *Inferno* 1).[22]

Comments on the Intelligibility of Tuscan Varieties

In the *Convivio* (1. 7. 12) Dante justifies his use of the vernacular by explaining that Latin would have been understood only by the 'litterati'.[23] Elsewhere, in the same work, he speaks of 'volgare italico' (distinguishing it, for instance, from Provençal) and claims to be using it to address 'quasi [...] tutti l'Italici' (*Conv.* 1. 6. 13).[24] Although Dante's written vernacular was open to various literary influences and aimed at being as 'italico' as possible, rather than narrowly municipal, its core lexicon and grammatical structures are essentially Florentine. So his remarks suggest that he expected this essentially Florentine language to be intelligible throughout Italy. A few decades later, Dante's reasons were expanded on by Boccaccio in his *Trattatello in laude di Dante*. Without restricting the potential audience of Dante's poetry to Florence or Tuscany, Boccaccio argues that Dante composed the *Commedia* in vernacular 'per fare utilità piú comune a' suoi cittadini *e agli altri italiani*'.[25] If the geographical scope is similar to the one implicit in Dante's *Convivio*, here Boccaccio seems to broaden the socio-cultural scope slightly by referring to the 'idioti' — that is, to illiterates in general, and not just those who were not 'literate in Latin' (which is probably the meaning of *litterati* in Dante's remarks). Even if they could not read Dante's text, illiterates in various parts of Italy could probably still enjoy it when it was performed or simply read out loud.[26]

With Boccaccio we have reached the second half of the fourteenth century, a period when Tuscan had already acquired a special status, particularly in literature. In an early vernacular translation of the Bible, which I shall quote from a fourteenth-century manuscript,[27] the anonymous translator — perhaps a Tuscan — explains that he has opted for 'uno chomune parlare toscano però che è il più intero e il più aperto e il più apto chomunemente di tutta Ytalia e il più piacevole e il più intendevole di ogni lingua'.[28] Similarly, in the first half of the century, the Paduan judge and poet Antonio da Tempo claimed that 'Lingua Tusca magis apta est ad literam sive literaturam quam aliae linguae, et ideo magis est communis et intelligibilis' [the Tuscan language is more suitable for writing or literature, and is therefore more common and intelligible than other languages].[29] These judgements must be taken with a pinch of salt. The growing prestige of Tuscan may have favoured its perceived intelligibility. Moreover, the intention here may have been of further promoting — rather than simply describing — the role of Tuscan.

Other comments present a different picture. On 27 October 1345, the Sienese merchant Francesco Bartolomei wrote to Pignol Zucchello, another Tuscan merchant who originally came from Pisa but was based in Venice. In his letter Francesco includes a few references to the reading difficulties of a friar called Pacino. This episode has been interpreted as an example of the difficulties which a Venetian would encounter when trying to understand a letter written in Tuscan.[30] The following passage from Bartolomei's letter is intriguing, though somewhat unclear for us today:

> Fra Pacino sì no' credo che sapia legiare e però io sì gli mando una lettara la quale sarà leghata con questa e però vi pregho che la diate bene in suo propia mano peroché v'è dentro una chomesione ch'è di gra' bisognio e quand'egli date, sì dite: Fraciescho scrive al modo toschano e però e' può essare che voi no' saprete be' legiare le suo lettare, e però e' mi scrive che se vi piacie io vi legha la suo lettara, acioché per altri no' si sapia quello che vi scrive.[31]

According to Morozzo della Rocca, Pacino was able to read.[32] However, even if we take an exceedingly cautious approach by assuming that this friar was illiterate, we still need to acknowledge that Bartolomei must have looked for a plausible excuse in order to help the friar without embarrassing him.[33] In other words, it must have been plausible to suggest that a non-Tuscan, such as Pacino, would find it difficult to understand a letter written in Tuscan.[34] Indeed, more than a century later — when Tuscan models had acquired a dominant role in many communicative domains, not only in literature — there were still people, such as the Friulian priest Pietro Edo, who considered 'la toschana lengua' to be 'troppo oscura' and scarcely intelligible in the north-eastern regions.[35]

Still in northern Italy, problems of intelligibility were not only experienced by clerics, but also by merchants in their correspondence with Tuscan firms. In two letters of 1398, the Milanese merchant Giovannino da Dugnano asked Francesco di Marco Datini and his partners to write in a more intelligible way.[36] Before drawing any conclusions about this evidence, however, we should recognize the possibility that on some occasions problems of intelligibility may have been due to a combination of linguistic and graphic differences. It is plausible to interpret the word *modo*, used by Bartolomei, as referring to language as such (see the *GDLI*, s.v. *modo*). Nonetheless, we should factor in the difficulties caused by different *modi* of representing language in letters and other written texts — according not only to individual ways of writing,[37] but also to different geographic and sociocultural backgrounds.[38] In the previously mentioned collection of letters to Pignol Zucchello, the only letter attributable to the indefinable Fra Pacino is written in a traditional chancery hand which is notably different from the mercantile script used by Bartolomei.[39]

The Early Commentary Tradition

Barriers to Italo-Romance intercomprehension clearly emerge from the early reception of the *Commedia*.[40] In their effort to ensure that the literal meaning of Dante's language was fully grasped, fourteenth-century commentators paid detailed attention to linguistic variation. Some of the Florentine names which Dante had used to designate animals and everyday objects required clarification even in geographically and linguistically contiguous areas, such as other Tuscan cities. Towards the end of the century, the Pisan Francesco da Buti explains *ramarro* 'European green lizard (Lacerta viridis)' (*Inf.* 25. 79) as 'lo *rogio*, che è uno serpente verde con quattro piedi';[41] likewise, Guido da Pisa has *rogus*, whereas Bartolomeo Nerucci da San Gimignano has *racanus* (both wrote their commentaries in Latin and adapted vernacular words to Latin). Guido also adds: 'Romani autem vocant ipsum "racanum" et Florentini "ramarrum"' [The Romans however call this *racanum* and the Florentines *ramarrum*].[42] Other equivalents for *ramarro* can be found in the glosses of commentators from other parts of Italy. The Bolognese Iacomo della Lana has 'magrassi overo liguri' [*magrassi* or *liguri*],[43] and Benvenuto da Imola explains that 'Ramarrus est serpens communis in Italia, qui alibi dicitur *marro*, alibi *ragano*, Bononiae vero dicitur *liguoro*' [*Ramarrus* is a common kind of snake in Italy, and in some parts it is called *marro*, in others *ragano*; in Bologna to be sure it is called *liguoro*].[44]

The following simile describing Lucifer also posed interesting challenges: 'Da ogne bocca dirompea co' denti | un peccatore, a guisa di maciulla' (*Inf.* 34. 55–56). In his Neapolitan commentary, Maramauro clarifies the meaning of these lines as follows: 'Qui fa comparatione de quello instrumento col qual se bate el lino o il canepo chiamato *maciulla*, che non taglia, ma dirompe'.[45] It is interesting that Maramauro repeats *maciulla* without providing an equivalent, probably because Neapolitan forms (the verb *maciulljà*, the noun *macìnələ*) are only partly different from Dante's form, with which they share the remote etymon MACHINULA, a diminutive of MACHINA.[46] Instead, in the north of Italy, comparisons had to be made with different tools used for breaking up flax or hemp, such as Lombard *spadula* in the commentary by the Anonimo Lombardo.[47]

As observed by Franceschini, who has extensively compared Dante commentaries with modern dialectological data, the richest lexical explanations are triggered by two factors: first, the absence of a common extra-linguistic referent, whereby words need to be explained not only because they are different in various parts of Italy, but also because they designate different objects or practices (as in the case of *maciulla/ spadula*); second, the absence of a clearly recognizable Latin antecedent (as in the case of *ramarro*). This second point suggests that comprehension problems were more readily perceived when the words involved came from different etyma or — even if they descended from the same Latin etymon — had been radically transformed by diachronic changes. The need to add explanatory glosses would seem to have been less pressing when cognate words from different Italo-Romance varieties had undergone sound changes which had not radically obscured their common origin. In synchronic terms, certain phonological differences must have been easy to work out and had little or no effect on overall intelligibility, especially if they gave rise to recurrent, recognizable correspondences — a relevant example being the presence of intervocalic *voiced* stops in northern Italy, instead of the *voiceless* stops found in Tuscan and southern varieties, as in *figo/fico* 'fig' (cf. *Inf.* 33. 120).

Finally, the early commentaries to the *Commedia* also show that certain words were more widespread in the Middle Ages than they are today. For example, *mo* is now typical of informal registers and mainly restricted to central and southern Italy, but in the Middle Ages it was used also in the north of Italy and in parts of Tuscany, and it was probably understandable, even if not actively used, in the rest of Tuscany. In the first half of the fifteenth century, when Guiniforte Barzizza explained Dante's *Inferno* at the Visconti court in Milan, he could go as far as to define *mo* as a 'general vocabolo italiano'.[48] In this respect, some lexical explanations contained in the early commentaries sit ill with widely shared assumptions about Italy's linguistic history as a process of linear progression from high levels of fragmentation, typical of the Middle Ages, to increasing unification and mutual intelligibility as we move into the modern period.

An Example

Further light on the question of intelligibility can be shed by linguistically analysing a textual sample. For this purpose I have chosen a passage dominated by the imperfect indicative, which, together with the present and past historic indicative (also represented in this passage), is one of the three most frequently used tenses in the *Commedia*.[49] This typically descriptive and narrative passage does not display particularly high degrees of encyclopaedic or stylistic complexity. Unlike other loci, where the main barriers to intelligibility are likely to be posed by the concentration of names (referring, for instance, to mythological figures) or by drawn-out similes, in the following lines we can presume that the ability to understand the literal meaning of the poem is largely determined by linguistic factors:

>   Già era in loco onde s'udìa 'l rimbombo
>   de l'acqua che cadea ne l'altro giro,

> simile a quel che l'arnie fanno rombo,
> quando tre ombre insieme si partiro,
> correndo, d'una torma che passava
> sotto la pioggia de l'aspro martiro.
> (*Inf.* 16. 1–6)

Vincent has emphasized the 'syntactic uniformity across medieval dialects', arguing that it allowed 'a greater degree of geographical intelligibility [...] than is usually supposed',[50] and Ledgeway has maintained that (unlike syntax) phonological differences are unlikely to have a particularly disruptive impact on cross-dialectal comprehension.[51] On the whole, these optimistic premises seem to be confirmed by the lines above — where *loco*, moreover, may have sounded clearer than Tuscan *luogo* in large parts of southern Italy (and to those familiar with Latin). The polymorphism of the imperfect endings (*-ia* and *-ea*, alongside *-ava*) was perhaps more inclusive than a uniform choice (cf. modern Italian *-ava*, *-eva*, *-iva*), given that *-v-* was dropped in some vernaculars but not in others.[52] The third-person plural past historic *partiro* was not hugely different — in form, and in the meaning it has in this passage — either from its Latin etymon or from its cognates in some of Italy's Romance varieties,[53] and the disappearance of this tense in northern varieties was not as advanced in the Middle Ages as it is today.[54] However, even if we skip other presumably inconsequential differences and continue to insist on elements whose form and function were probably widely intelligible (prepositions, numerals, *già*, *era*), we have to accept that some lexical features hindered comprehension. In the medieval corpus of the Opera del Vocabolario Italiano (OVI),[55] the form *arnia*, *-e* 'beehive' only appears in a small number of exclusively Tuscan texts. Francesco da Buti explained it as 'bugni delle lapi', and further away from Florence it would seem to have mislead readers:

> D[ante] dice che esso era in loco ove se audiva lo rimbombo etc., simele a quel rimbombo de Nargnie. Nargnie [i.e. Narni, in Umbria] è una cità de Patrimonio per la qual passa da lato el Tevere per stretissimo passo e fa un gran risono per altissime ripe ne la concavità ove cade, e non solo in una parte, ma in più lochi del dicto fiume che fanno un gran rombo, cioè le cadute fano un gran tumulto.[56]

This was not the only lexical explanation that Maramauro felt the need to provide for this passage: 'Primo è da sapere che cossa è rimbombo. E dico che "rimbombo" in toscano è a dir "risono" d'alcuna cossa che cade d'alto in basso e risona.'[57]

Creating (Partial) Comprehension

At first sight, the example in the previous section restricts quite drastically the plausible extent of popular dissemination of the *Commedia*. But this is true only if we imagine an ideal situation, in which audiences who are exclusively familiar with their own local varieties are suddenly exposed to Dante's poem in its genuine linguistic form. In reality, merchants, diplomats, political exiles, including their families and servants, and others, especially among city-dwellers, were in more or less direct contact with different varieties. At the same time, medieval society included groups such as itinerant preachers and minstrels who 'had every reason to modify their native dialects', as they 'depended on having their words immediately understood'.[58] For speakers (or writers) and hearers (or readers) who did not know Latin, adapting to different ways of speaking was at once more necessary and less embarrassing because of the lack of linguistic standardization in the vernacular.

In this context, the structural proximity of Italo-Romance varieties allowed speakers with 'active competence in one [variety] to acquire without problems passive competence in one or more of the others',[59] especially in a relatively conservative variety such as Tuscan, unreached by the most idiosyncratic innovations which had taken place in the south, and (even more) in the north, of Italy. The existence of recognizable, often systematic differences favoured the adaptation of one's speech to that of the interlocutor(s) — a phenomenon known today as 'accommodation'.[60] Indeed, modern linguists have observed these phenomena in cases of language contact,[61] particularly among speakers of closely related varieties (as in the case of Scandinavian languages).[62] Dante himself would seem to have exploited the already mentioned correspondence between intervocalic voiceless and voiced consonants, and that between Tuscan *-aio* and non-Tuscan *-aro*, as he occasionally used non-Tuscan variants such as *sego* [with himself] (*Purg.* 17. 57) and *ternaro, marinari, Notaro, paro* 'pair', etc.[63] Along these lines, his public could proceed further in mentally replacing Tuscan forms with local equivalents.

Evidence that the *Commedia* crossed linguistic boundaries in this way can be found in sources which show particularly high degrees of adaptation and distortion of the language of the poem. This evidence has for a long time been sidelined, given the dominant concern with reconstructing the text as accurately as possible. But in the light of what has been discussed in this chapter, its potential contribution to our understanding of the popular diffusion of the *Commedia* clearly stands out. We have already seen the word for 'beehives' turning into a place-name, Narni. Some fourteenth-century quotations from memory show metaphony and other non-Tuscan features, typical of the dialects of central Italy, as in 'quilli trunchi' instead of 'quei bronchi' (*Inf.* 13. 26);[64] while in a coeval note on a copy of the *Inferno*, which belonged to the Franciscan Matteo Porta, archbishop of Palermo, Sicilian 'li stilli' replaces Tuscan 'le stelle' (*Inf.* 34. 139).[65] Often considered as little more than passive corruption of Dante's language, these examples should be seen as the manifestation of a wider set of strategies through which people make sense of a language that is similar to their own and actively strive for communication, in writing as much as speaking. That we are not simply dealing with mistakes in the transmission of texts is confirmed by the fact that autographs, too, show signs of accommodation — especially in the lexicon, but also in phonological, and more generally grammatical, features.[66]

In conclusion, given the linguistic situation of late medieval Italy, could the *Commedia* have had a geographically wide audience at all levels of society? A possible answer is that it could not, and that outside Florence popular performances of the poem only existed in the exaggerated, polemical comments of Dante's elitist critics.

In fact, the references to mispronouncing and misunderstanding contained in such comments might be grounded in reality and thus suggest a somewhat different answer. The *Commedia* was difficult to understand, perhaps impossible for those who lived in isolated areas and only knew local varieties removed from Florentine; yet in an altered form — in which comprehensible words replaced unfamiliar ones, and various linguistic features were modified, overlooked or misunderstood — the language of the poem could still find an audience beyond the educated elites and beyond Florence.

Notes to Chapter 10

1. Ignazio Baldelli, *Conti, glosse e riscritture : dal secolo XI al secolo XX* (Naples: Morano, 1988), p. 127.
2. Giulio Lepschy and Laura Lepschy, 'Dante as a Native Speaker', in *'Legato con amore in un volume': Essays in Honour of John A. Scott*, ed. by John Kinder and Diana Glenn (Florence: Olschki, 2013), pp. 309–19 (p. 313).
3. Giulio Lepschy, 'How Popular is Italian?', in *Culture and Conflict in Postwar Italy*, ed. by Zygmunt Barański and Robert Lumley (London: Macmillan, 1990), pp. 63–75 (p. 64). Italo-Romance varieties (Venetian, Neapolitan, Florentine, etc.) come from Latin, so from this genetic point of view they are not dialects of Italian, but rather Latin dialects, as recently reaffirmed by Tullio Telmon, 'Dialects of Italy', in *Handbook of Dialectology*, ed. by Charles Boberg and others (Oxford: Blackwell, 2018), pp. 486–97. Italian language historians call them *volgari* 'vernaculars' with reference to the period up to the sixteenth century, before the literary codification of the old Florentine used by Dante, Petrarch and Boccaccio, whereas *dialetto* 'dialect' tends to be reserved for the period following the adoption of Florentine-based literary Italian throughout the entire peninsula. See for example Mirko Tavoni, 'Linguistic Italy', in *Dante in Context*, ed. by Zygmunt Barański and Lino Pertile (Cambridge: Cambridge University Press, 2015), pp. 243–59: 'the word "dialect" is used to refer specifically to vernaculars from the Cinquecento to modern times, the period during which the "Italian language", namely, the country's common literary language, reduced the prestige of the country's other vernaculars' (p. 245).
4. Shaped by the seminal contributions of Tullio De Mauro and Arrigo Castellani, this topic has recently been taken up by Pietro Trifone, *Pocoinchiostro: storia dell'italiano comune* (Bologna: il Mulino, 2017).
5. Tavoni, 'Linguistic Italy', p. 251.
6. See Charlotte Gooskens, 'Dialect Intelligibility', in *Handbook of Dialectology*, pp. 204–18. On intelligibility in linguistic history see Roger Wright, 'Early Medieval Pan-Romance Comprehension', in *A Sociophilological Study of Late Latin* (Turnhout: Brepols, 2002), pp. 175–90; Martin Maiden, 'The Definition of Multilingualism in Historical Perspective', in *Multilingualism in Italy: Past and Present*, ed. by A. L. Lepschy and Arturo Tosi (Oxford: Legenda, 2002), pp. 31–46; Kurt Braunmüller, 'Receptive Multilingualism in Northern Europe in the Middle Ages', in *Receptive Multilingualism*, ed. by J. D. ten Thije and Ludger Zeevaert (Amsterdam: Benjamins, 2007), pp. 25–47; Claire Blanche-Benveniste, 'Comment retrouver l'expérience des anciens voyageurs en terres de langues romanes?', in *S'entendre entre langues voisines: vers l'intercompréhension*, ed. by Virginie Conti and François Grin (Chêne-Bourg: Georg, 2008), pp. 33–51.
7. See e.g. Zygmunt Barański, 'Early Reception', in *Dante in Context*, pp. 518–37: 'one of the primary functions of especially non-Tuscan commentaries was to make Dante's language accessible to readers in different regions' (p. 523).
8. I began working on this topic during my time as an MHRA Research Associate at the University of Oxford (2017–18), within the 'Creative Multilingualism' programme funded by the Arts and Humanities Research Council. I remain grateful to this funder and to the Modern Humanities Research Association, as well as to the scholars who helped me with their suggestions and comments, especially Martin Maiden, Nick Havely and Simon Gilson. Responsibility for any mistakes contained in this chapter rests solely with the author.

9. See e.g. Francesco Guidi Bruscoli, 'I mercanti italiani e le lingue straniere', in *Comunicare nel medioevo: la conoscenza e l'uso delle lingue nei secoli XII–XV*, ed. by Isa Lori Sanfilippo and Giuliano Pinto (Rome: Istituto storico italiano per il medioevo, 2015), pp. 103–31, and Maria Elisa Soldani, '"E perché costui è uxo di qua e intende bene la lingua": remarques sur la communication entre marchands au bas Moyen Âge', in *Les langues de la négociation: approches historiennes*, ed. by Dejanirah Couto and Stéphane Péquignot (Rennes: Presses universitaires de Rennes, 2017), pp. 129–61.
10. See also Isabella Lazzarini, 'Orality and Writing in Diplomatic Interactions in Fifteenth-Century Italy', in *Voices and Texts in Early Modern Italian Society*, ed. by Stefano Dall'Aglio and others (London: Routledge, 2017), pp. 97–109, and John Ahern, 'Singing the Book: Orality in the Reception of Dante's Comedy', in *Dante: Contemporary Perspectives*, ed. by Amilcare Iannucci (Toronto: University of Toronto Press, 1997), pp. 214–39.
11. Peter Armour, 'The Comedy as a Text for Performance', in *Dante on View: The Reception of Dante in the Visual and Performing Arts*, ed. by Antonella Braida and Luisa Calè (London: Ashgate, 2007), pp. 17–22 (p. 21).
12. Armour, 'The Comedy as a Text for Performance', pp. 18–19.
13. Ibid., p. 20.
14. On Giovanni del Virgilio, see the essay by Jonathan Katz and Matthew Leigh in this volume (Chapter 1).
15. English translation from Barański, 'Early Reception', p. 519.
16. Franco Sacchetti, *Le trecento novelle*, ed. by Michelangelo Zaccarello (Florence: Galluzzo, 2014), pp. 260–63.
17. Anna Pegoretti, 'Early Reception until 1481', in *The Cambridge Companion to Dante's Commedia*, ed. by Zygmunt Barański and Simon Gilson (Cambridge: Cambridge University Press, 2018), pp. 245–58. See also Santa Casciani, 'Bernardino: Reader of Dante', in *Dante and the Franciscans* (Leiden: Brill, 2005), pp. 85–111, and Nick Havely, *Dante's British Public: Readers and Texts from the Fourteenth Century to the Present* (Oxford: Oxford University Press), pp. 8–29.
18. Francesco Guccini, 'Addio', in *Stagioni* (EMI Records, 2003). See also Havely's essay in the present volume (Chapter 9).
19. Carlo Dionisotti, *Geografia e storia della letteratura italiana* (Turin: Einaudi, 1967), p. 79. 'Dialect diversity is still so marked in Italy that it usually prevents intelligibility': Arturo Tosi, *Language and Society in a Changing Italy* (Clevedon: Multilingual Matters, 2001), p. 21; 'mutual intelligibility [is] generally impossible in Italy between people speaking dialects of two non-adjoining regions': Alberto Mioni and Anna Maria Arnuzzo-Lanszweert, 'Sociolinguistics in Italy', *International Journal of the Sociology of Language*, 21 (1979), 81–107. See also Paul Oskar Kristeller, 'The Origin and Development of the Language of Italian Prose', in *Studies in Renaissance Thought and Letters* (Rome: Edizioni di Storia e Letteratura, 1956), pp. 473–93; Adam Ledgeway, 'Understanding Dialect: Some Neapolitan Examples', in *Didattica della lingua italiana: testo e contesto*, ed. by Adam Ledgeway and A. L. Lepschy (Perugia: Guerra, 2008), pp. 99–111; Marco Tamburelli, 'Uncovering the "Hidden" Multilingualism of Europe: An Italian Case Study', *Journal of Multilingual and Multicultural Development*, 35 (2014), 252–70.
20. See Luca Serianni, *Viaggiatori, musicisti, poeti: saggi di storia della lingua italiana* (Milan: Garzanti, 2002), pp. 56–57.
21. See Maiden, 'The Definition of Multilingualism'; Nigel Vincent, 'Languages in Contact in Medieval Italy', in *Rethinking Languages in Contact: The Case of Italian*, ed. by A. L. Lepschy and Arturo Tosi (Oxford: Legenda, 2006), pp. 12–27, and 'Language, Geography and History in Medieval Italy', in *Ciò che potea la lingua nostra: Lectures and Essays in Memory of Clara Florio Cooper*, ed. by Vilma De Gasperin, special supplement to *The Italianist*, 30 (2010), 44–60; Alvise Andreose and Lorenzo Renzi, 'Dai volgari ai dialetti. Schizzo di storia linguistica dell'Italia medievale', *Laboratorio sulle varietà romanze antiche*, 4.1 (2011), 59–77; and the already mentioned chapter by Tavoni, 'Linguistic Italy'.
22. See Wright, 'Early Medieval Pan-Romance Comprehension', and Vincent, 'Language, Geography and History'.
23. Dante Alighieri, *Opere*, ed. by Marco Santagata, 2 vols (Milan: Mondadori, 2011–14), II, 144.

24. Ibid., II, 126–38.
25. Giovanni Boccaccio, *Tutte le opere*, ed. by Vittore Branca, 10 vols (Milan: Mondadori, 1964–98), III, 486 (my emphasis).
26. Boccaccio, *Tutte le opere*, III, 486.
27. See *Le traduzioni italiane della Bibbia nel Medioevo: catalogo dei manoscritti (secoli XIII–XV)*, ed. by Lino Leonardi, Caterina Menichetti and Sara Natale (Florence: Galluzzo, 2018), pp. 49–51.
28. Florence, Biblioteca Medicea Laurenziana, MS Palatino 3, fol. 1^r.
29. Antonio Da Tempo, *Summa artis rithmici vulgaris dictaminis*, ed. by Richard Andrews (Bologna: Commissione per i testi di lingua, 1977), p. 99.
30. See Teresa Poggi Salani, 'La Toscana', in *L'italiano nelle regioni. Lingua nazionale e identità regionali*, ed. by Fancesco Bruni (Turin: Utet, 1992), pp. 402–61 (p. 416).
31. In *Lettere di mercanti a Pignol Zucchello, 1336–1350*, ed. by Raimondo Morozzo della Rocca (Venice: Comitato per la pubblicazione delle fonti relative alla storia di Venezia, 1957), pp. 45–46.
32. *Lettere di mercanti*, p. ix.
33. The other reason mentioned by Bartolomei, in order to justify his help to Pacino, is that it was potentially damaging to disclose information to third parties. This was indeed a genuine and frequently felt concern, in business transactions as well as in diplomatic communication (cf. e.g. Francesco Novello da Carrara's letter to Uguccione dei Contrari of June 1402, in Andreose and Renzi, 'Dai volgari ai dialetti', p. 61).
34. Lexical barriers to communication between Tuscany and Venice also emerge from a letter of Giovanni Dominici of 28 January 1401 (see his *Lettere spirituali*, ed. by M. T. Casella and Giovanni Pozzi (Fribourg: Edizioni universitarie, 1969), p. 148).
35. *Costituzioni della patria del Friuli nel volgarizzamento di Pietro Capretto del 1484 e nell'edizione latina del 1565*, ed. by Anna Gobessi and Ermanno Orlando (Rome: Viella, 1998), p. 104.
36. See Lorenzo Tomasin, 'Sulla percezione medievale dello spazio linguistico romanzo', *Medioevo romanzo*, 39 (2015), 268–92.
37. See Federigo Melis, *Aspetti della vita economica medievale. Studi nell'Archivio Datini di Prato* (Siena: Monte dei Paschi, 1962), p. 26.
38. Cf. Armando Petrucci, *Writers and Readers in Medieval Italy*, ed. by C. M. Radding (New Haven: Yale University Press, 1995), esp. p. 198.
39. I have checked the originals at the Archivio di Stato di Venezia, Sant'Anna di Castello, busta 48, documents 19 and 64 respectively.
40. See Saverio Bellomo, *Dizionario dei commentatori danteschi* (Florence: Olschki, 2004), p. 21; Andrea Mazzucchi, 'Contributi dell'antica esegesi dantesca a un vocabolario storico del dialetto napoletano', in *Tra res e verba. Studi offerti ad Enrico Malato*, ed. by Bruno Itri (Padua: Bertoncello Artigrafiche, 2006), pp. 79–135; Spencer Pearce, 'Uses of Learning in the Dante Commentary of Iacomo della Lana', in *Interpreting Dante: Essays on the Traditions of Dante Commentary*, ed. by Paola Nasti and Claudia Rossignoli (Notre Dame: University of Notre Dame Press, 2013), pp. 53–83.
41. Quoted by Fabrizio Franceschini, *Tra secolare commento e storia della lingua: studi sulla Commedia e le antiche glosse* (Florence: Cesati, 2008), p. 162.
42. Guido da Pisa, *Expositiones et glose: declaratio super Comediam Dantis*, ed. by Michele Rinaldi, 2 vols (Rome: Salerno, 2013), II, 749.
43. Iacomo della Lana, *Commento alla Commedia*, ed. by Mirko Volpi, 4 vols (Rome: Salerno, 2009), I, 719.
44. Benvenuto da Imola, *Comentum Super Dantis Aldigherij Comoedia*, ed. by J. P. Lacaita, 5 vols (Florence: Barbèra, 1887), II, 241.
45. Guglielmo Maramauro, *Expositione sopra l'Inferno di Dante Alligieri*, ed. by P. G. Pisoni and Saverio Bellomo (Padua: Antenore, 1998), p. 490.
46. Franceschini, *Tra secolare commento e storia della lingua*, p. 168.
47. *Anonymous Latin Commentary on Dante's Commedia*, ed. by Vincenzo Cioffari (Spoleto: Centro italiano di studi sull'alto medioevo, 1989), pp. 138–40 ('spatula' in one of the manuscripts that have transmitted this commentary).

48. Guiniforte Barzizza, *Lo Inferno della Commedia di Dante Alighieri*, ed. by Giuseppe Zacheroni (Marseille: Mossy, 1838), p. 523.
49. I have checked this quantitative aspect in the DanteSearch database, <www.perunaenciclopediadantescadigitale.eu> [accessed 5 October 2019]. See also Riccardo Ambrosini and Franca Brambilla Ageno, 'Verbo', in *Enciclopedia dantesca: Appendice* (Rome: Treccani, 1978), pp. 215–332.
50. Vincent, 'Language, Geography and History', p. 57 and p. 46.
51. See Ledgeway, 'Understanding Dialect'.
52. Gerhard Rohlfs, *Grammatica storica della lingua italiana e dei suoi dialetti*, 3 vols (Turin: Einaudi, 1966–69), II, 286–92.
53. See e.g. 'se partiro' in Anonimo Romano, *Cronica: Vita di Cola di Rienzo*, ed. by Ettore Mazzali (Milan: Rizzoli, 1991), pp. 99 and 162. But in the variety of Verona, where we find infinitives such as *partiro* 'to leave' (see Nello Bertoletti, *Testi veronesi dell'età scaligera* (Padua: Esedra, 2005)), *partiro* 'they left' was potentially ambiguous, at least in isolation.
54. See Paola Manni and Lorenzo Tomasin, 'Storia linguistica interna: profilo dei volgari italiani', in *Manual of Italian Linguistics*, ed. by Sergio Lubello (Berlin: De Gruyter, 2016), pp. 31–61.
55. See <www.ovi.cnr.it> [accessed 5 September 2019].
56. Maramauro, *Expositione*, p. 279.
57. Ibid., p. 279.
58. Bruno Migliorini, *The Italian Language*, abridged, recast and revised by T. G. Griffiths (London: Faber, 1984), p. 59. See Bernardino da Siena, *Prediche volgari sul Campo di Siena (1427)*, ed. by Carlo Delcorno (Milan: Rusconi, 1989), p. 672: 'Quando io vo predicando di terra in terra, quando io giogno in uno paese, io m'ingegno di parlare sempre sicondo i vocaboli loro.'
59. Vincent, 'Languages in Contact in Medieval Italy', p. 20.
60. See Frans Hinskens, Peter Auer and Paul Kerswill, 'The Study of Dialect Convergence and Divergence: Conceptual and Methodological Considerations', in *Dialect Change: Convergence and Divergence in European Languages*, ed. by Peter Auer and others (Cambridge: Cambridge University Press, 2005), pp. 1–48; and Peter Auer, 'Mobility, Contact and Accommodation', in *The Routledge Companion to Sociolinguistics*, ed. by Carmen Llamas and others (London: Routledge, 2007), pp. 109–15.
61. See Uriel Weinreich, *Languages in Contact*, 2nd edn (New York: Linguistic Circle of New York, 1968), especially his notion of 'automatic conversion formula' (p. 2).
62. See *Receptive Multilingualism*, and Peter Trudgill, 'Comprehensibility', in *Dialects in Contact* (Oxford: Blackwell, 1986), pp. 21–23.
63. See Paola Manni, *La lingua di Dante* (Bologna: il Mulino, 2013), and Lorenzo Tomasin, 'Dante e l'idea di lingua italiana', in *Dante e la lingua italiana*, ed. by M. Tavoni (Ravenna: Longo, 2013), pp. 29–46, who also deal with the philological problems involved.
64. See Ignazio Baldelli, 'Citazioni dantesche in glosse cassinesi', in *Medioevo volgare da Montecassino all'Umbria* (Bari: Adriatica, 1971), pp. 179–81.
65. See Havely, *Dante's British Public*, p. 29 (cf. the OVI corpus for occurrences of *stilli* in texts from medieval Sicily).
66. See the recent studies by Joshua Brown, 'Language Variation in Fifteenth-Century Milan: Evidence of Koineization in the Letters (1397–1402) of the Milanese Merchant Giovanni da Pessano', *Italian Studies*, 68.1 (2013), 57–77, and *Early Evidence for Tuscanisation in the Letters of Milanese Merchants in the Datini Archive, 1396–1402* (Milan: Istituto Lombardo di Scienze e Lettere, 2017), and by Lorenzo Tomasin, 'Urban Multilingualism: The Languages of Non-Venetians in Venice during the Middle Ages', in *Mittelalterliche Stadtsprachen*, ed. by Maria Selig and Susanne Ehrich (Regensburg: Schnell und Steiner, 2016), pp. 63–76, and references therein.

CHAPTER 11

Notes on the Presence of Petrarch in the Dante Commentaries of Cristoforo Landino (1481) and Trifone Gabriele (1525–1527)

Simon Gilson

Comparisons between Dante and Petrarch have played an integral part in some of the most celebrated interventions in Italian literary criticism. One need only think of Ugo Foscolo's presentation of the 'conflict of opposite purposes' in his 'A Parallel between Dante and Petrarch', or of Gianfranco Contini's account of Petrarch's *monolinguismo* as opposed to Dante's *plurilinguismo*.[1] However, long before the nineteenth-century reinvigoration of Dante Studies and the burgeoning of new sets of Dante–Petrarch comparisons, the pursuit of parallels between the two poets had played a major role in the construction of their literary authority.

The history of such comparisons, from the 1370s to the early seventeenth century, offers a rich series of entry points by which to consider how Dante and Petrarch were interpreted, and to evaluate the broader critical and cultural dynamics of their reception. Of course, Petrarch himself had already developed — with great subtlety and agonistic charge — a concern, from the early 1350s, with 'comparing' himself to Dante in order to construct his own literary authority, and thereby to nuance, diminish, and even silence Dante's own.[2] From the 1370s onwards, however, the preoccupation with such comparisons begins to find space in commentaries on Dante, in biographies of the two poets, and, as we move into the later fifteenth and sixteenth century, in a swathe of other treatises, commentaries, works on poetics, and polemical writings. The most celebrated accounts include the remarks made by Dante commentators such as Benvenuto da Imola and Giovanni da Serravalle, by biographers such as Filippo Villani and Leonardo Bruni, and by authors who also functioned as what one might now call cultural operators, such as Angelo Poliziano, Lorenzo de' Medici and Lorenzo di Pico della Mirandola. Pico's own Latin letter to Lorenzo, with its teasingly polarized presentation — Dante's rough, harsh and untamed style but profound content is counterpoised to Petrarch's polished attractiveness but lack of profundity — offers perhaps the best-known earlier statement and one that continued to influence sixteenth-century writers.[3]

In the sixteenth century, Pietro Bembo's own critical remarks on Dante, in his *Prose della volgar lingua* (1525), cast the comparison into new and compelling forms. Bembo expressed his judgements on Dante's stylistic and grammatical deficiencies as part of discussions that almost invariably included mention of, or examples taken from, Petrarch. Moreover, when he formulates his famous strictures upon Dante, in Book II, Chapter 20, he does so within an extended comparison between the two poets.[4] After Bembo's intervention, almost all other sixteenth-century writings on the topic bear a degree of Bembist imprint, whether they endorse, oppose, nuance, or satirize his accounts. As Pier Francesco Giambullari was to put it in a related context in the 1550s, 'tutte le cose dette dagli altri sono scritte a la lanterna di esso Bembo'.[5] From the 1530s, then, a growing number and range of writings develop Dante–Petrarch comparisons of various kinds. By way of exemplification, one might signal in particular the following: (1) the responses produced by Florentines such as Giovan Battista Gelli, Giambullari himself, Carlo Lenzoni, Benedetto Varchi, Vincenzo Borghini and others; (2) the presentations put forward by non-Florentine academicians such as Bernardino Tomitano, Girolamo Muzio, and others, as well as those developed in academic literary quarrels; and (3) the parallels made by the so-called 'polygraphs', such as Lodovico Dolce, who were often also academicians and were active in editing and writing for the Venetian presses.[6]

Of course, each comparison needs to be studied with close attention to its precise critical context, its geographical setting and mode of cultural production, and its genre. We also need to interrogate the comparisons with due account taken of the close dialogue that is often developed with previous estimates. One lesser-known example that might help to illustrate the value of such an approach is found in Giovan Battista Giraldi Cinzio's *Discorsi intorno al comporre dei romanzi* (1554), his theoretical discussion of the romance or heroic poem that he composed in defence of Ariosto's *Orlando Furioso*. Here, Cinzio presents his playful comparison as part of a verbal account of a painting that presents Dante and Petrarch together in a luxuriant field as they assume quite different floricultural attitudes to their surroundings. The immediate context is a discussion of the extent to which licence may be taken when creating and using new words in contemporary romance. Cinzio signals the value of Petrarch's *Triumphi* as a model for creating acceptable neologisms, but at the same time he resolutely excludes the extreme 'licentiousness' of Dante:

> Di Dante non vi voglio parlare, perché o per vitio di quell'età o per essere egli di quella natura, fu tanto licentioso che passò in vizio la sua licenza. Laonde mi pare che molto giudiciosamente facesse quel dipintore, che volendo sotto bella imagine mostrare quel che valesse nello scrivere l'uno e l'altro di questi due poeti, gli finse amendue in un verde e fiorito prato che egli haveva dipinto sul colle d'Helicona, et diede in mano a Dante una falce, il quale (havendo la veste succinta alle ginocchia) la menava a cerco, tagliando ogni herba, ch'egli con la falce incontrava. Et gli dipinse di dietro il Petrarca, che vestito di veste senatoria giva scieglendo le nobili herbe, et i gentili fiori, et tutto fu per mostrarci la licenza dell'uno, et il giudicio, et la osseruatione dell'altro.[7]

Dante, scythe in hand, hacks through all he finds; Petrarch makes judicious, carefully calibrated choices from the grasses and flowers. Of course, the entire passage recalls Bembo's conceit in *Prose della volgar lingua*, Book II, chapter 20, where he compared Dante's poem to a vast field marred by tares and grasses. More significantly, though, Cinzio's comparison, with its use of terms such as 'giudicio', 'osservatione', and 'licenza', sends us back to the precise language used by Bembo in the *Prose* to describe the respective stylistic properties and (im-)proprieties of both Dantean and Petrarchan poetic language.[8] As this one example suggests, then, a study of the Dante–Petrarch comparisons helps to illuminate not only their critical reception, but also such matters as discussions on linguistic usage and poetic standards, the status and development of genres and genre theory, and literary disputes. Other parallels are valuable for how they inflect the relationship between the vernacular and Latin and issues raised by the *questione della lingua*. One could also extend the enquiry to other kinds of 'coupling' in a wide range of works, from encyclopaedias to grammatical writings. One might also want to include — as the example provided by Cinzio playfully suggests — the visual arts.[9]

Our aim here is more limited and circumscribed. In what follows, we will discuss some of the main findings that emerge from studying one small part of this rich body of material, by concentrating on the ways in which Dante commentators compare Dante and Petrarch and utilize quotations from Petrarch's vernacular poetry. The notes that follow are concerned primarily with two commentaries: the 1481 Florentine print edition and commentary by Cristoforo Landino; and the manuscript notes penned by pupils present at the oral lessons (*c.* 1525–27) of the Venetian patrician Trifone Gabriele. Before examining these commentators, let us first consider some relevant earlier background. The best starting-point for assessing the presence of Petrarch in Dante commentators before Landino and Trifone is a fundamental article published in 1996 by Luca Carlo Rossi.[10] Rossi studied the explicit references to Petrarch made by Dante commentators from the edition by Guglielmo Maramauro, who was active in Naples in the early years of the 1370s up to the Milanese edition prepared by Martino Paolo Nibia or Nidobeato printed in 1478. Rossi's study provides near-exhaustive documentation of the relevant passages, and offers us some excellent preliminary analysis. Three points emerge from his work that are noteworthy for our purposes. The first is the fact that — and this should not be surprising given what we know of the early reception of Petrarch's works both in Italy and outside — in Dante commentaries before Landino, Petrarch's authority as a Latin writer prevails quite decisively over any discussion of his vernacular poetry. Thus, for example, in the commentaries by both Boccaccio and Benvenuto, the quotations reproduced are almost invariably from Petrarch's Latin works. Second, as Rossi argues, commentators utilize Petrarch's authority in Latin letters in order to bolster their own cultural and intellectual credentials: once more, the examples of Boccaccio and Benvenuto, thoroughly documented by Rossi, pay eloquent testimony to this phenomenon. A third salient point is that we already find some precocious and important examples of full-scale comparisons between Dante and Petrarch in the exegetical tradition before Landino. In commenting on lines 34–46 of *Paradiso* 1, for example, Benvenuto da

Imola in the final redaction of his Latin commentary (*c.* 1378–80) underlines how the Dantean allusion to 'better voices' that may come after Dante-poet might be said to have come true with Petrarch. For Benvenuto, Petrarch is a poet whose rhetorical powers are greater than Dante's, even though the commentator takes care to stress that Dante is the superior poet:

> ut jam dictum est supra, con miglior voci, idest, facundiori sermone, quasi dicat: forte veniet alius poeta eloquentior me, qui magis movebit Apollinem; et dicit, forse, dubitative. Et hic nota quod poeta pro parte videtur dicere verum; nam tempore quo florebat Dantes novissimus poeta Petrarcha pullulabat, qui vere fuit copiosior in dicendo quam ipse. Sed certe quanto Petrarcha fuit maior orator Dante, tanto Dantes fuit maior poeta ipso Petrarcha, ut facile patet ex isto sacro poemate.[11]

> [As has already been said above, 'con miglior voci', that is, with more eloquent language, as if he were saying perhaps another poet will come who is more eloquent than I am and who will move still more Apollo; and he says, 'forse' in order to express this doubt. Note here that the poet in part seems to say the truth since in the time when Dante flourished a very recent poet — Petrarch — sprang forth who truly had greater rhetorical abundance than this one. But certainly, however much finer an orator Petrarch was than Dante by just as much was Dante a greater poet than Petrarch, as is easily seen in this sacred poem.]

Giovanni da Serravalle re-elaborates this passage, noting that it is a 'true prophecy' in his own later Latin commentary and translation prepared at the Council of Constance (*c.* 1416–17).[12] Later commentators, however, make no further reference to Petrarch when glossing these lines.[13]

Having set out some of the earlier background, let us now begin to examine more closely Cristoforo Landino's 1481 printed commentary, the *Comento sopra la Comedia*, that is, the most important and influential Renaissance commentary on Dante and one renowned for its philo-Florentine charge.[14] This is the first commentary to arrest, and indeed most decidedly reverse, the tendency found in the previous exegetical tradition of treating Petrarch almost exclusively as a Latin *auctoritas*. What Landino heralds throughout the commentary is instead Petrarch's authority as a vernacular poet (the parallels made by Benvenuto and Serravalle would still seem to celebrate Petrarch as a Latin poet). Not only does the reversal represent a major and highly strategic attempt to overturn the earlier commentary tradition, but, more significantly still, Landino probably targets an autochthonous Florentine tradition, one represented above all by the biographies of Filippo Villani and Leonardo Bruni, and which had stressed the excellence of Petrarch as a Latin poet and even signalled Dante's lesser abilities or deficiencies in that language.[15] In the extended prologue to his commentary, two passages in particular help us to appreciate the cultural and ideological factors that motivate Landino's comparisons. The first comes in the fourth chapter of the prologue ('Fiorentini eccellenti in eloquenzia'), where Landino asserts that eloquence has recently been brought back to life by Dante and Petrarch. Two Florentines, in fact, provide the chronological limits of this process of recovering poetry — Claudian, who is understood to be the first Florentine to assume the mantle of Latin poet, and then Petrarch himself. Significantly, however, Landino is explicit about Dante's priority in resurrecting poetry and his own patriotic motivations for not taking the laurel crown other than in Florence (Landino may well have in mind Dante's refusal of a Bolognese coronation in *Eclogue* 1. 42–44):

> l'ultimo poeta laureato, che in prezo rimanessi in lingua latina, fu el fiorentino Claudiano, et dipoi perché el primo che dopo la resurrexione della facultà poetica prendessi laurea corona fu el Petrarca, perché Danthe dinegò prendere tale honore se non lo prendessi nel baptisterio fiorentino. Fu adunque la nostra città l'ultima, nella quale si spegnessi tale facultà, et la prima nella quale si raccendessi [...].[16]

More important still is a passage in which Landino affirms Petrarch's vernacular eloquence in the eighth chapter of the prologue as part of the commentator's life of Dante. Here, when discussing Dante's works and the *Comedy* in particular, he addresses a paean to Dante's poetry. He stresses how Dante brought back to light rhetorical and poetic ornaments, and cultivated the elegance, compositional modes and dignity of the ancients. According to Landino, Dante had forged the Tuscan language almost without precedent by using his knowledge of Latin writers: he understood what to take from Latin oratory, and, by his own talent, he found new subject matter and adorned his poetry. The well-known passage offers us a remarkable statement of Landino's sense of the classicizing qualities of Dante's poetry, and of his own pro-Florentine cultural programme, in particular his desire to reinvigorate the Tuscan vernacular and assert its status as a language of learning and cultural sophistication. Having praised Dante as the foundational figure in the literary tradition, Landino turns his attention immediately to Petrarch, providing a judgement that is equally remarkable:

> lui decte principio, lui molto la riduxe inverso la perfectione [...] Lui primo dimostrò quanto fussi idoneo el fiorentino idioma, non solo ad exprimere ma ad amplificare, et exornare, tutte le chose che caggiono in disputatione. A Danthe successe Francesco Petrarcha. Che huomo, immortale Dio, et di quanta admiration degno!, el quale nelle sue canzone et sonetti, non dubiterò non solo agguagliarlo a' primi lyrici et elegiaci greci et latini poeti, ma a molti preporlo. E ne' versi lyrici per comune consenso di tutti supremo Pyndaro, el quale Oratio meritamente afferma essere inimitabile. [...] Considerate quanto spesso el Petrarca insurge, et come cygno si leva. Considerate quanto sia copioso di sententie, et quanto quelle in ogni parte quadrino. È acerbo nella invectiva et nel riprendere, et con quella vehementia che Alceo percuote e tyranni ne' suoi versi, lui persequita e vitii. È negli affecti amatori, hor lieto hor mesto, et in forma tutti gl'exprime, che nè o a Ovidio lo postpongo, nè a Propertio. Ma quello in che obtiene sopra tutti la palma, in ogni lasciva materia, benchè sia giocondissimo, nientedimeno observa lieta modestia, nè mai diviene obsceno; et nessuno de gl'eloquentissimi negherà trovare in lui, non solo expresse, ma dipincte molte chose, le quali innanzi giudicava essere impossibile dirle con alchuna elegantia in questa lingua.[17]

The passage is notable for many reasons. Of course we know that Landino, probably in the late 1460s, had made the radical move of choosing to lecture *not* on a classical author but on the vernacular poetry of Petrarch from his chair as Professor of Poetry and Eloquence at the Florentine *Studio*. The judgement in his later Dante commentary can be linked in part with views expressed earlier there, but new elements are added, such as the parallel with Pindar (for Horace the Greek poet was in part inimitable), the attention paid to Petrarch's use of *sententiae* and invectives, and the absence of any lascivious or obscene content. Landino may well be entering into dialogue and polemic here with early Petrarch commentaries such as that of Francesco Filelfo (*c.* 1440s; *editio princeps* Bologna 1476–77), which had emphasized the amorous dimension of Petrarch's lyric production.[18] As Roberto Cardini has indicated, moreover, Landino's judgement had a significant afterlife and traces of it can be found in the later Petrarch commentaries by Giovanni Andrea Gesualdo (1533), Bernardino Daniello (1541, 1549), and others.[19]

If we now examine Landino's use of Petrarch in the *chiosa* or glosses provided to Dante's poem, the first thing to note is that he pays unprecedented attention to his vernacular poetry. Landino mentions Petrarch by name some sixty-seven times, and provides over fifty quotations from his vernacular poetry. With only one exception, he takes all these citations from the vernacular works. That exception — a reference to Petrarch's *De remediis* in the gloss on *Purgatorio* 12. 25–26 (ed. Procaccioli, III, 1231) — is in fact entirely derivative: Landino transcribed it without attribution from Benvenuto's own Dante commentary *ad locum*.[20] Landino gives fifty-six quotations in all, and these are taken from both the *Rerum vulgarium fragmenta* (*Rvf*) and the *Triumphi*. Once more, this is not the place for a detailed study, which would need to document the references fully, analysing the quotations and variants in relation to known manuscript or print traditions and to the emerging commentary tradition, and assessing fully the ways in which Landino adapts them to various ends. What we offer here are some preliminary remarks regarding the main types of reuse that Landino makes of Petrarch's vernacular poetry in his quotations.

A first broad category is made up of quotations that Landino uses in order to illustrate both the historical and the mythological figures mentioned by Dante. Thus, for example, we find a quotation from *Triumphus Amoris/Cupidinis*, I. 138 ('et funne el mondo sobtsopra volto') in the *chiosa* that he provides for Helen of Troy in *Inferno* 5. 64–66 (ed. Procaccioli, I, 456). Other such examples, again derived from the *Triumphi*, include: another short quotation ('Alexandro ch'al mondo brigha diè': *Triumphus Famae*, I, 160) at the opening of a long historical note on *Inferno* 12. 106–08 (ed. Procaccioli, II, 632), discussing Alexander the Great; and the full tercet quoted from *Triumphus Famae* Ia. 148–50 on Marcus Crassus when discussing this figure at *Purgatorio* 20. 116 (ed. Procaccioli, III, 1359). Landino also uses the *Rerum vulgarium fragmenta* when glossing historical and mythological figures. For example, he quotes the opening two lines of *Rvf*, CIII, 1–2 ('vinse Hanibal ma non seppe usar poi Ben la victoriosa sua ventura') when discussing the 'lunga guerra', that is, the Second Punic War in which Hannibal defeated the Romans at Cannae in Apulia, a battle to which Dante alludes in *Inferno* 28. 10 (ed. Procaccioli, II, 923).

A second category is made up of parallel passages from Petrarch's poetry that are used as part of rhetorical or linguistic glosses. Landino's *chiosa* is steeped in such passages, and he uses Petrarch to clarify Dante's lexical choices, as is the case with his explanations of words such as 'schermo', 'orgoglio' (*Inf.* 6. 20; 8. 46), or the assistance he provides for his readers regarding locutions such as 'seggendo in piuma' (*Inf.* 24. 47) for which Landino sends his readers to *Rvf*, VII, 1: 'La gola, el sonno e l'otiose piume'.

A third grouping of quotations concerns those select passages in which Landino either comments upon features of Petrarch's poetry, or else offers judgements relating to it. A representative example here is the revealing aside Landino makes when commenting on *Inferno* 4. 145–47, stating that Petrarch 'tracta in ogni triompho solamente una specie d'huomini' (ed. Procaccioli, I, 442). Perhaps the most significant passage is, however, the discussion related to Virgil-guide's admonition that Dante-character keep a tight rein on the eyes in the terrace of the lustful (*Purg.* 25. 118–20). This elicits from Landino a moralizing lesson, beginning with a two-line quotation from 'Occhi piangete' (*Rvf*, LXXXIV, 1–2) and then a further comment on the moral value of the *Triumphus Amoris*. What is especially notable in this passage is the way he refers to Petrarch stressing his elegiac qualities and how quotations from Propertius and Virgil are interwoven with Petrarch's own. The equivalence of Petrarch's vernacular *auctoritas* with classical authors is a hallmark of Landino's re-evaluation of the vernacular poet:

> Nè si può con altro senso che con l'occhio giudicare della belleza; di qui Propertio: 'si nescis oculi sunt in amore duces'. Et el nostro fiorentino elego et lyrico poeta maraviglosamente questa sententia dichiara in questo sonecto: 'Occhi piangete a ccompagnare el chore, Che per vostro fallire morte sostiene' [...] Adunque dobbiamo sempre rifrenar gl'occhi, se non voglamo cadere in questa perturbatione, la quale vince ogni spetie di furore. Et spesso conduce l'amante a volontaria morte. Facci ciechi nel iudicio, fanciugli nella cupidità. Et per questo el già decto Propertio: 'quicunque ille fuit puerum, qui pinxit amorem, Nonne putas miras hunc habuisse manus? Is primus sentit sine sensu vivere amantem, Et levibus curis magna perire bona'. Molto prolipso sarebbe riferire quanto dannose, quanto gravi, quanto pericolose, quanto pestifere sieno le perturbationi dell'amore. Et similmente quanto leggieri, quanto mobili, quanto varie, quanto puerili, quanto simili al furore, le quali tutte da' poeti elegi, et lyrici, greci et latini, sono state non solamente expresse, ma dipincte. Ma el nostro Petrarcha nel *Trionpho dell'amore* in forma in un cumulo tutte le raguna, che non si posson leggere sanza sommo stupore. Et Virgilio con degna exclamatione in brevissime parole abbracciò el tutto. Dove dixe: 'improbe amor quid non mortalia pectora cogis?'.[21]

One final category in which Landino quotes from Petrarch is concerned with illustrating either a particular interpretative solution or discussing a doctrinal point or scientific idea. Significantly, in such instances, as in the previous example, Landino will often cite Petrarch's vernacular text as an *auctoritas* alongside other authorizing passages from classical authors (above all Ovid, Persius, and Cicero). Perhaps the best-known passage here, one with bearing on a contemporary philosophical dispute, is that on the relative status of Plato or Aristotle (*Inf.* 4. 132), where after invoking Cicero and Augustine he quotes three lines from the *Triumphus fame*:

> Conciosia che *etiam* buona parte de' comentatori d'Aristotele difendono Platone dove Aristotele lo danna. Cicerone lo chiama Homero de' philosophi, et Augustino dice havere electo e platonici chome quegli che hanno inteso meglio la divinità. Et altrove scrive: 'taccia Aristotile, el quale contro a Platone è sempre fanciullo'. Et el nostro Petrarcha lo prepone dicendo: 'volsimi da man dextra et vidi Plato Che'n quella schiera andò più presso al segno Al quale aggiunge chi dal cielo è dato. Aristotele poi pien d'alto ingegno'.[22]

A passage such as this one could not stand in more marked contrast with the citational and mental habits of the earlier commentary tradition. One final point to note is the fact that Landino also shows a keen interest in the so-called 'Babylonese' sonnets where Petrarch fulminated against the corruption of the Avignonese Church. The sonnet 'Fiamma dal ciel su le tue treccie piova' (*Rvf*, CXXXVI) is, for example, mobilized twice in discussing clerical dissoluteness and corruption (*Inf.* 7. 46–48; 19. 115–17 *ad loc.*).

Let us now turn briefly to consider Trifone Gabriele's *Annotationi sopra Dante*, that is, the oral lessons on Dante's poem that he delivered before a select circle of his followers (*c.* 1525–27) in the small town of Bassano del Grappa in the Veneto. His pupils, most notably Bernardino Daniello, helped to diffuse these lessons, and Daniello's own posthumous Dante commentary (1568) draws extensively on his master's teachings, including his references to Petrarch.[23] Trifone's lessons show us how he read Dante to his entourage with constant attention to rhetorical and linguistic matters, by means of a pithy yet learned paraphrase that elucidates the poet's lexical choices, grammar and rhetoric. Even though a friend and close correspondent of Bembo and familiar with his *Prose*, Trifone developed a different overall assessment of Dante's style and of the relationship between Petrarch and Dante. His Dante lessons provide us with still more references to the vernacular Petrarch than Landino. Trifone provides some 170 notes on Petrarch with quotations taken from both the *Rerum vulgarium fragmenta* and the *Triumphi*. He uses these passages for moral, doctrinal and antiquarian purposes, but above all they are deployed to explain Dante's lexical, grammatical, and stylistic choices with a strong emphasis on the parallels and equivalence between the two poets. Once more, this is not the place for an extended analysis, and we offer instead a summary overview of Trifone's approach with select examples. Four main points are worth noting.

First, we should signal the notable independence from Landino. Trifone knew Landino's commentary extremely well, and in his lessons often commented upon its strengths and weaknesses. With regard to Petrarch, he makes very little use of Landino, preferring instead to develop his own parallelisms. On several occasions we can in fact detect a strong implicit criticism of the earlier linguistic comments provided by the Florentine commentator. A representative example is Trifone's treatment of the word 'pieta' in *Inferno* 1. 21. Landino had argued that the Florentine vernacular distinguished semantically between two different forms of compassion. However, Trifone takes his Florentine predecessor firmly to task for this view, and quotes Petrarch in support of his own argument:

> LA NOTTE dice, e di sopra disse *tant'era pien di sonno in su quel punto*. PIETA: invano s'affatica il Landino in voler trovar differentia tra *pièta* e *pietà*, e non si ricorda che il Petrarca disse anch'egli 'cercandomi, e o pièta', e niuna altra differentia è se non che muta l'accento per la rima. *Pièta*, adunque, compassione ch'io di me stesso presi.[24]

A second related point concerns the accuracy and sophistication of these linguistic and stylistic glosses. One pertinent example is provided by Trifone's comments on *Inferno* 4. 25–26, where once again we see the care shown to provide precise grammatical annotations with examples offered from both Petrarch and Boccaccio, and a clear sense of what is common usage, on the one hand, and stylistically differentiated by an individual writer, on the other. The passage also contains a further critical comment on Landino's own earlier linguistic commentary:

> NON AVEA PIANTO: *avea*, idest, era. È da notare che l'antica lingua toscana usava per tre modi *sum, es, est*: l'uno per il medesimo verbo *io son, tu sei, quel è*; il secondo con questa voce *enno*, la quale non approvò il Petrarca, ancor che Dante la portasse in questa sua opera, come di sotto vedremo, cap. V, *enno dannati*. Usavano poi il verbo *ho, hai, ha* in vece di *son, sei, è*, come qui, e questa si prese il Petrarca, come ivi: 'Due fonti ha', e in molti altri luoghi, e il Boccaccio ancora più sovente. Ma è da notare che, quando questo verbo *ho* si piglia per il verbo *son*, o sia accompagnato con nome del numero del meno o con quelli del più, sempre esso si manderà fuori con la voce del n umero del meno, come l'exempio detto dal Petrarca e in questo del Boccaccio: 'molti v'ebbe di quegli', etc. MA CHE DI SOSPIRI: *ma che* tanto vale quanto 'se non', e se avesse il Landino detto che non solo lombardo ma bergamasco modo stato fusse, non arebbe detto male: è invero bassissimo.[25]

A third point relates to the ways in which Trifone responds to passages where Bembo had issued harsh judgements on Dante's language and style, and stakes out his independence from the *Prose*. In the *Annotationi*, the five main examples of Dantean grammatical licence which Bembo openly criticizes in Book III of the *Prose* are either passed over with little fuss, or else receive straightforward lexical explanations, often with the aid of supporting parallels in Petrarch.[26] One representative example is the gloss that deals with a passage (*Inf.* 32. 105) in which Dante had used 'lui' as the subject pronoun after a gerund, a usage roundly condemned by Bembo in the *Prose* (III, 48). Trifone by contrast notes the usage and offers an illustrative passage taken from Petrarch:

> LATRANDO LUI: ecco che si mette col caso obliguo il gerundio; il Petrarca: 'lasciando lei che come un' etc.[27]

Trifone does express some occasional reservations about Dante's harshness, and at least twice asserts that Petrarch had adopted a better expression or solution.[28] The best example is probably his account of the Latinism 'corollario' found at *Purgatorio* 28. 136, where he notes that:

> Il giudicio gentil del nostro Petrarca, accadendogli dire 'corellario', per fuggir questa voce, che è troppo rozza e forse non degna da elimato poema, l'espresse per circumlocutione in questi versi, posti nel fin del capitolo II di Morte: 'Più ti vo dir per non lasciarti senza' etc.[29]

Yet with an even-handedness quite alien to Bembo, Trifone also notes how Petrarch should himself be excused at times for some excesses, on account of the fact that Dante had used a similar word or locution (*Purg.* 30. 108; *Par.* 17. 27 *ad loc.*). More commonly, however, the many parallels Trifone offers to passages in Petrarch's vernacular poetry make it clear that Dante's linguistic usage and style is to be understood as entirely consistent with Petrarch's ('così l'usò il Petrarcha', i.e. 'Petrarch used it in this way': *Purg.* 19. 140 *ad loc.*).

Our fourth and final point is also original to Trifone. It concerns his awareness in his brief but critically alert note on *Paradiso* 33. 1 that imitative threads connect Petrarch's poetry to the *Comedy*:

> VERGINE, MADRE, FIGLIA etc., perchè dice la Scriptura: 'Genuisti eum qui te fecit in aeternum':[30] è bellissima e artificiosissima oratione questa, e quinci il Petrarca trasse molte cose della canzone sua alla Vergine.[31]

As we have seen, then, our two Renaissance Dante commentators provide us with a rich field of reference to, and quotation from, Petrarch, both before and after Bembo's judgements in the *Prose*. Of course, any future enquiry would need to extend these notes not only to consider more fully the relevant passages in Landino and Trifone, but also to study other commentators, lecturers, and writers on Dante in the sixteenth and seventeenth centuries.[32] Notwithstanding their very different overall aims and exegetical strategies, Landino and Trifone both illustrate how Dante commentary had begun to engage richly and extensively with Petrarch's vernacular poetry as ways of discussing Dante's classical and mythological references, his science and doctrine, and his linguistic, grammatical and lexical habits. In their differing ways, both commentators display a keenly felt concern to illustrate that there is a fundamental concord between Dante's language and Petrarch's own; and, again in differing ways, they are both preoccupied with asserting Dante's authority as a vernacular poet. For Landino, this is also a question of asserting Petrarch's authority as a vernacular poet. For Trifone, of course, the vernacular poet Petrarch needs no valorization, and his attention turns instead to ensuring that Dante's own authority will continue to be recognized.

Notes to Chapter 11

1. Ugo Foscolo, *Essays on Petrarch* (London: Murray, 1823), pp. 163–208 (quotation at p. 127); Gianfranco Contini, 'Preliminari sulla lingua del Petrarca' (1951), in his *Varianti e altra linguistica* (Turin: Einaudi, 1970), pp. 169–92.
2. See Paola Vecchi Galli, 'Dante e Petrarca: scrivere il padre', *Studi e problemi di critica testuale*, 79 (2009), 57–82; Simon Gilson, *Dante and Renaissance Florence* (Cambridge: Cambridge University Press, 2005), pp. 32–40; *Petrarch and Dante: Anti-Dantism, Metaphysics, Tradition*, ed. by Zygmunt G. Barański and Theodore J. Cachey, Jnr. (Notre Dame, IN: University of Notre Dame Press, 2009).
3. Pico della Mirandola's Latin epistle (15 July 1486), addressed to Lorenzo de' Medici; see Pico della Mirandola, 'Ioannes Picus Mirandula Laurentio Medico s.p.d.' [Epistle to Lorenzo de' Medici, 15 July 1484], ed. by Francesco Bausi, 'Giovanni Pico della Mirandola a Lorenzo de' Medici: testo, traduzione e commento', *Interpres*, 17 (1998), 7–57 (pp. 26–27). For the other comparisons mentioned here, see Filippo Villani, *De origine civitatis Florentie et de eiusdem famosis*

civibus, ed. by Giuliano Tanturli (Padua: Antenore, 1997), pp. 73–74; Leonardo Bruni, *Vita di Dante*, in *Opere letterarie e politiche di Leonardo Bruni*, ed. by Paolo Viti (Turin: UTET, 1996), pp. 550–51; Poliziano, *Epistola dedicatoria* to the *Raccolta Aragonese*, in *Prosatori latini del Quattrocento*, ed. by Eugenio Garin (Milan and Naples: Ricciardi, 1952), pp. 985–90 (p. 989); Lorenzo de' Medici, *Comento de' miei sonetti*, in *Tutte le opere*, ed. by Paolo Orvieto, I, 367–68.

4. For discussion, see Simon Gilson, *Reading Dante in Renaissance Italy: Florence, Venice and the 'Divine Poet'* (Cambridge: Cambridge University Press, 2018), esp. pp. 46–54.
5. Pierfrancesco Giambullari, *In difesa della lingua fiorentina, et di Dante. Con le regole da far bella et numerosa la prosa* (Florence: Torrentino, 1556), p. 45.
6. For these (select) examples, see: (1) Giovan Battista Gelli, *Letture edite e inedite sopra la Commedia di Dante*, ed. by Carlo Negroni, 2 vols (Florence: Bocca, 1887), I, 17; Giambullari, *In difesa*, pp. 115–17, 202; Benedetto Varchi, *L'Hercolano, dialogo di Messer Benedetto Varchi, nel qual si ragiona generalmente delle lingue, & in particolare della toscana, e della fiorentina/composto da lui sulla occasione della disputa occorsa tra 'l Commendator Caro, e M. Lodovico Castelvetro*, ed. by Antonio Sorella, 2 vols (Pescara: Libreria dell'Università, 1995), II, 845–46; Vincenzio Borghini, *Scritti su Dante*, ed. by Giuseppe Chiecchi (Padua and Rome: Antenore, 2009), pp. 61–62, 75; (2) Bernardino Tomitano, *Ragionamenti della lingua Toscana dove si parla del perfetto Oratore, et poeta volgari: dell'eccellente Medico et Philosopho Bernardin Tomitano* (Venice: Giovanni de Farri & Frat., 1545), lib. I, pp. 62–63, 232; Girolamo Muzio, *Battaglie [. . .] per difesa dell'italica lingua* (Venice: Pietro Dusinelli, 1582), fol. 80v; (3) Lodovico Dolce, *Dialogo della institution delle donne secondo li tre stati, che cadono nella vita humana* (Venice: Gabriel Giolito de' Ferrara, 1545), fol. 19r; *Dialogo della pittura [. . .] intitolato l'Aretino [. . .]* (Venice: Gabriel Giolito de' Ferrara, 1557), fol. 48v.
7. Giovan Battista Giraldi Cinzio, *Discorsi intorno al comporre de' romanzi* (Venice: Giolito, 1554), pp. 133–34.
8. For 'licenza' as applied to Dante, see Bembo, *Prose della volgar lingua*, III, 44, 50, 255, 263; and on Petrarch's 'osservatione', see *Prose della volgar lingua*, III, 48, ed. by Carlo Dionisotti (Turin: UTET, 1960), p. 260–61: 'fu osservantissimo di tutte non solamente le regole, ma ancora le leggiadrie della lingua'.
9. Some well-known examples of double portraits include those in the panel painting (*c.* 1430) by Giovanni da Ponte now at the Fogg Art Museum in Cambridge, Massachusetts, and on the beautiful *intarsio* doors to the Sala Gigli in Florence's Palazzo Vecchio (*c.* 1470s).
10. Luca Carlo Rossi, 'Presenze di Petrarca in commenti danteschi fra Tre e Quattrocento', *Aevum* 70 (1996), 441–76. See now Priolo's important study of Petrarchan references in Bernardino Daniello's 1568 *Esposizione* (cited in n. 32).
11. Benvenuto da Imola, *Comentum super Dantis Aldigherij Comoediam*, ed. by J. F. Laicaita, 5 vols (Florence, Barbèra, 1887), IV, 309.
12. Giovanni da Serravalle, *Translatio et comentum totius libri Dantis Aldighieri*, ed. by Marcellino Civezza and Teofilo Domenichelli (Prato: Giachetti, 1891), p. 824: 'Quasi dicat: Ego deficiam morte, et alius veniet post me, qui erit dignus coronari ramo tuo. Vere hec fuit vera prophetia, quia post hoc, idest post completum librum istum, satis cito mortuus est auctor, quem subito secutus est dominus Franciscus Petrarcha, qui fuit eloquentior Dante; sed Dantes erat sapientior eo. Dante non laureato, morte prevento, ipse dominus Franciscus fuit florens poeta et laureatus.' [As though he said: I will fail to do so on account of death and another one will come after me who will be worthy of being crowned with your branches. This was indeed a true prophecy for after this, that is, after this book was finished, quite soon after the author died there immediately followed lord Francis Petrarch who was more eloquent than Dante; however, Dante was more learned than him. Dante was prevented from being laureated by death and this lord Francis was a blossoming poet and laureate.]
13. The only comparable later passage known to me is found in the 1544 print Dante commentary by Alessandro Vellutello in discussing Dante's allusion, in *Purgatorio* 11. 97–99, to the birth of a person who might chase the two Guidos (Cavalcanti and Guinizelli) from the nest of poetic mastery, Vellutello understands the reference as prophetic of Petrarch's future poetic pre-eminence; see *La 'Comedia' di Dante Aligieri con la nova esposizione*, ed. by Donato Pirovano, 3 vols (Rome: Salerno, 2006), II, 917: 'Chi l'uno e l'altro caccerà del primo luogo, intendendo,

secondo alcuni, di se stesso. Ma chi sa, se forse mosso da profetico spirito, come talhor suol avenire, pronosticasse del Pet. che già era nato, quando egli scrisse queste cose.' For a further comparison between the 'Aristotelian' Dante and the 'Platonic' Petrarch, see also Vellutello, 'Vita e costumi', in *La 'Comedia'*, ed. Pirovano, I, 139.
14. The only previous treatment of the Petrarch passages is the valuable discussion and documentation found in *Scritti critici e teorici*, ed. by Roberto Cardini, 2 vols (Rome: Bulzoni, 1974), II, 190–203, who notes that Landino represents (p. 190) 'una data negli studi sul Petrarca', and signals the extensive presence of quotations for 'l'illustrazione linguistico-tematica del poema' and 'l'analisi di interi settori e nodi strutturali di esso (il canto di Paolo e Francesca e Beatrice)' (p. 192), as well as for 'l'illustrazione storico-mitologica' (pp. 194–96), and for offering 'conferme tematiche e contenutische' (pp. 193–94).
15. Bruni, *Vita di Dante*, pp. 46–49; Villani, *De origine*, p. 73.
16. Cristoforo Landino, *Comento sopra la Comedia*, ed. by Paolo Procaccioli, 4 vols (Rome: Salerno, 2001), I, 236. For essential bibliography on Landino, see the indications provided in Procaccioli's critical edition and now the essays in *Per Cristoforo Landino lettore di Dante: contesto umanistico, storia tipografica e fortuna del 'Comento sopra la Comedia'. Atti del Convegno internazionale, Firenze, 7–8 novembre 2014*, ed. by Paolo Procaccioli and Lorenz Böninger (Florence: Società dantesca italiana, 2017).
17. Landino, *Comento*, ed. Procaccioli, I, 252–53.
18. See Carlo Dionisotti, 'Fortuna del Petrarca nel Quattrocento', *Italian medioevale e umanistica*, 17 (1974), 61–113 (p. 69).
19. On this indebtedness, see the preliminary remarks in Cardini, *Scritti*, pp. 190–92 (also noting the influence on Beccadelli and Varchi).
20. Benvenuto, *Comentum*, III, 326 (with reference to *De remediis* 1. 10 10).
21. Landino, *Comento*, ed. Procaccioli, II, 1420–21 (see *Triumphus Cupidinis* 3. 100–84).
22. Landino, *Comento*, ed. Procaccioli, I, 434–35.
23. On Trifone Gabriele the essential studies are: Saverio Bellomo, 'Lettura delle "Annotazioni nel Dante" di Trifon Gabriele', in *Tra commediografi e letterati. Rinascimento e Settecento veneziano: studi per Giorgio Padoan*, ed. by Tiziana Agostini and Emilio Lippi (Ravenna: Longo, 1997), pp. 61–81; Deborah Parker, *Commentary and ideology: Dante in the Renaissance* (Durham, NC and London: Duke University Press, 1993), pp. 89–108; Lino Pertile, 'Trifone Gabriele's Commentary on Dante and Bembo's *Prose della volgar lingua*', *Italian Studies*, 40 (1985), 17–30. All subsequent references are taken from *Annotationi nel Dante fatte con M. Trifone Gabriele in Bassano*, ed. by Lino Pertile (Bologna: Commissione per i testi di lingua, 1993).
24. Trifone, *Annotationi*, p. 5.
25. Trifone, *Annotationi*, p. 23.
26. The other four passages are: *Annotationi*, p. 25; cf. *Prose*, III, 44, ed. Dionisotti, p. 255; *Inf.* 14. 86, in *Annotationi*, p. 64; cf. *Prose*, III, 50, p. 263; *Purg.* 12. 13; cf. *Prose*, III, 50, p. 263: 'troppa licenza'.
27. Trifone, *Annotationi*, p. 107.
28. Trifone, *Annotationi*, pp. 76, 106, 238.
29. Trifone, *Annotationi*, p. 227.
30. 'You brought forth him who made you and remain forever'.
31. Trifone, *Annotationi*, p. 360.
32. One notable recent study in the field concerns Bernardino Daniello and his Petrarchan references, see Giorgio Calogero Priolo, 'Petrarca in chiosa alla *Commedia*: il caso del Dante con l'*Esposizione* di Bernardino Daniello', *Rivista di letteratura italiana*, 36.3 (2018), 21–36. Future work might also include the presence of Dante in Petrarch commentary: the phenomenon would appear to be less extensive than the presence of Petrarch in Dante commentary, though one notable exception here is Lodovico Castelvetro's *Le rime del Petrarca brevemente sposte per Lodovico Castelvetro* (Basel: Pietro de Sedabonis, 1582) where Dante is mentioned more than 250 times.

CHAPTER 12

Dante and Islam, Islam and Dante

Valerio Cappozzo

Now listen to the words of the Lord: Should there be a prophet among you, in visions will I reveal myself to him, in dreams will I speak to him. (Numbers 12. 6)

Praised be He who called upon His servant to travel by night from the sacred temple to the far-off temple whose precinct We have blessed, in order to show him Our signs. Indeed, He is the Hearing, the Seeing. (Quran 17. 1)

After one hundred years, the debate on Dante and Islam has reached a point where one aspect that appears well defined is the argument itself. It is not yet evident which aspects of the *Kitāb al-Miʿrāj* (*The Book of Muhammad's Ladder*) Dante may have borrowed, but we now have a better understanding of the different positions adopted by scholars on that matter. Some are convinced the Italian author was influenced by the Muslim holy text; others, however, reject this possibility categorically. On this topic the bibliography is dense, and assessing today the *pro et contra* we still are where the debate started a century ago: was Dante inspired by the Islamic Prophet, or not? The question itself has possibly limited our inquiry and has created tensions between two scholarly positions. Indeed, these connections are difficult to document rigorously; that is why, in the recent past, they have brought the debate to a dead end.[1]

New studies aim to explore Islamic influences in Dante's works in a larger context, considering different traditions of the ascension of the Prophet as well as Sufi mystical writings, while looking also at precise narrative elements within the *Comedy* itself, which may bring the investigation onto a more fruitful and constructive path.[2] It is thus necessary to address the transnational dialogue Italy had with the Arab world which may have influenced vernacular authors such as Dante and, for example, his successor Boccaccio. According to Menocal and Mallette, a renewed direction of inquiry looks more broadly into the literary impact that Andalusian courts had on European poetry starting with Occitan authors, later on the Sicilian School at the court of Frederick II of Hohenstaufen, and on Dante's works.[3] If we focus on the cultural context between the eleventh and fourteenth centuries, it is noticeable how the Arabic and Latin worlds together established the foundations of modernity in literature through the following essential factors: the improvement of rhyme; the description of the afterlife as a mystical and didactic experience; and the inclusion and combination within the literary text of different fields of knowledge, such as, for example, astronomy, medicine, alchemy and divination. There are indeed many constructive connections between East and West during the Middle Ages, especially at a cultural, philosophical and scientific level, and it is worth outlining briefly the question discussed one hundred years ago by the Spanish Islamicist Miguel Asín Palacios.

Connections and Contentions: A Brief History of a Debate

At a time when historiography has participated in ideological opposition between two cultures by enhancing their contrast, it clearly becomes especially difficult to do the reverse: find connections. When it comes to analysing the influences of the Islamic world on Dante, several problems arise, particularly that of the availability of sources. The uncertainty of their identification does not allow us to proclaim any specific discovery and legitimizes caution and concern when evidence has been obtained through intuition and textual interpretation, rather than archival documentation. We may consider the concept of 'interdiscursivity', suggested by Maria Corti. According to the Italian scholar, certain aspects of culture become a shared heritage following interdiscursive interpenetration thanks to the circulations of those traditions, thus these connections appear surprisingly convincing.[4] It is with this aim that — decades before Corti — Asín Palacios proceeded in his ground-breaking study that opened up a century of debates.

The Spanish scholar found relevant commonalities between Islamic traditions of Muhammad's afterlife voyage and the *Divine Comedy*, especially regarding the general narrative structure, as well as between specific episodes that are almost identical. His revolutionary intuitive approach aimed to understand the inspiration behind the structural narrative of the *Comedy* by looking at the different traditions of Muhammad's ascensional voyage. Asín Palacios argued that Dante's inspiration came from the tale of the nocturnal flight of the prophet from Mecca to Jerusalem's Temple (the *isrâ*); his ascent to Paradise and descent to Hell (the *mi'râj*) and his journey back to the starting point, Mecca, where he recounted his mystical journey to those in his community. In Dante's journey, the Spanish Islamicist found several connections: the dream-vision condition in both; the presence of guides, Gabriel for Muhammad and Virgil in Dante; the ascent of an inaccessible mountain; the presence of fire on its slope, and the visualization of a funnel-shaped Hell in Dante. There are even more specific contacts that can be found in the tortures inflicted on the damned according to the law of retaliation (*contrappasso*), where they are tortured with a punishment appropriate to the vice they had in life. However, Asín Palacios did not have access to the text of *The Book of Muhammad's Ladder*, which was only discovered in 1949, independently, by Enrico Cerulli and by José Muñoz Sendino. The text was first translated into Castilian by the Jewish Abraham Alfaquín, then later translated by Bonaventura da Siena in Latin and old French at the Andalusian court of Alfonso X, around 1264. Brunetto Latini, one of Dante's most influential teachers, attended that very court as an ambassador in 1260. The 1949 discovery was therefore crucial for the subject, as was Maria Corti's hypothesis that Dante may have known the Islamic text through his mentor.[5] Corti claimed indeed that Brunetto Latini may have brought back to Florence news of the translation that Bonaventura da Siena was making in Toledo, thus allowing Dante to come into contact with the Islamic text. This discovery offered important material evidence and helped confirm Asín Palacios's intuitions.[6]

Cross-cultural studies, however, started even centuries before Asín Palacios's influential book, *La Escatología Musulmana en 'La Divina Comedia'*. The confluence of Arabic poetics with Franco-Spanish, and then Italian, was analysed as early as in the sixteenth century by Giovanni Maria Barbieri. The *Arte del rimare* (composed in 1572 but published by Girolamo Tiraboschi only in 1790) was written as an attempt to complete Dante's *De vulgari eloquentia* with the same aim of studying the roots of poetry. His chapter, 'Propagazion della Rima degli Arabi agli Spagnuoli e a' Provenzali',[7] focuses particularly on the connection between Arabic and Occitan poetry: 'né da' Greci, né da Latini antiqui né da' più moderni sia originato il modo delle Rime, ma dagli Arabi passando ad altre lingue e nazioni'.[8] As Menocal and Dainotto pointed out,[9] this inquiry was followed up closely by publications in the nineteenth century which looked at the Arabic origins of French and Italian courtly poetry, as a starting point for an analysis, first of the question of the Islamic sources, and secondly of the broader question of the origins of Italian literature that relates to the production of the *Comedy*. Works by Juan Andrés, *Dell'origine, progressi e stato attuale di ogni letteratura* (1785); by Esteban de Artega, *Dell'influenza degli Arabi sull'origine della poesia moderna in Europa* (1791); by Madame de Staël, *De la littérature considérée dans ses rapports avec les institutions sociales* (1812) and by Jean Leonard Simonde de Sismondi, *De la littérature du Midi de l'Europe* (1819), are considered in Italo Pizzi's *Storia della poesia persiana* (1884), where he states that between Arabic and Italian vernacular versification: 'sono molto evidenti certe somiglianze di soggetto, di forma e di concetto'.[10]

This is also when scholars started to trace oriental narrative elements in the *Comedy*, and connections with Indian and Persian literature.[11] Importantly, some publications reassessed the figure of the prophet Muhammad in other ways than through the lens of the 'theological hate' that was common up to that time.[12] In 1921, the eminent orientalist, Giuseppe Gabrieli summarized the question in his *Dante e l'Oriente*, while other scholars have investigated the similarities between the Muslim structure of the afterlife and the Italian medieval one, or more generally the oriental elements that can be found in Dante's writings.[13]

In the last century, debates on Dante and Islam have been intense in the West, and so were they on the other side, too. In Arab countries Dante was introduced at the end of nineteenth century and popularized since 1930 by Ṭāhā Fawzī and translated by ʿAbbūd Abī Rashīd and by Ḥasan ʿUthmān in prose, while the first translation in verse dates to 2002.[14] As we can easily imagine, Dante's placement of Muhammad and his cousin Alì in Hell (*Inferno* 28. 22–63) is controversial.[15] Arabic scholars have mostly called in question Asín Palacios's intertextual discourse; however, they acknowledge the circulation of oral Islamic literary traditions in Andalusian, French and Sicilian courts.[16]

Arabic poetry was born between the fifth and the sixth centuries CE at the Syrian and Mesopotamian borders, and with themes belonging to the nomadic and desert-based life of the Bedouins. The *qaṣīda*, a pre-Islamic poetic form, presents similar themes that will then be developed in European poetry: the melancholic remembering of a past meeting with the beloved woman, the attempt to break free from heartaches, the spiritual and physical path accomplished by the poet, the journey that brings the poet to maturity, and the discussion of morals. After the tenth century, the old genre of the *qaṣīda* was renovated by 'modernist' poets and becomes very popular in Arabic countries. It circulates in the West, through Spain, and gives way to the so-called *muwaššaḥ*, usually written in vernacular Arabic and Spanish Mozarabic, which reused the typical themes of Arabic poetry, with the addition of courtly life values. This poetic form also appears in Hebrew and in Spanish, and represents the evolution of Arabic poetic composition, which in troubadour versification finds its metrical precision, and in poems of the vernacular Italian has developed into the sonnet.[17]

The first 'school' of Italian poetry appears at the Norman court of the emperor Frederick II, who continued and expanded in Palermo the multicultural tradition started by his grandfather Roger II of Sicily. There, the themes of the Arabic-Spanish-French poetry develop greatly, by going beyond the schematism of the theme of the impossible, distant, and lost beloved. The Sicilian 'school' proposes a more elevated and spiritual conception of love from which Dante will take inspiration. Giacomo da Lentini, otherwise known as the inventor of the sonnet, introduces the element of the imaginative depiction of the woman: in his poetic composition, *Meravigliosa-mente*, he places the image of the beloved within. Instead of mourning the loss of the beloved, the poet 'depicts' her image in his heart. The depiction of the beloved within the poet's imagination brought the language to an unprecedented level of refinement that enabled the poet to go deeper into his own soul. The Florentine 'Dolce Stil Novo', led by Dante Alighieri with his *Vita Nova*, tells of falling in love through a vision, with a need — at the end — to find the right words to write about Beatrice and his transcendental journey to her: 'Appresso questo sonetto apparve a me una mirabile visione, ne la quale io vidi cose che mi fecero proporre di non dire più di questa benedetta infino a tanto che io potesse più degnamente trattare di lei' (42. 1).

Dream-books between East and West

One of the significant comparative elements between East and West is certainly the afterlife voyage, a motif which goes back to Homer, Ovid and Virgil, and which is foundational to the *miʿrâj* tradition as well as to Dante's work. Dante structures the entire *Comedy* as a vision, a specific condition in which every message that the character receives needs to be interpreted. Ancient literature offered important examples of afterlife voyages since Odysseus, who travels to the underworld to meet Tiresias and ask him about his destiny (*Odyssey*, 11. 90–137). Ovid describes the descent of Juno into hell to ask for the help of the furies (*Metamorphoses* 4, 432–85), and of Orpheus in an attempt to bring Eurydice back to life (10, 1–77). In the sixth book of the *Aeneid*, Virgil provided a description of the topography of 'Avernus' (*Aeneid* 6. 237–316), where Aeneas descended with the Sibyl, Apollo's prophetess, to meet his father Anchises. In these ancient texts, the underworld had prophetic possibilities, as provided by a meeting with an important person, a member of the family or a seer. This concept can be found in Cicero's *Somnium Scipionis* (*De re publica* 6, 15–19) and later inspired Dante's meeting with the crusader Cacciaguida in *Paradiso*, his great-great-grandfather who prophesies his exile (*Paradiso* 17. 31–99). The Bible, however, uses another way to 'see' the afterlife — or paradise — through the means of a mystical rapture: Saint Paul, in his biblical vision, provides no specific description of the 'third heaven', but says rather that it is impossible to find the words to describe what he saw: he 'was caught up into Paradise and heard ineffable things, which no one may utter' (II Corinthians 12.4).

Dante therefore develops the theme of the afterlife by visualizing and describing precisely its form and the different placements of the souls according to their levels of sinfulness or sainthood, adding new elements, either descriptive and moral. To this end, Dante uses a wide variety of sources. While it is still controversial to confirm his usage of Islamic sources for the structure of the *Inferno* and *Paradiso*, it has been established that Dante referred to Irish traditions of the afterlife, especially for the *Purgatorio*: the *Treatise on Saint Patrick's Purgatory*, the *Visio Tnugdali*, and *The Voyage of Saint Brendan*.[18] Indeed, medieval literature includes a number of texts that deal with travellers searching for the underworld, or more broadly consisting in fantastic travel reports. But Dante is unprecedented in the level of complexity and precision of his three ascending worlds and their structure. In order to express the 'mirabile visione', he draws upon the science of dream-interpretation, which endows his writing about a visionary journey with a prophetic character.

Dante followed the precepts of divinatory sciences and the categories of truthfulness and falsity established by Artemidorus Daldianus (second century CE). The diviner travelled through Greece, Asia Minor and Italy while collecting dream symbols for his encyclopaedia of dreams in five books.[19] This conceptualization is later commented upon by Macrobius and Calcidius and continued by the patristic and Neoplatonic traditions.[20] Arabic oneirocritical theories, circulated in the western world since the twelfth century, established a scientific framework for deciphering dreams. The dreamer should have command of different types of scientific knowledge to achieve the full interpretation of his or her own dreams, which were believed to come directly from God. Dream interpretation developed enormously under the influence of Arabic sciences such as medicine, in order to enhance knowledge about the physical conditions of the dreamer; astronomy, to localize the planets' influence over the dreamer; and alchemy, to connect earthly symbols with astrological ones.[21]

Oneiromancy, or the divinatory science related to dreams, develops alongside oneirocriticism, the evaluation of the validity and divinatory value of dreams. These sciences come together in a tradition of dream guides which drew upon Indian, Persian, Egyptian, Arabic, Greek, Byzantine and Latin dream theories.[22]

One of the most common and circulated dream-books is the *Somniale Danielis*, named after the biblical prophet. The *Somniale Danielis*, or *The Dream Book of Daniel the Prophet*, was the most popular of its kind in the Middle Ages. It consists of a list of dream symbols, arranged in alphabetical order and interpreted as portending something good or evil for a dreamer. The structural form of the *Somniale Danielis*, revealed in its manuscript sources, had its origins in early fourth-century CE Greek manuscripts and thrived in the Middle Ages mainly in Latin, Arabic and the European vernaculars.[23]

If we look closely into Dante's text, we find that dreaming occurs at three distinct moments in the *Purgatorio*. The symbols that appear to the pilgrim in his three dreams (*Purgatorio* 9. 13–33; 19. 1–33; 27. 94–114) — the eagle, the woman and the act of picking flowers as Leah does in the third dream — correspond to entries in the *Somniale Danielis*: 'Aghuglia sopra sé vedere honor significa'; 'Femmine vedere morte significa'; 'Fiori torre o cogliere il nimico guardarsi significa'. According to the dream-book, the vision of an eagle flying above your head means honour, something that Dante is pursuing in his ascent toward *Paradiso*. Dreaming about a woman means harm, damage, as Dante finds when he dreams of the stammering woman. Finally, dreaming of someone picking flowers means to beware of enemies, something that Dante well knows after the infernal and purgatorial experience, when he finally enters *Earthly Paradise*.[24]

Literary dreams helped to connect two cultures apparently opposite from one another: the first influenced by superstitions and popular beliefs shared by different people in time and places, and the second finding expression in the new poetry in vernacular Italian, exemplified by Dante's *Comedy*. Another example is in *Purgatorio* 19, where Dante refers to dream sciences and to geomancy, a further divinatory science of Arabic origins:

> Ne l'ora che non può 'l calor dïurno
> intepidar più 'l freddo de la luna,
> vinto da terra, e talor da Saturno
>   — quando i geomanti lor Maggior Fortuna
> veggiono in orïente, innanzi a l'alba,
> surger per via che poco le sta bruna — ,
>   mi venne in sogno una femmina balba,
> ne li occhi guercia, e sovra i piè distorta,
> con le man monche, e di colore scialba. (*Purgatorio* 19. 1–9)

In the above verses 'Maggior Fortuna', 'alba', 'via', may correspond to geomantic figures, whereas 'luna', 'Saturno' to the planets, and 'terra' to the natural elements and to their related qualities. In Arabic, geomancy — *'ilm al-raml* — means the science of the sand, and was introduced in the Latin world and Byzantium around the twelfth century. Like other divinatory practices, geomancy allows one to interrogate the past, understand the present and attempt to decipher the future. Far more widespread than astrology, geomancy used simple symbols and did not require any special instrument. It consisted in tracing dots haphazardly on the ground or on paper and finding their correspondence with the position of the planets and constellations. The presence of divinatory techniques within the Dantean text helps towards the understanding that these practices were well integrated in medieval literature without losing their scientific validity. If we consider the formation and diffusion of oneirocriticism, oneiromancy and geomantic treatises, it becomes clear that literary works, like the *Comedy*, use these prognostic practices in order to offer the reader a possible divinatory key to interpret the text.

In the above-cited passage, Dante offers specific astronomic conditions related to the meridian of Florence, through geomantic figures that allow us, according to Charmasson, to date the dream precisely to 12 April 1301.[25] It is perhaps worth noticing how common those practices were at the time; interestingly, Dante's son, Pietro Alighieri — also one of the first commentators on his father's work — proposed some interpretations for symbols that were then obscure. He offered an additional geomantic symbol, *Fortuna Minor*, to interpret the passage above, in which the traveller is about to have a dream.[26] In geomancy, this symbol is in opposition to *Fortuna Major*, which Dante uses in the text, and the association of the two symbols means danger during travel. Pietro Alighieri's interpretation of his father's poem in a divinatory key presupposes a familiarity with these practices. The danger to which Dante is exposed in his dream — and that Pietro has alluded to — was therefore anticipated by geomantic and astronomical symbols in the sky of the *Purgatorio*. They also coincide with what Dante saw in his dream, the *femmina balba* as a symbol of temptation, the same kind as we find in literature: Odysseus' Circe and Sirens; in the Bible, the adulterous woman in *Proverbs* 7; in Muhammad's ascension when his faith is tested by three attractive women calling the prophet away from his divine mission. The *Somniale Danielis* endorses this interpretation: 'seeing women means danger of death', confirming the presence of common cultural beliefs in this canto of the *Purgatorio*, as a way to ease the interpretation of the oneiric episode.

Conclusion: Considering Cultural Diplomacy

There are many ways to investigate the connections between Latin and Arabic cultures, by looking closely at Dante's writings or by analysing the cross-cultural exchanges like the circulation of dream sciences. However, in order to move research forward, the concept of cultural diplomacy needs to be considered, within the broader context of the history of crusades and of Spanish Andalusia, through the circulation of knowledge, political relationships and mutual understanding. If we consider the Arabic historians' evidence on the crusades, and look at the opposite point of view we may find documents that clarify the socio-cultural context. An example might be the case of the multicultural Norman courts in Palermo and Frederick II's in Apulia.[27] During the Sixth Crusade, Frederick travelled to Egypt and the court of the sultan al-Malik al-Kāmil, where both leaders reached a ten-year long peace treaty on 24 February 1229. Soon after, the historian Ibn Wāsil reports: 'al-Malik al-Kāmil and the emperor swore to observe the terms of the agreement and made a truce for a fixed term', ten years, five months and forty days.[28] The Muslim chronicler also relates the exchanges between the two rulers;

exchanges that went beyond political matters and touched on philosophy, geometry and mathematics:

> Many conversations and discussions took place between them, during which the emperor sent to al-Malik al-Kāmil queries on difficult philosophic, geometric and mathematical points, to test the men of learning at his court. The sultan passed the questions on to Sheikh 'Alam ad-Din Qaisar, a master of that art, and the rest to a group of scholars, who answered them all.[29]

It is well known that the religious, cultural, political and commercial conflicts between East and West shaped the thirteenth century. However, this type of dialogue also contributed to the circumstances that led to the *Comedy*. To be able to return to Dante it is necessary to leave Dante by looking at the historical periods before his work as well as the literature immediately after it, where aspects of science, culture and poetry of the Middle East continue to be integrated in the narrative structure of vernacular Italian literary works, as for example in Boccaccio's *Decameron*.

From both sides of the medieval world, it seems that interdiscursivity must remain a firm starting point for new inquiries about Dante beyond borders.[30]

Notes to Chapter 12

1. The debate began with the publication of Miguel Asín Palacios's *La Escatología Musulmana en 'La Divina Comedia'. Discurso leído en el acto de su recepción en la Real Academia Española por don Miguel Asín Palacios y contestación de don Julián Ribera Tarragó, el día 26 de enero de 1919* (Madrid: Impr. de E. Maestre, 1919); Miguel Asín Palacios, *Dante y el Islam* (Madrid: Voluntad, 1927). After the opposite reactions to his book, Asín Palacios added the 'Historia y critica de una polèmica' (Madrid and Granada: Imprenta de la Vda de E. Maestre, 1943) in his second edition to defend his work from criticism, which went well beyond academia into a more ideological level. On the development of the debate, see Ugo Monneret de Villard, *Lo studio dell'Islam in Europa nel XII e nel XIII secolo* (Vatican City: Biblioteca Apostolica Vaticana, 1944); Jacques Monfrin, 'Les sources arabes de la *Divine Comédie* et la traduction française du *Livre de l'ascension de Mahomet*', *Bibliothèque de l'École des Chartes*, 109.2 (1951), 277–90; Francesco Gabrieli, 'New Light on Dante and Islam', *Diogenes*, 2.6 (1954), 61–73; Enrico Cerulli, 'Dante e l'Islam', *Al-andalus: Revista de las escuelas de estudios árabes de Madrid y Granada*, 21.2 (1956), 229–53; Enrico Cerulli, *Nuove ricerche sul* Libro della Scala *e la conoscenza dell'Islam in Occidente* (Vatican City: Biblioteca Apostolica Vaticana, 1972); R. W. Southern, 'Dante and Islam', in *Relations between East and West in the Middle Ages*, ed. by Derek Baker (Edinburgh: Edinburgh University Press, 1973), pp. 133–45; Paul Cantor, 'The Uncanonical Dante: The Divine Comedy and Islamic Philosophy', *Philosophy and Literature*, 20 (1996), 138–53.
2. In the last decades scholars have analysed the Arabic texts upon which the *Kitab al-Mi'raj* was based, for example, the eleventh-century ascension narrative by Abu al-Hasan Bakri, or rediscovered sources of Dantescan inspiration in Sufi's writings, see Frederick S. Colby, *Narrating Muhammad's Night Journey: Tracing the Development of the Ibn 'Abbas Ascension Discourse* (Albany: State University of New York Press, 2008); Muhammad Abdul Haq, 'Significance of the 'Isra'-Mi'raj in Sufism', *Islamic Quarterly*, 34.1 (1990), 32–58. Studies that have recently investigated the question of Islamic influences in Dante's *Comedy* are: Andrea Celli, *Figure della relazione: il Medioevo in Asín Palacios e nell'arabismo spagnolo* (Rome: Carocci, 2005); Sabina Baccaro, 'Dante e l'Islam. La ripresa del dibattito storiografico sugli studi di Asín Palacios', *Doctor Virtualis*, 12 (2013), 13–33; *Dante and Islam*, ed. by Jan M. Ziolkowski (New York: Fordham University Press, 2015); *Sguardi su Dante da Oriente*, ed. by Carlo Saccone, special issue of *Quaderni di studi Indo-Mediterranei*, 9 (2016); Roberta Morosini, *Dante, il profeta e il Libro. La*

leggenda del toro dalla Commedia *a Filippino Lippi, tra sussurri di colomba ed echi di Bisanzio* (Rome: L'Erma di Bretschneider, 2018).
3. For new studies that aim to explore Islamic influences in Dante's works in a wider context, see María Rosa Menocal, *The Arabic Role in Medieval Literary History: A Forgotten Heritage* (Philadelphia: University of Pennsylvania Press, 2004); Karla Mallette, *The Kingdom of Sicily, 1100–1250: A Literary History* (Philadelphia and Oxford: University of Pennsylvania Press, 2005), and *European Modernity and the Arab Mediterranean: Toward a New Philology and a Counter-Orientalism* (Philadelphia and Oxford: University of Pennsylvania Press, 2010).
4. Maria Corti, 'La 'Commedia' di Dante e l'oltretomba islamico', *Belfagor*, 50 (1995), 301–14 (p. 301) [now in: Maria Corti, *Scritti su Cavalcanti e Dante* (Turin: Einaudi, 2003), 365–79]: 'Ci sono nella cultura processi di interdiscorsività per cui è impossibile rinvenire la fonte diretta di una notizia o di un dato in quanto ormai quella notizia o quel dato circolano nella cultura, sono patrimonio comune in seguito a una compenetrazione interdiscorsiva.' Other works by Maria Corti on the topic of Dante and Islam: 'La "favola" di Ulisse: invenzione dantesca?', in *Scritti su Cavalcanti e Dante*, 255–68; 'Dante e la cultura islamica', in *'Per correr miglior acque . . .': bilanci e prospettive degli studi danteschi alle soglie del nuovo millennio. Atti del Convegno di Verona-Ravenna, 25–29 ottobre 1999*, 2 vols (Rome: Salerno Editrice, 2001), I, 183–202.
5. Corti, *Scritti su Cavalcanti e Dante*, pp. 369–73.
6. Enrico Cerulli, *Il Libro della Scala e la questione delle fonti arabo-spagnole nella Divina Commedia* (Roma: Biblioteca Apostolica Vaticana, 1949); José Muñoz Sendino, *La Escala de Mahoma* (Madrid: Ministerio de Asuntos Exteriores, 1949). For a more recent edition of the text in the Latin and Old French, see *The Prophet of Islam in Old French: The Romance of Muhammad (1258) and 'The Book of Muhammad's Ladder (1264)*, trans. by Reginald Hyatte (Leiden: Brill, 1997).
7. Giovanni Maria Barbieri, *Dell'origine della poesia rimata* (1572), ed. by Girolamo Tiraboschi (Modena: Società tipografica, 1790), p. 43.
8. Giovanni Maria Barbieri, *Dell'origine*, p. 43.
9. Menocal, *The Arabic Role in Medieval Literary History*, pp. 71–90: 79–80; Roberto M. Dainotto, 'On the Arab Origin of Modern Europe: Giammaria Barbieri, Juan Andrés, and the Origin of Rhyme', *Comparative Literature*, 58 (2006), 271–92.
10. Italo Pizzi, *Storia della poesia persiana*, 2 vols (Turin: Unione Tipografico-editrice, 1894), p. 413. See also Menocal, *The Arabic Role in Medieval Literary History*, pp. 79–80; Dainotto, 'On the Arab Origin of Modern Europe'. Both approaches are summarized and discussed in Elisabetta Benigni, 'Dante and the Construction of a Mediterranean Literary Space: Revisiting a 20th Century Philological Debate in Southern Europe and in the Arab World', *Philological Encounters*, 2 (2017), 111–38; Juan Andrés, *Dell'origine, progressi e stato attuale d'ogni letteratura*, 8 vols (Parma: Stamperia Reale, 1785–1822), in particular: vol. I, cap. 11; vol. II, cap. 1; Esteban de Artega, *Della influenza degli arabi sull'origine della poesia moderna in Europa: dissertazione* (Roma: Nella Stamperia Pagliarini, 1791); Giammaria Barbieri, *Dell'origine della poesia rimata* (1572), ed. by Girolamo Tiraboschi (Modena: Società tipografica, 1790); Jean C. L. Simonde de Sismondi, *De la littérature du Midi de l'Europe*, 4 vols (Paris: Treuttel et Wurtz, 1813–19); Madame de Staël-Holstein, *De la littérature considérée dans ses rapports avec les institutions sociales* (Paris: Bibliothèque Charpentier, Eugène Fasquelle, 1800); Italo Pizzi, *Storia della poesia persiana*, 2 vols (Turin: Unione Tipografico-editrice, 1894). See also: Federico Diez, *Die Poesie der Troubadours* (Leipzig: Barih, 1883).
11. Antoine F. Ozanam, *Essai sur la philosophie de Dante* (Paris: Faculté des Lettres, 1838), pp. 197–204; Angelo De Gubernantis, 'Le type indien de Lucifer chez Dante', in Actes du Xe Congrès des Orientalistes: Dante e l'India, *Giornale della Società asiatica italiana*, 3 (1889), 3–19; Edgar Blochet, *Les sources orientales de la Divine Comédie* (Paris: Maisonneuve & Larose, 1901); Italo Pizzi, *Storia della poesia persiana*, 2 vols (Turin: Unione Tipografico-Editrice, 1894), II, 412–89. Modern studies on Dante's 'orientalism' can be found in: Brenda Deen Schildgen, *Dante and the Orient*, Illinois Medieval Studies (Urbana: University of Illinois, 2002); Andrea Celli, *Dante e l'Oriente. Le fonti islamiche nella storiografia novecentesca* (Rome: Carocci, 2013).
12. Alessandro D'Ancona, 'La leggenda di Maometto in Occidente', in *Studi di critica e storia letteraria*, 2nd edn, 2 vols (Bologna: N. Zanichelli, 1912), II, 165–308; Angelo De Fabrizio, 'Il 'Mirag' di

Maometto esposto da un frate salentino del secolo XV', *Giornale storico della letteratura italiana*, 49 (1907), 299–313.

13. Giuseppe Gabrieli, *Dante e l'Oriente* (Bologna: N. Zanichelli, 1921); Arturo Graf, *Miti, leggende e superstizioni del medioevo* (Turin: Giovanni Chiantore, 1925); René Guénon, *L'ésotérisme de Dante* (Paris: Ch. Bosse, 1925); Leonardo Olschki, 'Dante e l'Oriente', *Giornale Dantesco*, 39 (1936), 65–90.

14. Ṭāhā Fawzī, *Dāntī Alīğiyīrī. Dante Alighieri* (Cairo: Maṭbaʿat al-Iʿtimād, 1930). The first Arabic translations of the *Divine Comedy*, in prose, are: ʿAbbūd Abī Rashīd, *al-Riḥla al-Dāntīyya fī al-mamālik al-ilahiyya: al-Jaḥīm, al-Maṭhar, al-Naʿīm*, 3 vols (Tripoli: Plinio Maggi, 1930–33); Ḥasan ʿUthmān, *Kūmīdīyā Dāntī Alīghīrī* (Cairo: Dār al-Maʿārif, 1955–69). The first and recent Arabic translation in verse is: Kāẓim Jihād, *al-Kūmīdiyyā al-Ilahiyya* (Beirut: al-Muʾassasah al-ʿArabiyyah li-l-Dirasāt wa al-Nashr, 2002). On these translations and the Arab discussion on Asín Palacios' theories, see Benigni, 'Dante and the Construction of a Mediterranean Literary Space', pp. 128–35; Bartolomeo Pirone, 'Dante nell'editoria araba', in *Lectura Dantis 2002–2009. Omaggio a Vincenzo Placella per i suoi settanta anni*, ed. by Anna Cerbo, 4 vols (Naples: Università degli Studi di Napoli 'L'Orientale', 2011), I, 103–28.

15. For recent studies on the figure of Mohammed in the 28th canto of *Inferno*, see Heather Coffey, 'Encountering the Body of Muhammad: Intersections between *Miʿraj* Narratives, the Shaqq al-Sadr, and the *Divina Commedia* in the Age before Print (c. 1300–1500)', in *Constructing the Image of Muhammad in Europe*, ed. by Avinoam Shalem (Berlin and Boston: Walter de Gruyter, 2013) pp. 33–86; Andrea Celli, '"Cor per medium fidit": Il canto XXVIII dell'*Inferno* alla luce di alcune fonti arabo-spagnole', *Lettere italiane*, 2 (2013), 171–92; Andrea Moudarres, 'Beheading the Son: Muhammad and Bertran de Born in *Inferno* 28', *California Italian Studies*, 5.1 (2014), 550–65; Maria Esposito Frank, 'Dante's Muhammad: Parallels between Islam and Arianism', in *Dante and Islam*, ed. by Jan M. Ziolkowski, (New York: Fordham University Press, 2015), 159–77; M. Salem Elsheikh, 'Lectura (faziosa) dell'episodio di Muhammad', *Quaderni di filologia romanza*, 2 (2015), 263–99; Michelina di Cesare, 'From ʿAlī to Dante's Alì: a Western Medieval Understanding of Shīʿa', *Mediaevalia*, 19.2 (2016), 175–201; Roberta Morosini, 'Dante e Maometto: una lettura metaletteraria di *Inferno* XXVIII', *Bolletino dantesco*, 2 (2017), 6–32; Morosini, *Dante, il profeta e il Libro*, pp. 7–24, 165–255.

16. Arab discussion about Islamic influences on Dante's *Commedia* can be found in: Abdul Laṭīf aṭ-Ṭībāwī, *aṭ-Taṣawwuf al-Islāmī al-ʿArabī* (Cairo: Dār al-ʿAṣr li-l-Ṭibaʿa wa al-Nashr bi-Miṣr, 1928); Ḥasan ʿUthmān, 'Dante in Arabic', *Annual Reports of the Dante Society, with Accompanying Papers*, 73 (1955), 47–52. 'According to ʿĀʾisha ʿAbd al-Raḥmān, an Egyptian professor who devoted her efforts to the study of Abū ʿAlāʾ al-Maʿarrī's work, the first comparison between the *Commedia* and the *Risālat al-ghufrān* [*Epistle of Forgiveness*] dates back to 1886 and was published in the Egyptian journal *al-Muqtaṭaf*' (Benigni, 'Dante and the Construction of a Mediterranean Literary Space', p. 119), see Āʾisha ʿAbd al-Raḥmān, *al-Ghufrān min Abū ʿAlāʾ al-Maʿarrī* (Cairo: Dār al-Maʿārif, 1954), p. 312; Carlo A. Nallino, *Raccolta di scritti editi ed inediti* (Roma: Istituto per l'Oriente, 1940), p. 439.

17. On Arabic poetry in the medieval West, see Peter Dronke, *Medieval Latin and the Rise of European Love-Lyric* (Oxford: Clarendon Press, 1965); Rosa Trillo Clough, 'Gli studi intorno alle fonti islamiche in *Dante* e nelle poesie della scuola del Dolce Stil Nuovo', *Alighieri*, 9.2 (1968), 66–73; Samuel Miklos Stern, *Hispano-Arabic Strophic Poetry*, ed. by L. P. Harvey (Oxford: Clarendon Press, 1974); Flavio Catenazzi, *L'influsso dei provenzali sui temi e immagini della poesia siculo-toscana* (Brescia: Morcelliana, 1977); *Poeti arabi di Sicilia*, ed. by Francesca Maria Corrao (Milan: Mondadori 1988); James T. Monroe, '*Zajal* and *Muwashshaha*: Hispano-Arabic Poetry and the Romance Tradition', in *The Legacy of Muslim Spain*, ed. by Salma Khadra Jayyusi (Leiden and New York: E. J. Brill, 1992), pp. 398–419; Karla Mallette, 'Arabic and Italian Lyric in Medieval Sicily', in *The Future of the Middle Ages and the Renaissance. Problems, Trends, and Opportunities for Research*, ed. by Roger Dahood (Turnhout: Brepols, 1998), pp. 81–92; María Rosa Menocal, 'The Newest Discovery: the Muwashshahāt', in *The Arabic Role in Medieval Literary History*, pp. 91–113; Alexander E. Elinson, *Looking back at al-Andalus: The Poetics of Loss and Nostalgia in Medieval Arabic and Hebrew literature* (Leiden and Boston: Brill, 2009); J. A. Abu-Haidar, *Hispano-*

Arabic Literature and the Early Provençal Lyrics (London and New York: Routledge, 2013).
18. In-depth analysis of otherworldly journeys can be found in: *Visioni dell'aldilà in Occidente. Fonti modelli testi*, ed. by Maria Pia Ciccarese (Florence: Nardini, 1987); Eileen Gardiner, *Visions of Heaven and Hell before Dante* (New York: Italica Press, 1989); Eileen Gardiner, *Medieval Visions of Heaven and Hell: A Sourcebook* (New York and London, Routledge, 1993); Alison Morgan, *Dante and the Medieval Other World* (Cambridge: Cambridge University Press, 2007); Giuseppe Ledda, 'Dante e la tradizione delle visioni medievali', in *Letture classensi: le tre Corone. Modelli e antimodelli della Commedia*, ed. by Michelangelo Picone (Ravenna: Longo Editore, 2008), pp. 119–42.
19. Artemidorus Daldianus, *Artemidorus'* Oneirocritica: *Text, Translation, and Commentary*, ed. by Daniel E. Harris-McCoy (Oxford: Oxford University Press, 2012); Macrobius, *Commentary on the Dream of Scipio*, ed. by William Harris Stahl (New York: Columbia University Press, 1990); Calcidius, *On Plato's Timaeus*, ed. by John Magee (Cambridge, MA: Harvard University Press, 2016).
20. For an overview of dream interpretation in the Middle Ages, see Steven F. Kruger, *Dreaming in the Middle Ages* (Cambridge: Cambridge University Press, 1992).
21. For an overview of Islamic divination, see Yehia Gouda, *Dreams and their Meanings in the Old Arab Tradition* (New York: Vantage Press, 1991); Pierre Lory, *Le rêve et ses interprétations en Islam* (Paris: Albin Michel, 2003); Elizabeth Sirriyeh, *Dreams and Visions in the World of Islam: A History of Muslim Dreaming and Foreknowing* (London and New York: I. B. Tauris, 2015).
22. Two important examples are the *Liber thesauri occulti* by Pascalis Romanus, written in Latin in 1165 in Constantinople, and the pseudo-Achmet ibn Sīrīn's book, translated from Greek into Latin in 1176 by Leo Tuscus, also in Constantinople. Leo Tuscus's work assembled various traditions on dream interpretation in one volume, namely Indian, Persian and Egyptian. See Simone Collin-Roset, 'Le *Liber thesauri occulti* de Pascalis Romanus (un traité d'interprétation des songes du XIIe siècle', *Archives d'histoire doctrinale et littéraire du Moyen-âge*, 30 (1963), 111–98; Ambrogio Camozzi Pistoja, 'The Oneirocriticon of Achmet in the West: A Contribution towards an Edition of Leo Tuscus' Translation', *Studi medievali*, 55.2 (2014), 719–58. On the pseudo-Achmet's text and dream theory, see Steven M. Oberhelman, *The Oneirocriticon of Achmet: A Medieval Greek and Arabic Treatise on the Interpretation of Dreams* (Lubbock: Texas Tech University Press, 1991); Maria Mavroudi, *A Byzantine Book on Dream Interpretation: The Oneirocriticon of Achmet and its Arabic Sources* (Leiden and Boston: Brill, 2002).
23. On the transmission of dream manuals in the Middle Ages, see Lorenzo DiTommaso, *The Book of Daniel and the Apocryphal Daniel Literature* (Leiden and Boston: Brill, 2005), pp. 378–89; László Sándor Chardonnens, 'Dream Divination in Manuscript and early Printed Books: A Pattern of Transmission', in *Aspects of Knowledge: Preserving and Reinventing Traditions of Learning in the Middle Ages*, ed. by Marilina Cesario and Hugh Magennis (Manchester: Manchester University Press, 2018), pp. 23–52.
24. For the complete list of dream entries from the ninth century to 1550, and for a discussion on dream culture in medieval Italian literature, see Valerio Cappozzo, *Dizionario dei sogni nel Medioevo: il Somniale Danielis in manoscritti letterari* (Florence: Olschki, 2018).
25. Thérèse Charmasson, *Recherches sur une technique divinatoire: la géomancie dans l'Occident médiéval*. Centre de recherches d'histoire et de philologie, 4 (Geneva: Droz; Paris: H. Champion, 1980), pp. 241–42. For a recent overview of geomancy, see *Geomancy and Other Forms of Divination*, ed. by Andrea Palazzo and Irene Zavattero (Florence: SISMEL-Edizioni del Galluzzo, 2017).
26. Pietro Alighieri, *Petri Alleghierii super Dantes ipsius genitoris* Comoediam. *Commentarium, nunc primum in lucem editum* (Florence: Guglielmum Piatti, 1845), pp. 430–31: 'Quando geomantes suam geomantiam operantur, faciendo in alba diei suas figuras dictas fortunam majorem et minorem, somniasse se videre Sirenam. Ita ut dicit textus de ea; pro cuius figura adverte' [As when the geomancers practice their art at dawn, drawing their figures called Greater or Lesser Fortune, he seemed to see a Siren in his dream. Thus, as the text says of her: pay attention to her shape]. See also: Pietro Alighieri, *Comentum super poema* Comedie *Dantis. A Critical Edition of the Third and Final Draft of Piero's Alighieri's Commentare on Dante's* The Divine Comedy, ed. by Massimiliano Chiamenti (Tempe: Center for Medieval and Renaissance Studies, 2002), pp. 10–11: 'et in qua alba hora geomantes parant se ad videndum surgere in Orientem solem per

viam, idest per spatium breve inter lucem et obscurum, quem solem vocant 'maiorem fortunam' ex eo quod inter sedecim figuras geomantie duas ex eis attribuunt ipsi soli que per eos vocantur 'fortuna minor' et 'fortuna maior' — sic vidisse, idest contemplative percepisse, dictam triplicem attractionem in suo primo et proprio esse ut mulierem quandam ita turpem et informem, ut dicit textus.' [and at that hour of dawn, the geomancers prepare themselves to see the sun as it rises in the east — that is in the brief interim between light and darkness — and this sun they call 'the Greater Fortune' since among the sixteen figures of geomancy they attribute two of them to this sun, and they call these Greater and Lesser Fortune. Thus he saw — that is, perceived through contemplation — the said threefold temptation in its first and proper guise, thus as a certain woman initially ugly and deformed, as the text says.]

27. For biographical information on the Swabian emperor, see David Abulafia, *Frederick II: A Medieval Emperor* (Oxford: Oxford University Press, 1992). On the Norman court and the emperor's relationship with the middle eastern world, see Hiroshi Takayama, *Sicily and the Mediterranean in the Middle Ages* (New York: Routledge, 2019).
28. *Arab Historians of the Crusades*, ed. by Francesco Gabrieli, trans. from the Italian by E. J. Costello (New York: Barnes & Noble, 1993), p. 270.
29. *Crusade and Christendom: Annotated Documents in Translation from Innocent III to the Fall of Acre, 1187–1291*, ed. by Jessalynn Bird, Edward Peters and James M. Powell (Philadelphia: University of Pennsylvania Press, 2013), p. 256. To solve the emperor's queries, the Sultan reached out to scholars of his court. It is believed that among the group, the Arab Sufi philosopher Ibn Sab'în was able to give answers, known as the *Sicilian Questions*, on a variety of issues such as Aristotelian and Arabic philosophy, see *Le questioni siciliane: Federico II e l'universo filosofico*, ed. by Patrizia Spallino (Palermo: Officina di Studi Medievali, 2002); Anna Ayæe Akasoy, 'Ibs Sab'īn's Sicilian Questions: The Text, its Sources, and their Historical Context', *Al-Qantara*, 29.1 (2008), 115–46.
30. I thank Dr Louise Arizzoli for supporting me in giving shape to the complex thoughts in this chapter. I extend my thanks to the Dar al Athar al Islamiyyah (Kuwait City) for offering me the opportunity to travel to the Middle East and learn another point of view, and finally my gratitude goes to the editors of this volume and to my peer reviewers for sharing their critical and constructive opinions.

CHAPTER 13

Dante in Spain: Translations, Literary Theory and Canonizations

Paul Carranza

Dante's influence in Spain began in the early fifteenth century as the Iberian kingdoms of Castile and Aragon tried to assimilate Italian humanism and poetry. The *Commedia* played an important role in this assimilation, since Dante, in his role as the poem's author as well as its fictional protagonist, was put to a wide variety of uses: as a model of erotic dream visions; as model of allegorical poems with religious or political content; as a way to think about vernacular authors and their relation to tradition; and as a text to be translated — the translation of the poem into Castilian prose in 1428 was the first translation of the *Commedia* into another vernacular language.[1] This activity was more eclectic than systematic, but it will be the argument of this chapter that this eclecticism was extremely productive. Indeed, it is not an exaggeration to say that engagement with the *Commedia* was a key factor in the development of fifteenth-century Spanish humanism.

The figure connected to all these activities was Íñigo López de Mendoza, better known by his noble title, the Marquis of Santillana (1398–1458).[2] Santillana's political and literary activity spanned the courts of Alfonso V of Aragon and Juan II of Castile, both monarchs of the Trastamaran dynasty. Santillana was a prominent figure in the incipient humanism in Spain: he promoted translations and amassed a significant library, one of the largest in Medieval Spain. It was Santillana who commissioned the first Castilian translation of the *Commedia* and then used it to create his own compositions, as well as his theorizing of poetic canons. It is with Santillana that one must start to unravel the many strands of Dante's influence in fifteenth-century Spain.

One element of the *Commedia* that obviously impressed Santillana was the basic structure of the dream vision and journey by a poet-protagonist. His first sustained engagement with the *Commedia* as a model was a poem entitled the *Infierno de los enamorados*. In this poem Santillana adapts the *Inferno*'s basic structure of a poet-protagonist experiencing a dream vision and meeting sinners in hell. But as the title of the poem indicates, the sinners in his hell are all lovers, making this adaptation an expansion of *Inferno* 5. The poet-protagonist's guide is Hippolytus, who is there because he resisted love (that of his stepmother) and died because of it. And as in the case of the *Commedia*, there is an inscription over the gate of hell:

> El que por Venus se guía
> Venga a penar su pecado. (375–76)³
>
> [Let him who is guided by Venus
> Come and pay for his sin.]⁴

There follows a viewing of thirty-two lovers (four times more than the catalogue in *Inferno* 5),⁵ including Francesca da Rimini, 'la dona de Ravena, | de que fabla el florentino' [the woman of Ravenna | spoken of by the Florentine]. The catalogue ends with the appearance of the shade of the medieval Portuguese poet Macías, who is in Hell because of his excessive devotion to Love. Macías, in dialogue with the poet-protagonist, essentially translates the opening of Francesca's famous speech of lament: 'Nessun maggior dolore | che ricordarsi del tempo felice | ne la miseria (*Inf.* 5.121–23).

> 'La mayor cuita que haver
> puede ningún amador
> es membrarse del placer
> en el tiempo del dolor. [...]' (vv. 489–92)
>
> ['The greatest distress
> That a lover can have
> Is to remember pleasure
> In a time of pain.']

In the *Infierno de los enamorados*, Santillana reduces Dante's *Inferno* to, essentially, the condemned and suffering lovers of the fifth Canto. The inscription under which the poet-protagonist passes can stand for change the Santillana makes to Dante: the warning to all sinners in Dante becomes, in Santillana, an address to lovers only.

The Catalan poet Bernat Hug de Rocabertí also fashioned a Dantesque hell populated by lovers in his *Glòria d'amor* ('Glory of Love').⁶ Rocabertí's poet-protagonist meets a guide named Conaxença (Acquaintance) who takes him on a tour of a landscape populated by the souls of lovers. Some of the lovers in the *Glòria d'amor* have been virtuous in life, but others, like those in *Inferno* 5 (and in Santillana's *Infierno*), have transgressed the codes of love by being fickle, or cruel to their lovers. There are many from mythology, but also Beatrice (who is paired with her creator, Dante) and Macías, the poet who was also present in Santillana's *Infierno*. One element of Dante's *Inferno* that Rocabertí imitated quite closely, more so than Santillana, is the poet-protagonist's exchanges with sinners, in which the latter are invited to share their stories. Thus, in the course of his journey, the protagonist of the *Glòria d'amor* has conversations with many souls about their experiences with love while in life, whereas Macías is the only condemned soul to speak in Santillana's poem.

Because the underworld of both poems is populated only with the souls of lovers, it is tempting to criticize them as reductions of Dante's multifaced original, with its examination of all facets of human conduct and their theological implications.[7] But the poems can also be seen as sophisticated adaptations of the *Commedia* in the service of love casuistry. Indeed, in a recent analysis of the *Infierno* and the *Glòria d'amor*, Pau Cañigueral Batllosera argues that both poems succeed as adaptations of the codes of love poetry that provided the original background of *Inferno* 5 and the exchange between Dante-Protagonist and Francesca.[8]

Another area of the *Commedia*'s influence in Spain was a series of allegorical poems on both political and religious themes. These poems employ the *arte mayor* verse form, used by fifteenth-century Spanish poets to treat elevated themes, especially public or religious subject matter, and hence the reliance on the *Commedia* for structures and imagery. Santillana's entry in this genre was the *Comedieta de Ponza* [Little Comedy of Ponza], which he wrote in response to the defeat of the Aragonese fleet by the Genoese off the island of Ponza in 1435. As a result of the battle Alfonso V of Aragon and his brothers, Juan of Navarra and Enrique, Master of the Order of Santiago, were taken prisoner. The poet-protagonist of the poem, in a vision, sees four women dressed in black, who are the wives of the prisoners in addition to doña Leonor, the queen mother. Leonor recounts how she received news of the defeat and capture of her sons. The lady Fortune appears and prophesies that Spain will go on to greater glory and conquer more lands. Fortune ends with a prophecy that the prisoners will be freed.

The influence of Dante's *Commedia* on the *Comedieta de Ponza* is seen in the title itself, and was discussed by Santillana in a letter he sent, with the copy of the *Comedieta* and other poems, to the Catalan noblewoman Violante de Prades.[9] Here Santillana explains why he called his poem a *Comedieta* by drawing on Benvenuto da Imola's commentary on the *Commedia* and his discussion of tragedy, satire and comedy. The genre of comedy, notes Santillana, is not only for describing characters of humble origin, but also for stories that begin with painful episodes but end happily, as is the case with the defeat at Ponza and the subsequent release of Alfonso V and his brothers. This is the first example in Spain of this definition of comedy, so important to commentators on the *Commedia* such as Imola and, to a lesser extent, Pietro Alighieri. Santillana possessed Castilian translations of both commentaries, and his use of them, in writing the *Comedieta de Ponza* and commenting on it as an act of self-exegesis, illustrates how the poem and its commentaries entered Spain simultaneously and exerted influence on its authors, especially Santillana and his circle.[10]

Another poet who used the *Commedia* as the model for a long poem was Juan de Mena (1411–56). Born in Cordova, Mena became part of the court of Juan II and also a friend of Santillana.[11] The poem by Mena that shows Dante's influence is the *Laberinto de Fortuna* [Labyrinth of Fortune], his longest poem, and by far his most well-known. The *Laberinto* is a dream vision in which a first-person poetic persona journeys to the heavens and meets the allegorical character of Divine Providence. Providence shows the narrator a vision of the world that represents it as three wheels, representing the past, the present and the future. Each wheel contains seven circles in turn, and mythological and historical figures populate each circle. The ones who acted morally are on the top of the circles, while the ones who conducted themselves sinfully in life are on the bottom.

The poem begins by praising the power of Juan II, and the text was presented to the king himself in 1444. But the *Laberinto* is much more than a panegyric of Juan II. The poem laments the unsettled political situation in Castile, but it also, as its title suggests, reflects on the workings of Fortune in human affairs, although scholars debate the relationship in the poem between Fortune and Providence, the former a force of chance, while the latter adjusts human fate according to the merits and morality of each individual.

The influence of Dante on the *Laberinto* is less clear than in the case of Santillana's *Comedieta*. Unlike Santillana with the *Comedieta*, Mena did not affix any prefatory material to his poem explaining his aims or a theory of poetry. But Mena clearly follows the *Commedia* in placing exemplary figures from the past in a world beyond the living, seen by a poet-protagonist. And the *Laberinto* approaches the *Commedia* in the scope of its vision. As Daniel Hartnett says, in the *Laberinto* 'Mena, like Dante, creates an allegorical vision that encompasses the broad totality of culture to that point', much broader than Santillana's adaptations of the *Commedia*.[12]

The last allegorical poem to be considered is by Francisco Imperial and entitled *El dezir a las siete virtudes* [The Poem to the Seven Virtues]. Though chronologically it was the first of the Spanish allegorical poems to draw on Dante's *Commedia* (critics generally date the poem to 1407),[13] it deserves to be treated last because of its privileged place in the reception of Dante in Spain. Imperial was Italian, from Genoa, and he thus had a more direct access to Dante. Imperial's most audacious imitative manoeuvre in the *Dezir a las siete virtudes* is the choice of Dante himself as a guide to the first-person poet-protagonist. After an invocation modelled on that of *Paradiso* 1, the poet-protagonist falls asleep and dreams.[14] He sees a man identifiable as Dante because of the description of the book he is holding, especially its first verse: 'escripto todo con oro muy fino, | e començava; "en medio del camino"' [written entirely in very fine gold, | which began: 'In the middle of the journey'] (103–04). Dante then guides him as he sees the Seven Virtues in the form of stars.

In addition to choosing Dante as a fictional guide, Imperial's reliance on the *Commedia* extends to imitations of individual lines and vocabulary, to the point that at times it is difficult to understand the *Dezir a las siete virtudes* without comparing it to the *Commedia*.[15] Imperial's singular engagement with the *Commedia* was known to Santillana and it provided yet another connection between Santillana's circle and Dante's great poem, which explains why Santillana called Imperial 'poeta' as opposed to 'dezidor' or 'trobador', in a distinction that Dante himself also used.[16]

As we move beyond Dante's influence on allegorical narrative poems in fifteenth-century Spain, we see that he was in part responsible for spurring authors to think about canons of poets, and to make such canons and scenes of coronation subjects of poetic compositions. The quality of Dante's *Commedia* was without doubt a cause of this. But the acceptance of Dante-protagonist as the sixth author in the *bella scola* of poets in *Inferno* 4, comprising Vergil, Homer, Horace, Ovid and Lucan, also played a role.[17] This scene led to several compositions in Castilian in which a poet-protagonist goes on a journey and witnesses another poet crowned and accepted into group of canonical authors.[18]

The voyage of the poetic protagonist of the *Commedia* is combined with poetic canonization in Santillana's 'Defunssión de don Enrique de Villena' [Death of Don Enrique de Villena], a poem on the death of the Catalan noble who had translated the *Commedia* into Castilian (on which more below).[19] Here the poet-protagonist finds himself in a wild landscape with only one path forward. He passes through men in mourning until, 'non menos cansados que Dante [a] Acharonte, | allí do se passa la triste ribera' [no less tired than Dante at Acheronte, | where one crosses the sad bank].[20] It is at this point that the poet-protagonist sees the nine Muses, who bewail the loss of Villena.

Dante's influence is even more pronounced in Santillana's poem lamenting the death of the Catalan poet Jordi de Sant Jordi, the 'Coronación de Mosén Jordi de Sant Jordi' [The Coronation of Mosén Jordi de Sant Jordi].[21] The poem begins with a mythological dawn that is modelled on that of *Purgatorio* 9.1–18.

> e commo Aligeri reza
> do recuenta que durmió
> en sueños me paresçió
> ver una tal extrañeza. (12–15)

> [As Alighieri states
> Where he relates that he slept
> In dreams it seemed to me
> He saw such a wonder.]

Thus begins the vision in which the poet-protagonist sees a *locus amoenus* in which Venus appears. The poet Lucan, accompanied by Vergil and Homer, approaches Venus and requests that she crown the shade of Sant Jordi, a request which Venus grants, in an imitation of Dante-protagonist's acceptance into the *bella scola* of poets in *Inferno* 4.[22]

Santillana was also the subject of a poetic coronation modelled on part on the *Commedia*. The poem is the *Coronación* [Coronation] by Juan de Mena, written to honour Santillana for his capture of the town of Huelma from Muslim forces in 1428. Dante's influence on the poem is suggested even before it starts, as Mena uses one of the preambles to quote the theory of genres from Benvenuto da Imola's commentary on the *Commedia*, just as Santillana did in discussing his own *Comedieta de Ponza*. The *Coronación*, says Mena, will be satire, in that it excoriates vice. But it will also be comedy, because it begins by relating sad events but ends in happiness, that is, the news of Santillana's victory and his coronation.[23]

The poem itself divides into a vision of hell and heaven, and as such has a structural similarity to the *Commedia*.[24] The poet-protagonist begins by wandering in an inhospitable land before seeing mythological figures being tormented for their transgressions in life. The poet-protagonist escapes across the river Lethe and eventually reaches Parnassus, where he sees the nine Muses arrive with Santillana (who is not, however, dead) and crown him.

Santillana was also depicted in a poetic coronation after his death in an allegorical poem by his secretary, Diego de Burgos, entitled *El triunfo del Marqués de Santillana*.[25] The poem shows how the Dantean model of the allegorical journey, thanks in no small part to Santillana, had found a home in Castilian literature.[26] As in the case of Imperial, Dante appears as a character to guide the poet-protagonist on his journey. The role of Dante in this poem is to console Burgos the poet-protagonist for the death of Santillana. Dante leads Burgos past the mouth of hell and the mount of Purgatory before coming upon a collection of great heroes, followed by one of sages, including Juan de Mena. Burgos and his guide end up at the Temple of Grace, where they see Santillana's shade. The character Dante makes explicit Santillana's role in engaging with the *Commedia* and making it known in Spain:

> que si tengo fama, si soy conocido,
> es porque él quiso mis obras mirar. (189)
>
> [If I enjoy fame, if I am known,
> It is because he read my works]

In these poetic canonizations, Dante himself was enshrined as a model, as he hoped to do by including himself in the *bella scola* of poets in *Inferno* 4,[27] and the *Commedia* itself, as a text, became a model for further canonizations of poets. While Petrarch's coronation in Rome in 1341 was known in fifteenth-century Spain, even by Santillana,[28] by far the most influential image of a poetic coronation was that of Dante-protagonist in the *Commedia*.

In cases where fifteenth-century poets were not using Dantean images and motifs in order to crown other poets, they put Dante himself in a canon of poetry. At times, he was the only vernacular author mentioned in a list of Greek and Latin writers. Francisco Imperial, as would be expected, did this by placing Dante among Homer, Horace, Vergil and Ovid in one poem, and placing him with the same classical poets, plus Boethius and Lucan, in another.[29] Other poets pair Dante with Petrarch as the only two vernacular authors in a list of past poetic greats, as Santillana does in the 'Defunssión de don Enrique de Villena'.[30]

Dante's place in the history of poetry is also treated in Santillana's *Prohemio e carta* [Prologue and Letter], a preface to his complete works that he sent to the Constable of Portugal.[31] The *Prohemio e carta* is Santillana's statement on literary theory, as well as a history of poetry as he understood it. Dante is present in the *Prohemio e carta* as both another historian of poetry and an important figure himself in recent literary history. As Santillana traces the history of poetry from biblical examples to poetry in Greece and Rome, his examples of individual poets draw on Dante's presentation of them in the *Commedia*.[32] There is Homer, 'que Dante soberano poeta lo llama' [whom Dante calls *soberano poeta*], as Santillana notes, in yet another reference to the *bella scola* of poetry in *Inferno* 4.[33] And as Santillana moves to Latin poetry, his mention of Vergil is accompanied by a citation of Sordello's address to Vergil as Dante-protagonist's guide as 'gloria del Latin' in *Purgatorio* 7.[34] Later in the *Prohemio e carta*, as Santillana discusses vernacular poetry, Dante returns as an author who wrote the *Commedia* in *terza rima* 'elegantemente'.[35]

The last manifestations of Dante's influence in Spain that remain to be discussed are the translations of the *Commedia* made in the early fifteenth century. The Catalan nobleman Enrique de Villena — whom we have already met as the subject of Santillana's 'Defunssión' — translated the poem into Castilian prose in 1428, the first translation of Dante's *Commedia* into another vernacular language.[36] This translation was followed a year later by a translation of the poem into Catalan verse by the poet Andreu Febrer. The translation by Febrer is much the more polished product; it is a bold attempt to imitate the original *terza rima*.[37] The prose translation by Villena, by contrast, was much more workmanlike, and it was not designed to be widely circulated. Indeed, one has to be careful in calling Villena's version a translation; it might also be called an extended gloss on the original. Its importance, however, was that it was commissioned by Villena's friend Santillana. Villena's literal translation aided Santillana in understanding the *Commedia* and its vocabulary, allowing him to write the adaptations of the poem discussed earlier.[38]

Aside from Villena's translation, Santillana also had translations of commentaries on the *Commedia* text in his library: a Castilian translation of Benvenuto da Imola's commentary on the *Purgatorio* by Martin Gonçales de Lucena, and commissioned by Santillana; and a Castilian translation of Pietro Alighieri's commentary on the poem.[39] We have already discussed how these commentaries allowed Santillana and his friend Juan de Mena to theorize their own poetry by, for example, placing it within the hierarchy of styles. Daniel Hartnett has recently identified another function of Santillana's collection of Dante materials — Villena's translation, the commentaries, as well as *vitae* of Dante — as well as his adaptations of the *Commedia*: Santillana's association with Dante increased his own prestige as a court poet, even as his literary activity further publicized the importance of Dante among Castilian authors.[40] So while Andreu Febrer's was the more literary, polished translation, Villena's translation, because of its presence in Santillana's library, was much more influential, allowing Santillana and perhaps other authors access to the *Commedia* in unadorned Castilian, ready to be adapted in future compositions.

It is worth pausing over the figure of Villena and some of his other works for what they can tell us about fifteenth-century Spanish humanism and its relationship to Dante. Related by birth to the noble families of both Aragon and Castile, Villena was an utter failure as a courtier but a diligent and innovative scholar. He wrote a variety of works that combined medieval and more humanistic forms of interpretation, including an allegorical treatise on the Twelve Labours of Hercules, a treatise on carving at table, and a treatise on the evil eye. But his most significant contribution to early Spanish humanism, aside from his translation of the *Commedia*, was his translation of Vergil's *Aeneid* into Castilian prose — the first translation of the entire work into a vernacular language — with a commentary on the first three books. By the end of his life he had become the object of suspicions that he practised alchemy, necromancy and magic, and some of his library was burned by ecclesiastical authorities after his death. But within the circle of Santillana he continued to be revered, as shown by his depiction in Santillana's 'Defunssión', and as one of the shades in Mena's *Laberinto*.[41]

Villena's translation of the *Aeneid* has an interesting relationship to his version of the *Commedia*. Villena was originally commissioned to translate the *Aeneid* by Juan II, king of Navarre (and Villena's nephew). Juan II had become interested in the *Aeneid* after reading the *Commedia* and seeing Vergil as Dante's guide. Not knowing Latin, the king sought out Villena to do the translation, though because of political tensions between Navarre and Castile the king later broke off the relationship, and the translation ended up with Santillana, as had the translation of the *Commedia* before it.

Villena's work as translator highlights the conditions of fifteenth-century Spanish humanism that made Dante so important as an authority. For many enthusiasts like Juan II of Navarre, and even for writers like Santillana, difficulties in reading Latin made them uncomfortable engaging with Roman authors and holding them up as models to be emulated. In this atmosphere, Dante often functioned almost as a classical author. He was easier to read than a Roman author (though even Dante's Tuscan presented difficulties for authors such as Santillana, as Villena's translation of the *Commedia* attests); he arrived in Spain already having been canonized thanks to the commentaries by Benvenuto da Imola and Pietro Alighieri (both texts, like the *Commedia* itself, translated into Castilian and possessed by Santillana); and he staged what is essentially a self-canonization, creating a scene in his *Commedia* in which his poetic protagonist joins the ranks of five classical poets. We saw above how in the *Prohemio e carta* Santillana discusses Vergil as one of the great classical poets not by citing his poetry directly, but rather by quoting Dante's Sordello and his address to Vergil as a great poet in the *Purgatorio*. As Daniel Hartnett argues in his analysis of this passage, this manoeuvre allows Santillana to show Dante passing judgement on the poetry of Vergil; at the same time Santillana, by citing Dante, can share in the vernacular poet's status as an authority.[42]

In surveying the influence of Dante in Spain before the sixteenth century, one is struck by the variety of functions performed by both the *Commedia* and Dante as author of the text and character in it: as a model for allegorical poems and trips to the heavens; as an example of a vernacular author who has achieved canonization; and as a way to theorize literary genres, sometimes with the help of commentaries on the *Commedia*. The existence of two early translations of the *Commedia*, by Enrique de Villena and Andreu Febrer, has led some scholars to ask themselves why Spanish humanists did not develop a more systematic understanding of Dante's project in the *Commedia*, or why poets like Santillana did not engage with its major theological themes. What Santillana did instead was choose the features of the *Commedia* that would advance his poetic project, and the same could be said about Mena and Imperial. And if these poets did not understand Dante's more overarching concerns in the *Commedia*, they were not alone. As Zygmunt Barański has argued, even early commentators on the *Commedia* such as Boccaccio and Benvenuto da Imola — writers closer in time to Dante and, more importantly, from the same linguistic tradition — failed to see the features in the poem that modern readers find fundamental to its meaning and novelty.[43] Spain's engagement with Dante in the early fifteenth century demonstrates that intertextual relationships between literary traditions need not be systematic to be productive, and that Dante's *Commedia*, the great medieval poem of the cosmos, did not need to be fully understood or even read in its totality in order to advance late medieval Spanish literature and humanism.

Notes to Chapter 13

1. For a basic bibliography of earlier studies of Dante in Spain, see Margherita Morreale, 'Apuntes bibliográficos para el estudio del tema "Dante en España hasta el s. XVII"', *Annali del Corso di Lingue e Letterature Straniere dell'Università di Bari*, 8 (1967), 91–134. For basic surveys of the topic, see Morreale, 'Dante in Spain', ibid., pp. 3–21; Joaquín Arce, 'Spagna', *Enciclopedia Dantesca*, dir. by Umberto Bosco, ed. by Giorgio Petrocchi and others, 6 vols (Rome: Istituto della Enciclopedia Italiana, 1970–78), v, 355–62; Paola Calef, 'A proposito della ricezione di Dante nel Quattrocento spagnolo'; and Andrea Zinato, 'La ricezione di Dante nel medioevo spagnolo', the latter two in *Dante oltre i confini: la ricezione dell'opera dantesca nelle letterature altre*, ed. by Silvia Monti (Alessandria: Edizioni dell'Orso, 2018), pp. 61–75 and 185–207, respectively.
2. See Marco Boni, 'Santillana, Iñigo López de Mendoza, marchese di', in *Enciclopedia Dantesca*, v, 11–12. For an overview of Santillana's works in English, see Regula Rohland de Langbehn, 'Íñigo López de Mendoza, Marqués de Santillana (1398–1458)', in *Castilian Writers, 1400–1500*, ed. by Frank A. Dominguez and George D. Greenia, Dictionary of Literary Biography, 286 (Detroit, MI, Washington DC and London: Gale, 2004), pp. 233–54.
3. Quotations from Santillana are from Marqués de Santillana, *Poesías completas*, ed. by M. P. A. M. Kerkhof and Ángel Gómez Moreno (Madrid: Castalia, 2003). The inscription over the gate of Hell in *Inferno* is in 3. 1–9.
4. All translations into English are my own unless otherwise indicated.
5. Cinthia María Hamlin, 'El viaje dantesco y su funcionalidad metapoética en *El sueño* y el *Infierno de los enamorados* del Marqués de Santillana', *Letras*, 71 (2015), 117–28 (p. 123).
6. Text and study in H. C. Heaton, *The Gloria d'Amor of Fra Rocabertí: A Catalan Vision-Poem of the 15th Century* (New York: Columbia University Press, 1916).
7. See, for example, David William Foster, 'The Misunderstanding of Dante in Fifteenth-Century Spanish Poetry', *Comparative Literature*, 16.4 (1964), 338–47, especially pp. 342–43.
8. Pau Cañigueral Batllosera. 'La sentimentalització de Dante a la poesia cortesana del segle XV: La *Glòria d'amor* de fra Bernat Hug de Rocabertí i l'*Infierno de los enamorados* del marquès de Santillana', *La Corónica*, 45.1 (2016), 9–36, especially p. 14.
9. Marqués de Santillana, 'Carta a doña Violante de Prades', in Santillana, *Poesías completas*, pp. 637–40.
10. Miguel A. Pérez Priego, 'De Dante a Juan de Mena: sobre el género literario de "comedia"', *1616: Anuario de la Sociedad Española de Literatura General y Comparada*, 1 (1978), 151–58.
11. For a basic biography and description of Mena's works, see Philip Gericke, 'Juan de Mena (1411–1456)', in *Castilian Writers, 1400–1500*, ed. by Frank A. Dominguez and George D. Greenia, Dictionary of Literary Biography, 286(Detroit, MI, Washington, DC and London: Gale, 2004), pp. 109–26. On the relationship to Dante, see Joaquín Arce, 'Men, Juan de', in *Enciclopedia dantesca*, III, 894.
12. Daniel Hartnett, 'Biographical Emulation of Dante in Mena's *Laberinto de Fortuna* and *Coplas de los siete pecados mortales*', *Hispanic Review*, 79.3 (2011), 351–73 (p. 360).
13. For a review of attempts to date the poem, see Cinthia María Hamlin, 'Francisco de Imperial "leyendo" la *Commedia*: el *Dezir de las siete virtudes* y su legado (meta)poético y político', *Dicenda*, 37 (2019), 199–225 (p. 212). On Imperial and Dante generally, see Joaquín Arce, 'Imperial, Francisco', in *Enciclopedia dantesca*, III, 383.
14. For these and other parallels in the *Commedia*, see Marina S. Brownlee, 'Francisco Imperial and the Issue of Poetic Genealogy', *Poetry at Court in Trastamaran Spain: From the 'Cancionero de Baena' to the 'Cancionero General'*, ed. by E. Michael Gerli and Julian Weiss (Tempe, AZ: Medieval and Renaissance Texts and Studies, 1998), pp. 59–78; and Hamlin, 'Francisco de Imperial "leyendo"

la *Commedia*', ibid., pp. 199–225. The text of the poem is in Micer Francisco Imperial, *El dezir a las syete virtudes y otros poemas*, ed. by Colbert I. Nepaulsingh (Madrid: Espasa-Calpe, 1977), pp. 98–131.
15. Zinato, p. 196.
16. Santillana's *Prohemio e carta* in *Poesías completas*, p. 657 (a text that will be discussed below). Dante's distinction between *dicitore* and *poeta* is in *Vita nuova* 16.3. For Imperial's influence on Mena, see Hartnett, 'Biographical Emulation', pp. 360–61, 368–71.
17. *Inferno* 4. 85–96.
18. For a general discussion see Julio Vélez-Sainz, *El Parnaso español: canon, mecenazgo y propaganda en la poesía del Siglo de Oro* (Madrid: Visor, 2005), pp. 43–55.
19. Santillana, *Poesías completas*, pp. 285–94.
20. Vv. 131–32. As Kerkhof and Ángel Gómez Moreno note in their edition, the reference to the banks of Acheron is an allusion to *Inferno* 3. 78 (p. 292 n. 628).
21. Santillana, *Poesías completas*, pp. 215–24.
22. These parallels are discussed in Francisco Bautista, 'Santillana, Mena, y la coronación de los poetas'. *From the* Cancionero da Vaticana *to the* Cancionero general: *Studies in Honour of Jane Whetnall*, ed. by Alan Deyermond and Barry Taylor (London: Department of Hispanic Studies, Queen Mary, University of London, 2007), pp. 55–74 (p. 61).
23. Juan de Mena, *La coronación*, ed. by M. P. A. M. Kerkhof (Madrid: Consejo Superior de Investigaciones Científicas, 2009), p. 4.
24. See the discussion by Florence Street, 'The Allegory of Fortune and the Imitation of Dante in the *Laberinto* and *Coronaçion* of Juan de Mena', *Hispanic Review*, 23.1 (1955), 1–11 (pp. 6–8).
25. See the edition and study by Carlos Moreno Hernández, *Retórica y Humanismo: El triunfo del Marqués de Santillana (1458)* (Valencia: Universitat de València, 2008), <http://www.parnaseo.uv.es/Lemir/Textos/Carlos_Moreno.pdf> [accessed 2 April 2021].
26. For a detailed discussion of Dantean elements in the poem, see Joaquín Arce, 'El *Triunfo del Marqués* de Diego de Burgos y la irradiación dantesca en torno a Santillana', *Revista de la Universidad de Madrid*, 19.74 (1970), 25–39; Javier Gutiérrez Carou,'Dante en la poesía de Diego de Burgos', *Actes del VII Congrés de l'Associació Hispànica de Literatura Medieval (Castelló de la Plana, 22–26 de setembre de 1997)*, ed. by Santiago Fortuño Llorens and Tomàs Martínez Romero, 3 vols (Castelló de la Plana: Universitat Jaume I, 1999), II, 209–21; and the discussion by Zinato, pp. 201–02.
27. *Inf.* 4. 94f.
28. Iñigo Ruiz Arzalluz, 'Caminos de Petrarca en la España del siglo XV', *Boletín de la Real Academia Española*, 90.302 (2010), 291–310 (p. 297 n. 18).
29. Imperial, Micer Francisco. *El dezir a las syete virtudes y otros poemas*, p. 21; see Infantes, 'Espejos poéticos', pp. 25–26.
30. Vv. 159–60.
31. Text in Santillana, *Poesías completas*, pp. 641–60.
32. Santillana, *Poesías completas*, pp. 645–46, and see the notes by Kerkhof and Gómez Moreno.
33. *Inferno* 4. 88: 'quelli è Omero poeta sovrano'.
34. *Purgatorio* 7. 16–18.
35. Santillana, *Poesías completas*, p. 649.
36. Marta Marfany, 'Traducciones en verso del siglo XV', *Bulletin of Hispanic Studies*, 90.3 (2013), 261–73. The translation by Villena is Biblioteca Nacional de Madrid MS 10186. The most complete description of the MS is Paola Calef, *Il primo Dante in castigliano: il codice madrileno della* Commedia *con la traduzione attribuita a Enrique de Villena* (Alessandria: Edizioni dell'Orso, 2013). See also José A. Pascual, *La traducción de la* Divina commedia *atribuída a D. Enrique de Aragón: estudio y edición del* Infierno (Salamanca: Universidad de Salamanca, 1974). An edition of the entire translation can be found in Enrique de Villena, *Obras completas*, ed. by Pedro M. Cátedra, 3 vols (Madrid: Turner, 1994–2000), III, 515–1039. For more on Villena, see Joaquín Arce, 'Villena, Enrique de', in *Enciclopedia dantesca*, V, 1021.
37. The modern edition is *Divina comèdia*, ed. by Annamaria Gallina, 6 vols (Barcelona: Barcino, 1988).

38. On Villenas's translation and Santillana's use of it, see Calef, 'A proposito della ricezione di Dante nel Quattrocento spagnolo', pp. 64, 70–71.
39. See Francesco Ardolino, 'Dante Alighieri', in *Diccionario histórico de la traducción en España*, ed. by Francisco Lafarga and Luis Pegenaute (Madrid: Gredos, 2009), pp. 243–51 (pp. 282–86). See also Joaquín Rubio Tovar, 'Traductores y traducciones en la Biblioteca del Marqués de Santillana', *Medioevo y literatura: Actas del V Congreso de la Asociacion Hispánica de Literatura Medieval*, 4 vols (Granada: Universidad de Granada, 1995), IV, 243–51 (p. 245).
40. Daniel Hartnett, 'The Marques de Santillana's Library and Literary Reputation', in *Self-Fashioning and Assumptions of Identity in Medieval and Early Modern Iberia*, ed. by Laura Delbrugge (Leiden: Brill, 2015), pp. 116–43; Hartnett, pp. 122–25, has a full list of Dante manuscripts present in Spain in Santillana's time, including the ones in his library.
41. For an overview of Villena, see Sol Miguel-Prendes, 'Enrique de Villena (circa 1382–1384–15 December 1434)', *Castilian Writers, 1400–1500*, ed. by Frank A. Dominguez and George D. Greenia, Dictionary of Literary Biography, 286 (Detroit, MI, Washington DC and London: Gale, 2004), pp. 266–76. For more on Villena's translation of the *Aeneid*, see Donald Gilbert-Santamaría, 'Historicizing Vergil: Translation and Exegesis in Enrique de Villena's *Eneida*', *Hispanic Review*, 73.4 (2005), 409–30.
42. Hartnett, 'Santillana's Library', pp. 135–36.
43. Zygmunt Barański, 'La lezione esegetica di *Inferno* I: allegoria, storia e letteratura nella *Commedia*', in *Dante e le forme dell'allegoresi*, ed. by Michelangelo Picone (Ravenna: Longo, 1987), pp. 79–97 (p. 79).

CHAPTER 14

Dante and Death in Late Medieval France

Helen Swift

'Although Dante was known by name in fifteenth-century France, his influence was scant.'[1] *The Dante Encyclopedia*'s entry for 'Dante in France' offers an unpromising opening for thinking about and with Dante in late-medieval French literature. I do not argue here for hitherto grossly underestimated influence, but do wish to consider carefully how we retrospectively frame reception of and responses to the *Commedia* in particular. I should argue, for instance, for 'scattered' rather than 'scant' — meagre findings depend upon the sources in which one has searched, and, for the fifteenth century, there is much currently under-studied literature that was nonetheless popular at the time; the formerly maligned court writers dubbed *grands rhétoriqueurs* have found their way back into favour, but only emergently into circulation through modern critical editions.[2] Gauging scope of impact is challenging when there are localized pockets of evidence across France and Burgundy from across several decades — it is tempting, for profile-raising purposes, to extrapolate an unduly globalising narrative. In this chapter, by focusing on death as a key theme of fifteenth-century literature,[3] I unpick how both direct reference to and echoes of Dante contributed to writers' abiding concerns with the relationship between literature and morality, most especially the contemporary status and role of vernacular poets. After examining afresh the difficulties of defining Dantean influence in medieval France, I shall consider references to Dante by name as part of a literary genealogizing discourse, before discussing how the dead were represented in poetry and prose in ways that may productively be viewed in dialogue with the *Commedia*, interrogating the limits of representation through a reflection on the relationship between fiction and embodiment.

Dante in Medieval France

While the evidence is scattered and variable, we can nonetheless discern a multifaceted and multilingual relationship between Dante and Francophone medieval literature, not least given this relationship's beginnings in the Florentine's appreciation of Occitan verse of the troubadours. Linguistic reasons have been offered, however, as a significant constraint on dissemination of the *Commedia*, given its composition in vernacular Italian rather than Latin,[4] especially when compared to the substantial and widespread transmission of Boccaccio, above all *De casibus virorum illustrium* in Latin and in French translation;[5] though of course Dante himself features as a character within *De casibus*, so is nonetheless vicariously present.[6] The picture is complex.

Let us scrutinize first the manuscript record. While, for Boccaccio, Laurent de Premierfait and others have obligingly provided a rich fifteenth-century history of translation into French, the first known French translation of Dante's works, thought to date from the late fifteenth century, is now lost,[7] and the first published French translation of the entire *Commedia* only appeared in 1596.[8] It is believed that Italian texts appeared in France from the turn of the fifteenth century;[9] these manuscripts were a combination of the whole work, single books, and commentaries on the poem.[10] Printed editions, counterfeits of Aldine editions, began to be produced in Lyons in 1502.[11]

Encounters between individual authors and copies can sometimes be inferred or conjectured.[12] Study of fifteenth-century library inventories has revealed that René, Duke of Anjou, possessed 'ung livre en parchemin nommé *Dente de Fleurence*, escript en lettre ytalienne' [a parchment book called Dante of Florence, written in Italian script],[13] identifiable as Paris, BnF, MS it. 74, decorated with the arms of René's seneschal, Jean Cossa; when he came by this, however, is uncertain. The *Commedia* was translated into Latin during the Council of Constance in 1416–17, and the various ecclesiastical council meetings of the first half of the fifteenth century are more generally known to have been fora for rich intellectual and literary exchange.[14] Martin Le Franc, working in the service of Amadeus VIII of Savoy, was present at the Council of Basel in the later 1430s as the anti-pope's secretary; it is plausible that he accessed the *Commedia* and other Italian texts there, if, indeed, a copy of the former was not already available to him in the Savoyard ducal library.[15]

One important conjecture regarding an author-text encounter that has exercised scholars is that first made by Villani and Boccaccio: that the Florentine himself travelled to Paris, which Laurent de Premierfait elaborates into Dante's first reading of *Le Roman de la rose*. De Premierfait interpolates a biographical sketch of Dante into his second, highly popular, 1409 translation of *De casibus*. Dante appears already as a character in conversation with Boccaccio-persona, wishing not to have his own tale of misfortune included, but to direct the persona's attention to one who brought shame on Florence, Walter, Duke of Athens (IX.xxiii). Was De Premierfait's interpolation explicatory, to introduce a figure unfamiliar to his French court audience?[16] It is striking that, while De Premierfait praises the 'noble poete florentin',[17] and offers a moralising vision of Dante's poetic vocation that implicitly promotes him through alignment with (better-known) Boccaccio ('dampnoit et reprenoit les vices et les hommes vicieux', fol. 395^r [he condemned and sanctioned sins and sinful men]), the main focus of the interpolation is praise of Paris, which De Premierfait claims Dante sought out as a centre of learning, piety, and justice, and of Jean de Meun ('homme d'engin celeste', ibid. [man of divine intelligence]), continuator of the recently completed *Rose*, which purportedly furnished Dante with his model for the *Commedia*. Since:

> ou livre de la rose est descript le paradis des bons et l'enfer des mauvais en langaige françois, voult, en langaige florentin, soubz aultre maniere de vers rimoiez, contrefaire au vif le beau livre de la rose. (fol. 395^r)

> [in the *Book of the Rose* the paradise of the good and the hell of the bad are described in the French language, [he] wished to reproduce closely the fine *Book of the Rose* in the Florentine language in another manner of rhymed verse.]

De Premierfait unproblematically aligns the *Rose*'s and *Commedia*'s ethical projects as sharing the same didactic scheme, but it is a perception of irreconcilable differences between the two that characterizes Dante's principal channel of early-fifteenth-century reception, Christine de Pizan.[18]

It is important to recognize that Christine was not the first French writer to mention or cite Dante; in 1369 and then 1389, Jean Froissart and Philippe de Mézières demonstrated an acquaintance with his work that may have arisen from their extensive travelling.[19] The idea of travel, of physical *translatio*, has likewise been associated with Christine's knowledge and promotion of the Florentine, because she had moved from Venice to Paris in early childhood to join her father, court physician to Charles V.

Her intervention in Dante reception is construed as significant for a number of reasons. It was substantial and multiple, with explicit references occurring in four of her works. Such works were destined for prestigious audiences including nobles of the royal court (through the severally dedicated copies of her 1402 allegorical narrative *Le Chemin de longue estude*) and prominent clerics (through her engagement with Jean de Montreuil and others in an epistolary debate over the *Rose* between 1400 and 1402). Her involvement was also highly polemical.

Le Chemin recasts Dante's journey with Virgil by giving Christine-persona the Sibyl as guide, thereby itself revisiting Virgil's *Aeneid*, where she accompanied Aeneas to the Underworld. Christine seems to have read the *Commedia* primarily as a moral and theological, not political work,[20] and to have enlisted Dante to promote her vision of *poetrie*, a figurative mode of discourse embracing both verse and prose, as fostering the pursuit of learning ('science') and spiritual discernment, not erotic love.[21] The *Commedia* and its Virgilian roots thus serves as cogent counterpoint to an Ovidian line of literary descent via the *Rose*, commending Dante as ethical authority and denigrating Jean de Meun as propagator of immorality, which she expounds in a letter to Pierre Col, canon of Paris. Refuting Col's contention that de Meun urges his readers to follow 'paradis et [...] vertus' and to flee 'vices [et] enfer',[22] she argues that he seeks instead to reward sinners:

> Et pour ce mesle il paradis avec les ordures dont il parle: pour donner plus foy a son livre. Mais se mieulx vuelz oïr descripre paradis et enfer, et par plus subtilz termes plus haultement parlé de theologie, plus prouffitablement, plus poetiquement et de plus grant efficasse, lis le livre que on appelle le Dant, ou le te fais exposer pour ce que il est en langue florentine souverainnement dicté:

la oyras autre propos mieulx fondé plus subtilement [...] et cent fois mieux composé; ne il n'y a comparison, ne t'en courouces ja.[23]

[He mixes paradise in with the filthy acts of which he speaks for the following reason: in order to lend more credence to his book. But if you wish to hear a better description of paradise and hell using more subtle terminology, expressed more majestically from a theological perspective, more profitably, more poetically, and with greater efficaciousness, read the book attributed to Dante or have it explained to you since it is brilliantly written in the Florentine language. There you will hear another discourse, more wisely conceived and with a better foundation [...] — and a hundred times better written. Do not be angered by this, but there is no comparison.][24]

Contrary to De Premierfait's ethical alignment of *Commedia* and *Rose*, Christine deems them utterly incompatible. But the fifteenth-century writers' framing of the two works — as depicting heaven and hell — is notably similar: a common didactic template applied to both, or the possibility of De Premierfait implicitly responding to Christine, co-opting Col's point to enhance the lustre of Paris's intellectual splendour? Christine's remarks are, quite typically, predicated on an indissoluble link between literary form and ethical implication; casting de Meun as a confidence trickster, she opposes his having created 'a deceptive linguistic instrument that undercuts the moral value of poetic language'.[25] When she speaks of Dante writing 'plus poetiquement', she is ascribing a greater integrity, in all senses, to the *Commedia*'s allegorical fiction. 'Subtilz', a term that she deploys with polyptotonic emphasis, is often used by late-medieval writers to connote finesse of style and literary intricacy, subtlety, and sophistication. For Christine, that can carry either positive or negative moral value; she uses it elsewhere deprecatingly of De Meun (as connoting deceitful wiles), but employs it here in approbation to evoke a certain kind of refinement in Dante's poetry: its allegorical reach into theology,[26] evoking a particular role for the vernacular poet in conveying Christian truth.[27] The moralizing lens through which Christine views all literary endeavour inflects late-medieval reception of both Dante and Jean de Meun by positioning them as poles on an axis that measures 'grant scïence' [great erudition];[28] she thereby discards the romance narrative of the latter's 'rommant' [romance] to treat it more, in De Premierfait's denomination, as the '*livre* de la rose' [*book* of the rose] (my emphasis): 'on quitte le domaine de l'amour pour celui de la morale et de la connaissance' [we move from the domain of love to that of morality and knowledge].[29]

Studies of Dante in medieval France tend to stop at this chronological point, with Christine serving as both launch-pad and, for lack of another well-known name, end-point for defining his reception prior to the Renaissance. Pick-up thereafter occurs either at Charles VIII's Italian campaign in 1494,[30] or with poets of the early sixteenth century, starting with Clément Marot.[31] A whole century is thus usually elided, from 1430 to 1530, but, as we shall see below, a scattering of fifteenth-century interventions suggests a sustained conception of Dante as Christian moral authority, of the *Commedia* as a journey to be imitated, and of representation of the afterlife as a spur to virtuous living.

Living and Dying with Dante

> Le florentin poete Dante
> A escript merveilleusement
> La paine et la vie meschante
> Des espris dampnez justement.
> Mais mortel homme plainement
> Oncques n'entendy n'entendra
> La grandeur de cellui tourment
> Qui ja aux dampnez ne fauldra.
>
> Halas, que mal nous entendons
> La fin de la vie mortelle!
> Que mal les yeulx au ciel tendons
> Pensans a la joye immortelle!
> Nostre condicion est telle
> Que pour eternel bien conquerre
> Et eschiver paine eternelle
> Nous ne sçavons le chemin querre.[32]

[The Florentine poet Dante has depicted brilliantly the suffering and the wretched existence of souls justly damned. But mortal man plainly never heeded, nor will heed, the enormity of this torment which the damned will endure forever. Alas, that we fail to understand the end of mortal life! That we fail to direct our gaze to heaven in contemplation of immortal joy! Our condition is such that we do not know how to seek out the path towards attaining eternal good and avoiding eternal suffering.]

The Normandy-born poet Martin Le Franc, in a work dedicated to Philip the Good of Burgundy, cites Dante as a laudatory point of reference for evoking pains of infernal torment in his dream-vision debate poem *Le Champion des dames* (c. 1442). Four of the poem's five books pit a pro-feminine protagonist Free Will against delegates of his arch-misogynist adversary Ill Speaking. The first book, the source of this quotation, furnishes a narrative preamble in which the first-person persona is guided around the demesnes of Venus and Love, their pertinence to the forthcoming debate being that the Castle of Love houses the ladies whom Free Will will defend. Everything associated with Venus is set up as a perverted antithesis to Love: corrupted, worldly sensuality pitched against Love understood in a spiritual, Trinitarian sense — sinful vice vs Christian virtue. Dante is referenced when the persona is being shown the cemetery of Venus, a conduit to 'la caverne Lucifer' [Lucifer's cave] (l. 1403). The mention comes as the retrospective narrator steps back from what his experiential counterpart witnessed in the cemetery to reflect more broadly on humanity's ignorance and misdirection. Dante is thus invoked as a moral guide, but one whose audience are ill-equipped to follow the path that he lays out for them — Le Franc emphasizes through polyptoton the deficiencies of human understanding, which is unable to locate the correct 'chemin': this lexeme undoubtedly evokes the 'cammin di nostra vita' [our life's way] in *Inferno* I.1;[33] might it also nod to Christine's *Chemin*, suggesting, through plural layers of Dante reception, a further, French path to find?

The locus of a cemetery and issues of language arise in the French court writer Octovien de Saint-Gelais's reference to Dante, which also brings us back to the *Rose*. In the cemetery fiction of his *Sejour d'honneur* (1489–94), another didactic allegory about finding one's way, his persona encounters a 'divine precinct' in which a memorial site is dedicated to contemporary authors: Jean de Meun, Dante, Petrarch, Boccaccio, Alain Chartier, and Jacques Milet.[34] An interest in literary genealogizing, adumbrated already by Christine,[35] was often dramatized narratively in the fifteenth century, thereby assembling a kind of medieval canon — Le Franc's *Champion* commemorates Machaut, Froissart, Christine, and Chartier, and, perhaps most famously, the literary cemetery of René d'Anjou's *Livre du coeur d'amour épris* (1459) honours Jean de Meun, Ovid, Petrarch, Boccaccio, Chartier, and Machaut.[36] Saint-Gelais could thus be seen to be replacing Machaut with Milet (explicable chronologically, since Milet was still alive in 1459) and Ovid with Dante. One reason for these substitutions could be the different orientation of the two cemeteries: René's allegory concerns erotic desire, the graveyard of the Hospital of Love valorizing victims of love; Saint-Gelais's several memorial grounds structure the education of his persona away from sensuality and towards learning and the Hermitage of Understanding, aided by Divine Grace. The *Sejour*'s precinct is a 'lieux solacïeux, | Scïentifique et moult delicïeux' (III.xii.6–7 [a place of solace, learning, and delight]), a garden of knowledge and scholarship, not an amorous garden of sensual pleasure. The ordering of its commemorated authors is chronological:

> Aprés luy [Jean de Meun] vy ung noble Florentin
> Qu'on appelloit en commune voix Dente,
> Qui maintz œuvres en tresaorné latin
> A compillé par raison evidente.
> Il declaira de la vie presente
> Soubz fainct langaige et poëtiques vers
> Les accidens et tourbillons divers
> Et *si* descript de l'infernal repaire
> Le cas piteux et la grande misere. (*Séjour*, III.xii.118–26)

[After him [Jean de Meun] I saw a noble Florentine who was commonly called Dante, who compiled many works in very elegant Latin by clear reason. He revealed the contrary misfortunes and vicissitudes of contemporary life beneath disguised language and fictional verse, and thereby described the pitiable situation and the great wretchedness of the infernal domain.]

Le Franc presented Dante as 'le florentin poete Dante'; does Saint-Gelais's more expansive, indefinite naming, referring to the past rather than the present ('ung [...] qu'on appelloit [...]'), indicate lack of current knowledge of Dante for which he is therefore compensating? His depiction of the Florentine's work is pitched quite generally, but certain features are noteworthy. First, there is the matter of language — only Latin is mentioned, perhaps suggesting Saint-Gelais's acquaintance was solely with Latin translations, including of the *Commedia* given that he, like Le Franc, privileges mention of *Inferno*, and solely *Inferno*: did both writers necessarily know all three books? We recall Christine's advice to Pierre Col to have the

Commedia explained to him through translation from Italian — but did she mean into French or Latin? The second point of note is Saint-Gelais's spotlighting of Dante's allegorical method — the *poetrie* praised by Christine — and the didactic orientation of *Inferno*: like Le Franc, he portrays it functioning as an *ars moriendi*, using representation of posthumous suffering to prompt urgent moral and spiritual reformation in life, like doom paintings or the *Traicté des peines d'enfer et de purgatoire* [Treatise on the pains of hell and purgatory] (published 1492). It is interesting that Boccaccio follows immediately after Dante, in that Saint-Gelais's framing of the Florentine's enterprise is couched in terms redolent of the Certaldan's most numerously disseminated didactic text in late-medieval France, *De casibus*: the particular lexeme 'cas' gestures in this direction, as more broadly does proclaimed depiction of the misfortunes and vicissitudes of life, like the fates and turbulent fortunes enumerated by Boccaccio. Is it possible that Saint-Gelais knew Dante only from his appearance in *De casibus*? He brackets him as a moral authority alongside Boccaccio and Petrarch, who 'ont fait livres tresmoraulx et exquis' (III.xii.132 [have written morally excellent and remarkable books]).

Brief consideration of commemorative praise of Dante in the fifteenth century, representing him as a deceased author, points up the richly networked way in which his name is enlisted and his depiction of hell cited, and thus the importance of reading such references relationally and severally as carefully contextualized moments of reception. The Dante of Christine, for example, is in some of her works conditioned by being placed in dialogue with Jean de Meun, a pairing which is then crucial for De Premierfait, but is more simply a case of chronological contiguity for Saint-Gelais. The idea of a vision of hell is seized upon by didactic writers wishing to advise on paths to virtue, with the 'infernal repaire' of 'espris dampnez' valued more for its general moral implication (as the consequence of vicious living) than for its representational particularities. However, both Christine and Le Franc commend the manner as well as the matter of Dante's depiction, 'subtil' and 'escript merveilleusement', perhaps in part to encourage broader readership of a writer whom their commemoration seeks not to honour as an already established figure in the medieval canon but to inaugurate as a writer worthy of propagation.

Representing the dead with Dante

My final section, considering late-medieval French representations of the dead in light of *Inferno*, does not depend on our securely identifying direct Dantean influence. Given what we have seen of the richly networked scene of transmission and reception, it concerns itself more analogically with shared preoccupations, valorising concerns present in both the *Commedia* and texts by René d'Anjou and George Chastelain. The key principle at stake is the importance of morality underpinning the definition of posthumous identity: ontological status has an ethical implication, which we can expediently approach through two issues mobilised in how the dead get represented — on the one hand, reputation and judgement; on the other, the 'complex materiality of virtual bodies',[37] when the deceased are shown embodied and animated, walking and talking, as in Chastelain's *Temple de Bocace*.

A relationship between identity, reputation and judgement is developed by Dante in the liminality of *Inferno* 3 at the Gate of Hell, on which is written 'giustizia mosse il mio alto fattore' (3 .4 [Justice urged on my high artificer]), when he encounters the morally neutral, those souls 'che visser sanza 'nfamia e sanza lodo' (3. 36 [who lived without disgrace and without praise]). Having never truly lived (3. 64), they can never truly die (3. 46), and so Virgil advises that they will not be spoken of: 'Fama di loro il mondo esser non lassa' (3. 49 [The world will let no fame of theirs endure]). Moral worthiness determines judgement, which itself assesses moral worth, and moral status — for ill or for good — accords identity. This nexus of concerns is juggled in the Francesca and Paolo episode in *Inferno* 5, which is picked up in René's *Livre* in a manner that resonates intriguingly with Dante's drama of justice and compassion. In the Hospital of Love, *Livre*'s protagonists, Heart and Desire, attend a mass in memory of a lover and his lady 'apportez mors leans par ung cas piteux nouvellement advenu' (section CXX [brought here dead by a grievous accident recently occurred]). Desire asks Courtesy, a superintendent, for the truth of this case, which she proceeds to recount in very allusive terms, speaking anonymously of 'cest amoureux' (l. 1645 [this lover]), persecution by 'mesdisans' (l. 1652 [slanderers]), and how personified Jealousy took the couple's lives:

> Car d'une espëe par le corps
> A ung coup les a tous deux mors. (*Livre*, ll. 1657–58)
>
> [Piercing a sword through their bodies, she killed them both in a single blow.]

René's adulterous lovers are thus cast as sympathetic victims rather than as sinners meriting punishment; one could see this to be adopting Dante-persona's sympathetic response to *Inferno* Francesca's account of love's compulsion.[38] Alternatively, however, one could conjecture a response here, not to the *Commedia*, but to Boccaccio's version, which mentions explicitly the sword (Dante does not) and presents the pair as tragic lovers, betrayed by a deceitful Gianciotto more readily assimilable to the courtly 'mesdisans' trope than the betrayed husband of the *Commedia*.[39] René's presentation also carries Boccaccian resonance in the introductory framing of Paolo and Francesca as 'ung cas piteux' (incidentally, the same collocation used by Saint-Gelais in his cemetery transition between Dante and Boccaccio). Teodolinda Barolini has proposed that, more important than Dante placing Francesca in hell, is how he 'records her name and saves her from consignment to historical oblivion';[40] the significance of storytelling to shore up identity is also promoted by René. After Courtesy's allusive account, she lifts a sheet covering the bodies to reveal their corpses pierced by the sword that killed them. This act of uncovering, I propose, opens up the body as a space to be filled with narrative, with the sword as a prop for storytelling, a tool for activating a tale — a kind of cue to which *Livre*'s protagonists respond by kissing it, mobilizing its potential to serve as a relic, a preserving trace of the unnamed lovers. It is moreover a cue to the extratextual audience — not to determine a single identification so much as to juggle possible associations (does it matter whether this is or is not Paolo and Francesca, and, if it is, whose version it relays?) and thereby appreciate the very processes of identity construction, as when Dante invites us to read his readerly

Francesca's reading of herself.[41] A metatextual reflex is prompted. Courtesy speaks of 'mesdisans' as those 'qui plus que veoir | Dient et on dit mainteffoiz' (*Livre*, ll. 1652–53 [slanderers who very often say and have said more than the truth]), and who thus come reflexively to represent bad tale tellers, whereas Courtesy's account and the mass now being celebrated in *Livre* can be seen as recuperative recording opportunities: in the posthumous events commemorating their death, their life — in the sense of a positive identity narrative — can be restored.

Livre's treatment of Paolo and Francesca raises the issue of posthumous corporeality — a relatively straightforward matter for corpses depicted recumbent and inert, but more complicated when the fictional framework deployed requires physical movement and oral communication with the living, as with Dante's 'ombre triste smozzicate' (*Inf.* 29. 6 [lost and mutilated shadows]), and also with Boccaccio's processional dead in *De casibus*. Boccaccio is not concerned with defining his deceased characters ontologically; whenever a collective noun is used, they are classified, not as 'dead', but often as 'unfortunates' ('infelices') or 'mourners' ('fluentes') — their status defined by the import and tone of the story that they (and/or the persona) tell, the attitude that they have adopted posthumously towards their own life. Both Dante and late-medieval French respondents to *De casibus* are, by contrast, keen to explore the limits of representation through complex reflections on posthumous ontology. In *Inferno*, a clear distinction between living and dead is established when Charon upbraids the pilgrim:

> Et tu che se' costí, anima viva,
> Pàrtiti da cotesti che son morti. (*Inf.* 3. 88–89)

[And you approaching there, you living soul, keep well away from these — they are the dead.]

But there is nonetheless continuity between the two states, as when Capaneus states: 'Qual io fui vivo, tal son morto' (*Inf.* 14. 51 [That which I was in life, I am in death]), and this continuity is moral: an unrepentant sinner's ethical identity is eternally fixed (like Le Franc's 'paine eternelle' of the damned), so that sinful acts in life are expressed in the afterlife. Such expression somatically materializes sin, as in the physical dismemberment of the sowers of discord encountered in the ninth *bolgia*, most famously Bertran de Born:

> erch' io parti' così giunte persone,
> partito porto il mio cerebro, lasso!,
> dal suo principio ch'è in questo troncone. (*Inf.* 28. 139–41)

[Because I severed those so joined, I carry — alas — my brain dissevered from its source, which is within my trunk.]

his severed talking head representing his having ruptured the bond between father and son.

Chastelain's *Temple de Bocace* (1463–65), the most widely disseminated prose work by the Burgundian court historiographer, offers a dream-vision narrative of unfortunates from recent history (from Othon III de Grandson to still-living Margaret of Anjou, the work's dedicatee). The narrator witnesses them entering a temple dedicated to Boccaccio, who, we learn, is himself entombed there and resuscitated in order to advise Margaret that she cannot have her life recorded as wretched because she is not yet dead and her fate thus not yet fixed; as a punning rejoinder, Boccaccio offers her the 'plus vif exemple' [more cogent [lit. living] example] of her late uncle, Charles VII.[42] Some continuity between life and death is evidenced as the unfortunates appear bearing signs of their demise: Richard II is a dead man walking, entering multiply pierced with weapons; Jacques Chabot arrives in a state of dismemberment and speaks while decapitated: 'atout une doloire, sans teste, le troncq du corpz esquartelé, qui durement se complaingnoit de la honte que procuré on avoit a son parentage' (p. 75 [with a doloire, headless, the trunk of the body quartered, who was complaining bitterly of the shame that had been brought upon his kin]). The corporeality of the deceased is spotlighted by its flagrant impossibility — Richard II appears 'par ostention lamentable' (p. 27 [in a lamentable display]). Its paradoxicality draws attention to their ontology and also to their temporality: when someone speaks impaled by swords and daggers, recounting their life and its downward fall towards death, it is difficult to classify them according to any simple ontological or temporal binary: living or dead, past or present. Posthumous representation releases the body from any assumption of unitary integrity and inaugurates instead a mode of performance: the nouns by which Chastelain designates his characters qualify their substantiality — Richard II is 'l'image d'ung roy' (p. 27 [the image of a king]); Boccaccio directs Margaret to 'des personnages que tu vois droit cy' (p. 129 [characters whom you see here]). Like Dante's shades, whose 'simili corpi' [bodiless bodies] cast no shadow on the ground (*Purg.* 3. 32, 28), these are virtual embodiments, but nonetheless arresting for the impact on their viewing audience, not least insofar as they stand as projections of the viewer's imagination and the representational limits of their human understanding. Chastelain's persona offers an interesting retrospective reframing of the processional dead that prompts a metatextual reflection:

> vis je entrer en vif personnage une roine, atout couronne en teste, menant en main ung roy, son mary [Henry VI], en vie aussy par difference de toutes les aultres presentacions contees dont les ymages ne faisoient que fiction. (*Temple*, p. 79)
>
> [I saw enter in living person a queen, with a crown on her head, leading by the hand a king, her husband [Henry VI of England], also alive, in contrast to the other representations recounted whose appearances were only fiction.]

The 'living' status of Margaret and her husband, both still alive extratextually, is contrasted with the figures who have appeared before, not in terms of the latter being 'dead', but in relation to their status as 'fictions' or illusions. We are reminded of the illusory human reality of the shades whose physical form is revealed to the pilgrim as insubstantial when he tries to embrace Casella: 'Ohi ombre vane, fuor che ne l'aspetto' (*Purg.* II.79 [O shades — in all except appearance — empty]). On another level, of course, as literary constructs within a dream-vision narrative, Margaret, Henry, the dead and, for that matter, the persona, all share the same status as 'fictions', like the *Commedia*'s pilgrim and Virgil.

Conclusion

Sylvie Lefèvre asserts that 'la *Commedia* n'a d'abord été connue que grâce à des changements de perspective' [at first the *Commedia* was only known thanks to shifts in perspective],[43] meaning travels by a Mézières or Froissart, translations of Boccaccio, and Christine's critical approach to the established authority of Jean de Meun. To these movements, one could add French fifteenth-century literature's particular fascination with addressing life — moral conduct, identity formation, writerly vocation — from the perspective of death: posthumous genealogizing through cemetery fictions, and dramatizing communication between the living and the dead. In Dante's words, 'forti cose a pensar mettere in versi' (*Purg.* 29. 42 [to put in verses things hard to conceive]) or in prose, yields fruitful interrogation of the capacities of poetic fiction, which, translated into a late-medieval French context, involved debate about the rightful powers of *poetrie* as a figurative mode of discourse and its legitimate subtleties. Dante became cited in a network of references about the didactic role of literature, positioned in particular in relation to Jean de Meun and Boccaccio. In common with both those writers, mention of his name inevitably represented varying degrees of knowledge of his works (books of the *Commedia* or otherwise), variously transmitted (in part, in the original language, through translation, via another author, etc.). While undeniably scattered and not copious, fifteenth-century French engagements with Dante nonetheless attest a measure of influence insofar as his name clearly played an important rhetorical role for them, with their role in turn being in part to propagate it further. As Francesca 'became a cultural touchstone and reference point through the intervention of the fifth canto of the *Inferno*, [...] giving [her] a dignity and a prominence — a celebrity — that in real life she did not possess',[44] so Dante's 'reputation took hold'[45] though Christine de Pizan's and others' acts of promotion through commemoration.

Notes to Chapter 14

1. John A. Scott, 'Dante in France', in *The Dante Encyclopedia*, ed. by Richard Lansing (London and New York: Routledge, 2010), pp. 259–62 (p. 259).
2. See, in particular, the work of Adrian Armstrong, Florence Bouchet, Cynthia J. Brown, François Cornilliat, David Cowling, Nathalie Dauvois, Frédéric Duval and Jane H. M. Taylor.
3. See Helen Swift, *Representing the Dead: Epitaph Fictions in Late-Medieval France* (Cambridge: D. S. Brewer, 2016).
4. *Dante: The Critical Heritage, 1314–1870*, ed. by Michael Caesar (London: Routledge, 1989), p. 16.
5. Documented by Carlo Bozzolo's seminal *Manuscrits des traductions françaises d'œuvres de Boccace: XVè siècle* (Padua: Antenore, 1973), and articles on medieval reception in *Il Boccaccio nella cultura francese*, ed. by Carlo Pellegrini (Florence: Olschki, 1971), as well as art historical work by Vittore Branca (*Boccaccio visualizzato: narrare per parole e per immagini fra Medioevo e Rinascimento*, 3 vols (Turin: Einaudi, 1999)), Brigitte Buettner (*Boccaccio's 'Des cleres et nobles femmes': Systems of Signification in an Illuminated Manuscript* (Seattle: University of Washington Press, 1996)) and Anne D. Hedeman (*Translating the Past: Laurent de Premierfait and Boccaccio's 'De casibus'* (Los Angeles: J. Paul Getty Museum, 2008)).
6. And Boccaccio also wrote the *Trattatello in laude de Dante* and *Esposizioni sopra la 'Comedia' di Dante*: *Tutte le opere di Giovanni Boccaccio*, ed. by Vittore Branca, 10 vols (Milan: Mondadori, 1964–98), III, VI.

7. See Gianni Mombello's substantial article, 'I manoscritti delle opera di Dante, Petrarca e Boccaccio nelle principali librerie francesi del secolo XV', in *Il Boccaccio*, pp. 81–209 (p. 143).
8. Scott, p. 259. The first printing in France of the Italian text occurred in 1547 (Werner Friederich, *Dante's Fame Abroad, 1350–1850* (Rome: Edizioni di storia e letteratura, 1950), p. 72).
9. Nick Havely, *Dante* (Malden, MA and Oxford: Blackwell, 2007), p. 228.
10. For example, Paris, BnF, MS it. 534, housed in the library of Fontainebleau at the start of the sixteenth century, consisted of *Inferno* and an Italian translation of a Latin commentary (Lucien Auvray, *Les Manuscrits de Dante des bibliothèques de France: essai d'un catalogue raisonné* (Paris: Thorin, 1892), p. 46).
11. Scott, p. 259.
12. For the case of Alain Chartier, see Joan McRae, 'Alain Chartier's *Livre de l'Esperance*: A Remodeling of Dante's *Commedia*?', *Digital Philology*, 7.2 (2018), 230–49.
13. Mombello, p. 137.
14. On Serravalle's Latin translation and commentary, as well as the importance, from the fourteenth century, of the papal curia at Avignon for wider transmission of Dante's work, see Nick Havely, *Dante's British Public: Readers and Texts, from the Fourteenth Century to the Present* (Oxford: Oxford University Press, 2014), pp. 15–17, 24–32.
15. Mombello, p. 158.
16. McRae, p. 234.
17. Paris, BnF, MS fr. 226, fol. 394^v. Subsequent references to this manuscript are incorporated in the text.
18. William Burgwinkle, 'Dante and Medieval French Literature', in *Dante in France*, ed. by Russell Goulbourne, Claire E. Honess and Matthew Treherne, *La Parola del Testo*, 17.1–2 (2013), 21–29.
19. McRae, pp. 233–34.
20. Burgwinkle, p. 28.
21. Jacqueline Cerquiglini-Toulet, 'Introduction: l'amour de Sophie. Poésie et savoir du *Roman de la Rose* à Christine de Pizan', in *Poetry, Knowledge and Community in Late Medieval France*, ed. by Rebecca Dixon and Finn E. Sinclair (Cambridge: D. S. Brewer, 2008), pp. 1–14; Suzanne Conklin Akbari, 'The Movement from Verse to Prose in the Allegories of Christine de Pizan', in *Poetry*, pp. 136–48 (pp. 141–43).
22. *Le Débat sur 'le Roman de la rose'*, ed. by Eric Hicks (Paris: Champion, 1977), p. 141.
23. Ibid., pp. 141–42.
24. *The Debate of the Romance of the Rose*, ed. and trans. by David Hult (Chicago: University of Chicago Press, 2010), p. 184.
25. Sylvia Huot, 'Seduction and Sublimation: Christine de Pizan, Jean de Meun and Dante', *Romance Notes*, 25.3 (1985), 361–73 (p. 364).
26. See *Dante's Commedia: Theology as Poetry*, ed. by Matthew Treherne and Vittore Montemaggi (Notre Dame: University of Notre Dame Press, 2010).
27. Cerquiglini-Toulet, p. 13.
28. *Le Chemin de longue étude: édition critique du ms. Harley 3341*, ed. by Andrea Tarnowski (Paris: Librairie générale française, 2000), l. 996
29. Cerquiglini-Toulet, p. 13.
30. See Scott, p. 259; Caesar, p. 29.
31. Goulbourne, Honess and Treherne, 'Introduction', in *Dante in France*, pp. 15–19 (p. 16).
32. Martin Le Franc, *Le Champion des dames*, ed. by Robert Deschaux (Paris: Champion, 1999), ll. 1909–24.
33. References here and following are to *La Divina Commedia*, ed. by Giorgio Petrocchi (Milan: Mondadori, 1966–67) and, for the English translation, to *The Divine Comedy*, trans. by Allen Mandelbaum, Everyman's Library, 183 (London: David Campbell, 1995), both according to *Digital Dante*, <https://digitaldante.columbia.edu> [accessed 3 August 2019]
34. Octovien de Saint-Gelais, *Le Séjour d'honneur*, ed. by Frédéric Duval (Geneva: Droz, 2002), III. xii. Subsequent references to the *Séjour* are incorporated in the text.
35. See Kevin Brownlee, 'Literary Genealogy and the Problem of the Father: Christine de Pizan and Dante', *Journal of Medieval and Renaissance Studies*, 23.3 (1993), 365–87, and Huot.

36. René d'Anjou, *Le Livre du cœur d'amour épris*, ed. by Florence Bouchet (Paris: Librairie générale française, 2003), section CXIII. Subsequent references to *Livre* are incorporated in the text.
37. Timothy J. Welsh and John T. Sebastian, 'Shades of Dante: Virtual Bodies in *Dante's Inferno*', in *Digital Gaming Re-imagines the Middle Ages*, ed. by Daniel T. Kline (London and New York: Routledge, 2014), pp. 162–74 (p. 163).
38. For critical debate regarding Dante-author's position, arguing for willing ambiguity and suspension of judgement, see Elena Lombardi, *Wings of the Doves: Love and Desire in Dante and Medieval Culture* (Ithaca, NY: McGill-Queen's University Press, 2012), pp. 9–11.
39. Boccaccio, *Esposizioni*, ed. by Giorgio Padoan, *Tutte le opera*, VI (1965), p. 315.
40. Teodolinda Barolini, 'Dante and Francesca da Rimini: Realpolitik, Romance, Gender', in *Dante and the Origins of Italian Literary Culture* (New York: Fordham University Press, 2006), pp. 304–32 (p. 330).
41. On Francesca's reading, see Lombardi, pp. 217–23.
42. George Chastelain, *Le Temple de Bocace*, ed. by Susanna Bliggenstorfer, Romanica Helvetica, 104 (Bern: Francke, 1988), p. 131. Subsequent references to the *Temple* are incorporated in the text.
43. 'Dante Aligheri', in *Le Dictionnaire des lettres françaises: le moyen âge* (Paris: Fayard, 1992), pp. 369–70 (p. 369).
44. Barolini, p. 330.
45. Burgwinkle, p. 21.

CHAPTER 15

Illustrating Editions of Dante in France before Gustave Doré

Richard Cooper

The Dante illustrations by Gustave Doré continue to determine the vision of the *Commedia* of so many readers. It now seems hard to imagine how difficult it was for the artist to convince reluctant publishers to bring to fruition his ambitious and long-planned enterprise to give Dante a new visual dimension. Potential publishers might have argued that the keen French appetite for the poet, manifest in the many paintings of Delacroix, Ingres and others, was already well satisfied by editions produced in the first half of the nineteenth century, including several new translations into French, without needing to go to the expense of a luxury folio edition. This chapter seeks to explore, without revisiting Doré's only too well-known illustrations, what publishers in France had offered to their readers before Doré swept the board from 1861.

Fifteenth-century Manuscript Illustration

By the early fifteenth century, hundreds of manuscripts of the *Commedia* were in circulation in Italy and beyond. Dante was reaching a wider market, notably in France, where copies were being sought by members of the court, as witness the paper manuscript of the *Commedia* owned by Jean II de Bourbon (1426–88), Comte de Clermont. The count's only intervention seems to be the painting of the Bourbon arms (fol. 3) and other initials, before he presented the book in 1454 to his counsellor, the bibliophile Louis de la Vernade, Président de Forez:[1] marginal notes in French as well as in Latin indicate that the manuscript was being read attentively.[2] This initiative was matched by that of Jean II's cousin, Charles de France (1446–72), brother of Louis XI. While Duc de Berry from 1461 to 1466, he acquired a fourteenth-century vellum manuscript of the *Commedia* in Italian,[3] which left spaces for decoration. Like Jean II, he commissioned illuminated capitals, one with his own coat of arms, but added one illumination for each *cantica*, for which the artist was the Maître de Coëtivy, now generally identified as the prolific miniaturist Colin d'Amiens. These three landscape illuminations show considerable originality: *Inferno* (BnF, MS Italien 72, fol. 1ʳ) is depicted in greys and blues lit up by orange flames, showing chained souls on the left dragged by a demon, others thrown off a rock, others transpierced by nails, others boiled in a cauldron, the whole presided over by Lucifer devouring souls through both mouth and belly. The miniature for Purgatory (fol. 30^r) is another composite landscape of souls being purged but rescued by angels. The third miniature (fol. 60^r) shows a single vision of Christ in Majesty surrounded by circles of the blessed. This manuscript, in its early binding, passed into the royal collection.[4]

Dante Manuscripts under François Ier

Other members of the royal family were also collecting, notably Charles d'Angoulême, whose marriage to Louise de Savoie was to give birth to François I and his sister Marguerite, future Queen of Navarre.[5] Charles's collection included in 1496 an illuminated 'libvre de Dante' on vellum,[6] with what was the earliest example of French translation on facing pages. He also owned a fourteenth-century vellum copy of *Inferno*, which passed into the royal collection at Blois and Fontainebleau.[7] Following his entry to Florence in November 1494, Charles VIII was presented with a splendid vellum manuscript of Petrarch, commissioned by Lorenzo the Magnificent in 1476 for the Medici library.[8] Written by Antonio Sinibaldi, illuminated by Francesco di Antonio del Chierico, and with ornaments on the binding by Antonio del Pollaiuolo, this masterpiece was altered to overpaint the Medici arms with those of Charles VIII, incorporating his claim to Naples and Jerusalem. Whether a diplomatic gift or war booty, the manuscript was taken to the Blois library and proudly shown to visitors.[9] Apart from the miniatures of the *Trionfi*, it also includes the *Rime* of Dante (fols 202–37^v)[10] and Leonardo d'Arezzo's *Vita di Dante* (fols 238–48^v), each introduced by historiated initials portraying Dante, and the *Rime* by a partial decorative border of flowers, fruit, putti, vases and birds. Pursuing his campaign to Naples, Charles found other Dante manuscripts in the library of the Aragonese kings. Three complete *Commedie* on vellum from the early fifteenth century (BnF, MS Italien 70) and late fourteenth century (BnF, MS Italien 71, 69) were carried off in 1495, and taken first to Amboise, then to Blois and Fontainebleau. The incomplete illumination of the first is very simple, except for the title page in red and blue, where the initial includes a seated figure of Dante,[11] while the second uses puzzle initials,[12] and the third has an illuminated title page showing foliate margins with dragons, lion, angels and an initial representing Christ.[13]

A vellum *Inferno* had already entered France by a different route, through the court of René d'Anjou in Naples and Provence. After fighting for the king in Naples, the Neapolitan Giovanni Cossa (*c.* 1400–76) was appointed seneschal and lieutenant-general of Provence. His library included an early fourteenth-century Florentine *Inferno* with the Ottimo commentary, written by Jacopo Guido di Puccini, and with thirty-four miniatures painted by Bartolomeo di Fruosino and assistants. The volume is notable for the full-page portrait of Hell (fol. 1) and for the complex folio showing the seven liberal arts and their classical exponents, birds, insects, *putti*, flowers, scrolls, the arms of Cossa, and an historiated initial showing Dante writing (fol. 3). This fine volume passed into the French royal library in the sixteenth century.[14]

A clear case of continuing Valois interest in Dante is seen in the Milanese mid-fifteenth-century manuscript of the *Inferno*, with commentary by Guiniforte Barzizza,[15] presented to François I in 1519 by the Milanese jurisconsult and bibliophile Jacopo Minuti, appointed by the king as Senator in the Parlement of newly conquered Milan.[16] Minuti had had it bound in Milan, and embellished with a special title page framed in a rich foliate and historiated border. The white-vine decoration incorporates two coats of arms, Minuti's own, and those of his new royal patron, circled by the Order of St Michel, and supported by salamanders and wild men. It also includes a peacock and various *putti*, as well as a vignette of a seated Dante. The opening of each section is decorated with ornate initials in the same white-vine style covering seven lines of text, from which spring elaborate fronds.[17]

This is not the only illuminated vellum *Inferno* with the same commentary brought from Milan by an Italian benefiting from the patronage of François I. After entering French service in 1528, the condottiere Giovanni Caracciolo, prince of Melfi (1480–1555), became a major figure at court. In his library was an *Inferno* copied *c.* 1440 for Filippo Maria Visconti, and illuminated by an artist in the circle of the Master of the *Vitae Imperatorum*.[18] The volume has been mutilated, with only fifty-nine very fine miniatures remaining; it did not pass into the royal collection, but was kept by Caracciolo's descendants in the provinces.[19] François I himself was not just interested in the *Commedia*, but acquired a vellum *Convivio*, catalogued in the royal collection as 'Le Banquet et Convive de Dante Florentin en Prose', with a title page decorated with a white-vine pattern in the initial and margins, leaving a space for the royal arms, which were not inserted.[20]

The First Translations into French

Given the Valois' interest in collecting Dante manuscripts, whether as gifts or loot,[21] what original contribution was France to make to the illustration of Dante in the Renaissance? A royal secretary, François de Bergaigne, probably of Italian origin, was commissioned between 1515–24 by Claude de France to translate the *Commedia* into French *terza rima* — perhaps both as a literary exercise and to reach a new readership. Whether or not the whole poem was completed, all that survives are two fragments of *Paradiso*, both on vellum, one containing cantos 1–7 written for the Admiral, Guillaume Gouffier,[22] the second containing cantos 1–11 and 15–20, written for the Chancellor, Cardinal Antoine Duprat.[23] Besides the verse translation, of particular interest in these manuscripts are the miniatures, of which seven survive for MS 4119 and eight for MS 4530. They are attributed to two different Paris artists, one (MS 4530) from the Paris Entry Workshop, responsible for albums of various court festivals in Paris; and the other (MS 4119) to an assistant of Etienne Colaud.[24] I have shown elsewhere[25] that the miniatures, set in Italianate tabernacle frames, have been inspired from woodcut illustrations of Venetian editions of Dante from

1491 and 1497. The artists have corrected errors, made up for missing cuts, reduced the number of figures portrayed, and frenchified the costumes.

Venetian woodcuts inspired another illustrated French translation of Dante, of which part of *Inferno* survives.[26] It is written on French paper with facing Italian and French texts, which may suggest some connection with the parallel text copy owned by Charles d'Angoulême mentioned above. It is hard to date: the use of alexandrines and *terza rima* would seem to place it in the reign of François I, though some critics date it earlier.[27] Since one of the frames (fol. 82) contains the salamander of François I, that at least gives a date for some work on the drawings, which are in black pen with occasional brush work for modelling. Each canto was to have a small drawing illustrating it, but although all the frames were drawn, in varied styles, only six illustrations were executed, of which five survive. We can consider three drawings here. The one for canto 1 is a good example, set in a tabernacle frame embellished with scrolls and *putti*, with a vase and two winged phoenix-like beasts in the pediment (Figure 15.1). The illustration uses sequential narrative, snaking from bottom left to top right, tracing six scenes in the canto, from Dante waking, meeting the three *fiere*, being attacked by the *lupa*, being rescued by Virgil, and being accompanied by him into Hell. Of the illustrated Venetian editions published before 1530, all of which use sequential narrative, the ones that come closest to illustrating Dante's gestures in the foreground are those of Benali and Petrus de Plasiis of 1491. The French artist has then invented the background to take the narrative forward from Virgil's appearance.

Fig. 15.1. Turin, BNU, MS L.III. 17; *La Commedia* (Venice: Petrus de Plasiis, 1491), fol. i.1.

The miniature for canto 3, set in a tabernacle frame with vases in the spandrels and a foliate surround crowned by *putti*, also depicts six scenes from the canto, from the spirits crossing the Acheron, to Charon's barque into which spirits are thrown under lightning flashes, when Dante falls in a faint (Figure 15.2). Again, the French artist has taken the left foreground from the Venetian block, and then added a series of scenes to describe later events in the canto, leading up to the earthquake and fire shown in the background of the Venetian cut.

Fig. 15.2. Turin, BNU, MS L.III. 17; *La Commedia* (Venice: Petrus de Quarengiis, 1497), fol. xviii^v.

The miniature for Canto 4, set in a chivalric frame of shields and helmets, shows no fewer than nine scenes, from Dante waking, meeting the souls who had no faith, encountering Homer, Horace, Ovid and Lucan, then a group of warriors, then philosophers, then poets, whom Dante salutes (Figure 15.3). The influence is clear here of the woodcut seen in Venetian editions.

Fig. 15.3. Turin, BNU, MS L.III. 17; *La Commedia* (Venice: Petrus de Quarengiis, 1497), fol. xxiv[r].

The French artist has imitated the scene of the meeting with the ancient authors in the middle right of his narrative, and then reprised it for other meetings in two further crenellated enclosures before the poet exits at top right.

The Earliest Printed Editions in France

How far is this French interest in illustrated Dante in manuscript matched in printed editions?[28] Lyon was in the forefront of pirating Aldines, of which one was the 1502 counterfeit of Dante published by Balthasar Gabiano and Barthélemy Troth, unillustrated like the Aldine. The rivalry of two Lyon publishers in the 1540s led to editions with commentary coming out in Italian of the *tre corone*, Dante, Petrarch and Boccaccio. Jean de Tournes brought out his sextodecimo edition of Dante in 1547, with Landino's commentary, and with a dedication to Maurice Scève, the only illustration being the laurel-crowned medallion portrait on the title page. De Tournes had already placed a profile medallion of Petrarch in his 1545 edition; but, in this case, the models for the profile portrait of Dante seem to have been two woodcuts (Figure 15.4), one attributed to Giulio Clovio on the title page of the 1521 *Convivio*,[29] and one in an oval frame in Stagnino's edition of 1536,[30] the French artist having added cross-hatching to a circular frame to resemble a medal portrait.

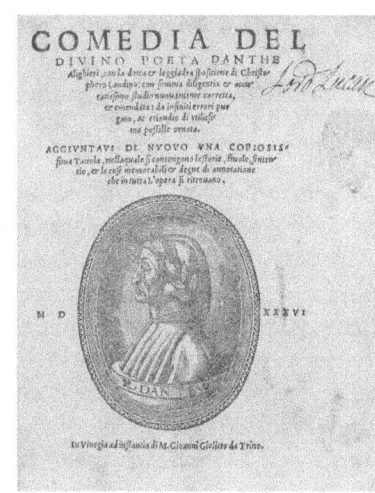

Fig. 15.4. *Il Dante* (Lyon: J. de Tournes, 1547); *Lo amoroso Convivio* (Venice: Z. A. da Sabio, 1521); *Comedia* (Venice: Bernardino Stagnino, 1536).

De Tournes's edition appears not to have been reprinted, and was rapidly superseded by that of Guillaume Roville, who published his Dante in 1551, also in sextodecimo, dedicated to the Florentine scholar Lucantonio Ridolfi. This too had a medallion portrait of Dante, imitated from that of De Tournes/Stagnino, and probably engraved by Pierre Eskrich, who was also responsible for the three illustrations in the text (Figure 15.5). These three woodcuts had been copied and reduced from among the eighty-seven illustrations to the quarto 1544 Marcolini edition, which inaugurated the new Vellutello commentary.

Fig. 15.5. *Dante, con nuove et utili ispositioni* (Lyon: G. Roville, 1551), pp. 11, 232, 442.

Roville's edition was a considerable publishing success, reprinted in 1552, 1571 and 1575, due in part no doubt to the draw of Vellutello's new commentary.

The first printed French translation of the *Commedia*, published in three volumes in Paris in 1596, made no attempt to illustrate the poem, other than in a patriotic architectural frontispiece: the publisher, Jean Gesselin, had commissioned it from the prolific engraver, Thomas de Leu, showing the oval portrait of Dante supported by winged cherubs and the figures of Religion and Justice, and embellished with the device and the arms of the new king, Henri IV.[31]

There was no equivalent in France of the three ambitious series of drawings by Federico Zuccari (1585–88), Jacopo Ligozzi (1587–88) and Giovanni Stradano (1585–87), allegedly intended for an illustrated edition. The only initiative by a French artist in this period was that by Jacques Callot, who was working for Cosimo II in Florence from 1611 to 1612 in the studio of Giulio Parigi. Seeing a new drawing of *Inferno* by Bernardino Poccetti, dedicated to the Duke on 30 May 1612, Callot undertook to etch it on copper. The large print, assembled from four plates, presents an inverted view of *Inferno*, where the structure is seen as a six-tiered pyramid, with Satan at the top, rather than as the traditional funnel-shaped pit. At the top right is the *limbus sanctorum patrum*, at the bottom left the *limbus infantium*, at the top left a view of *Purgatorio* with angels coming to save souls, and at the bottom left a new shipload of the damned arriving in Hell.[32]

Enlightenment Editions

There were no more editions or translations of Dante published in France before the eighteenth century, until a 1768 edition in Italian by the London and Paris publisher, Marcel Prault. This has a three-quarter bust of Dante (Figure 15.6), drawn and engraved in 1767 by Claude-Antoine Littret de Montigny, which clearly derives from the tradition seen in sixteenth-century panel portraits, of which one is in the Musée Condé, and one was recently sold at Sotheby's.[33]

Fig. 15.6. *La Divina Commedia* (Paris: Marcel Prault, 1768).

The more interesting illustration in this edition is the title page (also Figure 15.6), drawn by Jean-Michel Moreau, and engraved by François Godefroy in 1768, showing a tempestuous landscape of flames and clouds, with the damned to the right raising despairing arms. Above them all we note a glowing triangle, which may reflect the triad of *Par.* 28, or more likely the Masonic radiant triangle: a Masonic reading of the poem suggested by this symbol is supported by the facts that the artist Moreau was shortly to join the Masonic lodge, *Les Neuf Sœurs*, and that the edition is prefaced by two letters by Vincenzio Martinelli (1702–85), settled in London since 1748,[34] to his patron, Horace Walpole, a prominent Mason. If so, this anticipates by half a century the Masonic interpretations of Dante by Gabriele Rossetti[35] and Eugène Aroux.[36]

A burst of editions and translations followed over the next half-century, including a prose translation by Artaud de Montor (1811–13), which he illustrated with a full-page engraving for each cantica.[37] All three prints derive from earlier Italian editions, in this case probably the Rome 1791 edition: Artaud used the Manetti-inspired cross-section of *Inferno* engraved by a Swedish artist resident in Paris, Christian Didrik Forssell (1777–1852), that of *Purgatorio* drawn by Adolphe Roehn and engraved by Georges-Jacques Gatine (1773–1824), and the plan of the spheres of *Paradiso* copied without acknowledgement. These continued to appear in Artaud's subsequent editions, until he switched to Doré in the fourth.

The Influence of Flaxman

This inherent conservatism was to change once the impact was felt in France of the Flaxman drawings, completed in Rome in 1793.[38] They were first issued in Rome in 1802 for a French readership, etched by Flaxman's regular engraver Tommaso Piroli.[39] These images, recalling the style of bas-reliefs, inspired French engravers, notably Sofia Giacomelli, née Billet (Madame Chomel), also known as a sculptor and a singer,[40] who created and also engraved her line drawings for Dante, Milton and Sophocles. One of the few critics to study her illustrations describes her manner as in the 'Roman mode [...]: all the figures are as if drawn from statues', adding however that they are 'techically extremely weak', and examples of an 'advanced state of dilettantism'.[41] One could counter by arguing that her hundred plates for Dante, published in Paris in 1813,[42] deserve attention as the first attempt in France to illustrate the whole poem, and the first to use the style of Flaxman in original compositions, rather than in simply reproducing the English model, as would Pierre-Jacques Feillet (*c.* 1820) or Étienne-Achille Réveil (1836).[43] In her *Inferno*, a muscular Virgil, and later Statius, are always portrayed naked with laurel crown and pallium, whereas Flaxman had them swathed in a toga; the gate of Hell is a classical portico, and her centaurs and giant imitate classical statuary (Figure 15.7). Beatrice too will be arrayed in Roman stola and palla.

Fig. 15.7. Mme Giacomelli, *La Divina Comedia* (Paris: Salomon [1813]), *Inf.* 3 and 12.

Some plates are close to Flaxman: in *Inferno*, Eryon, the Simoniacs, Cacus, Ugolino, especially Lucifer; or in *Paradiso* the meeting with Cunizza or the Great Light in *Par.* 28, both of which Giacomelli has reversed, or the Eagle in *Par.* 19, or Christ triumphant in *Par.* 23. Some are more static than the dynamism of Flaxman, for instance her Centaur or the Harpies in *Inf.* 12–13. This had been noted in a contemporary review, which, while saluting her 'imagination vive et sensible', suggested she had shown 'plus d'adresse que de force', and only lifted 'la massue de l'Hercule italien [= Dante] que d'une main tremblante'.[44] But others show considerable vigour, such as the persecuting demons in *Inf.* 18 and 21, or the serpents in *Inf.* 24 (Figure 15.8).

Fig. 15.8. Mme Giacomelli, *La Divina Comedia* (Paris: Salomon [1813]), *Inf.* 21 and 24.

In each of the scenes, which are in portrait rather than landscape layout, she always includes Dante and his guide, which Flaxman often omits, for example *Purg.* 8 (fig. 20), where they witness the ritual of angels and snake. She also provides much more detail, whether with more crowded scenes, or by adding background and scenery, missing in Flaxman, such as the Avaricious in *Purg.* 19 (Figure 15.9).

FIG. 15.9. Mme Giacomelli, *La Divina Comedia* (Paris: Salomon [1813]), *Purg.* 8; *Par.* 27.

An example of her personal vision is the Hymn to the Trinity in *Par.* 27 (fig. 9), which in Flaxman shows angels looking up at a Masonic triangle, but in Giacomelli has the three figures of the Trinity within an aureola. In sum, within Flaxman's linear style, Sofia Giacomelli showed considerable originality throughout in her choice and treatment of illustration, as well as a close knowledge of the poem, but her prints were not republished.

The neo-classical simplicity of Flaxman's drawings continued to find later imitators in France. The poet Sébastien Rhéal (1814–63) received French government support to attempt a new translation, not just of the *Commedia*, but of the complete works, which was to appear in instalments from 1843 to 1852, in what would run to five octavo volumes, plus a sixth in 1856 on the *Monde Dantesque*.[45] The 1843 translation of *Inferno* is illustrated by close copies of Flaxman engraved by Desvignes. But it is preceded by a translation of *Vita Nuova,* with an illustration in the style of Flaxman by Rhéal's wife, Madame de Rhéal,[46] together with two other imaginary sentimental pieces at the end, drawn by her and engraved by a certain Bous, representing *La Mort de Béatrice* and *Vision du Jeune Dante* (Figure 15.10).

FIG. 15.10. Sébastien Rhéal, *Inferno* (Paris: À la Direction, 1843), last two prints.

Rhéal's *Inferno* translation met with sufficient success for him to bring out *Purgatorio* in 1845, again using Flaxman drawings, and then in 1846 *Paradiso*, with the Flaxman drawings engraved by a certain Albert, probably Alfred Albert (1814?–79).

When Rhéal undertook in 1852 to make the first translation of the minor works, for which he had no pictorial model, he used his imagination.[47] For Dante himself, his artist reversed the portrait in the Vatican *Disputa del Sacramento* (pl. 1); for Beatrice he used the Canova bust (pl. 3); in the *canzoni* section, he used two bust portraits of Beatrice and Dante engraved by Léon Mauduisson, loosely derived from Orcagna's frescoes in Santa Maria Novella (pl. 2). To illustrate his translation of the sonnet 'Guido, vorrei che tu e Lapo ed io', with its dream of a sea voyage, he chose a wholly anachronistic engraving entitled *Le Rêve* from a Morelli drawing of a modern warship and skiff (pl. 2bis). Another Morelli drawing of a modern pastoral view of Florence served to illustrate a group of sonnets called *Amours et Regrets* (pl. 5), as did his full-length portrait called *Exaltation de Béatrice*, placed between the sonnets 18 and 19 of the *Vita Nuova* (pl. 6). Another group, called *Rimes profanes*, is illustrated by female busts in modern dress, drawn by Mme Rhéal and engraved by Jean-Baptiste Fosseaume, representing *Primavera* ('Fresca rosa novella', pl. 7), *La Pargoletta* ('Io mi son pargoletta bella e nuova', pl. 8), *Pietra* ('Così nel mio parlar voglio esser aspro', pl. 9), and *La Montanina* ('Amor, dacché convien pur c'io mi doglia', pl. 10). The final group of *Rimes sacrées* is introduced by an engraving showing *La Récompense des Élus* (pl. 11), showing angels bearing up a redeemed woman, and the volume concludes with a copy (pl. 12) of the engraving by Giacomo Aliprandi of Dante sitting in the Grotto of Tolmino (now in Slovenia), from which he had supposedly drawn inspiration for the *Commedia*.[48] In the fifth and sixth volumes, Rhéal printed the first French translations of *Convivio*, *Monarchia* and *De vulgari eloquentia*, the latter two in a volume, *Le Monde Dantesque*, enlivened with a motley collection of prints of knights, fools, troubadours and the popes of Dante's time.[49]

Fig. 15.11. Antoine Étex, *La Divine Comédie* (Paris: J. Bry aîné, 1854), pp. 41 and 46–47.

Pupils of Ingres

The influence of Flaxman continued until 1854, when Rhéal's translation was reissued with a whole new set of very different illustrations by the sculptor, Antoine Étex (1808–88),[50] a pupil of Ingres, whose interest in Dante needs no comment here. The volume is presented as part of an abortive series of *Chefs d'œuvre européens illustrés par A. Étex*, though the sculptor makes no mention of this initiative in his personal *Souvenirs* (1877). The drawings may date from as early as 1847, following the artist's second trip to Rome,[51] and they mark an abrupt change in style from line drawing to picturesque romantic effects, using the new art of wood engraving. They were entrusted by the printer Joseph Bry to the studio of Noël-Eugène Sotain (1816–74), among the pioneers in France of wood engraving, who had in the same year 1854 engraved for the same printer 500 woodcuts of Russia drawn by Gustave Doré, as well as illustrations for an edition of Rabelais. Étex's drawings for Dante had been copied and engraved by Sotain on to endgrain blocks, using a graver or the tint-tool favoured by Doré (*gravure de teinte*). Étex's biographer is damning about the engravings, which he asserts were 'déplorablement gravées et aussi mal imprimées', adding that Étex possibly lacked experience in drawing for the new art of wood engraving.[52] Another critic regrets his lack of 'powerful fancy' and of 'technical excellence' compared with Doré, and damns the illustrations as 'often weak, and indeed mistaken in conception'.[53]

These criticisms do not do justice to the breadth and originality of Étex's ambition to create a whole new illustration for the *Commedia*, however unsuccessfully engraved. Most of the twenty-nine *Inferno* prints bear his signature and that of his engraver Sotain; there are only ten in *Purgatorio*, mostly signed Dumont, and only nine in *Paradiso*, all unsigned. Following the introductory print of the exile's ecstatic vision of a veiled Beatrice (p. 9), the style remains consistent throughout *Inferno*, with a series of sweeping, storm-tossed gothic landscapes (anticipating the style of Doré), populated by wraithlike figures, devils, snakes and monsters. Unlike Giacomelli's nude Virgil, the poet here is dressed in a toga with a laurel wreath. Étex goes further than Flaxman or Giacomelli in giving depth to the scenes, with rocky glades in *Inf.* 1 and 2, sea and riverscapes in *Inf.* 7, 8 and 14, vast plains in *Inf.* 12, 14 and 31, a gloomy forest in *Inf.* 13 (Figure 15.11), mountain scenes in *Inf.* 11, 18 and 19, and cemeteries in *Inf.* 10 and 11 (Figure 15.11).

Many scenes portray the dead, whether as the noble virtuous pagans of *Inf.* 4, or the elongated whirling skeletal ghosts in trailing white shrouds of *Inf.* 3, 6, 8, 15, 16, 17, 18, 20, 24, or quarrelsome figures in *Inf.* 7, or Greek warriors in heroic pose in *Inf.* 26–27 (pl. 12). Only two images describe events from the memory of a sinner: Paolo and Francesca in *Inf.* 5, as Gianciotto draws his sword, and Ugolino surrounded by his starving children in *Inf.* 33. *Inferno* opens with Manetti's cross-section of the circles, and concludes with a vision of the Malebolge, with its ten *bolgie*, and with Dante and Virgil flying on a griffin, as if escaping to the light (Figure 15.12).

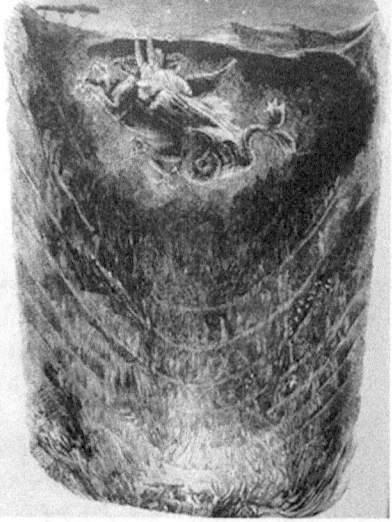

Fig. 15.12. Antoine Étex, *La Divine Comédie* (Paris: J. Bry aîné, 1854), pp. 69 and 82–83.

There are far fewer (10) illustrations in *Purgatorio*, mostly signed by Louis Dumont (b. 1822), who had already engraved for Doré, and which may not necessarily be from designs by Étex. The artist is mainly interested in Antepurgatory, where he portrays Cato, Casella, La Pia and Conrad, and then in the Earthly Paradise, where we meet Matelda, Statius and Beatrice, there being no prints between cantos 13 and 28. He distinguishes between Roman costume for Cato (*Purg.* 1) or Trajan (*Purg.* 10), and medieval costume for Casella (*Purg.* 2) or armour for Conrad (*Purg.* 8). Two prints are very static, the unrepentant (*Purg.* 4) and *invidiosi* (*Purg.* 13–14), while others show procession (*Purg.* 5) or flight (*Purg.* 8 and 31). One print for *Purg.* 10 combines in three tiers the annunciation to the Virgin, the relief of Trajan and the widow, and beneath them the *superbi* bowed down under heavy weights (fig. 24). Among the final cantos the artist chooses three river scenes: the picturesque pastoral vision of Matelda gathering flowers (*Purg.* 28, Figure 15.13); Dante seeing Beatrice on the Griffin (*Purg.* 31); and the prophecy of Beatrice, with Dante and Statius being taken by Matelda to bathe in the Eunoe (*Purg.* 33).

FIG. 15.13. Antoine Étex, *La Divine Comédie* (Paris: J. Bry aîné, 1854), pp. 105 and 132–33.

Paradiso only has nine wood engravings, none of them signed. Two prints for *Par.* 1 and *Par.* 15 exploit the theme of soaring upward, Beatrice leading Dante heavenwards, and (presumably) Cacciaguida rising with wife and child. Two prints evoke the whirling dance of the blessed, one for *Par.* 8 with Rahab as the brightest at the centre, and one for *Par.* 13, with St Thomas, the fifteen stars, and the circle of dancers, musicians and singers (Figure 15.14).

Fig. 15.14. Antoine Étex, *La Divine Comédie* (Paris: J. Bry aîné, 1854), pp. 156 and 165.

Two represent interviews, one with Piccarda (*Par.* 3) and one with St Benedict before the Ladder of Contemplation (*Par.* 22). The edition culminates with Christ in majesty (*Par.* 23), which the artist has interpreted freely by adding cherubs and angels swinging thuribles; and Beatrice's discourse on angels (*Par.* 29), who float in the middle ground against the background chorus of numberless blessed. One print in this series, however, simply does not fit (Figure 15.15). To accompany *Par.* 10, where Dante ascends and contemplates the *alte rote*, the artist has illustrated a figure in a balloon attended by two cherubs, high above a landscape depicting progress in mid-nineteenth century life: around a central monumental arch are set a factory with smoking chimney, a stately home, a distant steamship and sailing boats, a steam train crossing a long viaduct, and in the foreground a farmer ploughing, a stream and bridge, and a mother and children picnicking, one child pointing up at the balloon. If not an error by the publisher, this is an aberration which compromises what was otherwise an honest attempt to present Dante in a different aesthetic style.

Fig. 15.15. Antoine Étex, *La Divine Comédie* (Paris: J. Bry aîné, 1854), p. 161.

One more artist was to try his hand in France at the *Commedia* before Doré's monumental edition of 1861, the Swiss Franz Adolf von Stürler (1802–81)[54], another pupil of Ingres. He had lived in Florence till 1853, where he had prepared some drawings for *Inferno*, self-publishing in France in 1859 a portfolio edition of forty full-page engravings with the text on facing pages.[55] Few copies circulated, and it was not till after his death that a complete edition of 111 prints for the three *cantiche* was printed in 1884.[56] A few examples will illustrate his dramatic interpretation. Two engravings for Canto 5 (Figure 15.16) show Minos and various devils presiding over the punishment of the *lascivi*, with the second one depicting Paolo and Francesca, who embrace as they plunge headlong downwards, Francesca pierced by a sword.

FIG. 15.16. Adolf von Stürler, *L'Enfer de Dante Alighieri*, canto 5.

The prints for cantos 16 and 20 (Figure 15.17) introduce Dante as pilgrim, standing on a rocky ledge next to a statuesque Virgil, encountering in the first the twisting figures of the three Guelph noblemen, and in the second the weeping *indovini* crammed into a grotto, their heads wrenched back: in each case, Dante reveals his emotion at their punishment, and in canto 20 cannot hold back his tears.

Fig. 15.17. Adolf von Stürler, *L'Enfer de Dante Alighieri*, cantos 16 and 20.

Rather than portraying emotional involvement, the engravings for cantos 22 and 27 (Figure 15.18) give prominence to the horde of devils who are about to shred the inert Ciampolo, or to carry off the limp wraith of Guido da Montefeltro under the harsh gaze of Minos.

Fig. 15.18. Adolf von Stürler, *L'Enfer de Dante Alighieri*, cantos 22 and 27.

The final two examples here, for cantos 30 and 33 (Figure 15.19), offer a striking contrast in the engagement of Dante with the scene. From a distance the poet observes the writhing and gesticulating figures in the foreground of two *falsari*, with Gianni Schicchi biting into Griffolino's neck as they run along. In the later canto, Dante moves to the foreground as, in a vast bleak landscape of icy mountains and rocks, he looks on in horror at the two *traditori* locked in struggle, as Ruggiero gnaws at Ugolino's scalp, both clearly identified on scrolls.

FIG. 15.19. Adolf von Stürler, *L'Enfer de Dante Alighieri*, cantos 30 and 33.

These two pupils of Ingres offer a striking contrast in their illustration of Dante in the 1850s. Von Stürler's portfolio for *Inferno* has none of the gothic moodiness of Étex: it is characterized by the muscularity and dynamic movement of the damned, with their almost theatrical expressions of emotion. That both are now almost entirely forgotten arises from the initiative of their younger contemporary Doré, who was comprehensively to upstage them. By 1855, Doré had already conceived his ambition to publish a folio Dante, building on the success of his Rabelais (1854) and his Balzac (1855), both copiously illustrated with cuts by his team of wood engravers. It remains hard to believe that, despite French readers' keen appetite for Dante, despite the vogue for wood engraving, and despite Doré's own publishing record, Louis Hachette was unwilling to support his *Inferno*, which the artist was left to finance himself in 1861, as Von Stürler had done in 1859. It sold 3,000 copies in a few days, and transformed indelibly the public's vision of the *Commedia* right up to today.

Notes to Chapter 15

1. BnF, MS Italien 1470, f° 90, <https://www.gallica.bnf.fr/ark:/12148/btv1b100334004>; Lucien Auvray, *Les Manuscrits de Dante des bibliothèques de France, essai d'un catalogue raisonné* (Paris: E. Thorin, 1892), pp 39–45.
2. Gianni Mombello, 'I manoscritti delle opere di Dante, Petrarca e Boccaccio nelle principali librerie francesi del secolo XV', in *Il Boccaccio nella cultura francese*, ed. by Carlo Pellegrini (Florence: Olschki, 1971), pp. 139–46; *Censimento dei commenti danteschi. 1, I commenti di tradizione manoscritta, fino al 1480*, ed. by Enrico Malato and Andrea Mazzucchi, 2 vols (Rome: Salerno, 2011), II, 968–69.
3. Bibliothèque nationale de France (BnF), MS Italien 72, <https://gallica.bnf.fr/ark:/12148/btv1b55013333r>; Auvray, *Manuscrits*, pp. 24–25; Paul Durrieu, 'Dante et l'art français du XVe siècle', in *Comptes rendus des séances de l'Académie des Inscriptions et Belles-Lettres*, 65.3 (1921), 214–24.
4. Henri Omont, *Anciens inventaires et catalogues de la Bibliothèque Nationale*, I (Paris: E. Leroux, 1908), no. 378 and 1469; *Les Manuscrits à peintures en France: 1440–1520*, ed. by François Avril and Nicole Reynaud (Paris: Flammarion, 1993), notice 24; *Censimento dei commenti danteschi*, II, 940–41.
5. Maxence Hermant, 'Charles d'Angoulême et sa bibliothèque', in Maxence Hermant and Séverine Lepape, *Les Heures de Charles d'Angoulême* (Barcelona: M. Moleiro, 2016), p. 20; Marie-Pierre Laffitte, 'À propos de la librairie de la chambre du roi: manuscrits de la bibliothèque personnelle de François Ier hérités des comtes d'Angoulême (1445–1496)', *Bulletin du bibliophile*, 1 (2018), 11–52.
6. Not extant; see Arturo Farinelli, *Dante e la Francia dall'età media al secolo di Voltaire*, 2 vols (Milan: U. Hoepli, 1908), I, 235–36.
7. BnF, MS Italien 534, <https://www.gallica.bnf.fr/ark:/12148/btv1b85624748>; Auvray, *Manuscrits*, pp. 46–52; *Censimento dei commenti danteschi*, II, 955.
8. BnF, MS Italien 548, <https://www.gallica.bnf.fr/ark:/12148/btv1b105325942>; Léopold Delisle, 'Note sur un manuscrit des poésies de Pétrarque rapporté d'Italie en 1494 par Charles VIII', *Bibliothèque de l'Ecole des Chartes*, 61 (1900), 450–58.
9. Omont, *Anciens inventaires*, p. 46, no. 294.
10. Used in Dante Alighieri, *Rime*, ed. by Domenico De Robertis, I.1 (Florence: Le Lettere, 2002), pp. 570–72.
11. BnF, MS Italien 70, <https://gallica.bnf.fr/ark:/12148/btv1b8426803g>; Omont, *Anciens inventaires*, no. 1627, 2858; Auvray, *Manuscrits*, pp. 82–85; Marcella Roddewig, *Dante Alighieri, die göttliche Komödie: vergleichende Bestandsaufnahme der Commedia-Handschriften* (Stuttgart: A. Hiersemann, 1984), pp. 233–34.
12. BnF, MS Italien 71, <https://gallica.bnf.fr/ark:/12148/btv1b8426804w>; Omont, *Anciens inventaires*, no. 1468, 2860; Auvray, *Manuscrits*, p. 23; Roddewig, *Dante Alighieri*, p. 234.
13. BnF, MS Italien 69, fol. 1, <https://gallica.bnf.fr/ark:/12148/btv1b84268074>; Auvray, *Manuscrits*, pp. 21–22; Omont, *Anciens inventaires*, nos. 1626, 2861; Roddewig, *Dante Alighieri*, p. 233.
14. BnF, MS Italien 74, <https://gallica.bnf.fr/ark:/12148/btv1b10500687r>; Omont, *Anciens inventaires*, no. 2855; Auvray, *Manuscrits*, pp. 77–82; Peter Brieger, Millard Meiss and Charles S. Singleton, *Illuminated Manuscripts of the Divine Comedy* (Princeton: Princeton University Press, 1969), pp. 314–16; Roddewig, *Dante Alighieri*, pp. 235–36.
15. BnF, MS Italien 1469, <https://gallica.bnf.fr/ark:/12148/btv1b105251285>; Auvray, *Manuscrits*, pp. 112–14 and 170–75; Roddewig, *Dante Alighieri*, pp. 247–48; *Censimento dei commenti danteschi*, II, 968–69.
16. Léon Dorez, 'Le manuscrit de Dante offert au roi François Ier en 1519 par Jacques Minut', *Revue des bibliothèques*, 13 (1903), 207–23.
17. BnF, MS fonds italien 1469, fols 17, 27, 38, 57, 67^{r-v}, 75^v, 89, 97^v, 110^{r-v}, 118^v, 128, 142^v, 155, 166^v, 174^{r-v}, 180^v, 188, 196^v–197, 205^v, 216^{r-v}, 225, 232.
18. BnF, MS fonds italien 2017, <https://gallica.bnf.fr/ark:/12148/btv1b10509601v>; Auvray, *Manuscrits*, pp. 115–27 and pp. 170–75; Brieger, Meiss and Singleton, pp. 38–39 and 318–21; Sandra Bandera Bistoletti, 'La datazione del ms 'italien' 2017 della Bibliothèque Nationale di

Parigi miniato dal 'Magister Vitae Imperatorum'", in *Scritti di Storia dell'arte in onore di Roberto Salvini*, ed. by Cristina De Benedictis (Florence: Sansoni, 1984), pp. 289–92.
19. Camille Morel, *Une illustration de l'Enfer de Dante, 71 miniatures du XVe siècle* (Paris: H. Welter, 1896).
20. BnF, MS Italien 1014, <https://gallica.bnf.fr/ark:/12148/btv1b10033406t>; Omont, *Anciens inventaires*, n° 2819; Auvray, *Manuscrits*, p. 155.
21. Omont, *Anciens inventaires*, nos. 1468–69, 1623–28, 2852–64.
22. BnF, MS NAF 4119, <https://gallica.bnf.fr/ark:/12148/btv1b10540048h>.
23. BnF, MS NAF 4530, <https://gallica.bnf.fr/ark:/12148/btv1b53196537m>; Auvray, *Manuscrits*, pp. 129–36; partly published in Camille Morel, *Les plus anciennes traductions françaises de la Divine Comédie* (Paris: Librairie Universitaire, 1897), pp. 589–603.
24. Marie-Blanche Cousseau, *Etienne Colaud et l'enluminure parisienne sous le règne de François Ier* (Tours: Presses Universitaires François-Rabelais de Tours, 2016), pp. 85, 95, 167, 169–72, 216–20, 227, fig. 34, 93.
25. Richard Cooper, 'Dante sous François Ier: la traduction de François de Bergaigne', in *Pour Dante: Dante et l'Apocalypse; lectures Humanistes de Dante*, ed by Bruno Pinchard (Paris: Champion, 2001), pp. 389–406; Myra Orth, *Renaissance Manuscripts: The Sixteenth Century*, 2 vols (London: Harvey Miller, 2015), II, 99–102.
26. Turin, Biblioteca nazionale universitaria, MS L.III. 17; published by Camille Morel, *Les plus anciennes traductions*; Jules Camus, 'La première version française de l'*Enfer* de Dante: Notes et observations', *Giornale storico della letteratura italiana*, 37 (1901), 69–93.
27. Alessandro Bertolini, 'À propos de la première traduction de l'Enfer de Dante (Turin, Biblioteca nazionale universitaria, L.III. 17): quelques questions préliminaires', *Le Moyen Français*, 71 (2012), 3–32; Stefania Vignali, 'Le "cas" littéraire du manuscrit L.III.17 de la "Biblioteca Nazionale Universitaria" de Turin: une traduction ambitieuse', *Studi francesi*, 176 (2015), 221–34.
28. Richard Cooper, 'Praise and (more) Blame of Dante in Late Renaissance France', *Yale French Studies*, 134 (2019), 67–81.
29. *Lo amoroso Convivio di Dante* (Venice: Zuane Antonio & fratelli da Sabio, 1521).
30. *Comedia con la dotta & leggiadra spositione di Christophoro Landino* (Venice: Bernardino Stagnino, 1536).
31. *La Comedie de Dante*, tr. B. Grangier (Paris, J. Jesselin, 1596).
32. Print in the Fogg Museum, Harvard, <https://www.harvardartmuseums.org/art/280231>.
33. Sotheby's sale, New York, 30 January 2019; Collections des musées de France (Joconde) 00000104762.
34. *Dizionario biografico degli Italiani*, 100 vols (Rome: Istituto della Enciclopedia italiana, 1960–<2020>), LXXI, 133–36.
35. *La Divina Commedia di Dante Alighieri con comento analitico di Gabriele Rossetti*, 6 vols (London: John Murray, 1826).
36. *La Comédie de Dante (Enfer-Purgatoire-Paradis): traduite en vers selon la lettre et commentée selon l'esprit. suivie de la Clef du langage symbolique des Fidèles d'amour*, ed. by E. Aroux, 3 vols (Paris: héritiers J. Renouard, 1856–57).
37. *Le Paradis — L'Enfer — Le Purgatoire poëme du Dante, traduit de l'italien suivi de notes explicatives pour chaque chant par un Membre de la Société colombaire de Florence, de la Société royale de Gottingue et de l'Académie de Cortone* (Paris: Treuttel et Würtz, 1811); (Paris: Smith et Schoell, 1812); (Paris: Blaise & Pichard, 1813).
38. Corrado Gizzi, *Flaxman e Dante*, exhibition catalogue, Torre de' Passeri, Sept.–Oct. 1986 (Milano: Mazzotta, 1986).
39. *La Divine Comédie du Dante*, illustrated by John Flaxman, engravings by Piroli (Rome: s.n., 1802).
40. See a review in *Le Moniteur Universel*, 51 (1813), p. 1557.
41. Ludwig Volkmann, *Iconografia Dantesca* (London: H. Grevel, 1899), p. 149.
42. *Collection de cent figures dessinées et gravées par Mme Giacomelli; pour orner la Divine Comédie du Dante, traduite en français par M. Artaud* (Paris, J. J. Blaise, 1813); *La Divina comedia di Dante Alighieri: cioè l'Inferno, il Purgatorio, ed il Paradiso, composta ed incisa da Sofia Giacomelli* (Paris: Salmon [1813]).

43. *La Divine Comédie du Dante par Flaxman*, lith. de Feillet, (s.l., n.d., c. 1820); *Divine Comédie du Dante Alighieri gravés par Reveil* (Paris: Reveil Audot, 1836).
44. *Le Moniteur universel*, 51 (1813), p. 1557.
45. Paris: À la Direction, later Moreau: 1843 (*Enfer*), 1845 (*Purgatoire*), 1846 (*Paradis*), 1852 (*Œuvres mineures*), 1852 (*Banquet*), 1856 (*Monde Dantesque*).
46. See the dossier in BnF, Estampes, SNR-3 (Mme Rhéal).
47. Sébastien Rhéal, *Œuvres mineures* (Paris: Moreau, 1852).
48. Drawn by Giovanni Derif, and printed in the Udine edition of 1823. Dante had supposedly been the guest there of Patriarch Pagano della Torre. Rhéal appears to have deformed the engraver's name to make it Aldoprandi.
49. Signed by Tauxier and L. Bath.
50. *Œuvres de Dante Alighieri. La Divine Comédie. Traduction nouvelle, précédée d'une introduction contenant la vie de Dante et une clef générale du poème, par Sébastien Rhéal, avec des notes d'après les meilleurs commentaires, par Louis Barré. Illustrations par Antoine Étex* (Paris: J. Bry aîné 1854).
51. Paul-Emile Mangeant, *Antoine Étex peintre, sculpteur et architecte* (Paris: Plon, 1894), p. 43.
52. Ibid., p. 13.
53. Ludwig Volkmann, *Iconografia dantesca* (London: H. Grevel, 1899), p. 188.
54. See the exhibition by Marie Therese Bätschmann and Marc Fehlmann, *Adolf von Stürler (1802–1881)* (Bern: Kunstmuseum, 2002).
55. Adolf von Stürler, *L'Enfer de Dante Alighieri, quarante dessins composés par Stürler* (Paris: à l'auteur, 1859).
56. Adolf von Stürler, *La Divine comédie de Dante Alighieri: l'Enfer, le Purgatoire et le Paradis: recueil de cent onze compositions* (Paris: Firmin-Didot, 1884).

CHAPTER 16

A Poor Relation among French Dante Scholars: Abel-François Villemain's Public Classes at the Sorbonne 1828–1830

Franziska Meier

In the first half of the nineteenth century, Abel-François Villemain, a professor of rhetoric at the Sorbonne, enjoyed a remarkable celebrity in France and even beyond. However, after his death on 8 May 1870, his name slowly started to disappear. While Gabriel Vauthier in his book *Villemain 1790–1870: essai sur sa vie, son rôle, ses ouvrages* from 1913[1] — the only biography up to now — retraced Villemain's stunning academic and less successful political career, subsequently, historians or scholars of literature have paid him very little attention. If his name still rings a bell, this is due to his association with two colleagues at the Sorbonne, namely the historian François Guizot and the philosopher Victor Cousin. During the Restoration years, the three formed an intellectual triumvirate giving a series of well-attended open courses which the ultra-royalist government under Villèle even suspected to be hot spots of liberal opposition and would temporarily suspend in the middle of the 1820s.[2]

In 1830, Villemain, like his colleagues, stopped teaching at the university (he only spent a little time on editing his stenographed courses on the history of French Literature) and entered politics. It is not clear why his interests shifted so radically. First, he became a member of the Conseil royal de l'instruction publique. In December 1834, he was elected permanent secretary of the Académie française, and, in 1838, was appointed secretary of public instruction. In contrast to his two peers, he did not leave a mark on the French higher educational system. In 1844, he definitively resigned from office following an act of folly which, as Victor Hugo suggests, was down to paranoia.[3] Under the Second Empire he retired from politics, maintaining only his seat at the Académie. During the following two decades he edited his earlier articles, published his *Souvenirs contemporains d'histoire et de littérature* in 1854, and yielded to his enthusiasm for the Middle Ages. In 1860, his study *La France, l'Empire et la Papauté* — a defence of the medieval Popes' earthly politics and claims — caused a scandal. In 1873, three years after his death, the *Histoire de*

Grégoire VII appeared, whose first sketches can be traced back to Villemain's lectures on Dante Alighieri.

Through his public lectures at the Sorbonne Villemain had a deep impact on French culture. Although Lady Morgan does not explicitly name him in her *France in 1829–30*, where she fails to name any teacher, she is very likely to have attended Villemain's courses as so many other Parisians did in those years. In the chapter 'Mornings at Paris' she sketches how the great and the good spent their leisure time:

> Nothing can be more delightful, more instructive, more amusing, than our mornings at Paris. One goes through a course of literature, science, arts, politics, philosophy, and fashion, *tout en-courant*; laughing, arguing, gossiping, lounging on sofas, or jumping into carriages, running in and out of public and private edifices and collections.[4]

Lady Morgan's depiction gives a good insight into what these lectures at the Sorbonne were like. This type of 'cours publique', in which university professors addressed both students and the general public, had been introduced in the second half of the eighteenth century.[5] They reached their peak in the Restoration, turning into a high-profile event driven by the three gifted professors with cultural as well as political ambitions. More precisely, the professors used them as a platform to encourage critical reflection upon human rights and liberties. After this climax, the open classes increasingly came under fire for being *cours spectacle* instead of a serious academic training programme. In 1877 Jules Ferry's reform of the university system put an end to the practice by excluding all non-students.[6]

A good, ironic witness to the appeal that the three open courses exerted is Stendhal, who in a series of articles kept his English readers posted on what was going on in Paris between 1826 and 1829. In June 1828 he starts his account by saying that, because of the absence of any interesting recent publication, he cannot help speaking about the classes held at the Sorbonne. He then reveals to his readers the extent to which they had become fashionable among the rich, the literary groups and the middle class.[7] He also highlights the political direction that, under the Restoration, any interest in literature had taken.[8] Stendhal decides to focus his chronicle on Villemain because, as he puts it, Guizot, the later prime minister, was too boring and Cousin's presentation of German philosophy was altogether incomprehensible. Incidentally, the French review *Le Globe* also kept its readers posted about these classes and their suspension for political reasons. They seem to have been increasingly followed in other French cities and abroad.[9]

In his portrait of Villemain from 1836, Sainte-Beuve recalls the impact the professor's teaching had on the younger generation. Speaking of 'cette rapide jeunesse', he compares the way Villemain spoke about literature to an excited youth with a pioneer who enters a beautiful forest for the first time; in doing so, he clears three to four ways which were doomed to disappear should the youth not take up the task of demarcating and paving the faint paths. As Sainte-Beuve states, his generation, unfortunately, could no longer roam the woods like kings chasing game in their royal parks; they had to settle down as engineers or geometers who take measurements and secure the newly opened area.[10] It was Villemain who had the chance to discover new landscapes of literature.

From Stendhal's long account of Villemain's classes it is hard to tell what they were about. Villemain seems to have spoken indiscriminately about Dante, Shakespeare and, finally, on Richardson's impact on French literature. It may, of course, be that Stendhal's account was entirely fictitious, plundered from some of the professor's earlier publications, perhaps even intended to appeal to his English audience. It is also far from clear how many lectures Stendhal summarized in the two articles written in June 1828. From the reports that the prestigious review *Le Globe* published about Villemain's classes in December 1827 and the first months of 1828, we get the impression that the professor predominantly dealt with eighteenth-century French literature and had a very comparative, albeit encyclopaedic, approach.[11] In Sainte-Beuve's portrayal, Villemain turns out to have been also an expert on ancient Greek literature and the Fathers of the Church.[12] In any case, the only printed version we have[13] rather gives the impression that Villemain had been mainly interested in French literature. From 1830 to 1838 his voluminous *Cours de littérature française*, which is considered to be his masterpiece, was published.

Interestingly, the three volumes on the French eighteenth century are preceded by a *Tableau de la littérature au Moyen Âge en France, en Italie, en Espagne et en Angleterre*. However, according to his biographer, the classes on the Middle Ages had not been very successful.[14] Sainte-Beuve does not pay much attention to them at all except for the interest Villemain had always taken in Pope Gregory VII. Why, then, did the two volumes on the Romance Middle Ages, in which three lectures are dedicated to Dante Alighieri, end up in the *Cours de littérature française*?

Villemain's lectures have not yet stirred much curiosity among Dante scholars. In contrast to Claude Fauriel, Pierre-Louis Ginguené and the younger Frédéric Ozanam, the entry on Villemain in the *Enciclopedia dantesca* is rather dry. Remo Ceserani seems to be confused by the fact that an elegant yet superficial professor of rhetoric such as Villemain had been so much acclaimed in his lifetime and held in even greater esteem than Claude Fauriel.[15] The only exception to this general neglect is Michael Pitwood who, in the third chapter of his book on *Dante and the French Romantics*,[16] puts Villemain on the same footing as Fauriel; both championed the third and decisive period in French Dante scholarship. Whereas Jean-Charles-Léonard Simonde de Sismondi and Pierre-Louis Gingené, according to Pitwood, maintained the classicist bias towards Dante's barbarous language and bad taste,[17] Villemain and Fauriel, who were both more sympathetic to the ideas of romanticism, made a case for appreciating Dante's style on its own terms.[18] It is curious that Pitwood does not make any distinction between the two Dante scholars as far as the quality of their research[19] or its method is concerned. Nor does he take into account the contrary position held by the authoritative *Enciclopedia dantesca*. His positive assessment of Villemain as Fauriel's peer would find its way into the American *Dante Encyclopedia*. John Scott, though, in his entry on Dante reception in France, cites Villemain only once, whereas he allows more space for Fauriel's research.[20] But even this positive assessment has not triggered scholars' interest.

What makes Villemain's lectures on Dante specific and, in my view, intriguing is the extent to which he, contrary to his French predecessors Ginguené and Sismondi, as well as to Claude Fauriel, inserts the Florentine poet into the framework of French literature. It is true that Ginguené initially intended to write a comparative history of romance literatures and ended up narrowing his scope to Italian.[21] According to Paolo Grossi,[22] this had been due, first of all, to the fact that Ginguené knew it best and, second, because it had been less well known in France. His purpose had been to convince the French audience of Dante's 'rôle fondamental dans le progrès des lettres de l'Europe moderne' [leading role in the progress of modern European letters].[23] Fauriel, in turn, the first professor of foreign literature at the Sorbonne, gave two different classes: the first about his pioneering research on Provençal poetry, and the second, held between 1833 and 1835, on Dante and the origins of the Italian language. Obviously, he stressed the debt which Dante owed to the Provençal, but he did not mix up the two fields.[24]

To recap, the three Dante scholars share a commitment to the comparative method promoted by Madame de Staël, but Fauriel and Ginguené for different reasons decide to deal with Italian literature separately while Villemain places Dante within a general picture and, strikingly, under the heading of French literature. The issue is now to understand what impact this collocation had on the presentation of Dante.

A reader of a *Cours de littérature française*[25] is likely to expect that the author will indulge in celebrating the *Chanson de Roland*, the songs of the Troubadours, or the chivalric novels composed by Chrétien de Troyes as the first great monuments of French literature. Villemain, however, proceeds differently. He underscores the extent to which these texts[26] are of merely linguistic interest, which does not exclude the possibility that they give precious insights into the spirit of a people, as Villemain emphasizes.[27] He makes a clear-cut distinction between even the most sophisticated use of language in medieval France and a real work of literature. Unfortunately, he does not give a definition of what he means by literature.[28] From his lectures we only get the very standard view that a work of literature manages to touch human souls[29] and, thereby, frees itself from all historical bounds.

Admittedly, Villemain answers the question, 'où parut la première lumière de l'esprit moderne? où se leva la poésie?' [Where did the first gleams of the modern spirit appear? Where did poetry arise?](I, 13) positively by indicating the songs of the Troubadours. Yet, this is an assessment that he borrows from François Raynouard, the first authority in the field of Provençal poetry at that time. In the following paragraphs, Villemain actually turns to ranking the songs among the first examples of artistic expression and the first testimonies of a political and social criticism in rhyme which he considers to be typical of the French.[30] The best he can say about them is that they feature an 'élégance poétique qui se rapproche un peu de l'humanité des temps modernes' [poetic elegance which comes somewhat closer to the humanism of modern times] (I, 14). In his inaugural lecture, Villemain conveys the idea that the French Middle Ages lack a poet and literary composition. Apparently, no French text before Dante manages to touch human souls; thus they all fail the test of time. Dante's *Comedy* is the first literary text which is not bound to historical circumstances. As if wanting to make his listeners feel the longing of the Middle Ages for the emergence of such a Poet, Villemain delays the Florentine's first appearance until the last of his inaugural lectures.

While Jules Michelet will number the layman Dante among the most important gravediggers of the ever-dying Middle Ages,[31] Villemain, in the spirit of the eighteenth century, introduces him as 'le premier flambeau du génie européen' [the leading light of European genius] (I, 26). Significantly, in the first mention of his name, he sets the Florentine in a European context. Moreover, he almost wraps him up in a veil of mystery that enhances the impression of Dante's singularity and isolation:

> Une sorte d'obscurité est répandue sur la naissance poétique de ce phénomène qu'on appelle le Dante. Rien ne l'annonce. D'où vient-il? Cinquante ans auparavant, où était cette langue? (I, 27)
>
> [A kind of obscurity besets the poetical birth of this phenomenon that we call 'le Dante'. Nothing announces it. Where does he come from? Fifty years beforehand, where had this language been?]

According to this first entrance on the stage of Villemain's *Cours de littérature française*, Dante emerges from nowhere. He stands out alone and seems to be better acknowledged as a 'phenomenon' than as a human being.[32] He even had to forge his own linguistic tool, the Italian vernacular. In this representation of an isolated creative poet, Villemain is very close to the Romantics, or to what Sainte-Beuve in his portrayal calls the 'génies créateurs' [creative geniuses].[33] Likewise, Victor Hugo, around the same time in 1830, describes Dante in his novel *Notre-Dame de Paris* as one of the rare examples of 'le grand accident',[34] which means that a genius is suddenly thrown into a chance historical context. Similarly, Villemain presents Dante by almost stripping him of his historical and national features. In other words, it looks as if Dante just happens to have been born in Florence.

When Villemain, at the conclusion of his first lecture, lays out the programme of his class, he resumes the concept of an isolated genius, but then proceeds in another direction:

> Le génie du Dante est distinct et séparé de tout ce qui l'entoure. Rien ne le précède, et rien ne l'égale. Maintenant, par cette puissante commotion qu'un homme supérieur donne à ses contemporains, des génies secondaires naîtront à sa suite. Ainsi se présente le XIV siècle de l'Italie, avec son éclat, sa belle langue, son harmonie, que le Dante lui-même avait imitée des Troubadours provençaux, mais en les effaçant trop, pour qu'on les nomme après lui.
>
> Nous étudierons avec soin toute cette littérature italienne, où la France puisa beaucoup, et qui lui devait tant à elle-même. (I, 35–36)
>
> [The genius of Dante is distinct and separated from all that surrounds him. Nothing precedes him, nothing equals him. Now, through the powerful commotion that a superior man causes among his contemporaries, he will trigger the birth of secondary geniuses. This is what characterizes fourteenth-century Italy: its brilliance, its beautiful language, its harmony which Dante had copied from the Provençal Troubadours, although he erased them all too

> radically so that they should be referred to in his terms [i.e. in the terms of the *Commedia*].
>
> We shall closely study all of this Italian literature, which France drew from so much and to which he [Dante] indeed owed so much.]

The oral character of the printed version may account for some clumsiness in the sentences. However, there is more to it. The argumentation leaves little doubt that Villemain, in the inaugural lecture, does have a hard time coming to terms with the question of how to connect Dante to French literature. He seems to be torn between the assumption that Dante is a genius who composes all by himself and the idea of a literature that comes about within a continuous process of *imitatio* and *aemulatio*. In the case of the Troubadours, the chain of influences worked out rather negatively for the imitated models. Villemain almost complains about the extent to which Dante's poetry overshadows, even annihilates, its French predecessors, which Villemain himself did not consider as literature. Furthermore, the parallel between Dante having followers and Dante himself copying the Troubadours may contain a kind of *lapsus* since it suggests that the poet may have suffered the same fate at the hands of his heirs — a sense which would contradict Villemain's most firmly held opinion.

In the last sentence quoted above, the wording is also confusing. Apart from the fact that Villemain hints at 'all this Italian literature' (although he will exclusively focus on Dante), he now seems to be keen on understanding the mutually enriching relationship between France and Dante. In other words, after having introduced Dante as an outstanding genius, Villemain shifts the attention to the poet's special association with France. However comparative and all-encompassing the professor's approach to literature may have been — and taking into account the oddities of oral performances — the inconsistencies make us aware of some uneasiness about Dante's unquestioned predominance over medieval culture and, what is more, his eclipsing the cultural primacy of France. Unlike Ginguené, who showcased Dante's fundamental role at the beginning of vernacular national literatures, Villemain, conversely, may have sensed this assessment as a challenge to French superiority. The question now is whether, and to what extent, his lectures on Dante may be read as an attempt to give a French answer to this challenge without diminishing Dante's importance. The tenth lecture[35] embarks on a long passage about the thirteenth century characterizing it as one of the decisive moments in the history of the *esprit moderne*. Instead of shifting to Dante, Villemain starts by picking up again his discussion of two French writers, Thibaut de Champagne and Jean de Joinville. Unfortunately, they cannot really give an idea of why France had such an impact on Europe (I, 321). In other words, before tackling Dante, Villemain makes a foray into French culture and its supremacy in the Middle Ages. Thus he tends to convert Dante's work into a case-study concerning the ways in which the movement of minds and literary activity (I, 321), inspired by what was happening in France, reached other nations and came to fruition in other vernaculars. What makes Italy in the thirteenth century so particular, according to Villemain, is the fact that the powerful aristocrats and princes could not prevent social mobility, nor stop the people ('la force populaire' (I, 324)) from asserting their political ambitions. It was in the middle of the clash between the two medieval superpowers — the Pope and the Emperor — that the ancient concept of liberty, of democratic institutions, was restored in Italy. Whereas the movements of minds (I, 325) seems mainly to have resonated in France without producing any work of art there, political activity and the popular life had only been aroused in Italy, and thereby set the stage for Dante.

Contrary to the inaugural lecture, Villemain's first lecture on Dante draws attention to the extent to which essential literary, philosophical and intellectual inspirations, the engines powering progress, originated in France.

Villemain's picture of the medieval mainstreams that made the biggest impact on all European nations is multifaceted. He employs (or borrows) August Wilhelm von Schlegel's concept of the three mythologies which had come about in the popular collective imagination — the chivalric, the allegorical and the Christian — and which would find their first and most inspiring expressions in the French vernaculars. He adds the burgeoning of sciences, also rooted in France, or more precisely at the Sorbonne, that is at the very place where Villemain himself is giving his lectures. However, he hesitates to give all the credit for the early superiority of France of which the other nations, even Italy, had been aware (I, 328) to the Sorbonne. For instance, he brings into play the French *trouvères*, whose inventions had been admired, as well as the prosperous and highly civilized society under Saint Louis, which may have attracted people to France. He explains to his listeners that all those whose talents had been admired in their own countries had been tempted to move to Paris (I, 328). Villemain drops the names of Albertus Magnus, Thomas Aquinas and Roger Bacon as émigrés to the pinnacle of learning. Then he switches to Brunetto Latini, who came to Paris in 1266, apparently attended the 'cours célèbres' of two professors of Italian origin and, finally, wrote the *Trésor* in Old French, which Dante's master praised as the most delightful language, 'le plus délitable' (I, 329).

Finally, Villemain adds to this series of great scientists a man who is 'famous for very different reasons' (I 330). In a long passage he describes Dante's masterful performance at the university. In the tenth lecture, for the first time the Italian poet appears in person. Villemain evidently takes inspiration from Boccaccio's first redaction of the *Trattatello in laude di Dante*, but he modifies the anecdote of Dante's 'disputazione de quodlibet' in a school of theology in a significant way. Giovanni Boccaccio introduced it as an exemplum to prove Dante's memory as well as his intelligence.

> Quattordici quistioni da diversi valenti uomini e di diverse materie, con gli loro argomenti pro e contra fatti dagli opponenti, senza mettere in mezzo raccolse, et ordinatamente, come poste erano state, recitò; quelle poi, seguendo quello medesimo ordine, sottilmente solvendo e rispondendo agli argomenti contrarii. La qual cosa quasi miracolo da tutti i circustanti fu reputata.[36]

Villemain gives a slightly different version:

> C'était vers 1304. Beaucoup de monde, clercs et laïcs, étaient accourus dans la grande salle de l'Université pour entendre une thèse qui devait être soutenue

de quolibet, sur tout ce qu'on voudra. Le tenant était un étranger, jeune encore, d'une physionomie haute et grave. Il y avait quatorze champions attaquans. Chacun présentait sa question, sa difficulté, avec tous les argumens que la science du temps pouvait fournir. Lorsque ces quatorze chevaliers scolastiques eurent passé, le tenant reproduisit lui-même toutes les questions; puis il les reprit, et avec une infinie variété d'argumens, terrassa chacun de ses quatorze adversaires. Cet étranger était le Dante, qui, banni de son pays, voyageait alors en France pour son instruction. (I, 330–31)

[It was around 1304. Many people, clerics and laymen alike, rushed to the aula of the University to listen to a thesis in the form of a *quolibet* [sic], which means open to any topic. The discussant was a foreigner, still young, with a haughty and grave physiognomy. There were fourteen opposing champions. Each presented a question, a difficulty, with all the arguments that the science could offer at that time. After the fourteen scholastic knights had finished, the discussant reproduced all the questions raised; he then reformulated them, and, thanks to an infinite variety of arguments, managed to strike down each of his fourteen enemies. This foreigner was Dante who, banned from his country, travelled in France in pursuit of instruction.]

It is hard to tell if Villemain did not understand the Italian original, if he distorted it on purpose, or if this is just a striking lapse. Whereas Boccaccio speaks of a *disputatio* held at a school of theology, Villemain arguably prefers the more general term 'university' which is naturally reminiscent of the university where he lectures. It does not come as a surprise that he does not specify the discipline or the department. While Boccaccio distinguishes fourteen issues whose different arguments Dante manages to recap and to settle, Villemain stages a kind of battle, with Dante and fourteen adversaries represented as knights, as if the chivalric code characterized academic debates. While Boccaccio refers to a small number of people who attend the *disputatio*, Villemain evokes a large and mixed audience because the *disputatio*, or rather the 'thèse' — a term that is more equivocal — aroused a lot of interest in Paris, which, in turn, is strongly suggestive of the appeal the professor's own classes would have roughly six hundred years later. In the final sentence, Villemain resumes his guiding argument: Dante had been travelling in France in search of higher education. In other words, Villemain pays tribute to Dante's genius, but, at the same time, he proudly highlights Paris as the most accomplished place of learning, of intellectual progress. This is all the more puzzling since everywhere else in the *Cours* Villemain belittles scholasticism, which, according to him as well as to many other Dante scholars, is the very part of the *Divine Comedy* that bothers modern readers.[37]

Despite the probability of some linguistic misunderstandings, these modifications are consistent, and thus telling. They arouse suspicion about the professor's personal involvement. The choice of the year 1304, in which Dante is supposed to have turned thirty-nine, may imply another allusion, since in the winter of 1829/30, when the open course took place, Villemain was the same age. However, it is hard to figure out why he draws the parallel.[38] Should we put the blame on his limited knowledge of medieval philosophical teaching? Or may we take his distortions as an unconscious consequence of his teaching experience at the Sorbonne?

Once Villemain has established Dante's reverence for France's learning, he turns to sketching the Italian antecedents of Dante's poetry. While in his inaugural speech he had denied any antecedents (and from Stendhal's account in June 1828 we learn that he had presented Dante as an entirely isolated genius),[39] here he surprisingly comes up with a somewhat different and very vivid picture of the Italian context. Is the shift in perspective due to his fresh reading of *De vulgari eloquentia*? This would make sense, since Villemain had confessed in his inaugural lecture that he did not know much about the Middle Ages and, therefore, would study while preparing the lectures.[40] Or did he draw on other sources? For instance, he certainly read the article about burgeoning vernacular poetry in Italy published in *Le Globe* on 27 January 1830, since he cites Dante's questionable encounter with Fra Ilario; nevertheless, he did not just copy that account.

Whatever his sources may have been, Villemain gives his description of vernacular culture a peculiar twist. Again, he is adamant in stressing the extent to which early Italian poetry had been profoundly anchored in French antecedents, that is, in court life, in the chivalric code, and in religious enthusiasm (I, 346). In his view, the Sicilian school had merely transposed the Provençal songs into their dialect; subsequently, Italian wordsmiths trod in their footsteps, disremembering the model. Dante, therefore, rightly referred back directly to the Troubadours and, by doing so, almost obliterated the Italian poets in between. Moreover, Italian poetry was all about scholasticism and love, which may amount to yet more evidence for its debt to French culture. Consistent with this strategy is the delight that the professor takes whenever he comes across a quote in which Italians show respect for France. Northern Italians chose the Provençal language because of its harmony and good taste (I, 335). Dante appreciated Old French in *De vulgari eloquentia* (I, 334). While complaining about how impossible it is to translate the *Divine Comedy*, Villemain does not miss the opportunity to highlight the closeness of Occitan and the Italian vernacular and, thereby, again enhances the debt that Dante owes to the Troubadours.[41] However, in contrast to Claude Fauriel, he is not interested in upgrading the Troubadours' poetry to being at the origin of all national literatures in Europe, but simply in locating Italian and, in particular, Dante's poetry within a French-centred framework.

Contrary to his inaugural lecture, Villemain offers the surprisingly poignant insight that even the greatest genius cannot escape from the constraints of tradition or from historical pressures.[42] Italy in the thirteenth century ceases to provide a wild space in which a great man may create as he wishes. The classical heritage weighs heavily on all the emergent vernacular literatures.[43] Thus Villemain in the course of the three lectures moves away from both the romantic idea of a self-contained genius and Vico's concept of history that evolves along full cycles, each of them restarting from scratch (I, 364). Instead, he sketches a long tradition in which all the national literatures are placed and somehow united.

After having separated Dante's *Comedy* as the first real work of literature from all the other medieval linguistic testimonies, Villemain surprisingly sets out to isolate the poetical moments in Dante's rather scholastic masterwork. He emphasizes the extent to which these poetical islands had to be gained, albeit conquered from the oppressing 'amas de souvenirs',[44] the mass of recollections that ancient traditions, as well as historical circumstances, had accumulated. Hence his reading turns out to be another instance of the nineteenth-century tendency to fragmentize the *Comedy* and to focus exclusively on specific passages. Moreover, it is striking that Villemain describes Dante's poetical islands as being close to the simplicity and naturalism of the Greek Homer,[45] or the densest moments of inspiration as being 'germanique'.[46] In other words, where Dante's poetry is at its best, Villemain brings into play the stereotyped features of other, non-Italian nations. This might be seen as a specifically French 1830s perception of the universality of literature that Herder and Goethe had claimed. Whereas Rivarol, in 1785, could promote his translation of the *Inferno* into French as a way of shifting Dante's outdated Italian into the universality of eighteenth-century French,[47] Villemain is torn between his nationalist French endeavours, which leave a mark on all his historical and biographical reconstructions, and the commitment to a literature that stands above time and on its own to a literature that, in its respective specific idioms, claims universality because it speaks to all human beings.

Notes to Chapter 16

1. Gabriel Vauthier, *Villemain 1790–1870: essai sur sa vie, son rôle, ses ouvrages* (Paris : Perrin, 1913).
2. In his *Chroniques parisiennes* (27 August 1843), Sainte-Beuve claimed: 'Trois hommes éminents ont exercé la plus grande influence sur la direction des esprits et des études en France depuis vingt-cinq ans, et on peut dire qu'ils ont été véritablement les régents de cet âge' ["Three eminent figures have exercised the greatest influence on the direction of minds and studies over the past twenty-five years, and one could say that they have been the true rulers of the age"]. Quoted in Anne Martin-Fugier, *La vie élégante ou la formation du Tout-Paris 1815–1848* (Paris: Fayard 1990), p. 244.
3. Cf. the conversation with Villemain recollected by Victor Hugo: *Choses vues*, 7 December 1845, <https://fr.wikisource.org/wiki/Choses_vues/1845/Villemain> [accessed 7 May 2021].
4. Lady Sidney Morgan: *France in 1829–30* (London: Saunders and Otley, 1831), p. 318. For further details, see Martin-Fugier, pp. 202–14.
5. See Bruno Belhoste, 'Un espace public d'enseignement aux marges de l'université : les cours publics à Paris à la fin du XVIII siècle et au début du XIX siècle', in *Les universités dans la ville, XVI–XVIII*, ed. by Thierry Amalou and Bloris Noguès (Rennes: PUR, 2013), pp. 217–33.
6. For more information see Louis Liard, 'L'enseignement supérieur pendant la restauration', *Revue des deux mondes*, 109 (1892), 823–53, <https://fr.wikisource.org/wiki/L'Enseignement_supérieur_pendant_la_restauration> [7 May 2021].
7. See Stendhal, *Esquisses de la société parisienne de la politique et de la littérature 1826–1829* (Paris: Sycamore, 1983), p. 278.
8. See ibid., p. 279.
9. See Charles Dejob, *L'instruction publique en France et en Italie au dix-neuvième siècle* (Paris: Armand Colin 1894), pp. 84–85. See also Johann Peter Eckermann, *Gespräche mit Goethe in den letzten Jahren seines Lebens*, ed. by Fritz Bergemann (Frankfurt: Insel, 1955). On 18 February 1829, Goethe states: 'Villemain steht in der Kritik gleichfalls sehr hoch. Die Franzosen werden zwar nie ein Talent wieder sehen, das dem von Voltaire gewachsen wäre. Von Villemain aber kann man sagen, daß er in seinem geistigen Standpunkt über Voltairen erhaben ist, so daß er ihn in seinen Tugenden und Fehlern beurteilen kann.' [Villemain also ranks very high as a critic. The French will, it is true, never again witness a talent such as that which sprang from Voltaire. Yet one can say of Villemain that in his intellectual and spiritual position he is rasied above Voltaire, so that he can judge the latter's faults and virtues.]

10. Sainte-Beuve, *Portraits contemporains*, ed. by Michel Brix (Paris : PUBS 2008), pp. 689–713 (p. 704).
11. See the articles in *Le Globe : recueil philosophique et littéraire*, 11 December 1827, p. 41 ; 23 April 1828, pp. 353–60; 26 April 1828, pp. 316–68; and 30 April 1828, pp. 369–76.
12. Cf. Sainte-Beuve's portrait of Villemain, p. 707.
13. At the end of the 1820s, the interest in these courses had rocketed so much that editors had them stenographed and, after a short revision by the lecturer, published. From Stendhal we also know the financial circumstances of the book-project, p. 279.
14. See Vauthier, p. 78.
15. Ceserani states: 'nonostante un'eccessiva pomposità dell'eloquio e una non sempre buona informazione (e anche, a quanto pare, una non sempre attenta revisione degli appunti delle lezioni), le pagine del V. ebbero nell'Ottocento un successo straordinario e furono assai più note di quelle dell'Ampère e del Fauriel.' (*Enciclopedia Dantesca*, v (Rome: Instituto dell'Enciclopedia Italiana, 1976), p. 1021) The disparity as far as public renown is concerned may be due to Fauriel's notorious shyness. See Michael Pitwood, *Dante and the French Romantics* (Geneva: Droz, 1985), p. 51.
16. Pitwood, pp. 41–65.
17. See ibid., p. 47.
18. According to Pitwood (ibid., p. 51): 'Both men considered it essential to look at Dante as a personification of the spirit of the age in which he lived. He was seen as the product of the conflicting tendencies of the Middle Ages, shown in the mixture of Christian and Classical and in the dichotomy in his work between a desire to philosophize and the inspiration derived from love of Beatrice. Both Villemain and Fauriel discuss Dante's sources, but conclude that they are unimportant once subjected to the power of Dante's genius.'
19. Villemain's superficiality was already noted by contemporaries such as Stendhal and Goethe. In *Gespräche mit Goethe* on 3 February 1829, Goethe claims that Villemain 'besitzt die Kunst einer gewandten Entwickelung aus dem Grunde, er ist nie verlegen um schlagende Ausdrücke, wodurch er die Aufmerksamkeit fesselt und seine Hörer zu lautem Beifall fortreißt; aber er ist weit oberflächlicher als Guizot und weit weniger praktisch' [Villemain has a gift for clever exposition of an argument; he is never at a loss for a striking expression which commands attention and moves his hearers to applause; but he is much more superficial and much less practical than Guizot].
20. John A. Scott takes up Pitwood's concept in a more radical way: 'Dante scholarship was inaugurated in France by the work of Villemain and Fauriel', *The Dante Encyclopedia*, ed. by Richard Lansing (New York: Routledge, 2010), p. 260.
21. Ginguené's *Histoire littéraire d'Italie*, published between 1811 and 1824, is also based on notes taken during his open classes and revised by the author, in this case carefully.
22. Paolo Grossi, *Pierre-Louis Ginguené, historien de la littérature italienne* (Bern: Peter Lang, 2006), p. 151.
23. See ibid., p. 156.
24. Fauriel's former student Jules Mohl, who in 1854 edited the notes taken in Fauriel's classes along with his professor's manuscripts, also kept the two fields separated.
25. I use the first two volumes of the edition of the *Cours de littérature française* republished in 1846. The volumes and the pages will be indicated in the text.
26. Villemain omits the *Chanson de Roland*, which, some years later, Michelet praises as an outstanding literary and historical testimony of a free people. Jules Michelet, *Renaissance et Réforme : histoire de France au XVIe siècle* (Paris : Robert Laffont, 1982), pp. 40–41.
27. Like Herder, Villemain appreciated linguistic documents as testimonies to the particularities and the development of the 'Volksgeist'.
28. As Stendhal pointed out, p. 289 : 'D'un bout à l'autre de son cours, M. Villemain n'a rien dit de nouveau sur la théorie des beaux-arts, et il a même embrouillé les idées qu'il avait empruntées' [From one end of his course to the other Villemain has said nothing new on the theory of the fine arts and has muddled up those ideas that he borrowed].
29. Cf. Villemain, I, 26 : 'Mais ce n'est qu'au génie qu'il est donné d'agir sur les âmes, d'élever ces monuments qui rayonnent au loin dans les siècles, et enfin de créer une littérature' [But it is only

to genius that it is given to work upon the spirit, to raise those monuments that shine through the distance of the ages, and, in short, to create a literature].
30. See Villemain, I, 26; concerning the peculiarity of rhymed criticism, I, 17 and 22–23.
31. Cf. Michelet, p. 36 : the Middle Ages end 'au XIVe siècle, quand un laïque, s'emparant des trois mondes, les enclôt dans sa comédie humaine, transfigure et ferme le royaume de la vision' [in the fourteenth century, when a layperson takes the three worlds of the afterlife and puts them into his human comedy, transforming and closing off the realm of vision].
32. Later, Villemain adds that Dante neither followed any model nor had a school of followers (I, 39).
33. Sainte-Beuve, p. 690.
34. Victor Hugo: *Notre-Dame de Paris 1482*, ed. by Benedikte Andersson (Paris: Gallimard, 2009), p. 295.
35. Dante is briefly mentioned in the second lecture. Villemain apologizes for all the dry philological material which he will lay out in the following lectures. The material, that is the analysis of the French vernacular documents, however, is necessary if the audience wants to understand how a poet uses similar linguistic tools. See I, 97.
36. Giovanni Boccaccio, *Vite di Dante* (Milan: Mondadori, 2002), p. 33.
37. Pitwood (p. 42) highlights a similar dichotomy in Ginguené.
38. Villemain certainly felt great sympathy for the uncompromising Dante who refused to come back to Florence on humiliating terms (I, 356). *Le Globe* reports that Villemain showed the same uncompromising attitude when he resumed his class after the suspension, *Le Globe* of 26 November 1828.
39. Stendhal, p. 281 : Villemain's 'connaissances sont extrêmement bornées et, lorsqu'il remonte au moyen âge ou seulement au XVIe siècle, il commet les bévues les plus singulières que l'on puisse imaginer' [learning is extremely limited and in dealing with the Middle Ages or even the sixteenth century he commits the most egregious blunders that one could imagine].
40. At the beginning of the 13th lecture he tells his audience that he ignored even the name of Jacopone da Todi, a listener had pointed out to him (II, 3).
41. See Villemain, I, 383.
42. See ibid., I, 368: 'Quelle que fût la liberté de son génie, la nouveauté de son langage, il n'a pas été libre du joug de toute imitation. Il n'a pas échappé à cette forme érudite qui est imprimée à toute la littérature moderne; il naissait dans un siècle qui déjà pliait sous le poids des souvenirs.' [However free his genius was and however original his language, he was not entirely free from the yoke of imitation. He did not escape that tendency to erudition which is stamped upon all modern literature; he was born in an age which was already bowing under the weight of memory.]
43. See ibid., I, 378 : 'Quelle que soit la native et indomptable originalité de son génie, il écrit d'après des règles et des modèles. Il est disciple de la Bible et d'Aristote, de Virgile et des scolastiques' [However natural and untameable was the originality of his genius, he still wrote according to rules and models. He is a student of the Bible, Aristotle, Virgil, the Scholastics].
44. See Villemain, I, 401: 'C'est du milieu de cet amas de souvenirs et de faits que le poète s'élance pur et nouveau' [Out of the midst of this heap of recollections and circumstances the pure, new poet springs forth].
45. See Villemain, I, 401: 'il a les goûts naïfs; il a la voix jeune et argentine du poète grec; comme lui, il aime toutes les images simples de la nature, des champs, de la vie domestique; elles reviennent sans cesse dans ses vers. [...] ce grand poète primitif.' [he has the simplicity, the youthful and silvery voice of the Greek poet; like him he prefers natural and simple images of rural and domestic life; they recur constantly in the verse of this great primitive poet.]
46. Concerning Dante's *Vita Nuova*, Villemain states: 'le génie de ce grand poète n'est pas italien, mais rêveur, triste, exalté. S'il était moins naturel, je le dirais germanique' [the genius of this great poet is not Italian but dreamy, melancholy, exalted. Were it not that he is more natural, I should call him Germanic] (I, 372).
47. Whereas in the *Discours préliminaire* Rivarol praises the benefits of translating that always enrich a language, it is only in the comments on the cantos that he hints at the necessity to transpose

Dante's medieval Italian into a more civilized form of modern French. Aida Audeh, in fact, bases her statement (according to which in Rivarol the act of 'translation' is a means of both appropriating and 'correcting' Dante's Italian and thereby asserting the superiority of the French language at a time when the growth of nations and the sharp demarcation of languages were closely related processes) on a telling glossing of the 27th canto: 'Au treizième siècle la langue toscane était républicaine, et chaque mot y participait de la souveraineté; mais quatre ou cinq cents ans d'intervalle, la familiarité que le temps nous fait contracter avec certaines expressions, et surtout le changement du gouvernement ont fait d'une langue républicaine un langage de populace.' [In the thirteenth century the Tuscan language was republican and all its expressions had to do with sovereignty; but in the four or five centuries since our dealings through time with certain terms — and above all, political change — turned a republican language into a popular one.] (quoted in 'Dufau's Mort d'Ugolin: Dante, Nationalism, and French Art, c. 1800', in *Dante in the Long Nineteenth Century: Nationality, Identity and Appropriation*, ed. by Aida Audeh and Nick Havely (Oxford: Oxford University Press, 2012), pp. 141–63 (p. 145)).

CHAPTER 17

Dante Alighieri and German Romanticism

Alfred Noe

At the very beginning of the second volume of Goethe's *Wilhelm Meisters Lehrjahre* (Berlin, 1795) Mignon, the mysterious young girl abducted as a child from somewhere in Italy, recites a poem that was soon to become the most famous literary expression of the so-called nostalgia for Italy in German speaking countries:

> Kennst du das Land, wo die Citronen blühn,
> Im dunkeln Laub die Gold-Orangen glühn,
> Ein sanfter Wind vom blauen Himmel weht,
> Die Myrthe still und hoch der Lorbeer steht.
> Kennst du es wohl?
> Dahin! Dahin!
> Mögt ich mit dir, o mein Geliebter, ziehn.

> [Do you know the land where the lemon-trees grow,
> In darkened leaves the gold-oranges glow,
> A soft wind blows from the pure blue sky,
> The myrtle stands mute, and the bay tree high?
> Do you know it well?
> It's there I'd be gone,
> To be there with you, O, my beloved one!]

In his book *Das klassische Land. Wandlungen der Italiensehnsucht* (Leipzig, 1927), Wilhelm Waetzoldt observes that the perception of Italy, not so much as a real country but more as an idea, starts with Renaissance humanism but changes over the centuries, resulting in an interesting mirror of the German mentality. Those changes are, of course, embedded in European cultural history and begin, in the German-speaking countries, with Albrecht Dürer, who sojourned twice in Italy, first as a young man in 1494 and later, as an acclaimed artist, in 1509. His early watercolours show that he was aware of, and interested in, the cultural differences he observed at the German–Italian linguistic border near Trento. He found the land extending beyond the southern border of his 'Germania' to be very much what Petrarch described in his poem 'Italia mia' (*Canzoniere*, 128), that is, God's own beloved country:

> Rettor del Cielo, io cheggio
> che la pietà che ti condusse in terra
> ti volga al tuo diletto almo paese.

During the Carolingian dynasty, in what is known as the *translatio imperii*, the Roman Empire was revived north of the Alps. The German humanists thus never thought of Italy simply as one more neighbouring country; Italy was where a blend of Antiquity and Christianity had laid the foundation of European culture, arts and politics. Wilhelm von Humboldt defined Rome as the symbol of transience and, at the same time, of universal connectedness, and we may still agree with Waetzoldt when he affirms in the introduction to his book that Italy remains crucial to everyone for whom culture is an object worth attaining.[1] Previously, pilgrimages to Rome had been made mostly for spiritual reasons. The new pilgrims, however, wished to see with their own eyes in Italy, and most of all in Rome, the marvels of the perfect union of ancient paganism and the Christian Middle Ages, the loveliness of nature and the wonders of human architecture. As early as the middle of the seventeenth century, Andreas Gryphius in his poem 'Als Er auß Rom geschieden' meditates on Rome as a symbol of decadence and resurrection, declaring that nothing can ever be equal to the eternal city, the meeting point between East and West and South and North.

Italian travels were not infrequent during the Middle Ages and the Renaissance, but the real boom was triggered around 1700 by the fashion for the Grand Tour, and lasted for around two centuries. From the late Middle Ages onwards, a universal admiration for Italian culture led to increased travelling among members of the German nobility. Those early tourists undertook extended excursions to culturally interesting regions of the peninsula, and would spend some time in Padua or Bologna studying in one of the famous law faculties. They were supposed not only to learn the language but also to improve certain other skills such as conversation, dancing, riding and fencing, as well as acquiring the elegant, urbane manners defined in the various educational treatises which, since their publication in Italy in the sixteenth century, had been setting standards of civilized behaviour throughout Europe. The person making the Grand Tour was typically male, between 17 and 21 years old, accompanied by a tutor, and financially well provided for by his family.[2]

The Grand Tour gave rise to a substantial service sector. Knowledgeable guides could be hired in every important city; these guides kept reference books and put their clients in contact with local artists offering souvenir paintings, engravings, etc. Most of the young travellers possessed their own *barouche* and relied on the postal service alone for coachmen and horses; this allowed them greater freedom of movement than the stagecoach, while posthouses provided the necessary accommodation. Obligatory stages were Venice, Florence, Milan, Padua, Bologna and Siena, though the ultimate destination was of course Rome, where the young gentlemen spent the winter in order to visit the famous sights. Apart from the various religious festivals, special highlights for northern Europeans seeking entertainment were the Roman Carnival and the Venice opera season. Because of the danger of banditry, few travellers ventured further south, though Naples was found very attractive, being at that time one of the most populous European cities and the capital of a kingdom renowned for its exotic splendour. Vesuvius was also a great attraction, as were the excavations at Pompeii from the middle of the eighteenth century.

There are many personal chronicles of the Grand Tour, though few of them rank as works of literature. Johann Caspar Goethe's *Viaggio per l'Italia* (1740) was long known only through his famous son's quotations. A work of some literary value is *Hercules Prodicius* (Antwerp, 1587) by Stephanus Vinandus Pighius, tutor to Prince Charles Frederick of Jülich-Cleves-Berg, who died of smallpox in Rome in 1575 at the age of nineteen. In this work Pighius created for his pupil a literary monument that became the basis of the first tourist guide to Italy. Two other texts are worth mentioning for their literary merits. The travelogue of a trip to the Orient undertaken in 1587 by an Austrian Protestant, the Baron Hans Christoph Teufel (1567–1624), after the obligatory studies in Padua, Bologna and Siena, was written in Italian with the title *Viaggio fatto di Constantinopoli verso il Levante* and published in Vienna in 1598. And a diary was written by Augustus the Younger, Duke of Brunswick-Lüneburg (1579–1666); on 6 October 1598 Augustus started out on his Grand Tour, which lasted two years and took him as far as Sicily. The most interesting features of this diary are descriptions of the cabinet of curiosities in Florence and of the public libraries of Bologna, Siena and Rome.[3]

The earliest professional guides start to appear around 1600, their number increasing considerably in the second half of the seventeenth century because of a fast-growing demand. The most popular guide in the German-speaking area was Franciscus Schott's *Itinerarium Italiae*, first published for the 1600 jubilee in Antwerp; this is for the most part a simple compilation from the above-mentioned *Hercules Prodicius*. There were many reissues and translations of the Schott *Itinerarium*, for example *Itinerario, ovvero Nova descrittione de' viaggi principali d'Italia* (Padua, 1629), and it remained a work of reference until the eighteenth century.[4] One of the most popular guidebooks in the German-speaking area was François Maximilien Misson's *Nouveau voyage d'Italie, faite* [!] *en l'année 1688*, first published in 1691 in The Hague. J. W. Goethe's father Johann Caspar owned the fifth edition published in Utrecht in 1722.

In 1755, after publishing his monumental work on ancient Greek art, *Gedancken über die Nachahmung der griechischen Wercke in der Mahlerey und Bildhauer-Kunst*, in Dresden, Johann Joachim Winckelmann set foot on Roman soil for the first time. This saw the beginning of his creative approach to the study of ancient Greek and Roman, as well as Italian, art and culture. His work profoundly influenced German romanticism, and in particular the reception of Italian literature in German-speaking countries. On 7 July Winckelmann wrote to his friend Hieronymus Dietrich Berendis:

> I believe, in coming here it was my mission to open the eyes of those who will come to see Rome after me. Of course, I only speak of artists. On their arrival here, all the noblemen are fools, and they are donkeys when they depart. They do not deserve to be instructed.[5]

Winckelmann gradually acquired an unrivalled knowledge of ancient art, culminating in his famous descriptions of the Belvedere-Apollo, the Laocoön-group and the temples at Paestum. But his writings also convey the liberating effect Italy had on his mind, which was to become the stereotype for Italy:

> I do not desire anything. And he who, like myself, has neither fears nor wishes, is freer and happier than a king. I am so content and so pleased with my fate that, upon my returning to Germany, I plan to go on a trip to Greece.[6]

Winckelmann's *History of Ancient Art* appeared in 1764 in Dresden, two years after the German painter Anton Raphael Mengs's treatise *Gedanken über die Schönheit und über den Geschmack in der Malerey* (Zurich, 1762). Unsurprisingly, given their close relationship, there is a great similarity of thought between the two works. Winckelmann describes and analyses the aesthetics of ancient Greek art, juxtaposing it to the artistic achievements of the ancient Egyptians and Romans. He concludes that it is the Hellenic aesthetic canon that reaches the highest degree of perfection. The Enlightenment, striving for political emancipation, regarded the ancient Hellenic city-states as the realm of freedom, where art in its ideal form, based on nature and rationality (what Winckelmann called *noble simplicity and quiet grandeur*), could flourish and perfect itself. This highest form of artistic expression is celebrated simultaneously as the material appearance of the divine and the manifestation of the perfect human principle. Gotthold Ephraim Lessing (1729–81) contributes to this train of thought with his treatise *Laokoon, oder über die Grenzen der Malerei und Poesie* (1766). Lessing argues against Horace's thesis *ut pictura poesis* (as painting, so poetry) as a basis for literature. Poetry and painting must maintain their own character, the former being extended in time, the latter in space.

As librarian at the ducal library of Wolfenbüttel since 1770, Lessing had for several years cherished a wish to visit Italy. Eventually, in 1775, he was invited to accompany Prince Leopold of Brunswick-Lüneburg on his Grand Tour. The party started out from Vienna (where Lessing had sought employment as court librarian) and travelled via the Tyrol to Milan, the first stage of an eight-month sojourn in Italy. On 7 May 1775, in a letter to his brother Karl, Lessing declared that, at least in part, the journey made his dreams come true. He liked everything he saw and heard, so that his old plan of living permanently in Italy seemed once more very attractive. In subsequent letters Lessing does not tell us much about Italy, but writes mainly about his professional future and about obtaining a satisfactory income after his return to Wolfenbüttel. He does, though, supply detailed records of all the cities the party visited, and notes on Italian literature and the lives and oeuvre of various Italian scholars, as well as the history of Italian theatre. He also provides a list of the books he wishes to buy for the Wolfenbüttel library.[7] He has purchased in total 264 books on various subjects, ranging from theology to political science, medicine and literature. He has bought only one book on Dante, but this is noteworthy in itself: *Le similitudini della Commedia di Dante Alighieri: trasportate verso per verso in lingua latina da Carlo d'Aquino della Compagnia di Gesù* (Rome, 1707). This is d'Aquino's Latin translation of 490 rhetorically interesting passages from the *Divine Comedy*, and is a preliminary step towards his main work, the Latin translation of the entire *Commedia* in three volumes (Naples; resp. Rome, 1728). In his commentary, d'Aquino attempts a synoptic interpretation of the metaphors in the Italian original and in his Virgilian hexameter version. He also deals with the importance of rhetorical figures in the *Commedia*, underlining the vitality and variety of Dante's poetic images, their visionary depth and their prodigious number.

At the end of the Enlightenment and in the early years of Romanticism, the image of Italy depended to a large extent on the reception of Italian literature, and especially on the leading names such as Dante, Petrarch, Boccaccio, Ariosto and Torquato Tasso. Most of the important works of Italian literature had been translated between 1470 and 1630, during the period of Renaissance humanism and the early Baroque, a period when the German language went through a transitional phase. A consciously sought side benefit of these translations was thus the perfection of the German literary language. In the second half of the seventeenth century, the focus shifted towards more contemporary texts, especially in the field of music. The Italian *drammi per musica*, in their original Italian versions and in their German adaptations, attracted the greatest attention in all the culturally active German-speaking cities, from Vienna to Hamburg. Towards the middle of the eighteenth century the interest in Italian literature reverted to the sacred monuments of the past, triggering a second wave of translations of the great classics which continued until the beginning of the twentieth century. In the German-speaking area, ever since the sixteenth-century printing houses and publishing companies had been editing Italian literature in the original, but in the second half of the eighteenth century literary magazines also began to take an interest. Perhaps the best known of these magazines is the monthly *Gazzetta di Weimar*, edited by Christian Joseph Jagemann (1735–1804), who, as a member of the Accademia della Crusca, published an Italian–German dictionary and two anthologies of Italian poetry, each of them in two volumes: *Antologia poetica italiana* (Weimar, 1776) and S*celta delle migliori prose e poesie dei più chiari scrittori Italiani — Italiänische Chrestomathie* (Weimar, 1794–96). In the two years of its existence (1787–89), the *Gazzetta di Weimar* regularly issued essays on Dante, Petrarch, Machiavelli, Ariosto, Tasso and Goldoni.

Nevertheless, the reception of Italian classics encountered a certain degree of prejudice, mostly because of the admiration the French classics enjoyed in Germany. This is particularly true of the works of Dante. During the first half of the eighteenth century, the reception of Dante's oeuvre was sparse, and impeded by incomprehension, mostly owing to the considerable influence of Johann Christoph Gottsched, the last, and totally uncompromising, philosopher, author and critic of the neoclassical school. The only aspects of Dante's oeuvre held in high regard were his technical innovations in Tuscan versification;[8] his poetic visions were totally alien to this intellectual current.

The situation changed with the Swiss author, academic, critic and poet Johann Jakob Bodmer. In 1734 Bodmer began to engage with Dante in two of his essays: *Critische Betrachtungen über die Poetischen Gemählde der Dichter* (Zurich, 1741) and *Über das dreyfache Gedicht des Dante* (Zurich, 1763). In his *Critische Betrachtungen* he emphasizes that, in order to understand Dante rightly, the critic must keep in mind the intellectual and social circumstances of his time. Bodmer juxtaposes the normative notion of art coined by the Enlightenment and Neoclassicist writers with the idea of historical and national relativity, thus preparing the ground for an adequate comprehension of medieval poetics. According to Bodmer, literary critics only reveal their own lack of understanding when they unthinkingly conclude that Dante's poetry offends against all the rules that the classical school has laid down for the (mechanical) construction of a poem.

From our modern standpoint the idea of reducing a work like the *Divina Commedia*, on account of its poetic flaws, to an anthology of its most attractive passages seems absurd, but we must remember that Antoine Houdart de La Motte did exactly this in his 1714 transposition of the *Iliad* into French, as did Anne-Marie Du Bocage in her version of Milton, *Le Paradis terrestre, poème imité de Milton* (1748). Both compilers made what they deemed rational choices, cutting down the *Iliad* to twelve of its original twenty-four books, and much the same with *Paradise Lost*. Bodmer harshly criticized this scholarly and eclectic approach, demanding unconditional respect for the entirety of a work of literature; otherwise, what the reader gets is only a skeleton. These considerations were of course meant to challenge the classical principle of never mixing literary genres, an idea which originated in the sixteenth-century interpretations of Aristotle's *Poetics*: for 'if Dante was able to use all the genres in one poetic composition, why should he be condemned, for not limiting himself to only one?'[9] Bodmer's writings successfully countered the negative opinion Gottsched's school held on Dante, allowing for the first time an unbiased analysis of the *Commedia* in the original and in German translations.

Nicolò Ciangulo (1680–1762), author of an Italian grammar,[10] poet laureate and teacher of Italian in Leipzig and Göttingen, published an edition of Dante's *Inferno* in 1755, and thereby helped to increase the prestige of the Italian language in comparison with French.[11] Strictly speaking, the first rendering in German of a major episode in the *Commedia* was the translation of an English version. This is to be found in Moses Mendelssohn's translation of Joseph Warton's essay on Alexander Pope, which contains the famous Ugolino episode of *Inferno* 33.

The first true translator of Dante into German was Johann Nicolaus Meinhard. Although being something of a commercial failure, Meinhard's principal publication, *Versuche über den Charackter und die Werke der besten italiänischen Dichter* (Braunschweig, 1764; later edition 1774), had the merit of making extracts from many highlights of Italian literature accessible in German translation. Only a few years later, between 1767 and 1769, the lawyer Leberecht Bachenschwanz published in Leipzig the first complete German translation of the *Divina Commedia*. His contemporary critics rightly found fault both with the author's literary taste and with the accuracy of his translation.

Neither Johann Nicolaus Meinhard nor Leberecht Bachenschwanz attempted a verse translation. The first to do so was the above-mentioned Christian Joseph Jagemann, who, in the first volume of his history of Italian arts and science, *Geschichte der freyen Künste und Wissenschaften in Italien* (Leipzig, 1777), included a verse translation of several parts of the *Inferno*.[12]

The translations, and the esteem in which the *Divina Commedia* was held, converge in one respect; there was much greater interest in the *Inferno* and its dramatic scenes than in either *Purgatorio* or *Paradiso*. The story of Count Ugolino seems to have exerted the most attraction. In this respect, taste in the second half of the eighteenth century is in agreement with the later nineteenth-century Romanticism, which continues to see in Dante the poet of sublime horror and eternal torments of hell. A good example of this tendency is Heinrich Wilhelm von Gerstenberg's tragedy *Ugolino* (1768); the play, which still respects the three classical unities, tells the story of Count Ugolino's horrible imprisonment, his growing stoicism and finally his death by starvation. The play's almost brutally realistic rendering of Ugolino's inner conflict was no doubt influenced by Shakespeare and, importantly for the history of German literature, the play stands at the beginning of the expressive drama genre created by the 'Sturm und Drang' movement. Ugolino's story also inspired poets of the Romantic movement: Casimir Ulrich Böhlendorff, whose *Ugolino* appeared in 1801, Karl August Buchholz with *Ugolino Gherardesca's Fall* in 1807 and Ferdinand von Biedenfeld with *Ugolino oder Der Hungerthurm* in 1822.

As for Goethe, we can simply say that he was not greatly fascinated either by Dante or by the *Divina Commedia*. He abhorred the *Inferno*, and thought the *Purgatorio* ambiguous and the *Paradiso* boring. But he did admire Dante's realistic descriptions:

> Dante's imagination is so lively, and his description of even the most abstruse and strange objects so perfect, that we get the impression of having actually seen them. This trueness to life is almost nightmarish; it was not easy to banish those eerie monsters from my mind.[13]

Goethe's remarks on the *Inferno* are especially interesting:

> The conception of the space occupied by hell is most confusing. Dante wants us to imagine, from upside down, one circle within the other; but this reminds us of an amphitheatre and, being as it is a theatre, we will always perceive it as limited, even in its horrors. [...] His images are more rhetorical than poetical; our imagination is stirred but not satisfied.[14]

It is interesting to see that Goethe's objections anticipate those of much more recent literary critics, especially Benedetto Croce. Goethe's conclusion is rather more conciliatory: 'I do not want to praise the whole thing, but the great variety we find in the single locations of the *Inferno* surprises, confounds us and commands our admiration.'[15]

There are two main reasons why Dante was important for the German Romantic movement: first, in writing the *Divina Commedia* Dante created his own Christian mythology, and secondly, the force of his imagination allowed him to surmount the bleakness of reality through poetry, transcendence and the pursuit of infinity in content and form.

In Gottfried August Bürger's collection *Akademie der schönen Redekünste* (1791) August Wilhelm Schlegel published his essay *Über des Dante Alighieri Göttliche Komödie*, in which he summarizes the journey through the three metaphysical worlds and deals also with a hitherto neglected aspect, namely the form of the *Divina*

Commedia. He regards the tercet as the perfect rhyme scheme for the spiritual content of the *Commedia*: since each strophe is connected to the next one through the middle verse, the composition can never actually come to an end, and so stretches out into eternity. Bearing in mind these considerations, Schlegel attempted a translation, a part of which was published between 1794 and 1795 in Schiller's literary magazine *Die Horen*. In 284 tercets from the *Inferno* (*Die Hölle*), 153 from the *Purgatorio* (*Die Büßungswelt*) and 122 from the *Paradiso* (*Das Himmelreich*), Schlegel tried to maintain the form of the Italian tercet, but he did not succeed in maintaining the rhyme of the middle verse, simply because there not as many rhymes in German as there are in Italian. The initial verses of the *Paradiso* are particularly intense; the metaphysical notion of the various shades of light anticipates the *Commedia*'s final verses, which describe how the divine glory shining over the world changes into the divine love that moves 'the sun and all the other celestial bodies':

> La gloria di colui che tutto move
> per l'universo penetra e risplende
> in una parte più e meno altrove.
> Nel ciel che più della sua luce prende
> fu' io, e vidi cose che ridire
> né sa né può chi di là su discende;
>
> Die Hoheit dessen, welcher für und für,
> Was ist, bewegt, durchdringt das All der Dinge,
> Und leuchtet stärker dort und schwächer hier.
> Im Himmel, den sein vollstes Licht belebet,
> War ich und sah, was, wer von jener Höh'
> Herniedersteigt, umsonst zu nennen strebet.[16]

The scholastic style and the brevity of the original are certainly unattainable in a translation. But compared to the two first *Commedia* translations of Bachenschwanz and Meinhard, Schlegel's version in verse is a great deal more elegant.

Friedrich Wilhelm Joseph Schelling, inspired by A. W. Schlegel, also tried his hand at translating the *Divina Commedia*. The starting point for his translation was his own study, *Über Dante in philosophischer Beziehung* (1803), which greatly contributed to the appreciation of Dante's oeuvre in the German-speaking world. Schelling is the first critic who actually comprehends the *Commedia*'s unity of content and form; he expounds Dante's aesthetic principles, shows his eminent place in the history of poetry, and, being a true Romantic, envisages a profound union between life and art through a poeticizing of all aspects of human existence. Schelling compares the *Divina Commedia* to a Gothic cathedral, on the grounds that medieval architecture deployed innumerable symbols in its endeavour to imitate the multiplicity of the divine creation, in contrast to the Greek temple, which was based on only one aesthetic principle.

Karl Friedrich Ludwig Kannegießer's[17] translation of the *Divina Commedia* (1809–21) was based on Schlegel's considerations. The result, however, was no more satisfactory than preceding versions or the slightly later one by Karl Streckfuß (Halle, 1824–26). In 1849, a person calling himself Philalethes ('lover of truth') published in Dresden what is still today considered one of the best German translations of the

Divina Commedia. The person hiding behind this pseudonym was none other than King John of Saxony. A particular feature of Philalethes's translation is the choice of blank verse, the regular metrical, but unrhymed, iambic pentameter generally used in the Romantic tragedies. King John (among whose friends were the poet Ludwig Tieck and the translator Karl August Förster) was a lover of everything literary, as well as a good scholar. He founded the German Accademia Dantesca, and with it initiated the lively interest German philologists have taken ever since in Dante. Germany now becomes the classic country of Dante studies, occasioning the ironic remark that, essentially, Dante is a German invention. Theodor Ostermann's bibliography *Dante in Deutschland* (Heidelberg, 1929), which covers the years from 1416 to 1927, contains 4,062 entries, most of them from the nineteenth century. Karl Witte, professor of Roman law in Halle, was a major figure in the reception of Dante's works in nineteenth-century Germany. He founded the German Dante Society, which exists to this day, wrote a text-critical essay on the *Convivio*, and edited Dante's Latin letters. His two greatest achievements came in his critical edition of the *Divine Comedy*, *La Divina Commedia di Dante Allighieri, ricorretta sopra quattro dei più autorevoli testi a penna* (Berlin, 1862) and in a *Commedia* translation in blank verse in 1865, the year of Dante's 600th anniversary, in competition with Karl Eitner.[18]

Keen interest in Dante extended also to the poet's person, his biography, and the ways in which his life and work could be illustrated. In his novella *Der Tod des Dichters* (1823), for instance, Ludwig Tieck describes the last hours of Dante's life in his exile in Ravenna, inventing a kind of symmetry between the lives of Dante and of his venerated predecessor Virgil. In 1800, the Tyrolean landscape painter Joseph Anton Koch started to take an interest in Dante, and over the following years created various illustrations for the *Divina Commedia*. By 1807 he had completed twenty-five drawings for the *Inferno*, and between 1825 and 1828, together with several other German artists, all members of the Brotherhood of St Luke or *Lukasbund* (Peter von Cornelius, Friedrich Overbeck and Johannes Veit, Dorothea Schlegel's son), painted the Dante frescoes in the Roman Villa Massimo. For the Gallery of Karlsruhe, Anselm Feuerbach painted *Dante and the Noble Women of Ravenna* (1858) and *Paolo and Francesca* (1864), the famous episode of the secret love between Paolo Malatesta and Francesca da Rimini, situated in the second circle of the *Inferno*.

The already mentioned A. W. Schlegel published a widely acclaimed collection of translations of Italian, Spanish and Portuguese poems, *Blumensträusse italiänischer, spanischer und portugiesischer Poesie* (Berlin, 1804). In a poem of his own, which he placed at the end of the collection, Schlegel gave a somewhat far-fetched reason for his choice; the lineages of the poets he translated had sprung from romanized Germanic tribes, and it was Schlegel's wish somehow to bring them back into the German language. He deplores the now lost unity of Europe and its former creative spark in a second strophe, and in the third the decline of artistic creativity. In the fourth strophe he fervently appeals to his fellow poets to draw inspiration from the past for the creation of new poetry. In Schlegel's collection there are four poems by Dante, all of them from his *Rime*, which, together with the poems of the *Vita*

Nuova, became also the inspiration for Franz Schubert's so-called 'Sonett Dante', D. 630 (which is really Petrarch in the Schlegel collection) and Hans von Bülow's 'Meine Liebste ist so sanft: Sonett von Dante Alighieri', Op. 22.

In summary, we can identify three reasons why German Romanticism was so attracted to Dante. First is the theme of love and passion. Dante's eternal love for Beatrice, which gives an autobiographical touch to his texts, continues, as does Petrarch, the Troubadour tradition of courtly love. In this setting, the poet himself becomes a literary character as a dramatic interpretation of his own work.[19] Secondly, Dante's main work, the *Divina Commedia*, contradicts the neoclassical rules of poetry, with neither its form nor its content fitting into any of those categories. It is also visionary and, as such, tells of horrors, the grotesque, the dark and the monstrous, as in the aforementioned depiction of Ugolino.[20] Thirdly, the poetic form, the *terza rima* and, in general, the great variety of stylistic devices, are an enormous challenge for German translators and an incentive for German poets to imitate Dante's style in a modern and contemporary form.[21] It is no wonder, therefore, that Dante was among the Romantic movement's most venerated great old masters.

Notes to Chapter 17

1. Wilhelm Waetzoldt, *Das klassische Land. Wandlungen der Italiensehnsucht* (Leipzig: Seemann, 1927), p. 4: 'Italien hat die Phantasie Europas seit der Antike gefesselt: als Herz des römischen Weltreiches, als Thronsitz der Nachfolger Petri, als Zentrum der großen kaiserlichen Politik, als Schatzkammer klassischer Kunst, als Quellgebiet wiedererwachender Wissenschaft, als Mutterland freien Menschentums."
2. Cf. Lucia Tresoldi, *Viaggiatori Tedeschi in Italia 1452–1870* (Roma: Bulzoni, 1975); Eberhard Haufe (ed.), *Deutsche Briefe aus Italien: von Winckelmann bis Gregorovius* (Munich: C. H. Beck, 1987); Eva Bender, *Die Prinzenreise: Bildungsaufenthalt und Kavalierstour im höfischen Kontext gegen Ende des 17. Jahrhunderts* (Berlin: Lukas, 2011); Peter Gendolla, *Die Erfindung Italiens. Reiseerfahrung und Imagination* (München: Fink, 2014); Golo Maurer, *Italien als Erlebnis und Vorstellung. Landschaftswahrnehmung deutscher Künstler und Reisender, 1760–1870* (Regensburg: Schnell & Steiner, 2015).
3. Maria von Katte, *Enge Grenzen — weiter Horizont. Die Bildungsreisen August des Jüngeren zu Braunschweig und Lüneburg von 1598 bis 1603* (Wolfenbüttel 2004). Digital edition: http://diglib.hab.de/edoc/ed000225/startx.htm [accessed 26 March 2020].
4. Numerous guidebooks to Italy are edited in Latin, French, English and German. For the latter language there are: Georg Kranitz von Wertheim, *Delitiæ Italiæ, Das ist: Eigentliche Beschreibung was durch gantz Welschland in einer jeden Statt vnd Ort von Antiquiteten Pallästen Pyramiden Lustgärten Begräbnüssen vnd andern denckwürdigen Sachen zu sehen ist* (Frankfurt am Main: Bassaeus, 1601); Johann Heinrich von Pflaumern, *Mercurius Italicus* (Augsburg: Apergerus, 1625); Hieronymus Welsch, *Warhafftige Reiß-Beschreibung auß eigener Erfahrung von Teutschland, Croatien, Italien, denen Insuln [...]* (Nürnberg: Endter, 1658); Martin Zeiller, *Topographia Italiæ, Das ist: Warhaffte und Curiöse Beschreibung von gantz Jtalien* (Frankfurt am Main: Merian, 1688); Heinrich von Huyssen, *Curieuse und vollständige Reiß-Beschreibung von gantz Jtalien* (Freiburg: Groschuff, 1701); Joachim Christoph Nemeitz: *Nachlese besonderer Nachrichten von Jtalien* (Leipzig: Gleditsch, 1726); Johann Georg Keyßler: *Neüeste Reisen durch Teütschland, Böhmen, Ungarn, die Schweitz, Jtalien, und Lothringen*, 2 vols (Hanover: Förster, 1740–41).
5. 'Ich glaube, ich bin nach Rom gekommen, denenjenigen, die Rom nach mir sehen werden, die Augen ein wenig zu öffnen: ich rede nur von Künstlern: denn alle Cavaliere kommen als Narren her und gehen als Esel wieder weg; dieses Geschlecht der Menschen verdienet nicht,

daß man sie unterrichte und lehre.' (Johann Joachim Winckelmann, *Werke*. 9. *Band. Welcher die Briefe Winckelmanns von 1747–1761 enthält* (Berlin: Schlesinger, 1824), p. 178)

6. Johann Joachim Winckelmann, *Werke*. 11. *Band. Welcher die Briefe Winckelmanns von 1766–1768 und biographische Beiträge enthält* (Berlin: Schlesinger, 1825), p. 167.

7. Cf. *Eine Reise der Aufklärung: Lessing in Italien 1775*, ed. by Lea Ritter Santini, 2 vols (Berlin: Akademie-Verlag, 1993).

8. Despite his profound hostility to the author, Gottsched ranks Dante among the greatest and oldest poets of Italy in his *Handlexikon oder Kurzgefasstes Wörterbuch der schönen Wissenschaften und freien Künste* (Leipzig: Fritsch, 1760, col. 493s.), but criticizes his insufficient knowledge of Latin versification in *Versuch einer critischen Dichtkunst vor die Deutschen* (Leipzig: Breitkof, 1730), p. 66: 'So hoch Dante und Petrarcha in Welschland, Ronsard und Malherbe in Frankreich, wegen der durch sie gesäuberten Poesie ihres Vaterlandes, geschätzet werden: so seltsam muß es einem Verständigen vorkommen, daß diese grosse Geister ihren Landesleuten nicht gewiesen, wie man auch im Welschen und Französischen die lateinische Art zu Dichten nachahmen, und verschiedene Arten der Abwechselung langer und kurtzer Sylben einführen könnte. Sie blieben nehmlich bey der blossen Abzehlung der Sylben und dem Reime.' [The esteem in which Dante and Petrarch were held in Italy was matched by that of Ronsard and Malherbe in France, because they had purified the poetic techniques in their respective countries; it will therefore seem all the more surprising to the informed reader that those eminent minds should not have been able to teach their countrymen how to imitate Latin poetry in Italian and French by introducing the various ways of using long and short syllables; for they never went further than mere syllable-counting and rhyme.] While the article on Petrarch, for example, in *Großes vollständiges Universal Lexicon Aller Wissenschaften und Künste*, 64 vols (Halle and Leipzig: J. H. Zedler, 1732–54) contains a long list of his works, this encyclopaedia offers only an offensively short commentary about Dante's *Commedia*: 'Er schrieb Italiänische Gedichte, worunter die Comödie von der Höllen, Fege-Feuer und Paradieß, welches eine hefftige Satyre ist, gelesen zu werden, wohl verdient' (vol. I, col. 1216).

9. Johann Jakob Bodmer and Johann Jakob Breitinger, *Schriften zur Literatur* (Stuttgart: Reclam, 1980), p. 285.

10. His thesis at the University of Göttingen was *Novum Tyrocinium Lingua Italicae* (Göttingen: Vandenhoeck, 1735); later: *Italiänische und Deutsche Gespräche*; trans. by L. Bachenschwanz (Leipzig: Jacobi, 1757).

11. *La Divina Comedia di Dante Alighieri. Dell'Inferno. Poemetto morale, e filosofico. Colle annotazioni distinte, ch'esplicano chiaramente il testo* (Leipzig: Heinsius, 1755). This edition comes highly recommended by Johann Friedrich Christ, professor of poetics and history at the university of Leipzig: 'Einen DANTE kann niemand entbehren, wer im Italienischen nur ein wenig mit einigem Grunde sich will umgesehen haben, es ist hier die Rede von einem, der fein correct, und mit kurzem, aber guten und nützlichen Anmerckungen, wie die Probe davon sich erzeiget, hier soll gedruckt werden. Leipzig am 22. Iulii 1755.' (verso title page) [No one who wishes to study the Italian language in any depth can dispense with Dante; what concerns us here is the production of an edition that combines precision with brief, but reliable and useful, annotations that are self-sufficient for the reader.] Dedicated to Christian Gottlieb von Holzendorf and Johann Gottlieb von Globig, both members of the ecclesiastical council in Saxony, Ciangulo's work seeks, in his introductory life of Dante and the commentaries, educational purposes, especially in his analysis of *Inf.* 1–4: 'Ho scelto quattro canti della Divina Comedia del dottissimo Dante, utilissimi ai studiosi d'ogni sorte di scienze, non intesi da molti di questo nostro paese, mentre questi parlano meglio il Tedesco, o Francese, che l'italiano' (A 2^r).

12. These early German translations are discussed by W. P. Friederich, *Dante's Fame Abroad* (Chapel Hill, NC: UNC Studies in Comparative Literature, 1950), pp. 358–66.

13. Part 1: 'Er [Dante] faßte die Gegenstände so deutlich ins Auge seiner Einbildungskraft, daß er sie scharf umrissen wiedergeben konnte; deshalb wir denn das Abstruseste und Seltsamste gleichsam nach der Natur gezeichnet vor uns sehen' (Johann Wolfgang von Goethe, *Gedenkausgabe der Werke, Briefe und Gespräche*, ed. by Ernst Beutler, 24 vols (Zurich: Artemis, 1948–54), XIV, 862); Part 2: 'ich genug zu tun hatte, die gespensterhaften Ungeheuer nach und nach aus der Einbildungskraft zu vertilgen' (ibid., , XI, 938).

14. 'Die ganze Anlage des Danteschen Höllenlokals hat etwas Mikromegisches und deshalb Sinnverwirrendes. Von oben herein bis in den tiefsten Abgrund soll man sich Kreis in Kreisen imaginieren; dieses giebt aber gleich den Begriff eines Amphitheaters, das, ungeheuer wie es sein möchte, uns immer als etwas künstlerisch Beschränktes vor die Einbildungskraft sich hinstellt. [...] Die Erfindung ist mehr rhetorisch als poetisch, die Einbildungskraft ist aufgeregt, aber nicht befriedigt.' (ibid., xiv, 862)
15. 'Indem wir das Ganze nicht rühmen wollen, so werden wir durch den seltsamen Reichtum der einzelnen Lokalitäten überrascht, in Staunen gesetzt, verwirrt und zur Verehrung genötigt' (ibid., xiv, 862).
16. *Sämmtliche Werke. Poetische Übersetzungen und Nachbildungen* (Leipzig, 1846), I, 363.
17. Kannegießer also translates some of Dante's prose, *Dante Alighieris prosaische Schriften mit Ausnahme der* Vita nuova. *Erster Teil* (Leipzig: Brockhaus, 1845) and Giacomo Leopardi's *Canti — Gesänge* (Leipzig: Brockhaus, 1837).
18. On Kannegießer, Streckfuß, 'Philalethes' and Witte, see Friederich, *Dante's Fame Abroad*, pp. 394–402, 408–13 and 416–21.
19. For instance, Ignaz Kollmann shows in his drama *Dante: Ein dramatisches Gedicht in fünf Aufzügen* (Graz: Kienreich, 1826) the political turmoil in Florence before Dante's exile and his unfulfilled love for Beatrice Portinari who dies at the end.
20. Among the later literary transpositions of this character is August Werg, *Der Thurm der sieben Straßen oder der Untergang des Hauses Gherardesca: Eine Erzählung aus den Zeiten der Gibellinen- und Guelfen-Kämpfe* (Berlin: Lüderitz, 1836). Meanwhile, German authors seem more fascinated by the character of Francesca da Rimini, especially in the dramatic genre, such as Paul Heyse, *Francesca von Rimini: Tragödie in fünf Acten* (Berlin: Hertz, 1850), Hans Koester, *Paolo und Francesca: Trauerspiel in fünf Akten* (Leipzig: Brockhaus, before 1874), Martin Greif, *Francesca da Rimini. Tragödie in fünf Akten* (Berlin and Vienna: DVA 1892) and Hermann Goetz, *Francesca von Rimini: Oper in drei Akten* (Leipzig: Kistner, 1874).
21. The most famous examples of *terza rima* in German are several ballads by Adelbert von Chamisso (e.g. *Die Ruine*, 1834) and four poems by Hugo von Hofmannsthal (1892).

CHAPTER 18

Dante's Presence in Weimar around 1800

Karl Philipp Ellerbrock

Taking as a point of departure the Duchess Anna Amalia Library in Weimar, this chapter explores some of the material conditions that made it possible for Dante Alighieri to enter German letters as an epitome of 'modern' literature in the years around 1800.[1] Founded by William Ernest, Duke of Saxe-Weimar, in 1691, the library received its current name in 1991 as a homage to Anna Amalia of Brunswick-Wolfenbüttel (1739–1807), who is remembered as a patron of literature and credited with attracting to her court key figures of contemporary intellectual life.[2] It was during Anna Amalia's reign that her family's library, which contained a substantial number of Italian volumes, moved to the sixteenth-century 'Green Castle' on the river Ilm, adapted in the 1760s to house the ducal collection of books and to make it accessible to the public.[3] In 2015, an exhibition was opened in the historic building's 'Renaissance hall' to mark the 750th anniversary of the birth of Dante. Showcasing a selection of the library's distinguished Dante-related holdings, the exhibition *Dante, ein offenes Buch* ['Dante: an Open Book'] presented an opportunity to draw attention once more to the italophilia of Anna Amalia's court and to the affinities of both Classicist and Romantic Weimar with the Italian literary tradition.[4] More specifically, it shed light on the role that the library played in the rediscovery of Dante not so much as an historically distant figure, but rather as an intellectual presence perceived as 'contemporary'. In what follows, I shall revisit *Dante, ein offenes Buch* in order to trace the origins of Dante's presence in Weimar and to show how the format of the book exhibition could be an effective way to introduce a present-day public to Dante's life and works.[5]

Situated on the ground floor beneath the famous 'Rococo hall' of the historic building, the smaller 'Renaissance hall' was restored to its 1565 condition and transformed into an exhibition space after the opening of the library's modern study centre in 2004.[6] The exhibition, which ran from August 2015 to June 2016, presented some sixty exhibits ranging in date from 1502 to 1921. The exhibits — predominantly Italian editions and German translations of Dante's works, but also drawings, maps and musical scores, as well as certain Dante-related objects in Goethe's possession — were grouped in sixteen thematic cabinets for the purpose of the display, but documented in chronological order in the accompanying book.[7] The main curatorial challenge was one of selection. In 2015 the library held 360 Dante editions in 570 volumes and 286 German Dante translations, including duplicates.[8] A catalogue search under the keyword 'Dante' yielded more than 2,000 entries of primary and secondary literature.[9] In its final form, the exhibition as documented in the catalogue presented 45 items from the library itself, complemented by nine objects from the museum collections of the Klassik Stiftung Weimar,[10] five loans from the University Library in Jena[11] and one document from the Thuringian State Archive in Weimar.[12] In addition to the intrinsic interest of the exhibits as library and museum holdings, another important aim was to show how they could be used to familiarize visitors and readers with Dante's works themselves. Despite their chronological arrangement, the one-page descriptions of the objects in the catalogue sought to avoid formulating an overarching 'narrative' of Dante's reception in Weimar, and instead allowed the exhibits to interact with each other and to stimulate reactions in ways unforeseen by the curators.

What follows is a virtual tour of the exhibition, moving between the cabinets in their original arrangement.[13] Turning to the left after entering the 'Renaissance hall', visitors first saw, in the main display case, Joseph Anton Koch's 1809 drawing 'Francesca and Paolo surprised by Gianciotto Malatesta', featuring at its centre the open book chosen as the exhibition's leitmotiv.[14] Koch, a member of a reading circle convened in Rome by the Italianist and later Weimar librarian Carl Ludwig Fernow, first encountered Dante in the translation published by August Wilhelm Schlegel in Friedrich Schiller's journal *Die Horen* in 1795.[15] His illustration of the famous reading scene in *Inferno* 5 is remarkable in several ways. Koch departs from a centuries-old iconographic tradition, which from the earliest illuminated manuscripts had shown the souls of the two *lussuriosi* encountered by Dante and Vergil in the second circle of hell.[16] Instead, like the Swiss painter Johann Heinrich Füssli before him, Koch chooses to illustrate the contents of Francesca's confession, her secret encounter with Paolo.[17] Artfully condensing the elements of her story into a tableau of simultaneity and tension, Koch imagines the moment in which the lovers, who are just about to become one with their reading and to kiss in imitation of Lancelot and Guinevere, are 'surprised' — and will in an instant be stabbed to death — by Francesca's husband and Paolo's brother Gianciotto Malatesta.[18] While Füssli foregrounds a dark and overwhelming passion in his rendering of the scene,[19] Koch depicts precisely that precarious moment in which the boundary between text and reader, between literature and life, becomes unstable. This is why, unlike Füssli, and more like John Flaxman before him,[20] Koch places in Francesca's hands the open book which, rather than serving as a mere attribute, now becomes the central vanishing point of the drawing. The pages of the book do not contain any trace of writing, but are left tellingly blank. They form a *Projektionsfläche*,[21] the kind of 'screen' or empty space that imaginative readers such as Francesca and Paolo can animate with ideas of their own.

By giving such centrality to the blank pages of the 'open book', Koch, perhaps unintentionally, draws attention to the key role that 'indeterminacy' as a feature of fictional texts plays in the act of reading, though this was theorized only much later, in twentieth-century literary criticism.[22] Mainly known for his landscape paintings, Koch was praised as an intimate connoisseur of Dante's works by Wilhelm von Humboldt.[23] As late as 1830, he was depicted reciting the *Commedia* in the streets of Rome, where he had contributed to the Dante frescoes in the Casino Massimo, in a sketch drawing by Friedrich Preller, the director of the Weimar Free Princely Drawing School.[24] Whether intentionally or not, Koch's 'Francesca and Paolo surprised by Gianciotto Malatesta', one of several renderings of the episode that he produced, makes a strong exegetical statement about *Inferno* 5. How is it possible for the lovers from Rimini to identify with the characters from the Arthurian cycle? As the whiteness of the pages suggests, the reason why the text they are reading can become a 'Galeotto'[25] in the first place lies in the textual vagueness of the passage recalled so eloquently by Francesca:

> Quando leggemmo il disïato riso
> esser basciato da cotanto amante,
> questi, che mai da me non fia diviso,
> la bocca mi basciò tutto tremante. (*Inf.* 5. 133–36)

To the eager readers, the lines from the Lancelot romance present themselves as a proliferation of gaps waiting to be filled. Did the knight kiss the queen or vice versa?[26] In their lustful act of reading, a parody of Augustine reading Paul's Epistle to the Romans,[27] Francesca and Paolo proceed to determine the indeterminate ('questi' for 'cotanto amante'), to turn passive into active ('mi basciò' for 'esser basciato'), to make concrete what so far had remained abstract ('la bocca' for 'il disïato riso').[28] With consummate craftsmanship, Dante presents the recalled description of the kiss between Lancelot and Guinevere as a textual artwork that draws its life-changing potential from the 'meaningful omissions'[29] typical of courtly literature. Francesca's own speech ends with a famous example of reticence, 'quel giorno più non vi leggemmo avante',[30] which in turn has an overwhelming effect on the pilgrim. As Koch's drawing so ably illustrates, the fifth canto exhibits the production of lacunae, and the filling-in of these, as a potentially dangerous dynamic inherent in any act of reading.

Given the close attention it pays to the fifth canto and the aspect of 'indeterminacy', Koch's drawing can be regarded to a certain extent as characteristic of Dante's early reception in Weimar. As in the illustration, which apparently singles out the episode of Francesca and Paolo as a scene representative of Dante's art, the fifth canto in particular became the object of translations, commentaries and literary appropriations around 1800. It is the only canto rendered in full by A. W. Schlegel in his 1795 contribution to *Die Horen*.[31] Schlegel, who taught at the University of Jena from 1795, can be seen as a pioneer through whose work Dante 'entered the mainstream of German letters'.[32] In his notes to *Inferno* 5, Schlegel shows an awareness that this episode is particularly prone to imitation or even to what he calls involuntary parody.[33] Above all, he does not hesitate to make explicit the space that Francesca's final words leave for interpretation: 'Dieser Schluß mag eben sowohl Fülle des verstummenden Gefühls seyn, als ein Schleyer, den die

Sittlichkeit wirft' [This conclusion may signal at once the very brimming of that secret emotion and a veiling of it by moral rectitude].[34] According to Schlegel, the fact that Francesca leaves in the dark the consequences of the kiss can be explained by her sense of chastity (*Sittlichkeit*) as well as by an overwhelming excess of emotion (*Gefühl*). Against this backdrop of semantic ambiguity, Schlegel supplies a dramatic reinterpretation of the scene's female protagonist. While in the original the pilgrim Dante's pity for Francesca is marked by his death-like swoon, which is commonly interpreted as a sinful inclination that has to be overcome in order not to endanger the project of the *Commedia* as a whole, there is no such restraint of sympathy on Schlegel's part. On the contrary, Francesca becomes an embodiment of authenticity and innocence: 'Aus allen Reden Francesca's athmet Weiblichkeit, Unschuld, Liebe, Seele, eine zarte Seele der Liebe' [From Francesca's every utterance there breathes femininity, innocence, love, soul, a tender soul of love].[35] As is well known, it is this perceived authenticity in the portrayal of individuals such as Francesca da Rimini that makes Dante a 'romantic', that is a 'modern', poet in the eyes of Schlegel and his contemporaries, leading up to his appraisal as a 'realist' author by Erich Auerbach.[36] It seems safe to assume that Dante's own technique of producing *Projektionsflächen*, 'surfaces of textual openness', was a key factor in his reception as a voice capable of speaking with great immediacy to every generation of readers.[37]

Among the first and most prominent figures to engage with the fifth canto in its ability to provoke divergent readings is Johann Wolfgang von Goethe, who may have read it in the translations by Johann Nicolaus Meinhard and Leberecht Bachenschwanz.[38] In *Die Leiden des jungen Werthers*, first published in 1774, Lotte asks Werther to read to her from his translations of Ossian, kept in her drawer awaiting a moment of privacy. Like Francesca and Paolo, the two lovers are drawn to one another by the story they are reading: 'Sie fühlten ihr eigenes Elend in dem Schicksale der Edlen, fühlten es zusammen und ihre Thränen vereinigten sie' [They felt their own suffering in the fate of their heroes, felt it together, and were united in their tears].[39] However, unlike in the fifth canto, their union is not to be. When Werther starts covering her trembling lips with raging kisses, Lotte, albeit hesitatingly and almost unwillingly, pushes him away. Eventually Werther sinks to the floor motionless, a narrative prolepsis to his suicide that is soon to follow. While the echoes of Dante's fifth canto are quite clear, Goethe does not simply update the medieval story to suit the taste of a modern readership. It is as though he were preparing his lovers to re-enact *Inferno* 5 only to let them fail in the attempt.[40] While Francesca and Paolo are inseparable in death ('quei due che 'nsieme vanno'[41]), a higher power prevents Lotte and Werther from being united in life, as is shown in engravings by Daniel Berger and Vincenz Raimund Grüner.[42] By bringing premature closure to the story of Francesca and Paolo, Goethe expands the range of creative reactions to the fifth canto, while at the same time indicating their limits.

In the field of translation, a sense of open-endedness prevails.[43] In 1865, Reinhold Köhler, then director of the Weimar library, published a collection of twenty-two German translations of the fifth canto, admitting in his preface that there had been no time to edit one further one that had begun to circulate in the meantime.[44] If this proliferation of different German versions of one passage can be explained in part by the challenges posed to translators by poetic texts in general, and by Dante's *terza rima* in particular, the fifth canto especially continues to spark controversy with regard to the most appropriate contemporary translation.[45] However, the translation activity that began to flourish in Germany in the second half of the eighteenth century and is documented in the library's collection history was not limited to the story of Francesca and Paolo. The exhibition featured, in chronological order: the first full German rendering of the *Commedia* into German prose, published in Leipzig by Leberecht Bachenschwanz in 1767;[46] the first metrical translation of the *Inferno* by Christian Joseph Jagemann in 1780;[47] the already mentioned 1795 instalment of A. W. Schlegel's translation for *Die Horen*;[48] the first volume of Karl Ludwig Kannegießer's 1809 integral and rhymed *Commedia* translation (the first of its kind in Germany);[49] the first German translation of Dante's *Vita Nuova*, published by Friedrich von Oeynhausen in 1823;[50] a copy of the first volume of Karl Streckfuß's translation of the *Commedia* with a handwritten dedication to Goethe dated 1824;[51] an 1827 bilingual edition of Dante's lyric poetry by Kannegießer;[52] the metrically translated *Goettliche Comoedie* that the later king John of Saxony published under the pseudonym of Philalethes between 1828 and 1849;[53] a copy, again dedicated to Goethe, of Antoni Deschamps's partial verse translation into French which appeared in 1829;[54] and finally the German translation of the *Commedia* published by Karl Witte in 1865, the 600th anniversary year of the poet's birth, when Witte founded the German Dante Society.[55]

While the early modern period had seen an interest in Dante's political writings,[56] the increasing translation activity around 1800 reveals above all an aesthetic fascination with the *Commedia* and with Dante's lyric poetry. An important condition for this deepened dialogue with Dante the poet was the availability of reliable Italian editions, which abounded in Anna Amalia's library. Of the editions of the *Commedia* exhibited,[57] the earliest was a 1502 Venetian 'Aldina',[58] followed by eight other *cinquecentine* of note,[59] a number of editions complete with the humanist commentaries of Cristoforo Landino (first published in 1481)[60] and Alessandro Vellutello (first published in 1544).[61] The strong presence of eighteenth-century editions of the *Commedia* in the library's present-day holdings is due in part to Carl Ludwig Fernow, who succeeded Christian Joseph Jagemann as librarian in 1804 and brought with him a substantial collection of Italian books. Consisting of 957 volumes and incorporated into the library in 1808, Fernow's 'Italienische Bibliothek' contained several noteworthy Dantiana ranging in date from 1629 to 1760,[62] including a *Commedia* printed in Bergamo in 1752 with the critical apparatus of Lodovico Dolce[63] and an illustrated *Inferno* printed in Venice in 1784.[64] Goethe, who personally owned some sixty titles in the field of Italian literature,[65] inherited three Dante editions from his father, among them a 1739 *Commedia* based on the Crusca edition of 1595[66] and a 1741 two-volume annotated edition of *Opere*,[67] both printed in Venice.[68] Anna Amalia herself owned a *Commedia* printed in Paris in 1768, bound in leather and adorned with her personal coat of arms in plated gold,[69] and a three-volume edition of *Inferno*, *Purgatorio* and *Paradiso* printed in Rome by Antonio Fulgoni in 1791, which features engraved schematic depictions for each cantica on blue-tinted paper.[70] Right from its foundation in 1691, the ducal library had been acquiring Italian books, with a major contribution made at the outset by an endowment of the 'Fruchtbringende Gesellschaft' [Fruitbearing Society], which had been founded in Weimar in 1617 on the model of the Accademia della Crusca in Florence.[71]

Given the number and quality of editions,[72] of Dante portraits,[73] illustrations,[74] schematic renderings of Dante's imaginary topographies,[75] as well as other Dante-related materials that the library made available,[76] the small town of Weimar was well equipped to become, metaphorically speaking, one of Dante's 'Heimatstädte' [home towns] in Germany.[77] As early as 1766, Christoph Martin Wieland had inserted an echo of the first canto in his Bildungsroman *Geschichte des Agathon* [The Story of Agathon].[78] In 1776, one year after being appointed librarian to Anna Amalia, Christian Joseph Jagemann had published, in Italian, a selection of passages from the *Commedia*.[79] In 1780, he began to circulate his translation 'Die Hölle des Dante Alighieri' [The Inferno of Dante Alighieri] in his own *Magazin der italienischen Litteratur und Künste* published with Hoffmann in Weimar,[80] followed by his 1785 Dante essay.[81] In 1798, three years after A. W. Schlegel's translation for *Die Horen*,[82] his brother Friedrich Schlegel expressed his admiration for the *Commedia* as 'das einzige System transzendentaler Poesie' [the only true system of transcendental poetry] in the *Athenaeum* journal, a mouthpiece of the 'Jenaer Frühromantik' [Jena or early Romantics].[83] In 1803, another member of the early romantics' circle, Friedrich Wilhelm Joseph Schelling, who was teaching at Jena at the time, published his essay 'Ueber Dante in philosophischer Beziehung' [On Dante in Relation to Philosophy] in *Kritisches Journal der Philosophie*, co-edited with Georg Wilhelm Friedrich Hegel.[84] And in 1807, Carl Ludwig Fernow, who in the meantime had succeeded Jagemann as director of the library, published a full Italian edition of the *Commedia* with Frommann in Jena.[85] Fernow, whom Johanna Schopenhauer recalls as working on a Dante biography until hours before his death,[86] was also instrumental in bringing to Weimar's library the artistic legacy of the painter Asmus Carstens, whose works on Dante were inspired by A. W. Schlegel, and among whose students in Rome was Joseph Anton Koch.[87]

With the sustained activity of Philalethes, who brought together a circle of translators, artists and scientists to comment on, and translate, the *Commedia* starting in 1826, the centre of interest in Dante shifted from Weimar to the castles of Weesenstein and Pillnitz, near Dresden.[88] It was in Dresden that Karl Witte, who had become known for his groundbreaking 1862 edition of the *Commedia*,[89] reprinted in Milan in 1864,[90] founded the German Dante Society in 1865. Meanwhile the Dante fever in Weimar had not subsided completely, but intensified once more around the middle of the century when the town's court musical director, Franz Liszt, was working to finish his two well-known Dante compositions.[91] In 1846, Adele Schopenhauer, who had grown up in the Weimar of Goethe, published a noteworthy essay on the tradition of Dante illustrations in the journal *Kunstblatt*.[92]

To return to the motif of hermeneutic openness, mention should be made of the sonnet 'Wess ist das Lied, das mit geweihten Zungen' [Whose is the song that with sacred tongues] published in 1800 by A. W. Schlegel, certainly one of the main protagonists in the Weimar reception of Dante.[93] In this poem, Dante, exiled from his native Florence in life, is granted new civic rights 'im Reich der Geister' [in the spiritual realm], where he occupies a permanent place among the figures of outstanding intellect. Schlegel's text opens with a question ('Wess ist das Lied?' [Whose is the song?]) over the author of a poetic creation which is described in sweeping periphrastic terms over two stanzas. It is clear that the universal song, evoked in its movement through the three spheres of the cosmos, is Dante's *Commedia*. In his rhetorical question, however, Schlegel does not make explicit the title of the text, but refers to it obliquely, allowing himself effectively to delay naming the author of the 'Lied' until the very last line ('der grosse Dante' [the great Dante]). Crucially, this technique of *retardatio nominis* is also typical of Dante's own style, used for example to great effect in *Inferno* 5, where the pilgrim pauses before responding to a still nameless soul's highly circumlocutory self-presentation: 'Francesca, i tuoi martìri | a lagrimar mi fanno tristo e pio'.[94] It becomes evident that Schlegel's 'naturalization' of Dante in German letters[95] goes hand in hand with a subtle appreciation of the Italian poet as a master of 'Leerstelle' [ellipsis] and 'Konkretisation' [concretization]. Schlegel is in excellent company; the art of periphrasis, as a recurrent stylistic trait of the *Commedia*, had been noted by readers as early as Giovanni Boccaccio, who uses it in his celebration of Dante as a 'gran poeta'.[96]

The form of an exhibition offering little more than books opened, sometimes fortuitously, at certain pages proves strikingly apt in capturing some of the fascination that Dante's works generated around 1800. It would be misleading to think that the engagement with Dante in Weimar was limited to his monumentalization, as is suggested by the imposing juxtaposition of the Dante and Goethe busts in the gallery of the 'Rococo hall'.[97] While not entirely lost on contemporaries, as Schlegel's sonnet shows, the interest in Dante as a monument ('Tempel') in literary history was counterbalanced by a receptiveness to the finer shades of Dante's text, the specific formal qualities of his poetic works. To what extent the appreciation of stylistic 'indeterminacy' highlighted here was reflected in translations, commentaries and literary appropriations of the *Commedia* at large is a question that has not been pursued systematically to my knowledge. To be sure, it is a question that presents a certain affinity with the essentially open character of libraries as such. Jürgen Kaube recently suggested that what makes libraries attractive and irreplaceable is not only their function as repository for books, but also their capacity to allow their users to find what they had not been explicitly looking for.[98] Perhaps this was the sensation that overcame Anna Amalia herself when in 1806 she was copying onto a sheet of paper a passage from *Purgatorio* that deals with the futility of earthly fame,

> Non è il mondan rumore altro ch'un fiato
> Di vento, ch'or vien quinci, ed or vien quindi,

> E muta nome perchè muta stato
> Dante

and when she found herself responding with an Italian stanza of her own on the constancy of friendship:

> L'amicizia sola è quel che non muta,
> e che con animo tranquillo ci mantiene
> fra le turbolezze di tempi
> Amalia D[uchessa] di S. W.[99]

As Anna Amalia's verses show, the efforts of Jagemann, the dedicated promoter of Italian literary culture who had compiled an *Antologia poetica italiana* as early as 1776, 'to ease Her Highness's study of the Italian language' ('per agevolare lo studio della Poesia italiana a *Vostra Altezza Serenissima*'), had borne fruit.[100] If Dante came to Weimar as a 'revelation', it was a revelation of a different sort from the apotheosis of the prophet in Domenico di Michelino's famous painting, which is reproduced on a bronze medal owned by Goethe.[101] In the handwritten pseudo-terzina composed by Anna Amalia, the medieval poet is not primarily retained as a public authority,[102] but his voice makes itself heard in the more intimate sphere of friendship. Rather than being museumized, Dante becomes an interlocutor in dialogue with contemporary readers.

Notes to Chapter 18

1. The works of Dante experienced a renaissance in Germany in the second half of the eighteenth century. See Eva Hölter, *'Der Dichter der Hölle und des Exils': Historische und systematische Profile der deutschsprachigen Dante-Rezeption* (Würzburg: Königshausen & Neumann, 2002), p. 27: 'Aus dem bis dahin relativ unbekannten und vor allem ungelesenen italienischen Autor wird um die 1760er Jahre ein vielzitierter Dichter, der an der Schwelle des nächsten Jahrhunderts schon zum deutschen Literaturkanon gehört' [The 1760s saw the emergence of a much-cited poet from the hitherto relatively unknown, and above all unread, Italian author; by the turn of the next century he was already a member of the German literary canon]; Werner P. Friederich, 'Dante in Germany', in *Dante's Fame Abroad: The Influence of Dante Alighieri on the Poets and Scholars of Spain, France, England, Germany, Switzerland and the United States* (Rome: Edizioni di Storia e Letteratura, 1950), pp. 341–495; Johannes Bartuschat, 'Dante in Germania in età romantica', in *Letture e lettori di Dante: l'età moderna e contemporanea*, ed. by Marcello Ciccuto (Ravenna: Longo, 2011), pp. 47–70. Cf. also Alfred Noe's article 'Dante Alighieri and German Romanticism' in the present volume.
2. Annette Seemann, *Anna Amalia: Herzogin von Weimar* (Frankfurt am Main and Leipzig: Insel Verlag, 2007).
3. On the history of the library, see Michael Knoche, *Die Herzogin Anna Amalia Bibliothek: Ein Portrait* (Berlin: Otto Meissners Verlag, 2016).
4. See the contributions in the collected volume *Herzogin Anna Amalia von Sachsen-Weimar-Eisenach und die Italien-Beziehungen im klassischen Weimar*, ed. by Peter Kofler, Thomas Kroll and Siegfried Seifert (Bozen: Edition Sturzflüge, 2010).
5. On the question whether book exhibitions can be a means to stimulate authentic experiences of the literary, see the special issue 'Ce que le musée fait à la littérature. Muséalisation et exposition du littéraire', ed. Marie-Clémence Régnier, *Interférences littéraires* 16 (2015).
6. Claudia Kleinbub, 'Thematische Jahresausstellungen in der Herzogin Anna Amalia Bibliothek: Das Buch in seiner zeitlichen, inhaltlichen und künstlerischen Dimension', in *Praxishandbuch Ausstellungen in Bibliotheken*, ed. by Petra Hauke (Berlin and Boston: De Gruyter, 2016), pp. 381–89.

7. *Dante, ein offenes Buch*, ed. by Edoardo Costadura and Karl Philipp Ellerbrock (Berlin: Deutscher Kunstverlag, 2015). In what follows, the catalogue section in *Dante, ein offenes Buch*, pp. 76–194, is quoted as 'Cat.' followed by the italicized number of the exhibit in question. The rest of the book is also referred to as 'Cat.', but with regular page numbers.
8. Cf. Knoche, 'Vorwort', Cat. 6.
9. Ibid. The catalogue of the Herzogin Anna Amalia Bibliothek is available online, <https://www.lhwei.gbv.de/DB=2/>, as is the one of the Thüringer Universitäts- und Landesbibliothek, <https://www.kataloge.thulb.uni-jena.de/>.
10. Cat. *4, 25, 26, 31, 32, 41, 42, 43, 50*.
11. Cat. *81, 87, 89, 95, 105*.
12. Cat. *60*.
13. The display cabinets were entitled as follows: (1) Francesca and Paolo; (2) Portrayals of the Poet; (3) Surveying Hell; (4), (5) Dante and Goethe; (6) Early Italian Editions of the *Commedia*; (7) Dante's Theoretical Writings on Language and Politics; (8) Italian Editions of the Eighteenth Century; (9) Dante's Teachers; (10) German Translations; (11) Duchess Anna Amalia; (12) Dante and German Early Romanticism; (13) Dante in Dresden; (14) Between Jena and Rome; (15) Franz Liszt; (16) From Goethe's Library.
14. Cat. *41*.
15. Cat. *30*.
16. An example of this, the *c*. 1450 miniature by Priamo della Quercia in the British Library's Codex Yates Thompson 36, is reproduced in Cat. *70*, ill. 7. For other illustrations that follow the traditional pattern, see Peter Brieger, Millard Meiss and Charles Singleton, *Illuminated Manuscripts of the Divine Comedy*, 2 vols (London: Routledge and Kegan Paul, 1969), II, 79–91.
17. See Wolfgang Hartmann, *Die Wiederentdeckung Dantes in der deutschen Kunst. J. H. Füssli, A. J. Carstens, J. A. Koch* (doctoral thesis, University of Bonn, 1969). On Füssli's 'Dante in seiner Studierstube' (1778–79) see Cat. *25*.
18. A similar rendering can be found in an illuminated manuscript of Petrarch's *Triumphi* dating from the early sixteenth century. See Lucia Battaglia Ricci, *Dante per immagini: dalle miniature trecentesche ai nostri giorni* (Turin: Einaudi, 2018), p. 131 and fig. 80.
19. Füssli's 1785 painting is reproduced and briefly discussed in Cat. *15*, ill. 3.
20. *La Divina Comedia di Dante Alighieri, cioè L'Inferno, il Purgatorio, ed il Paradiso, composto da Giovanni Flaxman Scultore Inglese ed inciso da Tommaso Piroli* (Rome: n.p., 1802), p. [16]. On Flaxman, see Cat. *35*.
21. Peter von Becker, 'Bei Ehebruch: Hölle', *Der Tagesspiegel*, 1 November 2015, p. 26.
22. On the notions of 'Unbestimmtheitsstelle' and 'Konkretisation' see Roman Ingarden, 'Konkretisation und Rekonstruktion. Grundbehauptungen über den wesenseigenen Aufbau des literarischen Kunstwerks', in *Rezeptionsästhetik. Theorie und Praxis*, ed. by Rainer Warning (Munich: Fink, 1975), pp. 42–70, and Wolfgang Iser, *Der Akt des Lesens. Theorie ästhetischer Wirkung* (Munich: Fink, 1976).
23. For the Humboldt quote, see Otto Lutterotti, *Joseph Anton Koch, 1768–1839: Leben und Werk. Mit einem vollständigen Werkverzeichnis* (Vienna: Herold, 1985), p. 45: 'Den Dante kennt vielleicht kaum einer in Italien genauer und wenige sind in seine Poesie so eingedrungen' [There can scarcely be a single reader in Italy who knows Dante better, and few have fathomed his poetic art so well].
24. Cat. *50*.
25. *Inf.* 5. 137. On the figure of Galehaut, cf. Cat. *16–17* and ill. 4.
26. For an overview of this long-standing philological debate, see Anna Hatcher; Mark Musa, 'The Kiss: Inferno V and the old French prose Lancelot', *Comparative Literature*, 20 (1968), 97–109.
27. Robert Hollander, 'Inferno V, 138: Francesca's confession', *L'Alighieri*, 40 (2012), 115–19.
28. See Elena Lombardi, 'Francesca lettrice di romanzi e il "punto" di Inferno V', *L'Alighieri*, 43 (2014), 19–39 (p. 38).
29. Ingrid Kasten, 'Die doppelte Autorschaft. Zum Verhältnis Sprache des Menschen und Sprache Gottes in mystischen Texten des Mittelalters', in *'. . . wortlos der Sprache mächtig'. Schweigen und Sprechen in der Literatur und sprachlicher Kommunikation*, ed. by Hartmut Eggert and Janusz Golec (Stuttgart: Metzler, 1999), pp. 9–30 (p. 24).

30. *Inf.* 5. 138.
31. Cf. Cat. *30*. Schlegel's translation of *Inferno* 5 is edited in Cat. 197–200.
32. Donald Lee, 'The Divine Comedy, a German Classic: On Dante's German debut', see *The Art Newspaper*, 1 (May 2016).
33. Cat. 200, n. 10.
34. Cat. 198.
35. Ibid.
36. On Schlegel's view of Dante as 'the first great romantic poet' see Peter Kuon, 'Die kreative Rezeption der *Divina Commedia* in Klassik und Romantik', in *'Italien in Germanien': Deutsche Italien-Rezeption von 1750–1850*, ed. by Frank-Rutger Hausmann, Michael Knoche and Harro Stammerjohann (Tübingen: Narr, 1996), pp. 300–17. On Friedrich Wilhelm Joseph Schelling's 1803 essay 'Ueber Dante in philosophischer Beziehung', which also inspired the works of Georg Wilhelm Friedrich Hegel and Erich Auerbach, see Cat. *36*.
37. I would like to refer in this context to my Jena habilitation *Die Poetik des Ungesagten in Dantes Commedia* (Paderborn: Wilhelm Fink, 2021).
38. Gian Paolo Marchi, 'Appunti su alcune presenze di Dante nella cultura tedesca', in *La presenza di Dante nella cultura del novecento*, ed. by Alberto Castaldini e Vasco Senatore Gondola (Verona: Accademia di Agricoltura Scienze e Lettere di Verona, 2017), pp. 27–48 (p. 32). For the translations of Meinhard (1763) and Bachenschwanz (1767), see Brigitte Heymann in Cat. 48–49 and Cat. *22*.
39. The text is quoted in the so-called 'Fassung B' from Johann Wolfgang von Goethe, *Die Leiden des jungen Werthers. Die Wahlverwandtschaften. Kleine Prosa. Epen*, ed. by Waltraud Wiethölter in collaboration with Christoph Brecht (Frankfurt am Main: Deutscher Klassiker Verlag, 1994), pp. 231–47.
40. Robert Stockhammer, *Leseerzählungen. Alternativen zum hermeneutischen Verfahren* (Stuttgart: Metzler, 1991), p. 157 speaks of 'kalkulierte Zeremonie' and 'scheinbare Spontaneität'.
41. *Inf.* 5. 74.
42. Presented in the main display cabinet, these engravings are inserted into the introductory essay, Cat. 12–13, ill. 1 and 2.
43. On the various attempts to do justice to the original, see Edoardo Costadura, 'Übersetzungen der Göttlichen Komödie in der Goethe- und Philalethes-Zeit', *Palmbaum. Literarisches Journal aus Thüringen*, 1 (2016), 35–48.
44. The volume edited by Köhler to mark the 1865 Dante anniversary was presented in the main display cabinet along with Koch's illustration. A reproduction of the title page can be found in Brigitte Heymann's essay 'Dante für Liebhaber und Gelehrte', Cat. 54, ill. 3.
45. Cf. Gerhard Regn, 'Himmelsdisko. Anmerkungen zum Dante von Kurt Flasch', *Scientia poetica*, 18 (2014), 260–76.
46. Cat. 22.
47. Cat. 27.
48. Cat. *30*. On the particular technique known as 'Schlegel-Terzine', see Stefan Matuschek, Cat. 41–43.
49. Cat. *40*. Kannegießer also translated Silvio Pellico's 1815 drama *Francesca da Rimini*.
50. Cat. 44.
51. Cat. *45*. The dedication reads: 'Sr Excellenz dem Herrn Staatsminister von Göthe ehrfurchtsvoll überreicht vom Uebersetzer. Berlin, den 7. Jul. 1824' [To his excellency, the state minister von Göthe, reverentially presented by the translator. Berlin, 7 July 1824].
52. Cat. *46*.
53. Cat. *47, 51, 53*.
54. Cat. *49*. The dedication reads: 'à l'illustre Goethe son très humble admirateur Antoni Deschamps' [To the illustrious Goethe, his humble admirer Antoni Deschamps].
55. Cat. *58*. On the Society's decision to move its seat to Weimar in 1921, see Cat. *60*.
56. See the 1559 translation of *De Monarchia* by Johann Basilius Herold, Cat. *11*. See also Walter Pauly, 'Irdische Universalherrschaft und göttliche Gerechtigkeit: Zu Dante Alighieris (1265–1321) Stellung in der spätmittelalterlichen Publizistik', *Der Staat*, 53 (2014), 509–31.
57. It is not possible, in the context of this essay, to address in detail the question of when exactly a

certain book entered the library's collections. Wherever known, the provenances are indicated in the catalogue headings.
58. Cat. *1*.
59. Cat. *3, 5, 6, 9, 10, 12, 13, 15*.
60. Cat. *3* (loan from Thüringer Universitäts- und Landesbibliothek Jena), *9, 12, 5*.
61. Cat. *12, 13*.
62. *Italienische Bibliothek. Die Sammlung Carl Ludwig Fernows in der Herzogin Anna Amalia Bibliothek, Weimar*, ed. by Lea Ritter-Santini, in collaboration with Katrin Lehmann and Anneke Thiel, 2 vols (Göttingen: Wallstein, 2014), II, 402–07.
63. Cat. *19*. Dolce was the first, in his 1555 edition, to use the title *Divina Commedia*, cf. Cat 10 (loan from Thüringer Universitäts- und Landesbibliothek Jena).
64. Cat. *28*.
65. Hans Ruppert, *Goethes Bibliothek* (Weimar: Arion, 1958).
66. Cat. *17*. Goethe mentions this edition explicitly in a letter to Streckfuß when he talks about his translation of the beginning of *Inf.* 12, cf. Cat. *50–51*. A copy of the 1595 edition of the Crusca was among the loans from Thüringer Universitäts- und Landesbibliothek Jena, Cat. *15*.
67. Cat. *18*.
68. Goethe also owned a Dante medal pre-dating 1514 (Cat. *4*), and a *c.* 1811 *intaglio* showing a portrait of Dante (Cat. *42*), as well as a copy of Dante's alleged death mask (Cat. *43*).
69. Cat. *23*.
70. Cat. *29*.
71. See Michael Knoche, 'Vorwort', in *Italienische Bibliothek*, I, 13–23.
72. In addition to the editions of the *Commedia* mentioned above, the library's holdings made it possible to put on display some of Dante's other works: the *Vita Nuova* in an illustrated Venetian edition of 1758 (Cat. *21*), the *Convivio* in Goethe's copy of 1741 (Cat. *18*), and the *De Monarchia* in a German translation of 1559 (Cat. *11*). While Dante's linguistic treatise *De vulgari eloquentia* could be displayed in Fernow's *c.* 1529 copy of the Italian translation by Gian Giorgio Trissino (Cat. *8*), Jacopo Corbinelli's first print of the Latin text, which was published in Paris in 1577, once in the library, was probably lost in the fire that broke out in the 'Rococo hall' in 2004 (Cat. *14*). In an effort to contextualize Dante's works further, one of the display cabinets was dedicated to two major texts that Dante refers to in the *Commedia*: Vergil's *Aeneid*, in an edition published in Straßburg by Johannes Grüninger with woodcarvings by Sebastian Brant in 1502 (Cat. *2*), and Brunetto Latini's *Tesoro*, in an Italian edition dating 1528 (Cat. *7*, loan from Thüringer Universitäts- und Landesbibliothek Jena).
73. Entries in the catalogue section reproducing sole portraits of Dante are: Cat. *4, 25, 26, 31, 38, 42* (?), *43, 58*.
74. Illustrations of individual scenes from Dante's works reproduced in the catalogue section are: Cat. *3* (loan from Thüringer Universitäts- und Landesbibliothek Jena), *9, 20, 21, 28, 32, 35, 41, 47, 57*.
75. Cat. *4, 5* and front jacket, *29, 48, 51, 53, 59*.
76. A *rimario* of verse endings (Cat. *16*) and a glossary explaining rare words and neologisms (Cat. *19*) were both owned by Fernow.
77. Edoardo Costadura, 'Dantes deutsche Heimatstädte Weimar, Jena und Dresden', *Dresdner Hefte*, 122 (2015), 49–57.
78. Giorgio Padoan, 'Un'eco della 'Comedìa' nell''Agathon' di Wieland', in *Il lungo cammino del 'poema sacro'. Studi danteschi* (Florence: Olschki, 1993), pp. 283–85.
79. Cat. *24*.
80. Cat. *27*.
81. 'Von der Divina Commedia des Dante', *Neuer Teutscher Merkur*, July 1785. See also Cat. *24*.
82. Cat. *30*.
83. Cat. *33*.
84. Cat. *36*.
85. Cat. *39*. As early as 1788, Giuseppe de Valenti, who taught Italian at the University of Jena, had published an Italian edition of the *Commedia* with the Jena-based printer Heller, in the series

La sublime scuola italiana. A copy is in the Thüringer Universitäts- und Landesbibliothek (8 Art. lib.XI,5). The Weimar library owned a copy, which was presumably lost in the 2004 fire (8° XXXVIII: 293 (e)). On Giuseppe de Valenti and his son Agostino, see Margrit Glaser, 'Jagemanns Beitrag zur Entwicklung der italienischen Grammatikographie in Deutschland', in *Die Italianistik in der Weimarer Klassik: Das Leben und Werk von Christian Joseph Jagemann (1735–1804)*, ed. by Jörn Albrecht and Peter Kofler (Tübingen: Gunter Narr, 2006), pp. 143–67 (p. 163). The first Italian edition of the *Inferno* to appear in Germany was published in Leipzig by Nicolò Ciangulo in 1755. See also Ernst Behler, 'Dante in Germany', in *The Dante Encyclopedia*, ed. by Richard Lansing (New York: Garland, 2000), pp. 262–69 (p. 266).

86. 'Seine liebste Arbeit aber war das Leben Dante's, welches er mit großer Liebe aus den ersten Quellen zusammensetzte [...]. Leider ist Dante's Leben nur ein Fragment geblieben; wenige Stunden vor seinem Tode beschäftigte er sich noch damit' [However, his favourite work was the life of Dante, which he composed with great love from the first sources. [...] Regrettably, his life of Dante remained a fragment; a few hours before his death he was still working on it]. Johanna Schopenhauer, *Carl Ludwig Fernow's Leben* (Tübingen: Cotta, 1810), pp. 422–23.
87. Cat. *31, 32*.
88. See Brigitte Heymann's essay 'Dante für Liebhaber und Gelehrte', Cat. 51–55.
89. Cat. *56*.
90. Cat. *57*.
91. Cat. *54, 55*.
92. See Francesca Fabbri, 'Illustrare Dante dal medioevo all'ottocento: un saggio dimenticato di Adele Schopenhauer e il suo contesto', *Letteratura & Arte*, 14 (2016), 111–36.
93. Cat. *34*. The text is also in Friederich, *Dante's Fame Abroad*, p. 384.
94. *Inf.* 5. 116–17. See, by contrast, the beginning of Francesca's speech ('Siede la terra dove nata fui. . .') in verses 97–107.
95. Cf. Costadura, 'Dantes deutsche Heimatstädte'.
96. In the *Amorosa visione*, 5. 70–75: 'Dentro del coro delle donne adorno, | in mezzo di quel loco ove faciemo | li savii antichi felice soggiorno, | rimirando, vid'io di gioia pieno | onorar festeggiando un gran poeta, | tanto che 'l dire alla vista vien meno.' Giovanni Boccaccio, *Amorosa visione*, trans. by Robert Hollander, Timothy Hampton, Margherita Frankel, with an introduction by Vittore Branca (Hanover, NH: University Press of New England, 1986), p. 24. On Boccaccio's response to Dante's use of the ineffability topos, see Giuseppe Ledda, 'Retoriche dell'ineffabile da Dante a Boccaccio', *Studi sul Boccaccio*, 39 (2001), 115–37.
97. On the problematic consequences of such monumentalizing forms of literary historiography, see the essay by Stefan Matuschek, 'Dante als deutscher Klassiker', Cat. 29–45, where the busts are reproduced as ill. 1 and 2.
98. Jürgen Kaube, speech to mark the 325th anniversary of the Herzogin Anna Amalia Bibliothek, Weimar, 30 September 2016, <https://www.youtube.com/watch?v=871gnZ_oLSY>.[99] Cat. *37*.
99. The passage transcribed is *Purg.* 11. 100–02.
100. Cat. *24*.
101. Cat. *4*.
102. On Domenico di Michelino, see Friederike Wille's essay 'Dante in der bildenden Kunst', Cat. 60–62 and ill. 2.

CHAPTER 19

'How the Young Women Take to It!': Italian Exiles and Women Readers of Dante in Nineteenth-Century New England

Christian Y. Dupont

On 20 February 1892, Samuel Gray Ward wrote to Charles Eliot Norton:

> Just sending off to one of my grandchildren a copy of your translation of the Inferno. I am reminded how long it is since I have heard from you though I have often thought of you in connection with Lowell's death, and the satisfaction I felt on learning that you were to be his literary executor.[1]

Norton had succeeded James Russell Lowell and Henry Wadsworth Longfellow as president of the Dante Society that they had founded a decade earlier at Harvard, and had just published his prose translation with notes of the first two *cantiche* of the *Commedia*, with the third to follow later in the year. Ward continued:

> I still keep up my Dante whenever I have a chance of a new hand to read a few cantos with. How the young women take to it! I read the Purgatorio with my granddaughter last summer, in a week's visit she paid us; — and the Inferno this winter at Santa Barbara with Ellen Hale.

Ellen Day Hale, daughter of the historian and Unitarian minister Edward Everett Hale, was a notable printmaker and painter who lived and worked between Paris, London, and Boston. She was in her mid-thirties when she sojourned in Santa Barbara to enjoy its more temperate coastal climate, like Ward and his wife. The Wards were then in their mid-seventies, and their granddaughter, Elizabeth Howard Ward, eighteen. Born to elite if not Brahmin families into which they sometimes married,[2] these intelligent and talented, moneyed, and mobile young women represented those whom Ward witnessed 'taking to Dante' so readily and passionately. Perhaps this should come as no surprise, for by the close of the nineteenth century, the study of the works and life of the medieval Florentine poet in America were becoming increasingly institutionalized as well as democratized through the diffusion of university courses and public lectures, the formation of reading groups and library collections, the publication of translations and study aids, and even children's books.[3] For its part, the Dante Society encouraged many of these kinds of activities, and supported some of them directly.[4]

Kathleen Verduin cites the above passage from Ward's letter in the conclusion to her 1996 article on Margaret Fuller's ambivalent attractions to Dante and to Ward.[5] Through that ground-breaking study and subsequent essays, Verduin has done more than Angelina La Piana and other scholars who have studied Dante's reception in America to observe how women in nineteenth-century New England engaged with the medieval poet and his works.[6] The present chapter aspires to continue Verduin's lines of inquiry into the reading of Dante by women from prominent New England families, focusing ultimately on those who discovered him earlier in the century through their encounters with exiled Italian revolutionaries, who tutored them in their language and literature.[7]

Seeking to explain to Ralph Waldo Emerson why she could not take up his suggestion to translate Dante's *Vita Nuova*, Fuller confessed that she taught herself Italian on her own ('unassisted, except as to the pronunciation'), and keenly felt the lack of more formal training and exposure. 'I have used all the means within my reach, but my not going abroad is an insuperable defect in the technical part of my education', she confessed with moderated vexation and regret in a letter dated December 1842.[8] Five years later she would travel, and marry, in Italy.

Yet Fuller was already offering instruction in Italian, or at least Italian literature, by the autumn of 1836. In addition to teaching Latin and French at Bronson Alcott's Temple School in Boston, she also formed classes of her own to introduce young women to French, German, and Italian.[9] In a letter to a friend, presumably James Freeman Clarke, she reported success in educating her students to read German, and noted that 'with my Italian class, I read parts of Tasso, Petrarch, — whom they came to almost adore, — Ariosto, Alfieri, and the whole hundred cantos of the Divina Commedia, with the aid of the fine Athenaeum copy, Flaxman's designs, and all the best commentaries'.[10] It is not clear what the 'fine Athenaeum copy' of the *Commedia* would be, unless Fuller were referring to an edition held by the Boston Athenæum, which is possible, since its 1827 catalogue indicates that its collection included a 3-volume set of Henry Francis Cary's translation published in London in 1778.

Modelled on the Athenæum and Lyceum of Liverpool, the Boston Athenæum had been established in 1807 as a membership library in Boston's Beacon Hill neighbourhood. It added an art gallery in 1827, and began that year to host an annual art exhibition. The inaugural exhibition included a painting by Washington Allston titled *Beatrice* that presented an idealized portrait of Dante's muse. Fuller visited the exhibition with her friend Elizabeth Palmer Peabody, with whom she would later hold her famous 'conversations' at Peabody's West Street bookstore. Both women, teenagers at the time, were enthralled with Allston's portrait, especially Peabody, who would return to see it day after day.[11]

There is no evidence that Peabody's absorption with Beatrice led her to read Dante, yet it seems likely. Fuller certainly did, though it is difficult to say how early.

Verduin conjectures that Fuller was probably acquainted with Dante by 1828, if not by 1825, when she began studying Italian and read Sismondi's *De la littérature du midi de l'Europe*.[12] By 1837, when Fuller was having the young women in her tutelage read the *Comedy*, she was also reading and discussing it at length with the 'apostle of Unitarianism', William Ellery Channing.[13]

Despite the lack of explicit references in their correspondence, one imagines that Fuller also read and discussed Dante with fellow Italophile Samuel Gray Ward, whom she courted around this time, albeit unsuccessfully. Ward would later read Dante with his wife, Anna — evidently in translation, as Anna, at least, had studied French and German but not Italian.[14]

Perhaps embittered by losing Ward to a woman she considered less cultivated than herself and by the recognition of her own limitations, Fuller asserted in a review of the Flaxman-illustrated 1845 edition of Henry Francis Cary's translation of the *Commedia* that the only use for such volumes is to help the translators themselves and others who endeavour to improve their understanding of the original. From this assertion she turned to decrying what she claimed had become a common educational practice, admittedly even her own:

> We must say a few words as to the pedantic folly with which this study has been prosecuted in this country, and, we believe, in England. Not only the tragedies of Alfieri and the *Faust* of Goethe, but the *Divina Commedia* of Dante, — a work which it is not probable there are upon earth, at any one time, a hundred minds able to appreciate, — are turned into school books for little girls who have just left their hoops and dolls, and boys whose highest ambition it is to ride a horse that will run away, and brave the tutor in a college frolic. This is done from the idea that, in order to get acquainted with a foreign language, the student must read books that have attained the dignity of classics, and also which are 'hard.' Hard indeed it must be for the Muses to see their lyres turned into gridirons for the preparation of a school-girl's lunch.[15]

The reference to Alfieri in conjunction with Dante suggests that Fuller may have had in mind the methods of Lorenzo Da Ponte, the famous librettist for Mozart who emigrated to New York in 1805 to escape creditors, and who later began teaching Italian language and literature at Columbia College and privately, using the works of Italian poets and dramatists, in particular, Dante, Tasso, Monti, Metastasio, Petrarch, and Alfieri. Commenting on Da Ponte's method, one of the young women who studied with him reported that she began by learning verbs, then by translating a story from French into Italian, 'and in this way, without actually studying it, I learnt almost all of the grammar', adding that 'at the same time I began to read with him the lovely plays of Metastasio, the easiest of the Italian poets, and little by little in six months I read almost all the classics'.[16] By the time of his death in 1838, Da Ponte had become well known, even to New Englanders, through the influence of his teaching, his operatic endeavours, and the publication of his memoirs.

Though this was probably never his intention, Da Ponte nevertheless became the forerunner of a number of Italian expatriates who came to the United States and supported themselves, at least initially, as language teachers. Most arrived between the mid-1820s and mid-1830s as political exiles.

One such figure was Antonio Gallenga, who became a fugitive on account of his involvement in revolutionary factions in his native Parma in 1831. After taking refuge in France, Corsica, and Switzerland, he attempted re-establish himself in Italy under the assumed name Luigi Mariotti, but soon fled again. After nearly two years in Malta and Morocco, he arrived in New York and then proceeded to Boston in the autumn of 1836. American diplomats had provided him with letters of introduction to Massachusetts Governor Edward Everett and Harvard president Josiah Quincy, suggesting that he could teach at Harvard, which had established a modern languages department. Harvard, however, had already named an instructor of Italian some years earlier: a Sicilian who had likewise been forced to flee due his association with the Carbonari and their pursuit of Italian independence, namely Ignazio Batolo, or, as he came to be known thereafter in America, Pietro Bachi. Bachi's courses in Italian language prepared Harvard's undergraduates (then all male, of course) to study Dante with George Ticknor and his successor, Henry Wadsworth Longfellow.

Bachi and yet another Sicilian exile, Pietro d'Alessandro, who offered private Italian lessons and occasionally exchanged books with Everett,[17] welcomed Gallenga upon his arrival in Boston, but could not provide much assistance in settling him. For that, Gallenga relied initially on Everett, who hired him to tutor his two eldest daughters in Italian, Anne Gorham, then thirteen, and Charlotte Brooks, age eleven.

In his spirited memoir, Gallenga describes Anne as 'an infant prodigy' whose 'precocious talents' had been 'forced with so much more zeal than discretion' by her father such that she was 'stunted in growth and spoilt in temper; a poor, thin, sallow, peevish thing, sickly as a hot-house plant, and, as it was easy to foresee, and actually happened, doomed to an early grave'.[18] Edward Everett had purchased an Italian grammar for Anne shortly after her eleventh birthday and had been reciting lessons in Italian (which he both read and spoke) and Latin with her almost daily since, in order to supplement her learning of French at school, a routine that seems to have pleased her, judging by the attention she gives it in her meticulous diaries.[19] She likewise refers appreciatively to Eliza Ware Farrar's manual of advice and instruction for young ladies, which assumed the value of studying the French, Italian, and Latin languages and literary classics.[20] In her entry for 21 November 1836, Anne refers to the precipitous appearance of Gallenga at the family home in Charlestown:

> We are not going to town to school, as I thought we should, but we are to have a private teacher at home, whose name is M. de Mariotti [Gallenga continued to use the pseudonym after fleeing Italy]. He is to teach us French, Italian, and Latin, and came first this morning.

By then, she had already begun reading Tasso's *Gerusalemme liberata*, which she continued with Gallenga. 'As to the foreign languages', she reported in her diary entry for 8 February 1837, 'I am getting on very well. I am reading Caesar's Commentaries in Latin, and Tasso's Gerusalemme Liberata in Italian, and I am learning to speak a little Italian'.

Gallenga, on the other hand, had complained to her father in a letter the day before that the sisters did not like him and lacked confidence in him as a teacher.[21] By April, the situation had not improved, and the girls were sent to an aunt's house on the North Shore for a respite.[22] Yet it was not enough: by June, Gallenga resigned.[23] To make up for the lost income and pride, 'Mr. Everett volunteered to become himself my pupil', Gallenga confided in his memoir, 'and went with me through a course of readings of Dante in the evenings, in which he persevered with great steadiness.'[24] Meanwhile, Marianne Dwight,[25] whom Gallenga had befriended, brought him to Providence and introduced him to Margaret Fuller, who subsequently found him 'ample employment' as a tutor of Italian, 'if not in Charlestown or Boston, at least in the neighbouring towns of Salem, Lowell, etc.', to which he travelled 'almost every day in the week, either by rail, or on horseback, or as the winter set in, by sledge'.[26]

For her part, Anne Gorham Everett continued her study of Italian at home. She evidently made good progress, for in an entry from November 1838, she reported:

> We went on with our lessons today, and I began to learn German. I can hardly tell whether I shall like it yet, for it looks rather hard, but I think I shall. We say about the same lessons now as last summer to papa, and have added geography and history. I learn Dante now in Italian, and have about half finished 'L'inferno', the first part of the poem. I also read Virgil, which I have three fourths finished.[27]

Since her father was then her primary teacher, one may presume that his reading of Dante with Gallenga had some influence on the selection of a text for her Italian recitations. Nevertheless, the novelty and difficulty of German seems have engaged the better part of her attention, for she does not explicitly refer to her Italian lessons, much less Dante, in her diary entries until the following September, and then only in passing,[28] whereas her German lessons receive nearly daily mentions. When she had opportunities to visit the retrospective exhibition of William Allston's paintings at Harding's Gallery in Boston in the spring of 1839, she singled out paintings of biblical subjects, whereas *Beatrice* was the focus of reviews published by Fuller and Peabody — not surprisingly, perhaps, given their enraptured impressions as teenagers.[29] And yet in a letter to a girlfriend she wrote in June 1839, Anne gave the upper hand to Italian over German, and Dante over Tasso:

> I get on very well with my studies now; just as well, indeed, as if I went to school. I am learning German, and though I found it very hard at first, yet now I like it very much. I am reading a very pretty little book, by Goëthe, called 'Hermann and Dorothea.' I hope you study Italian now, for it is, I think, the most beautiful of all the foreign languages, that I have ever studied; and when you know more of it, and read Dante and Tasso, you will take still greater pleasure in it than now.[30]

The mention of Tasso alongside Dante is intriguing in light of Fuller's curricular critiques cited earlier, for in the same passage she went on to chide:

> In Italian have you not Tasso, Ariosto and other writers who have really a great deal that the immature mind can enjoy, without choking them with the stern

politics of Alfieri, or piling upon a brain still soft, the mountainous meanings of Dante.[31]

That Tasso was considered an easier and more suitable Italian master to forge the linguistic development of young ladies may be attested by his primacy and presence, and Dante's absence, from the reading list of other New England girls who were receiving tutoring. In a letter to a cousin written in 1841, Elizabeth Payson Prentiss, then twenty-three years old, confessed: 'As to my Italian and Tasso, I am ashamed to tell you how slow I have been. Between company and housework and sewing I have my hands about full, and precious little time for reading and study.'[32]

Some years earlier, Lydia Huntley Sigourney drew her own contrast between Dante and Tasso that anticipated Fuller's. In the third edition of a volume of *Letters to Young Ladies*, first published in 1833, Sigourney enriched her discussion of the qualities that polite and intellectual conversation should take with references to 'men of genius and wisdom' who were often found 'deficient in its graces': 'Neither Buffon or Rousseau carried their eloquence into society. The silence of the poet Chaucer was held more desirable than his speech. [...] Dante was taciturn, and all the brilliance of Tasso, was in his pen.'[33]

Like Sigourney, Farrar, and other women of the period who penned practical advice for their younger counterparts, Catharine Maria Sedgwick held up the value of learning French, Italian, German, as well as English literature and language in her domestic novels, including *Hope Leslie* (1827) and *Clarence* (1830), and a guide addressed to young women for their personal cultivation titled *Means and Ends, or, Self-training* (1839). Yet for as much as she extolled the ideals of Republican motherhood, Sedgwick preferred to remain unmarried and expend her pedagogical energies on her niece and namesake, who came to spell her name with a 'K' and call herself 'Kate', and her aunt, 'Kitty'.

Kate was born in 1820 to Catharine's brother Charles, a lawyer raised in Stockbridge, Massachusetts, who settled in nearby Lenox following his marriage in 1819 to Elizabeth Buckminster Dwight, with whom he had four other children. Elizabeth founded a well-regarded school for young ladies and authored several books on education. She shared not only a common purpose but a close friendship with her sister-in-law, and enjoined her assistance in educating Kate. As early as 1832, Kate attended a school in New York, where she studied French, Italian, and music, as well as mythology, history, philosophy, and even astronomy, supplemented by dancing and drawing lessons.[34] It is not clear whether she boarded at school or stayed with her aunt, but Catharine did arrange for tutoring in music and Italian in August 1834,[35] and welcomed her to stay for extended periods in subsequent years, during which they would also visit family friends around Philadelphia. In 1839, Catharine brought her on a year-long tour of Europe with her brother Robert and his family.[36] Upon their arrival in London, they met Gallenga, who had lately decided to leave Boston after failing to find secure and satisfactory employment.[37]

Like many girls at the time, Kate kept an autograph album in which family members and acquaintances would inscribe inspirational thoughts or poems, and sometimes drawings. An unsigned entry from 1831 records a quotation from

Anna Brownwell Jameson's *Loves of the Poets*, a compilation of romantic verse and commentary that she published in London in 1829 after leaving her husband. The selection, attributed to Dante, reads: 'We know that the heavens shine on in eternal serenity and that it is only our imperfect vision & the rising vapours of the earth that make the ever-beaming stars appear clouded at times to our eye.'[38] This passage is not translated or adapted from the *Commedia*, nor even the *Vita Nuova*, but rather from the third treatise of the *Convivio*, in which Dante glosses his canzone 'Amor che ne la mente mi ragiona'.

If this were the only evidence of Kate's knowledge of Dante, it would hardly be worth mentioning, but in another notebook she compiled in the mid-1830s, one finds a detailed commentary in English on the first fourteen cantos of *Inferno* that runs to some twenty pages of neatly lined text.[39] The content of the commentary is unlike any other published up to that time, or even since. It begins innocently enough with the factual statement that 'Dante was born in 1265 of a Guelph family' but quickly moves into abstruse speculations concerning the origins and names of the political parties that then divided Italy. 'Before they became sufficiently numerous and strong to declare themselves openly', the Ghibelline sects that attempted to reform the Church from within with the support of emperors

> were obliged to invent signs and mystic language by means of which they communicated with one another without being understood by their enemies. [...] Some of these sects, or secret societies called themselves Katharos (pure), or Lambs — and as Wolves are the natural enemies of Lambs, they called the opposite party Wölf, bywölf, Guelph.

The commentary goes on to assert that Boccaccio, Petrarch, Dante, and other distinguished men of the time belonged to these secret societies. In the case of Dante, as soon as he could reason for himself, he 'abandoned the party of the Pope, (the Neri of Florence) in strict allegiance to whom he had been brought up, and joined the Bianchi and the heretics'. Glossing the second line of *Inferno*, the commentator asserts, 'The *selva oscura* in which Dante found himself was the party of the *Bianchi*, who professed themselves honest Ghibellines, but were so corrupt, that the Guelphs themselves were but little worse — "Tanto è amara che poco è più morte".'

A systematic search of the seventy-five historical commentaries on the *Commedia* included in the Dartmouth Dante Project database for the word 'Bianchi' in relation to the opening lines of *Inferno* yields a match in only one commentary, published by Giuseppe Campi in 1889–93, almost fifty years after Kate transcribed the above passages into her notebook. Interestingly, Campi refers to a lecture given some decades earlier by a self-taught yet precocious scholar of Dante manuscripts, the attorney Jacopo Ferrari of Reggio Emilia. Ferrari claimed that the image of the *selva oscura* comprised all of the political factions that divided Florence in Dante's day: the Guelphs and Ghibellines, the Bianchi and Neri, the Grandi and Popolani, the Popolo grosso and Popolo minuto, adding that 'the Bianchi, in sum, with respect to this forest, refers to the moral and political disorder of Italy, especially Florence, which Dante calls a "trista selva" ("a sad and wretched wood") in Purgatorio (14:64).'[40]

A scant reference to Ferrari in the newspaper published during the sexcentenary celebrations of Dante's birth in Florence indicates that he was 'an exile of 1821'.[41] Ferrari's association with the pro-republican, anti-papal, secretive networks of the Carbonari that were forced underground or into exile following the collapse of their uprisings in 1821 fits with the esoteric tenor of the commentary copied down by Kate: 'Dante's poem is all mystic — it veils under Catholic language the strongest animosity toward the Pope, and the firmest loyalty towards the emperor.' Several still more obscure interpretations relying on strained etymologies and dubious prophecies, including forced anagrams (e.g., 'Veltro/Ueltro' in *Inferno* 1. 101 as an anagram and prophecy of the birth of 'Lutero/Luther') and acrostics ('EN-RI-C-O' from the first and last syllables of *Inferno* 9. 67–69, evidently taken as a reference to Emperor Henry VII), confirm the hermetic political nature of the exegesis. Yet there is no evidence that Ferrari sought refuge in America, nor it is possible that a sixteen-year-old girl bred in New England could have contrived such conspiratorial theories. So where did she encounter them?

The notebook itself provides a clue. Turned over and opened from the back cover, it contains copies of a series of letters between Kate and Giovanni Albinola, an Italian patriot who was invited to join the Carbonari in 1830 by one of its leaders, Felice Argenti, and who was arrested by the Austrians the following year with Argenti when one of their letters was intercepted. Both were subsequently incarcerated in the infamous Spielberg castle memorialized by Silvio Pellico in his 1832 memoir, *Le mie prigioni*.

Argenti and Abinola were initially condemned to death, but their sentences were commuted to life in prison. Later, they were granted refuge in the United States. In August 1836, they sailed from Trieste to New York with other exiled compatriots, including Eleuterio Felice Foresti, Luigi Tinelli, Pietro Borsieri, and Gaetano de Castillia.

Kate's correspondence with Albinola copied into the notebook with the Dante commentaries includes five letters they exchanged between 20 and 29 November 1836, while Albinola was visiting her relations in Stockbridge.[42] The premise was that each would provide practice in the other's language, but instead both wrote in Italian and argued about grammatical points Kate had been taught by the tutor her aunt had arranged during extended stays with her in New York: Piero Maroncelli.[43]

Maroncelli was yet another of the Spielberg prisoners who had been offered exile in lieu of continued imprisonment. He arrived in New York in September 1833, together with his wife, a German opera singer whom he had married during his prior sojourn in Paris. In New York, he soon met Catharine Maria Sedgwick, possibly through Lorenzo da Ponte.[44] In August 1834, Maroncelli visited Boston with his wife for a concert.[45] The opportunity enabled him to meet Andrews Norton, with whom he had been corresponding about the publication of a new translation of Pellico's memoir that had been prepared by Norton's wife along with Sedgwick's translation of Maroncelli's own recollections of their imprisonment. This new edition appeared in two volumes in September 1836.[46]

On 31 October 1836, Maroncelli sent a letter to Kate announcing that Albinola, his friend and fellow expatriate, would soon come to stay with her family in

Stockbridge, being desirous to spend time in the countryside and learn English.[47] In a postscript, he added that he was sorry that Kate would not be returning to take his lessons, for she had been the 'chief ornament'. 'I hope to have you back next year', he remarked, 'so we can continue reading Dante or something else.'

In the diary Kate irregularly kept that year, some pages have been cut from the end, but the last leaf definitively identifies Maroncelli as the source of the mysterious commentary she had transcribed in her notebook: 'I have been taking from Maroncelli a very interesting course of lessons on Dante's Inferno. Aunt Kitty, Miss Watts + Agnes Smedberg were my companions.'[48] The beginning of the entry is missing, but it must have been added sometime after the date of the previous entry, 9 July 1836, in which she mentions having spent several months in New York.

Beginning her research on Maroncelli in the 1920s, Angeline Lograsso was the first scholar to attempt to track down letters and documentation concerning the exiled patriot.[49] Besides the newly discovered evidence cited here, other surviving witnesses may yet be found who will further illuminate his tutoring in Italian and Dante, as well as the sources of his esoteric and politicized readings of the *Commedia*, which probably include fellow Carbonari, such as Jacopo Ferrari, or even Gabriele Rossetti.[50]

However improbable it may seem that young women in nineteenth-century New England were studying Dante in the original under the tutelage of Italian political exiles, clearly they were doing so, and earlier and more seriously and in greater numbers than may have been previously recognized.

Notes on Chapter 19

1. Cambridge, Massachusetts, Houghton Library, Charles Eliot Norton Papers, bMsAm 1088 (7723). Lowell died on 12 August 1891 following a protracted illness. For a discussion of Lowell's personalized reading and impressionistic teaching of Dante and its influence, see Kathleen Verduin, '"Why Do You Rend Me?" Dante and the Pain of James Russell Lowell', which appears as Chapter 20 in this volume.
2. Following her grand tour of Europe, Elizabeth Howard Ward (1873–1954) married the somewhat older Boston architect Charles Bruen Perkins (1860–1929); see University of California Santa Barbara, 'Guide to the Ward-Perkins Family Papers, ca. 1788–1954', MS 129, <https://www.oac.cdlib.org/findaid/ark:/13030/kt4v19s0sj/> [accessed 10 October 2020].
3. With regard to children's books based on Dante's *Comedy*, see Carol Chiodo, 'Dante for Mothers', which appears as Chapter 21 in this volume.
4. Christian Y. Dupont, 'Collecting and Reading Dante in America: Harvard College Library and the Dante Society', *Harvard Library Bulletin*, 22.1 (2011), 1–57.
5. Kathleen Verduin, '"The Inward Life of Love": Margaret Fuller and the *Vita Nuova*', *Dante Studies, with the Annual Report of the Dante Society*, 114 (1996), 293–309 (p. 306).
6. Angelina La Piana, *Dante's American Pilgrimage: A Historical Survey of Dante Studies in the United States 1800–1944* (New Haven, CT: Yale University Press, 1948). Among other studies of Dante's American reception, one must mention Theodore W. Koch, *Dante in America: A Historical and Bibliographical Study* (Boston: Ginn and Company, 1896), several essays by J. Chesley Mathews, as well as Kathleen Verduin, 'Dante in America: The First Hundred Years', in *Reading Books: Essays on the Material Text and Literature in America*, ed. by Michele Moylan and Lanes Stiles (Amherst, MA: University of Massachusetts Press, 1996), pp. 16–51.
7. It should be noted that the studies of the teaching of Italian in the United States by Bruno Rosselli, Howard Marraro, and Joseph Fucilla were consulted but not cited because they did

not furnish any primary evidence concerning the topics examined in this essay. Preliminary research was presented by the author at a panel session organized by the Dante Society of America for the 2016 annual meeting of the Renaissance Society of America, held in Boston. The role of political exiles as teachers of Italian (sometimes including Dante) to young women in early nineteenth-century Europe also deserves further and comparative study. Examples include Giuseppe Pecchio and Niccolo Giosafatte Bagioli. On Pecchio as a teacher in England in the 1820s, see C. P. Brand, *Italy and the English Romantics: The Italianate Fashion in Early Nineteenth-Century England* (Cambridge: Cambridge University Press, 1957, 2011), pp. 38–39, and as a political and economic commentator, Maurizio Isabella, *Risorgimento in Exile: Italian Émigrés and the Liberal International in the Post-Napoleonic Era* (Oxford: Oxford University Press, 2009), pp. 113–14, 159–69, 182–85 and 240. On Biagioli as teacher of Frances Kemble in Paris in the 1820s and as an editor and commentator of Dante, see Nick Havely, *Dante's British Public: Readers and Texts, from the Fourteenth Century to the Present* (Oxford: Oxford University Press, 2014), pp. 139–40 and 156–57. I am grateful to Nick Havely for signalling this vein of inquiry and these references, as well as for the editorial guidance that he and an anonymous reader provided in the preparation of this essay.
8. *Letters of Margaret Fuller*, ed. by Robert N. Hudspeth, 6 vols (Ithaca, NY: Cornell University Press, 1983–94), III (1984), 103: 'Besides, the translating Dante is a piece of literary presumption, and challenges a criticism to which I am not sure that I am, as the Germans say, *gewachsen*. Italian, as well as German, I learned by myself, unassisted, except as to the pronunciation. I have never been brought into connection with minds trained to any severity in these kinds of elegant culture.'
9. *Memoirs of Margaret Fuller Ossoli*, ed. by William Henry Channing, 2 vols (Boston: Phillips, Sampson, & Co., 1852), I, 171.
10. Ibid., p. 174. The full text of the letter appears in *Letters of Margaret Fuller*, I (1983), 278–79; Hudspeth does not identify a correspondent but suggests that it was written 'ca. Summer 1837'. The first portion of the *Memoirs*, however, was compiled by James Freeman Clarke and mainly comprises extracts of letters Fuller addressed to him (see Barbara Packer, 'Dangerous Acquaintances: The Correspondence of Margaret Fuller and James Freeman Clarke', *English Literary History*, 67.3 (2000), 816, n. 1). It is therefore reasonable to assume the letter was addressed to Clarke. Clarke's older sister Sarah attended Fuller's 'conversation' classes, which began in 1839, and contributed a poem on Dante to *The Dial*, which Fuller edited; see: '"The Impulses of Human Nature": Margaret Fuller's Journal from June through October 1844', ed. by Martha L. Berg and Alice De V. Perry, *Proceedings of the Massachusetts Historical Society*, 102 (1990), 38–126 (p. 59, n. 23). Verduin, 'Inward Life', p. 295, presumes that the letter refers to Fuller's subsequent teaching at the Greene Street School in Providence, but context and content suggest that it instead refers to her teaching in Boston, hence the probable reference to the Boston Athenæum.
11. Elizabeth Palmer Peabody, 'Exhibition of Allston's Paintings in Boston in 1839', in *Last Evening with Allston and Other Papers* (Boston: D. Lothrop, 1886), pp. 30–61 (pp. 46–47): 'I used to go and sit before it day after day, and it unlocked streams of thought and feeling which, as unuttered presentiment, had burdened me before. I felt in it the power of genius to unfold the soul's treasures to itself.' Fuller mentions first seeing the painting, when she was sixteen, in the review she wrote for the June 1940 issue of *The Dial* in which she offered her 'Record of Impressions Produced by the Exhibition of Mr. Allston's Pictures in the Summer of 1839', being the exhibition mounted that year in Harding's Gallery in School Street (see p. 74). The painting now hangs in Boston's Museum of Fine Arts. See also Diana Strazdes, 'Washington Allston's Beatrice', *Journal of the Museum of Fine Arts, Boston*, 6 (1994), 63–75, esp. 73, where Strazdes mentions Fuller and Peabody.
12. Verduin, 'Inward Life', p. 294.
13. Ibid., p. 295, citing a letter of Fuller to Ralph Waldo Emerson, 11 April 1837, *Letters of Margaret Fuller*, I (1983), 269: 'Dr Channing meant to go [to the party] but was too weary when the hour came. I spent the early part of the eveg [sic] in reading bits of Dante with him and talking about the material sublime till half past nine, when I went with Mrs C. and graceful Mary.'
14. See Anna Hazard (Barker) Ward, transcript of diary, Lenox, 1 January 1845–Boston, 28

September 1852, Houghton Library, Samuel Gray Ward and Anna Hazard Barker Ward Papers, bMS Am 1465 (1340); several entries for March 1849 mention reading Dante, including that for 13 March: 'I enjoy highly my canto of Dante every morning with Sam', while entries for 1845 and 1846 attest to her study of German and French. Verduin, 'Inward Life', pp. 305–06 cites the 1849 entries but mistakenly places them in January.

15. Margaret Fuller, 'Italy', in *Margaret Fuller, Critic: Writings from the New-York Tribune, 1844–1846*, ed. by Judith Mattson Bean and Joel Myerson (New York: Columbia University Press, 2000), pp. 262–66 (pp. 262–63).

16. Sheila Hodges, *Lorenzo Da Ponte: The Life and Times of Mozart's Librettist* (Madison, WI: University of Wisconsin Press, 2002), p. 197.

17. See letters of d'Alessandro to Everett dated 14 March, 26 June, and 28 June 1837 for examples of their book exchanges: Boston, Massachusetts Historical Society, Edward Everett Papers, Ms. N-1201, Series I, Correspondence, June 1835–May 1838, box 8, microfilm reel 6. For biographical information on d'Alessandro, see S. Eugene Scalia, 'Figures of the Risorgimento in America: Ignazio Batolo, Alias Pietro Bachi and Pietro D'Alessandro', *Italica*, 42.4 (1965), 311–57 (p. 336 refers to his private teaching).

18. Antonio Gallenga, *Episodes of my Second Life, by Antonio Gallenga (L. Mariotti)*, 2 vols (London, Chapman and Hall, 1884), I, 135.

19. Boston, Massachusetts Historical Society, Edward Everett Papers, Ms. N-1201, Anne Gorham Everett diaries. In the entry for 17 March 1834, Anne writes: 'Papa sent over to Boston today for an Italian grammar for me. He is going to teach me Italian. I think I shall like very much to study it.' In her entry for 16 September 1836, she refers to her father conversing in Italian with a Greek visitor, an ability later demonstrated when the family sojourned in Italy. Edward Everett commissioned the publication of a memoir with excerpts from Anne's diaries and letters following her premature death in 1843 at age 20, possibly a consequence of a malarial fever she had contracted two years before; see *Memoir of Anne Gorham Everett, with Extracts from her Correspondence and Journal*, ed. by Philippa C. Bush (Boston, MA: Privately published, 1857), esp. pp. 314–15. The *Memoir* (p. 39) mistakenly states the year of the grammar purchase as 1835.

20. Anne Gorham Everett diary entry for 7 November 1836: 'There has been a new book lately written by Mrs Farrar, called the young lady's Book [sic], which is full of useful advice to a young lady, and we have been reading it. I like it very much, though we have not read a great deal in it.' See Eliza Ware Farrar, *The Young Lady's Friend, by a Lady* (Boston: American Stationers' Co., 1836), pp. 4–5, and especially 259–60: 'Much good might be done to girls who have left school, if they could form classes and get highly cultivated persons to read the English, French, and Italian classics with them, pointing out the peculiar merits of each author, and lecturing upon them as they went along.' In a footnote, Farrar remarks: 'This has been done by a gifted individual in Boston to large classes of ladies, and has been attended by the best results' — almost certainly a reference to Fuller.

21. Edward Everett Papers, Correspondence, L. Mariotti to E. Everett, 7 February 1837.

22. See Anne Gorham Everett diary entry for 17 April 1837 and Gallenga, p. 138.

23. Edward Everett Papers, Correspondence, L. Mariotti to E. Everett, 7 June 1837.

24. Gallenga, pp. 135–36.

25. Renzo Dionigi, *An Italian Exile in Brahmin Boston, 1836–1839: Antonio Gallenga* (Varese, Italy: Insubria University Press, 2006), p. 59. Gallenga mentions 'Miss Dwight' frequently in his memoir. It is possible that she was the same 'Miss Dwight' who operated the school the Everett sisters attended in 1835–36; see *Memoir of Anne Gorham Everett*, p. 32. Dwight would be remembered later for her letters detailing life at the Brook Farm community.

26. Gallenga, p. 139.

27. 6 November 1838, quoted with commentary in *Memoir of Anne Gorham Everett*, p. 60.

28. See entries for 12 September 1839 ('I learnt my lesson in Italian'); 24 September 1839 ('I did a good deal of work [i.e., sewing], and read and learnt my lesson in Dante'); and 15 October 1839 ('I sewed a good deal in the course of the morning, read to myself, and learnt a lesson in Dante').

29. In her entry for 26 April 1839, Anne recorded: 'I went today with Papa and Mamma to see a collection of pictures, by a distinguished artist, Mr. Allston. They were very handsome. There

was one of Jeremiah, dictating his prophecy of the destruction of Jerusalem to Baruch the scribe, which was very fine; and another, of the witch of Endor calling up Samuel, which was also very striking.' She mentions returning to see the exhibition again on 30 April and 9 May without further comment. See note 11 above for citations to the reviews by Fuller and Peabody.
30. Letter to Philippa Call, 20 June 1839, quoted in *Memoir of Anne Gorham Everett*, p. 62.
31. Fuller, 'Italy', p. 263.
32. Elizabeth Payson Prentiss, Letter to George E. Shipman, 22 December 1841, in *The Life and Letters of Elizabeth Payson Prentiss*, ed. by George Lewis Prentiss (New York: Randolph, 1882), p. 573.
33. Lydia Huntley Sigourney, *Letters to Young Ladies*, 3rd edn (New York: Harper and Brothers, 1837), pp. 174–75.
34. Boston, Massachusetts Historical Society, Charles Sedgwick Papers, Ms. N-853, box 4, folder 25, Katharine Sedgwick letter to Charles Sedgwick, New York, 15 January 1832.
35. Boston, Massachusetts Historical Society, Catharine Maria Sedgwick Papers, Ms. N-852.1, Correspondence, 1798–1837, box 1, folder 21, Catharine Maria Sedgwick letter to Katherine Sedgwick, [n.p., n.d.], August 1834.
36. See Charles Sedgwick Papers, vol. VI, Katharine Sedgwick's diary, 1835–36 (in which she also references her German teacher, Madame Gérard, a native of Poland, in her entry for 9 July 1836) and vols VII–X, Katharine Sedgwick's travel diaries, May 1839–June 1840.
37. Kate mentions learning Italian 'charades' [i.e. riddles] from Mariotti [i.e. Gallenga] in her diary entry for 31 May 1839.
38. Charles Sedgwick Papers, vol. I, Katharine Sedgwick Minot's album, 1828, pages unnumbered; compare Anna Brownwell Jameson, *The Loves of the Poets*, 2 vols (London: H. Colburn, 1829), I, 114.
39. Charles Sedgwick Papers, vol. III, Katharine Minot Sedgwick's notebook, n.d., with letters from 1836. A heading for *Inferno* 15 with nothing following suggests that the project broke off unexpectedly.
40. Cited from the commentary to *Inferno* I. 2 by Giuseppe Campi (Turin: UTET, 1888–93), as found in the Dartmouth Dante Project, <https://www.dante.dartmouth.edu> [accessed 10 October 2020], my translation. Other commentators refer to the Bianchi and Neri parties in relation to the allegory of the leopard in *Inferno* 1.32.
41. *Giornale del centenario di Dante Allighieri celebrato in Firenze nei giorni 14, 15 e 16 Maggio 1865* (Florence: Cellini, 1864–65), p. 73.
42. In fact, Kate managed to copy the first four letters and only part of the fifth into her notebook. These and the rest of their correspondence which extended, along with Albinola's stay in Stockbridge, into March 1837, and possibly later; see Charles Sedgwick Papers, box 18, General Correspondence 1828–1850.
43. That Sedgwick had engaged Maroncelli to tutor Kate may be substantiated by Charles Sedgwick Papers, box 4, folder 1, Letter of Catharine Maria Sedgwick to Henry Dwight (Hal) Sedgwick, New York, 21 January 1834: 'I suppose you know that Kate + I take lessons of Maroncelli.'
44. Angeline H. Lograsso, *Piero Maroncelli*, Quaderni del Risorgimento, 11–12 (Rome: Edizioni dell'Ateneo, 1958), p. 189. See also Angeline H. Lograsso, 'Poe's Piero Maroncelli', *Publications of the Modern Language Association*, 58.3 (1943), 780–89 (p. 785).
45. Lograsso, *Piero Maroncelli*, p. 202.
46. Silvio Pellico, *My Prisons, Memoirs of Silvio Pellico of Saluzzo*, trans. by Piero Maroncelli, ed. by Andrews Norton (Cambridge, MA: C. Folsom, 1836). For additional background on the publication of this volume, see Angeline H. Lograsso, 'Due Lettere Inedite di Silvio Pellico (Con una lettera inedita di Andrews Norton)', *Italica* 20.3 (1943), 135–40. The original Italian edition was published in Turin in 1832 under the title *Le mie prigioni*. An earlier English translation by Thomas Roscoe was published in New York in 1833.
47. Charles Sedgwick Papers, box 18, General Correspondence 1828–1850.
48. Charles Sedgwick Papers, vol. VI, Katherine Sedgwick's diary, 1835–1836.
49. Angeline H. Lograsso, 'Piero Maroncelli: Poet and Patriot-musician and Exile' (unpublished doctoral dissertation, Radcliffe College, 1927).

50. The commentaries on *Inferno* and *Purgatorio* by Carbonari founder Gabriele Rossetti, published in 1826–27 after he settled in London as an exile, include speculative glosses that are similar to those found in the commentary transcribed by Kate Sedgwick from her studies with Maroncelli. In particular, Rossetti discusses the 'Ueltro/Lutero' anagram mentioned above; see: Gabriele Rossetti, *Commento analitico al 'Purgatorio' di Dante Alighieri*, ed. by Pompeo Giannantonio, Biblioteca dell' 'Archivum romanicum', 87 (Florence: Olschki, 1967), p. 353.

CHAPTER 20

'Why Do You Rend Me?' Dante and the Pain of James Russell Lowell

Kathleen Verduin

> Among them is one figure before which every scholar, every man who has been touched by the tragedy of life, lingers with reverential pity. The haggard cheeks, the lips clamped together in unfaltering resolve, the scars of lifelong battle, and the brow whose sharp outline seems the monument of final victory, — this, at least, is a face that needs no name beneath it. (Lowell, 'Dante' (1876))

And the shaggy visage of James Russell Lowell was once as recognizable as Dante's, if only by inclusion in framed portraits of the Fireside Poets formerly ubiquitous in American schoolrooms and now a staple of the junk shop. Like Oliver Wendell Holmes, John Greenleaf Whittier, and even Longfellow — 'a group united', Christoph Irmscher reminds us, 'by the scholarly disdain they have experienced' — Lowell upon his death fell victim to cultural rustication, his reputation withering in inverse proportion to that of Walt Whitman and his identity as a Harvard professor devolving into liability.[1] 'One forgot his poems', Van Wyck Brooks could write confidently in the 1930s, and the New Critical deprecation of Lowell's verse as 'thin and mechanical' resurfaces in a more recent censure of his long poem *The Vision of Sir Launfal*: 'its excruciating metric is overshadowed only by the incoherence of its structure and its intrusive moralisms'.[2]

Yet the outpouring of memoirs that followed Lowell's passing in 1891, conventional to his era as such tributes were, call into question his negligibility for American literary history, particularly when one encounters the reminiscences of young men with whom he read Dante. 'One of my most cherished experiences', Robert Todd Lincoln reported. 'When I now take up my Dante, Mr. Lowell seems to be with me'.[3] 'My pleasantest memory of Harvard College', wrote Frederick M. Holland, and for Barrett Wendell the Dante classes 'opened to some of us a new world'.[4] All of Lowell's students bore witness to his erudition, but more immediately they acknowledged Dante's integration into their teacher's humanity: the handwritten glosses in the Fraticelli edition from which he read comprised a testament to years of contemplation. 'We young men, eager and willing, but crude, if not callow, must have bored him', William Roscoe Thayer reflected, 'but whatever pleasure Mr. Lowell got was rather the echo of earlier pleasure, and the glow kindled his memory rather than swept his imagination, as when Dante was new to him'.[5]

Appointed to the Harvard faculty in 1855 and teaching the *Commedia* until 1877, when he began his diplomatic career in Spain and England, and then again from 1885 to 1886, Lowell published relatively little on the Italian poet: aside from two poems, 'Paolo to Francesca' and 'On a Portrait of Dante by Giotto', there was only his learned contribution to *Appleton's New American Cyclopaedia* in 1859 and a long critique for the *North American Review* in 1872, subsumed eventually into a single essay, titled simply 'Dante', that he incorporated into the volume *Among My Books* in 1876. Nevertheless, Lowell's engagement with Dante emerges as a compelling record of literary reception, especially against the poignant vicissitudes of his personal life. Despite his popular image as a humorist, creator of the likes of Hosea Biglow and Birdofredum Sawin, Lowell was no stranger to the darker recesses of human experience; he turned to Dante first at the loss of his young wife, then in the face of suicidal impulse, but finally as a mighty example of high character and self-control, holding tight against pain and resisting the dubious consolations of melancholia. This authentically private appropriation empowered Lowell's idiosyncratic mode of instruction — but also, and with more far-reaching effect, informed his vision of the uses of modern literature in the changing academy of his time.

M. L. M. L. M. L.

Matriculating as a Harvard student in 1834, Lowell studied under the institution's Italian instructor Pietro Bachi; in a letter of 1836 he reports a copy of Dante 'in Bob's room'.[6] Over his adult life he scattered his correspondence with references to the *Commedia* — some playfully flippant, as in his complaint (22 December 1839) that 'the belowzeroish sufferings of your unfortunate friends' outdid the ninth round of Dante's Hell. 'I read your advertisement in the *Nation*', Lowell joked with his publisher James T. Fields in 1868, 'and discovered with some surprise what a remarkable person I was. It is lucky for Dante and them fellers that they got their chance so early' (*Letters*, II, 13). Dante's influence hit home, however, when the young Lowell became enamored of Maria White: with rising attention to the *Vita Nuova* at mid-century Dante's beloved was easily superimposed on contemporary constructions of feminine ideality, and to their friends, Nathaniel Hawthorne's son Julian observed, James and Maria seemed 'a modernized Petrarch and Laura, or even Dante and Beatrice'.[7] Educated at an Ursuline convent, Maria was 'beautiful — so pure and spiritlike', Lowell rhapsodized in May of 1840, and by winter was exulting, 'Maria *fills* my ideal [. . . .] And I mean to live as one beloved by such a woman should live. She is in every way noble' (*Letters*, I, 59, I, 61).

The two married in 1844, but Lowell continued to envision his wife as inviolate, even within the bonds of conjugal intimacy. 'Though Maria bears such a blessed burthen close under her dear heart there', he wrote on the occasion of her first pregnancy, 'yet I love to call her (as she is) a virgin still. [. . .] I thank God that

I never go to our bed with less reverence, or less joy than to our bridal bed and I believe it will be so to the end of my days'.[8] Maria gave birth to four children, but three of them — Blanche, Rose, and Walter — died in early childhood, Walter in Rome during the Lowells' sojourn there in 1852; and Maria herself soon manifested signs of advancing tuberculosis. 'I cannot bear to write it but she is very dangerously ill', her husband admitted on 6 October 1853, 'it is only within the last week that I have realized the danger' (*Letters*, I, 203–04). On October 27 Maria died; Lowell's surviving daughter Mabel saw him hunched over a tree and sobbing.[9] A month after Maria succumbed he avowed bravely, 'But oh it is a million times better to have had her and lost her, than to have had and kept any other woman I ever saw' (25 November 1853); yet from January of 1854 until November of the same year the initials 'M. L.' are scratched obsessively on the pages of his private diary. In mid-October, days before the 'Black Anniversary' of her death, Lowell entreated, 'Sancta Maria, ora pro me'.[10]

Most of Lowell's notations about his departed wife are in Italian; a screen of privacy, perhaps, but Lowell's loss of his *gentilissima donna* could hardly fail to recall the grieving lover of the *Vita Nuova*. In January of 1854 Lowell recorded a dream in which Maria appeared with their dead son on her knee: 'E disse, guardi che bel bambino e come è cresciuto!' Similar dreams visited him throughout the year. On 12 March Lowell invoked Francesca da Rimini: 'Ahi, nessun maggior dolore che ricordarsi dei tempi felice nell' miseria' (*Inf.* 5. 121–23). The heartfelt inscription confirms the era's imperviousness to Francesca's guilt, the general apprehension of her fate as merely tragic. But clearly Maria's transformation from flesh to spirit invited her conflation with Dante's saint. Many years later, in a fireside conversation with Wendell, Lowell would muse that it was

> the dead, unbodied Beatrice that lives forever in the lines of Dante. We can watch among our friends the growth of their own Beatrices that such as have had the happiness to know them make amid the agonies of bereavement, each for himself.[11]

The Velleities of Suicide

Scholars of our own time have approached Lowell's spiritualization of his wife with suspicion: Maria was a poet herself, complains one, but 'blocked by her domestic duties from activity in the public world'.[12] In 1855 Lowell commissioned fifty copies of a private edition of Maria's poems; when the volume was reissued in 1907 the poet Amy Lowell, his near relative, lighted on 'An Opium Fantasy' and cried, 'That is *poetry*! It is better than her husband ever wrote [...]'.[13] The record indicates, however, that Maria embraced her prescribed role with serenity, guiding Lowell to alliance with the abolitionist cause. And it was in her office as moral exemplar that he most missed her. 'It *is* lonely and bad is it not', he confessed a few months after Maria's death: 'But I have learned to pray and I try to keep my soul pure and sweet, and sometimes I feel as if something were near me, but oftener not. And then I lie awake for hours, thinking of my razors and my throat, and that I am a fool and a coward not to end it all at once' (8 February 1854).

Incited here by his immediate deprivation, suicidal fantasy was not new to Lowell. In 1840 he had ruminated on Goethe's classic novel on the theme: 'Goethe wrote his "Sorrows of Young Werther" and I will mine. Alas! the young soul is full of sorrows at that time [...] it only sees written over the gate of life, "Per me si va in eterno dolore"' (*Inf.* 3. 2; *Letters*, I, 60). In his classic meditation *The Savage God*, Al Alvarez pronounces that Romantic dreams of self-obliteration added 'a dimension of drama and doom, a fine black orchid to the already tropical jungle of the period's emotional life', and to some extent suicidal ideation for the young Lowell functioned similarly, a self-dramatizing affectation validated by its origin in literature.[14] In 1866 he read with interest *The Life and Letters of James Gates Percival*, the account of an aspiring American poet troubled by a chronic impulse to self-harm.

Lowell's friend and fellow Dante scholar Charles Eliot Norton responded to Percival's story with sympathy: 'His nerves were all on the outside, and our climate is very cruel to such a nature [. . .]'.[15] In his own reaction, however, Lowell indulged his characteristic blend of analytical and wry:

> What first disgusted me with him was the pretended attempt at suicide. [...] It gives a flavor of insincerity to all the rest that follows. I suppose scarce a young man of sensibility ever grew his shell who didn't, during the process, meditate suicide a great many times. I remember in '39 putting a cocked pistol to my forehead — and being afraid to pull the trigger, of which I was heartily ashamed, and am still whenever I think of it. Had I been in earnest, of course, you would never have had the incomparable advantage of my friendship. (*Letters*, I, 375)

Yet suicidal depression, like a 'clot of black blood' (*Letters*, II, 289), continued to plague Lowell, even in his later years. To Norton, whose unfailing rationality rendered him more than once a father confessor to the dejected, Lowell was most open, admitting in 1886 (23 November),

> I hate to remember how many times in my life I have been haunted by the velleities of suicide — so many times that the humorous lobe of my brain has amended the proverb 'Threatened men live long' by 'men who threaten themselves live longest.' But this is my reason for never buying a revolver. Once in Madrid, once in London and once here, had I owned one, I should not be writing to you now.

And in 1888 (30 March) Lowell again confided to Norton, 'There was one day last week when if I had had strychnine in my pocket I could have walked off quietly and seemed to die of an honest apoplexy'.

In the presence of such disclosures, Lowell's references to *Inferno* 13 take on a suggestive coloration. The 'gigantic olive trees' with their 'wildest contortions' that he saw in Italy in the aftermath of Maria's death put him naturally in mind of Dante's poem:

> It was some such wood that gave Dante the hint of his human forest in the seventh circle, and I should have dreaded to break a twig, lest I should hear that voice complaining, 'Perchè mi scerpi? Non hai tu spirto di pietate alcuno?' (ll. 35–36).[16]

Given the grief still rending Lowell, the words must have reverberated with the anguish he sensed in Keats's last letter, 'which is so deeply tragic that the sentences we take almost seem to break away from the rest with a cry of anguish, like the branches in Dante's lamentable wood'.[17] The image hovered: in 1861, even the Virginia creeper 'that I planted against the old horse-chestnut stump trickles down in blood as if its support were on Dante's living wood' (*Letters*, 1, 315).

When he came to review Percival's book, however, Lowell denounced its author, and in words that imply an inkling of the narcissism that modern exegesis now attributes to Dante's sinners. Conceding the probable frustration of a creative artist 'in a country not ripe for literary production', Lowell nonetheless finds Percival's self-pity illegitimate. 'But Percival seems to have satisfied himself with a syllogism something like this: Men of genius are neglected; the more neglect, the more genius; I am altogether neglected, — *ergo*, made up of the priceless material'. By contrast, Lowell demands, 'Dante, Shakespeare, Cervantes, Calderon, Molière, Goethe, — in what conceivable sense is it true of them that they wanted' — that is, lacked — 'the manly qualities that made them equal to the demands of the world in which they lived?'[18] Restored to biographical context, the lines may plausibly be read as a willed repudiation of whatever depressive tendencies afflicted Lowell; but they serve as well to instal the *maestri* of literary history as docents in the conduct of life.

The Results of Assiduous Study

The position of Professor of the French and Spanish Languages at Harvard had been endowed by the Boston merchant Abiel Smith in 1815; Edward Everett Hale, who published a life of Lowell in 1899, praised Smith as 'the first person in the English-speaking world to recognize the value of the systematic study of the modern languages in any university in England or America'.[19] The chair was first occupied by George Ticknor, who taught courses on Dante *ad libitum* until his resignation in 1835, after which Longfellow made the *Commedia* a regular feature of the curriculum: along with 'the late Mr. Smith', as Lowell's humorous couplet had it, these were 'the men but for whom, as I guess, sir, | Modern languages ne'er could have had a professor'.[20] 'Longfellow's place has been offered to him,' Norton rejoiced, 'and I think there is no doubt that he will accept it'.[21]

The great twentieth-century *littérateur* René Wellek identified Lowell as 'the first American critic who was also an academic scholar', and although its obligations frequently irked him, Lowell's accession to professional status accelerated his literary studies and positioned him at the centre of enthusiasm for Dante then radiating from Harvard.[22] 'What an extraordinary threefold nature was that of Dante's', he exclaimed to Norton in 1857. 'The more you study him the more sides you find, and yet the ray from him is always white light' (*Letters*, 1, 276). In addition to offering a regular round of courses, he participated in the 'Dante Club' that gathered from 1865 to 1867 to vet Longfellow's translation, then attended the Saturday meetings on Norton's version of the *Vita Nuova*, and upon Longfellow's death assumed the presidency of the fledgling Dante Society. The *Appleton Cyclopaedia* essay of 1859, reprinted in the *Annual Report of the Dante Society* in 1886, consists of an extensive historical biography, a detailed account of the reception of the *Commedia* up to Lowell's own time, and an introductory survey of Dante's other writings.[23] The 1872 contribution to the *North American Review*, at that time co-edited by Lowell and Norton, was occasioned by the appearance the previous year of Maria Francesca Rossetti's *A Shadow of Dante*.[24] 'Tell Charles the article on Dante was written in all the distraction of getting away, with the thermometer at 95 degrees, and keeping abreast of the printers, so that I could not arrange and revise it properly', Lowell apologized, but acknowledged later that it 'contained the results, at least, of assiduous study' (*Letters*, II, 84, II, 138; see also II, 80).

Rossetti's monograph was a representative product, Nick Havely points out, of Dante's dissemination to a broader readership in the latter decades of the nineteenth century, and her intention was expressly pedagogical: 'How many young people could we name,' she questions in her introduction, 'as having read Dante as part of their education? [...] The few pore over such works, but what of the many?'[25] 'As to the Rossetti', Lowell told Norton in 1879 (18 October), 'I use it every day I hear my class in Dante. It is just what I wished for'. For the ultimate iteration of his research in 1876, he expanded the biographical material from the Appleton piece and incorporated additional details, such as the question of Dante's birth date, the significance of his astrological sign, and the range of his post-exilic wanderings; he made a few verbal emendations, substituting for example the more accurate 'bit' for 'bridle', replacing 'folly' with 'unwisdom', and adding the phrase 'the right of private judgment with the condition of accountability' — a probable sign of conversations with Norton, who would later preface his prose translation of the *Commedia* with the identical words.[26]

Over the evolution of his three-stage disquisition Lowell displays only minimal interest in medieval theology, barely addresses the poem's allegory, attempts no analysis of its characters, and quotes very little from Dante's actual text; the benefits of close reading were still to come. What commands attention, however, is his actively subjective response; and indeed, the essay conspicuously intersects his engagement with the poet in previous decades. This is evident first of all in his insistence on the centrality of Beatrice. In his earlier commentary on Chaucer, Lowell had written of the troubadours,

> Without them we could not understand Dante, in whom their sentiment for woman was idealized by a passionate intellect and a profound nature, till Beatrice became a half-human, half-divine abstraction, a woman still to memory and devotion, a disembodied symbol to the ecstasy of thought.

No Provençal bard, Lowell continues, 'so much as dreamed of that loftier region native to Dante, where the woman is subtilized into *das Ewig-Weibliche*, type of man's finer conscience and nobler aspiration made sensible to him only through her'.[27] Accordingly, Lowell dates Dante's individuation to his youthful encounter with Beatrice: 'In 1274 occurred what we may call his spiritual birth, the awakening in him of the imaginative faculty, and of that profounder and more intense consciousness which springs from the recognition of beauty through the antithesis of sex' (pp. 8–9). The only opinion for which he chides Rossetti is in fact her scepticism regarding Dante's fidelity:

> We think Miss Rossetti a little hasty in allowing that in the years which immediately followed Beatrice's death Dante gave himself up 'more or less to sensual gratification and earthly aim.' The earthly aim we in a certain sense admit; the sensual gratification we reject as utterly inconsistent, not only with Dante's principles, but with his character and indefatigable industry. (p. 62)

Nor will Lowell countenance the theory that Beatrice was a merely allegorical fabrication. 'But surely we must be content to believe that she who speaks of "the fair limbs wherein I was enclosed which scattered are in earth" [*Purg.* 31. 50] was once a creature of flesh and blood [...]'. At the same time, however,

> She early began to undergo that change into something rich and strange in the sea of his mind which so completely supernaturalized her at last. [...] As his love had never been of the senses (which is bestial), so his sorrow was all the more ready to be irradiated with celestial light, and to assume her to be the transmitter of it who had first awakened in him the nobler impulses of his nature [...].

'Take *her* out of the poem,' Lowell remonstrates, 'and the heart of it goes with her; take out her ideal, and it is emptied of soul' (pp. 67–68, 78).

The Benign Ministry of Sorrow

Here we sense Lowell's investment, his unwillingness to relinquish a parallel between Dante's love story and his own. At a deeper substratum, however, Lowell remains most transfixed by the poem's author, like Beatrice once a mortal being but transubstantiated now into a deathless consciousness laid open for examination. Dante himself, of course, had invited such scrutiny: indeed, Lowell points out, Dante was 'the first great poet who ever made a poem wholly out of himself' (p. 119). Lowell was alert to Dante's poetic dexterity: 'He drags back by its tangled locks the unwilling head of some petty traitor of an Italian provincial town, lets the fire glare on the sullen face for a moment, and it sears itself into the memory forever' (p. 120). But what engrosses him is consistently subtextual: the *Commedia* materializes as a monstrance for its author's human pain. The appeal to pathos is already discoverable in the 1859 essay, where Lowell declares that 'the poem comes nearer to us than this. It is the real history of a brother man, of a tempted, purified, and at last triumphant human soul; it teaches the benign ministry of sorrow, and [...] of the cross manfully borne'.[28] Additions from 1872 reveal a drive to enter Dante's mind amid the woes of exile and isolation, but also to asseverate their absolute necessity for his attainment of wisdom:

> To him, longing with an intensity which only the word *Dantesque* will express to realize an ideal upon earth, and continually baffled and misunderstood, the far greater part of mature life must have been labor and sorrow. We can see how essential all that sad experience was to him, can understand why all the

> fairy stories hide the luck in the ugly black casket, but to him, then and there, how seemed it?
>
> *Come sa di sale* [*Par.* 17. 57]! Who never wet his bread with tears, says Goethe, knows ye not, ye heavenly powers! Our nineteenth century made an idol of the noble lord who broke his heart in verse every six months, but the fourteenth was lucky enough to produce and not make an idol of that rarest earthly phenomenon, a man of genius who could hold heartbreak at bay for twenty years and would not let himself die until he had done his task. (pp. 19–20)

It is Dante's incontrovertible pain that exposes Byron's posturing and in fact claims the poem as Christian. For Christianity, Lowell points out, 'finds enemies in those worldly good fortunes where Pagan and even Hebrew literature saw the highest blessing, and invincible allies in sorrow, poverty, humbleness of station, where the former world recognized only implacable foes'; the *Commedia*, it follows, 'is truly a cathedral, over whose high altar hangs the emblem of suffering, of the divine made human to teach the beauty of adversity, the eternal presence of the spiritual, not overhanging and threatening, but informing and sustaining the material' (pp. 99, 101). To live is to suffer, Lowell tacitly insists — a conviction that his father's stroke, his mother's psychosis, the demise of a beloved wife and three cherished offspring, and then the agony of the Civil War and the sacrifice of three young nephews had immured in his bones; his second wife Frances Dunlap would precede him in death in 1885. But suffering is the redemptive essence of Christianity, epitomized in the immolation of the Saviour.

> In the company of the epic poets there was a place left for whoever should embody the Christian idea of a triumphant life, outwardly all defeat, inwardly victorious, who should make us partakers of that cup of sorrow in which all are communicants with Christ. (p. 124)

'Thou also hast had thy crown of thorns', Sir Launfal tells a mendicant leper.[29] Despite its reverence for the Crucifixion, however, Lowell's treatise on Dante should not be taken as a covert confession of faith; he espoused no form of orthodoxy, and notwithstanding an evident nostalgia for the bracing sternness of Puritanism acknowledged, 'I don't think a view of the universe from the stocks of any creed is a very satisfactory one' (*Letters*, II, 167). Nowhere in Lowell's presentation is Dante indebted to the grace of God. Instead, he remains the 'indomitably self-reliant man' (p. 17) that Lowell would have him: a *figura* of consummate self-mastery and an admonishing sentry against despond.

The Modern Languages

Lowell is properly situated among a secularized New England intelligentsia for whom literature was perceptibly modulating into a substitute for religion. In 1887, moreover, he was elected president of the newly established Modern Language Association of America, and the outlines of his engagement with Dante stand in sharper relief against the concurrent incorporation of modern literature into the university curriculum. Lowell was aware that Abiel Smith had bestowed his gift 'rather with an eye to commerce than to culture', but under Ticknor the position had moved from pragmatic considerations to philological inspection of language as the storied scat of bygone peoples, conceived as the only justification for the study of post-classical texts at all.³⁰ Lowell himself, of course, was multilingual; even his affectionate reproduction of the idiom of rural Massachusetts in *The Biglow Papers* and elsewhere betrays attention to the spores and rhizomes of an organic English vernacular. Yet already in his essay on Chaucer he chafes against overzealous attention to language as such.

> No matter how complete its vocabulary may be, how thorough an outfit of inflections and case-endings it may have, it is a mere dead body without a soul until some man of genius sets its arrested pulses once more athrob, and shows what wealth of sweetness, scorn, persuasion, and passion lay there awaiting its liberator.³¹

The historic transition from philology in fact coincides exactly with Lowell's academic career; Charles William Eliot, the Harvard president under whom he served, approvingly registered Lowell's conviction 'that language should always be taught primarily as the vehicle of beautiful literature, where most language teachers were using it as a means of teaching grammar and philology'.³² In his presidential address to the Modern Language Association in 1889, therefore, Lowell takes on the reigning practice of philological analysis and effectively signs the order of execution:

> If I did not rejoice in the wonderful advance made in the comparative philology of the modern languages, I should not have the face to be standing here. But neither should I if I shrank from saying what I believed to be the truth, whether here or elsewhere. I think that the purely linguistic side in the teaching of them seems in the way to get more than its fitting share. I insist only that in our college courses this should be a separate study, and that, good as it is in itself, it should, in the scheme of general instruction, be restrained to its own function as the guide to something better. And that something better is Literature, for there language first attains to a full consciousness of its powers and to the delighted exercise of them.³³

In the estimation of Gerald Graff, Lowell was a pivotal figure not only in the advance of literary studies but in resultant shifts in pedagogical practice: 'Teachers who deviated from the usual textbook approach to literature tended toward the other extreme of impressionism' — a word, Graff observes, that 'seems fairly to characterize the popular courses on Dante' given by Longfellow and Lowell.³⁴ Doffing the *Tarnhelm* of professorial distance, Lowell impressed his classes, Horace Scudder perceived, as

> an older friend who knew in a large way the author they were studying, and drew upon his own knowledge and familiarity with the text for comment and suggestion. [...] Toward the close of the hour, question and answer, or free discussion yielded to the stream of personal reminiscence or abundant reflection upon which Lowell would by this time be launched. [...] And the listeners? They went away, a few carelessly amused at the loose scholastic exercise and complacent over the evasion of work, but some stirred, quickened in their thought, and full of admiration for this brilliant interpreter of life as seen through the verse of Dante.³⁵

For those students who were among his last, Lowell's casually unmethodical manner took on most of its aura when he relocated his discussions of Dante from University Hall to the intimacy of his home, Elmwood, and could appear before a self-selected group of postulants in slippers and a nimbus of tobacco smoke. 'He never, from the beginning', Wendell remembered, 'bothered us with a particle of linguistic irrelevance'. Instead,

> Here before us was a great poem — a lasting impression of what human life had meant to a human being, dead and gone these five centuries. Let us try, as best we might, to see what life had meant to this man; let us see what relation his experience, great and small, bore to ours. [...] Let us read, as sympathetically as we could make ourselves read, the words of one who was as much a man as we; only vastly greater in his knowledge of wisdom and beauty.[36]

Firelight

In what now seems a collective *Vatermord*, the wave of American literary scholars immediately following Lowell hastened to unfrock him. Lowell's forte was really the after-dinner speech, said W. C. Brownell, and even the Dante essay, though the best of his efforts, fell short by a damning absence of critical principles; Joseph J. Reilly dismissed the Dante piece as 'rapt devotion' and proposed similarly that 'so far as criticism approaches a science [...] Lowell is not a critic'.[37] For V. L. Parrington, Lowell was 'a bookish amateur'; Norman Foerster, laboriously dissecting him in 1928, concluded rather sadly that Lowell remained 'a man of shreds'.[38] These attempts to retire Lowell imply a resolute subordination of the humanities to the presumptive rigour of scientific method, a transparently defensive manoeuvre as the study of American literature aspired towards professional status. But Lowell had in fact thought seriously about how to approach literature, as confirmed by the uncollected lecture that Norton quoted before the Dante Society in 1892. 'If I may be allowed a personal illustration', Lowell had written, 'it was my own profound admiration for the "Divina Commedia" of Dante that lured me into what little learning I possess'. He had then set himself, he continues, a list of questions:

> What are his points of likeness or unlikeness with the authors of classical antiquity? In how far is either of these an advantage or defect? What and how much modern literature had preceded him? How much was he indebted to it? How far had the Italian language been subdued and suppled to the uses of poetry or prose before his time? How much did he color the style or thought of the authors who followed him? Is it a fault or a merit that he is so thoroughly impregnated with the opinions, passions, and even prejudices not only of his age but his country?[39]

Such an agendum, straightforward and unpretentious, appears arguably more serviceable than the dated reproaches of the early twentieth century, and one intuits why, to those students who came to love him, Lowell was most often visualized in a transfiguring chiaroscuro of hearth and lamplight. 'The turning of the leaves and crackling of the fire are the only things that break its stillness', was Henry James's memory of Lowell's library; and Wendell's painterly tableau of youths gathered before 'a flickering wood-fire whose ashes were crumbling down into a great bed' enshrines Lowell finally as a magus, a shaman, initiating his followers into the mysteries of existence.[40] Inscribing his seemingly artless discourse with immemorial themes of love, death, and pain, Lowell succeeded in passing down the *Commedia* to a new generation of readers, perhaps achieving something of what he himself had revered in Dante: 'that compressed force of life-long passion which could make a private experience cosmopolitan in its reach and everlasting in its significance'.[41]

Notes to Chapter 20

1. Christoph Irmscher, 'The Fire This Time: Longfellow, Lowell, Holmes, Whittier', in *The Cambridge Companion to American Poets*, ed. by Mark Richardson, Cambridge Companions to Literature (Cambridge: Cambridge University Press, 2015), pp. 47–60 (p. 48); on Lowell and Whitman, see William A. Pannapacker, *Revised Lives: Walt Whitman and Nineteenth-Century Authorship* (New York: Routledge, 2004).
2. Van Wyck Brooks, *The Flowering of New England*, new edn (New York: Dutton, 1937), p. 319; Cleanth Brooks and Robert Penn Warren, *Understanding Poetry*, 3rd edn (New York: Holt, Rinehart, and Winston, 1960), p. 241; Shira Wolosky, 'Poetry and Public Discourse 1820–1900', in *Nineteenth-Century Poetry 1800–1910*, ed. by Barbara Packer, vol. IV of *The Cambridge History of American Literature*, ed. by Sacvan Bercovitch (Cambridge: Cambridge University Press, 2004), pp. 147–480 (p. 290).
3. Quoted in Edward Everett Hale, *James Russell Lowell and his Friends* (Boston: Houghton Mifflin, 1899), p. 126.
4. Frederick M. Holland, 'Reading Dante with Mr. Lowell', *New England Magazine*, January 1896, pp. 575–76 (p. 575); Barrett Wendell, 'Mr. Lowell as a Teacher', in *Stelligeri and Other Essays Concerning America* (New York: Scribner's, 1893), pp. 203–17 (p. 207).
5. William Roscoe Thayer, 'James Russell Lowell as a Teacher', *Scribner's Magazine*, October 1920, pp. 473–80 (p. 476).
6. *The Letters of James Russell Lowell*, 2 vols, ed. by Charles Eliot Norton (New York: Harper and Brothers, 1894), I, 11. Quotations from Lowell's correspondence are either from this edition, cited hereafter as *Letters*, or from letters in the James Russell Lowell Papers 1835–1919 at the Houghton Library of Harvard University, b MS Am 765, and cited by date. For a calendar of Lowell's references to Dante, see J. Chesley Mathews, 'James Russell Lowell's Interest in Dante', *Italica*, 36.2 (1959), 77–100. On Bachi, see the essay by Christopher Y. Dupont, Chapter 19 in this volume.
7. *The Memoirs of Julian Hawthorne*, ed. by Edith Garrigues Hawthorne (New York: Macmillan, 1938), p. 136.
8. Quoted ibid., p. 137.
9. Nina Sankovitch, *The Lowells of Massachusetts: An American Family* (New York: St. Martin's, 2017), p. 199.
10. 'Diary 1854 Private and Purely Personal', James Russell Lowell Papers, Houghton b MS Am 1234.2; quotations in the paragraph below are from this document as well.
11. Wendell, pp. 213–14.
12. Angus Fletcher, 'James Russell Lowell', in *The Encyclopedia of American Poetry: The Nineteenth Century*, ed. by Eric L. Haralson (New York: Routledge, 1998), pp. 271–77 (p. 273).
13. Quoted in Cheryl Walker, 'Maria White Lowell', in *The Encyclopedia of American Poetry*, ed. by Haralson, pp. 278–80 (p. 279).
14. A. Alvarez, *The Savage God: A Study of Suicide* (1971; reprinted New York: Norton, 1990), p. 156.
15. *Letters of Charles Eliot Norton*, 2 vols, ed. by Sara Norton and M. A. DeWolfe Howe (Boston: Houghton Mifflin, 1913), I, 293.
16. 'Leaves from My Journal in Italy and Elsewhere' (1854), in *The Complete Writings of James Russell*

Lowell, Elmwood edition, 16 vols, ed. by Charles Eliot Norton (Boston: Houghton Mifflin, 1904), I, 119–221 (p. 166). Unless otherwise indicated, all quotations from Lowell's published works are from this edition and cited hereafter as *Writings*.

17. 'Keats' (1854), *Writings*, V, 315–47 (p. 336).
18. 'Life and Letters of James Gates Percival' (1867), *Writings*, II, 103–27 (pp. 103, 112, 121–22).
19. Hale, p. 126.
20. 'At the Commencement Dinner' (1866), *Writings*, XIII, 266–69 (p. 269).
21. *Letters of Charles Eliot Norton*, I, 119.
22. Renée Wellek, *A History of Modern Criticism 1750–1950*, IV: *The Later Nineteenth Century* (New Haven: Yale University Press, 1965), p. 201.
23. 'Dante', in *New American Cyclopaedia: A Popular Dictionary of General Knowledge*, ed. by George Ripley and Charles A. Dana, 16 vols (New York: Appleton, 1859), VI, 247–58, reprinted in *Annual Report of the Dante Society*, 5 (1886), 15–38.
24. Review of Maria Francesca Rossetti, *A Shadow of Dante*, *North American Review*, July 1872, pp. 139–209.
25. Nick Havely, *Dante's British Public: Readers and Texts from the Fourteenth Century to the Present* (Oxford: Oxford University Press, 2014), pp. 264–67; Maria Francesca Rossetti, *A Shadow of Dante: Being an Essay toward Studying Himself, His World, and His Pilgrimage* (London: Rivington, 1871), p. 2. On the popular dissemination of Dante, see the essay by Carol Chiodo, Chapter 21 in this volume.
26. 'Dante' (1876), in *Among My Books*, Second Series (Boston: Houghton Mifflin, 1881), pp. 1–124 (p. 102), page numbers cited hereafter in text (I quote from this volume because the *Complete Writings* reproduces only the 1872 version); Charles Eliot Norton, 'Introduction', in *The Divine Comedy of Dante Alighieri*, I: *Hell*, trans. by Norton, rev. edn (Boston: Houghton Mifflin, 1902), p. xvi.
27. 'Chaucer' (1870), *Writings*, II, 181–269 (pp. 197–98).
28. *New American Cyclopaedia*, VI, 256.
29. *The Vision of Sir Launfal* (1848), *Writings*, IX, 301–24 (p. 312).
30. 'The Study of Modern Languages' (1889), *Writings*, VII, 305–36 (p. 306). On Ticknor's philological approach, see my '"Living Voices": Letters, Language, and the Dante Studies of George Ticknor', *Massachusetts Historical Review*, 20 (2018), 33–73.
31. 'Chaucer', *Writings*, II, 181–269 (p. 226).
32. Charles William Eliot, 'James Russell Lowell as a Professor', *Harvard Graduates Magazine*, June 1919, pp. 492–97 (p. 495).
33. 'The Study of Modern Languages', *Writings*, VII, 305–36 (pp. 335–36).
34. Gerald Graff, *Professing Literature: An Institutional History* (Chicago: University of Chicago Press, 1987), p. 40.
35. Horace E. Scudder, *James Russell Lowell: A Biography*, 2 vols (Boston: Houghton Mifflin, 1901), I, 393–94.
36. Wendell, pp. 206–07.
37. W. C. Brownell, 'Lowell', *American Prose Masters* (New York: Scribner's, 1909), pp. 271–72, 306–07; Joseph J. Reilly, *James Russell Lowell as a Critic* (New York: Putnam's, 1915), pp. 129, 214.
38. Vernon Louis Parrington, *Main Currents in American Thought: An Interpretation of American Literature from the Beginnings to 1920*, II: *The Romantic Revolution in America* (1927; reprinted New York: Harcourt, Brace, 1930), p. 461; Norman Foerster, *American Criticism: Studies in Literary Theory from Poe to the Present* (Boston: Houghton Mifflin, 1928), p. 150.
39. 'Annual Report', *Annual Report of the Dante Society*, 11 (1892), 10–11.
40. Henry James, *Essays in London and Elsewhere* (New York: Harper and Brothers, 1893), p. 74; Wendell, p. 211.
41. 'Shakespeare Once More' (1868), *Writings*, III, 215–320 (p. 242).

CHAPTER 21

Dante for Mothers

Carol Chiodo

American public interest in Dante and his *Comedy* comes alive in an advertisement in a Sears Roebuck and Company mail order catalogue from 1893. For forty-five cents, a reader in Wichita, Kansas could purchase the poetry of Dante along with the work of distinguished American poets such as John Greenleaf Whittier and Edgar Allan Poe. These were books destined to burnish backcountry bookshelves: printed in duodecimo format on toned paper with gilded pages, clothbound, and stamped in black and gold. This mail-order Dante marked just one of the ways that the *Comedy* circulated as a bound bauble, both novelty and commodity, in the midwestern United States at the close of the nineteenth century. Sears customers were not the only readers to value Dante's poem. Lest we imagine that the poem merely decorated the parlours of aspiring book-collectors, other editions imagined American mothers and their children to be the ideal recipients of the poem's message. The year before Dante appeared in the mail order catalogue, a kindergarten educator from Chicago, Elizabeth Harrison, published his poetry in *The Vision of Dante: A Story for Little Children and a Talk for Their Mothers*. This slim volume was printed by the same printer of the Sears Roebuck catalogue, R. R. Donnelley & Sons, on behalf of the Chicago Kindergarten College.[1] A bauble of a different sort, Harrison's *Story* was artfully made, with woodcut illustrations by English artist Walter Crane and a softcover of creamy handmade paper featuring embossed ornamental type. The preface announced the book's aims, calling the *Comedy* a 'world poem' whose truths make 'the great poem of Dante one of the masterpieces of the world of art'. Then, the author adds, 'May not it. . . be given to little children in a simple way?'

While today's readers of the *Comedy* may quickly recognize the *Comedy*'s explicit didactic aims, less apparent is how the poem might find itself pedagogically reconfigured for late nineteenth-century college-educated kindergarten instructors in the midwestern United States. How did Dante's *Divine Comedy* shed its stern habit of Thomistic scholasticism to re-clothe itself with the playful trousers of kindergarten pedagogy? Dante — for mothers and their children? Really?

Along this seemingly unlikely path to early childhood education, a wide range of textual transformations emerge. With a growing number of translations, the poem provided a point of departure for all sorts of acculturations, adaptations, and transformations in the United States, 'from the most benign to the most venal'.[2] From Boston to San Francisco, Dante's *Divine Comedy*, particularly the *Inferno*, was avidly read, rewritten, adapted and repackaged in the late nineteenth century. It found its way into songs, ditties, plays, sketches, pantomimes, and lantern slide lectures. Its imagery inspired bronzes, paintings, medallions, tapestries, jewellery, bookends, wax museums, pageants and tableaux vivants. Experts and amateurs alike contributed the countless essays, articles, poems and tributes[3] which appeared in periodicals ranging from the *Southern Literary Messenger*, the *Bostonian Atlantic Monthly*, the *Century*, the *Critic*, and the *Dial*, to the *Journal of Speculative Philosophy*, a publication to which we will return. The Chautauquan, a monthly news magazine devoted to the adult education movement then sweeping the nation, featured Dante's work extensively;[4] so too the popular *Ladies Home Journal*. This publication urged its readers to ignore

> the picket fence of intellectual superiority [...] erected by scholars around certain books [...] Any bright woman of keen sympathies can read Longfellow's version of Dante's Divine Comedy [...] The beauty and the passion [...] will burn in her mind with such a pure flame that it will make the tawdry sentiment of inferior writers appear like the sputtering flame of a tallow candle.[5]

Scholars have noted how the transatlantic crossing of people and goods shaped nineteenth-century literature in ways that are insufficiently explained by the study of separate national literary traditions. Lurking behind assumptions linking people, place and culture is the Romantic idea of an organic relationship between a population, its geographic and political boundaries, and the organization of meaningful forms into something known as culture.[6] The enduring legacy of this idea has prompted a critical reinvestigation of a number of dominant national-historical scholarly narratives, including those associated with the field-coverage model of departmental organization in North American higher education[7] or the cultural capital of literature within society.[8] In this latter category, both Nancy Glazener and John Guillory have explored the idea of super-canon or a transnational canon.[9] For Guillory, the easy appropriation of Dante's *Comedy* into English for an American public acts as a powerful institutional buttress of an imaginary cultural continuity while suppressing the specificity of the poem's production and consumption. While we may view the *Comedy* as part of a deracinated transnational canon, to use Guillory's terms, its reproduction and transmission, particularly in educational contexts during the nineteenth century, inhabit unique historical and regional conditions. Harrison's pedagogical primer presents an unusual case study for exploring them.

The nineteenth century saw over 400 editions and reprints of editions of the *Comedy*. If we include translations, the number quickly exceeds the total editions of all of the previous centuries combined.[10] Many of these relied heavily on the early print tradition of the *Comedy*, particularly the 1595 Crusca edition.[11] Yet, textual variants propagated like daisies as more and more manuscript witnesses of the *Comedy* were tallied and examined. Nineteenth-century American readers experienced Dante predominantly through English-language translations. Henry

Francis Cary's blank verse translation, entitled *The Vision of Dante*, would provide Harrison with the first part of the title for her later volume. The translation was first published in England in 1814.[12] In spite of a number of competing translations in both England and the United States, it remained the dominant translation until Henry Wadsworth Longfellow's translation was published in 1867.

As the number of material ways American readers could experience Dante grew, so too did Dante's communities of readers[13] and Elizabeth Harrison counted herself among them. Born in Kentucky, educated in St Louis, Boston and Chicago, she was a pioneer in creating new professional standards and promoting early childhood education. She studied in Chicago with Alice Putnam, whose ideas on education drew from the educational theories of Friedrich Froebel, the German creator of the kindergarten. She would go on to study with Susan Blow, a pioneer in American idealist philosophy, participating in one of her advanced teacher training courses held in St Louis. Harrison's interest in Dante was far from cursory. Her copy of the Longfellow translation, today held at the National Louis University, is littered with notes that include references to Susan Blow's commentaries and Thomas Davidson's adaptation of a Dante handbook published by the Swiss Protestant pastor Johann Scartazzini.[14] Harrison's subsequent publications on early childhood education make frequent mention of Dante and the ideas associated with a philosophical movement then gaining steam in St Louis. There, Harrison experienced first-hand the development of Blow's unique synthesis of pedagogy and philosophy, in which her study of Dante played a central role.

A major figure in what became known as the St Louis philosophical movement, Susan Blow joined educators, regional and national policy-makers and other public intellectuals in their interest in German idealism and their attempts to 'make Hegel talk English'.[15] In 1860, the group founded the first American philosophy periodical, the *Journal of Speculative Philosophy*. In it, Blow and other intellectuals such as Anna Brackett, Bronson Alcott, Henry Brockmeyer, Thomas Davidson, Charles Sanders Peirce, and its editor William Torrey Harris, explored the Kantian aftermath in German philosophy. The group was explicit in both their attempt to transplant Hegel in the United States and to apply and adapt his philosophy to the real and practical demands of society, politics and ethics. The group held fast to their commitment to *Bildung*, supporting free public education and lifelong learning. Many held public office. William Torrey Harris, for example, first served as Superintendent of the public schools in St Louis and would later go on to serve as U.S. Commissioner for Education, while Henry Brockmeyer would become lieutenant governor of Missouri.

Hegel never wrote a systematic theory of education, but the St Louis Hegelians, as they were also known, posited collective life as both the product and the basis for individual action and development. Blow, with her interest in early educational theory, found the work of idealist philosopher Friedrich Froebel[16] in alignment with this interpretation of idealism. When she returned to St Louis from an extended stay in Germany, her advocacy for early childhood education took a practical turn when she founded Des Peres School in 1873. She taught children in the morning, trained fellow teachers in the afternoon, and leveraged her contact with the superintendent of schools and her editor at the journal, William Torrey Harris, at every opportunity. By 1883, every St Louis public school boasted a kindergarten. In April 1884, Blow published the first of a series of reflections on Dante's *Comedy*. She took a Hegelian theme developed in Froebel's educational theory which resonated among the St Louis idealists, self-activity,[17] and applied it to Dante's *Inferno*. She writes,

> If we try to think the creative principle of the world, we come at once face to face with the idea of self-activity. By self-activity is meant an activity that acts upon itself: as a creative principle logically antedates all creation, it must be self-active, for the obvious reason that there is nothing but itself for it to act upon. Its acuity, therefore, begins from and comes back to itself. It is a circular process, and therefore necessarily an eternal process.

And, to underscore her point, Blow quotes Longfellow's verses from Canto 33 of the Paradiso: O Light Eterne, sole in thyself that dwellest, | Sole knowest thyself, and, known unto thyself | And knowing, lovest and smilest on thyself!'[18] Dante's journey, as a pilgrim gaining knowledge through his journey, and as a poet retrospectively retelling it with the assimilation of that knowledge, stands as an emblem for Blow, and for Harrison, of a Hegelian 'Selbsttätigkeit'.

From these formative experiences with Susan Blow and the St Louis Hegelians, Harrison began to develop her own definition of early education, one which aimed to draw out the child physically, mentally and morally through this creative principle. She looked to literature and myth, and to the importance of the imagination. This was a daring move at a time when educational reforms, bolstered by recent scientific and analytic trends, were roiling both higher and lower educational systems in the United States and elsewhere. One such theory, from British scientist Herbert Spencer, drew a connection between post-Darwinian theories of recapitulation and the pedagogical directive that education repeats human evolutionary history. Applying this theory to elementary education, Spencer declared that:

> if there be an order in which the human race has mastered its various kinds of knowledge, there will arise in every child an aptitude to acquire these kinds of knowledge in the same order [...] and hence the fundamental reason why education should be a repetition of civilization in little.[19]

For educators embracing such a theory, the aesthetic, the poetic and the artistic were quickly trampled by the inexorable march of the scientific, the technological and the industrial. Elizabeth Harrison found this view incongruous with her own experience. She viewed this inclination to map individual development onto an evolutionary schema as a reduction of educational theory, foreshadowing a misguided turn to vocationalism.[20] She would go on to rebuke these theories in a number of pamphlets she published on the relationship of great literature to kindergarten.[21] For her, the connection between the study of the great poets of the world, on the one hand, and the nursery and the kindergarten on the other, was essential to developing children's symbolic thought. In her accompanying 'Talk for Mothers,' Harrison, cites Froebel, 'easily a symbol teach | what thy reason cannot reach'. She calls the poem a 'pictured form of truth' which provides a poetic form of expression for the human soul.

For Harrison, mothers played a crucial role in mediating between children's play and symbolic thought. While the Chicago Kindergarten College aimed to prepare early childhood educators, its courses and certifications were also offered to mothers. These courses aimed at 'teachers, mothers and nurses' provided 'special, needed training to all women who have the care of children'. Prerequisites for coursework included a high-school education or its equivalent, and first-year students were required to complete the foundational course taught by Harrison. The course drew entirely upon Froebel's method, but the focus on literature reflected the idealist philosophical movement from which it sprang:

> The highest value of the great literature in the world is the portrayal of man in some form of conflict with the institutional world and the reconciliation of that conflict by the bringing of man into harmony with those laws that are greater than his individual will.[22]

The line from the St Louis Hegelians to Froebel is swiftly drawn: 'this is also what Froebel means by "the unity of the laws of the world and of man."' For Harrison and her colleagues, the aim of kindergarten is to educate children so that they 'may realize the relationships of life and the duties arising from them'.[23] They view this as 'the supreme object of literature' and, through Froebel, they bring this to children by means of play. The study of Dante — in company with Shakespeare, Homer, and others — is a crucial part of the kindergartner instructor's training, as it helps 'keep alive in the heart this most important part of her work'.[24] And it was women's work, by both mothers and teachers, united in a maternal embrace of belle-lettrism that justified the women's active, critical engagement with world poetry.

Harrison begins her 'story for little children' much in the same way all stories for little children might begin, with a 'once upon a time'. After speaking about the importance of the poem, its age, and its influence, Harrison, in the first person, attempts to 'tell it to-day as a short story'. The parallels with the popular fairy tales of the Grimm brothers are pronounced, as these were familiar to young readers:[25] the dark forest, the three beasts, an ominous crevasse, a steady guide and the pilgrim's hope of seeing Beatrice make up the core of the expurgated narrative of the *Inferno*. Harrison then centres her narrative on Purgatory, where redemptive opportunities abound. Susan Blow had viewed that canticle as an extended lesson, where individual spiritual energies grow:

> the more thought communicates itself, the more truly it possesses itself […] only through membership and the communion which membership implies does man make actual his ideal nature; only in so far as he becomes universal is he in any true sense individual.[26]

As to *Paradiso*, 'of this I cannot tell you', Harrison exclaims, 'no words of mine could make you see that glorious vision as Dante then beheld it'. She concludes her story admonishing her young listeners, 'your own little hearts must be freed from all wrong thoughts, from all evil motives, from all selfish desires, must be filled with a love of others, and with generous willingness for others', so that they too may come upon a similar vision as Dante.

Harrison's epilogue, an address to children's mothers, also gets to the point quickly: 'the last two centuries', she writes, 'have been largely scientific and analytic. The effort has been to get away from the pictorial and symbolic, to get at the *exact facts*' (her emphasis). This is an oblique rebuke of the post-Darwinian pedagogy of rational utilitarianism espoused by Herbert Spencer and his acolytes. Harrison counters this with an alternative view for education, an extended reflection on the importance of the imagination in instructional endeavours and how play provides insight into higher things. She references the pedagogical power of the parable and other 'pictured forms of truth'. For Harrison, the study of Dante underscores the value of poetry as a form of expression for human experience. She reflects on the multiple layers of interpretative meaning that are found in Dante's verses, and how politics, art and ethics intersect. She also reminds her mothers that the truth of the poem does not lie in its facts, but in its affect.

Some commentators have explained the poem to be the political disappointment of Dante, pouring itself out in bitter though brilliant imagery. The leopard is Florence, the lion is France, the she-wolf is the Papal power of Rome. But Florence and France and Rome have passed out of their supremacy in the minds of men, and the Divine Comedy still keeps its hold upon the affections of mankind. Some other meaning must lie in the poem [...] else we would not be studying it to-day.[27] The poem's longevity is 'the picture which every great poet holds up — man's soul in a state of estrangement and the struggle to get back to the peace of God'.[28]

One year after publishing this volume, Harrison would bring a number of 'kindergartners', as the teachers were known, to exhibit their work in Children's Building at the World's Columbian Exposition in Chicago. With nearly 27 million visitors coming to the fair, they had ample opportunities to demonstrate their methods of imaginative play and story-telling, and the power of 'self-activity' as a means for educating the nascent freedom of the individual for the good of the community. The following year, her story of Dante would go into a second printing. In those same years, following a national trend, the Chicago Board of Education voted to incorporate ten privately sponsored kindergartens which had been operating in the public schools. Yet for a number of historians of early education, Chicago would only emerge as the centre of professionalization of the field when John Dewey began his progressive kindergarten experiment at the University of Chicago.

As Belinda Jack has noted, the history of the woman reader is the history of a neglected minority; a history of readers who have left very few traces and marks of their existence, who are downplayed as secondary and subordinate.[29] It is a history of denied access to education. It is also a history of staged female readership or unexamined modes of reading. Reading Harrison, reading Dante, as a 'story for little children and a talk for their mothers', we see how she infused the poem with pedagogical philosophy in order to ask questions that were meaningful to her and her readers. How might early education move towards reconciling the freedom of the individual and the good of the community? What is women's role in society if tasked with delivering such an education? Dante's trajectory among such readers invites us to reread his Comedy and revise our understanding of its reception in light of the social organization of readership and the possibilities such an organization engenders. The scholarly emancipation of this woman reader of the *Comedy* and those who came before her sheds new light not only on reading Dante in North America, but on the important role played by Dante's poem in shaping an American education.[30]

Notes to Chapter 21

1. In the second half of the nineteenth century, R. R. Donnelley & Sons were one of the largest book, directory, and periodical printers in the West. The volume I refer to here is the 1892 edition, housed at Beinecke Rare Book and Manuscript Library, BEIN J18 C8512 +892Hr. My thanks to the staff there for their kind and attentive assistance.
2. Bella Brodzki, *Can These Bones Live? Translation, Survival and Cultural Memory* (Stanford: Stanford University Press, 2007), p. 2. For an outline of the importance of historical context and the ways in which texts travel across borders and are received in new cultural contexts, see Itamar Even-Zohar, 'The Position of Translated Literature within the Literary Polysystem', in *Literature and Translation: New Perspectives in Literary Studies*, ed. by James S. Holmes, J. Lambert and R. van den Brooeck (Leuven: Acco, 1978), pp. 117–27. Susan Bassnett has explored how an institutional emphasis on the national basis for literary production shunts translations to the wrong side of the tracks, viewing them as 'immigrants, not quite worthy of the status accorded to texts produced within a given literary tradition'. In her essay, 'From Cultural Turn to Translational Turn: A Transnational Journey', Bassnett views the growth of world literature as an opportunity for a reappraisal of the cultural significance of translation and it is in this spirit that I offer this research. See *Literature, Geography, Translation*, ed. by Cecilia Alvstad and others (Newcastle upon Tyne: Cambridge Scholars Publishing, 2011), pp. 67–80, republished in *World Literature in Theory*, ed. by David Damrosch (New York: Wiley, 2014), pp. 234–42.
3. Angelina LaPiana, drawing on T. W. Koch's bibliography, lists around fifty Dantean poems published between 1881 and 1905 in *Dante's American Pilgrimage* (New Haven, Yale University Press, 1948), pp. 150–51. This of course predates the readers outlined by Christian Dupont elsewhere in this volume in his essay, 'How the Young Women Take to It!' drawing upon Kathleen Verduin's 1996 article on Margaret Fuller's engagement with Dante. Any examination of Dante's reception in North America during this later period, beyond Verduin's essay on Lowell and Dupont's work in this volume, must also take into account the African American readers outlined by Dennis Looney in *Freedom Readers*, and particularly his research on the Dantean poetry of Cordelia Ray.
4. For an overview of the Chautauqua movement and the liberal tradition it embodied, see Andrew C. Rieser, *The Chautauqua Moment: Protestants, Progressives, and the Culture of Modern Liberalism* (New York: Columbia University Press, 2003).
5. Droch's 'Literary Talks II: Some Old Favorites', *Ladies Home Journal*, 14.2 (1897), p. 15.
6. See Benedict Anderson, *Imagined Communities* (London: Verso, 1983).
7. See for example, Gerald Graff's introduction 'The Humanist Myth' in the anniversary edition of *Professing Literature: An Institutional History* (Chicago: University of Chicago Press, 1987), pp. 1–15. The fall 2020 decision by the English Department at Cornell University to change its name to Literatures in English might be seen as a recent salvo in exploding this myth.
8. As John Guillory has argued, 'there can be no general theory of canon formation that would predict or account for the canonization of any particular work, without specifying first the unique historical conditions of that work's production and reception', in *Cultural Capital: The Problem of Literary Canon Formation* (Chicago: University of Chicago Press, 1995), p. 85.
9. Glazener offers an examination of the foundational components of literature and literary studies in North America, from modern literature's earliest emergence as an infrastructure, subject to market forces, public engagement, and institutionalization. See *Literature in the Making: A History*

of U.S. Literary Culture in the Long Nineteenth Century (New York: Oxford University Press, 2015). Guillory details the process of deracination from the actual cultural circumstances of a textual artifact's production and consumption.

10. See Giuliano Mambelli, *Gli annali delle edizioni dantesche* (Bologna: Zanichelli, 1931). Also, Aldo Vallone, *La critica dantesca nell'Ottocento* (Florence: Olschki, 1958); Colomb de Batines, *Bibliografia dantesca, ossia Catalogo delle edizioni, traduzioni, codici manoscritti e commenti della Divina Commedia e delle opere di Dante, seguito dalla serie dei biografi di lui*, 2 vols (Prato: Tipografia Aldina, 1845–46).

11. *La Divina Commedia di Dante Alighieri ridotta a miglior lezione dagli Accademici della Crusca* (Florence: Domenico Manzani, 1595).

12. His blank verse translation of the *Inferno* initially appeared in 1804 with little success. The 1814 publication of all three canticles, with facing page translation, was financed by Cary himself after publisher James Carpenter refused it on the basis of the poor sales of the *Inferno*. For more on the Carey translation in Great Britain and its use in Romantic art and poetry, see Antonella Braida, *Dante and the Romantics* (Basingstoke: Palgrave Macmillan, 2004).

13. Aida Audeh and Nick Havely have noted the many 'Dantes' during the long nineteenth century, each characterized by a malleability within different economies of meaning. Their overarching concern, however, is firmly rooted in the relation of these to national identity. See their introduction to the volume *Dante in the Long Nineteenth Century: Nationality, Identity and Appropriation* (Oxford: Oxford University Press, 2012), pp. 1–12.

14. Davidson's translation of Scartazzini's manual *A Handbook to Dante* was published in Boston in 1887 by Ginn & Company. Scartazzini had published the manual in Italy for Ulrico Hoepli, but Davidson's translation takes considerable liberties with the text, including a flurry of footnotes that express outright disagreement with the author.

15. See Denton J. Snider, The *St. Louis Movement in Philosophy* (St Louis, MO: Sigma, 1920), p. 279. There are a number of publications on the St Louis movement, including *St. Louis Hegelians*, ed. by Michael DeArmey and James A. Good, 2 vols (Bristol: Thoemmes Continuum, 2001); *The Ohio Hegelians*, ed. by James A. Good, 3 vols (Bristol: Thoemmes Continuum, 2004); and Dorothy G. Rogers, *America's First Women Philosophers: Transplanting Hegel, 1860–1925* (New York: Continuum, 2005).

16. Friedrich Froebel's first work, *The Education of Man*, boasted two translations in the United States, one by Josephine Jarvis featuring an introduction by Elizabeth Palmer Peabody and the other by W. N. Hallman (St Louis: International Education Series, 1892). Froebel's *Pedagogics of the Kindergarten* would also be translated by Jarvis and published by Appleton in 1899.

17. William Torrey Harris, in his translation of Hegel's 'Selbsttätigkeit', used self-activity, that is the power of individuality to do away with the difference between subject and object. See his 'Outlines of Hegel's Phenomenology', *Journal of Speculative Philosophy*, 3.2 (1869), 166–74. For more on self-activity, and the themes associated with this form of American idealism, see Dorothy G. Rogers, *America's First Women Philosophers* (New York: Continuum, 2005).

18. Susan Blow, 'Dante's Inferno', *Journal of Speculative Philosophy*, 18.2 (1884), 121–38.

19. Herbert Spencer, *Education: Intellectual, Moral, and Physical* (New York: Appleton, 1861), p. 76.

20. See for example her address to the Chicago Kindergarten College's incoming class of 1891, *The Kindergarten as an Influence in Modern Civilization* (Chicago: Chicago Kindergarten College, 1893).

21. *The Relationship between the Kindergarten and Great Literature: Dante* (Chicago: Chicago Kindergarten College, 1893); *The Relationship between the Kindergarten and Great Literature: Homer* (Chicago: Chicago Kindergarten College, 1893); *The Relationship between the Kindergarten and Great Literature: Shakespeare* (Chicago: Chicago Kindergarten College, 1893).

22. From the *Chicago Kindergarten College Course Catalog, 1892–1893* (Chicago: Chicago Kindergarten College, 1892), p. 21.

23. Ibid.

24. Ibid., pp. 21–22.

25. Between 1881 and 1900, dozens of editions of the fairy tales were published in English. Of note, *Grimm's Household Tales*, 2 vols, trans. and ed. by Margaret Hunt (London: George Bell and Sons, 1884); *German Popular Stories and Fairy Tales, as Told by Gammer Grethel*, trans. by Edgar Taylor

(London: George Bell and Sons, 1888); *Household Stories from the collection of Grimm Brothers*, trans. by Lucy Crane (Chicago and New York: Rand, McNally, & Company, 1889); *Grimm's Fairy Tales: Volume 1*, ed. by Mara L. Pratt (Boston, New York, and Chicago: Educational Publishing Company, 1892). *Grimm's Fairy Tales: Part 1*, ed. by Sara E. Wiltse (Boston, New York, Chicago, and London: Ginn and Company, 1894); *Classic Stories for the Little Ones: Adapted from the Tales of Andersen, Grimm Brothers, and Others,* Mrs. Lida Brown McMurry (Bloomington, Illinois: Public School Publishing Company, 1894).

26. Susan Blow, 'Inferno', *The Journal of Speculative Philosophy*, 18 (1884), 121–38.
27. Elizabeth Harrison, *The vision of Dante: A Story for Little Children and a Talk to their Mothers* (Chicago: Chicago Kindergarten College, 1892) [unpaginated].
28. Ibid.
29. Belinda Jack, *The Woman Reader* (New Haven, CT: Yale University Press, 2012).
30. I would like to express my gratitude to Joe Stadolnik for his perceptive comments and spirited defence of Dewey.

PART IV

Modern and Contemporary Readings

CHAPTER 22

Hidden Presence: Dante's *Commedia* in Proust's *À la recherche du temps perdu*

Karlheinz Stierle

Dante is the poet of poets. If this holds true for a long tradition of outstanding works of poetry, the presence of Dante's *Commedia* in *À la recherche du temps perdu*, Marcel Proust's saga of time lost and time refound, is of a particular quality both in the originality of its intertextual references and in its affinity to the narrative structure of Dante's work.[1] Yet Dante's part in Proust's literary masterpiece has remained for a large part a *terra incognita* waiting to be explored.[2]

Proust indeed makes Dante a central figure in the perspective of his first-person narrator, who has no name but whom we suggest calling Marcel. Marcel sometimes seems to be identical with the real author Marcel Proust, but often also 'I' (*je*) seems to be purely fictional. At first glance, however, the occurrence of Dante's name in the *Recherche* is not very marked, and does not give an idea of his importance for Proust's work. In total it appears five times. Three times the name simply indicates that referring to Dante is fashionable in the Parisian society of the *belle époque*.

Dante's name appears when Madame de Villeparisis, aunt of the Duchess de Guermantes, reminds her guests at one of her *matinées* that the famous Italian tragic actress Adelaide Ristori 'in her great days' (S. 3, 199; R. 2, 202) had come to her salon, where she recited Dante: 'Ristori came here once — the Duchesse d'Aoste brought her — to recite a canto of Dante's Inferno' (ibid.). This occurrence of Dante's name is only part of the gossip of a society of the happy few. In a conversation with Marcel during wartime in Paris, Baron Charlus remarks, regarding the role of women in the Middle Ages, 'that the "ladies" of knights in the Middle Ages and Dante's Beatrice, were perhaps placed on a throne as elevated as the heroines of M. Becques' (S. 6, 106; R. 3, 798). Once again the reference to Dante has no further significance. Apparently more interesting is the case of Charles Swann, who makes a sarcastic comment about the Wagner enthusiast Madame Verdurin and her circle: 'It really is, he said, the lowest thing on the social ladder, Dante's last circle' (S. 1, 290; R. 1, 289). Swann, pretending to be a connoisseur of Dante, in reality confounds Dante with Balzac, the *Commedia* with Balzac's *Comédie humaine*. It is in fact Balzac who, in the introduction to his novel *La fille aux yeux d'or*, takes the circles of Dante's *Inferno* as a metaphor for the social layers of Paris: 'Nous voici donc amenés au troisième cercle de cet enfer, qui peut-être, un jour, aura son DANTE' [Behold us here, brought to the third circle of this hell, which perhaps perhaps one day will find its Dante].[3]

Marcel's own explicit or hidden references to Dante are of a radically different kind: 'For a long time, I went to bed early' (S. 1, 7; R. 1,3). This simple phrase, opening a work of thousands of pages, is highly emblematic. Who is the first person speaking here? What is that state of remembering which 'I' actually remembers? How is that presence situated in time and in space? Why has Marcel gone to bed early? And what could the presence of Dante be in that context? The first sentence is a piece that has to be replaced in the whole puzzle. In the long series of nights that he remembers, Marcel particularly focuses on the nights passed at Tansonville, when he was invited by Madame de Saint-Loup, the wife of his friend Robert de Saint-Loup:

> I was in my room at Mme de Saint Loup's, in the country; good Lord! It's ten o'clock or even later, they will have finished dinner! I must have overslept in the nap I take every evening when I come back from my walk with Mme de Saint-Loup, before putting on my evening clothes. For many years have passed at Combray, where, however late we returned, it was the sunset's reflections I saw in the panes of my window. It is another sort of life one leads at Tansonville, at Mme de Saint-Loup's, another sort of pleasure I take in going out only at night, [...] (S. 1, 10 f.; R. 1, 6–7)

At the beginning of the last part of the *Recherche* Marcel returns to his visit at Tansonville, which now is situated more precisely. We now see him immediately before the outbreak of war in 1914, when Marcel is forced to give up his social life in Paris and retire to a sanatorium. He must 'break with society, give up travelling and visiting museums in order to enter a sanatorium and undergo treatment' (S. 6, 29, R. 3, 723). During the first years of the war Marcel stays in this sanatorium until it is closed in 1916 and he returns to Paris. In the same year he moves to a second sanatorium, where he stays for several years before his final return to Paris. Thus, when Marcel says 'Longtemps je me suis couché de bonne heure' he is remembering in the second sanatorium his nights of remembering in the first sanatorium. The first cycle of his recollections is restricted to the young Marcel's evenings and nights of insomnia at the house of his grandparents in Combray. All other reminiscences of that time, however, are totally blocked. 'For many years already, everything about Combray that was not the theatre and drama of my bedtime had ceased to exist for me' (S. 1, 47; R. 1, 44). But this obstacle is overcome when, in Paris between his two stays at the sanatoria, one day in winter his mother offers him a madeleine, of the kind he used to eat in Combray at the house of his aunt Léonie. The taste of this pastry all of a sudden opens up, in a 'souvenir involuntaire', a past world that had been inaccessible to him up to that moment (S. 1, 47; R. 1, 45). Marcel's stay at the second sanatorium remains an absolute void, and yet we can presume that during this time he becomes a fascinated reader of Dante. In fact, Marcel's first memories of Combray are free of any reference to Dante. But there is a clear allusion to the

Commedia, when in sanatorium II Marcel remembers his own state of remembering in sanatorium I. Looking back, Marcel remembers the moments of night-time insomnia and the confused fragments of remembering coming to his mind. What Marcel has retained especially is the moment of confusion immediately following the first moment of awakening:

> when I woke in the middle of the night, since I did not know where I was, I did not even understand in the first moment who I was; all I had in its original simplicity, was the sense of existence as it may quiver in the depths of an animal; I was more bereft than a caveman. (S. 1, 9; R. 1, 5)

It seems to me to be of structural importance that the *Recherche* begins with a passage that clearly refers to Dante's *Commedia*. In canto 25 of *Paradiso* Dante, by looking too intensely into the light that emanates from the soul of the apostle St John, loses his sight. When it slowly returns, passing through all the membranes of the eye, Dante finds himself at first, like a man awaking, in a world of confusing immediacy:

> E come a lume acuto si disonna
> per lo spirto visivo che ricorre
> allo splendor che va di gonna in gonna,
> e lo svegliato ciò che vede aborre,
> sì nescia è la sùbita vigilia
> fin che la stimativa non soccorre
> [...] (*Par.* 26. 70–75)[4]

The data of the senses remain void before *vis estimativa* ('la stimativa') can bring them to his judgement, and thus to conceptual clarity. This passage is undoubtedly a first reference to Dante and to his analytical ingenuity. Right from the beginning, then, Dante is present in the *Recherche*.

When in an enlarged circle of remembering Marcel recalls his walks with his parents around Combray, a memory of the little river Vivonne once again recalls Dante. Marcel, the Dante-reader in sanatorium II, recalls his fascination with the nymphaeas (water-lilies) and their movement to and fro in the current:

> This water-lily was the same and it was also like one of those miserable creatures whose singular torment, repeated indefinitely throughout eternity, aroused the curiosity of Dante, who would have asked the tormented creature himself to recount its case and its particularities at greater length had Virgil, striding on ahead, not forced him to hurry after immediately, as my parents did me. (S. 1, 170; R. 1, 169)

What Marcel has in mind is canto 7 of *Inferno*, where the wasteful and the mean are eternally confronted with each other:

> poi si volgea ciascun, quand' era giunto,
> per lo suo mezzo cerchio a l'altra giostra.
> [...] (*Inf.* 7. 34–35)

This reference to Dante gives a mythic aura to a snapshot of memory, but it also vivifies a memory of reading though a personal recollection of childhood. It is not Marcel remembered, but the voice of Marcel remembering.

A new chapter of Marcel's memories begins with his summer vacations in the seaside resort, Balbec. Waiting for his train at the Gare Saint-Lazare young Marcel, who has no experience of travel, is in a state of deep despair, which Marcel the narrator again characterizes in Dantean terms when in a general reflection he evokes the atmosphere of stations: 'as soon as we venture outside the waiting-room, we must abandon all hope of returning to the familiar bedroom which we left only a moment before' (S. 2, 224; R. 1, 645). 'Lasciate ogne speranza, voi ch'entrate' is the last verse of the inscription Dante reads at the entrance into the first circle of hell (*Inf.* 3. 9). When Marcel, together with his grandmother, arrives at the Grand Hotel of Balbec, he takes a look at its reading-room, and on this occasion Dante is present once again:

> behind a glass partition, people sat in a reading-room to describe which, if I had borrowed colours from Dante, I would have had to use first those with which he depicts Paradise, then those with which he depicts Hell. (S. 2, 242; R. 1, 664)

This new reference to Dante corresponds once again to Marcel's perspective of reminiscence, as he seeks to give a deeper significance to this initial moment of encountering a new world.

Alone in his room, Marcel feels miserable in the face of all the unknown objects which surround him. But when his grandmother appears, he suddenly feels as if he is in Paradise. When Dante, in the company of Beatrice, enters the lowest sphere of heaven, which is that of the moon, he still believes himself to be on earth and takes the souls approaching him to be mirrored images. Conversely Marcel, being still on earth, believes in the immediate transparency of communication with his grandmother, as if they were already in heaven: 'my thoughts became hers without alteration, passing from my mind to hers without changing medium or person' (S. 2, 246; R. 1, 668). And 'like [...] a dog snapping at the flittering shadow misled by the appearance of the body, as we are in this world where souls are not directly perceptible, I fell into my grandmother's arms' (S. 2, 246 f.; R. 1, 668). In Dante's Paradise there is an immediacy of loving communication which no longer needs language. However, whereas Dante in Paradise believes himself to be still on earth, Marcel, being on earth, believes for a moment that he is in Paradise. After the death of his grandmother Marcel returns to Balbec for a second time. Encountering for the first time the experience of *souvenir involuntaire*, he suddenly realizes that he will never meet his grandmother again, and yet the desire and vain hope remain that in Paradise, if it existed, he would be with her for eternity, only separated from her by a thin wall, as on their first vacation:

> And I asked nothing more of God, if there is a Paradise, than to be able to give there the three little taps on that partition that my grandmother would recognize anywhere [...] and that he should let me remain with her for all eternity, which would not be too long for the two of us. (S. 4, 165; R. 2, 763)

Extreme modernity and myth confront each other in a dramatic way, when one day during Marcel's second stay at Balbec, in order to see the 'Verdurins' he rides his horse through wild countryside along the sea, while two paintings by the painter Elstir come to his mind, both of them evoking scenes of a Greek mythic prehistory.

More and more the landscape around him and Elstir's evocation of mythical Greece merge together, when suddenly a strong noise frightens his horse and Marcel looks up and sees, and is deeply affected by, one of the new aeroplanes moving in the sky as if gravity no longer existed. 'I was moved as might a Greek have been setting eyes for the first time on a demigod' (S. 4, 423; R. 2, 1029). The pseudo-Greek setting of this scene once again evokes the hidden presence of Dante. When in *Paradiso* 33 Dante recalls the moment of God's presence, he explains that the overwhelming intensity of this moment wiped out any possibility of true recollection. He compares this astonishment with that of the Greek god Neptune when he admired the shadow of the ship Argo, a miraculous achievement of Greek technical skill:

> Un punto solo m'è maggior letargo
> che venticinque secoli a la 'mpresa
> che fé Nettuno ammirar l'ombra d'Argo. (*Par.* 33. 94–96)

The deep emotional identification of Dante with Neptune helps to give an idea of Marcel's amazement at the latest invention of modern technology.

The aeroplane which appears over a quasi-mythic landscape is but a prelude to the military formation of aeroplanes appearing in the sky over Paris in wartime. Marcel, having returned from his first sanatorium, admires the celestial spectacle of the fighting French and German planes: 'Meanwhile the aeroplanes took up their places among the constellations and looking at those "new stars" one might easily have believed oneself to be in another hemisphere' (S. 6, 110; R. 3, 801 f.). Without any doubt Marcel is thinking here of the first canto of *Purgatorio*, where Dante, arriving with Virgil on the shore of Mount Purgatory, observes the four stars which after Adam's expulsion from Earthly Paradise have never again been seen by human eyes.

> I' mi volsi a man destra, e puosi mente
> a l'altro polo, e vidi quattro stelle
> non viste mai fuor ch'a la prima gente. (*Purg.* 1. 22–24)

But the previously unseen stars in the sky of Paris are not the stars of the southern hemisphere; they are the new and fatal stars of modern technology.

At the end of his work Marcel refers once again to the *Commedia*, when Marcel (Proust or Marcel?) gives Time itself the last word. An emblem of time before Proust starts his work is the figure of the old Duc de Guermantes. Marcel has kept in mind the Duc's appearance at the Guermantes *matinée* when, years later, he is confronted with the faces of his old friends cruelly disfigured by time. The Duc, having got up,

> could not move forward without shaking like a leaf, on the scarcely manageable summit of his eighty-three years, as if all men are perched on top of living stilts which never stop growing, sometimes becoming taller than church steeples, until eventually they make walking difficult and dangerous, and down from which, all of a sudden, they fall. (S. 6, 357; R. 3, 1048)

Once again this emblem of time has a corresponding emblem in the *Commedia*. In canto 14 of *Inferno* Virgil tells Dante that in the mountains of Crete, which has become a waste land, 'sta dritto un gran veglio' (*Inf.* 14. 103). This emblematic figure of old age, composed of the ages of mankind, has fallen into ruin and his tears are the origin of all the rivers of hell. For Proust, the Duc de Guermantes is the mythic figure of time itself. Thus the beginning of the *Recherche* as well as its end is marked by a Dante reference; Proust's work is framed by a programmatic Dante-presence.

When, after a stay of several years, Marcel has definitely decided to return to Paris, his train stops in the open country. Looking at the scenery around him, he has a bitter feeling of absolute incapacity as a writer. Next day he acts on an invitation to the Guermantes *matinée*. On arriving in their courtyard, his stumbling over a paving stone releases in his mind, as did his formerly eating the madeleine, a flood of *souvenirs involuntaires*. His mother's madeleine had already given him the idea of 'the immense edifice of memory' (*l'édifice immense du souvenir*) (S. 1, 50; R. 1, 47) without bringing this experience into any relation with his ambitions as a writer in search of his subject. In the Guermantes' library, waiting for the end of the musical performance taking place in the *salon*, Marcel, working through his new experience, all of a sudden discovers his real vocation as a writer who will create an outstanding literary work on the basis of his experience of the liberation of *souvenir* from the constraints of temporality. But this project is to be unrealizable, and Marcel is also wrong in his conviction that Charles Swann would have been the true origin of his new project for a great work that he had been contemplating for so long. In fact, Marcel affirms: 'The raw material [Proust simply says *matière*] of my experience, which was to be the raw material (*matière*) of my book, came to me from Swann' (S. 6, 223; R. 3, 915). And:

> my very presence at this moment in the house of the Prince de Guermantes, where the idea for my work had just suddenly come to me (which meant that I owed Swann not just the material but the decision, too), also came to me from Swann. (S. 6, 224; R. 3, 915)

But as if slightly regretting his exaggerated affirmation, Marcel adds:

> rather a slender stem, perhaps, to support in this way the whole span of my life [...] But this source of the different aspects of our life is frequently a person much inferior to Swann, somebody of complete insignificance. (S. 6, 224; R. 3, 915)

What is the reason for this homage to Swann, the embodiment of mediocrity, as connoisseur of art? Could the name of Swann not be a cover for quite another inspiration, namely that of Dante?[5]

Immediately after his reflections about his future work, in which he thinks he has finally found his vocation, Marcel enters the *salon*, where the musical performance has now ended. This is the moment when Marcel discovers, assembled around him, the faces of his old friends and acquaintances, cruelly deformed by time. Thus, from eternity Marcel falls back into the rudest temporality. This new experience of time will radically change the project of his work. It will contain in itself eternity and temporality at once. This, however, leads back to Dante and his silent presence. Might not Marcel, perhaps without knowing it, during the long period of his second stay in a sanatorium, have learnt from Dante the very essential idea of his own future work, before it entered his consciousness at the Guermantes *matinée*? Not only do we find correspondences with the *Commedia* throughout *Recherche*, but the project of Proust's work as a whole is clearly inspired by the structure of Dante's *Commedia*. Reading Dante in Sanatorium II must have prepared Marcel for the discovery of his own vocation.[6]

In giving the title 'Comedia' to his work (*Inf.* 16. 128 and 21. 2, Dante seems to have placed it in a generic frame. In fact, Dante's *Commedia* is a work that stands alone; it does not fit into any pre-established genre. It is unique in form, but also unique as the art work into which Dante concentrates all his poetic energy after having, through his exile from Florence, lost his reputation, social standing, family and political influence. The *Commedia* is a work of profound solitude, as is the *Recherche*. Proust's extraordinary work resembles Dante's *Commedia* in combining extratemporality and temporality. Like the *Commedia*, the *Recherche* is dominated by the figure of a first-person narrator who is either the author or a fictive person, or both in mutual transparency. This ambiguity underlies the instability of genre common to the two works. But Proust also follows a particular narrative technique that Dante has taken from the *De Consolatione Philosophiae* of Boethius. Here for the first time the path towards the accomplishment of the work and the work itself coincide in a circular movement. The reader has to take on two roles: he follows the path towards the realization of the work, and he perceives it as the work itself. Thus, in the *Commedia* we follow Dante's 'altro viaggio' from the crisis of the 'selva oscura' to the proximity of God himself. But then, falling again from eternity into temporality, Dante consummates his work in such a manner that eternity and temporality converge in a third dimension, that of the highest poetry. Proust, too, narrates the long approach to a vocation which is fulfilled by a work evoking the long path towards the vocation itself. With the word 'Temps', Proust's work is closed before it begins with the word 'Longtemps'. This is Proust's circle of temporality, by which temporality itself is destroyed.

Both the *Commedia* and *Recherche* pass from temporality to eternity, from eternity to temporality, and from time and eternity to poetic work. This raises the question of the work's own temporality or extratemporality. In canto 10 of *Purgatorio*, at the threshold between *antipurgatorio* and *purgatorio*, Dante is confronted with God's own work of art, destined to lead the souls from arrogance to humility. Dante, however, is more fascinated by the art of the divine artist than by its moral intention. God's art of *visibile parlare* (*Purg*. 10. 55) is in fact 'novello a noi perché qui non si trova' (*Purg*. 10. 26). It seems that Dante himself, the real *superbo* in art, considers how to approach divine art in his own poetry. In the following canto, however, the soul of Oderisi d'Agobbio, the then famous illuminator, insists upon the temporality of human art, destined as it is to pass away in the very moment that brought it forth. Fame for human art is 'vana gloria dell' umane posse' (*Purg*. 9. 1), and

> Non è il mondan romore altro ch'un fiato
> di vento, ch'or vien quinci e or vien quindi
> (*Purg*. 11. 100–01)

Dante, however, after a short hesitation, knows that he will stay on the side of the *superbo*, striving for the highest achievement in art worthy of Apollo's laurel. Thus, at the beginning of *Paradiso* he invokes Apollo himself:

> O buono Appollo, a l'ultimo lavoro
> fammi del tuo valor sì fatto vaso,
> come dimandi a dar l'amato alloro.
> (*Par.* 1. 13–15)

The question of the temporality and extratemporality of art is of fundamental importance in the *Recherche* too. Like Oderisi, Marcel, after having met the writer Bergotte, reflects on the temporality of art:

> Such is the new and perishable universe that has just been created. It will last until the next geological catastrophe unleashed by a new painter or writer with an original view of the world. (S. 3, 325 f.; R. 2, 327)

and:

> Perhaps, on the contrary, art was now like science in this respect; each new writer of originality seemed to me to have progressed beyond his predecessors. (S. 3, 326; R. 2, 328)

The heroine of this doctrine is Madame de Cambremer, the incarnation of Parisian art-snobbery. Her ideology of progress in art, and her absolute lack of taste, are portrayed with merciless irony.

Whereas Dante's and Oderisi's conceptions of art are in complete contradiction, Marcel has a long way to go through a world of social and artistic mediocrity, which reflects a sense of his own lack of gifts as a writer. Marcel is in fact a phenomenologist of mediocrity in all its hues. And like Diderot's 'neveu de Rameau', he is also a master of its pantomime. In order to oppose to each other great art and art which is trapped in mediocrity, Marcel inserts a legend about art itself (S. 5, 169–70; R. 3, 186–88). Bergotte is visiting an exhibition of paintings by Vermeer van Delft. A little detail, the 'petit pan de mur' in his painting *Vue sur Delft* opens his eyes to the absolute difference between great and mediocre artistic achievement and, seeing his life-work ruined, he breaks down and dies. When a short time later, at a concert in the house of the Verdurins, Marcel hears the *Septuor* of the deceased composer Vinteuil, he experiences for the first time an 'overwhelming masterwork' (Proust says 'chef-d' œuvre triomphal') (S. 5, 231; R. 3, 252), produced by a 'perpetual innovator' (S. 5, 233, R. 3, 254) whose work is of 'enduring novelty' (S. 5, 233; R. 3, 254). Could it be pure coincidence that this new experience for Marcel corresponds to Dante's impression of 'cosa nova', the 'visibile parlare', 'novello a noi perché qui non si trova' (Purg, 10, 96), that is to say God's own art, which Dante aspires to imitate?

The *Septuor* is Vinteuil's masterwork. But is not Vinteuil too a mediocre artist, such as Elstir the painter and Bergotte the poet? It seems in fact that the real composer of the *Septuor* is the female friend of his daughter, who remains nameless. Out of some confused notes left by Vinteuil she has made a glorious piece of music. Corresponding to the nameless composer is an almost absent Dante, whose traces have to be reconstructed. The *Commedia*, it seems, in the years of the second sanatorium has become a model for Marcel's own writing. When in the Guermantes *matinée* Marcel suddenly discovers his long-sought-for vocation, he returns, perhaps unconsciously, to what he has learnt from Dante, namely the idea of a great and singular work. From this moment on Marcel will live in absolute solitude, dedicated only to his work, as was Dante. Only the *Commedia* could help Marcel to find his own way, and to create a work which is more than a sum of snapshots of memory.

The poetic world of Dante and the poetic world of Proust have their focus in the singularity of a solitary consciousness. However, the opposite is equally true. Consciousness turned upon itself becomes receptive to a legend of times leading back to the origins of sea and land, or to the beginning of humanity.[7] Time, both in Dante and in Proust, is layered time, or a palimpsest of times. Both Dante and Proust seem to follow the poetic programme of Ovid's *Metamorphoses*: *Ad mea perpetuum deducite tempora carmen* [Lead, ye gods, an unbroken thread of song from the very beginnings down to my own times] (1. 4).

'Perpetuum carmen' — would this not be the generic formula both for Dante and for Proust? The *Metamorphoses* are not only a great model for both. Ovid's poem is also the place where, for the first time, the arts in their unity and plurality are represented.[8] Painting, sculpture, music, and poetry are the media of metamorphosis. Both in Dante's and in Proust's work the arts have a place of their own. In the *Commedia* the ascension to the earthly, and then to the celestial, Paradise is also a world of encounter with the arts as media of transition from the material to the ideal world. The threshold between *antipurgatorio* and *purgatorio* is the place of divine art, which gives Dante an idea of what supreme art can achieve. Immediately after this revelation comes the encounter with Oderisi, the modest artist of illumination, and his melancholic ideas about the futility of all human ambition in art. On the shore of the isle of Purgatory Dante meets the soul of his friend, the musician Casella, who with his song enchants Virgil, deeply moved by his encounter with Purgatory, to which he will never have access by himself. In his encounter with the souls of the Italian and Provençal poets Bonagiunta da Lucca, Guinizelli and Arnaut Daniel, Dante explains the principles of his own lyric poetry. But after their encounter with the supposedly Christian epic poet Statius, Dante listens to their conversation in order to learn something about the principles of epic poetry. The fine arts are present in the *Recherche* too, in their twofold appearance as works of mediocrity and those of outstanding achievement, represented by the painter Vermeer van Delft, the nameless friend of Mademoiselle Vinteuil, and in particular by an almost invisible Dante. Elstir, Bergotte and Vinteuil, conversely, remain artists of mediocrity. Only Marcel himself, under the influence of Dantes's *Commedia*, is passing from artistic mediocrity to a work of highest ambition.

At the beginning of canto 25 of *Paradiso* Dante looks forward to the end of his almost finished work:

> Se mai continga che 'l poema sacro
> al quale ha posto mano e cielo e terra,

> sì che m'ha fatto per molti anni macro,
> vinca la crudeltà che fuor mi serra [...] (*Par.* 25. 1–4)

This is, as it were, the most advanced point in time in the *Commedia*. After years of work in the loneliness of his exile, Dante can foresee the end of his work, his *poema sacro*, saved from the contingencies of time. Heaven and earth, time and eternity, come together in the creation of Dante's work. Marcel too, at the end of his work, looks forward to its achievement. It will be a battle against time narrowing down: 'Yes, the idea of Time that I had just formed was telling me that it was time to apply myself to the work. It was high time' (S. 6, 344; R. 3, 31035). However, the beginning is already the end, and the end is the beginning. Contingent time is needed if what is beyond contingency is to be created. Thus Dante meets Marcel, and through Marcel he meets Proust.[9]

Notes to Chapter 22

1. My quotations will follow Marcel Proust, *In Search of Lost Time*, general editor Christopher Prendergast (London: Penguin Classics, 2003), 6 vols: I: *The Way by Swann's*, trans. with an introduction by Lydia Davis; II: *In the Shadow of Young Girls in Flower*, trans. with an introduction and notes by James Grieve; III: *The Guermantes Way*, trans. with an introduction and notes by Marc Trehane; IV: *Sodom and Gomorrah*, trans. with an introduction and notes by John Sturrock; V: *The Prisoner*, trans. with an introduction and notes by Carol Clark (pp. 1–384), *The Fugitive*, trans. with an introduction and notes by Peter Collier (pp. 387–658); VI: *Finding Time Again*, trans. with an introduction and notes by Jan Patterson. References to the French text follow Marcel Proust, *A la recherche du temps perdu*, ed. by Pierre Clarac and André Ferré, 3 vols (Paris: Bibliothèque de la Pléiade, 1954). References to translation are marked by S., references to the original by R.
2. For initial approaches, see Gemma Pappot, 'L'*Inferno* de Proust à la lumière de Dante', *Marcel Proust aujourd'hui*, 1 (2003), 91–118, Anne Teulade, 'Proust et l'èpopée de Dante', in *Proust l'étranger*, ed. by K. Haddad-Wotling and L. Ferré (Amsterdam and New York: Rodopi 2010), pp. 15–36, and my book *Zeit und Werk in Dantes 'Commedia' und Prousts 'A la recherche du temps perdu'* (Munich: Hanser Verlag, 2008).
3. *La fille aux yeux d'or*, in Balzac, *La Comédie humaine*, V, ed. by Pierre Georges Castex (Paris: Bibliothèque de la Pléiade, 1977), p. 1046.
4. The quotations are taken from Dante Alighieri, *Commedia*, ed. by Anna Maria Chiavacci Leonardi, 3 vols (Milan: Mondadori 1997).
5. It is true that Marcel 'colouring' his *souvenirs* with reminiscences of his reading of the *Commedia* seems to follow Swann's manic urge to colour the image of his love Odette with a postcard reproduction of Botticelli's Zipporah (see 'A Love of Swann's', S. 1, pp. 225–28), but Marcel's response to Dante is incomparably more complex.
6. Our argument, that the main lines of the *Recherche* are essentially inspired by Dante, can be illustrated only in a very concentrated form. It will be explained in more detail in another study.
7. See Karlheinz Stierle, 'Land und Meer in Prousts *À la recherche du temps perdu*', in *Marcel Proust: Die Legende der Zeiten im Kunstwerk der Erinnerung*, ed. by Karlheinz Stierle and Patricia Oster (Frankfurt: Insel Verlag, 2007), pp. 25–45.
8. On the relation between Ovid, Dante and Proust, see Karlheinz Stierle, 'La fable du monde et le système des beaux-arts: Ovide, Dante, Proust', *Rassegna europea di letteratura italiana*, 12 (1998), 9–35.
9. For a different approach to Proust's reception of Dante, see Jennifer Rushworth, *Discourses of Mourning in Dante, Petrarch, and Proust* (Oxford: Oxford University Press, 2016). [*Eds*]

CHAPTER 23

Allen Tate's Flight from Racism: Dante and 'The Swimmers'

Dennis Looney

Allen Tate's Interest in Dante

In the early 1950s, Allen Tate, the Southern U.S. poet and critic, composed a sequence of poems in the metrical pattern of Dante's *Divine Comedy*, the *terza rima*. The poems, in English, constitute a kind of poetic autobiography of the author. He never gave a title to the incomplete longer poem of which they were to be a part, but we know that the original longer piece was to contain a sequence of nine shorter poems of around seventy to ninety lines each, which the poet then reduced to a design of six poems.[1] In the end, however, he only managed to finish and publish three: 'The Maimed Man', 'The Swimmers' (both finished in 1952 and published in 1953) and 'The Buried Lake' (finished and published in 1953). A footnote to 'The Swimmers', first published in the winter 1953 issue of *Hudson Review*, refers to it as 'Part III of a poem of some length, now in progress'.[2] These three poems are connected not only by the Dantesque metre they share, but by a series of themes, which point allusively to Dante's poem: water, light, reflections, music, baptism, divinity, blood, mutilation, among other topics. 'The Maimed Man' and 'The Buried Lake', which in the final arrangement are the first and third poems of a loosely configured trilogy, use an entanglement of dreamy reveries to create modernist poetic compositions that are in certain passages very difficult to parse. 'The Swimmers', by contrast, is a more straightforward narrative retelling of the childhood experience of coming upon a lynched body of an African American in the Kentucky backwoods. The eleven-year-old narrator who identifies himself by name as 'Tate, with water on the brain' (18) — his parents had worried incorrectly that he was hydrocephalic — is separated from his playmates when they are out for a day's fun at the local swimming hole in the woods, hence the poem's title. The young Tate witnesses the county sheriff's posse ride in and out of the woods and is able to piece together what has just happened to the victim, whose body the sheriff and one of his henchmen then drag into the main square of the town nearby.

Just who exactly was Allen Tate and what precisely was his connection to Dante? In their critical survey of *African American Writers and Classical Tradition*, William W. Cook and James Tatum label him 'the white racist poet and critic' and they are certainly justified in calling him that.³ Born in 1899, Tate was an outstanding student in the English Department at Vanderbilt University in the early 1920s when John Crowe Ransom held sway over a group of students and young professors devoted to literature, mostly male, who called themselves the Fugitives. They wrote poetry and prose, fiction and non-fiction, and practised a brand of criticism that came to be called New Criticism, famous for its direct focus on the text itself. In their literary work, they took refuge from encroaching industrialization, promoting a return to an idyllic agrarian past. In the 1920s that kind of conservatism meant a nostalgia for the Antebellum South, inequalities and all. From his early writings, which include biographies of the Confederate heroes Stonewall Jackson and Jefferson Davis, it is easy to identify Tate as one of those unreconstructed southerners still apparently unwilling in the 1920s to accept the social and economic changes institutionalized by Reconstruction after the Civil War. The Fugitives morphed into the Southern Agrarians of the 1930s, whose collective publication, a book of controversial essays that came out in 1930, *I'll Take My Stand*, made an appeal to the pre-industrialized, feudal, aristocratic culture of Old Europe. They believed that their romanticized Old South was the link to that past. But as Robert H. Brinkmeyer, Jr., has convincingly argued in *The Fourth Ghost: White Southern Writers and European Fascism, 1930–1950*, the world of courtesy and curtsies that these men imagined had much more in common with New Europe, with Nazi Germany and fascist Italy of the 1930s. The project of Agrarianism was unambiguously racist.⁴

Tate read Dante at Vanderbilt in English courses in the translations of Cary and Longfellow and his professors in a variety of courses promoted the Italian poet.⁵ In the 1920s and 1930s he would, in the spirit of T. S. Eliot, teach himself enough Italian to grapple with Dante's text in the original, and like Eliot read Dante in the Temple Classics edition. Eliot became a friend in letters with Tate in the 1940s and 1950s, corresponding with him regularly to discuss the state of poetry in English in the post-war years. Like many other modernist American poets, Tate received his Dante through the filter of T. S. Eliot, who maintains that 'more can be learned about how to write poetry from Dante than from any English poet'.⁶ And while Eliot is careful to say that one does not need to embrace Christianity to understand Dante's poem, he admits that 'it may be in practice easier for a Catholic to grasp the meaning, in many places'.⁷ Tate consequently became interested in Dante as a Catholic poet with Eliot, Jacques Maritain and Etienne Gilson guiding his reading in these directions, along with his devout wife, Caroline Gordon.⁸ Accordingly, he was as interested in Dante's *Purgatorio* and *Paradiso* as the *Inferno*. In fact, he was more open to Dante the metaphysical poet of the divine than to Dante the poet of the secular world whose writing about hell affected the work of so many interpreters in the post-war period. In February of 1951, Tate delivered two lectures at a Jesuit institution, Boston College, which outline his interpretation of the metaphysical Dante: 'The Angelic Imagination' and 'The Symbolic Imagination'. In these two essays, generally acknowledged to be among his best (of over fifty published essays), he juxtaposes the writing of Edgar Allen Poe and the theory of language embedded in his prose with the theory of language 'reflected', to use Tate's word, in Dante's poetry.⁹ In 'The Symbolic Imagination', the critic offers an interpretation of the final images of Dante's poem in *Paradiso* 33 in the context of previous images of light in *Paradiso* 2, 28, 29, and 30.

In the same year, 1951, he assumed a position at the University of Minnesota (held previously by fellow Fugitive and lifetime friend Robert Penn Warren from 1942–50), where he taught till retiring in 1968. A student's published recollection of Tate's powerful presence in the classroom emphasizes the straightforward New Critical approach of the teacher before a text, who had his students interpret literary texts guided by four simple questions: Where? What? How? Why? Tate taught his class to approach literature following a fourfold method of interpretation that emphasized the literal, logical, dramatic, and spiritual levels of meaning in the text, moving from one to the next in an attempt to arrive at the comprehensive significance of the literary work of art. This fourfold method is none other than a version of the approach to interpretation outlined in the *Letter to Can Grande*, which Tate assumed was written by Dante.¹⁰ The student, Warren Kliewer, explains that the master had them examine a literary text for its literal meaning, then its allegorical significance, its tropological meaning, and its anagogical symbolism. In other words, Tate (whether or not he acknowledged his source in the classroom is unclear) taught his students to read following the dictates of Dante. We could say that Tate turned Dante into a New Critic, and that Tate turned his students into New Critical readers via Dante. For his essays, for his teaching, for his poetry, the Dante Alighieri Society in Florence, Italy, awarded him its Gold Medal in 1962.

In the late 1940s and early 1950s, as he turned fifty, 'nel mezzo del cammin', we might say, Tate was going through a midlife crisis during which he tried subtly and consistently to distance himself from racist positions he had articulated as a younger man.¹¹ His conversion to Roman Catholicism in 1950 was part of this move to redefine himself.¹² In these years he was estranged from his wife Caroline Gordon; they divorced then remarried, then divorced a second time. Charles Scribner's, Tate's publisher, commissioned him to write an autobiography in 1966, but he gave up soon after he started, confessing in a late publication: 'unlike Ernest Hemingway in *A Moveable Feast*, I couldn't bring myself to tell what was wrong with my friends — or even mere acquaintances — without trying to tell what was wrong with myself'.¹³ Lewis Simpson, in *The Fable of the Southern Writer*, suggests that Tate quit the memoir 'in his struggle to come to terms with the fate of the self in the history, or the inner history, of the rise and fall and subsequent historical situation of the last great modern slave society'.¹⁴ Tate turns to Dante to make this point obliquely in an essay of 1972, 'A Lost Traveller's Dream':

> Should one be immodest enough to try to tell all? That would be shameful. Let the authenticity of fact remain shadowy, as Henry James might have said, for however truthful the memorialist may try to be, his anecdotal recollections will be closer to fiction than history.
>
> One's awareness of this dilemma, history or fiction, or the treacherous interplay of both, is one's *selva oscura*. In the Dark Wood modern man may scarcely hope to find Vergil [...]¹⁵

If Tate abandoned that commissioned editorial project, his poetry gave him a different venue through which to approach his complicated past and nowhere is this more visible than in his poem most inspired by Dante, 'The Swimmers'. There is archival evidence to indicate that Tate worked hard to perfect the poem over the course of its initial composition.[16] In addition, he reportedly continued to imagine possible revisions even into his latter years. Poet and professor of creative writing at the University of the South, Wyatt Prunty, who was a student when Tate taught at Sewanee in the latter years of his life, has commented that Tate presented 'The Swimmers' to his classes at Sewanee with striking frequency, as if he still wanted to perfect it.[17]

Before I consider the poem, I would like to sketch out a literary-historical context in which to understand Tate's Dantesque poem more broadly. There is a tradition of turning to Dante on the part of African American artists from the nineteenth century to today for help in negotiating the complexities of race relations, which I explore in my study *Freedom Readers*.[18] Perhaps unexpectedly, Allen Tate's poem on the aftermath of a lynching, inspired by his understanding of Dante's poetics, makes most sense in this thoroughly African American context.

Freedom Readers

Freedom Readers is a literary-historical study of the ways in which Dante — the historical figure and the character in the poem — assumed a position of importance in African American culture, especially literary culture. I argue that it is unique to African American readings and rewritings of Dante to suggest that the man is a kind of abolitionist and that the *Divine Comedy* is itself a kind of slave narrative. African American adaptations of Dante have frequently used the medieval author and his work to comment upon segregation and integration, exile and migration.[19] This consistent response to Dante's life and poem in a political vein, this dependence on Dante to make sense of perceived injustice and to effect a change in politics to which one is opposed, underlies the play on words in the book's title, *Freedom Readers*. African American authors use Dante as if he were a 'freedom rider' accompanying them on a journey through a harsh landscape of racial inequality.

The book explores this ongoing reception through the following chronological categories in separate case studies: (1) Coloured Dante; (2) Negro Dante; (3) Black Dante; (4) African American Dante. My starting place is frontier Cincinnati, in a wax museum created in 1828 by Frances Trollope and Hiram Powers, which featured the unusual representation of a black man in hell alongside white sinners, a spectacular sight that caught the attention of many visitors who comment on it in journals, diaries, letters, and published articles. And if hell is integrated, what about heaven?

The pilgrim's passage from hell to heaven, it turns out, like the narrative of the children of Israel fleeing Egypt in search of the Promised Land, was of heightened interest to a people with an experience and, later, a memory of slavery. In fact, Dante's journey recalls in many ways the exodus of the children of Israel. Moreover,

Dante, the historical man in addition to the character in the *Divine Comedy*, had become an important symbol of freedom for many of the Anglo-American abolitionists, some of whom maintained close ties to the new Italy, 'la giovine Italia', during the period of the Risorgimento, from the 1840s to the foundation of the unified Italian state in the 1860s. Many of the New England intellectual elite who promoted the study of Dante's life and works — Emerson, James Russell Lowell, Norton, and Longfellow, first among them — were closely connected with abolitionists.[20] Italian nationalists who argued that their compatriots were enslaved to the Austrians in the north, Spanish in the south, and to the Vatican throughout the middle of the peninsula promoted Dante's unflinching criticism of the papacy in an attempt to convince their contemporaries to struggle for self-rule and determination. Giuseppe Mazzini made this case forcefully in the middle decades of the nineteenth century and it was none other than William Lloyd Garrison, the most important American abolitionist, who edited Mazzini's writings for readers of English in 1872. Mazzini's political Dante, inherited from Ugo Foscolo, is handed on to Garrison and through him to general readers on both sides of the Atlantic. Out of this heady political mix in the mid-nineteenth century, Cordelia Ray (my prime example of an author of a Coloured Dante), whose father, Charles Bennett Ray, was a close associate of Frederick Douglass, turns the medieval Italian poet into a constitutional activist lawyer, an abolitionist, in her charged 52-line poem, 'Dante' (1885).

The connection between Dante and African American culture has its origins in these political links between abolitionists and Italian nationalists in the nineteenth century. The politicized readings of Dante promoted by these two groups depend in turn, at least partially, on sixteenth-century interpretations of his work by English Protestant intellectuals. The historical Dante's political career and eventual exile, as well as his criticism of the papacy, his steadfast support of the Holy Roman Emperor, and his belief that the two powers, spiritual and temporal, should be separated and distinct, made him into an idiosyncratic symbol of liberty and gave him currency as a radical political thinker among English Protestants as early as the sixteenth century. Dante's subsequent rise in popularity in the Anglo-American world depends in part on this earlier radical anti-establishmentarian Protestant Dante.[21]

Spencer Williams, an independent filmmaker who worked from the 1920s into the 1950s, uses Dante's allegory of good and evil to shed light on the daily existence of the Negro's segregated world in the first half of the twentieth century. Williams splices cuts from the first feature length film in Italian cinematic history, the silent film, *L'inferno* (1911), into his own *Go Down, Death!* (1944), and in so doing he uses Dante-the-character to integrate his 'All-Negro Production' (to borrow from the film's publicity poster). Of note for my comments below on Tate's poem is how Williams has his character hallucinate a lynching rope. His conscience goads him: 'See that tree over yonder? I'm going to tell you something about that tree. Now listen. They once hung a man on it for killing a woman.' The imagined noose represents a potential flashback that the director does not have to give us, for we know how that scene from race relations looks. And if we did not know, the reaction shot of Jim's terror amply fleshes out the picture for the viewer's imagination. There was arguably nothing more hellish for an African American audience, even as late as the 1940s, than the diabolical administration of retribution and vengeance through lynching.

Richard Wright and Ralph Ellison also use Dante to striking effect at this moment around the middle of the twentieth century. But perhaps more important for my argument here is Melvin B. Tolson's *Libretto for the Republic of Liberia*, published in 1953 with a preface by Allen Tate.[22] *Libretto* alludes to Dante's poem in three passages, including one on the fatigue of exile, which Tolson refracts through Dante Gabriel Rossetti's *Dante in Verona*, itself a poem by an author whose sensibility of deracination characterized his work and life. By promoting Tolson's work and perhaps even orchestrating its publication, Tate inserts himself directly into the African American tradition of using Dante as a commentary on the challenges of quotidian existence.

During the Black Revolution, Dante retains his potential as a powerful model of emancipation, exemplified by LeRoi Jones, who uses the medieval poet as a model for a modern slave narrative making himself out to be a Black Dante. Using Dante as a foil for his own life in *The System of Dante's Hell* (1965) liberates LeRoi Jones, turning him into a new man with a new name, Amiri Baraka, who becomes, then, a model for the hip-hop poets of the urban ghetto in Gloria Naylor's novel *Linden Hills* (1985). The African American artists she creates follow in Dante's footsteps, although they are wary of writing's potential to enslave them, opting instead for a new tradition of oral poetry, which takes its inspiration in part from Dante's poem.

This chronology of reception at first glance would seem at odds with Edward Said's claim that Dante's *Divine Comedy* is the foundational text in the imperial — to use his word — project of comparative literature as it developed in the twentieth century across Europe and the United States under the influence of a group of independent but like-minded Romance philologists such as Erich Auerbach and Ernst Curtius.[23] According to Said, comparative literature emerged as a discipline at the same time that a colonial Eurocentric geography was being imposed on much of the world. He argues that the conceptual framework underlying comparative literature that privileges a certain body of texts for a certain kind of comparative study is analogous to the mentality that prompted Europeans to take their administrative cultures into what seemed to them undeveloped areas and colonize them. Dante's encyclopaedic summation of much of what had preceded him in medieval European culture and his idiosyncratic response to the classical tradition made his texts extremely useful in the scholarly attempt to articulate the western literary tradition from its classical origins to the revival of classicism in the Renaissance. Thus Dante's work, especially the *Divine Comedy*, becomes a central privileged site of investigation in the modern comparatist's configuration of the literary tradition.

Despite the keen attention to Dante on the part of the founding fathers of comparative literature, there has been little notice of the African American tradition of reading Dante. This tradition that embraces the canonical Dante but is often anti-imperial, using Dante to critique the very structures of power that promote a hierarchy that keeps one group in control of another. In the American South, these groups are not colonizers and colonized; they are, rather, masters and slaves. There is, then, a dual appropriation of Dante and his work by writers of colour, which holds it up as a foundational text of the western tradition, on the one hand, and uses it to critique the system that produces and values that sort of canonical thinking, on the other.

Dante designates his *epic* poem as a *comedy* to recognize its hybrid status as a genre. The art of fiction itself is figured as a mixed hybrid creation in the first of the two passages in the *Comedy* in which the word *comedía* occurs, *Inferno* 16. 128. As Geryon, the embodiment of fraud, which is presented as the counterpoint to fiction, flies up from the depths of hell to fetch the pilgrim and his guide in order to carry them down into the eighth circle of the fraudulent, the poet feels the need to swear by the sound of the notes of his *comedía* that what he is reporting to have seen, he really and truly saw. Geryon — part dragon, snake, scorpion, with the face of a just man — is a hybrid creature *in malo*, a symbolic representation of fraud, which looks honest but will sting when it gets a chance. Fiction, the counterpoint to fraud, works in an opposing way: it looks false but is, in fact, true. In the case of Dante's poem, it may appear that he did not do any of the things he claims to have done, but he wants the reader to believe that he actually did. If fraud is false but appears honest at first glance, fiction by contrast is truthful though it might appear false. In other words, like the hybrid beast Geryon, the art of fiction is also hybrid. Dante's fiction, it turns out, is true. Or, as one critic has put it memorably, 'The fiction of the *Comedy* is that it is not fiction.'[24]

Allen Tate, like the African American authors discussed in *Freedom Readers*, uses Dante to critique the dominant culture of his racist past, which he first wants to come to grips with and then, I believe, overcome in 'The Swimmers'.

A Reading of Tate's 'The Swimmers'

After the publication of 'The Swimmers' in 1953, Tate continued to alter the poem. I cite the opening lines of the poem from the final version published during Tate's lifetime, from *Collected Poems, 1919–1976*.[25]

> SCENE: *Montgomery County,*
> *Kentucky, July 1911*
>
> Kentucky water, clear springs: a boy fleeing
> To water under the dry Kentucky sun,
> His four little friends in tandem with him, seeing
>
> Long shadows of grapevine wriggle and run
> Over the green swirl; mullein under the ear
> Soft as Nausicaä's palm; sullen fun
>
> Savage as childhood's thin harmonious tear:

The year before he died, Tate wrote the following lengthy note in one of his last published pieces:

> I will end this series of free associations with a brief account of the writing of one of my poems in *terza rima* — 'The Swimmers.' In Princeton, New Jersey, in the summer of 1951, a boyhood experience began to come back to me in considerable detail. In July, 1911, I saw the end of a lynching about a mile from the town of Mount Sterling, Kentucky. The four boys who were with me on the way to the swimming hole also saw the dead body of the black man lying in the road. But in the poem I eliminated them because I didn't know how to dramatize five boys. What I actually saw is what I describe in the poem. I learned some years later, but not from any member of my family, that that lynching was not the result of the standard lynching situation: the rape of a white woman by a black man. A black tenant farmer learned that his white landlord had cheated him out of his share of the tobacco crop. When the landlord refused to pay the man, the man shot the landlord. The sheriff and his posse arrived too late to save the black man from the lynching mob.[26]

It is noteworthy for one of the founding practitioners of New Criticism, that approach to the literary text that adamantly rejects historical and biographical interpretation, to provide us with detailed personal information on the composition of one of his poems. All the more strange to admit that the details are altered for the sake of the poem: five boys are reduced to one at the end of the poem, to Tate himself. Poets can take such licence, of course. Dante, too, in the Ugolino episode of *Inferno* 33, alters the historical fact of a grandfather, two sons, and two grandsons imprisoned to a father with four young children. With this reconfiguration Dante could, to borrow Tate's word, 'dramatize' the horrific scene better. Tate wants to emphasize his eye-witness testimony, as if it were unique (but he tells us it is not), so much so that he repeats it: 'I saw the end of a lynching' and 'What I actually saw is what I describe in the poem.' It could be that the elderly Tate plumbing the depths of his memory works hard to re-envision what it was that inspired his composition. Or could it be that the rhetorical overstatement of repeating what he saw, and excluding the fact that others saw it too so as to privilege his own perspective, is a clue that suggests an invented fiction? The reader is invited to apply the same compositional logic to Tate's poem that Charles Singleton applies to Dante's when he posits that what the *Comedy* is most about — its fiction — is that it is not fiction, that is, it describes a true story. While meant to establish his authorial veracity as witness, does the reconstruction of Tate's memory actually have the opposite effect? Does his way of remembering cast doubt on the truthfulness of the memory? One dutiful positivist critic who has researched the archives is convinced that there was no lynching in Kentucky's Montgomery County in 1911 for Tate to claim as his source.[27] Whether or not Tate actually experienced this event in the manner he recounts, does not really matter. We are moving into the workshop of the artist.

The first decision the artist has to make is about poetic form. Tate chooses *terza rima* in order to propel the poem's narrative forward. The first rhyme word is one of motion, 'fleeing' (1), and the next rhyme turns on the verb 'run' (4). These opening tercets form an invocation in which the poet asks the source of creativity, here identified as the 'fountain' (8), to give him back his eye, to give him back the ability to see and to recall what he saw. His eye, which has 'fled' (10), needs to be caught and made to look and see again. In fact, that initial rhyming word of the poem, 'fleeing', is in rhyme with 'seeing' (3); this poem is about the traumatic difficulty of trying to confront and overcome the fear of seeing the horrendous.

The narrator is young, the fuzz on his ear as soft as the hand of Nausicaä, the nubile Phaiakian princess who rescues Odysseus/Ulysses from shipwreck in the sixth book of Homer's *Odyssey*. Tate and his companions are themselves on an 'odyssey' (15). In fact, the protagonist himself is a youthful version of Odysseus, or Ulisse as Dante names him in the *Inferno*. Dante the poet establishes a series of parallels between his protagonist, Dante the pilgrim and Homer's Ulysses, with one crucial difference: in Homer's version Ulysses survives; in Dante's rewriting of Homer in *Inferno* 26, Ulysses dies. If Tate's character is a figure like Ulysses on an adventure, like Ulysses his adventure can end tragically. The coiled copperhead at the end of the invocation eerily anticipates other more dangerous coils to come. And is that copperhead an anxious reminder that the poet, himself a creature of the South, has taken his distance from the region, which he now prepares to critique?[28]

Like Dante's pilgrim as he descends into hell in *Inferno* 3, our protagonist looks but sees nothing; instead he hears: 'Peering, I heard' (25ff.). The sheriff's men ride by. Then a Dantesque-sounding simile describes how the boys scoot down an embankment to get to the edge of the creek along which they walk in fear (28–33). The poem implies that the sheriff's posse, which one might think has been dispatched to save the victim from an enraged mob, is actually the group that kills him. In *Inferno* 22, a troop of devils is dispatched to lead Dante and Vergil safely through the fifth ditch of the eighth circle. Like the posse, the devils intend to do the opposite of what they are supposed to do; but they fail as Vergil quickly grabs Dante and slides down into the next ditch just out of their reach. Continuing the theme of false appearances, the sheriff's men are Jesus-Christers (38), which ought to be a good thing, but Tate's description (which the drafts in Princeton's archives show he laboured over) recalls, rather, a lynching party of Klansmen dressed in robes.

The reference to the sacrifice of Christ is a periphrasis to describe the lynching of the African American victim: 'Whose Corpse had died again in dirty shame' (39). A commonplace among representations of lynching is that the lynched body resembles Christ on the cross. Claude McKay, a Jamaican immigrant who was the first significant writer of the Harlem Renaissance in the 1920s, in a powerful sonnet called simply 'The Lynching', makes this comparison. Countee Cullen, another important poet of the Harlem Renaissance, is more explicit in describing the victim's suffering in 'The Black Christ'. Richard Wright, too, has a poem on lynching that does not mince words, 'Between the World and Me'. It is Ralph Ellison in a late essay, 'An Extravagance of Laughter' (1984), who reflects on lynching as a kind of sacrifice. The lynching, he writes, is 'a ritual drama that was usually enacted [...] in an atmosphere of high excitement and led by a masked celebrant dressed in a garish costume who manipulated the numinous objects (lynch ropes, the American flag, shotgun, gasoline and whiskey jugs) associated with the rite as he inspired and instructed the actors in their gory task'.[29] Tate's protagonist had not stumbled upon a gathering for such an elaborate ceremonial lynching; what he saw was the aftermath of a lynching that was quick and dirty.

The hangman's knot around the dead man's neck is loosened (56ff.). The sheriff then puts a noose around the dead man's feet and he and his partner drag the body to town in a cloud of dust, the three of them forming a kind of unholy trinity: 'three figures in the dying sun' (77). From the protagonist's youthful perspective, it is now 'the Negro's body' (64) — contrast the sheriff's disparaging remark at line 48 — and 'our town' (70); and the narrator is left alone to face 'the faceless head' (81) once the other two leave. The poem ends with a reflection on the moral shortcomings of the town where no one ever mentions the lynching; the word 'town' is repeated as the final new rhyme in the metre that is left hanging in the next to last verse. The juxtaposition of private and public, specifically in the context of crime and responsibility — it is a 'private thing' (83) in which the public has ownership — recalls many passages in the *Inferno*, where the poem unfolds around the tension between the individual and community, between 'I' and 'we'. A telling emendation in the poem's penultimate line, 83, which Tate ultimately does not keep, reflects this tension: 'I owned it.'[30] At the end of *Inferno* 13, one sinner from Florence asks another Florentine: 'What responsibility do I have for your wicked life?' (135). The answer is simple in Dante's world: the individual citizen must take responsibility for the moral rectitude of his fellow citizens. Not so for the town of Tate's youth. But he seeks to rectify things in writing the poem and situating it in place and time with the epigraph at the very beginning: 'SCENE: *Montgomery County, | Kentucky, July 1911*'. The epigraph was one of Tate's emendations as he revised the poem for publication in the volume of collected poems. Moreover, 'SCENE' is surely also a pun that calls to mind 'SEEN'. This is about what was actually seen, what was witnessed, to which the poem now and forever testifies. Or is it a performance on a poetic stage with Tate in the wings giving his reader directions?

If the poem is written and submitted to set the record straight about an unrecorded lynching, perhaps it is fitting that the poet call on Dante's *terza rima*, which tightens its own coils around the subject matter as it pushes the reader deeper and deeper into a scene of hell. When the poem opens under the thrust of the metre, the protagonist flees and runs; as the poem concludes with its condemnation of the moral inadequacies of the town's citizens, the protagonist 'could not run' (81) and he has no place to hide, but stands '[a]lone in the public clearing' (82). 'Alone in the public clearing' actually generates meaning on several levels in the poem's final lines. It refers first to the lynched body that has been unceremoniously dumped before the county court house. The poet then adds the substantival phrase 'this private thing' (83), which refers to the secretive actions of the sheriff and his men that culminate in the murder of the victim. And then finally the protagonist himself 'stood. Alone' (82). Tate as poet, in a position analogous to that of his youthful character in the poem, has decided to stand alone, to stand apart from his Fugitive and Agrarian peers, to take a different kind of stand and break their silence about racial violence.[31] The poem opens with a concern about private poetic seeing, but it ends with a plea to re-examine what the community hears. The *terza rima* neatly ties the knot with its final rhymes: what was seen in the *clearing* must be discussed and claimed, Tate says, in the *hearing*. As do so many of Tate's lexical choices, the poem's final word carries extra semantic weight. 'Hearing' is not only a reference to audibility but also a session at which testimony is taken from a witness as the basis for a judgment. Tate judges and asks to be judged.

The African American authors who constitute a tradition of responding to Dante that I discuss in *Freedom Readers* use Dante to negotiate crucial transitions in their private lives and in the lives of their people. Allen Tate too. At a moment of conversion — not just his literal conversion to Catholicism but also his attempt to move away from the ideology of segregation to an acceptance of the inevitability of integration and the changes to come in American culture in the 1950s and beyond — he too turns to Dante to help him negotiate and rewrite a racist past, his own and his people's. It may or may not be a successful move: but the fiction of the fiction is that it is not a fiction.[32]

Notes to Chapter 23

1. Radcliffe Squires, *Allen Tate* (New York: Pegasus, 1971), pp. 201–02.
2. Allen Tate, 'The Swimmers', *Hudson Review*, 5.4 (1953), 471–73 (p. 471).
3. William W. Cook and James Tatum, *African American Writers and Classical Tradition* (Chicago: University of Chicago Press, 2010), p. 250.
4. Robert H. Brinkmeyer, Jr., *The Fourth Ghost: White Southern Writers and European Fascism, 1930–1950* (Baton Rouge: Louisiana State University Press, 2009).
5. See Thomas A. Underwood, *Allen Tate: Orphan of the South* (Princeton: Princeton University Press, 2000), on Tate's professor of logic, Charles Herbert Sanborn: 'A transplanted New Englander who [...] quoted freely from the Dante he had memorized as a young man' (p. 40) and Pierre E. Briquet, professor of Romance languages, who tried to have Tate expelled for an impertinent response prompted by a question about Dante (p. 45).
6. 'Dante', in T. S. Eliot and others, *The Complete Prose of T. S. Eliot: The Critical Edition: Literature, Politics, Belief, 1927–1929* (Baltimore: Johns Hopkins University Press, 2015), pp. 700–45 (p. 712), Project MUSE muse.jhu.edu/book/41952. First published as *Dante* (London: Faber & Faber, 1929), No. 2 in 'The Poets on the Poets' series.
7. Eliot, p. 718.
8. Gordon's novel, *The Women on the Porch* (New York: Charles Scribner's Sons, 1944), on the complicated relationship between the protagonist, Kit, and her husband, Jim, who is teaching and reading Dante throughout the narrative, deserves attention as another response to the medieval poet in not just Southern, but also Catholic, literary explorations.
9. For the essays, see Allen Tate, 'The Angelic Imagination' (pp. 401–23) and 'The Symbolic Imagination' (pp. 424–26) in *Essays of Four Decades* (Chicago: The Swallow Press, 1968). For critical response to the essays, see, for example, Radcliffe Squires's laudatory praise in 'Will and Vision: Allen Tate's *terza rima* Poems', *Sewanee Review*, 78.4 (1970), 543–62 (pp. 546–47).
10. See Tate, 'The Symbolic Imagination', p. 440. For the student's recollection, see Warren Kliewer, 'Allen Tate as a Teacher', *Descant*, 7 (Autumn 1962), 41–48.
11. See Underwood, pp. 149–50, p. 209, p. 291, for some examples of Tate's racist rhetoric. Hayden Carruth opened a short piece in response to the publication of an edition of Tate's essays mentioned in the note above with this declaration: 'To the mind of a northern radical existentialist, some parts of Allen Tate's philosophy must seem unacceptable.' See his 'A Debt to Allen Tate', *Poetry*, 99.2 (1961), 123. For a remembrance of Tate that takes him to task for his racism, see Lem Coley, 'Memories and Opinions of Allen Tate', *Southern Review*, 25.2 (1992), 944–64.
12. Lewis P. Simpson, *Fable of the Southern Writer* (Baton Rouge: Louisiana State University Press, 1994), p. 115. Like many readers before and after him, Tate depends on Dante as a spiritual guide. See the essay by Elizabeth Coggeshall (chapter 25 in this volume), which includes an examination of this tendency.

13. Allen Tate, *Memoirs and Opinions, 1926–1974* (Chicago: The Swallow Press, 1975), p. ix.
14. Simpson, p. 29.
15. Tate, *Memoirs and Opinions*, pp. 3–23 (p. 4).
16. See the extensive revisions of 'The Swimmers', in the Allen Tate Papers, CO 106, Manuscripts Division, Rare Books and Special Collections, Princeton University Library. And see, for example, the letter of 19 November 1952, to Andrew Lytle, which accompanies an early draft of the poem: 'This is the only copy I have, and I'm sick of typing it; so please mail it back at your convenience.' *The Lytle–Tate Letters: The Correspondence of Andrew Lytle and Allen* Tate, ed. by Thomas Daniel Young and Elizabeth Sarcone (Jackson: University Press of Mississippi, 1987), p. 231.
17. In a verbal communication after a lecture I delivered at Sewanee on Tate and Dante, 1 February 2018.
18. Dennis Looney, *Freedom Readers: The African American Reception of Dante Alighieri and the* Divine Comedy (Notre Dame: University of Notre Dame Press, 2011).
19. By comparison, one might consider the translation of the Inferno by Ciaran Carson, which casts the action in terms of the ongoing tension between Protestants and Catholics on the edges of Northern Ireland (London: Granta, 2002), pp. xi–xii. In fact, Irish authors, most noticeably Joyce, Beckett and Heaney, also seem attuned to Dante's 'subversive power', to borrow from the provocative, if brief, discussion of Pascale Casanova, *World Republic of Letters*, trans. M. B. DeBevoise (Cambridge, MA: Harvard University Press, 2004), p. 329.
20. Emerson was the first to translate *Vita Nuova* into English (*c.* 1842); Lowell wrote a famous biographical sketch on Dante for the *Appleton New American Encyclopedia* (1859); Norton was the first to publish a complete translation of *Vita Nuova* (1859); and Longfellow's translation of the *Divine Comedy* came out in 1865.
21. See Nick Havely, "An Italian Writer against the Pope?" Dante in Reformation England, c. 1560–c. 1640', in *Dante Metamorphoses: Episodes in a Literary Afterlife*, ed. by Eric G. Haywood (Dublin: Four Courts Press, 2003), pp. 127–49.
22. Melvin B. Tolson, *Libretto for the Republic of Liberia* (New York: Twayne, 1953). Allusions to Dante are at lines 142, 507, and 554. The penultimate section of the poem and Tate's preface were first published in *Poetry*, 76.4 (July 1950), 208–18.
23. Edward Said, 'Connecting Empire to Secular Interpretation', in *Culture and Imperialism* (New York: Vintage Books, 1993), pp. 43–61.
24. Charles S. Singleton, 'The Irreducible Dove', *Comparative Literature*, 9 (1957), 124–35 (p. 129).
25. For the complete poem reprinted from Tate's *Collected Poems 1919–1976* (New York: Farrar, Straus, Giroux, 1977), pp. 132–35, see John Frederick Nims, 'In Honor of Allen Tate', *Poetry*, 135.2 (1979), pp. 63–75. Tate died on February 9, 1979, and Nims, the editor of *Poetry*, dedicated the issue that came out in November to him.
26. Allen Tate, 'Speculations', *The Southern Review*, 14 (1978), 226–32.
27. Jennings Mace, 'The Lynching in Allen Tate's "The Swimmers"', *ANQ: A Quarterly Journal of Short Articles, Notes, and Reviews*, 18.4 (2005), 42–48.
28. Copperhead is a term used to describe a northern Democrat during the Civil War, that is, a northerner who was pro-South. Richard O. Curry, 'Copperheadism and Continuity: Anatomy of a Stereotype', *Journal of Negro History*, 57.1 (1972), 29–36.
29. In Ralph Ellison, *Collected Essays*, ed. and intro. by John F. Callahan (New York: Modern Library, 2003), pp. 617–62 (pp. 644–45).
30. See the typescript with emendations published in *Poetry*, 135.2 (1979), 63–75 (p. 74). On responsibility for moral action and the lack thereof, see the essay by Kristina M. Olson (chapter 24 in this volume) on the reception of *Inferno* 3 from the nineteenth century to today.
31. Concluding his reading of this passage, Lem Coley claims: 'in "The Swimmers" he tacitly acknowledged the structural importance of terror' (p. 955).
32. I would like to acknowledge the support of the William C. Mullen Memorial Fund, Bard College.

CHAPTER 24

'Maintaining Neutrality in a Period of Moral Crisis': Appropriations of *Inferno* 3 in Twentieth- and Twenty-First-Century America

Kristina M. Olson

Despite the numerous sins punished in Dante's *Inferno*, twentieth- and twenty-first-century anglophone authors, politicians and clerics frequently reference the condition of the neutral angels and cowards in *Inferno* 3, the antechamber to Hell — and not one of the sins of Hell proper. Three influential and noteworthy examples in this canto's poetic and fictive *fortuna* include T. S. Eliot, Mikhail Bulgakov and Dan Brown.[1] Eliot's *The Waste Land* (1922) urges us to consider the large population of this group, and the possibility that we might find such souls on earth: 'A crowd flowed over London Bridge, so many, | I had not thought death had undone so many' (vv. 62–63).[2] Here, Eliot's interpretation transposes the infernal souls of the cowards to modern-day London, blurring the distinctions between the living and the dead and showing the relationship between 'the medieval inferno and modern life', which was his intention.[3] On the other hand, Mikhail Bulgakov's *Master and Margarita* (1967) enters into the debate on the identity of the nameless coward 'who made the great refusal' ('colui | che fece per viltade il gran rifiuto', *Inf.* 3. 59–60), variously identified within the commentary tradition as an anonymous soul, Pontius Pilate or Celestine V.[4] In *Master and Margarita*'s novel within a novel (Book Two of 'The Burial'), Pontius Pilate corrects Yeshua Ha-Nostri's claim, stating that cowardice is the greatest of all vices, implying his own guilt.[5] Finally, the epigraph and the epilogue of Dan Brown's *Inferno* (2013) display the cross-fertilization of political discourse and mainstream literature in the proverbial reception of *Inferno* 3: 'The darkest places in hell are reserved for those who maintain their neutrality in times of moral crisis.'[6] The protagonists of this novel espouse a relentless sense of moral imperative, of what Teodolinda Barolini has called, Dante's 'commitment to commitment'.[7] As Brown adds to this phrase in the Epilogue, 'For Langdon, the meaning of these words had never felt so clear: In dangerous times, there is no sin greater than inaction.'[8]

As in the case of Dan Brown's novel, the afterlife of *Inferno* 3 depends upon the cross-contamination and accretion of literary, political and religious interpretations over many decades. The *ignavi* [cowards] of *Inferno* 3 have been cited and appropriated in literary and political discourse through the twentieth and twenty-first centuries, particularly in the American political arena. This chapter aims to connect Dante's poem with this interpretative afterlife by focusing on Dante's vision of cowardice as a civic sin, namely as the refusal to act in a time of crisis. Such an interpretation of Dante's text allows us to draw a line, albeit not a linear one, from *Inferno* 3 to present incarnations of this canto within modern and contemporary public discourse in America.

Though unfaithful in the characterization of the cowards' location in hell, these appropriations resonate faithfully with the political nature of Dante's definition of cowardice.[9]

This chapter begins by examining the critical tradition on the *ignavi* of *Inferno* 3, the nature of their failing, and the theological basis for their punishment. It then surveys a variety of references made by American political leaders and preachers to the *ignavi*, appropriations which display varying degrees of familiarity with Dante's poem. I then consider the positions of American philosophers and gender theorists on the *ignavi* within debates over feminism and Western-centric social and civil rights movements. In my conclusion, I consider two contemporary examples from twenty-first-century American politics: one, which begs the 'application' of Dante's definition of cowardice as a civic sin, and the other, the most recent political appropriation of *Inferno* 3.

Cowardice in Dante's *Inferno*

Cowardice is introduced in Dante's poem as a personal and emotional condition experienced by the pilgrim. Cowardly sentiments begin to permeate the language of the poem in *Inferno* 2, conveying the personal nature of this sin for our poet.[10] Dante refers to cowardice as 'viltà', and 'viltade', in verses that lead up to the encounter with the throngs of neutral angel and cowardly souls, namely as a reflection upon the pilgrim's own spiritual state. Assailed by fear, the pilgrim is uncertain if he can embark upon the journey. Vergil notices and comments upon the pilgrim's cowardly state both at the beginning of the canto, 'l'anima tua è da viltade offesa' ('your soul has been assailed by cowardice', *Inf.* 2. 45), and at the end, 'perché tanta viltà nel core allette' ('why does your heart host so much cowardice?', *Inf.* 2. 122).[11] Hence when viewing the inscription on the Gate of Hell, Vergil seems to say that the pilgrim, and not just every soul, must abandon his cowardice: 'Qui si convien lasciare ogne sospetto; | *ogne viltà* convien che qui sia morta. | Noi siam venuti al loco ov' i' t'ho detto | che tu vedrai le genti dolorose | c'hanno perduto il ben de l'intelletto' ('Here one must leave behind all hesitation; | here every cowardice must meet its death. | For we have reached the place of which I spoke, | where you will see the miserable people, | those who have lost the good of the intellect', *Inf.* 3. 14–18). Vergil's definition of the 'gente dolorosa' include both those who dwell in hell as well as those in the antechamber: they have lost the good of the intellect ('il ben de l'intelletto'). Radiating outwards, cowardice is first enacted by the pilgrim, but soon can be identified in the damned population that the pilgrim encounters.

Elsewhere, in the *Convivio,* Dante defines the 'good of the intellect' as the truth, following Aristotle: 'sì come dice lo Filosofo nel sesto dell'Etica, quando dice che 'l vero è lo *bene dello 'ntelletto*' (*Conv.* 2. 13); ('as the Philosopher says in the sixth book of the Ethics when he says that truth is the *good of the intellect,*' Lansing translation, emphasis added).[12] Yet Dante appears to offer a variation upon this Aristotelian definition in the *Inferno*: the 'good of the intellect' may be what the cowardly souls have lost, because they missed the opportunity to set their minds to the good and take action. Dante articulates one's intellectual and ethical potential as a citizen in *Inferno* 6 with this vocabulary. When the pilgrim asks Ciacco as to the whereabouts of Farinata, Tegghiaio Aldobrandi and others, he reprises the language of *Inferno* 3.18, noting that their minds were bent towards the good: 'Farinata e 'l Tegghiaio, che fuor sì degni, | Iacopo Rusticucci, Arrigo e 'l Mosca| e li altri *ch'a ben far puoser li 'ngegni*' ('Farinata and Tegghiaio, who were so worthy, Iacopo Rusticucci, Arrigo, and Mosca, | and the others *whose minds bent towards the good*', *Inf.* 6. 79–80, emphasis added). Most of these individuals (Ghibellines or Black Guelphs) were on the opposite side of political divide from Dante, not fulfilling their 'ben fare', but acting in evil, as remembered in the 'mal fare' (*Inf.* 25. 12) of the Black Guelph Vanni Fucci. In contrast, Dante conveys that he himself executed good deeds in the political arena, civic acts that would lead to his exile, as Brunetto Latini describes: 'ti si farà, *per tuo ben far,* nimico' ('[the Florentine people] for your good deeds, will be your enemy', *Inf.* 15. 64, emphasis added).[13] 'Ben far' and 'mal far' should be understood alternately as civic acts for good or for evil.

Cowardice is unique, for it describes inaction, not a 'fatto' or a deed, but the lack of a decisive action in a time of urgency, or civic crisis. This is unlike many sins of incontinence, violence or fraud, in which an action, albeit a sinful action, is committed. While it could be said that the cowardly souls share a similar disposition with the sullen, the difference is the implication that the former group ignored a civic or public imperative to act during a moment (or crisis) that required it. For this reason, the cowards are those who 'lived without disgrace and without praise' ('l'anime triste di coloro | che visser sanza 'nfamia e sanza lodo', *Inf.* 3. 35–36), neither meriting the grace of salvation nor the eternal suffering of divine justice throughout their exemplary works. The category of the cowards is Dante's invention, just as their shared population with the neutral angels is his poetic innovation: those angels did not rebel or stand with God, and consequently were purged from heaven and rejected by hell.[14] Because they have been banished by both heaven and hell, these souls chase a meaningless banner at a fast clip while being stung repeatedly by horseflies and wasps, as their blood and tears mingle together and fall at their feet, being gathered up by worms. Since they failed to make a name for themselves through exceptional deeds, their contrapasso also lies in their lack of posthumous fame, a fitting retribution: 'The world will let no fame of theirs endure; | both justice and compassion must disdain them; | let us not talk of them, but look and pass' ('Fama di loro il mondo esser non lassa; | misericordia e giustizia li sdegna: | non ragioniam di lor, ma guarda e passa', *Inf.* 3. 49–51). The historical record will not name those who did not act when the unfolding of history required it.

Dante not only invents this category of sinners which remains separate from those who enter hell or heaven, but he decides to make them a large population, as Eliot reminds us in the *The Waste Land*. Yet the mysterious identity of one who 'made, though cowardice, the great refusal' ('che fece per viltade il gran rifiuto', *Inf.* 3. 60) — an historical personage who has been variously identified as scholars as Celestine V, the pope who abdicated and opened the way for Pope Boniface VIII, or Pontius Pilate — confirms the identity of this population as those who did not act in the civic arena. Upon recognizing this one individual, the pilgrim immediately understands with certainty that these are the cowards, 'hateful to God and His enemies' ('a Dio spiacenti e a' nemici sui', *Inf.* 3. 63), who 'never were alive' ('che mai non fur vivi', *Inf.* 3. 64).[15] Dante leaves the identity of this soul open to interpretation for posterity; his readers can understand that the souls condemned here could be anyone who refused to act in the universal history of the church or the state, as scholarship and the commentary tradition have shown. By leaving the soul's identity unclear, Dante also allows us to entertain the potential for other souls in his time, as well as in ours, to face eternity for their cowardice. It is a fertile textual moment for the elaborate *fortuna* — of interpretation and of appropriation — that has materialized in its wake.

Importantly, Dante draws upon Aquinas in his definition of the cowards. In the poem, the cowards are not 'ignavi' but 'vili'. This sense of 'viltà' comes from Aquinas's *Summa Theologica*:

> Now just as presumption makes a man exceed what is proportionate to his power, by striving to do more than he can, so pusillanimity makes a man fall short of what is proportionate to his power, by refusing to tend to that which is commensurate thereto.[16]

Cowardice is a *recusatio tensionis*, a refusal to strive towards a goal within the limits of one's natural capabilities. As Dante writes in the *Convivio*, 'the coward [...] always considers himself less than he truly is' ('lo pusillanimo [...] sempre si tiene meno che non è', *Conv.* I. II. 18). To elaborate upon Aquinas's thought, Dante posits the low self-esteem of the coward, who does not comprehend his full potential. In the *Inferno*, this lack of self-awareness translates into the refusal to exercise the good of the intellect commensurate with one's powers, namely in the civic sphere.

That cowardice is a failure to act in the civic sphere can be seen as well in the case of Brunetto Latini in *Inferno* 15. Here we can find the poetic elements of the same contrapasso — the race after a banner, in this case, a cloth — together with a soul whose personal record of civic participation might have been viewed ambivalently by Dante. Latini, the poet's father figure and master, a Guelph leader of Florence from the thirteenth century who abandoned Italy after his mission to France, ends his encounter with the pilgrim as he 'turned and seemed like one of those | who race across the fields to win the green | cloth at Verona; of those runners, he |

appeared to be the winner, not the loser' ('Poi si rivolse, e parve di coloro | che corrono a Verona il drappo verde | per la campagna; e parve di costoro | quelli che vince, non colui che perde', *Inf.* 15. 121–24). It is possible that Dante saw Latini as an individual who failed in following through on his political commitment, his *impegno*: one who looks like he will win on his own, but must run with an anonymous crowd of souls. Cowardice effaces individual identity and distinction within the nameless collective.

Cowardice in America: Nineteenth- and Twentieth-Century Politicians and Preachers

It would be something of a poetic irony if Dante were able to see the afterlife of *Inferno* 3 today. I think, namely, of the posting on demonstration boards and banners of the creative appropriations of the statements made by John F. Kennedy or the Reverend Martin Luther King, Jr. Ignoring for a moment that we know these to be 'unfaithful' interpretations of his poem, we should take into consideration what we see in these images: the empty banner of *Inferno* 3 has become thousands of 'banners' meant to rouse the collective masses into political action. If only Dante could have known how his poetic and political vision would be fulfilled in our lifetime.

The source for this omnipresent appropriation of *Inferno* 3 is taken to be President John F. Kennedy, who uttered on several dates: 'Dante once said that the hottest places in hell are reserved for those who in a period of moral crisis maintain their neutrality.' Kennedy kept a book of memorable quotes which he began collecting in his youth.[17] He cited this phrase which he attributed to Dante more than twenty-five times during his career, but probably never read the *Commedia*. As Deborah Parker convincingly argues, the former president incorporated this quote into his speeches as a rhetorical measure, in order to persuade his audience with greater moral conviction.[18] The quotation, first included in his speech delivered at the meeting of the National Conference of the Christians and the Jews on 16 February 1956, appears to come directly from Henry Powell Spring's book of aphorisms, *What Is Truth?* (1944). Spring's book, inspired by Steiner's esoteric field of anthroposophy, features this quotation on a page together with authors as diverse as Voltaire and Harriet Beecher Stowe.[19] It is clear that Spring's book was a source for political and journalistic references to *Inferno* 3 before Kennedy's repeated appropriation, as newspaper archives document for 1944 (*The Pampa News*) and 1954 (*The Milwaukee Sentinel*).[20]

Two elements of Spring's quotation strike the reader of Dante. First, the phrase 'hottest places of hell' incorrectly locates the cowards, according to Dante's infernal topography. Secondly, and most significantly, Spring adds the phrase 'moral crisis' to his interpretation of *Inferno* 3, something which one might *infer* from reading Dante, but which cannot be found in the text itself. This particular quotation — including the two phrases 'lowest places of hell' and 'moral crisis' — also came to influence the Revered Martin Luther King, Jr. Speaking out against the war in Vietnam on 30 April 1967, King said:

> Now, I've chosen to preach about the war in Vietnam because I agree with Dante, that the hottest places in hell are reserved for those who in a period of moral crisis maintain their neutrality. There comes a time when silence becomes betrayal.[21]

While King says that he agrees with Dante, he clearly agrees with Kennedy (and Spring) as well. The addendum of 'moral crisis' is the distinctive modification that one can find in the appropriation of this quotation beginning with Spring's book.[22]

However, Spring's book would not have been the only source for Kennedy and King. President Theodore Roosevelt condemned Wilson and other 'ultrapacifists' who turned their backs on the First World War, when he wrote:

> The kind of 'neutrality' which seeks to preserve 'peace' by timidly refusing to live up to our plighted word and to denounce and take action against such wrong as that committed in the case of Belgium, is unworthy of an honorable and powerful people. *Dante reserved a special place of infamy for those base angels who dared side neither with evil nor with good.*[23]

Unlike Kennedy, Roosevelt truly studied Dante's *Inferno*, as Akash Kumar has documented.[24] Therefore Roosevelt's reference to the antechamber of hell gains a certain amount of specificity that is lacking in Kennedy's appropriation: it is a 'special place of infamy', where the 'base angels' reside. While Roosevelt would implicitly refer to the dangers of neutrality with Dantean overtones in his 1910 speech at the Sorbonne, as Kumar as argued, Roosevelt never explicitly refers to the 'hottest places in hell', nor to a 'moral crisis' — trademarks of his sophisticated reception of Dante's ideas — before the times of Spring's influence.

The tradition to which Roosevelt and others belong in their evocations of *Inferno* 3 harkens back as early as the debates surrounding slavery during the American Civil War. As Joshua Matthews has observed, in a 4 July 1859 speech, George Sumner compared compromisers in the North with the 'indifferent angels' from *Inferno* 3. Matthews writes: 'for Sumner, these northern "conservatives" — because they compromised with southern politicians — were supporting the causes of "barbarism" and "liberticide," "backing down before every presumptuous aggression [...] until they fall among the lost ones whom Dante describes." '[25] It appears that the Sumner family was well-read in Dante. Dennis Looney has shown how George's brother, Charles Sumner — the Massachusetts senator and one of the founders of the Radical Republican Party, who had travelled to Italy several times — had earlier demonstrated his deep knowledge of Dante that allowed him to refer extensively to *Inferno* 3 in his denunciations of slavery. In his speech, 'The Antislavery Enterprise: Its Necessity, Practicability, and Dignity with Glances at the Special Duties of the North', delivered in New York on 9 May 1855, he exhorts his fellow Americans to take a stand, quoting *Inferno* 3. 37–39 in full:

> Better strive in this cause, even unsuccessfully, then never strive at all. The penalty of indifference is akin to the penalty of opposition, — as is well pictured by the great Italian poet, when, among the saddest on the banks of Acheron, rending the air with outcries of torment, shrieks of anger, and smiting of hands, he finds the troop of dreary souls who had been ciphers in the great conflicts of life: —

> 'Mingled with whom, of their disgrace the proof,
> Are the vile angels, who did not rebel,
> Nor kept their faith to God, but stood aloof.'[26]

Charles Sumner again referred specifically to *Inferno* 3, likening those who do not stand against someone to the one who 'made the great refusal' (*Inf.* 3. 60), in his May 1856 speech to the Senate, 'The Crime against Kansas: The Apologies for the Crime; and the True Remedy'.[27] Here, Sumner unleashes the hortatory power of this canto, using *Inferno* 3 as a warning to the living to take a stand, much as we will later see in the political speeches of Kennedy and King.

The early decades of the twentieth century witness an interest in *Inferno* 3 in religious and political discourse. In 1917, a preacher named W. M. Vines stated that Dante had placed neutral individuals in 'the lowest place in hell', as he believed that ministers could never be neutral: 'The Christian minister must have convictions on all great issues [...] Dante, in his *Inferno*, put those who are neutral in the everlasting fight between right and wrong in the lowest place in hell.'[28] Earlier, in 1913, Reverend John H. Hutton gave the most accurate understanding of the topography of *Inferno* 3:

> In Dante's great poem, the neutrals, those who in this world had never taken a side, occupy the mouth and vestibule of Hell. There they swirl unceasingly in clouds of red sand, their faces bitten by wasps and hornets. They pursue in a blind fatal way a flag which never stays for a moment in one place.
>
> Dante denies them the moral dignity of a place even in hell itself. 'Heaven will not have them, and the deep Hell receives them not lest the wicked there should have some glory over them' — lest the wicked, that is, looking at these neutrals, should be able to feel that there were souls worse than themselves.
>
> And what was the sin of these neutrals? Oh, simply this: they had never taken a side. They had spent God's precious moment, which is our life, they had spent it watching which way the wind was likely to blow.[29]

While Hutton's accuracy could be considered superior to Vines's lack of fidelity to Dante's infernal topography, this tendency is nonetheless faithful to the poet's location of the cowards in an extremity of hell. The hyperbolic claims of heat or depth mean to convey that these are the worst places of hell. Such a sense resonates with the poet's damning treatment of these souls in other ways: namely, their exclusion from the rings of hell, but in an abstract sense, their anonymous fate. There is nothing worse than being damned to Dante's hell and not being remembered by name in his book of eternity. Their exceptional status is also conveyed by Dante in an adjective, 'cattivi' ('the evil ones') which he uses only *once* in all of the *Inferno*, remarkably: 'questa era la setta d'i *cattivi*' ('this company contained the evil ones', *Inf.* 3.62, my translation). 'Cattivo,' the singular form of this adjective, is employed in the same canto to describe the neutral angels: 'Mischiate sono a quel *cattivo* coro | de li angeli che non furon ribelli' ('They now commingle with the evil angels', *Inf.* 3. 37, my translation). That 'cattivo' can be taken to signify 'vile' in Italian, but also 'misero' (v. 34) or 'triste' (v. 35), as Umberto Bosco and Giovanni Reggio claim, conveys here the unique nature of these damned souls as repugnant to Dante in their misery and their evil.[30] The exceptional status of the cowards in Dante's poem is conveyed in their location, their psychic state, and the permanent erasure of their identity, the loss of fame and reputation. These variations within sermons and political discourse attempt to convey the exceptional nature of cowardice by mistaking Dante's infernal topography in ways that are consonant with the poet's contempt for these souls.

Cowardice in America: Philosophers and Gender Theorists

Whether to rouse their listeners to action, or to criticize colleagues in the Senate or world leaders on the international stage, the speeches that appropriate *Inferno* 3 which have been explored so far share one common characteristic: they are intended for an audience of their peers. Attacking one's colleagues in the field by means of *Inferno* 3 is also in the spirit of what we find in the American academy at the turn of the twenty-first century. This is the spirit in which Martha Nussbaum, writing her book *Sex and Social Justice*, would take up Dante again, when bringing up the issue of how Westerners address injustice against women in non-Western cultures. On the one hand, she writes, one cannot rush to judge traditions of other cultures as necessarily retrograde, as this resonates with colonialism. Yet, to say that a certain practice is fine because it is endorsed locally, is to risk withholding critical judgement where real evil and oppression are present. She writes:

> To avoid the whole issue because the matter of proper judgment is so fiendishly difficult is tempting but perhaps the worst option of all. It suggests the sort of moral collapse depicted by Dante when he describes the crowd of souls who mill around in the vestibule of hell, dragging their banner now one way, now another, never willing to set it down and take a definite stand on any moral or political question. Such people, he implies, are the most despicable of all. They cannot even get into hell because they have not been willing to stand for anything in life, one way or another. To express the spirit of this chapter very succinctly, it is better to risk being consigned by critics to the 'hell' reserved for alleged Westernizers and imperialists — however unjustified such criticism would in fact be — than to stand around in the vestibule waiting for a time when everyone will like what we are going to say. And what we are going to say is: that there are universal obligations to protect human functioning and its dignity, and that the dignity of women is equal to that of men. If that involves assault on many local traditions, both Western and non-Western, so much the better, because any tradition that denies these things is unjust. [...] The situation of women in the contemporary world calls urgently for moral standtaking.[31]

What was Dante's anonymous mass of individuals following a collective banner becomes the listless, feckless individuals of Nussbaum's moment of 'moral collapse', dragging their own individual banners.

In the same year that *Sex and Justice* was published, Nussbaum reviewed Judith Butler's work *Excitable Speech* in *The New Republic*. In it, she criticizes Butler for her 'quietism', a word that is used six times in her review. She writes:

> The big hope, the hope for a world of real justice, where laws and institutions protect the equality and the dignity of all citizens, has been banished, even perhaps mocked as sexually tedious. Judith Butler's hip quietism is a

comprehensible response to the difficulty of realizing justice in America. But it is a bad response. It collaborates with evil. Feminism demands more and women deserve better.[32]

It is a review that earned Nussbaum the ire not only of Butler, but of Spivak and several others, who published their rebuttals in a subsequent issue.

Nussbaum's take on *Inferno* 3 is both close to and far from Dante's poem in several ways. She misunderstands the contrapasso entirely, especially as regards the presence of multiple banners. Yet her understanding that silence and quietism are a form of intellectual and political inaction resonates strongly with the poem, especially with the Reverend King's modification of Spring's quotation ('There comes a time when silence becomes betrayal'). It does not mention the element of 'moral crisis' which Spring introduced into its afterlife, but the idea of 'moral collapse', of meaningless individual political conviction, is close. Applying these words to moments of moral crisis is the postmodern mode of appropriating Dante to urge justice and to expedite its realization.

Cowardice in America: Responding to Political and Racial Injustice during the Trump Administration

The long afterlife of the *ignavi* in American discourse begs a question: would *Inferno* 3 have gained as much traction in our modern political imagination without Spring's introduction of the idea of moral crisis? Certainly the phrase 'moral crisis' endows it with a power of persuasion which lends it to political rhetoric. I will illustrate the persuasive force of a 'moral crisis' through a specific example from American politics — one from the beginning of the Trump administration — and probe how the political imperative of *Inferno* 3 can be used as a lens for judging action within the civic sphere.[33]

It was hard not to hear the dilemma presented by *Inferno* 3 — that of the absolute responsibility to act within the civic realm for the public good — in the words of James Comey, former director of the FBI, when he testified: 'No action was the most important thing I could do to make sure there was no interference in the investigation' (8 June 2017).[34] Comey's decision not to act in the moment he describes here (namely as regards Russian interference) and, alternatively, to act (as in the disclosure of the Clinton emails, as well as in his decision to testify) were judged in the public sphere variously as cowardice and courage. It raises the question: was Comey's decision not to act in that precise moment — in what many would call a moment of moral crisis — a missed opportunity to act in the name of the civic good? Or was it an example of how Comey 'bent his mind towards the good', and is the former FBI director more of a Farinata degli Uberti than the Pontius Pilate of our times? While Comey's role in the turbulent beginnings of the Trump administration will most likely ensure the permanence of his name in American history, one rightly wonders if his decision not to act at a crucial moment in the American democratic process would be judged by Dante in the same harsh terms.

Four years later, Dante's idea of cowardice can still be found in the American political sphere — this time, in an explicit, literal fashion. While the appropriation of *Inferno* 3 appeared in resistance efforts and demonstrations protesting against the 2016 American presidential election, it has resurfaced in the Black Lives Matter movement, as politicians and protestors speak against acts of violence and murder in the policing of African-American citizens. An example of this most recent appropriation can be found in the words of California Governor Gavin Newsom when he spoke against the carotid restraint, a type of chokehold that compresses the carotid artery resulting in unconsciousness, brain injury, or death, during a press conference on 5 June 2020.[35] Addressing the broader systemic racism that leads to acts of brutality, Governor Newsom exhorted his Californians to bring about change and reform promptly through deeds, and not just words: 'The black community does not need to change. We need to change [...] We can't be long on rhetoric and short on results.'[36] To convey the urgency of this request, Governor Newsom reiterated JFK's famous words: 'Dante infamously said that the hottest place in hell is reserved for those in a time of moral crisis that maintain their neutrality. This is not the time to be neutral.'[37] Governor Newsom's speech bears authority in its adherence to the tradition of American political speeches citing *Inferno* 3. Its force lies in its fidelity to that literally unfaithful, yet 'spiritually' correct, interpretation of Dante's cowards, one that has gained authority over generations of its usage. It is a rhetorical tradition that pits individualism versus collectivism, and thought versus action, in ways that resonate with Dante's original poem — and in ways that are heard. Like the early debates on slavery during the nineteenth century, which were revived in the words of JFK and MLK, Dante's definition of cowardice has become America's final word on the perils of neutrality during racial injustice. Across centuries and borders, Dante's political ethics have become America's call to social justice — whether or not such calls are effective.

Notes to Chapter 24

1. To this list, one might also add Samuel Beckett's play *Waiting for Godot*. See Lois A. Cuddy, 'Beckett's "Dead Voices" in *Waiting for Godot*: New Inhabitants of Dante's *Inferno*', in *Modern Language Studies*, 12.2 (1982), 48–60, who reads the sense of futility in this existential play in light of Dante's neutral angels and cowards.
2. Eliot features the following note for verse 63 of the *Wasteland*: 'Cf. *Inferno* III, 55–57: "si lunga tratta | di gente, ch'io non avrei mai creduto | che morte tanta n'avesse disfatta."' See Eliot, *The Waste Land* (New York: W. W. Norton, 2001), p. 22. Also see Nick Havely, *Dante's British Public: Readers and Texts, from the Fourteenth Century to the Present* (Oxford: Oxford University Press, 2014), pp. 269–70, and Michael Aeschliman, 'The Heirs of Canto III of Dante's *Inferno*', *Lectura Dantis*, 2 (1988), 5–14, which takes inspiration from Eliot.
3. As Eliot himself notes in his essay, 'What Dante Means to Me', he meant for the reader to understand his allusion to *Inferno* 3: 'Certainly I have borrowed lines from him, in the attempt to reproduce, or rather to arouse in the reader's mind the memory of, some Dantesque scene, and thus establish a relationship between the medieval inferno and modern life. Readers of my *Waste Land* will perhaps remember that the vision of my city clerks trooping over London Bridge from the railway station to their offices evoked the reflection 'I had not thought death had undone so many' [...] And I gave the references in my notes, in order to make the reader who recognized the allusion, know that I meant him to recognize it, and know that he would have missed the

point if he did not recognize it.' (*To Criticize the Critic and Other Writings* (Lincoln: University of Nebraska Press, 1965), p. 128)

4. Some landmark contributions to this debate include Francesco Mazzoni, *Saggio di un nuovo commento alla 'Divina Commedia': 'Inferno'* — *Canti I–III* (Florence: Sansoni, 1967), pp. 390–415; Giorgio Padoan, 'Colui che fece per viltà il gran rifiuto', *Studi Danteschi*, 38 (1961), 75–128; and Maria Simonelli, *Lectura Dantis Americana: 'Inferno' III* (Philadelphia: University of Pennsylvania Press, 1993), pp. 41–58.
5. 'They had as much time as they needed, and the thunderstorm would only come towards evening, and cowardice was, undoubtedly, one of the most terrible of vices. Thus spoke Yeshua Ha-Nostri. *No, philosopher, I disagree with you: it is the most terrible vice!*' (Mikhail Bulgakov, *Master and Margarita*, trans. by Diana Burgin and Katherine O'Connor (New York: Vintage, 1996), p. 272 (emphasis added))
6. Dan Brown, *Inferno* (New York: Doubleday Books, 2013), p. 1.
7. Barolini writes: 'This vestibule of Hell dramatizes Dante's commitment to commitment.' Teodolinda Barolini, *'Inferno* 3: Crossings and Commitments', *Commento Baroliniano*, Digital Dante (New York, NY: Columbia University Libraries, 2018), <https://www.digitaldante.columbia.edu/dante/divine-comedy/inferno/inferno-3/> [accessed 28 September 2019].
8. Brown, *Inferno*, p. 463.
9. *Inferno* 3's afterlife thus adheres with how Elizabeth Coggeshall describes the faithful, or amplified, 'acoustics' in Dante's *fortuna* that exist alongside unliteral, unfaithful, or distorting sounds generated by later appropriations, in here contribution to this volume. She writes: 'New audiences expose and respond to the text in unforeseeable and generative ways, filling in or creating new meanings according to the ambient noise of their own environments. These unpredictable resonances can both enhance and destabilize the text's original sound.' The many examples surveyed in this chapter affirm the poet's definition of cowardice, though their incorrect characterizations of the canto's depiction of the cowards are often jarring.
10. For a wide-ranging history of cowardice which takes inspiration from Dante's poem, especially how Dante's idea of cowardice differs from what can be found in William Shakespeare, Søren Kierkegaard and Henry James, see Chris Walsh, *Cowardice: A Brief History* (Princeton, NJ: Princeton University Press, 2014), pp. 181–83.
11. All citations are taken from the Giorgio Petrocchi edition of Dante's *Commedia*, and all English translations are by Allen Mandelbaum.
12. Dante Alighieri, *Convivio*, ed. by Cesare Vasoli and Domenico de Robertis, in *Dante Alighieri, Opere minori*, II.I (Milan and Naples: Ricciardi, 1995), p. 218. English translations of the *Convivio* by Richard Lansing: see Dante Alighieri, *Il Convivio (The Banquet)*, trans. by Richard H. Lansing (London: Taylor & Francis, 1990).
13. Teodolinda Barolini, '*Inferno* 6: The City', *Commento Baroliniano*, Digital Dante (New York, NY: Columbia University Libraries, 2018), <https://www.digitaldante.columbia.edu/dante/divine-comedy/inferno/inferno-6/> [accessed 9 April 2021].
14. John Freccero, 'Dante and the Neutral Angels', *Romanic Review*, 51 (1960), 3–14. Freccero argues that Dante here departed from medieval theological tradition by arguing that the neutral angels did not rebel, but were for themselves 'per sé fuoro' (*Inf.* 3. 39), thereby not siding with the angels who were with God nor those who rebelled from God.
15. Marc Cogan argues that these souls were never alive, according to Dante, since they never acted upon their appetites, the defining characteristic of animal life. See Marc Cogan, *The Design in the Wax* (Notre Dame, IN: University of Notre Dame Press, 1999), pp. 297–98.
16. 'Sicut autem per praesumptionem aliquis excedit proportionem suae potentiae, dum nititur ad maiora quam possit; ita etiam pusillanimus deficit a proportione suae potentiae, dum recusat in id tendere quod est suae potentiae commensuratum' [Now just as presumption makes a man exceed what is proportionate to his power, by striving to do more than he can, so pusillanimity makes a man fall short of what is proportionate to his power, by refusing to tend to that which is commensurate thereto] (St Thomas Aquinas, *Summa Theologica*, 3 vols (New York: Benziger Bros, 1941), II-II, quaestio 133, 1). Translation by Fr. Laurence Shapcote, ed. and rev. by The Aquinas Institute, 2020, <https://www.aquinas.cc/la/en/~ST.II-II> [accessed on 9 April 2021].

17. Arthur M. Schlesinger, Jr., states that Kennedy wrote 'The hottest places in Hell are reserved for those who, in a period of moral crisis, maintain their neutrality' in a loose-leaf notebook of quotations Kennedy kept in 1945–46, attributing the phrase to Dante. See Schlesinger, *A Thousand Days: John F. Kennedy in the White House* (New York: Greenwich House, 1983), p. 105.
18. Deborah Parker, 'The Historical Presidency: JFK's Dante', *Presidential Studies Quarterly*, 48.2 (2018), 357–72. Parker examines the numerous contexts in which JFK spoke this phrase. See 'Kennedy, Cutler, Wolfson Feted by Anti-Bias Group',' *Boston Globe*, 17 February 1956, p. 4 (quoted by Parker, p. 361 n. 6), for the account of the event hosted by the National Conference of the Christians and the Jews. Also see *The Yale Book of Quotations*, ed. by Fred R. Shapiro (New Haven, CT: Yale University Press, 2006), p. 420, which locates this phrase in a speech JFK delivered in a speech given in Tulsa, Oklahoma on 16 September 1959, which was printed in John F. Kennedy, *The Strategy of Peace*, ed. by Allen Nevins (New York: Harper & Brothers, 1960).
19. See Henry Powell Spring, *What is Truth?* (Winter Park, FL: The Orange Press, 1944), p. 272.
20. According to the Google News Archives, the quotation appears in a letter to the editor titled 'Is Bipartisanship Leaving Voter without a Choice?' on 30 November 1954, in the *Milwaukee Sentinel*. See 'Letters to The Sentinel', pt 1, p. 10, col. 5: 'The hottest places in hell are reserved for those who, in a period of moral crisis, maintain their neutrality.' The date of this letter, which precedes Kennedy's first public use of the quotation in 1956, demonstrates that the president was not the only source for the mainstream public. It also appears even earlier, in 1944, in a newspaper from Pampa, Texas, dated July 10, 1944: 'Dante is quoted as saying, "The hottest places in Hell are reserved for those who, in a period of moral crisis, maintain their neutrality." No one would contend that this column or this newspaper has been neutral.' *The Pampa News*, 'Common Ground' column, by R. C. Hoiles: 'No Neutrality', p. 4, col. 2. Found by the 'Quote Investigator', <https://www.quoteinvestigator.com/2015/01/14/hottest/#note-10413-7> [accessed 1 October 2019].
21. King delivered this speech at the Ebenezer Baptist Church in Atlanta, Georgia, on 30 April 1967. He also gave a version of this speech in Riverside Church, New York, on 4 April 1967. The audio transcript of the Reverend's speech from 30 April 1967, is held in the Martin Luther King, Jr. Research and Education Institute in Stanford University, <http://www.okra.stanford.edu/en/permalink/document670430-002> [accessed 1 October 2019].
22. Future research should determine whether or not the phrase 'moral crisis' is combined with this reference to the 'lowest places of Hell' before Spring's book.
23. Theodore Roosevelt, *America and The World War* (New York: Charles Scribner's Sons), p. xi (emphasis added). See Parker's discussion of Franklin D. Roosevelt's 1936 speech which cites Dante; 'The Historical Presidency', pp. 367–68.
24. See Akash Kumar, 'Teddy Roosevelt, Dante, and the Man in the Arena', for a discussion of Roosevelt's profound and long-term engagement with Dante's poem. *Digital Dante* (New York, NY: Columbia University Libraries, 2018), <https://www.digitaldante.columbia.edu/history/teddy-roosevelt-dante-kumar/> [accessed 9 April 2021].
25. Joshua Matthews, 'The Divine Comedy as an American Civil War Epic', *J19: The Journal of Nineteenth-Century Americanists*, 1.2 (2013), 315–37.
26. See Dennis Looney, *Freedom Readers: The African American Reception of Dante Alighieri and the Divine Comedy* (Notre Dame, IN: University of Notre Dame Press, 2011), pp. 30–32. See Charles Sumner, *His Complete Works,* (New York: Negro Universities Press, 1900), p. 48. As Looney notes, Sumner cites a translation of Dante by Thomas Brooksbank.
27. Looney, *Freedom Readers*, p. 32. Sumner stated: 'Let it [Congress] now take stand between the living and dead, and cause this plague to be stayed. All this it can do; and if the interests of Slavery were not hostile, all this is would do at once, in reverent regard for justice law, and order, driving far away all alarms of war; nor would it dare to brave the shame and punishment of the "Great Refusal."' (Sumner, *His Complete Works*, p. 245) See also Looney's contribution to this volume, which outlines how Dante and African American culture were linked politically between abolitionists and Italian nationalists in the nineteenth century.
28. *The Wilmington Morning Star*, 1 July 1917, p. 10, col. 1.

29. Rev. John A. Hutton, *At Close Quarters* (London: Robert Scott, 1913), p. 101.
30. See Dante Alighieri, *La Divina Commedia*, ed. by Umberto Bosco and Giovanni Reggio (Florence: Le Monnier, 1988), pp. 37–38 n. 34.
31. Martha Nussbaum, *Sex and Social Justice* (Oxford: Oxford University Press, 1999), pp. 30–31.
32. 'The Professor of Parody', *The New Republic*, 22 February 1999.
33. As I was completing the final revisions on this essay, I encountered Laura Ingallinella's engaging survey of *Inferno* 3 and American politics in her blog post, 'The Hottest Place in Hell: Neutrality and the Politicization of Dante in the United States', 8 June 2020, <https://www.lauraingallinella.org/2020/06/08/hottest-place-in-hell-dante-neutrality/> [accessed 9 April 2021].
34. The redacted transcript of Comey's testimony on 8 June 2017: <https://www.assets.documentcloud.org/documents/5470646/Comey-Interview-12-7-18-Redacted.pdf> [accessed 9 April 2021].
35. Also see Guy Raffa's essay on Governor Newsom's speech, 'There's a Special Place in Dante's *Inferno* for Wafflers and Neutral Souls', *Zócalo*, 31 August 2020, <https://www.zocalopublicsquare.org/2020/08/31/dante-divine-comedy-2020-neutrality/ideas/essay/> [accessed 9 April 2021].
36. 'Gov. Gavin Newsom calls for end of carotid artery restraint by police', by Sue Dremann, *Palo Alto Weekly*, 5 June 2020, <https://www.paloaltoonline.com/news/2020/06/05/gov-gavin-newsom-calls-for-end-of-carotid-artery-restraint-by-police> [accessed 9 April 2021].
37. 'Gov. Gavin Newsom directs California police officers to stop training use of carotid chokehold', by Alix Martichoux, ABC News, 5 June 2020, <https://www.abc7news.com/governor-press-conference-today-time-newsom-george-floyd-black-lives-matter-phase-3/6233198/> [accessed 9 April 2021].

CHAPTER 25

Dante Today: Tracking the Global Resonance of the *Commedia*

Elizabeth Coggeshall

No fictional text has resonated across global cultures quite like Dante's *Commedia*. The poem emits different frequencies within each unique cultural chamber in which it resounds, its music mingling with the sounds of the culture through which it echoes. New audiences expose and respond to the text in unforeseeable and generative ways, filling in or creating new meanings according to the ambient noise of their own environments. These unpredictable resonances can both enhance and destabilize the text's original sound. Recuperating the benefits of the 'noise' of transhistorical and transcultural difference on the reception of a text, Wai Chee Dimock argues that a text's acoustics are enriched by the ambient sounds of the new interpretative contexts it reaches, as the text resounds across time and space.[1] The trouble with textual resonance, though, is that it undermines the stability of a text's intended meaning. Dimock explains, 'Across time, every text must put up with readers on different wavelengths, who come at it tangentially and tendentiously, who impose semantic losses as well as gains. Across time, every text is a casualty and a beneficiary.'[2] This development might not please all authors themselves, who may wish to insulate their texts against this kind of instability, preserving the clarity of their resounding voices, so that the text 'sounds' precisely as they meant it to.

As a poet with a clear moral agenda, Dante was particularly attuned to the problem of his audience's potential for mishearing. His direct addresses to the reader and his frequent instruction for proper readerly disposition act as safeguards against lapses of attention or understanding. As the mastermind behind the world of the *Commedia*, Dante appears to have desired his poem to have one clear, discoverable meaning, a lesson that would be communicated through a single channel, to a particular reader, who would unveil the unified substance of the text's language. Indeed, if we are to attribute the Epistle to Cangrande to the poet, we see exacting measures on the poet's part to exert control over the meanings that could be received through a correct hearing of the text, with nothing less at stake than the very salvation of his listener's soul.

Pace Dante and his fourfold allegorical mode of reading, this is not what the afterlife of the *Commedia* bears out. For all his efforts to channel the way his poem would resonate, he also built into the *Commedia* an incompleteness that insists upon its audience's active participation. The mechanisms of the poem that ask us to complete them — its allegory and figurality, its explicit addresses to the reader, its multisensorial appeal, and its insistent forward motion, looking back as it spirals ahead — are some of the same mechanisms that enable an open-ended and seemingly endless string of adaptations, translations, appropriations, and remixes of the work.

The holdings of the digital archive *Dante Today: Citings and Sightings of Dante's Works in Contemporary Culture* signal the consequences and the reach of this transmedial, transhistorical and transnational phenomenon. The website, created in 2006 by Arielle Saiber of Bowdoin College, and co-directed by Saiber and me since 2012, is a curated and crowd-sourced digital repository that catalogues references to Dante and his works in twentieth- and twenty-first-century culture. Although the holdings currently number over 1,400 posts, the archive is not exhaustive; it is in continual evolution as new works are discovered and generated. Because it relies on crowdsourcing and is curated by two American scholars, the materials collected in the archive thus far have a bias towards European and American content, but we actively solicit submissions from regions currently underrepresented in the archive. The goals of the site are twofold: first, to provide a central access point for this eclectic and ever-changing body of references; and second, to offer data that students and scholars can use to think about the enduring afterlife of Dante's works in relation to reception theory, resonance, and cultural studies.

Using the archive's holdings as my point of departure, I will present an overview of how Dante's works — especially the *Commedia* — resonate across contemporary media and cultures. In what follows, I will focus on two vectors offered by the archive: first, the site's tags, which give an indication of the Dantesque trends that are particularly resonant across contemporary cultural spaces, and which occasionally even generate their own feedback loops. Second, I will look at the site's map, where we track the origin of our posts, and which gives an (incomplete) idea of which contemporary cultural spaces are most sensitive to the resonant effects of Dante's poem. Ultimately, I aim to show how the archive records the amplifications produced by the *Commedia*'s resounding, its generative reverberations enabled by what I would argue is the incompleteness of the poem's form.

Dante Today: The Tags

Looking over the archive's tag cloud (Figure 25.1), one immediately sees — as would be expected — that *Inferno* dominates. The current count on the site (as of the writing of this chapter) is 485 posts, compared to only fifty-seven for *Purgatorio* and sixty-three for *Paradiso*. Many of those posts tagged 'Inferno' are also tagged 'Hell' (256 posts), a label we use to differentiate the place from the canticle. 'Circles of Hell', with 190 posts, is on the rise, as I will discuss below. The most popular

> FREQUENT TAGS
>
> 2004 2006 2007 2008 2009 2010 2011
> 2012 2013 2014 2015 2016 2017 2018
> 2019 2020 Abandon All Hope America Art
> Artists Beatrice Blogs Books California Children
> Circles of Hell Comics Dance Dark Wood
> Divine Comedy England Fiction Films Florence
> France Games Gates of Hell Hell History
>
> Humor Illustrations Inferno Internet
>
> Italy Journalism Journeys Literature Love
> Music Mystery New York New York City Non-
> Fiction Novels Paintings Paradise Paradiso
> Performance Art Poetry Politics Purgatorio
> Purgatory Religion Restaurants Reviews Rock
> Science Fiction Sculptures Sins Social Media
> Technology Television Tenth Circle Theater
> Translations United Kingdom United States
> Universities Video Games Virgil

FIG. 25.1. Tag Cloud, *Dante Today* [image captured 2 October 2020].

genres we see are Journalism (128), Novels (ninety-three), Films (ninety-one), Fiction (eighty-two), Reviews (seventy-one), Comics (seventy), Illustrations (sixty-nine), Theater (sixty-six), Poetry (sixty-two), Music (fifty-seven), Blogs (thirty-eight), Video Games (thirty-eight), Sculptures (thirty-one), Social Media (thirty-one), Games (thirty), and Non-Fiction (twenty-eight).

Most often the title 'Inferno' or 'Dante's Inferno' comes to stand in as a metonym for heat and fire, as is the case with the UK's fire home protection system 'Dante', the flame-coloured iris called 'Dante's Inferno', or 'Dante's Inferno Room', the flame-topped (but notably air-conditioned) nightclub featured in the 1988 film *Beetlejuice*. The heat of hellfire is used as a marketing tool to sell 'Dan•T's Inferno' hot sauces and the cinnamon candies 'Dante's Inferno Balls'. On a sombre note, we find references to Dante in blogposts and journalistic coverage of fires around the globe. An evacuee of the 2018 Camp Fire that ravaged Paradise, California, commented, 'It looked just like Dante's *Inferno*.'[3] A March 2017 fire in a Guatemalan youth home evoked a similar comparison, as have fires in Santa Olga, Chile (2009); in Nairobi's open-air market (2018); on the savannah in the Serengeti desert (2017); and in a bar called 'Dante's' in Seattle, Washington (2015).[4] In each of these cases, not only was the word 'inferno' invoked to describe the fires, but each also contains pointed invocations of the poet and his particular vision of the underworld.

Indeed, many natural disasters and other calamities invoke Dante's name and title as a descriptor for suffering on a grand scale. The title of the poem resonates with the catastrophic imaginations of late twentieth- and twenty-first-century thought, as Dante's name and title are applied to scenes of war and devastation, both manmade and not: migrants' camps in Turkey and Congo, for example;[5] a rubbish heap in Cambodia;[6] Indonesian slaughterhouses;[7] Venezuelan prisons;[8] the Soviet Gulag.[9] In the 1977 *New York Times* review of Michael Herr's *Dispatches*, a book of literary reportage covering the Vietnam War, the reviewer compares the reporter to the pilgrim, claiming, 'It is as if Dante had gone to hell with a cassette recording of Jimi Hendrix and a pocketful of pills: our first rock-and-roll war, stoned murder.'[10] The paradigm that informs Dante's political invectives in the *Commedia* stimulates similar critique among contemporary political commentators.[11]

One of the most striking political catastrophes to be given extensive treatment along the lines of Dante's *Commedia* is the punitive structure of the American prison system, in Columbia University law professor Robert A. Ferguson's comprehensive study *Inferno: An Anatomy of American Punishment*. Ferguson dives deeply into the theory of punishment that undergirds both Dante's *Inferno* and *Purgatorio*, calling for penal reforms that would model justice on purgatorial rather than infernal modes of thought, a framework that would give way to rehabilitation, treatment, and a reinvestment in human dignity. The tendency to compare the *Inferno* to cataclysmic events and circumstances wrought by humans on other humans, or on their world, is justified by the poem itself. The *Inferno* is, in many ways, a sociological and psychological study on the levels of injustice to which we willingly subject our fellows, our cities, and ourselves, and, even if the contemporary recollections of the poem's title relate to it in name only, they chart a path that follows the agenda set by the poet, an invective motivated by hope for change.

These are not the only modern 'hells' to which Dante's name is applied: on the lighter side of doom we find the *Inferno* called forth as a comparison for office meetings,[12] cubicles,[13] difficult puzzles,[14] and zombie apocalypse.[15] From the data gathered so far in the archive, the tendency to use the title *Dante's Inferno* to satirize all manner of hells-on-earth flourishes in the irreverent American cultural environment. The vast majority of our posts tagged 'Humor' (currently numbering 241 posts) come primarily from American authors, and Saiber has recently contributed an essay to a volume on satire in Dante that uses the materials from *Dante Today* to comment on Dante's role in American humour. Americans, it seems, enjoy repurposing Dante's schemata as a vehicle for satire about contemporary life, for a number of reasons that Saiber suggests in her essay: its inclusion of the reader in its world-building, its easy straddling of high and low cultures, its highly visual nature, its authority as part of the world canon, its neat-and-tidy system of punishment.[16]

The hierarchical and meticulous system of Dante's hell, where each crime is met with its precise punishment, is among the features most frequently extracted from the text and manipulated to humorous effect. Consider, for example, the punishments inflicted on abusers of technology in Con Chapman's so-called 'Three

Lost Cantos from Dante's *Inferno*'.[17] Writing in rhymed couplets, Chapman subjects his sinners to punishments meted out in a measure that equals their technological crimes: loud-mouthed braying for incessant cell-phone-users, crowds of 'fast-talking mimes' for email users who indiscriminately 'replied-all', and boiling coffee for those who clogged up the line at Starbucks. Even more explicit in its repurposing of Dante's theory of contrapasso is *The Simpsons*' episode 'Treehouse of Horror IV' (28 October 1993), in which Homer Simpson, after losing his soul to the devil (in the person of Ned Flanders) in a bargain over a doughnut, is banished to hell for a day, pending his trial. In hell, he enters the Ironic Punishment Division of Hell Labs — a clear marker of Dante's direct influence — and is subjected to a machine that force-feeds him doughnuts. Even the demon that oversees his 'punishment' is stunned at Homer's bottomless capacity, as he smilingly gulps stack after stack of the demon's pink-glazed rings.

In stark contrast to those posts which highlight 'The Devil', 'Demons', 'Punishment', and 'Hell', is an ever-growing number of materials that use Dante's works to meditate on love and desire, such as the stunning Valentino dress donned by Rachel McAdams at the 2016 Met Gala, adorned with swirling verses from *Inferno* 5; Dolce & Gabbana's 'Alta Moda' collection of Fall 2015, designed to remix Homer's augury, Shakespeare's humour, and Dante's beauty; jeweller Donna Distefano's 'Elixir of Love' ring, featuring a griffin in honour of Beatrice and the ascent to Paradise; the San Francisco Ballet Company's performance of Yuri Possokhov's original choreography for Tchaikovsky's symphonic poem *Francesca da Rimini*; or Petra Greule-Bstock's 2013 painting entitled *Beauty Awakens the Soul to Act*, a common English interpretation of *Purgatorio* 18. 19–21 ('L'animo [...] dal piacere in atto è desto'), which can be found all over lists of inspirational quotations attributed to Dante across the Internet.[18]

There is a long-standing American tradition of reading the *Commedia* in an inspirational key, the poem itself acting as Virgil for the reader's individualized inner spiritual pilgrimage.[19] One of the most memorable of these cases from the archive is the blog *Daily Dante*, a collaborative project undertaken by a self-described 'motley band of Dantophiles living in the Princeton, NJ, area'.[20] As a Lenten practice, the authors of the blog undertook a three-part reading exercise, in which they collaboratively read and commented on one canto per day (excluding Sundays) for each of the days of Lent. They completed *Inferno* during the Lenten season of 2010, *Purgatorio* in 2011, and *Paradiso* in 2012. Following in the steps of the poet, the commentators critique the sins of the contemporary world while at the same time performing examinations of their own consciences, assigning culpability where it is due, and seeking to eradicate it by a proper, thoughtful reading of the text. In effect, these bloggers are performing precisely what the poem asks of its reader: to meditate thoroughly on the allegories and figures it presents, to think by analogy with one's own local circumstances, and to apply the lessons of this meditation to train oneself gradually towards correct behaviour.

The *Daily Dante* blog is one of many contemporary examples that appear to think of the *Commedia* as a type of self-help manual. One of the most unabashed of these is Rod Dreher's *How Dante Can Save Your Life: The Life-Changing Wisdom of History's Greatest Poem* (2015).[21] Identifying with Dante's pilgrim in his personal losses, Dreher finds in the *Commedia* a practical manual for overcoming grief. Throughout, Dreher addresses his reader in the second person, dispensing the 'life-changing wisdom' he unearthed in his study of the poem. Dreher has elsewhere described the *Commedia* as 'the ultimate self-help book', claiming that the salvific power of the poem's moral wisdom may draw the reader from despair.[22] Many readers, like Dreher, view the *Commedia* as a guidebook away from grief or depression, or towards inner wisdom and a deeper understanding of one's 'personal myth'.[23] These books, articles, and blogs emphasize the first-person voice of the *Commedia* — the narrative giving landscape to an inward examination of conscience — whose guided self-reflection they choose to imitate. Such readings are divorced from the poem's concerns with language and nation, and invested in a one-to-one identification with the pilgrim, interpreting the allegory through the lens of personal duty towards a moralizing self-improvement project.

A third example of this reading trend (albeit in a different vein) is Joseph Luzzi's memoir *In a Dark Wood: What Dante Taught Me About Grief, Healing, and the Mysteries of Love*. Luzzi, a Dante scholar and professor of *italianistica* in the United States, approaches the poem from a biographical perspective, weaving episodes in the poet's biography together with an intimate portrait of his own personal grief and life experiences. Rather than abstracting the pilgrim from his historical circumstances, as do many of the works that read the poem as a manual for self-discovery and healing, Luzzi's memoir reads his own mourning in analogy with Dante's. Unlike Dreher, Luzzi is adamant: 'The *Divine Comedy* was not a self-help manual.'[24] For Luzzi, the seductive beauty of the poetry is a necessary counterpart to the wisdom it dispenses. The poem marries personal memoir with wise counsel, and employs beauty to disarm readers and dispose them toward receiving its guidance. In all of these cases, the poem's incompleteness is project-oriented, setting for the reader a quest towards the achievement of moral wisdom and inner peace, facilitated by its aesthetic power.

The title of Luzzi's memoir, *In a Dark Wood*, calls to mind another trend we notice in the archive: the variety of Dante 'memes' popular in contemporary discourse, some of which we have begun to track. The Dark Wood is one such meme: the notion of finding oneself in a dark wood has become a cultural touchstone, and references to the dark wood take it as an allegory for sin, surely, but also for grief and depression, general malaise, the solitude of urban life, political injustice, or midlife crisis. Another common place-based meme is the Gate of Hell, which, according to our archive, might be located in Japan, Turkey, Turkmenistan, or Clifton, New Jersey. Other memes we track on the site include verses, like *L'amor che move il sole e l'altre stelle*, or the perennially popular *Lasciate ogne speranza voi ch'intrate*, often shortened to 'abandon all hope', which currently boasts fifty-six posts in English and only eight in Italian (with the caveat that our data skew towards American phenomena).[25] The topography of hell has also generated its own loop that has become particularly resonant in the blogosphere, so much so that it seems to have migrated away from its point of origin. This is the Circles of Hell meme, of which we have currently archived 192 spin-off versions, some of which make reference to Dante's original poem or scheme, others of which blithely ignore it.

Frequently, these transpositions of hell amount to updated visions of hell for the twenty-first century, as we see in the 'Nine NEW Levels of Hell' by *CollegeHumor*'s Nat Towsen.[26] Towsen retains the original number of circles (revising them as 'levels', as is frequently seen across these engagements with the circles meme), but his nine new circles reflect the concerns of his college-aged and educated, middle-class, politically correct readership, who would condemn the behaviour of 'internet commentators' (level four) and those who 'make life harder for homosexuals, ethnic minorities, transgendered people, vegetarians, vegans, intellectuals, German-style board game players, and/or furries' (level eight). Towsen also seems to want to redeem the hipster, or, at least, to move on from the joke cycle surrounding this much-maligned group. His third level is reserved for those 'who use the word "hipster" as an insult', where they are upbraided for their lack of creativity.

Hipsters are not saved from damnation, however; in fact, their own special version of hell awaits them in German webcomic artist Adrian vom Baur's 2013 storyline *Hipsters in Hell*, part of his series *Hipsters*. Here, the hipsters find their own personalized vision of hell, complete with a 'Hell of Ironic Mustaches'[27] and a 'Hell of Fake Vintage Clothes'.[28] Personalized versions of hell such as that built for hipsters is a variant of the 'Circles of Hell' meme that seems to be particularly popular among American authors. Certain peculiarities of Dante's resonance in America contribute to this widespread phenomenon among writers, illustrators, and bloggers. First, American popular culture broadly treats the first canticle as if its full title were *Dante's Inferno*, not *Inferno*, by Dante Alighieri. *Hell is Empty*, a novel in Craig Johnson's Longmire mystery series, gives a version of the hackneyed joke: early in the novel, as one character sits reading the poem, another character inquires after it, saying, 'That book, that *Dante's Inferno*; who wrote that?'[29] The joke, in all its triteness, points to a long treatment of the poem in American mass culture: the presumption that the 'Dante' whose *Inferno* we are witnessing refers not to the author of the text, but only to its pilgrim, whose idiosyncratic vision of hell is narrated across these verses.

According to this assumption, Dante's vision is not a universal one, but is his alone, populated with historical individuals whose identities resonate in a specific way for the particular traveller who encounters them. Each character the pilgrim encounters is both an individual grounded in a distinct historical reality, and an Auerbachian 'figure' of universal and timeless patterns of human existence. Together, these characters become another aspect of the text's incompleteness, a thought experiment for the reader to pursue. The contingency that governs the poem's figural mechanism invites each reader to imagine what his or her own 'inferno' might look like, so readers encounter 'Dante's Inferno' as merely one inferno among many. And so, in addition to Dante's inferno, we find Jimbo's,[30] Anton's,[31] Danton's,[32] another for Stig,[33] one for academics,[34] a few for parents,[35] and a number for Los Angelenos, including Ron Bassilian's graphic novel *Inferno Los Angeles*[36] and Wallace Zane's *Taxi Inferno*,[37] both of which locate hell in twenty-

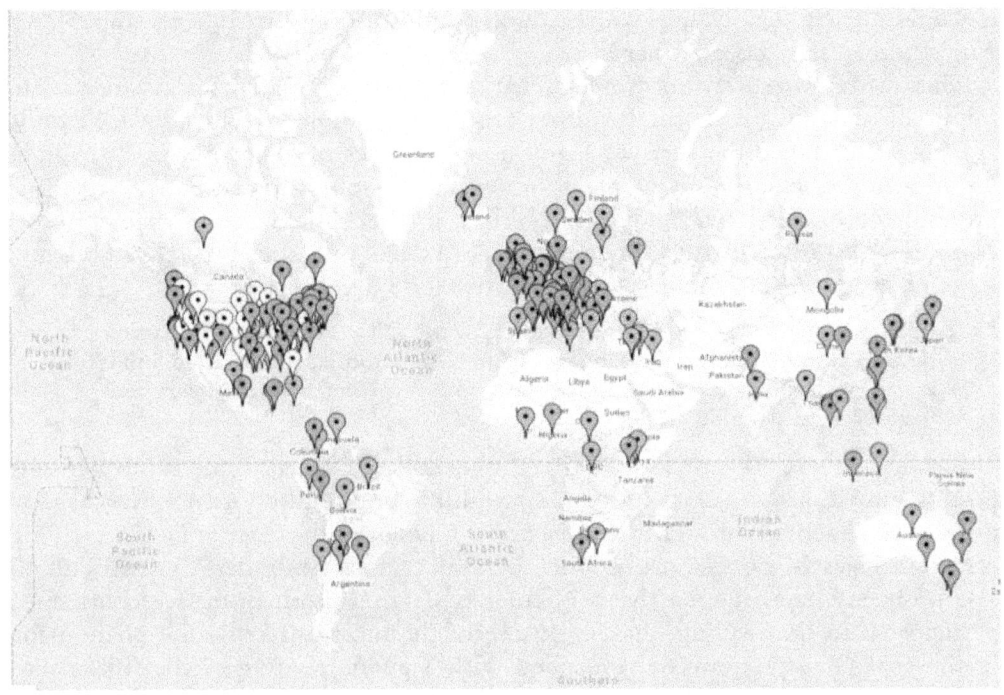

FIG. 25.2. Map of Sightings, *Dante Today* [image captured 2 October 2020].

first-century Los Angeles, and Sandow Birk's *Inferno*,[38] which takes L.A. as the model for a twenty-first-century hell.[39]

Dante Today: The Map

Los Angeles is not the only city that seems to have a particular relationship to Dante and his *Commedia*. In the tag cloud, New York City dwarfs the other cities, with its eighty-five posts.[40] It is followed in the list of cities by Florence (thirty-seven), Los Angeles (sixteen), San Francisco (sixteen), London (fifteen), Rome (thirteen), Boston (ten), Buenos Aires (eight), Bologna (five), Cambridge, Massachusetts (five), Chicago (five), Naples (five), and Venice (four). Beyond these most frequently cited cities, the map feature on *Dante Today* gives a glimpse of the furthest extent of Dante's reach. A glance at Figure 25.2 shows that the map of sightings is dominated by Europe and America. There are a number of factors that contribute to the predominance of European and American sightings: the patterns of Italian migration, both around Europe and into the Americas, especially the United States; the dominance of the notion of a canon of so-called 'Great Books' or *Weltliteratur* in school curricula in Europe and North America; or the mundane facts that the site is housed in the server space of an American university, and its authors and most frequent contributors are American. The practical limitations around crowd-sourced, non-mechanized data collection prevent us from knowing accurately how far Dante's works resonate in the global sphere, but, given the data thus far collected it would appear that Dante's works resonate more loudly in Europe and North America than they do elsewhere.

This picture is surely incomplete. Latin America, with its history of Italian migration and of Catholicism, furnishes a range of examples of which we have only, as of now, scratched the surface. Many new examples have been brought to light — or even generated — by a recent viral phenomenon, initiated by an Argentine professor of Comparative Literature residing in the United States, that lit across Latin America in early 2018. With a series of tweets in Spanish in November and December 2017, Pablo Maurette called for what he described as an

> open, simultaneous, and massive reading of the *Divine Comedy*. One canto per day, beginning on the 1st of January [2018]. One hundred cantos. One hundred days. To participate, you need: 1) the book 2) a brief moment every day 3) Twitter 4) to abandon all hope.[41]

Using the hashtag #Dante2018, Twitter users collectively read one canto per day, posting quotations, illustrations, comments, links, and photos (often selfies) as they progressed together through the *Commedia*. Copies of the *Commedia* were flying off the shelves in bookstores in Buenos Aires.[42] Exact numbers are difficult to assess, but estimates suggest that thousands of Twitter users, from five continents, participated in the reading, making it one of the most unlikely viral phenomena of the year. The programme concluded with a public reading of the final canto in Ravenna on 10 April 2018, with the collaboration of Maurette, the Comune di Ravenna, and Ludovica Ripa di Meana, the poet and widow of esteemed *dantista* Vittorio Sermonti.[43]

In addition to being itself an example of engagement with the poem in the twenty-first century, #Dante2018 also generated its own resonance. Participants responded to their reading with graffiti, comics, Tumblr blogs, public readings and lectures, sketches and doodles, art exhibitions and performances. In sum, the open, simultaneous, massive reading of the poem turned up the volume on Dante's voice: the poem's calls to active readerly engagement coupled with the participatory force of social media made the *Commedia* one of 2018's hottest trending topics in Latin America.

Dante's presence in Latin America is, of course, not a new trend. The archive contains references to Dante from across the region and across diverse media. We are aware of two restaurants that bear the name *Divina Comedia*, in Cusco, Peru, and in Bogotá, Colombia; there are almost certainly more. Argentina offers a stunning architectural example: Palacio Barolo, a 1923 palazzo designed to give architectural form to Dante's cosmology, much like Giuseppe Terragni's projected-but-not-executed plans for the Danteum in Rome (commissioned by Mussolini in 1938);[44] and the ARoS Museum in Denmark, opened in 2004, and explicitly modelled on the tripartite structure of the *Commedia*.[45] From Brazil, hardcore band Sepultura gives us *Dante XXI*, a 2006 album that represents one of many examples of Dante references within the heavy metal subgenre. From Chile comes the work of Raúl Zurita, a political poet and winner of the Chilean National Prize for Literature, whose collections *Purgatorio, Anteparaíso*, and *La vida nueva* take titles (and more) directly from Dante. Again, there are countless other Latin American literary examples that could be cited, with Borges topping the list. These sightings from Latin America, with their broad range of engagement from cursory to extensive, might result from the importation and imposition of (and often resistance to) European cultural frameworks, the traditions of the 'Great Books' and of Roman Catholicism, as well as the long history of Italian migration to the Americas, all of which make Latin America a particularly fertile region for generating creative engagements with Dante's poem.

What, then, can one make of the collections of sightings in East Asia? China, for one, has furnished a few high-concept visual engagements that we see in the archive. Most recently, in 2016, documentary filmmaker Zhao Liang released *Behemoth*, a film commenting on the costs of rapid industrialization in China, as Zhao moves through coalmines in Inner Mongolia using the *Inferno* as a visual reference. Famed Chinese artist and activist Ai Weiwei also used the *Commedia* to comment on current conditions in China, in his 2013 musical album *The Divine Comedy*. Yi Zhou, a Chinese multimedia artist raised in Rome, has released several short films that weave Dante's works through their surrealist visual storytelling: in Yi's seven-and-a-half-minute video short *The Ear* (2009), for example, pop star Pharrell Williams descends through his own severed ear into a hell resembling Cocytus, his descent set to a score by Ennio Morricone. The earliest of the references on the site is the enigmatic work *Discussing the Divine Comedy with Dante*, a 2006 oil-painting-turned-viral-Internet-sensation, co-created by three artists known as Dai Dudu, Li Tiezi and Zhang An. In the style of the eighteenth-century conversation piece, the painting features 103 identifiable figures from political and cultural history, becoming, as one art critic called it, 'a vision of Celebrity Hell'.[46]

Taiwan and China are not the only East Asian nations to engage with Dante in transmedial forms. Much like the video game industry, the anime and manga traditions from Japan and Korea offer a host of characters named after figures from the *Commedia*, especially Dante and Virgil.[47] In contrast to the Chinese examples, which deeply mine their source for visual and thematic inspiration, many of the Japanese and Korean posts we have collected thus far tend to make passing reference to the *Commedia*, littering their texts with character and place names drawn from Dante's world, but with little to no discernible relationship to the original.[48] One case in point is the animated series *Fullmetal Alchemist*, which gives us a female antagonist named Dante who governs seven beings named after each of the seven deadly sins. Likewise, the *Yu-Gi-Oh!* franchise released a set of trading cards with characters named Graff of the Malebranche; Dante, nicknamed 'Traveler of the Burning Abyss'; and Virgil, 'Rock Star of the Burning Abyss'. The visual novel *When Seagulls Cry* features two witches named Beatrice and Virgilia, and a parallel universe called Purgatorio. South Korean webcomic *Refund High School* — in which students earn karma to reincarnate as better versions of themselves — presents an infernal spirit named Dante, who is a fan favourite in spite of his limited appearances in the comic. Each of these examples ostensibly derives from an abstract connection between the name 'Dante' and the notion of evil, and they generally engage the original poem with a light touch.

One exception to the rule of superficiality in the anime-manga reception of Dante's poem is the collected work of Go Nagai, beginning with *Maō Dante* (in English, *Demon Lord Dante*), a 1971 manga inspired by Doré's illustrations of the *Commedia* (as were many examples categorized as 'visual art' on *Dante Today*). Nagai, having been haunted from childhood by Doré's image of Lucifer trapped in an icy hell, envisions an ancient demon named Dante, who had been encased in ice in the Himalayas, only to be resurrected by a young student, Ryō Utsugi.[49] *Maō Dante* was short-lived, running only for the first six months of 1971 and ending suddenly when the magazine in which it was serialized was abruptly discontinued. But Nagai revisited the characters and themes for his classic manga *Debiruman* (*Devilman*), which was serialized between 1972 and 1973. In both works, Nagai treats the ancient dualistic conflict between the forces of Good and those of Evil, often in violent and psychologically troubling ways. Much like Dante's pilgrim, Nagai's protagonists are not heroes, but rather timid or weak figures who must learn to battle inner demons, often figured as external forces that possess the characters. The connections to Dante's original poem are tenuous, perhaps, but the impact of Nagai's importation into Japanese manga of Judaeo-Christian and Dantesque themes, mediated through the visual language of Doré's illustrations, cannot be underestimated.[50]

Conclusion

In spite of the limitations around non-mechanized and crowd-sourced data curation, the *Dante Today* archive documents the rich variety of spaces in which the *Commedia* has resounded around the globe. Each of these specific times and spaces boosts the *Commedia*'s frequencies in disparate ways, allowing these frequencies to stretch further to reach new, differently attuned audiences. The interfering 'noise' of other cultural spaces need not be considered an impediment to but an amplifier of the sounds of a text: 'even as it impinges on texts', Dimock claims, 'even as it reverberates through them, it thickens their tonality, multiplies their hearable echoes, makes them significant in unexpected ways'.[51] This is a desirable, democratizing outcome, tapping into participatory modes in a repetitive, affirmative exercise of generation and destruction.

The *Dante Today* archive attests to the participatory culture engendered by the *Commedia*'s call. For all of Dante's attempts to control the *Commedia*'s reception, he also repeatedly invites — or, better, insists — that his audience listen carefully and respond. The poem calls its hearer to an active engagement, as she fights her way through what is now an archaic vernacular to understand how the figures Dante selects from local Duecento Tuscan history stand in as metonyms for universal conditions of sin. But listening does not end here: in order to accomplish the soul-saving function the poem prescribes, the reader must also reflect on the corresponding habits of thought and mind that characterize such vices in her contemporary age. This reflection stimulates the sort of tangential and tendentious nuances that can undermine textual stability, but which ultimately enhance the text's dynamic range. It is thanks to the poem's built-in incompleteness — its reliance on user participation to respond creatively to its call — that the poem resonates so expansively.⁵²

Notes to Chapter 25

1. Wai Chee Dimock, 'A Theory of Resonance', *PMLA* [*Publications of the Modern Languages Association*], 112.5 (1997), 1060–71.
2. Ibid., p. 1061.
3. Trevor Hughes, '"Like the Gates of Hell Opened Up": Thousands Fled Paradise Ahead of the Camp Fire', *USA Today*, 10 November 2018, <https://www.usatoday.com/story/news/nation-now/2018/11/10/california-fires-thousands-fled-paradise-flames-roared/1962141002/> [accessed 25 September 2020].
4. Each of these cases, with corresponding links, can be found under the tag 'fire' on *Dante Today*: <https://www.research.bowdoin.edu/dante-today/tag/fire/>.
5. Niki Kitsantonis, 'Migrants Reaching Greece Despite Efforts to Block Them', *New York Times*, 18 November 2009, <https://www.nytimes.com/2009/11/19/world/europe/19iht-greece.html> [accessed 25 September 2020]; Tom Miles, 'Congo faces "Dante's Inferno" but shuns U.N. aid effort', *Reuters*, 13 April 2018, < https://www.reuters.com/places/africa/article/us-congo-violence-un/congo-faces-dantes-inferno-but-shuns-u-n-aid-effort-idUSKBN1HK1NL> [accessed 25 September 2020].
6. Nicholas Kristof, 'Where Sweatshops Are a Dream', *New York Times*, 14 January 2009, < https://www.nytimes.com/2009/01/15/opinion/15kristof.html> [accessed 25 September 2020].
7. Emma McDonald, 'A Hero Speaks Up for the Voiceless', *Canberra Times*, 2 July 2011.
8. 'The Fifth Circle of Hell; Prisons in Venezuela', *The Economist*, 16 July 2011, <https://www.economist.com/the-americas/2011/07/14/the-fifth-circle-of-hell> [accessed 25 September 2020].
9. Saul Austerlitz, 'The Highest and Best Circle of Hell', review of Alexander Solzhenitsyn, *The First Circle* (1968), *The Second Pass* (blog), 4 August 2009, <http://www.thesecondpass.com/?p=2165> [accessed 25 September 2020].
10. John Leonard, review of Michael Herr, *Dispatches* (1977), *New York Times*, 28 October 1977, <https://www.nytimes.com/1977/10/28/archives/books-of-the-times.html> [accessed 25 September 2020].
11. On American political commentators' use of Dante to inveigh against moral cowardice, see Kristina Olson's contribution on the reception of *Inferno* 3, chapter 24 in this volume.
12. Ben Brantley, 'Review: "Miles for Mary," a Sendup of the Interminable Meeting from Hell', *New York Times*, 9 October 2016, <https://www.nytimes.com/2016/10/10/theater/review-miles-for-mary-a-sendup-of-the-interminable-meeting-from-hell.html> [accessed 25 September 2020].
13. Carl L. Harshman and Ryan D. Harshman, *Dante's Cubicles* (Bloomington, IN: AuthorHouse, 2015).
14. Tim Depopulos, *Dante's Infernal Puzzle Collection* (London: Carlton Books, 2013).
15. Kim Paffenroth, *Valley of the Dead: The Truth Behind Dante's* Inferno (Brentwood, TN: Permuted Press, 2010).
16. Arielle Saiber, 'Hell, Yes! Dante in Contemporary American Satire', in *Dante satiro: The Concept of Satire in the Middle Ages and in Dante's Works*, ed. Fabian Alfie and Nicolino Applauso (Lanham, MD: Lexington Books, 2020), pp. 171–86.
17. Posted to the blog *Fictionaut* on 2 July 2010, <http://www.fictionaut.com/stories/con-chapman/three-lost-cantos-from-dantes-inferno> [accessed 25 September 2020].
18. For more examples, see the tags 'Love' (<https://www.research.bowdoin.edu/dante-today/tag/love/>) and 'Lust' (<https://www.research.bowdoin.edu/dante-today/tag/lust/>), as well as those items tagged 'Beatrice' (<https://www.research.bowdoin.edu/dante-today/tag/beatrice/>) or 'Paolo and Francesca' (<https://www.research.bowdoin.edu/dante-today/tag/paolo-and-francesca/>).

19. For a related example of the transformative spiritual power of Dante's poem, see Dennis Looney's discussion of Allen Tate's poem 'The Swimmers', chapter 23 in the present volume.
20. Jeff Vamos, 'Welcome, pilgrim', *Daily Dante | Dante as Lenten Spiritual Discipline* (blog), Wordpress <https://www.dailydante.com> [accessed 25 September 2020].
21. See also the volume of the same title, recently published in Italy: Enrico Castelli Gattinara, *Come Dante può salvarti la vita: conoscere fa sempre la differenza* (Florence: Giunti, 2019).
22. Rod Dreher, 'The Ultimate Self-Help Book: Dante's *Divine Comedy*', *The Wall Street Journal*, 18 April 2014, <https://www.wsj.com/articles/the-ultimate-self-help-book-dantes-divine-comedy-1397832431> [accessed 25 September 2020].
23. See, for example, Daniel Dorman, *Dante's Cure: A Journey Out of Madness* (New York: Other Press, 2003); Bonney Gulino Schaub and Richard Schaub, *Dante's Path: A Practical Approach to Achieving Inner Wisdom* (New York: Gotham Books, 2003); and Dennis Patrick Slattery, *Day-to-Day Dante: Exploring Personal Myth Through the* Divine Comedy (Bloomington, IN: iUniverse, 2011). See more at < https://www.research.bowdoin.edu/dante-today/tag/self-help/>.
24. Joseph Luzzi, *In a Dark Wood: What Dante Taught Me About Grief, Healing, and the Mysteries of Love* (New York: HarperCollins, 2015), p. 130. I have elsewhere discussed pedagogical approaches to the works by Dreher and Luzzi in a contribution on 'Dante's Afterlife in Popular Culture', in *Approaches to Teaching Dante's* Divine Comedy, ed. Christopher Kleinhenz and Kristina Olson, 2nd edn (New York: Modern Language Association of America, 2020), pp. 185–91.
25. See the heading 'Important: Quirks to Keep in Mind' on the *User's Guide* page (<https://www.research.bowdoin.edu/dante-today/users-guide/#3>).
26. Nat Towsen, 'The 9 NEW Levels of Hell', *College Humor*, 22 April 2014, <http://www.collegehumor.com/post/6966006/the-9-new-levels-of-hell> [accessed 28 January 2019]; the image is no longer accessible but can be partially visualized at <https://www.collegehumor.tumblr.com/post/83540108288/click-to-see-5-more-the-9-new-levels-of-hell> [accessed 25 September 2020].
27. Adrian vom Baur, *Hipsters in Hell* 22, 2 December 2013, <https://www.hipsters-comic.com/comic/hip151/> [accessed 26 September 2020].
28. Adrian vom Baur, *Hipsters in Hell* 29, 13 January 2014, <https://www.hipsters-comic.com/comic/hip159/> [accessed 26 September 2020].
29. Craig Johnson, *Hell is Empty* (New York: Viking Penguin, 2011), p. 5.
30. Gary Panter, *Jimbo's Inferno* (Seattle: Fantagraphics Books, 2006).
31. Anton Brzezinski, *Anton's Inferno: Dante's Inferno Revisited* (Delirium Publishing, 2008).
32. Danton Walker, *Danton's Inferno: The Story of a Columnist and How He Grew* (New York: Hastings House, 1955).
33. Ty Templeton, *Stig's Inferno*, iss. 1–5 (Vortex Comics, 1984–1986) and iss. 6–7 (Eclipse Comics, 1987).
34. Jorge Cham, 'Dante's Inferno (Academic Edition)', *PhDComics* (2015), <http://www.phdcomics.com/comics.php?f=1813> [accessed 26 September 2020].
35. See, for example, 'Dante's Nine Circles of Hell If He Were a Parent Today', *This Michigan Life*, 8 October 2013, <https://www.thismichiganlife.com/2013/10/modern-parents-take-dantes-nine-circles-hell/> [accessed 26 September 2020]; Meredith Gordon, 'The 9 Circles of Hell for Moms', *Mom.me*, 14 May 2015, <https://www.mom.com/kids/19558-9-circles-hell-moms/> [accessed 26 September 2020]; WandC(D), '9 Circles of Parent Hell', *Wine and Cheese (Doodles)*, 6 March 2015, <https://www.wineandcheesedoodles.com/2015/03/06/9-circles-of-parent-hell/> [accessed 26 September 2020]; Sarah Woodard, 'The 9 Circles of Parenting Hell, Illustrated', *Motherly* (2015), <https://www.mother.ly/parenting/the-9-circles-of-parenting-hell-illustrated/> [accessed 28 January 2019; now partially visible at <https://www.parent.com/the-9-circles-of-parenting-hell-illustrated/> (25 September 2020)]. For more, see the tag 'Parenting' on *Dante Today*, <https://www.research.bowdoin.edu/dante-today/tag/parenting/>. There are currently fifteen examples, all of which play on the 'Circles of Hell' theme.
36. Ron Bassilian and Jim Wheelock, *Inferno: Los Angeles* (Los Angeles: NeoClassics Press, 2013).
37. Wallace Zane, *Taxi Inferno* (CreateSpace Independent Publishing Platform, 2014).
38. Sandow Birk and Marcus Sanders, *Dante's Divine Comedy* (San Francisco: Chronicle Books, 2004–2006). See Akash Kumar's discussion of Birk and Sanders in Chapter 26 of the present volume.

39. On hell and Los Angeles, see also Saiber, 'Hell, Yes!', p. 177.
40. This is, in part, due to the activity of some of our earliest contributors to the crowd-sourced archive. For other peculiarities of the collection, see the heading 'Important: Quirks to Keep in Mind' on the *User's Guide* page (<https://www.research.bowdoin.edu/dante-today/users-guide/#3>).
41. Pablo Maurette (@maurette79). '#Dante2018 será una lectura abierta, simultánea y masiva de La Divina Comedia. Un canto por día empezando el 1° de enero. Cien cantos. Cien días. Para participar necesitan: 1) el libro 2) un ratito todos los días 3) tuiter 4) abandonar toda esperanza.' 5 December 2017. My translation. To see all posts related to #Dante2018, see <https://www.research.bowdoin.edu/dante-today/tag/dante2018/>.
42. 'Una Divina Commedia-maratona social con #Dante2018, 100 canti in 100 giorni', *Ravenna Today*, 5 April 2018, <http://www.ravennatoday.it/cronaca/una-divina-commedia-maratona-social-con-dante2018-100-canti-in-100-giorni.html> [accessed 26 September 2020].
43. Ibid.
44. On the Danteum, see Thomas L. Schumacher, *Terragni's Danteum* (Princeton: Princeton Architectural Press, 2004).
45. Nicolai Hartvig, 'A Bold New Art World Is Lighting Up Western Denmark', *New York Times*, 14 October 2011, <https://www.nytimes.com/2011/10/15/arts/15iht-scdenmark15.html> [accessed 26 September 2020].
46. Alastair Sooke, cited in Matthew Moore, '103 Faces in one Painting', *Telegraph*, 16 March 2009, <https://www.telegraph.co.uk/news/newstopics/howaboutthat/5001462/103-famous-faces-in-one-painting.html> [accessed 26 September 2020]. See also Saiber, 'Hell, Yes!', p. 175.
47. For references to Dante across East Asian anime and manga, I am indebted to the research of Florida State University undergraduate student Savannah Mikus (FSU, '20).
48. Notable exceptions are the writers Kenzaburō Ōe and Natsume Sōseki and visual artist Kazumasa Chiba. See the tag 'Japan' on *Dante Today*, <https://www.research.bowdoin.edu/dante-today/tag/japan/>.
49. Gianluca di Fratta, 'Il fumetto in Giappone: 1) L'evoluzione del manga dagli anni settanta agli anni ottanta', *Il Giappone* 40 (2000), 127–55 (p. 138).
50. See also Go Nagai's *Dante Shinkyoku*, a 1994–95 serialized manga adaptation of the *Divine Comedy*, also inspired by Doré's illustrations.
51. Dimock, 'A Theory of Resonance'., p. 1063.
52. This chapter owes a great debt to the team that has built and maintains the *Dante Today* archive, especially my co-PI on that project, Arielle Saiber. I would also like to acknowledge our IT master, David Israel, and our staff of undergraduate students who have helped to write, categorize, tag, and map the more than 1,400 posts in the archive. A modified version of this work appeared in the 2020 issue of the journal *Italianistica*. My sincere thanks to the issue's editor, Giuseppe Sangirardi, and the editorial team at *Italianistica* for permission to reprint.

CHAPTER 26

Vernacular Hybridity Across Borders: Dante, Amīr Khusrau, Sandow Birk

Akash Kumar

Scholars who have considered a relationship between Dante and India have tended to focus on internal references in the *Commedia* or on reception within and among Indian authors of later periods (especially those of the Bengali Renaissance).[1] In this regard, the work of Ananda Coomaraswamy stands out. A prolific scholar and long-serving curator of the Museum of Fine Arts in Boston in the early part of the twentieth century, Coomaraswamy played an important role in increasing the knowledge of Indian art in the Western world. His scholarship on medieval literature and art regularly featured Dante and put the poet of the *Commedia* in dialogue with the religious traditions of India.

As a representative example, a 1936 article that he published in *Speculum*, 'Two Passages in Dante's Paradiso', makes the case that certain obscure points such as *Paradiso* 27. 136–38 are made more readily accessible by a turn to the Vedic tradition. A *terzina* that is still regarded, in the words of Anna Maria Chiavacci Leonardi's commentary, 'di difficile comprensione' [of difficult comprehension], it describes the daughter of the sun whose white skin turns dark as part of the gradual effect of corruption due to greed. Coomaraswamy first turns to Meister Eckhart as an intertext (an oft-cited reference in his scholarship of the soul's union with God that is likened to the sun swallowing up the dawn), and then to the Hindu mythological tradition that offers up sources that say Dawn is the daughter of the Sun as opposed to its sister. Here is his conclusion:

> We think it has been shown that the references of an exponent of orthodox Christian principles, writing at the end of and as it were resuming all the doctrine of the Middle Ages can actually be clarified by a comparison with those scriptures that were current half the world away and three millenniums earlier in time.[2]

Coomaraswamy's conclusion goes in the direction of a universal language of religion, and while we might rightly quibble with his reductive definition of Dante as 'an exponent of orthodox Christian principles", he does so to argue compellingly that moving out beyond the cultural horizons of Dante's work can have the paradoxical effect of shifting our approach to the *Commedia* itself.

Coomaraswamy's move is both temporal and geographical. In *Amor che move*, Manuele Gragnolati makes use of Donna Haraway's concept of diffractive reading to argue that reading the temporally removed work of Pier Paolo Pasolini and Elsa Morante alongside Dante allows for a model of textual interaction that is not based on linear and material connections, but instead permits a nexus to emerge on issues of the body, performativity, and desire. Far from Coomaraswamy's proposal of a common core of religious meaning and cross-cultural mythologies, Gragnolati uses diffractive reading to, for example, see the final verses of *Paradiso* as reflecting Elsa Morante's concept of the body that 'contenga una profondità affettiva legata alla costituzione intersoggettiva dell'individuo che non si dissolve ma continua a essere parte integrante della gloria'.[3] This refining of perspective to emphasize the affective depth and intersubjective identity of the individual even in the face of a totalizing vision of reality is a stunning result of the practice of diffractive reading that, in a sense, uses insights gained from the reading of twentieth-century Italian texts to reread even the most canonical of moments in Dante's *Commedia*.

I propose to use a combination of Coomaraswamy and Gragnolati's approaches in order to consider first a mode of reading Dante through the lens of the fourteenth-century Indian poet Amīr Khusrau and then to consider in closing how we might modulate our reading of the *Commedia* through select parts of Sandow Birk's visual and textual twenty-first-century American adaptation. In this, I am also guided by the idea of the Global Middle Ages that seeks to expand across cultural borders to study literature, art, history and the like from the period 500–1500 CE. As Geraldine Heng and Lynn Ramey make clear, this does not require giving up fields of national literature in favour of the global, but enhancing them: 'For those of us trained in particular national literatures, languages, and histories, the investigation of globalities yields rewarding glimpses into how the national and global interlock, in literature, and in history.'[4]

It is in this spirit of a global perspective and an interlocking of the local and global that I would like to turn to a fourteenth-century Indian contemporary of Dante. The life of the Delhi poet Amīr Khusrau (1253–1325) aligns almost as neatly with Dante's life (1265–1321) as can possibly be. He was an important poet of the Delhi Sultanate, and an incredibly prolific one at that, so the attention he devoted to matters as varied as astrology, social history, mysticism, politics, linguistics, and beyond makes for an easy affinity with the poet of the *Commedia*. My intention is not to argue for any specific influence or direct connection between the two poets, but rather to suggest a way to expand our critical approach with respect to the historical period in which Dante lived.

I am particularly taken with Amīr Khusrau's insistent lyric hybridity: his necessary adoption of Persian as the language of high culture and court poetry in the Sultanate, but also his apparent continued writing in Hindavi, an Indian language that brought together Persian, Arabic, Turkish, and the local Indian vernacular. His mixing of cultures at the level of vernacular literary production serves as an important paradigm for a pluralistic view of Indian culture with regard to religious and cultural interactions of the age. Alyssa Gabbay calls attention to his mixed ancestry (which she terms 'hybrid') and claims that his 'intimate familiarity with crucial aspects of both Islamicate and Indic life, ranging from language and poetry to the more abstruse elements of their natural sciences, religions, and philosophies, caused him to be a proponent of a new, third culture'.[5] Sunil Sharma points out that the Hindavi corpus of Amīr Khusrau is based in oral tradition and has probably been contaminated over the centuries to include inauthentic compositions, but the fact remains that the poet himself wrote of 'his pride in primarily being a poet in his mother tongue'.[6] One of his most famous couplets forcefully asserts his poetic identity as based in his vernacular work: 'I am a parrot of India if you ask me candidly | Ask me in Hindavi so that I can answer you correctly.' Through this perspective, I believe we can be drawn in far more to certain radical features of Dante's poetic output, especially with regard to the mixing together of languages to create a new kind of vernacular.

Such a focus on vernacular mixing resonates with Dante's thoughts on language as found in his incomplete treatise on vernacular eloquence, *De vulgari eloquentia*. In a stance most telling of his exilic status, he writes, 'Nos autem, cui mundus est patria velut piscibus equor' [To me, however, the whole world is a homeland, as the ocean is for fish].[7] And he proceeds to make clear that he does not believe Florentine to be the most perfect or beautiful vernacular, but rather that there are many people and places ('nationes et gentes') that have more pleasant and useful ('delectabiliori atque utiliori') language than that of Italians ('latinos'). This is a single moment in a larger though incomplete whole of Dante's search for the illustrious vernacular in this text, but it does open up a wider horizon of his thoughts on language beyond Florence and how the pleasure and utility of other languages might serve to craft a new kind of poetic language.

Indeed, most telling of the peculiar nature of Dante's search is the metaphor deployed in *De vulgari eloquentia* 1. 16 of a hunt for an elusive panther:

> Postquam venati saltus et pascua sumus Ytalie, nec pantheram quam sequimur adinvenimus, ut ipsam reperire possimus rationabilius investigemus de illa ut, solerti studio, redolentem ubique et necubi apparentem nostris penitus irretiamus tenticulis.
>
> [Now that we have hunted across the woodlands and pastures of all Italy without finding the panther we are trailing, let us, in the hope of tracking it down, carry out a more closely reasoned investigation so that, by the assiduous practice of cunning, we can at last entice into our trap this creature whose scent is left everywhere but which is nowhere to be seen].[8]

The image of Dante as a hunter after a panther who leaves a scent but is nowhere to be found is an interesting reversal from the more standard trope of the panther being the one who is doing the hunting by way of luring its prey through a scent, as seen in Aristotle's *Historia animalium* and in some telling precedents of Duecento poetry. As we will see in looking at these vernacular precedents, there is also a geographical link to India that stands out precisely because we are reading through the lens of Amīr Khusrau.

The likening of the lady to a panther is a trope that comes up in two poems by Inghilfredi, in the *Mare amoroso*, and in four separate poems by Chiaro Davanzati.

There is, however, also a geographical component to consider. We find in Guido Guinizzelli's *Lo fin pregi' avanzato* the image of the panther who lives in the exotic East as a point of reference to make clear that his lady's visage is even more fragrant and alluring: 'D'un'amorosa parte | mi vèn voler ch'è sole, | che inver' me più sòle | che non fa la pantera, | ched usa in una parte | che levantisce sole: | ché di più olor s'ole | su' viso che pantera' (*Lo fin pregi' avanzato* 40–43).[9] Guinizzelli plays upon the word 'sole' as referring to the sun of his desire, the geographical point of sunrise to indicate the panther's origin, and as a form of the verb 'olere' to dwell upon scent. By indicating a geography, he also perhaps shows that he is drawing on Guido delle Colonne's 'Gioiosamente canto', in which the poet praises his lady for having a more fragrant mouth than the panther: 'e la bocca aulitosa | più rende aulente aulore | che non fa d'una fera | c'ha nome pantera, | che 'n India nasce ed usa' ('Gioiosamente canto', 16–20).[10] Guido delle Colonne specifies India as the realm of the panther and makes clear that it draws in wild animals with its alluring scent, perhaps with the tacit understanding that it will consume them.

Because we are reading through the lens of Amīr Khusrau, this line of vernacular lyric that is played upon by Dante in *De vulgari eloquentia* 1.16 takes on a heightened significance, asking us to observe how the hunter has now become the hunted and how the Indian origins of the creature have been transposed into the woodlands and pastures of Italy. In doing so, we might come away with a more complicated, worldly notion of the illustrious vernacular that Dante seeks.

Another aspect that might be emphasized through this practice of diffractive reading is that of gender ambiguity and the confluence of the language of love and the language of mercantile trade. In one of the Hindavi poems attributed to Amīr Khusrau, there is a witty conflation of the consumption of fruit and the visit of a lover:

> He visits my town once a year.
> He fills my mouth with kisses and nectar.
> I spend all my money on him.
> *Who, girl, your man?*
> No, a mango.[11]

The poem partakes of a genre that involves two female friends talking about one of their lovers, interesting in and of itself in thinking about play with gender in medieval Italian genres like the *tenzone fittizia*, but what is striking to me here is the valuing of the mango/lover to such a degree that the third line declares, 'I spend all my money on him.' This draws my attention to a point in Cielo d'Alcamo's *Contrasto* (itself a play on gendered voices and roles) that likens the woman to cloves in a highly specific way that implicates economic trade and value. This alimentary connection emphasizes a real-world connection between medieval Italy and India in the form of the trade of spices; it asks us to ground moments of Duecento poetry and the poetry of the *Commedia* in a lived history that is by no means limited to the boundaries of peninsular Italy.

As a point of context for the medieval trade of cloves, we might look to Marco Polo's *Il Milione* that goes to southern and western India as well as the islands of the

Indian Ocean not in the vein of orientalizing fantasy but with a kind of sociological interest and mercantile perspective that defies its categorization as a travel narrative. Sharon Kinoshita emphasizes that the work is a 'textual witness' to the world of transcontinental travel, trade, and communication made possible by the so-called *pax mongolica*.[12]

Cloves come up in the world of Marco Polo in Jiandu (in present-day Sichuan province), and on the islands of Java and Nicobar. They are referenced as an exported commodity in the description of Malabar and Gujarat. The Malabar description in particular makes clear how the materials flow, with merchants importing what is not otherwise found in the kingdom and participating in a global trading network:

> They bring cloth of gold and cloth of silk, *sendal*, gold, silver, cloves, spikenard, and other spices they don't have and they trade these things for the merchandise of this country. Know that ships come here from many places — that is, from the great province of Mangi — and the merchants take things to several areas; but things going to Aden are subsequently taken to Alexandria.[13]

The extent of this network is made clear both by the catalogue of goods as well as by the emphasis on 'many places'', but that last point of geographical specificity, from Mangi in China to Malabar to Aden to Alexandria, makes clear the Red Sea route that will bring such goods into the Venetian mercantile orbit.

All this can be taken as highly compelling background to inform our reading of moments like the mention of cloves in Cielo d'Alcamo's *Contrasto* and Dante's *Inferno* 29. In the *Contrasto*, the woman's beauty is commodified by way of reference not just to 'garofano' in an abstract sense as a highly prized spice but in a specific economic mode of weight and price: 'Molti so' li garofani, ma non che salma 'nd'ài; | bella, non dispregiàmi s'avanti non m'assai' (*Rosa fresca aulentissima* 91–92).[14] This woman may have many desirable qualities (i.e. cloves), but their gathered weight does not rise to the level of a 'salma'. According to Margherita Beretta, most recent editor of the *Contrasto*, this was a widely diffused measure in medieval Sicily and amounted to the large quantity of 300 litres.[15]

By the time we come to Guittone d'Arezzo's sonnets 'Ahi, chera — donna' and 'Non già me greve fa d'amor la salma', the term 'salma' appears to have lost its highly specific quantitative value but is still being used to quantify love and desire in some concrete sense of a weight or burden. When we come to Dante's singular usage of the term in *Paradiso* 32, it has risen in significance to stand for Christ's desire to bear the burden of our human flesh ('carcar si volse de la nostra salma', *Paradiso* 32. 114). Through the perspective of the lyric history of a term like 'salma', we can see how Dante refigures language so that a commonplace measurement can assume the role of representing all that we are as human beings. This says much about the poetry of the *Commedia* that creates new vernacular meaning by elevating the quotidian. But more than that, by opening the *Commedia* out to the world of spice trade and history evoked in Cielo d'Alcamo's poem, we might find even greater meaning in Dante's embrace of a term like 'salma' as one that asks us to look out to the interconnected world beyond European borders.

'Garofano', on the other hand, remains an incredibly potent marker for luxury culture to the extent that Dante specifically uses the spice to critique the material excesses of the Sienese *brigata spendericcia* in *Inferno* 29. 127–29. Dante attributes to Niccolò de' Salimbeni the custom of using cloves to flavour meat and in so doing, 'isolates a key feature of the male social club, namely its devotion to extravagant eating and "la cucina."'[16] As Paul Freedman makes clear, cloves were less common than other spices like pepper, ginger, and saffron, but more prestigious and valuable.[17] This valuing persists well into the fifteenth century when, Freedman recounts, 'Venetians were able to sell cloves for 72 percent more than they had paid for them in the Levant[. . .]'[18] What such focus on material and economic history brings forth is an emphasis on the vital connections between India and medieval Italy, and so in a sense we have the worlds of Amīr Khusrau and Dante drawing closer together. Mangoes and cloves complement each other quite well in this respect.

They also complement each other in their specific poetic uses of linking the allure of gustatory pleasure to the amatory. In this regard, I would like to turn to the dimension of ambiguity in Amīr Khusrau's poetry that blurs the boundaries between *eros* and spirituality and might be taken up as a lens with which to read Dante a little differently. In framing Khusrau's writing of Persian *ghazals*, Losensky and Sharma dwell on the profound sense of ambiguity present in these songs of heartbreak and separation:

> The setting of a *ghazal* could be either the ruler's court or the Sufi cloister and the object of desire either an earthly beauty or a sacred divine. The difficulty of categorizing Khusrau's *ghazals* as either amatory or mystical is all the greater since he was active in courtly and Sufi circles at once and the ethos of courtly love that informs his poetry can conventionally be read as an allegory of longing for the divine.[19]

It is not much of a leap to emphasize how this ambiguity might resonate with a Stilnovist approach to the love lyric and the articulated language of desire throughout the *Commedia* that elides the boundary between the amatory and spiritual. Perhaps more interestingly, the translators dwell on the gender ambiguity in Persian that is very difficult to render in English translation. While Khusrau uses grammatical gender in his Hindavi poetry to vacillate between gender roles, 'this remains a moot point in his *ghazals* since Persian has no grammatical gender and the beauty of this work, to some extent, relies on sexual ambiguity'.[20] Their proposed solution is to vacillate between male and female pronouns in their translation to promote such ambiguous reading even at a remove from the original text. Dante's Italian of course is inflected by gender, but we are inevitably drawn to flashes of fluidity such as Virgil being described as a mother saving her child from a burning house in *Inferno* 23, Beatrice described as an 'ammiraglio' in *Purgatorio* 30, and Dante turning to the just-vanished Virgil to quote *Aeneid* 4. 23 to him, thus putting himself in the role of Dido.

In this vein of sexual ambiguity, we might enhance our approach to a dynamic often found in *Purgatorio* that plays upon anonymity, the terming of all those encountered as shades or souls, and our readerly expectation of a reunion with Beatrice. We know from *Inferno* 1. 121–23 that Virgil will leave Dante in the hands of Beatrice, that they will be reunited at some point in Purgatory, but it is not exactly clear when that will occur. When we first encounter Casella in *Purgatorio* 2, our initial impression is that of an anonymous, yet clearly intimate female individual because of its identification as an 'anima': 'Io vidi una di lor trarresi avante | per abbracciarmi con sì grande affetto, | che mosse me a far lo somigliante' (*Purgatorio* 2. 76–78). We are caught up in a passionate reunion and a poignant attempt at an impossible embrace, a redeployment of the language of love lyric, and an unabashed declaration of an amorous bond that endures beyond death. It is only twelve verses later, when Dante addresses the soul as 'Casella mio', that we are attuned to the dynamic of this encounter as one of intimate male friendship. Similarly, when we first encounter Sordello in *Purgatorio* 6, our initial impression is of a lady who waits alone ('posta | sola soletta', *Purgatorio* 6. 58–59) and her disdainful air ('altera e disdegnosa' *Purgatorio* 6. 62) is modulated only by the slow, dignified movement of the eyes ('e nel mover de li occhi onesta e tarda!', *Purgatorio* 6. 63). It is almost as though we are confronted with a lady of lyric tradition who was often characterized by such terms of resistance and alterity. This image only dissolves and transforms into a civic, fraternal embrace when Virgil says the word 'Mantua'.

This ambiguity presents problems in translation. Stanley Lombardo, for example, gives up the game in both of these episodes long before the naming and gendering male of these individuals, translating the ambiguous female pronouns with male English 'he' and 'him', while Robert Durling opts for the gender neutral 'it' in his rendition.[21] Durling's version no doubt more accurately captures the ambiguous state of expectation, but we might enhance it even more by following the translation strategy adopted by Losensky and Sharma and alternating between masculine and feminine pronouns. Such a move would alter the reader's experience to more fully embody and enliven this mode of poetic ambiguity that marks an important statement by Dante about the interconnectedness of gender, love, and desire in all of their forms.

The final aspect I would like to focus on in positing a link between Khusrau and Dante is that of linguistic mixing to create a new kind of poetry. One of the poems that Losensky and Sharma select for their edition blends together Indian and Persian elements in verse form and 'combines Hindavi and Persian literary tropes and metaphors in the form of a dialogue between a Persian lover (*'āshiq*) and pining Indian heroine (*virahinī*)'.[22] Here are the first few lines, as translated by them:

> Don't be heedless of my sorry state
> *He rolls his eyes, he makes excuses.*
> For I cannot bear this separation
> *Why won't he take me in his arms?*[23]

Khusrau vacillates between Persian courtly identity and a female Hindavi persona to remarkable effect, fusing languages together to create a new form of poetic harmony. And we might highlight a similar poetic practice on the part of Dante. The *rime petrose* remain a striking and revolutionary series of lyric compositions when considering the whole of Dante's poetic oeuvre. This is clear not just at the level of content in which the experimental verve comes through in harsh and wintry poetry and in the channelling of natural philosophy into the poetic vernacular, but also on the level of form. Dante's move to import the Occitan form of the sestina invented by Arnaut Daniel bears recognition not just for the single sestina that Dante produces, 'Al poco giorno e al gran cerchio d'ombra', and for the way that this act of translation sets the stage for Petrarch's later and far more ample use of the form. In fact, Dante's move, like that of Giacomo da Lentini translating Folquet de Marselha or Immanuel of Rome being the first to write a sonnet in a language other than Italian, is an act of new vernacular creation.[24]

If *Al poco giorno* can be seen as relatively benign at the level of formal adaptation, that is certainly not the case with the new form of the canzone-sestina *Amor tu vedi ben che questa donna*. In this poem Dante takes his cue from Arnaut's invention of the sestina and innovates considerably in creating a five-stanza poem in which five rhyme words cycle through in a similar pattern to those of the sestina but rhyme with each other as well through the course of a twelve-line stanza. Dante is highly aware of the stakes in creating this new form, claiming at the end of the *congedo* that he has dared to do what has never been done before: 'sì ch'io ardisco a far per questo freddo | la novità che per tua forma luce, | che non fu mai pensata in alcun tempo' (*Amor tu vedi ben* 64–66).[25]

But if the formal experiments of the *petrose* are unprecedented, we can find still more of an emphasis on lyric hybridity in the trilingual canzone *Ai faus ris, pour quoi traï aves* [O false smile, why have you betrayed] that alternates French, Latin, and Italian verses in a carefully modulated metre. At the level of content, the polyglot canzone shows links to the language of the *petrose*, with expressions like 'cuor di ghiaccio' (line 27) and individual words like 'fioretto' (line 13) and 'spina' (line 42). At the level of form, what first appears to be a somewhat standard canzone instead reveals, as shown by Furio Brugnolo, that the three languages alternate in similar fashion to the *retrogradatio cruciata* that governs the rhyme words of the sestina.[26]

This attention to lyric hybridity in a global key lends itself naturally to moments of the *Commedia* such as Plutus' utterance in *Inferno* 7. 1 that sounds like Greek and Hebrew, Nimrod's babble in *Inferno* 31. 67 that seems derived from Hebrew in some form, and the harmonizing of Hebrew and Latin in the opening of *Paradiso* 7 to create a new music. Key features in the beginning of *Paradiso* 7 include the identity of the speaker as the Eastern Roman emperor Justinian, himself a cultural hybrid, and Dante's ranging to create the Latin neologism 'superillustrans'. But far and away the most sustained move of vernacular alterity in the poetry of the *Commedia* is Arnaut Daniel's Occitan speech at the end of *Purgatorio* 26.

I will turn now in closing to considering the California artist Sandow Birk's early twenty-first-century illustrations of the *Commedia* that situate the poem in a modern American urban setting yet also seek to embrace a wider world-view in dwelling on other languages and religious traditions. In three volumes published between 2004 and 2005, Birk not only put out his canto-by-canto illustrations that relied on Gustave Doré's work as a foundation but also adapted the text of the poem with his collaborator Marcus Sanders into a simplified, contemporary version that Peter Hawkins has termed 'California-inflected youth-speak'.[27] Birk's interest in expanding the poem's linguistic and cultural frames of reference is announced early in his work: the illustration of *Inferno* 4 makes of Limbo's castle an encampment of homeless individuals who sit by a fire below an LA highway overpass. In the upper left corner, there is a billboard with Korean script that might provoke us to dwell on the multilingual nature of the denizens of Limbo: once there were Hebrew speakers, now there remain speakers of ancient Greek, Latin, Arabic, and Persian.

When we come to Birk's illustration of *Purgatorio* 26, it not only captures the instance of poetic hybridity that has Arnaut Daniel speak in Occitan, but accentuates it all the more. On the visual plane, Birk's Arnaut is no court poet but a taco stand line cook. This provocative move asks us to lend greater attention to Dante's poetic style as embracing all levels of language, from the sublime and sweet to the harsh and filthy. And perhaps Birk is reflecting the ambiguity of this gesture of linguistic inclusion. It is true that Arnaut is the only non-Italian character afforded the opportunity to speak his own language, but the style of this Occitan is not that of Arnaut's notoriously obscure *trobar clus*; it is simple and pleading — in fact by the terms of the lyric tradition, it puts the Dante character in the position of the beloved lady being entreated by the poet.

But Birk and his collaborator Marcus Sanders go still further in their telling choice to render Arnaut's Occitan speech into Spanish that stands apart from their California slang renderings of Dante's Italian. This appropriately highlights Dante's radical poetic move and provides an incisive way to extend Dante's reflections on languages in a diverse ecosystem of cultural production to the here and now. Birk and Sanders reflect the bold heterodoxy of this poetry, seeing it both as a product of its own period and one that can and should be 'translated' to the vernacular ecosystem of twenty-first-century America. As Kristina Olson puts it,

> we are reminded not only of racialized linguistic realities in America — namely, the perceived prevalence of Spanish among food stand workers — but also of vernaculars other than English across the Americas. It is the pilgrim's task to orient himself in such multilingual realities.[28]

One such mode of orientation is Birk's move to decentre Christian theology in the later sequence of his illustrations, and it is here that we might return to Coomaraswamy and Khusrau as diffractive lenses through which we can appreciate how Birk's illustration of the gate of Purgatory as a Hindu temple in *Purgatorio* 9 considers sacred space and ritual in a globalized fashion. We might thus reflect that the frontispiece of *Paradiso* 23 that depicts the unified Hindu godhead of Brahma, Vishnu, and Shiva capitalizes on a shared feature of unity and trinity that binds two disparate religions together. And finally, in what may be the most provocative illustration, we see how transforming the vision of Mary in *Paradiso* 32 into the Hindu goddess of knowledge Sarasvati might provoke not only an insight with regard to the man born on the banks of the Indus river of *Paradiso* 19, but also a way of insisting upon the intellectual nature of the final moments of the *Commedia* that draws poets like Dante and Amīr Khusrau up to the stars in the first place.

Notes to Chapter 26

1. Chief among these in recent memory is of course the work of Brenda Deen Schildgen. See, for example, *Dante and the Orient* (Urbana: University of Illinois Press, 2002) and 'Dante and the Bengali Renaissance', in *Dante in the Long Nineteenth Century: Nationality, Identity, and Appropriation*, ed. by Aida Audeh and Nick Havely (Oxford: Oxford University Press, 2012), pp. 323–38.
2. Ananda Coomaraswamy, 'Two Passages from Dante's *Paradiso*', *Speculum*, 11.3 (1936), 327–38 (p. 338). Coomaraswamy's more open approach to Dante earns him a place of exception in Francesco Benozzo's satirical pamphlet *Appello all'UNESCO per liberare Dante dai dantisti* (Alessandria: Edizioni dell'Orso, 2013).
3. Manuele Gragnolati, *Amor che move: Linguaggio del corpo e forma del desiderio in Dante, Pasolini e Morante* (Milan: Il Saggiatore, 2013), pp. 160–61.
4. Geraldine Heng and Lynn Ramey, 'Early Globalities, Global Literatures: Introducing a Special Issue on the Global Middle Ages', *Literature Compass*, 11.7 (2014), 389–94 (p. 392). The ideological construct of 'Global Middle Ages' is of course not without its issues. Though I have no compunction in offending flat-earthers with the imposition of a 'global' model, the notion of 'medieval' and 'Middle Ages' is certainly not shared by all and can be quite meaningless when considering a place and a history outside Europe.
5. Alyssa Gabbay, *Islamic Tolerance: Amīr Khusraw and Pluralism* (New York: Routledge, 2010), p. 18. As can be seen from the title, transliterated spelling of the poet's name vacillates between 'Khusrau', 'Khusraw', or sometimes 'Khusro'. Gabbay continues to endorse the view of Amīr Khusrau's pluralism throughout her work, although she also acknowledges instances of polemical disparaging of Hindus in other parts of his poetic corpus. Her general approach of framing Khusrau as embodying the 'internal conflicts and multiple loyalties of his age' (19) is a fine balance that allows both his radical stances to shine and his grounded historicity to remain ever-present.
6. This critical assessment as well as the cited couplet below it are found in Sunil Sharma, *Amīr Khusraw: The Poet of Sultans and Sufis* (Oxford: Oneworld, 2005), p. 78.
7. *De vulgari eloquentia* 1.6. I cite from *Dante: De vulgari eloquentia*, ed. and trans. Stephen Botterill (Cambridge: Cambridge University Press, 1996), pp. 12–13.
8. Ibid., pp. 38–39.
9. For the text of this poem, I cite from Guido Guinizzelli, *Rime*, ed. by Luciano Rossi (Turin: Einaudi, 2002).
10. For the text of this poem, I cite from *I poeti della scuola siciliana*, II, ed. by Costanzo di Girolamo (Milan: Mondadori, 2008).
11. I cite from *In the Bazaar of Love: The Selected Poetry of Amīr Khusrau*, ed. and trans. by Paul Losensky and Sunil Sharma (Gurgaon: Penguin India, 2013), p. 114.
12. Sharon Kinoshita, 'The Painter, the Warrior, and the Sultan: The World of Marco Polo in Three Portraits', *The Medieval Globe*, 2.1 (2015), 101–28 (p. 102).
13. I cite from the Kinoshita translation, Marco Polo, *The Description of the World*, ed. and trans. by Sharon Kinoshita (Indianapolis: Hackett, 2016), p. 174.
14. For the text of this poem, I cite from *I poeti della scuola siciliana*, II.
15. *I poeti della scuola siciliana*, II, 543.
16. Teodolinda Barolini, 'Sociology of the *Brigata*: Gendered Groups in Dante, Forese, Folgore, Boccaccio — From *Guido i' vorrei* to Griselda', *Italian Studies*, 67.1 (2012), 4–22 (p. 12).
17. Paul Freedman, *Out of the East: Spices and the Medieval Imagination* (New Haven: Yale University Press, 2008), p. 22.
18. Ibid., p. 115.
19. Losensky and Sharma, p. xli
20. Ibid., p. xlii
21. See Dante, *Purgatorio*, trans. by Stanley Lombardo (Indianapolis: Hackett, 2016) and *The Divine Comedy of Dante Alighieri*, II: *Purgatorio*, ed. and trans. by Robert M. Durling (Oxford: Oxford University Press, 2003). While I have not been exhaustive in checking every English translation

of *Purgatorio*, I have checked a good number (Mandelbaum, Hollander, Esolen, Kirkpatrick, Merwin, Longfellow) and have not found any that include a female pronoun for the passages in question.
22. Losensky and Sharma, p. xxxii
23. This is the first stanza of poem 54 in Losensky and Sharma, p. 98.
24. For more on Giacomo da Lentini's vernacular translation as a form of innovation, see my Introduction in *The Complete Poetry of Giacomo da Lentini*, trans. by Richard Lansing (Toronto: University of Toronto Press, 2018) and Michelangelo Picone, 'Aspetti della tradizione/traduzione nei poeti siciliani', in *Percorsi della lirica duecentesca* (Florence: Cadmo, 2003), pp. 17–31. For Immanuel of Rome and issues of cultural identity, see Fabian Alfie, 'Immanuel of Rome, alias Manoello Giudeo: The Poetics of Jewish Identity in Fourteenth-Century Italy', *Italica*, 75.3 (1998), 307–29. On his status as the first poet to import and translate the form of the sonnet into another language (in his case, Hebrew), see Isabelle Levy, 'Immanuel of Rome and Dante', *Digital Dante* (New York, NY: Columbia University Libraries, 2017), <http://www.digitaldante.columbia.edu/history/immanuel-of-rome-and-dante-levy/>.
25. For the text of this and other Dantean lyric poems, I cite from Dante Alighieri, *Rime*, ed. by Claudio Giunta (Milan: Mondadori, 2018).
26. For the expanded version of Brugnolo's original 1978 essay, see Furio Brugnolo, *Plurilinguismo e lirica medievale* (Rome: Bulzoni, 1983). The work of Brugnolo, Massimiliano Chiamenti and Domenico De Robertis has been key in bringing *Ai faus ris* out of the category of dubious attribution and firmly assigning it a place in Dante's lyric corpus. For more on this process and the cultural narrowness of previous editors and scholars, see especially Massimiliano Chiamenti, 'Attorno alla canzone trilingue "Aï faux ris" finalmente recuperata a Dante', *Dante Studies*, 116 (1998), 189–207. On plurilingualism as a mode of reading Dante, see *Dante's Plurilingualism: Authority, Knowledge, Subjectivity*, ed. by Sara Fortuna, Manuele Gragnolati, and Jürgen Trabant (Abingdon: Legenda, 2010).
27. See Peter S. Hawkin's introductory essay 'Moderno Uso' in Sandow Birk and Marcus Sanders, *Dante's Paradiso* (San Francisco: Chronicle Books, 2005), pp. vi–xiv (p. viii). The prior two volumes of *Inferno* and *Purgatorio* were also published by Chronicle Books in 2004. Hawkins rightly points out that neither Birk nor Sanders knows Italian; their adaptation of the text is a prose rendering of English translations they consulted, typeset as though it were free verse.
28. Kristina Olson, 'Dante's American Urban Vernacular: Sandow Birk's "Comedy"', *Dante Studies*, 131 (2013), 143–69 (p. 160).

CHAPTER 27

Translating Dante 1966–2019

Peter Hainsworth and David Robey

This chapter offers a broad preliminary survey of the number and nature of the translations of the *Divina Commedia* that appeared in English between 1966 and 2019, and draws comparisons with translations into French, German and Spanish over the same period. For while translating Dante poses similar problems for translators working in all four languages, British and American practice during this period is in many ways distinctive, as regards both the sheer number of translations produced and the evolution of translating practice. Some of the main reasons for this distinctiveness will be discussed.

Our starting point is 1966, because that is the end-point of Gilbert Cunningham's *The Divine Comedy in English*,[1] as well as, conveniently, the year following the last centenary celebrations. Cunningham presents a comprehensive survey and discussion of translations into English beginning with the *Inferno* of Charles Rogers of 1782, the first English version of a whole *cantica* of the *Comedy*; he also, without aspiring to quite the same comprehensiveness, discusses translations into other European languages. Cunningham himself gives figures only for the total number of published translations of each *cantica*: 183 in all, whether translated separately or together, of which 124 were by British translators, fifty-eight by Americans and one by an Italian. Using his historical list we can arrive at figures for English translations of the whole *Comedy* and for each *cantica*: forty-eight of all three *cantiche*, two of both *Inferno* and *Purgatorio*, and two of *Purgatorio* and *Paradiso*, all published either separately or together; twenty-three solely of *Inferno*, six solely of *Purgatorio*, three solely of *Paradiso*. In two cases the translations are incomplete.

That separate *Inferno* translations are well over double those of *Purgatorio* and *Paradiso* put together is not surprising. What is surprising is the sheer number of translations, and the fact that they appeared irregularly but frequently, with no significant surges or troughs in the rate of production, from the mid-nineteenth century onwards.

This trend has continued in terms of numbers and preferences since 1966. If anything, it has strengthened. Section 1 of the Appendix below gives what aims to be a full list of versions in English that have been published between 1966 and 2019, including versions by a group of translators (usually poets) and anthologies of existing translations. Altogether 26 translations of the whole *Comedy* have appeared over the half century since 1966 (as against 48 over the whole period from 1782 to 1965). The relative proportion of translations just of the *Inferno* has increased further still, while numbers for the other two *cantiche* have diminished: 20 of *Inferno* alone against 2 of *Purgatorio* and 1 of *Paradiso*. The rate of translation has also been accelerating, since more than half of the translations over the whole period have been produced from 2000 onwards. Another notable change, perhaps related, is that the balance between UK and US translations has shifted in favour of the United States. Translations first published in the United States comprise fifteen of the whole *Comedy* and twelve just of *Inferno*, against ten UK publications of the *Comedy* and six just of the *Inferno*. Only three English translations have been published elsewhere in the world.

The sheer numbers become all the more striking when we compare the production of translations in France, Germany and Spain as shown in sections 2–4 of the Appendix. Cunningham had calculated that 'there are now [1965] about 60 versions of one or more *cantiche* in both French and German, and nearly 30 in the Hispanic languages'.[2] Some disparity with English was thus already evident; the equivalent figure extrapolated from Cunningham for English is eighty-four. Since 1966 it has increased very considerably. Altogether there are twelve French translations of the whole *Comedy* plus one just of *Inferno*, twelve full German versions (none of single *cantiche*), fifteen Spanish versions plus two of *Inferno* alone published in Spain (and at least two published in South America — see Appendix, section 4 below). The fact that there are far more translations into English than into any of the other three languages obviously has a lot to do with the role of English as a world language and the size of the English-language market. Spanish has the next largest number of translations; but if we bear in mind that there are rather more first-language speakers of Spanish than of English in the world, the fact that there have been so many more English translations does require some further explanation, especially when those of single *cantiche*, above all *Inferno*, are taken into account. We shall return to this shortly.

One further point is to be made, though its importance is not to be overstated given the small numbers involved. Of the forty-eight translations into English listed in our Appendix, only two are solely by women (Lindskoog and Bang), with another by a husband-and-wife team (Robert and Jean Hollander). That is much fewer than the ten out of eighty-four translators in Cunningham's list. It is also much fewer proportionately than the number of women translators into French (three out of thirteen: Risset, Portier and Robert), German (two out of twelve: Urban and Christa Renata Köhler) and Spanish (two out of seventeen: Díaz-Corralejo and Akram). The numbers do increase in the collective volumes we discuss below, but it is hard to avoid the impression that translating Dante into all four languages has been largely a man's game over the last half century, and particularly so in the United States and the United Kingdom. However it is also worth adding that the translation by Jacqueline Risset has become almost the standard French version, and in this respect resembles that by Dorothy Sayers and Barbara Reynolds into English in the mid-twentieth century.[3]

Despite all these disparities it is notable how strongly the need for new translations has been felt in all four languages. After all, older translations continue to be serviceable; indeed many remain available or at least easily obtainable. These range from nineteenth-century versions (such those of Cary and Longfellow in English, Philalethes and Stefan George in German, the Conde de Cheste in Spanish) to highly regarded successors from the earlier twentieth century, such as the Penguin version by Sayers and Reynolds that dominated the mid-century English market,[4] the 1965 Pléiade version of Dante's complete works by the prominent Dante scholar André Pézard,[5] the German version by Karl Vossler.[6] But the limitations of any of these versions, whatever the language, are evident. They all tend to be literary in their idiom and can thus be perceived as old-fashioned and unappealing, particularly to the important student market. Interestingly, perhaps symptomatically, we have only found one translation in any of the four languages that overtly presents itself as the modernization of an earlier version: Douglas Neff's 2014 revision of Longfellow.[7]

There are also general questions regarding the actual business of translating Dante that need to be clarified. After all, translation into other European languages is not necessarily easier than it is into English.[8] Even Spanish, which might be thought to pose fewer problems given its closeness to Italian, seems to have to confront much the same difficulties as the other languages. First of all there is the question of rhyme and metre. If kept, the rhymes of *terza rima* can easily seem forced, uninteresting and distorting, and all too often to lead to padding or omissions. If adapted as half or imperfect rhyme, the result at best is a nod towards the original's sound texture. If removed, an essential element of Dante's poetry is felt to be lost, though with the possibility of gains in readability and greater closeness to the literal sense of the original. Over and above the difficulty of finding enough rhymes, there is that presented by Dante's distinctive use of the rhyme-word position as the focus of effect in the line, often characterized by bold, energetic and unusual forms of expression.

One might expect the Italian hendecasyllable to be relatively easily retainable in Spanish, in which it is the normal line of high lyric poetry. In fact modern Spanish translators have often opted for other forms, and in a surprising number of instances have eschewed verse altogether (ten out of seventeen translations published in Spain). Historically the hendecasyllable has normally been rendered in English as an iambic pentameter, though the fact that this is the traditional and therefore potentially dated metre of high poetry has increasingly led to its being abandoned in favour of one form or another of free verse. In French the traditional twelve-syllable alexandrine poses particular difficulties both because of its greater length and because it normally appears in rhyming couplets; consequently translators have generally opted for lines of ten syllables or fewer when they have not adopted freer patterns. In German, as in English, translators have tended, as a commentator has observed, to opt either for a replication of *terza rima*, despite German's 'notorious shortage of rhymes', or for blank verse, a form 'familiar to the German ear', when (like the Spaniards) they do not resort to prose.[9]

Overall, verse translators into all the four languages have used a variety of solutions. But it is small wonder that, given verse in any form may seem uncomfortable or unsatisfactory, there has also been widespread resorting to prose, some translators breaking off at the end of each line, others organizing the text into paragraphs. In any language, assuming that the translation follows the original more or less closely, the losses are likely to be not simply of sound and rhythm but also of the depths and complexities of meaning inscribed in the texture of Dante's verse. The result may easily seem quite unpoetic in itself, though of course it may be extremely useful as an aid to reading the original.

Alongside the determining formal choices, and inseparably from them, the translator has always to make choices regarding style and idiom. André Pézard had notoriously opted for a form of French of his own devising. The overwhelming tendency of more recent translators has been to aim at a contemporary idiom of one sort or another which can be followed without difficulty by the literate reader and hopefully with a degree of pleasure. It may even reproduce or imitate some of the stylistic features of the original (alliteration, metaphor, simile, etc.). What proves insuperably difficult for translators is to recreate in any language Dante's *plurilinguismo*, the variations in language and style that occupy all the gradations between the two extremes of the vulgarity of the devils in *Inferno* and the high poetry of much of *Paradiso*, and to retain throughout a distinctive balance between stylistic elevation and realism. Older translations generally privilege the aspect of elevation, and therefore seem old-fashioned to modern readers. But modern translations can shift too far in the opposite direction, and therefore betray the fundamental character of Dante's style. Steve Ellis's translation of *Inferno* has some striking examples: for instance 'then he's brass down to his crotch' for Dante's characteristic periphrasis 'poi è di rame infino a la forcata' (*Inf.* 14. 108).

The stylistic question is in turn connected with questions of historical reference. Most translations include notes identifying and clarifying characters and events mentioned in the text, or aspects of Dante's thinking that are felt to be remote from modern experience, not to mention allusive periphrases and other tropes. These in turn may prove problematic: notes as much as references in the text itself can have a distancing effect, not to say an off-putting one, that is particularly felt by the inexperienced or casual modern reader.

A number of English versions have attempted to deal with this latter problem as well as with problems of form and idiom by radical modernization. This seems not to be true to anything like the same extent in French, German and Spanish. The late Clive James, who wrote in regular rhyming quatrains with much enjambement in imitation of Dante's energetic forward movement, eliminated footnotes as such, and either eliminated references that a modern reader might find obscure or incorporated and glossed them in the body of the text. For instance, the last figure mentioned in Brunetto Latini's list of fellow sodomites is only identified in the original by an allusively complex periphrasis. James radically both simplifies and supplements the original:

> And if you like scum you might see the man
> Sent to Vicenza by the Pope, before
> Florence should see his sin-worn nerves collapse:
> Andrea de' Mozzi. Bishop in your youth.

> [...] e vedervi,
> S'avessi avuto di tal tigna brama,
> Colui potei che dal servo de' servi
> Fu trasmutato d'Arno in Bacchiglione,
> Dove lasciò li mal protesi nervi. (*Inf.* 15. 111–14)

The problem that James is grappling with leaps into relief if we compare the Durling-Martinez version of these lines:

> [...] and, if you had desired to see such scurf, you could see there
> him who by the Servant of the servants was
> transmuted from Arno to Bacchiglione, where he
> left his ill-protended muscles.

Arguably, however accurate and concise, this literal prose rendering (set out in paragraphs corresponding to the *terza rima* divisions) is unintelligible, which James certainly is not, nor is it easily graspable even with the aid of notes.

James's translation is nevertheless governed by a consistent spirit of fidelity to Dante's text; unlike some other recent English and American translators it does not introduce overt or deliberate anachronisms. We may contrast three versions of *Inferno* 1. 88–90. J. G. Nichols has:

> You see the beast that made me turn in flight,
> Save me from her, O famous fount of wisdom,
> She makes the blood run from my veins in fright.

Robin Kirkpatrick, unlike Nichols, eschews rhyme but attempts to capture more of Dante's expressive vigour:

> See there? That beast! I turned because of that.
> Help me — your wisdom's known — escape from her.
> To every pulsing vein she brings a tremor.

In their different ways both versions stay close to the original:

> Vedi la bestia per cu'io mi volsi;
> Aiutami da lei, famoso saggio,
> Ch'ella mi fa tremar le vene e i polsi.

In contrast Mary Jo Bang makes some major modifications:

> Can you see the beast I had to flee? Can you save me
> From her? You, Mr. Übermensch, you Mr. Man
> Of the World. I'm shaking with fear.

There is of course no *Übermensch* or 'Man of the World' in Dante's 'famoso saggio' (l. 89), but Bang's updating of the cultural reference, together with the highly conversational tone, jolt the reader into a modern world. Yet in assuming that *Übermensch* will be intelligible, Bang is obviously drawing a limit to her popularization; indeed she retains many of Dante's references (for instance to the Roman Empire in canto 1), just as she retains a visual memory at least of the Dantesque tercet. On the sliding scale between translation and adaptation, Bang is still in the area of translation.

On the other hand a number of versions, particularly but not only in English, are very much in the area of adaptation (and for this reason have not been included in the Appendix below). Sandow Birk and Marcus Sanders, for instance, delete Marsyas from the appeal to Apollo in *Paradiso* 1. 19–21 and instead have:

> I'll need your music to flow through me, like
> When Johnny won the golden fiddle in that
> *Devil Went Down to Georgia* country-western song.

Birk is still writing mostly ten- or twelve-syllable verse arranged in tercets. Frank Samperi reduces each canto to a brief free-verse poem, each line consisting of one or two words. Philip Terry, on the other hand, still sets out his version in tercets, but transfers the setting and action to the University of Essex and replaces Beatrice with Marina Warner. From here it is not a large leap to recent cartoon or graphic retellings aimed primarily at a younger readership, such as those by Seymour Chwast, John Agard and Satoshi Kitamura, and Kevin Jackson and Hunt Emerson.[10]

Such adaptations of the *Comedy* do exist in the other languages, but to a less conspicuous extent. Their presence in English is a pointer to the peculiar place that Dante has in the modern English-speaking world. There is no intrinsic reason why the flood of nineteenth- and early twentieth-century translations should have been prolonged and extended as it has been. As with many another non-English author, translations might have been produced from time to time which updated what had previously been produced and the limits of which were recognized but accepted. Such has been the case with Ariosto and Tasso: the number of modern English translations of the *Orlando furioso* and the *Gerusalemme liberata* is exiguous compared with those of the *Comedy*. It is already evident in the nineteenth century that Dante was not containable within such limits. Individuals (especially in the United Kingdom) again and again took upon themselves the herculean task of producing new versions, independently of the demands of publishers or the market, and often one feels out of personal compulsion as much as from a perception that a new Dante was actually needed. This tendency has continued in both the United Kingdom and the United States, with publishers now able to publish small print-runs easily, and translators themselves able to publish their versions on line (we have not included on-line-only versions in our counts).

There have, however, been important new developments. Most earlier translators were not professionals or established poets or writers, the most notable exceptions being Longfellow and Dorothy Sayers. In the early twentieth century Dante's reputation reached new heights with T. S. Eliot and Ezra Pound. Dante became one of the supreme authors of the past and at the same time a supreme model. In 1929 Eliot wrote:

> In writing of the *Divine Comedy* I have tried to keep to a few very simple points of which I am convinced. First that the poetry of Dante is the one universal school of style for the writing of poetry in any language. There is much, naturally, which can profit only those who write Dante's own Tuscan language; but there is no poet in any tongue — not even in Latin or Greek — who stands so firmly as a model for all poets.[11]

That remarkable claim has continued to be reasserted. William Cookson, the editor of a selection of translations of the *Comedy* published in *Agenda* in 1996–97,[12] wrote in his Introduction: 'I believe it is as true today as it was for Pound and Eliot when they began writing, that Dante is the best model for a young poet learning his or her craft' (p. 2). Whether or or not all poets would have agreed, the fact is that Dante has become a presence in English and American poetry to an extent that was not the case in the past. Since at least the mid-1960s he has been a figure to be discussed, assimilated, adapted and, of course, translated.[13]

Poets have become some of the most numerous translators. Of the names listed in the Appendix, C. H. Sisson, W. S. Merwin, Robert Pinsky, Peter Dale, Ciaran Carson, Sean O'Brien, Mary Jo Bang and Clive James are all well known as poets in their own right, while various other translators have also published poetry of their own. What is more, other well-known poets have published smaller sections or selections. The 1966 *Inferno* edited by Terence Tiller consists of translations by eleven English poets, each translating three canti. The list includes some of the best-known names of the time, in order, Ronald Bottrall, Robert Gittings, John Heath-Stubbs, Hugh Gordon Porteus, Vernon Watkins, G. S. Fraser, Patric Dickinson, Elizabeth Jennings, G. W. Ireland, Denis Goacher and Tiller himself (who also translates the numerically aberrant final canto). Daniel Halpern's *Dante's Inferno: Translation by Twenty Contemporary Poets* (1993) comprises versions of one or more canti by Seamus Heaney, Mark Strand, Daniel Halpern, Galway Kinnell, Cynthia Macdonald, Amy Clampitt, Jorie Graham, Charles Wright, Richard Howard, Stanley Plumly, C. K. Williams, Susan Mitchell, Carolyn Forché, Richard Wilbur, W. S. Merwin, Robert Pinsky, Alfred Corn, Sharon Olds, Deborah Digges and Robert Hass. And the 1996 *Agenda* anthology contains translations by twenty-three contemporary poets: John Burnside, William Cookson, Peter Dale, Richard Dove, James Harpur, Daniel Huws, Rosalind Ingrams, Alan Jenkins, Marius Kociejowsky, Peter Levi, Alan Massey, W. S. Milne, John Montague, David Moody, Alan Neame, Desmond O'Grady, Robin Robertson, Tom Scott, Matthew Sweeney, Charles Tomlinson, Alan Wall and Clive Wilmer. Nick Havely and Bernard O'Donoghue have recently edited a set of translations of *Purgatorio* by contemporary poets published this year (2021). We might finally add versions or adaptations of selections that appear elsewhere: for instance, 'Ugolino' in Seamus Heaney's *Fieldwork* (1979) includes a version of the Ugolino episode from the end of *Inferno* 32 to its conclusion in the middle of the next canto, and Don Paterson's 'Suicides' in *Landing Light* (2008) is a version of *Inferno* 13. In other words Dante has become a massive presence in English and American poetry and almost all poets (female as well as male) feel obliged to come to terms with some portion of his work directly, whether or not they have to rely to some degree on previous translations[14] and whatever the quality of the results.[15]

Such versions by poets of extracts from the *Comedy* are often primarily of interest as part of the oeuvre of the poet rather than as ways into the work of Dante for the reader without Italian. Often they insert, omit, rewrite and at times misunderstand the sense of the original. That is by no means always the case. Certainly the Terence

Tiller 1966 *Inferno* plainly did aim to introduce Dante to the English listener (the series was commissioned and broadcast by BBC radio) while implicitly recognizing that any translation would reflect the voice of the translator. In fact the poets who contributed to that collection did stay close to the original and by and large were conservative in their choice of verse forms, most of them opting for a form of *terza rima* and the iambic pentameter. Other poets who have more recently completed translations of a whole *cantica* or of the whole *Comedy* have tended to opt for other metres, with a sparing use of rhyme, if they have used it all, and a generally modern idiom. In terms of accuracy it is doubtful whether any are comparable with versions by scholars such as Robin Kirkpatrick and Robert Hollander.[16] It is worth pointing out, however, that the sober blank-verse *Inferno* by the artist Tom Phillips, which accompanies his illustrations to the *Comedy*, closely follows the original.

There is little indication that a similar cult of Dante engages the poets of France, Germany and Spain, though Dante's greatness is of course acknowledged and his work analysed and discussed at an academic level in all three countries. An exception is Jacqueline Risset, who was a highly respected poet and critic, associated with the *Tel Quel* group that included Philippe Sollers and Julia Kristeva.[17] Her highly readable free-verse version became almost the standard French Dante in the later twentieth century. Jean-Charles Vegliante (himself one of the translators we list) went so far as to say that:

> the critical and popular success of Risset's translation — such a success, in fact, that a thoroughgoing renewal of interest in reading Dante at the end of the twentieth century can reasonably be attributed to it — is in all likelihood due to this hybrid character — rhythmically varied and occasionally prose-like verse, simple semantic solutions, modern lexical choices — in which the clear text of the philosopher Masseron has passed through the pen of one of our best stylists.[18]

However, the only other poet-translator on our French list is the Belgian William Cliff. Of the German translators Hans Werner Sokop has published poems in Viennese. Of the Spanish Ángel Crespo is a respected poet and the very well-known Chilean Raul Zurita is apparently engaged on a Spanish translation which has not yet appeared. However, when an interviewer observed to him that 'not many Hispanics are seduced by Dante and that there is no Dantesque tradition [in modern poetry]', Zurita agreed and added, 'The direct marks of his poetry are insignificant, almost non-existent.'[19] In general poets writing in all three languages do not seem to feel the need to assimilate him to their own practice as if he were an intimate part of their own culture, though translators may feel the need to modernize him for contemporary consumption. In comparison with English and American practice, it appears that a majority of translators in the three languages aim to respect historical distance, however relevant in some sense Dante may be felt to be.

Finally there is the market. There are of course in many countries lovers of literature without Italian who wish to read Dante in much the same way as they might read Proust if they have no French or Goethe if they are without German. Some of those readers will be university students specializing in other national literatures than Italian or in some other subject than literature (most obviously European history and thought). But the peculiar status of Dante in the United States has led to the establishment of numerous university courses specifically focused on teaching Dante in English, thereby extending the translation market immensely.[20] It is evident from the number of on-line queries asking for recommendations that no one translation is now dominant. Indeed a recent anthology by Tim Smith and Marco Sonzogni of *Inferno* translations by seventy translators from Charles Rogers onwards celebrates the sheer diversity of what is on offer.[21] All major publishers have their Dante and in the case of Penguin more than one. The Penguin website currently (October 2019) lists five full modern versions of the *Comedy* — in chronological order, Dorothy Sayers and Barbara Reynolds, Allen Mandelbaum, Mark Musa, Robin Kirkpatrick and Steve Ellis. There are grounds for praising any or all of these versions, and quite how the uninformed potential reader (or consumer) is to make a choice between them remains unclear. Rightly or wrongly, French, German and Spanish readers, with a much more limited range before them, may well feel less bewildered.

Appendix: Translations of the whole *Divine Comedy* and of individual *cantiche* 1966–2019 (excluding partial selections and translations published only on-line)

1. **English**: 49; 26 of the *Comedy*, 20 of *Inferno*, 2 of *Purgatorio*, 1 of *Paradiso*[22]

1966: Louis Biancolli, *Comedy*, blank verse (USA)
1966: Terence Tiller (ed.), *Inferno*, various (UK)
1969: Allan Gilbert, *Inferno*, prose (USA)
1970–75: Charles Singleton, *Comedy*, prose (USA)
1971–84: Mark Musa, *Comedy*, blank verse set as tercets (USA)
1979: Kenneth Mackenzie, *Comedy*, blank verse (UK)
1980–82: Allen Mandelbaum, *Comedy*, blank verse (USA)
1980: C. H. Sisson, *Comedy*, blank verse (UK)
1983: Tom Phillips, *Inferno*, blank verse (UK)
1985: Nicholas Kilmer, *Inferno*, iambic tetrameters set as tercets (USA)
1986: Derrick Plant, *Inferno*, prose (Italy)
1987: James Finn Cotter, *Comedy*, loose blank verse (USA)
1993: Daniel Halpern (ed.), *Inferno*, various (USA)
1993: James Torrens, *Paradiso*, blank verse (USA)
1994: Stephen Arndt, *Comedy*, terza rima (USA)
1994: Robert Pinsky, *Inferno*, terza rima (USA)
1994–2019: Steve Ellis, *Comedy*, iambic tetrameters set as tercets (UK)
1996: Benedict Flynn, *Comedy*, blank verse (written for radio) (UK)
1996: Peter Dale, *Comedy*, terza rima (UK)
1996–2010: Robert Durling, *Comedy*, prose (USA)
1997–98: Kathryn Lindskoog, *Comedy*, prose (USA)
1998: Elio Zappulla, *Inferno*, blank verse (USA)

2000: A. S. Kline, *Comedy*, prose (UK)
2000: Derek Philcox, *Comedy*, blank verse (S Africa)
2000: W. S. Merwin, *Purgatorio*, blank verse (USA)
2000–07: Robert and Jean Hollander, *Comedy*, mixed verse set as tercets (USA)
2002: Ciaran Carson, *Inferno*, modified *terza rima* (UK)
2002: Michael Palma, *Inferno*, *terza rima* (UK)
2002–04: Anthony Esolen, *Comedy*, blank verse set as tercets (USA)
2003: Seth Zimmerman, *Inferno*, *terza rima* (USA)
2005–11: Paul S. Bruckman, *Comedy*, *terza rima* (USA)
2005–12: J. G. Nichols, *Comedy*, modified *terza rima* (UK)
2006: Leon Stephens, *Comedy*, free verse (USA)
2006: Sean O'Brien, *Inferno*, blank verse set as tercets (UK)
2006–07: Robin Kirkpatrick, *Comedy*, blank verse set as tercets (UK)
2007–17: Tom Simone, *Comedy*, 4-stress lines set as tercets (USA)
2007: Frank Salvidio, *Inferno*, free verse set as tercets (USA)
2009–17: Stanley Lombardo, *Comedy*, 4-stress lines set as tercets (USA)
2010: Anthony Cristiano, *Inferno*, prose (Canada)
2010: Burton Raffel, *Comedy*, blank verse set as tercets (USA)
2010–12: John Lambert, *Comedy*, iambic tetrameters (UK)
2011: Robert Mitchell Torrance, *Inferno*, *terza rima* (USA)
2012: Declan Moran, *Inferno*, rhyming octosyllabics (USA)
2012: Mary Jo Bang, *Inferno*, mix of tetrameters, pentameters etc. (USA)
2013: Clive James, *Comedy*, rhyming quatrains (UK)
2014: Douglas Neff, *Inferno*, unrhyming free verse (revision of Longfellow's translation) (USA)
2016: Peter Thornton, *Inferno*, blank verse (USA)
2018–19: Alasdair Gray, *Inferno* and *Purgatorio*, modified *terza rima* (UK)

2. **French**: 13, all of the whole *Comedy* except one of *Inferno* (as indicated; all published in France except where indicated)

1968: Alexandre Cioranescu, unrhyming alexandrines set as tercets (Switzerland)
1985–90: Jacqueline Risset, free verse set as tercets
1987: Lucienne Portier, free verse set as tercets
1992–97: François Mégroz, free verse set as tercets, with intercalated commentary (Switzerland)
1996: Marc Scialom, unrhyming decasyllables
1996–2007: Jean-Charles Vegliante, *terza rima* with mixed ten- and eleven-syllable lines
1998: Kolja Micevic, rhyming tercets in various metres
2003: Didier Marc Garin, polymetric
2013: Claude Dandréa, unrhymed alexandrines set as tercets
2014: William Cliff, *Inferno* only, unrhymed decasyllables
2017: René de Ceccatty, unrhymed octosyllables
2016–18: Danièle Robert, mixed ten- and eleven-syllable lines in part-rhyming

tercets

2019: Michel Orcel, unrhyming decasyllables (Switzerland)

3. **German**: 12, all of the whole *Comedy* (all published in Germany except where indicated)

1966: Christa Renate Köhler, *terza rima*
1983: Hans Werner Sokop, *terza rima* (Austria)
1984: Salo Weindling, blank verse
1986: Nora Urban, mostly blank verse (Austria)
1995: Hans Georg Hees, prose
1997: Hans Schäfer, *terza rima*
1997: Georg Peter Landmann, prose
2003: Walter Naumann, prose set as tercets
2003: Thomas Vormbaum, *terza rima*
2011: Kurt Flasch, prose
2012: Hartmut Köhler, prose
2015: Alfred Anderau, prose set as tercets

4. **Spanish**: 17 published in Spain (see below), all of the whole *Comedy* except two of *Inferno* alone (as indicated)

1967: Francisco José Alcántara, prose
1968: Rodríguez Vilanova y Sales Coderch, prose
1969: Enrique de Montalbán, prose
1970: Juan Godó Costa, prose
1973: Rafael Pérez Delgado, prose
1973: J. Ribera, prose
1973–77: Ángel Crespo, *terza rima*
1979: Ángel Chiclana Cardona, prose
1983: Julio Úbeda Maldonado, *terza rima* with rhyme or assonance
1988: Luis Martínez de Merlo, unrhymed 11-syllable lines
1999: Abilio Echeverría Pagola, *terza rima*
2001: Montserrat Oromí, prose
2012: Pedro Navarro Ainoza, *Inferno* only, *terza rima* mainly in alexandrines
2012: Violeta Díaz-Corralejo, prose
2014: Celia Akram, prose
2018: Javier S. Gálvez, *Inferno* only, part-rhymed 11-syllable lines
2018: José María Micó, unrhymed 11-syllable lines with some assonances

The list above does not include translations published only in South America, for which systematic details are very difficult to obtain: we have found those by Enrique Martorelli Francia (Mexico, 1969) and Ángel J. Battistesse (Argentina, 1972). We have also omitted from the list the translation attributed (in the front matter) to Luis Gil Fernández (Barcelona, Orbis: 1991 and 1994), since the version is the much older, and much republished, *terza rima* translation by the Conde de Cheste. A website attribution of *La divina comedia* (Palencia: Simancas, 2010) to

Fernando Mata Saez also appears to be mistaken (<https://www.archivero.es/isbn/autor/Fernando-Mata-Saez.317733/>): no translator's name is given in the edition, and the translation is that by Ángel Chiclana Cardona (1979). During the period two new translations were published in Catalan, by Joan Mira (2000: unrhyming hendecasyllables) and Jorge Carrión (2000, *Inferno* only, described as a prose adaptation).

5. Studies and Bibliographies

For general studies of English Dante translations with chapters or sections on the 1960s and later, see: Luciana Giovanetti, *Dante in America. Bibliografia 1965–1980* (Ravenna: Longo, 1987), chapter 13; Theodore Cachey, 'Between Hermeneutics and Poetics: Modern American Translation of the *Commedia*', *Annali d'Italianistica*, 8 (1990), 144–64; David Wallace, 'Dante in English', in *The Cambridge Companion to Dante*, ed. by Rachel Jacoff (Cambridge: Cambridge University Press, 1993), pp. 237–58; John Ahern, 'Translations into English', in *The Dante Encyclopedia*, ed. by Richard Lansing and Teodolinda Barolini (New York and London: Garland, 2000), pp. 824–30; *Divine Comedies for the New Millennium: Recent Dante Translations in America and the Netherlands*, ed. by R. de Rooy (Amsterdam: Amsterdam University Press, 2003); Nick Havely, *Dante's British Public: Readers and Texts from the Fourteenth Century to the Present* (Oxford: Oxford University Press, 2014), ch. 8. For bibliographies of translations, see the Dante Society of America's *American Dante Bibliography by Year*, <https://www.dantesociety.org/publications/american-dante-bibliography>.

For discussions regarding French see Marc Scialom, 'Répertoire chronologique et raisonné des traducteurs françaises de la *Divina commedia* (XVe–XXe siècles)', *Lingua e letteratura*, 78 (1986), 121–62; idem, 'Travail sur la langue/Travail sur le texte dans quelques *Divines comédies* en français', *Revue de Littérature Comparée*, 61.2 (1987), 167–84; idem, 'La traduction de la "Divine Comédie", baromètre de sa réception en France?', *Revue de Littérature Comparée*, 63.2 (1989), 197–207; Christian Bec, 'Le Dante en langue française au XXe siècle', in *L'opera di Dante nel mondo: edizioni e traduzioni nel Novecento. Atti del Convegno Internazionale di Studi, Roma, 27–29 aprile, 1989*, ed. by Enzo Esposito (Ravenna: Longo, 1992), pp. 83–92; Martine Van Geertruijden, 'Le traduzioni francesi della *Comedia* nel Novecento', in *Dante oggi*, III, ed. by Roberto Antonelli, Annalisa Landolfi, Arianna Punzi (Rome: Viella, 2011), pp. 203–25; *Dante in France*, ed. by Russell Goulborne, Claire Honess and Matthew Traherne, *La parola del testo*, 17.1–2 (Pisa: Viella, 2013); Stefania Vignali, 'Bibliographie des études sur Dante en France', *Studi Francesi*, 59.2 (2015), 319–34.

On German see Remo Fasani, 'Zur Übersetzung der *Göttlichen Komödie*', *Deutsches Dante-Jahrbuch*, 57 (1982), 137–44; Marcella Roddewig, 'Deutsche Ausgaben und Übersetzungen der Werke Dantes im zwanzigsten Jahrhundert', in *L'opera di Dante nel mondo*, pp. 102–13; Esther Ferrier (ed.), *Deutsche Übertragungen der Divina commedia Dante Alighieris 1960–1983: Ida und Walther von Wartburg — Benno Geiger — Christa Renate Köhler — Hans Werner Sokop. Vergleichende Analyse: Inferno XXXII, Purgatorio VIII, Paradiso XXXIII* [Quellen und Forschungen zur Sprach- und Kulturgeschichte der germanischen Völker, N.F. 105 (229)] (Berlin and New

York: de Gruyter, 1994). See also the *Vollständige Liste der deutschen Übersetzungen der 'Göttlichen Komödie' in chronologischer Reihenfolge nach Erscheinungsdatum des abschließenden Bandes*, <http://www.dante-gesellschaft.de/dante-alighieri/divina-commedia/>.

On Spanish see Joaquín Arce, 'La *Divina Comedía* en la literatura española', in *La Divina Comedía*, trans. by Francisco José Alcántara (Barcelona: Nauta, 1968), pp. 745–60 (revised as 'Dante en España', in *Divina comedía*, trans. by L. Martínez de Merlo (Madrid: Catedra, 1988), pp. 748–61); Carlos Alvar, 'El texto y sus traducciones: a propósito de la *Divina comedía*', in *Traducir la edad media: la traducción de la literatura medieval románica*, ed. by Juan Paredes and Eva Muñoz Raya (Granada: Universidad de Granada, 1999), pp. 133–52; Rossend Arqués, 'Traduzioni e irradiazioni ispaniche novecentesche della *Commedia* di Dante (Ángel Crespo, Luis Martínez de Merlo, Abilio Echevarría e María Zambrano)', in *Dante oggi* III, 119–48; Carlos Alvar, *Traducciones y traductores* (Madrid: Centro de Estudios Cervantinos, 2010), pp. 488–91.

Notes to Chapter 27

1. Gilbert F. Cunningham, *The Divine Comedy in English: A Critical Bibliography* 2 vols (Edinburgh: Oliver and Boyd, 1965–66). See Section 5 of the Appendix for studies of Dante translations into English.
2. Cunningham, *The Divine Comedy in English*, I, p. 1.
3. Considerations of ethnicity and regional characteristics fall outside the scope of this chapter.
4. *The Comedy of Dante Alighieri, the Florentine*, trans. by Dorothy L. Sayers and Barbara Reynolds (Harmondsworth: Penguin, 1949–63).
5. Dante, *Oeuvres complètes*, trans. by André Pézard (Paris: Gallimard, 1965).
6. Karl Vossler, *Die göttliche Komödie* (Zurich: Atlantis, 1942).
7. Douglas Neff, *Dante's Inferno in Modern English* (CreateSpace Independent Publishing Platform, 2014).
8. See Section 5 of the Appendix for further studies of translations into French, German and Spanish.
9. Reinhard Klesczewski, review of Georg Hees's Dante translation, *Deutsches Dante-Jahrbuch*, 72 (1997), 161–67.
10. *Dante's Divine Comedy*, adapted by Sandow Birk and Marcus Sanders (San Francisco: Chronicle Books, 2006); Frank Samperi, *Samperi–Dante* (London: Form Books, 1993); Philip Terry, *Dante's Inferno* (Manchester: Carcanet, 2014); Seymour Chwast, *Dante's Divine Comedy Adapted by Seymour Chwast* (London: Bloomsbury, 2010); John Agard, *The Young Inferno*, illustrated by Satoshi Kitamura (London: Frances Lincoln, 2008); Kevin Jackson and Hunt Emerson, *Dante's Inferno* (Stratford, Ontario: Fanfare Books, 2012).
11. *The Complete Prose of T. S. Eliot*, III: *Literature, Politics, Belief 1927–1929*, ed. by Ronald Schuchard, Frances Dickey and Jennifer Formichelli (Baltimore: Johns Hopkins University Press, 2015), p. 727.
12. *Agenda*, 34 (1996–97), special issue 'Dante, Ezra Pound and the Contemporary Poet'.
13. See, for example, the essays anthologized in *The Poets' Dante*, ed. by Peter S. Hawkins and Rachel Jacoff (New York: Farrar, Straus and Giroux, 2001), and the selection of poetic texts in *Dante in English*, ed. by Eric Griffiths and Matthew Reynolds (London: Penguin, 2005).
14. Heaney said in interview with Maria Cristina Fumagalli that for his versions of *Inferno* 1–3 he used Sinclair, Singleton and the old Temple Classics version, and also 'dipped into' Binyon ('Seamus Heaney and Dante', *Agenda*, 34, 204–34 (p. 209)).
15. On Dante and English poetry, see in particular Griffiths and Reynolds, and *Dante's Modern Afterlife*, ed. by Nick Havely (Basingstoke: Macmillan, 1998).

16. For an interesting comparison of fifteen English translations of *Inferno* 26. 112–20, see 'Boisterous beholding. A blog by Wm Jas Tychonievich. Fifteen Translations of Dante Compared', 7 February 2010, <https://www.wmjas.wordpress.com/tag/dante/> [accessed 7 April 2021].
17. Philippe Sollers's interest in Dante led to his *La Divine Comédie* (Paris: Desclée de Brouwer, 2000). On the *Tel Quel* group's interest in Dante and the emergence and nature of Risset's translation, see Sara Svolacchia, 'Storia di una riscoperta: Dante, la Francia e Jacqueline Risset', *Lingue e letterature d'Oriente e d'Occidente*, 7 (2018), 371–90.
18. Jean-Charles Vegliante, 'Afterword: Rereading Dante's *Commedia* in French Today', in *Dante in France*, ed. by Russell Goulborne, Claire Honess and Matthew Traherne, *La parola del testo*, 17.1–2, pp. 133–38.
19. '[Interviewer] No hay muchos hispanos seducidos por Dante. No hay una tradición dantesca. [Zurita]: Sí, no hay una tradición dantesca. Las marcas directas de su poesía son insignificantes, casi inexistentes'. <http://www.letras.mysite.com/rzur190613.html> [accessed 7 April 2021].
20. Hence various aids to teaching Dante in English, such as Carole Slade, *Dante's Divine Comedy, Approaches to Teaching World Literature*, 2 (New York: MLA, 1982); Milton Burke, *Teaching Dante's Inferno in the High-School Classroom* (Fayetteville: University of Arkansas, 2017).
21. Tim Smith and Marco Sonzogni (eds), *To Hell and Back: An Anthology of Dante's Inferno in English Translation (1782–2017)* (Amsterdam and Philadelphia: John Benjamins, 2017).
22. The lists that follow are derived partly from OPAC searches and partly from sources listed in section 5 of the Appendix. The geographical indications refer to place of first publication, not necessarily to the nationality of the translator. We have also received valuable assistance regarding English translations from Professor Martin McLaughlin.

GENERAL INDEX

ʿAbbūd Abī Rashīd 159

Académie Française 215
Accademia Fiorentina 124, 126
Accademia Dantesca 236
Accademia degli Umidi 124
Accademia della Crusca 232, 245
Achaemenides 15
Acheron 122, 173, 197, 316
Acis 15
Adam 124, 293
Aden 342
Adriatic 14, 15
Aeolian Mode 105
Aeneas 15, 21–22, 161, 182
Afrodisias, Alexander of 108
Agapetus 57
Agrarianism 300
Agard, John 354
Ahern, John 121–22, 360
Ai Weiwei 333
Akram 350, 359
Albert, Alfred 204
Albertano da Brescia 36
Alberti, Antonio degli 110
Alberti, Niccolò degli 110
Albertus Magnus 221
Albinola, Giovanni 259
Alcamo, Cielo d' 341–42
Alceo 149
Alcimus 51
Alcott, Bronson 253, 279
Aldrovandi, Giovanni Francesco 124
Aldus Manutius 181, 198, 244
Alessandro, Pietro d', 255
Alexander the Great 150
Alexandria 342
Alexandrianism 109
Alexis 15
Alfaquím, Abraham 158
Alfieri, Vittorio 253–54, 257
Alfonso V 169, 171
Alfonso X 158
Alì, 159
Alighieri, Jacopo 122
Alighieri, Pietro 121–22, 163, 171, 175–76
Aliprandi, Giacomo 204

Allston, Washington 253
Allston, William 256
al-Malik al-Kāmil 163–64
Alphesibeus 13, 15–16
Alvarez, Al 268
Amadeus VIII 181
Amaduzzi, Luigi xxxi
Amboise 194
Amiens, Colin d', 193
Aminadab 49, 51, 54, 56–57
Anchises 161
Andalusia 157–59, 163
Andrea da Firenze 101
Andrés, Juan 159
Anonimo Lombardo 137
Anton's Inferno 330
Antwerp 230
Aonia 13
Aoste, Duchesse d' 289
Apocalypse, 68
Apollo 14, 148, 161, 296, 354
Apulia 163
Aquileia, Rufinus of 89
Aquinas, Thomas, St 26, 35, 64, 221, 314
Aquino, Carlo d' 231–32
Arabic 157, 159, 161–63, 339, 346
Arachne 65–66
Aragon 169, 171, 175, 194
Arcadia 14
Ardissino, Erminia 92
Arena Chapel 66–68
Arezzo, Guittone d' 43, 342
Arezzo, Leonardo d' 194
Argenti, Felice 259
Argentina 332
Argo 22–25, 293
Ariosto 146, 232, 253, 256, 354
Aristotle 29, 40–41, 43, 56, 64, 108–09, 151–52, 233, 313, 340
Armour, Peter 133–34
Arno 13–14, 119, 353
ARoS Museum, Denmark 332
Aroux, Eugène 201
Arrigo 313
Artega, Esteban de 159
Artemidorus Daldianus 161
Ascoli, Albert R. xxv

Ashmolean Museum xxxi
Asín Palacios, Miguel 158–59
Assyria 55
Auerbach, Erich 243, 304, 330
Augustine, St 55, 89–94, 108, 110, 151–52, 242
Augustus 54–57
Augustus the Younger, Duke of Brunswick-Lüneburg 230
Auvergne, William of 90, 94
Averroism 108–09
Avernus 161
Avignon 152

Babylon 11, 47–48, 50, 55–57, 152
Bacchiglione 353
Bachenschwanz, Leberecht 233, 235, 243–44
Bachi, Pietro 255, 266
Bacon, Francis 74
Bacon, Roger 221
Balbec 292
Baldelli, Ignazio 132
Balliol College xxx
Balzac, Honoré de 4, 211, 289–90
Bang, Mary Jo 350, 353, 355, 358
Baraka, Amiri 304
Barański, Zygmunt 108, 176
Barbi, Michele xxix
Barbieri, Giovanni, Maria 159
Barolini, Teodolinda 187, 311, 360
Barolo, Palacio 332
Bartolomei, Francesco 136–37
Barzizza, Guiniforte 138, 195
Basel, Council of 181
Bassano del Grappa 152
Bassilian, Ron 330
Batolo, Ignazio 255
Baur, Adrian vom 330
Beatrice 22, 23, 47, 54, 57, 76–79, 92, 95–96, 110–11, 125, 160, 170, 201, 204, 206–08, 237, 253, 256, 266, 269, 270–71, 281, 289, 292, 328, 333, 343–44, 354
Becchi, Gianni Buiamonte de', 66–67
Beck, Friederich xxix
Becque, Henri 289
Bede 52, 58
Bedouin 160
Belgium 316
Belvedere-Apollo 231
Bembo, Pietro 146–47, 152–54
Benacus, Lake 15
Benali, Bernardino 196
Bene, Carmelo 127
Bene da Firenze 9
Benedict, St 52, 208
Benedict XI 53
Bengal 338

Benigni, Roberto 119, 124–25, 127
Benvenuto da Inola 137, 145, 147–48, 171, 173, 175–76
Berendis, Hieronymus Dietrich 230
Beretta, Margherita 342
Bergaigne, François de 195
Bergamo 244
Berger, Daniel 243
Bergotte 296–97
Bernard of Clairvaux, St 22, 24–25, 27, 30–31, 93
Bibliografia Dantesca Internazionale xxiii
Biedenfeld, Ferdinand von 234
Biglow, Hosea 266
Bini, Carlo 126
Birk, Sandow 331, 339, 345–46, 354
Black Lives Matter 320
Blake, William 75–77
Blois 194
Blow, Susan 279–81
Boccaccio 100, 108–09, 119, 122–24, 126, 135–36, 147, 153, 157, 164, 176, 181, 185–90, 198, 221–22, 232, 246, 258
Bodleian Library xxx, xxxi
Bodmer, Johann Jakob 232–33
Böhlendorff, Casimir Ulrich 234
Boethius 37, 44, 174, 295
Bogotá, Colombia 332
Bologna 2, 9, 11, 13–16, 124, 132, 149, 150, 229–30, 331
Bonandrea, Giovanni di 9
Bonaventura 28, 53, 57
Bonaventura da Siena 158–59
Boniface VIII 53, 67, 314
Borges, Jose Luis 332
Borghini, Vincenzo 146
Born, Bertran de 188
Borsieri, Pietro 259
Bosco, Umberto 317
Boston xxiii–xxv, 252, 253, 255–57, 259, 269, 278–79, 331
Bostonian Atlantic Monthly 278
Boston Athenæum 253
Boston College 300
Boston, Museum of Fine Arts 338
Bottrall, Ronald 355
Bourbon, Jean II de 193
Bous, engraver 203
Bowdoin College 325
Brackett, Anna 279
Brahma 346
Brazil 332
Brendan, St 161
Brescia, Albertano da 36
Briccio, Giovanni 125
Bridges, Robert xxx
Brinkmeyer, Robert H. Jr 300
Brockmeyer, Henry 279

Brooks, Van Wyck 265
Brown, Dan 311–12
Brownell, W. C., 274
Brugnolo, Furio 345
Bruni, Leonardo 145, 148
Brunswick 233
Brunswick-Lüneburg, Augustus the Younger, Duke of 230
Brunswick-Lüneburg, Leopold of 231
Brunswick-Wolfenbüttel, Anna Amalia of 240, 244–47
Bry, Joseph 205–08
Buchholz, Karl August 234
Buck, August xxii
Bülow, Hans von 237
Buenos Aires 331–32
Bürger, Gottfried August 234
Buffon 257
Bulgakov, Mikhail 311
Burgos, Diego de 174
Burgundy 180, 188
Burnside, John 355
Buti, Francesco da 103, 137, 139
Butler, A.J. xxvii
Butler, Judith 318
Byron 272
Byzantium 161–62

Cacciaguida 161, 207
Cacus 202
Cadiz 10
Caesarea, Basil of 29, 88–90, 92
Cahors 88
Calboli, Fulcieri da 16
Calcaterra, Carlo 108
Calcidius 161
Calderon, Pedro 269
California 320, 345–46
Callimachus 14
Callot, Jacques 200
Cambodia 327
Cambremer, Madame de 296
Cambridge, Massachusetts xxiii 331
Campi, Giuseppe 258
Canada xxv
Can Grande della Scala 12, 301, 324
Cañigueral Batllosera, Pau 171
Cannae 150
Canova, Antonio 204
Cán Prunera 76–77
Capaneus 188
Cappelli, Carlo 107
Caracciolo, Giovanni, Prince of Melfi 195
Carbonari 255, 259–60
Cardini, Roberto 150
Carroll, Lewis xxx
Carstens, Asmus 245

Carruthers, Mary 123
Carson, Ciaran 355
Cary, Henry Francis 77, 253–54, 279, 300, 351
Casella 297, 344
Castillia, Gaetano de 259
Casale, Ubertino da 53
Casella 189, 207
Casella, Mario 108
Castel Sant'Angelo 67
Castile/Castilian 169, 171–76
Catalan 133, 170–71, 173, 175, 360
Cato 56, 207
Cavalcanti, Guido 95, 100–02, 105–09
Cavalchini, Rinaldo 122
Celestine V 311, 314
Centenary Essays on Dante xxxi
Century, The, 278
Cerulli, Enrico 158
Cervantes, Miguel 269
Ceserani, Remo 217
Chabot, Jacques 189
Champagne, Thibaut de 220
Channing, William Ellery 254
Chapman, Con 327
Charlemagne 53
Charles V 182
Charles VII 189
Charles VIII 183, 194
Charles de France 193
Charles d'Angoulême 194, 196
Charlestown 255–56
Charlus, Baron 289
Charmasson, Thérèse 163
Charon 122, 188, 197
Chartier, Alain 185
Chartier, Roger 123–24
Chastelain, George 186, 188–89
Chaucer, Geoffrey 121, 257, 270, 273
Chautauquan, The 278
Cheste, Conde de 351
Chicago 277, 279, 282, 335
Chicago Board of Education 282
Chicago Kindergarten College 277, 281
Chicago, University of 282
Chile 332
China 333
Christopher, St 49
Chwast, Seymour 354
Ciacco 313
Ciampolo 210
Ciangulo, Nicolò, 233
Ciccia 27
Cicero 38–39, 44, 151–52, 161
Ciconia, Johannes 103
Cincinnati 302
Cinna 10

Cione, Jacopo di 110
Cistercian 27, 51
Clampitt, Amy 355
Clanchy, Michael 123
Clareno, Angelo of 53
Clarke, James Freeman 253
Claude de France 195
Claudian 148–49
Cliff, William 356
Clifton, New Jersey 329
Clinton, Hillary 319
Clovio, Giulio 198
Cocytus 333
Coëtivy, Maître de 193
Col, Pierre 182, 185
Colaud, Etienne 195
Coleridge 126
Colonne, Guido delle 341
Columbia College 254
Columbia University 327
Combray 290
Comestor, Petrus 58
Comey, James 319
Compagni, Dino 36–37
Conaxença 170
Congo 327
Contini, Gianfranco xxxi
Cooke, G.A. xxx
Cookson, William 355
Coomaraswamy, Ananda 338–39, 346
Conrad 207
Constance, Council of 148, 181
Constantine 51, 57, 68
Constantinople 230
Contini, Gianfranco 109, 145
Cook, William W., 299
Cordoba 171
Corn, Alfred 355
Cornelius, Peter von 236
Cornish, Alison xxvi
Corsi, Giuseppe 107
Corsica 255
Corti, Maria 108, 158–59
Corydon 13, 15
Cosimo II 200
Cossa, Giovanni 181, 194–95
Cossiga, President Francesco xxxi
Cousin, Victor 215–16
Crane, Walter 277
Crassus, Marcus 150
Crespo, Ángel 356
Crete 293
Critic, The, 278
Croce, Benedetto 234
Cullen, Countee 307
Cunizza 202

Cunningham, Gilbert 349–50
Curtius, Ernst 22, 304
Cusco, Peru 332
Cyclops 15
Cyrus 52, 55–57

Daffner, Hugo xxi
Dainotto, Robert M. 159
Dale, Peter 355
Damascus 26
Daniel 52, 57, 162–63
Daniel, Arnaut 297, 345–46
Daniello, Bernardino 150, 152
Dante Alighieri Society, Florence 301
Dante and Governance xxxi
Dante Beyond Borders xxxi
Dante Club xxiii, 269
Dante in Oxford xxxi
Dante Notes xxv
Dante Society of America xxiii–xxv
Dante Studies xxv
Danton's Inferno 330
Danube 10
Da Ponte, Lorenzo 254, 259
Darius 52, 57–58
Darwin 280, 282
Datini, Francesco di Marco 137
Davanzati, Chiaro 340
David 49, 54, 57, 88, 93
Davidson, Thomas 279
Davis, Jefferson 300
Delacroix, Eugène 193
Del Chierico, Francesco di Antonio 194
Delhi 339
Della Lana, Iacomo 137
Della Rocca, Morozzo 136
Del Virgilio, Giovanni 9–16
Demetrius 51
Deschamps, Antoni 244
Des Peres School 279
Desvignes, engraver 203
Deutsche Dante-Gesellschaft xxi–xxii, xxxi
Deutsches Dante-Jahrbuch xxii
Dewey, John 282
Dial, The 278
Díaz-Corralejo, Violeta 350
Dickinson, Patric 355
Diderot, Denis 296
Dido 343
Digges, Deborah 355
Dimock, Wai Chee 324, 334
Dis 63
Distefano, Donna 328
Dolce, Lodovico 146, 244
Dolce & Gabbana 328
Dominicans 54

Donati, Forese 93
Doni, Antonio Francesco 124
Doré, Gustave 4, 75, 193, 201, 205–07, 209, 211, 334, 345
Dorian Mode 105
Douglass, Frederick 303
Dove, Richard 355
Dreher, Rod 329
Dresden 231, 235, 245
Du Bocage, Anne-Marie 233
Dudu, Dai 333
Duèse, Jacques 88
Dugnano, Giovannino da 137
Dumont, Louis 206–07
Dunlap, Frances 272
Duprat, Antoine, Cardinal 195
Dürer, Albrecht 228
Durling, Robert M. xxv, 344
Durling-Martinez 353
Dwight, Elizabeth Buckminster 257
Dwight, Marianne 256

Eckhart, Meister 338
Eco, Umberto 119
Eden, Garden of 79
Edinburgh University 75
Edo, Pietro 136
Egypt 10, 55, 161, 163
Ehrenzweig, Anton 77
Einstein, Albert 23
Eitner, Karl 236
Elijah 50–54, 57–58
Eliot, Charles William 273
Eliot, T. S., 86, 300, 311, 314, 354–55, 300
Elisha 57
Ellis, Steve 352, 357
Ellison, Ralph 304, 307
Elphinstone, Mountstuart 126
Elstir 292–93, 296–97
Emerson, Hunt 354
Emerson, Ralph Waldo 253, 303
Emilia 15
Emiliano 135
Enciclopedia Dantesca xxix
Engels, Friedrich 75
Enrique, Master of the Order of Santiago 171
Epicureanism 108
Erasmus, Desiderius 135
Ercole, Pietro 108
Eridanus 13
Eryon 202
Eskrich, Pierre 199
Esdras 55
Esther 53
Étex, Antoine 205–08, 211
Etna, Mount 15

Eunoe 207
Eurydice 161
Eusebius 58
Everett, Anne Gorham 255–56
Everett, Charlotte Brooks 255
Everett, Edward Hale 252, 255–56
Exodus 49
Ezekiel 48–52, 54–55, 57
Ezra 52, 55

Farinata 313, 319
Farrar, Eliza Ware 255, 257
Fauns 14
Fauriel, Claude 217–18, 223
Favati, Guido 108
Febrer, Andreu 175–76
Feillet, Pierre-Jacques 201
Fenzi, Enrico 42
Ferdinando I de' Medici 125
Ferguson, Robert A., 327
Fernow, Carl Ludwig 241, 244–45
Ferrari, Jacopo 258–60
Ferry, Jules 216
Feuerbach, Anselm 236
Fields, James T., 266
Filelfo, Francesco 150
Fiore, Gioacchino da 27–30, 51–53, 57
Firenze, Andrea da 101
Firenze, Paolo da 101–02
Flanders, Ned 328
Flaxman, John 201–04, 206, 241, 253–54
Florensians 51
Förster, Karl August 236
Foerster, Norman 274
Foligno, Cesare xxx
Fontainebleau 194
Foresti, Eleuterio Felice 259
Forché, Carolyn 355
Foscolo, Ugo 303
Fraser, G. S., 355
Freedman, Paul 343
Froebel, Friedrich 279–81
Fuller, Margaret 253–57
Forssell, Christian Didrik 201
Foscolo, Ugo 126, 145
Fosseaume, Jean-Baptiste 204
Francesca da Rimini 121, 170–71, 187–88, 190, 206, 209, 236, 241–44, 246, 265, 267, 328
Franceschini 138
Francis of Assisi, St 53, 132
Franciscans 50–51, 53–54
François Ier 194–96
Frederick II of Hohenstaufen 53, 157, 160, 163
Froissart, Jean 182, 185, 190
Fruosino, Bartolomeo di 194
Füssli, Johann Heinrich 241

368 INDEX

Fulgoni, Antonio 245

Gabbay Alyssa 339
Gabiano, Balthasar 198
Gabriel, archangel 44, 158
Gabrieli, Giuseppe 159
Gagliardi, Antonio 108
Galatea 15
Gallarati-Scotti, Duke Tommaso xxx
Gallenga, Antonio 255–57
Garbo, Dino del 108
Gardner, Edmund xxix
Gare Saint-Lazare 292
Garrison, William Lloyd 303
Gatine, Georges-Jacques 201
Gazzetta di Weimar, 232
Gelli, Giovan Battista 124, 146
Genoa 135, 171–72
George, Stefan 351
Gerstenberg, Heinrich Wilhelm von 234
Geryon 63–67, 305
Gesselin, Jean 200
Gesualdo, Giovanni Andrea 150
Giacomelli, Sofia 201–03, 206
Giamboni, Bono 35–38
Giambullari, Pier Francesco 124, 146
Gianciotto 187, 206, 241–42
Gianfigliazzi family 66
Giles of Rome 37
Gilson, Etienne 300
Ginguené, Pierre-Louis 217–18, 220
Giotto 67–68, 266
Giraldi Cinzio, Giovan Battista 146–47
Girolami, Remigio de' 37
Gittings, Robert 355
Giunta, Claudio 92
Gladstone, William xxvii, 126
Glazener, Nancy 278
Globe [Le], 216–17, 223
Goacher, Denis 355
Godefroy, François 200
Goethe xxi, 4, 224, 228, 234, 240, 243–44, 246–47, 254, 256, 268–69, 272, 356
Goethe, Johann Caspar 230
Göttingen 233
Goetz, Walter xxi
Goldoni, Carlo 232
Goldsmiths' College 74
Go Nagai 334
Gonçales de Lucena, Martin 175
Gordon, Caroline 300–01
Gottsched, Johann Christoph 232–33
Gouffier, Guillaume 195
Graff, Gerald 273
Gragnolati, Manuele 339
Graham, Jorie 355

Grandgent, Charles Hall xxv
Grayson, Cecil xxxi
Gregorian chant 91
Gregory VII 216–17
Greule-bstock, Petra 328
Griffolino d'Arezzo 210
Grossi, Paolo 218
Grüner, Vincenz Raimund 243
Gryphius, Andreas 229
Guatemala 326
Gubbio, Bosone da 122
Gubbio, Oderisi da 86
Guccini, Francesco 135
Guermantes, Duc de 293–94
Guermantes, Duchesse de 289
Guermantes 293–95, 297
Guerrieri, Elisabetta 100
Guillory, John 278
Guinevere 241–42
Guinizelli, Guido 35, 297, 341
Guizot, François 215
Gujarat 342
Guston, Philip 74

Hachette, Louis 211
Haggadah 54
Haggai 53, 57
Hague, The 230
Hainsworth, Peter xxxi
Hale, Edward Everett 269
Hale, Ellen Day 252
Halpern, Daniel 355
Hamburg 232
Hannibal 150
Ha-Nostri, Yeshua 311
Haraway, Donna 339
Hardie, Colin xxxi
Harding's Gallery, Boston 256
Harlem 307
Harpur, James 355
Harris, William Torrey 279–80
Harrison, Elizabeth 277–82
Hartnett, Daniel 172, 175–76
Harvard xxiii, xxvi, 252, 255, 265–66, 269, 273
Ḥasan ʿUthmān 159
Hass, Robert 355
Havely, Nick xxxi, 270, 355
Hawkins, Peter 345
Hawthorne, Julian 266
Hawthorne, Nathaniel 266
Heaney, Seamus 355
Heath-Stubbs, John 355
Hebrew 47, 160, 272, 345–46
Hegel, Georg Wilhelm Friedrich 245, 279–80
Heidelberg 236
Helen of Troy 150

Hemingway, Ernest 301
Hendrix, Jimi 327
Heng, Geraldine 339
Henri IV 200
Henry VI 189
Henry VII 259
Hercules 22, 175
Herder, Johann Gottfried 224
Herr, Michael 327
Hirsch-Reich, Beatrice 28
Hezekiah 53
Hindavi 339–41, 343
Hinshelwood, Sir Cyril xxx
Hippolytus 170
Hoffmann, E.T.A 245
Holland, Frederick M. 265
Hollander, Robert and Jean xxv, 350, 356
Holmes, Oliver Wendell 265
Holywell Music Room xxxi
Homer 10, 152, 160, 172–74, 197, 224, 281
Hood, Lady 126
Horace 9–10, 150, 172, 174, 197, 231
Horden, Peregrine 91
Horen, Die 235, 241–42, 244–45
Howard, Richard 355
Hrabanus Maurus 48, 50, 55
Hudson Review, 299
Huelma 173
Hugo, Victor 215, 219
Humboldt, Wilhelm von 229, 242
Hutton, Reverend John H., 317
Huws, Daniel 355

Ibn Wāsil 163
Ilario, Fra 223
Immanuel of Rome 345
Imola, Benvenuto da 137, 145, 147–48, 171, 173, 175–76
Imperial, Francisco 3, 172, 174, 176
India 338–42
Indonesia 327
Indus 346
Inghilfredi de Lucca 340
Ingrams, Rosalind 355
Ingres 193, 205, 209, 211
International Congress of Medieval Studies xxv
Iolas 16
Ireland, G.W., 355
Irish 161
Irmscher, Christoph 265
Isaiah 48
Israel 49, 51, 302

Jack, Belinda 282
Jackson, Kevin 354
Jackson, Stonewall 300

Jagemann, Christian Joseph 232–33, 244–47
Jamaica 307
James, Clive 352–53, 355
James, Henry 274, 301
Jameson, Anna Brownwell 258
Jason 22
Japan 329, 333
Java 342
Jena 4, 241–42, 245
Jenkins, Alan 355
Jennings, Elizabeth 355
Jeremiah 47–52, 54–55, 57, 58
Jerusalem 47–55, 58
Jesse 54
Jesus/Jeshua, High Priest 53, 54, 57
Jiandu, Sichuan 342
Jimbo's Inferno 330
Job 48
John, King of Saxony xxi, 4, 236, 244
John the Baptist 52
John, St 52, 291
John XXII 88, 91
Johnson, Craig 330
Joinville, Jean de 220
Jones, LeRoi 304
Journal of Speculative Philosophy 278–79
Jove 54
Juan II 169, 171–72, 176
Judah 47–49, 52–53, 55
Judas 68
Judith 53
Jülich-Cleves-Berg, Prince Charles Frederick of 230
Juno 160
Justinian 53, 55, 57, 345

Kannegießer, Karl Friedrich Ludwig 235, 244
Kansas 317
Karlsruhe Gallery 236
Kaube, Jürgen 246
Keats 269
Kennedy, John F. 5, 315–17, 320
Kentucky 279, 299, 305–06, 308
Khusrau, Amīr 338–46
King, Reverend Martin Luther Jr 315–17, 319–20
Kinnell, Galway 355
Kinoshita, Sharon 342
Kirkpatrick, Robin 353, 356–57
Kitāb al-Miʿrāj, 157
Kitamura, Satoshi 354
Kliewer, Warren 301
Koch, Joseph Anton 236, 241–42, 245
Kociejowsky, Marius 355
Köhler, Christa Renata 350
Köhler, Reinhold 243
König, Bernhard xxii
Korea 333

Korean 346
Krefeld xxi
Kristeller, Paul Oskar 108
Kristeva, Julia 356
Kumar, Akash 316

Ladies Home Journal, 278
Lamentations, 47–51, 54, 57
La Motte, Antoine Houdart de 233
Lancelot 241–42
Landini, Francesco 101–10
Landino, Cristoforo 95, 145, 147, 150–54, 198, 244
Lane, William Coolidge xxiii
Laocoön 231
La Piana, Angelina 253
Lateran Council (1215) 28, 96
Latini, Brunetto 35, 38–39, 40, 42–44, 86, 158–59, 221, 352
Laura 266
La Vernade, Louis de 193
Leah 162
Lebanon 55
Ledgeway, Adam 139
Lefèvre, Sylvie 190
Le Franc, Martin 181, 184–86, 188
Leipzig 233
Lentini, Giacomo da 160, 345
Lenzi, Domenico 123
Lenzoni, Carlo 146
Leonardi, Anna Maria Chiavacci 95, 338
Léonie, Tante 290
Leonor, doña 171
Lessing, Gotthold Ephraim 231
Lessing, Karl 231
Lethe 13, 95, 173
Leu, Thomas de 200
Levi, Peter 355
Lewis, C.S. xxx
Libya 10
Ligozzi, Jacopo 200
Liguria 13
Liszt, Franz 245
Liverpool Lyceum & Athenaeum 253
Lograsso, Angeline 260
Lombard, Peter 90
Lombardo, Marco 56
Lombardo, Stanley 344
Longfellow, Henry Wadsworth xxiii 252, 255, 279–80, 300, 303, 351, 354
Los Angeles 330, 331
Losensky, Paul 343–44
Lotte 243
Louis XI 193
Lovati, Lovato 9
Lowell, James Russell xxiii, xxvii, 252, 265–75, 303
Lucan 9, 10, 172–74, 197

Lucca, Bonagiunta da 297
Lucifer 184, 194, 202, 334
Luke, St 50, 52
Luzzi, Joseph 329
Lyceum, Mount 14
Lycidas 10
Lydian Mode 88

Macdonald, Cynthia 355
MacEwan, Geoff, 74–86
Machaut, Guillaume de 185
Machiavelli, Niccolò, 232
Macrobius 161
Mahrt, William Peter 92
Malabar 342
Malato, Enrico 93
Mandelbaum, Allen 357
Manetti, Antonio 201, 206
Mantua 344
Maramauro, Guglielmo 137, 147
Marcolini, Francesco 199
Marco Polo 341–42
Marguerite de Navarre 194
Margaret of Anjou 188
Mariotti, Luigi 255
Maritain, Jacques 300
Mark, St 52
Maroncelli, Piero 259–60
Marot, Clément 183
Marselha, Folquet de 345
Marsyas 354
Marti, Mario 108–09
Martinelli, Vincenzio 201
Mary, Virgin 24, 54, 67, 207, 346
Masini, Lorenzo 101
Masons 201, 203
Massey, Alan 355
Matelda 96, 207
Matthew, St 52, 54, 90
Matthews, Joshua 316
Mauduisson, Léon 204
Maurette, Pablo 332
Mazzini, Giuseppe 126, 303
McAdams, Rachel 328
McKay, Claude 307
Mecca 158
Medici, Lorenzo de', 135, 145, 194
Meinhard, Johann Nicolaus 233, 235, 243
Melchisedek 57
Melibeus 12–15
Mena, Juan de 171–76
Menalcas 13
Menalus, Mount 13–14
Mendelssohn, Moses 233
Mendoza, Íñigo López de, Marquis of Santillana 169–76

Menocal, Maria Rosa 157, 159
Mercury 55
Merwin, W. S., 355
Metastasio, Pietro 254
Meun, Jean de 182–83, 185–86, 190
Mézières, Philippe de 182, 190
Michelangelo Buonarotti 124
Michelet, Jules 219
Michelino, Domenico di 247
Mignon 228
Milan 195, 229, 231
Milet, Jacques 185
Milne, W.S., 355
Milotti, Fiducio de', 13
Milton, John 201, 233
Milwaukee Sentinel, The, 315
Minnesota, University of 301
Minos 209–10
Minuti, Jacopo 195
Misson, François Maximilien 230
Mitchell, Susan 355
Modena, Gustavo 125–26
Modern Language Association of America xxv, 272–73
Moeris 13
Moggi, Moggio de', 121–22
Molière, Jean-Baptiste 269
Momigliano, Arnaldo 66
Montague, John 355
Montaperti 39
Montefeltro, Guido da 210
Monteverdi, Claudio 125
Monti, Vincenzo 254
Montigny, Claude-Antoine Littret de 200
Montor, Artaud de 201
Montreuil, Jean de 182
Moody, David 355
Moore, Edward xxv, xxvii
Mopsus 11–13, 15–16
Morante, Elsa 339
Moreau, Jean-Michel 200–01
Morricone, Ennio 333
Mosca 313
Mozarabic 160
Mozart, Wolfgang 91, 254
Mozzi, Andrea de', 352
Muhammad 157–59, 163
Munich xxxi
Musa, Mark 357
Musée Condé, 200
Muso 14
Mussato, Albertino 9, 14
Mussolini, Benito 332
Muzio, Girolamo 146

Nachon 51

Nairobi 326
Naples 13, 147, 194, 229
Nardi, Bruno xxx, 108–09
Narni 139–40
National Louis University 279
Nausicaä, 305, 307
Navarre 176
Naylor, Gloria 304
Neame, Alan 355
Nebuchadnezzar 55, 58
Neff, Douglas 351
Nehemiah 52
Neoplatonism 108, 161
Neptune 25, 293
Nerucci da San Gimignano, Bartolomeo 137
New England 252–53, 259, 272
Newsom, Gavin 320
New York School 74
Nibia Nidobeato, Martino Paolo 147
Niccolosa (Cosa), 100–02, 107, 110–11
Nichols, J.G., 353
Nimrod 345
Nisa 15
Noah 29
Norton, Andrews 259
Norton, Charles Eliot xxiii, xxvii, 252, 268–70, 274, 303
Novo Giorno, Il xxii
Nussbaum, Martha 318–19

Oberlin College xxv
Obriachi family 66
O'Brien, Sean 355
O'Donoghue, Bernard 355
O'Grady, Desmond 355
Occitan 157, 159, 180, 223, 345–46
Ockham, William of 105
Oderisi d'Agobbio 295–96
Odysseus/Ulysses 160, 163
Oeynhausen, Friedrich von 244
Olds, Sharon 355
Olivi, Pierre de Jean 53–54
Olson, Kristina 346
Orcagna 110, 204
Orcus 12
Origen of Alexandria 25
Orpheus 161
Ossian 243
Ostermann, Theodor 236
Othon III de Grandson 188
Ottimo Commento, 95, 194
Ovid 9, 10, 15, 36, 149, 151, 160–61, 172, 174, 182, 185, 197, 297
Oxford, Bishop of xxx
Oxford Dante Society xxvii, xxx, xxxi
Oxford Dante, The xxix, xxx

Ozanam, Frédéric 217

Pacino, Fra', 136
Padua 9, 13, 65–66, 103, 229–30
Palermo 160, 163
Pampa News, The, 315
Panciatichi, Bartolomeo 124
Paolo Malatesta 187–88, 206, 209, 236, 241–42, 244, 266
Paradise, California 326
Parigi, Giulio 200
Paris Entry Workshop 195
Parker, Deborah 315
Parma 255
Parnassus 173
Parrhasia 14
Parrington, V. L., 274
Parthenope 13
Pasolini, Pier Paolo 349
Paterson, Don 355
Patrick, St 161
Paul, St 21–22, 25, 26, 30–31, 161
Peabody's Bookstore 253
Peabody, Elizabeth Palmer 253, 256
Pecham, John 50–51
Peirce, Charles Sanders 279
Pellegrini, Anthony L. xxv
Pellico, Silvio 125, 259
Pelorus 15
Pepoli, Romeo de', 16
Percival, James Gates 268–69
Perini, Dino 13
Persian 159, 161, 339, 343–44, 346
Persius 151
Petrarch 106, 121, 123–24, 134, 145–54, 174, 185–86, 194, 198, 228, 232, 237, 253–54, 258, 266, 345
Pézard, André, 351–52
Phaeton 51, 54
Pharisees 49, 56
Philalethes (King John of Saxony) 235, 236, 244–45, 351
Philip the Good 184
Philistines 49, 58
Phillips, Tom 75, 356
Phrygian 88
Pia de' Tolomei 121, 207
Piccarda 121, 208
Pico della Mirandola, Lorenzo di 145
Pierides 12
Pighius, Stephanus Vinandus 230
Pindar 149–50
Pinsky, Robert 355
Piroli, Tommaso 201
Pisa, Guido da 137
Pistoia, Jacopo da 108
Pitwood, Michael 217

Pizan, Christine de 182–86, 190
Pizzi, Italo 159
Planck, Max 23
Plasiis, Petrus de 196
Plato 151–52
Plotinus 90
Plumly, Stanley 355
Plutus 345
Po 13–15
Poccetti, Bernardino 200
Poliphemus 15
Poliziano, Angelo 125, 145
Pollaiuolo, Antonio del 194
Ponte alla Carraia 119
Pontius Pilate 311, 314, 319
Pope, Alexander 233
Porta, Matteo 140
Porteus, Hugh Gordon 355
Possokhov, Yuri 328
Princeton 328
Pound, Ezra 108, 354
Prades, Violante de 171
Prato, Francesco Gherardi da 100–02, 107, 109–10
Prault, Marcel 200
Preller, Friedrich 242
Premierfait, Laurent de 181, 183, 186
Prentiss, Elizabeth Payson 257
Proclus 90
Propertius 149, 151
Proust, Marcel 289–98
Provençal 37, 135, 159, 218–19, 223, 270, 297
Provence 194
Providence 256
Prudentius 38
Psalms, 88–89, 91, 93–94
Pucci, Antonio 123
Puccini, Jacopo Guido di 194
Putnam, Alice 279
Pythagoras 88

Qaisar, Alam ad-Din, Sheikh 164
Quarengiis, Petrus de 197–98
Quincy, Josiah 255

Rabelais, François 205, 211
Radbertus, Paschasius 48
Radical Republican Party 316
Rahab 207
Rajna, Pio xxix
Ramey, Lynn 339
Rauschenberg, Robert 75
Ravenna xxxi, 10, 13, 14, 122, 170, 236, 332
Raynouard, François 218
Reeves, Marjorie 28
Reggio Emilia 27, 29, 258
Reggio, Giovanni 317

Reilly, Joseph J., 274
Renaissance Society of America xxv
René d'Anjou 181, 185–87, 194
Reno 14–15
Revelation, 48, 51–54
Réveil, Étienne-Achille 201
Reynolds, Barbara 350–51, 357
Rhéal, Madame de 203–04
Rhéal, Sébastien 203–05
Rheinfelder, Hans xxii
Richard II 189
Richardson, Brian 123
Richardson, Samuel 217
Ridolfi, Lucantonio 199
Riedel, Otto xxii
Rinuccini, Cino 102, 106, 109
Ripa di Meana, Ludovica 332
Ripheus 56
Risset, Jacqueline 350, 356
Ristori, Adelaide 289
Rivarol, Antoine de 224
Robertson, Robin 355
Robey, David xxxi
Rocabertí, Bernat Hug de 170
Roehn, Adolphe 201
Roger II 160
Rogers, Charles 349, 357
Roman de la Rose, 181–83, 185
Roosevelt, Theodore 316
Rosciate, Alberigo da 122
Rossetti, Gabriele 201, 260
Rossetti, Maria Francesca 270
Rossetti, William Michael xxvii
Rossi, Luca Carlo 147
Rothko, Mark 74
Rousseau, Jean-Jacques 257
Roville, Guillaume 199
Rubicon 15
Ruffini, Agostino 126
Ruggiero (Archbishop) 211
Ruskin, John xxvii
Rusticucci, Iacopo 313
Ryō Utsugi 334

Sacchetti, Franco 123, 134
Sacks, Oliver 91
Saiber, Arielle xvi, 325, 327
Said, Edward 304
Sainte-Beuve 216–17, 219
Saint-Gelais, Octovien de 185–87
Saint-Louis 221
Saint-Loup, Madame de 290
Saint-Loup, Robert de 290
Salimbeni, Niccolò de', 343
Salvadori, Giulio 108
Salvini, Tommaso 127

Samperi, Frank 354
Samuel 88
Sanders, Marcus 345, 346, 354
San Francisco 278, 331
San Francisco Ballet Company 328
San Pietro, Rome 30, 67
Santa Croce, Florence 27, 53
Santagata, Marco 92
Santa Maria Novella 124, 204
Santa Olga, Chile 326
Santi, Antonio xxix
Santillana, *see* Mendoza
Santi Maria e Zanobi, Capella, Fabroro 110–11
Sant Jordi, Jordi de 173
Sapegno, Natalino xxx
Sarasvati 346
Saturn 162
Saul 88
Savena 14–15
Savoie, Louise de 194
Savoy 181
Sawin, Birdofredum 266
Saxe-Weimar, William Ernest, Duke of 240
Sayers, Dorothy 350, 351, 354, 357
Scartazzini, Giovanni xxix
Scève, Maurice 198
Schelling, Friedrich Wilhelm Joseph 235, 245
Schicchi, Gianni 211
Schiller, Friedrich 235, 241
Schlegel, August Wilhelm von 221 234–37, 241–46
Schlegel, Dorothea 236
Schlegel, Friedrich 245
Schlüter, Friedrich xxi
Scholasticism 108
Schopenhauer, Adele 245
Schopenhauer, Johanna 245
Schott, Franciscus 230
Schubert, Franz 237
Scipio Africanus 54
Scott, John 217
Scott, Tom 355
Scribner, Charles 301
Scrovegni, Enrico degli 67
Scrovegni, Reginaldo (Rinaldo) degli 65–67
Scudder, Horace 273
Sears Roebuck and Company 277
Seattle, Washington 326
Sedgwick, Catharine Maria 257, 259–60
Sedgwick, Charles 257
Sedgwick, Kate 257–60
Sendino, José Muñoz 158
Seneca, Lucius Annaeus 108
Serengeti desert 326
Serianni, Luca 135
Serengeti desert 326
Sermonti, Vittorio 332

Serravalle, Giovanni da 145, 148
Servius 12, 13, 15
Sewanee 302
Shadwell, Charles L. xxix
Shakespeare xxii, 217, 234, 269, 281, 328
Sharma, Sunil 340, 343–44
Shaw, James E., 108
Shelley, Percy Bysshe 126
Shiva 346
Sibyl 27, 161, 182
Sicilian, dialect and school of poetry 37, 140, 157, 159, 160, 223, 255
Sicily 15, 159–60, 230, 342
Siena 229, 230, 343
Siena, Bonaventura da 158–59
Sigourney, Lydia Huntley 257
Simpson, Homer 328
Simpson, Lewis 301
Sinclair, John D., 77, 84
Singleton, Charles 306
Sinibaldi, Antonio 194
Sirens 163
Sismondi, Jean-Charles-Leonard Simonde de 159, 217–18, 254
Sisson, C.H., 355
Slade School of Fine Art 74
Smedberg, Agnes 260
Smith, Abiel 269, 272
Smith, Tim 357
Società Dantesca Italiana xxiii, xxx, xxxi
Sodano, Rossana 108
Sodom 95
Sokop, Hans Werner 356
Sollers, Philippe 356
Sóller, Mallorca 77
Solomon 49, 106
Song of Songs, 48–51, 54, 57, 101
Sonzogni, Marco 357
Sophocles 201
Sorbonne 4, 215, 216, 218, 221–22, 215–16, 221–22, 316
Sordello 174, 176, 344
Sotain, Noël-Eugène 205, 206
Southern Agrarians 300
Southern Literary Messenger, 278
Spain 169–77
Spalato, Tommaso da 132
Spanish 3, 159, 160, 346
Spencer, Herbert 280, 282
Spivak, Gayatri 319
Spring, Henry Powell 315–16, 319
Staël, Germaine de 159, 218, 223
Stagnino, Bernardino 198–99
St Andrews University 126
Starbucks 328
Statius xxx, 9–10, 201, 207, 297

St Edmund Hall xxvii
St Louis Movement 279–81
Steiner, Rudolf 315
Stendhal, Marie-Henri Beyle 216–17
Sterling, Mount 306
Stig's Inferno 330
Stillers, Rainer xxii
Stockbridge, Mass., 257, 259–60
Stowe, Harriet Beecher 315
Stradano, Giovanni 200
Streckfuß, Karl 235, 244
Striggio, Alessandro 125
Styx 63–64
Stürler, Franz Adolf von 209–11
Sufi 157, 343
Sumner, Charles 316–17
Sumner, George 316
Sunamite 49
Swann, Charles 289, 294
Sweeney, Matthew 355
Switzerland 126, 255, 358, 359
Syria 160

Ṭāhā Fawzī, 159
Taiwan 333
Tansonville 290
Tartars 64, 67
Tartarus 12
Tasso, Torquato 232, 253–57, 354
Tate, Allen 299–309
Tate Gallery xiii, 76–77
Tatum, James 299
Tavoni, Mirko 133
Taylorian Institution Library xxvii
Tchaikovsky, Peter 328
Tegghiaio Aldobrandi 313
Temple School, Boston 253
Tempo, Antonio da 136
Terragni, Giuseppe 332
Terry, Philip 354
Testilis 13
Teufel, Hans Christoph 230
Thaïs 68
Thayer, William Roscoe 266
Theocritus 15
Thomas Aquinas, St 207
Thomism 108, 277
Thoreau, Henry David 75
Ticknor, George xxiii, 255, 269, 272
Tieck, Ludwig 236
Tiller, Terence 355–56
Tinelli, Luigi 259
Tiraboschi, Girolamo 159
Tiresias 160
Titus, Emperor 55
Tityrus 11–16

Tivoli, Vitale de xxix
Todi, Jacopone da 120
Toledo 159
Tolkien, J.R.R. xxx–xxxi
Tolmino, Grotto 204
Tolson, Melvin B., 304
Tomitano, Bernardino 146
Tomatis, Alfred 91
Tomlinson, Charles 355
Tondelli, Leone 28
Tournes, Jean de 198
Towsen, Nat 330
Toynbee, Paget xxv, xxvii–xxxi
Tozer, Henry F. xxix
Trajan, Emperor 54, 56, 207
Trento 228
Trieste 259
Trifone, Gabriele 145, 147, 152–54
Trollope, Frances 126, 302
Troth, Barthélemy 198
Troubadours, *trouvères*, 180, 204, 218–21, 223, 237, 270
Troyes, Chrétien de 218
Turkish 339
Turkey 327, 329
Turkmenistan 329
Turks 65, 67
Tyrrhenian 13

Uffizi Palace 125
Ugolino 125, 202, 206, 211, 233–34, 237, 306, 355
Ulysses 15, 22, 307
University College London xxvii
Urban, Nora 350
Uzzah 51, 54

Valois 195
Vanderbilt University 300
Varchi, Benedetto 146
Varius, Lucius 10
Varus, P. Alfenus 14
Vasari, Giorgio 124
Vauthier, Gabriel 215
Vedic tradition 338
Vegetius, Publius 38
Vegliante, Jean-Charles 356
Veit, Johannes 236
Vellutello, Alessandro 199, 244
Venezuela 327
Venice 124, 136, 182, 229, 244, 331
Venus 170, 173, 184
Verduin, Kathleen 253–54
Verdurin, Madame 289
Verdurins 292, 296
Vergil/Virgilio 9–10, 12–13, 14, 15–16, 36, 57, 65, 78, 93, 120, 151, 158, 160–61, 172–76, 182, 186, 189, 196, 201, 206, 209, 236, 241, 256, 291, 301, 307, 312, 333, 343–44
Verini, Francesco 124
Vermeer van Delft 296–97
Vernon, William Warren xxvii
Verona xxxi, 121–22, 304, 314–15
Veronica, St 30–31
Vespasian, Emperor 55
Vicenza 352
Vickers, Nancy J. xxv
Vico, Giambattista 223
Vienna 230–32
Villani, Filippo 108–09, 145, 148
Villani, Giovanni 36–37, 119–20, 181
Villèle, Joseph de 215
Villemain, Abel-François 215–24
Villena, don Enrique de 173, 174, 175–76
Villeparisis, Madame de 289
Vincent, Nigel 135, 139
Vines, W.M., 317
Vinteuil 296–97
Virgilio, Giovanni del 9–16, 122–23, 134
Visconti court 138
Visconti, Federico da Pisa 132
Visconti, Filippo Maria 195
Vishnu 346
Visio Tnugdali, 161
Vitaliano di Iacopo Vitaliani 65, 66
Vivonne, River 291
Voltaire, François-Marie 315
Vossler, Karl 108, 351

Waetzoldt, Wilhelm 228–29
Wagner, Richard 289
Wall, Alan 355
Walpole, Horace 201
Walter, Duke of Athens 181
Ward, Anna 254
Ward, Elizabeth Howard 252
Ward, Samuel Gray 252–54
Warner, Marina 354
Warren, Robert Penn 301
Warton, Joseph 233
Weesenstein 245
Wehle, Winfried xxii
Weimar xxi, 4, 232, 240–47
Wellek, René, 269
Wendell, Barrett 265, 267, 274
Werther 4, 228, 243, 268
Wesselofsky, Alessandro 100
White, Maria 266, 268
Whitman, Walt 265
Whittier, John Greenleaf 265, 277
Wichita, Kansas 277
Wicksteed, Philip H. xxix
Wieland, Christoph Martin 245

Wilkins, Ernest Hatch xxv
Williams, Charles xxx
Williams, Pharrell 333
Williams, Spencer 303
Wilson, Woodrow 316
Winchester, Dean of xxx
Winckelmann, Johann Joachim 230–31
Witte, Karl xxi, xxvii, 236, 244–45
Wolfenbüttel 231
World of Dante, The xxxi
World's Columbian Exposition 282
Wright, Richard 304, 307

Yi Zhou 333

Zachariah 52, 57
Zane, Wallace 330
Zerubbabel 52, 54, 57, 58
Zhang An 333
Zhao Liang 333
Zibaldone Laurenziano 13
Ziino, Agostino 101
Zuccari, Federico 200
Zucchello, Pignol 136–37
Zurita, Raúl 332

REFERENCES TO DANTE'S WORKS

Commedia:
  early commentaries 3, 122, 124, 137–38, 145–54,
    171, 175, 194
  early editions (up to c. 1700) xxix, 145–54, 198–
    200, 240–41, 244
  films 126, 303–04, 326
  illustrations 2, 4, 5, 74–87, 193–211, 236, 326, 334,
    345–46, 354
  manuscripts xxvii, 133, 181, 193–95
  performance 3, 9, 119–27, 134–35, 289, 326, 328, 332
  translations 3, 4, 5, 6, 169–70, 175–76, 181, 193,
    195–98, 203–04, 224, 231–32, 233–34, 235–36,
    240–41, 243–44, 269, 278–79, 349–61
Inferno:
  general 44, 64, 120, 170, 185, 186, 202, 234, 252,
    300, 304, 316, 325–26, 327–28, 330–31, 333,
    349
  canto 1: 127, 135, 152–53, 206, 258, 329, 343–44,
    353
  canto 2: 22, 106, 206, 312
  canto 3: 5, 173, 187, 188, 197, 206, 292, 307,
    311–20, 329
  canto 4: 10, 151, 153, 172–73, 174, 197–98, 206,
    346
  canto 5: 170, 187–88, 190, 206, 209, 241–44, 246,
    266, 267
  canto 6: 151, 206
  canto 7: 152, 206, 291, 345
  canto 8: 151, 206
  canto 9: 259
  canto 10: 206
  canto 11: 206
  canto 12: 202, 206
  canto 13: 140, 202, 206, 268–69, 308, 355
  canto 14: 188, 206, 293–94, 352
  canto 15: 43, 86, 206, 313, 314–15, 352–53
  canto 16: 64, 138–39, 209, 295, 305
  canto 17: 63–68, 206
  canto 18: 202, 206
  canto 19: 152, 206
  canto 20: 206, 209
  canto 21–22: 120, 352
  canto 21: 202, 295
  canto 22: 121, 210
  canto 24: 151, 202, 206
  canto 25: 137, 313
  canto 26–27: 206
  canto 26: 307
  canto 27: 210
  canto 28: 150, 159, 188
  canto 29: 342–43
  canto 30: 210
  canto 31: 206
  canto 32: 153, 211
  canto 32–33: 355
  canto 33: 125, 206, 210, 234, 237, 306, 345
  canto 34: 80, 137, 140, 194
Purgatorio:
  general 3, 10, 88–96, 120, 162, 163, 234, 252, 300,
    325–26, 343–44, 349, 355
  canto 1: 56, 78, 92, 207, 293
  canto 2: 78, 189, 207, 297, 344
  canto 3: 189
  canto 4: 207
  canto 5: 92, 207
  canto 6: 47, 344
  canto 7: 174
  canto 8: 203, 207
  canto 9: 93–94, 162, 173, 295, 346
  canto 10: 54, 207
  canto 11: 86, 246–47, 295–96, 297
  canto 12: 150
  canto 13–14: 207
  canto 14: 258
  canto 16: 56, 58, 84, 89–90
  canto 17: 140
  canto 19: 94, 162, 163, 203
  canto 20: 92
  canto 23: 92, 93, 94
  canto 24: 297
  canto 25: 151
  canto 26: 95, 297, 345, 346
  canto 27: 57, 95, 162
  canto 28: 153, 162, 207
  canto 29: 54, 190
  canto 29–32: 58
  canto 30: 95, 154
  canto 31: 57, 95, 96, 207, 271
  canto 32: 43, 44, 54–55
  canto 33: 58, 92, 109, 110, 207

Paradiso:
  general xxix, 12, 93, 109, 120, 162, 234, 281, 300, 325–26, 349, 352
  canto 1: 23, 92, 147–48, 207, 296, 354
  canto 2: 22, 106, 301
  canto 3: 208
  canto 8: 207
  canto 10: 32
  canto 13: 207
  canto 15: 207
  canto 17: 154, 272
  canto 19: 56, 202
  canto 20: 56
  canto 22: 208
  canto 23: 12, 202, 346
  canto 24: 32
  canto 25: 31, 106, 291, 297–98
  canto 26: 124, 291
  canto 27: 203, 338
  canto 28: 201, 202, 301
  canto 29: 208, 301
  canto 30: 301
  canto 31: 23, 30, 109, 110
  canto 32: 24, 342
  canto 33: 2, 21, 23, 24, 25, 26–31, 110, 154, 280, 293, 301, 329, 339

Convivio 11, 42, 43–44, 135, 195, 198, 204, 258, 313, 314

De vulgari eloquentia 11, 43, 204, 223, 340

Eclogues xxix, 2, 11–12, 13–14, 15–16, 149

Epistolae 49–51, 56, 324

Monarchia 55–56, 204

Quaestio de Aqua et Terra xxvii, xxix

Rime xxix, 42, 194, 236–37, 345

Vita nuova xxix, 47, 107, 108, 110, 160, 203, 204, 236–37, 244, 253, 258, 267, 269

www.ingramcontent.com/pod-product-compliance
Lightning Source LLC
Chambersburg PA
CBHW081823230426
43668CB00017B/2353